Why Do You Need This New Edition?

1. New sections have been added to expand the scope of the text. For example, "Stages in Critical Thinking" provides a framework to guide students toward becoming sophisticated critical thinkers. The section "Criteria for Evaluating Philosophical Theories" equips students with an assessment rubric for critically evaluating philosophical points of view.

2. New sections on the birth of philosophy have been added. For example, in Chapter 2 the section "Hesiod, Homer, and the Birth of Philosophy" and the reading "The Axial Period" by Karl Jaspers provide students with a historical context for the development of philosophical thought. This perspective is enriched by the expanded treatment of the "pre-Socratic" thinkers in Chapter 5.

3. Chapter topics have been extended by the inclusion of new sections and readings. For instance, the thinking and writing of St. Augustine, Sigmund Freud, and Gilbert Ryle have been added to Chapter 3. And in Chapter 7, the treatment of the problem of evil in religion has been deepened by the inclusion of readings by J.L. Mackie "Evil Shows There Is No God" and Edward Madden and Peter Hare "A Critique of Hick's Theodicy."

4. Contemporary work in philosophy has been highlighted in Chapter 3, in sections like "Functionalism" where essays by Jerry Fodor, "The Mind/Body Problem" and Richard Brown, "Contemporary Issues in Philosophy of Mind" introduce students to current trends and controversies in philosophy today.

5. MySearchLab is an interactive and instructive multimedia site that offers access to a wealth of resources geared to meet the individual teaching and learning needs of every instructor and student. Within MySearchLab, MyThinkingLibrary contains the complete version of all the readings found in the text. Combining an ebook, video, audio, multimedia simulations, research support, and assessment, MySearchLab engages students and gives them the tools they need to enhance their performance in the course.

PEARSON

FOURTH EDITION

THE PHILOSOPHER'S WAY

A TEXT WITH READINGS

THINKING CRITICALLY ABOUT PROFOUND IDEAS

JOHN CHAFFEE

City University of New York

PEARSON

Boston   Columbus   Indianapolis   New York   San Francisco   Upper Saddle River
Amsterdam   Cape Town   Dubai   London   Madrid   Milan   Munich   Paris   Montreal   Toronto
Delhi   Mexico City   São Paulo   Sydney   Hong Kong   Seoul   Singapore   Taipei   Tokyo

Editorial Director: Craig Campanella
Editor in Chief: Dickson Musslewhite
Executive Editor: Ashley Dodge
Editorial Project Manager: Carly Czech
Development Editor: Maggie Barbieri
Editorial Assistant: Nicole Suddeth
Director of Marketing: Brandy Dawson
Senior Marketing Manager: Laura Lee Manley
Marketing Assistant: Paige Patunas
Managing Editor: Melissa Feimer
Senior Production Project Manager:
    Lynne Breitfeller
Senior Operations Specialist: Diane Peirano
Senior Art Director: Pat Smythe
Text and Cover Designer: Lisa Delgado

Manager, Visual Research: Ben Ferrini
Manager, Rights and Permissions:
    Charles Morris
Interior Permission Coordinator: Sue Brekka
Cover Photo: Galina Barskaya/Shutterstock
Digital Media Director: Brian Hyland
Digital Media Editor: Rachel Comerford
Full-Service Project Management:
    PreMediaGlobal, Lindsay Bethoney
Composition: PreMediaGlobal
Printer/Binder: R.R. Donnelley/Willard
Cover Printer: Lehigh-Phoenix Color/
    Hagerstown
Text Font: 10/12, ITC New Baskerville

Credits and acknowledgments borrowed from other sources and reproduced, with permission, in this textbook appear on appropriate page within text (or on pages 626–638).

Library of Congress Cataloging-in-Publication Data
Cataloging-in-Publication data is on record at the Library of Congress

10 9 8 7 6 5 4 3 2 1

Student Edition ISBN-10: 0-205-25469-1
                    ISBN-13: 978-0-205-25469-9

Exam Edition   ISBN-10: 0-205-39960-6
                    ISBN-13: 978-0-205-39960-4

For Heide,
Jessie & Joshua

brief contents

chapter

contents

6   what is real? what is true?

FURTHER EXPLORATIONS   281

10 what is social justice?

CREATING A JUST STATE 555

resources for teaching and learning with *The Philosopher's Way*

MySearchLab is an interactive and instructive multimedia site designed to help students and instructors save time and improve results. It offers access to a wealth of resources geared to meet the individual teaching and learning needs of every instructor and student. Combining an ebook, video, audio, multimedia simulations, research support, and assessment, MySearchLab engages students and gives them the tools they need to enhance their performance in the course. Please see your Pearson sales representative or visit www.mysearchlab.com for more information.

Common Philosophical Terms (013189661X) This glossary is a useful reference and guide for students. It glossary includes important terms with definitions.

Instructor's Manual with Test Item File [www.pearsonhighered.com/irc] This resource includes suggestions for teaching every chapter of the text, including chapter summaries, activities, and hundreds of sample test questions. For easy access, this manual is available within the instructor section of MySearchLab for *The Philosopher's Way,* Fourth Edition, or at www.pearsonhighered.com/irc.

MyTest Test Generator [www.pearsonhighered.com/irc] This computerized software allows instructors to create their own personalized exams, to edit any or all of the existing test questions, and to add new questions. Other special features of this program include random generation of test questions, creation of alternate versions of the same test, scrambling question sequence, and test preview before printing. For easy access, this software is available within the instructor section of MySearchLab for *The Philosopher's Way,* Fourth Edition, or at www.pearsonhighered.com/irc.

PowerPoint™ Presentation Slides [www.pearsonhighered.com/irc] New to this edition, these slides contain chapter outlines, critical thinking and philosophical statements that can be used for classroom discussion. Also included will be some selected images from the book. For easy access, these slides are available within the instructor section of MySearchLab for *The Philosopher's Way,* Fourth Edition, or at www.pearsonhighered .com/irc.

Custom Publishing Modify, adapt, and combine existing Pearson books to suit your course needs. Visit www.pearsoncustom.com to begin building your ideal text.

I was midway into my freshman year of college—and my very first philosophy course—when I suddenly announced to everyone's astonishment (including my own) that I was changing my major to philosophy. It didn't concern me that I had never taken a philosophy course, nor even read a philosophy book: Somehow I *knew* that I was destined to study this extraordinary discipline. It is a decision I have never regretted. Philosophy has enriched my life in countless ways, both personally and professionally, and I have witnessed it change the lives of many of my own students. I am confident that its study will do the same for you.

We are all the artists of our lives, with our brushstrokes being the choices we make each day as we gradually create our life portraits. Philosophy encourages us to follow Socrates' exhortation to examine our lives and to "know ourselves" so that we can make the most informed choices possible and create the most enlightened portraits. The study of philosophy provides the impetus and the thinking tools to confront the most fundamental questions in life: *Who am I? Who should I become? What is the meaning of my life?* More significantly, philosophy helps us craft an approach to living and develop a reflective attitude toward every aspect of our lives. These are invaluable, life-transforming gifts that only philosophy can provide. On a personal level, philosophy has served as a beacon in my life, helping to illuminate a path for me to follow while clarifying and informing my choices.

Professionally, philosophy has provided me with a framework for thinking critically and creatively. This has helped me perform my best in every job that I've held, ranging from cabinetmaking to teaching to writing. The study of philosophy trains our minds to think in powerful and analytical ways, enabling us to understand complex issues, reason cogently, and make intelligent decisions. These are foundational abilities that enhance our success in whatever career we choose.

My goal in writing *The Philosopher's Way* is for you to capture the spirit of philosophy, to experience the passion and adventure of engaging in the philosophical exploration of the core dimensions of our lives. In Western culture, philosophy traces its roots to ancient Greece where philosophers like Socrates, Plato, and Aristotle engaged in thoughtful reflection and energetic, rigorous discussions. Your "Introduction to Philosophy" course is your opportunity to become a part of this philosophical conversation that has spanned millenia, as you engage in philosophical discourse with your professor and your classmates.

Features

The Philosopher's Way has been designed to help you become a more accomplished critical thinker and to develop the analytical tools needed to think philosophically about important issues. It engages you in the process of doing philosophy in multiple ways: through reading, writing, discussing, and looking.

The Philosopher's Way Introduces You to the Big Questions of Philosophy

- Organized by the questions central to the main branches of philosophy, *The Philosopher's Way* examines the profound ideas of philosophers both past and present. Each chapter offers a historically organized survey of perspectives on the chapter question, while encouraging you to use these perspectives to develop your own philosophical answers. The chapters have a modular organization so that your instructor can assign parts within a chapter or follow a different sequence than that of the text. Because the sections are self-contained, the instructor has greater flexibility in choosing readings for his or her syllabus.

The Philosopher's Way Deepens Your Understanding of Primary Texts

- This book combines substantial readings from major philosophical texts with commentary that guides you through the readings. The commentary is designed to help you think your way through the philosophers' texts; it doesn't substitute for reading them. You will be able to come to class ready to understand your instructor's discussion of the works and contribute your own ideas.

- **Reading Critically** boxes offer questions that challenge you to think deeply about the philosopher's writing. Some questions ask you to critically evaluate a philosopher's claim while others help you improve your comprehension of difficult passages. Some ask you to compare the ideas of philosophers or apply their ideas to different situations. Instructors may use these questions to generate class discussions or writing assignments.

> **< READING CRITICALLY >**
>
> **Analyzing Streng on Definitions of Religion**
>
> - Describe your concept of *religion* as specifically as possible. Where did the concept originate for you? How did it evolve as you have matured? Explain the reasons or experiences that support your concept.
> - Evaluate your concept of *religion* by answering the four questions posed by Streng:
>   1. "Does your definition *reduce* religion to what you happen to be acquainted with by accident of birth and socialization?"
>   2. "Does your definition reflect a *bias* on your part—positive or negative—toward religion as a whole, or toward a particular religion?"
>   3. "Does your definition *limit* religion to what it has been in the past, and nothing else, or does your definition make it possible to speak of emerging forms of religion?"
>   4. "Does your definition have sufficient *precision*?"
> - Compare your definition of religion to the definitions of other students in your class. What are the similarities? What are the differences? How do you explain these similarities and differences?
> - Streng defines religion as a "means toward ultimate transformation." What do you think this definition means? Explain how this definition relates to your definition.

The Philosopher's Way Invites You to "Do Philosophy"

- **Thinking Philosophically** boxes challenge you to critically examine your own beliefs and assumptions while applying the ideas of philosophers to your experiences. The study of philosophy takes on greater meaning when it changes the way you see the world. Some "Thinking Philosophically" questions ask you to consider a recent event or experience through a philosophical lens. Other questions ask you to articulate your ideas about a philosophical problem or think about the source for your assumptions. By working through the questions in the "Thinking Philosophically" boxes, you will clarify your ideas and learn how to think philosophically.

- **Making Connections** essays at the conclusion of each chapter suggest how the chapter themes can apply to your own life. From Viktor Frankl's search for meaning in the midst of a Nazi concentration camp to Robert Coles's story of a young woman's frustration with the unethical behavior of her fellow students, these essays underscore the value of philosophy beyond the classroom.

> **thinking philosophically**
>
> **WHAT ARE YOUR RELIGIOUS BELIEFS?**
>
> As you respond to the following questions, express your ideas thoughtfully and articulately. If you have no religious beliefs at this time, you can respond to these questions with reference to a religion with which you are familiar or simply from your own perspective on religion, whatever that might be.
>
> - What is your definition of religion? What do you think is the purpose of religion?
> - How would you describe your religious beliefs? Does it include a belief in "God"? If so, describe your concept of God.
> - What was the origin of your religious beliefs (or lack of religious beliefs)? If your beliefs are different from those you were raised with, explain what caused you to change your religious views.
> - What religious activities do you engage in (for example, worship, prayer, meditation, communion, singing, chanting, liturgy)?
> - Describe the role that religious leaders and "holy books" play in your religion.
> - Describe some of the "symbols" and "myths" of your religion.
> - How does your religion view other religions?

Bernini, *Ecstasy of Saint Theresa*. One of the most famous mystics in the Christian tradition is Saint Theresa of Avila, depicted here in a mystical state of union with God. How does this image relate to the kind of religious experience that Søren Kierkegaard proposes that we strive to achieve?

The Philosopher's Way Uses Images to Communicate Philosophical Ideas

- The images in *The Philosopher's Way* are meant to add another layer of meaning to your study of philosophy. Selected from the world of art and journalism, the images go beyond mere illustration, offering instead a kind of "visual philosophy." In addition, portraits put a face with the words of classic and contemporary philosophers.

The Philosopher's Way Offers Resources to Help You Learn

- Each chapter opens with a **Concept Map**, which shows how the ideas and thinkers in each chapter relate to each other. In addition, interior concept maps illustrate relationships among ideas and provide a conceptual framework for visual learning.

- **Visual Summaries** at the end of each chapter provide helpful summaries of chapter concepts, and key terms are defined in the text and margin glossaries. These resources are useful for reviewing for tests and checking your comprehension of the chapter.

- An annotated list of **Film and Literature** offers engaging ways to further explore chapter concepts. This feature, which is at the end of every chapter, suggests works of fiction that dramatize philosophical themes and questions.

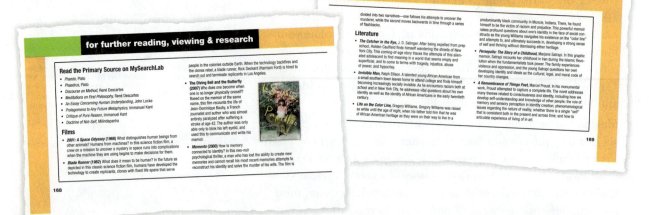

- **Writing About Philosophy** sections challenge you to express your ideas about philosophy in writing. An assignment, suggestions for approaching the topic, and a sample student response offer support as you develop critical thinking skills through writing.

Acknowledgments

I have been privileged to work on this new edition with a stellar team of people at Prentice Hall who are exemplary professionals and valued friends. Yolanda de Rooy, President, has continued to be steadfast in her personal and professional support of *The Philosopher's Way,* and I am deeply grateful. I would like to acknowledge the support of the Editorial Director, Craig Campanella, who with the other executives at Pearson has made *The Philosopher's Way* one of Pearson's flagship texts. Ashley Dodge, Executive Editor, provided the kind of passion and strategic guidance needed to successfully ensure that this fourth edition will achieve the ambitious goals set for it. Editor-in-Chief Dickson Musslewhite infuses every edition with his creative vision and his patented inexhaustible energy, insistent that the book achieve excellence in every area. The Developmental Editor, Maggie Barbieri was a delight to work with: fully committed, effective, and warmly professional. Senior Production Project Manager Lynne Breitfeller skillfully guided every element of the production process along through its seemingly endless details and decisions. The talented Project Managers Carly Czech and Lindsay Bethoney were at the center of the revision process, bringing their experience and intelligence to the multitude of editorial responsibilities. The stunning art program of *The Philosopher's Way* has dramatically distinguished this text from all others in the field, and this sterling quality has continued under the creative direction of the Art Director, Pat Smythe. My thanks also go to Senior Marketing Manager Laura Lee Manley for her dedicated efforts in marketing the text, as well as to Director of Marketing, Brandy Dawson. I am also indebted to Digital Media Editor Rachel Comerford for her work on behalf of the text. I would also like to express my gratitude to Nicole Suddeth for her ongoing service as a member of the team. Finally, I would like to acknowledge and thank the outstanding individuals who invested so much of themselves in the earlier editions of *The Philosopher's Way,* including Sarah Touborg, Charlyce Jones Owen, Ross Miller, Kathy Sleys, Kara Kindstrom, Deb O'Connell, Leslie Osher, Robert Farrar-Wagner, Kathy Boothby-Sestak, Nancy Roberts, Cynthia Ward, and Rochelle Diogenes.

The chapter-ending essays are one of the key features of *The Philosopher's Way,* and it is with my deepest appreciation that I acknowledge the people who contributed these superb pieces which have so greatly enriched the text: Gina Szeto, Jessie Lange, Sonja Tanner, and Susan Martin. A special thanks goes as well to Jessie Chaffee for her superb work on the Film and Literature sections at the conclusion of each chapter.

I am grateful to the many scholars and teachers whose thoughtful and detailed comments helped shape *The Philosopher's Way* over three editions: Nicoleta Apostle, College of Dupage; Mike Awalt, Belmont University; Philip Ayers, Virginia Western Community College; Marina P. Banchetti, Florida Atlantic University; Stephen Barnes, Northwest Vista College; Michael Booker, Jefferson College; Marshell Bradley, Sam Houston State University; Jaymes Buick, Broward Community College; Claudia Close, Cabrillo College; Timothy Davis, Baltimore County Community College;

Emma Easteppe, Boise State University; Miguel Endara, Los Angeles Pierce College; Byron Eubanks, Ouachita Baptist University; Brett Fulkerson-Smith, Eastern Kentucky University; Robert Gall, West Liberty State University; Mark Hillringhouse, Passaic County Community College; Randall Horton, San Jacinto Community College; Elaine Hurst, St. Francis College; Stella Ireland, Skagit Valley College; David Irvine, Community College of Baltimore County–Catonsville; Larry L. Kollman, North Iowa Area Community College; John Latourell, Delaware County Community College; Stephen Levy, County College of Morris; David Lopez, American River College; Robert M. Louis, Naugatuck Valley Community College; Brian Merrill, Brigham Young University, Idaho; Mark Michael, Austin Peay State University; Genevieve Migely, Mount San Antonio College; Peter Morton, Mount Royal College; Eric Mullis, Queens University of Charlotte; Christian Perring, Dowling College; Michael Potts, Methodist College; Mike Prahl, University of Northern Iowa; Joseph Profio, Southern University; Renton Rathbun, Owens State Community College; Henry Rinne, University of Arkansas–Fort Smith; Rayka Rush, Metropolitan Community College; Allen Shotwell, Ivy Tech Community College; Frederic L. Shuman, Pikes Peak Community College; Kent Slinker, Pima Community College; Robert Thomas, Brookdale, The County College of Monmouth; Jerome Van Kuiken, Vennard College; and Steve Young, McHenry Community College.

In addition, I would like to give my special thanks to Professors Richard Brown, Wayne Alt, Timothy Davis, and Dana Johnson for their important suggestions and clarifications. I would like also to thank Emmanuel Nartey for his lucid explication of Aristotle's concept of hylomorphism. I am particularly indebted to Richard Brown for his expert contributions to the sections dealing with physicalism, functionalism, and current issues in the philosophy of mind.

Finally, I wish to thank my wife Heide Lange and my children, Jessie and Joshua, for their complete and ongoing love, support, and inspiration. Throughout their lives, Jessie and Joshua have continually taught me the truth of Socrates' statement, "All philosophy has its origins in wonder," for they have been models of both wonder and wisdom. Heide has consistently inspired me to achieve the best of which I am capable and provided unwavering support in my efforts to do so. And her extraordinary talents in publishing have provided me with clear professional direction when it was most needed. It is these closest relationships that make life most worth living, and the threads of love that tie us together are woven into the fabric of this book. I also wish to remember my parents, Charlotte Hess and Hubert Chaffee, who taught me lasting lessons about the most important things in life. They will always be with me.

Although this is a published book, it continues to be a work in progress. In this spirit, I invite you to share your experiences with the text by sending me your comments. I hope that this book serves as an effective support for your own philosophical explorations in living an examined life. You can contact me online at JCthink@aol.com.

John Chaffee

John Chaffee, Ph.D., is a Professor of Philosophy at The City University of New York, where he has developed a Philosophy and Critical Thinking program that annually involves thirty faculty and 4,500 students. He is a nationally recognized figure in the area of Critical Thinking, having authored leading textbooks like *Thinking Critically*, as well as many professional articles. In developing programs to teach people to think more effectively in all academic subjects and areas of life, he has received grants from the National Endowment for the Humanities, the Ford Foundation, the Annenberg Foundation, and the Corporation for Public Broadcasting. He was selected as New York Educator of the Year (1992) and received the Distinguished Faculty Award for Diversity in Teaching in Higher Education (1998).

Defining Philosophy
- Pursuit of wisdom
- Begins with wonder
- Is a dynamic process
- Ultimate aims

Becoming a Critical Thinker
- Qualities of a critical thinker: Open-minded, curious, self-aware, analytical, creative, knowledgeable
- The critical-thinking model
- Stages in critical thinking

what is philosophy?

THINKING PHILOSOPHICALLY ABOUT LIFE

Understanding Arguments
- Structure of arguments
- Evaluating arguments
- Types of arguments:

  Deductive and Inductive

- Informal fallacies

Branches of Philosophy
- Metaphysics
- Epistemology
- Ethics
- Aesthetics
- Logic

chapter 1

◀ **What do you hope to learn?** These monolithic figures from Easter Island suggest the contemplative nature of philosophy, which can help you grapple with the big questions of life. This chapter introduces the scope and methods of the discipline.

1.1 Why Study Philosophy?

You are about to embark on a thrilling journey: the study of philosophy. Reading this book and taking a philosophy course is likely to be a memorable, life-altering experience for you. Why? One student explains:

> *In general, we as people don't usually think critically about the important areas of life, but it's these areas that help us to create a meaningful life. As an individual I was also one of those who didn't take the time to examine, ask questions, and think deeply about different perspectives on serious issues. As a result, studying Philosophy has helped me to become more open-minded and reflective about everything in my life.*

Tanya Louis

As Tanya notes, many of us get so caught up in the details and demands of life—deadlines, responsibilities, all the little tasks of living—that we don't make the time to step back and look at the whole picture. Why am I doing the things that I'm doing? In what direction am I headed? What does it all mean? Who am I? Who do I want to become? These questions penetrate the surface of life to confront the deeper currents lying beneath. But to achieve this more profound level of understanding, we need to recognize the need to go beyond the obvious. And we also need to be willing and open-minded enough to do this.

That's the unique mission of philosophy. Philosophy provides us with the motivation and the intellectual abilities required to explore life's most challenging issues. What *is* the meaning of my life? To what extent am I free and responsible for my choices? Facing moral dilemmas, what is the "right" thing to do? What is the relationship between my religious beliefs and other areas of my life? How do I gain genuine knowledge and ascertain truth? These questions, and others like them, are the core questions of life, and philosophy provides the map, compass, and tools needed to explore them.

In what ways will taking this philosophical journey affect your life? Here's one student's analysis:

> *Before taking this course I really never explored my thinking abilities: I only explored the obvious. Now that I've almost completed this introductory course in Philosophy, I feel I am more sophisticated in both thought and action. I realize that I react differently to situations; I think twice and evaluate circumstances more closely before I make decisions. Philosophy has helped me in my other courses, as it helped me to express myself more clearly in essays and speeches. From taking this course, I have grown as a person, and my mind is definitely not what it used to be.*

Ryan Malley

Studying philosophy in a serious and reflective way will *change you as a person.* Learning to think philosophically will inspire you to be more thoughtful, more open-minded, more attuned to the complexities and subtleties of life, more willing to think critically about yourself and all of life's important issues, and less willing to accept superficial interpretations and simplistic answers. It is very tempting for people *not* to think, to remain submerged in reality rather than aware of it, to be carried along by the current of events rather than creating their destiny through thoughtful, independent choices.

Philosophy is a training guide for your mind, showing you how to think in clear, analytic, and powerful ways. And, as Ryan notes, this high-level, sophisticated thinking will enable you to make thoughtful decisions, communicate more effectively, and grow as a person.

Studying philosophy will help you develop the understanding and insight you will need to make intelligent choices and fulfill your potential as an individual. To use a metaphor, you are an artist, creating your life portrait, and your paints and brush-strokes are the choices you make each day. How do you feel about the portrait you have created so far? Have you defined yourself as the person you always wanted to be, or are you a "work in progress"? Are you achieving your full potential as a human being, "actively exercising your soul's powers"—the ancient Greek definition of happiness (*eudaemonia*)? Do you possess a clear philosophy of life that acts as a guiding beacon, illuminating the whole of your life and showing you the path to wisdom and personal fulfillment? Creating an enlightened self-portrait is your preeminent responsibility in life, and though it is challenging work, it is well worth the effort. Your portrait is your contribution to the world, your legacy to present and future generations.

This is the special power of philosophy: to provide the conceptual tools required to craft a life inspiring in its challenges and rich in its fulfillment. Philosophy is *not* intended to limit your options or dictate your choices. Your responsibility as a student of philosophy is to explore, to reflect, to think critically—and then to create yourself in the image you have envisioned.

"Man is asked to make of himself what he is supposed to become to fulfill his destiny," the theologian Paul Tillich wrote. But how do we discover our destiny, the unique meaning of our lives? We must embark on a philosophical journey, a process of self-exploration and discovery, seeking answers to profound questions about our lives and illuminating the mysteries of our existence. Each of us strives to live a life of purpose, to fulfill our unique potential, and to achieve stellar accomplishments. It is the remarkable capability of our minds to reflect deeply and thoughtfully—to *think philosophically*—that enables us to pursue these goals. As the philosopher Bertrand Russell passionately expressed, "Thought is great and swift and free, the light of the world, and the chief glory of man."

What is the meaning of life? Hamlet, one of William Shakespeare's most famous characters, illustrates the philosophical mind at work. The character poses questions and searches for answers throughout the play. In this scene, he reflects upon the meaning of life and death. What gives your life meaning?

1.2 Defining Philosophy

Providing a precise definition of philosophy is not a simple task, in part because of the complex nature of philosophy's mission and in part because that mission has evolved over time. As we have begun to see, philosophy deals with the most complex, challenging, and profound questions in human life, questions that by their nature resist simple answers. In addition, the scope of philosophy has changed over the centuries. It began in ancient Greece as the "mother of all disciplines," encompassing the entire breadth of inquiry about humans and the universe they inhabit. Over time, as human knowledge expanded, distinct disciplines were established that specialized in understanding various dimensions of human experience. In the natural sciences, physics, biology, chemistry, and geology seek understanding of the natural world. The social sciences (psychology, sociology, anthropology, linguistics, political science, economics) seek to analyze, explicate, and propose better models for individual and collective human behavior. Philosophy has retained distinct areas of study that we will explore later in the chapter: *metaphysics, epistemology, ethics, social/political philosophy, aesthetics,* and *logic.* In addition, the evolving role of philosophy has been to continue examining the underlying principles and methodologies of other academic disciplines through the study of "philosophy of science," "philosophical psychology," "medical ethics," and so on.

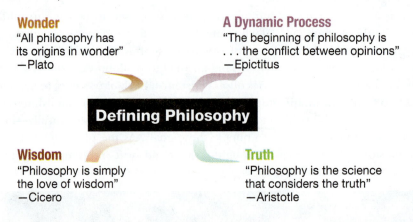

Wonder
"All philosophy has its origins in wonder" —Plato

A Dynamic Process
"The beginning of philosophy is . . . the conflict between opinions" —Epictitus

Defining Philosophy

Wisdom
"Philosophy is simply the love of wisdom" —Cicero

Truth
"Philosophy is the science that considers the truth" —Aristotle

Philosophy Is the Pursuit of Wisdom

> **Rightly defined, philosophy is simply the love of wisdom.**
> **CICERO**

The actual word *philosophy* is Greek in origin, and it is the composite of two Greek roots: *philein,* a Greek word for "love," and *sophia,* the Greek word for "wisdom." Taken together, they mean "the love or pursuit of wisdom." This definition is a good starting point for understanding the distinctive nature of philosophy. Philosophy is not merely a static compendium of great thoughts espoused by great thinkers—it is an activity that reflects passion, commitment, and intellectual ambition. The ultimate goal of this passionate activity is not mastering a certain amount of information but rather the achievement of "wisdom." What exactly is "wisdom"? Think of several people you know whom you would consider to be "wise": What qualities do they possess? It's likely that although they are knowledgeable regarding certain areas of life, it's their ability to *use* and *apply* this knowledge with great intelligence that distinguishes them. They are likely the kind of people who can get to the heart of a complex issue, who are able to generate genuinely creative solutions to challenging problems, who exhibit an insightful understanding of what it means to be human. These are undoubtedly people who are thoughtful and reflective, who are not afraid to confront the most difficult questions in life, who strive every day to develop themselves as astute thinkers and honorable individuals. These are people whom you admire and whom you would like to emulate. At the same time, wise people are usually intellectually humble: They don't fall under the spell of believing that they have all the answers, and instead approach the world with a childlike curiosity and eagerness to learn.

Viewing philosophy as the pursuit of wisdom was given eloquent expression by the female philosopher Perictione, who is thought to have lived around 300 B.C.E.:

> *Humanity came into being and exists in order to contemplate the principle of the nature of the whole. The function of wisdom is to gain possession of this very thing, and to contemplate the purpose of the things that are. Geometry, of course, and arithmetic, and the other theoretical studies and sciences are also concerned with the things that are, but wisdom is concerned with the most basic of these. Wisdom is concerned with all that is, just as sight is concerned with all that is visible and hearing with all that is audible. . . . Therefore, whoever is able to analyze all the kinds of being by reference to one and the same basic principle, and, in turn, from this principle to synthesize and enumerate the different kinds, this person seems to be the wisest and most true and, moreover, to have discovered a noble height from which he will be able to catch sight of God and all the things separated from God in serial rank and order.*

In this inspiring passage, Perictione gets right to the heart of being human and the nature of wisdom. Human life has a central purpose—to contemplate the profound essence of the universe—and wisdom is, in her mind, the divine gift we have to accomplish this. While various disciplines such as mathematics and science are concerned with determining specific knowledge of the universe, wisdom has a grander mission: understanding how and why the universe is the way it is, the core principles that underlie and govern the whole of experience. This Western concept of philosophy originated in ancient Greece in the work of Socrates, Plato, and Aristotle. We will be exploring their ideas in some depth as we journey through the history of philosophical thinking.

Of course, there have been many important thinkers since Socrates, Plato, and Aristotle, and there were even a number of insightful thinkers before them, the "pre-Socratics" who were known as *Sophos*, wise men and women who posed sophisticated and penetrating questions regarding the essential principles of human life and the natural world. In addition, there have been many significant thinkers in non-Western cultures. Although the primary focus of this text is on Western philosophy, we will also be examining key ideas from philosophers in non-Western cultures.

The *School of Athens*, painted by the Renaissance artist Raphael for the Vatican in Rome and reproduced on page 48, depicts the ancient Greek philosophers who first embodied the spirit of philosophy in the West. In the center of the painting, under the arch, Plato points toward the heavenly realm of the ideal while Aristotle gestures toward the earth. On the left, Socrates debates Xenophon. The "pre-Socratics" are also represented, including Epicurus, Pythagoras, Diogenes, and Ptolemy. These individuals are considered to be "heroes of philosophy" by professionals in the discipline. Although the "wise" people you know may not be professional philosophers, they may very well embody the *spirit* of philosophy that we will be considering in this book. Who are your intellectual heroes?

" **The beginning of wisdom is to desire it.**
SOLOMON IBN GABIROL

((• Listen to the **Podcast** *Alain DeBotton on Philosophy Within and Outside the Academy* on **mysearchlab.com**

" **He who knows he is a fool is not a great fool.**
CONFUCIUS

" **Let no young man delay the study of philosophy, and let no old man become weary of it; for it is never too early nor too late to care for the well being of the soul.**
EPICURUS

" **Philosophy means liberation from the two dimensions of routine, soaring above the well known, seeing it in new perspectives, arousing wonder and the wish to fly.**
WALTER KAUFMANN

Philosophy Begins with Wonder

Some definitions of philosophy focus on the *source* of philosophical thinking, the way philosophy encourages us to look both *deeper* and *wider*. Philosophy stimulates us to penetrate beneath the surface of daily experience while seeking a comprehensive, inclusive vision of reality.

The catalyst for thinking philosophically about one's life is often *wonder*, a search for *unity of knowledge*, a desire to answer the *great questions* of life. As Plato and Aristotle observe, philosophy begins with *wonder*, speculation, considering "what if?," asking that powerful question, "Why?" Instead of simply accepting life as it presents itself, philosophy seeks to probe beneath the surface, question the familiar, challenge "accepted wisdom." Where can we look for models of philosophical wonder? Children! Young children are brimming over with intellectual energy, blending innate curiosity, passionate convictions, and imaginative speculation: not coincidentally, the essential ingredients required for thinking critically and developing a philosophical perspective on the world. "Why?" is perhaps the most penetrating question in human language and thought, and children use it liberally, sometimes driving adults to distraction. Asking "Why?" shakes up complacent attitudes, forcing us to expose hidden assumptions and to articulate the rationale for our conclusions. And other questions can help us probe beyond the surface of everyday consciousness. Here's a brief sampler provided by my children, Jessie and Joshua, at very young ages: *Why did God create life? What is at the end of space? What happens after forever? Do people still love after they die? Suppose that animals could think just as well as we could, what would the world be like? Imagine that stuffed animals had feelings, how would you treat them? Why are bad people bad?*

Another catalyst for philosophy is the human desire for *synthesis* and *integration*, to "put all of the pieces together." As the contemporary American philosopher William Halverson observes, this drive toward integration is reflected in our concept of our world as a *uni* verse, the conviction that there are underlying principles of thought and reality that form the structure of our experience. Philosophy has always been driven by the desire to discover these primal principles and then to apply them to make human existence more intelligible. All of us have the responsibility to confront and try to answer these profound questions as we work to craft lives of meaning and purpose.

Philosophy Is a Dynamic Process

This definition probes the *dynamic* nature of philosophical thinking, a process that is *dialectical* in the sense that ideas are continually analyzed in terms of their opposites, with the ultimate goal of creating a more enlightened *synthesis*.

As Epictetus observes, the philosophical process is powered by conflict, bringing divergent opinions together into a dynamic interaction. Which ideas make most sense? Which are clearer? Best supported? Have greater explanatory power? Are consistent with other beliefs we know to be true? Are most comprehensive? *Why?* As we will see in the next chapter, this ongoing process of comparing and contrasting, analyzing and synthesizing, is at the heart of the Socratic Method, a powerful approach developed and used by Socrates that is characterized by relentless questioning, clear definitions, dialectical analysis, and critical evaluation. It is the process by which we can disentangle complex issues and distinguish more informed ways of thinking from less informed. Language is a key partner of thinking, as Wittgenstein notes: A confused, illogical, and sloppy use of language leads to confused, illogical, and sloppy thinking—and vice versa. Analogously, clarity and precision in our use of language contributes to clarity and precision in our thinking—and vice versa.

In its crusade to enlighten minds and inform choices, philosophy is not confined to the classroom or "ivory towers." The conclusions we reach by thinking philosophically have direct applications for how we live our lives in the real world. And because philosophy is committed to the truth rather than popular opinion, prevailing norms, or conventional wisdom, it means that we may indeed find ourselves, in the words of Spinoza, as "disturbers of the peace." In the case of Socrates, and other truth-seekers like him throughout the centuries, this passion for intellectual integrity and authentic lives had grave personal consequences.

The Ultimate Aim of Philosophy

Finally, philosophy can be defined in terms of the goal of philosophical thought, which is to improve the quality of our lives by enlightening our minds. Philosophy has grand and lofty aspirations, and this undoubtedly accounts for the fascination and high regard with which it has been held. Here is a brief sampling of some of the goals proposed by philosophers:

Are you willing to become a "disturber of the peace"? Philosophy gives us the tools to analyze complex issues and develop informed beliefs. These beliefs have direct applications for how we want to effect change in the world. What social issues are important to you? Are you ready to subject them to critical analysis and discussion?

- The complete liberty of the mind
- Freedom from all social, political, or religious prejudice
- To care for the well-being of the soul
- Answer the question, "What is it all about?"

Can philosophy really deliver on this ambitious promise? Perhaps a better question is, "Can any other discipline or approach to life do a more effective job than philosophy?" Philosophers—and many others—believe that philosophy is the one best hope we have to discover the truth to these profound questions and intimidating challenges. Philosophy is uniquely qualified, because of the historical scope of its vision and the conceptual and language tools that it employs, to help each person find his or her way to the truth of these issues. Virtually all people desire a liberated mind, an enlightened consciousness, a well-cared-for soul, a rich and fulfilling life. Philosophy provides the equipment you need to construct such a path for yourself: You need only to commit yourself to taking the philosophical journey.

1.3 Thinking Philosophically: Becoming a Critical Thinker

Socrates probably came closest to capturing the essence of philosophy when he issued a startling challenge that has reverberated through the centuries: "The unexamined life is not worth living." The ability to reflect on one's life and one's self is a distinctly human ability. Philosophy provides us with the intellectual tools to reflect with clarity and discipline, to critically evaluate the choices we have made, and to use this

> **Philosophy means the complete liberty of the mind, and therefore independence of all social, political, or religious prejudice.**
> **HENRI FREDERIC AMIEL**

> **Philosophy asks the simple question, what is it all about?**
> **ALFRED NORTH WHITEHEAD**

> **Philosophy should be responsive to human experience and yet critical of the defective thinking it sometimes encounters.**
> **MARTHA NUSSBAUM**

knowledge to make more enlightened choices in the future. The stakes are high: If we fail to make use of this unique ability to think philosophically about ourselves, then, according to Socrates, our lives have diminished potential.

To begin our journey of philosophical discovery, we must first distinguish between "having" a philosophy and "doing" philosophy. Every person "has" a philosophy of life—a collection of beliefs used to guide his or her thoughts and actions. For example, you may believe that it's wrong to needlessly kill living things, or you may believe that it's good to be kind to people in difficult circumstances. Such beliefs—and countless others that you have formed over the years of your life—influence the way you see the world and the choices that you make. You may not be aware of all your beliefs—some may be deeply buried in your unconsciousness—but they can still influence you. For instance, you may instinctively help an elderly person cross the street, without being consciously aware that your action reflects a deeply imbedded belief of yours.

Of course, an individual's philosophy of life can also contain beliefs that are wildly inaccurate, biased, or destructive. For example, racist or sexist beliefs can be factors in a person's philosophy of life—although many people would consider such beliefs to be unenlightened and destructive. Or someone might be convinced that aliens are living among us, planning to take over the human race—a belief that most of us would consider highly questionable.

"Doing" philosophy—thinking philosophically—means thinking critically about your beliefs to ensure that they are the most accurate and enlightened beliefs possible. For example, if your philosophy of life includes stereotyped beliefs about other races or genders, thinking critically about them would involve asking such questions as:

- What is the factual evidence or reasons for these beliefs? Do I have a compelling rationale for saying that I "know" them to be true?
- How did these beliefs originate? What circumstances gave rise to these beliefs?
- Are these beliefs logical or illogical, rational or irrational?
- If I were a member of this racial group or gender, would I still endorse these beliefs? Why or why not?
- Are there more enlightened, accurate beliefs than mine that I should consider?

> **Philosophy is the science which considers the truth.**
> ARISTOTLE

> **The first step toward philosophy is doubt.**
> DENIS DIDEROT

Thinking philosophically—"doing" philosophy—involves many advanced forms of thinking that we will be exploring in this book and that you will be developing in your philosophy class. But a productive place to begin is with *your* philosophy of life. The questions included in the following "Thinking Philosophically" box are designed to help you articulate some of the basic building blocks of your philosophy of life. You should record your responses in a philosophy journal or notebook that you keep for this course. Or your professor may request that the activity be completed in a form to be handed in or e-mailed. Here is a sample student response to the question, "What moral beliefs influence your choices?"

I firmly believe that all animals are sentient beings, and therefore I am opposed to their being used as inanimate raw material in our

"Who am I?" "What is a self?" The philosophical journey requires self-examination. Your responsibility as a critical thinker is to explore, reflect, and then create yourself in the image you have envisioned.

mass-production agricultural system. This matter spans a much broader area than simply eating meat. Although all animal suffering is deplorable, it is important to realize that there are degrees of suffering, and in many cases animals used for the production of milk or eggs endure more pain and distress, for longer periods of time, than those raised primarily for slaughter. Many people fight against animal experimentation based on principle, and although I think they are to be commended, very often they are unaware of the strict husbandry rules that strive for humane treatment in the research field, while the hens that lay their breakfast eggs are awarded no such luxury and live in dark, dirty, overcrowded battery cages, debeaked and unable to move, laying an average of 250 eggs per year versus a natural 25, all awaiting their final two-week fast (water withheld in addition to food) to induce a final molt and lay prior to slaughter. For anything less would be quite uneconomical. I have been a vegetarian for ten years, and vegan for the last four, yet I struggle with issues of animal welfare daily. Although I sometimes fantasize of myself as Jainist, I am aware of the impossibility of leading a completely cruelty-free life and so strive to make choices that will reduce the amount of animal suffering for which I am directly responsible.

Kasia Zarebska

> **I don't know what I think until I see myself write.**
> ANNIE DILLARD

> **The relation of word to thought, and the creation of new concepts, is a complex, delicate, and enigmatic process unfolding in our soul.**
> LEO TOLSTOY

> **I write to understand as much as to be understood.**
> ELIE WIESEL

You may be wondering why it is necessary to record your thoughts in writing if thinking is a mental activity. The answer is that writing is a vehicle for creating and communicating your ideas, a catalyst for your intellectual development. The process of writing stimulates your mind, helps shape your thinking, and enlarges your understanding of the world. Just as significantly, writing creates a permanent record—a "snapshot"—of your thinking process at a specific point in time. You can return to your thinking snapshot as often as you wish, evaluate its logic and coherence, and use it as a foundation on which to build a more insightful understanding. The **Thinking Philosophically** boxes in this book are designed as springboards for your "thinking in writing" about profound ideas.

Your philosophy notebook can be an actual book or a computer file; what matters is developing the discipline and commitment to engage in the process, thinking deeply, and expressing your ideas as clearly and specifically as possible. Once you have established this pattern of thinking and writing, you will find that it will become integrated into your life in a natural and profound way, leading you to deeper insights, creative ideas, and enriched meaning. Make your philosophy notebook an integral part of your life; let it remind you

---

thinking philosophically

WHAT IS YOUR PHILOSOPHY OF LIFE?

Everybody has a philosophy of life. Identify some of the foundation beliefs that form your philosophy of life, using these questions as a guide. Express your ideas as completely and clearly as you can. Think deeply and beyond superficialities and refuse to be satisfied with the first idea that you have.

- What do you most value in life? Why?
- What moral beliefs influence your choices and your behavior toward others? How do you determine the "right" thing to do?
- What role do religious beliefs play in your life? Do you believe in "God"? Why or why not? Is there an afterlife? If so, what is the path to it?
- What gives your life meaning? What is the purpose of your life? What do you hope to achieve in your life?
- How do we find truth? How do you know when you "know" something is true? What is an example of something you know to be true?
- Do you believe that your choices are free? Do you hold yourself responsible for your choices?
- What do you consider to be "beautiful"? Why? What is the function of art? Should "extreme" forms of artistic expression be censored? Why or why not?
- Are all people entitled to basic human rights? Why? What is justice?
- What are other important beliefs in your life?

to strive to think well. Expressing your ideas in your philosophy notebook should provide a stimulating, liberating experience and help you formulate and articulate your thinking.

Qualities of a Critical Thinker

> **He who will not reason is a bigot; he who cannot is a fool; and he who dares not is a slave.**
> **WILLIAM DRUMMOND**

> **Most people would rather die than think—in fact they do!**
> **BERTRAND RUSSELL**

Your responses to the previous Thinking Philosophically activity are a sampler of your "philosophy of life." To "do" philosophy, you have to question, scrutinize, explore, evaluate, analyze, synthesize, and apply these beliefs. You have to use higher-order thinking abilities and sophisticated language skills to determine the worthiness of these beliefs. Becoming a *critical thinker* changes qualitatively the way a person views the world, processes information, and makes decisions.

The word *critical* comes from the Greek word for "critic" (*kritikos*), which means to question, to make sense of, to be able to analyze. It is by questioning, making sense of, and analyzing that you examine your thinking and the thinking of others. These critical activities aid us in reaching the best possible conclusions and decisions. The word *critical* is also related to the word *criticize*, which means to question and evaluate. Unfortunately, the ability to criticize is often used destructively, to tear down someone else's thinking. Criticism, however, can also be *constructive*—analyzing for the purpose of developing a better understanding of what is going on. You need to engage in *constructive criticism* as you develop your ability to think critically.

The best way to develop a clear and concrete idea of the critical thinker you want to become is to think about people you have known who can serve as critical thinking models. For example, I've been fortunate to have studied with a number of teachers who taught me what it means to be a critical thinker through the example of their lives. I considered them to be brilliant critical thinkers because of the power of their minds and their commitment to excellence. Here are some qualities that characterized these and other expert critical thinkers:

- *Open-minded:* In discussions, they listen carefully to every viewpoint, evaluating each perspective carefully and fairly.
- *Knowledgeable:* When they offer an opinion, it's always based on facts or evidence. On the other hand, if they lack knowledge of the subject, they acknowledge this.
- *Mentally active:* They take initiative and actively use their intelligence to confront problems and meet challenges, instead of simply responding passively to events.

- *Curious:* They explore situations with probing questions that penetrate beneath the surface of issues, instead of being satisfied with superficial explanations.
- *Independent thinkers:* They are not afraid to disagree with the group opinion. They develop well-supported beliefs through thoughtful analysis, instead of uncritically "borrowing" the beliefs of others or simply going along with the crowd.
- *Skilled discussants:* They are able to discuss ideas in an organized and

thinking philosophically

WHO ARE YOUR MODELS OF CRITICAL THINKING?

Whom would you identify as an expert critical thinker? What qualities from the list on this page does he or she exhibit? For each critical thinking quality, write down a brief example involving the person. Identifying such people helps us visualize the kind of people we'd like to emulate. As you think your way through this book, you will be creating a *portrait* of the kind of critical thinker you are striving to become, a *blueprint* you can use to direct your development and chart your progress.

intelligent way. Even when the issues are controversial, they listen carefully to opposing viewpoints and respond thoughtfully.

- *Insightful:* They are able to get to the heart of the issue or problem. While others may be distracted by details, they are able to zero in on the essence, seeing the "forest" as well as the "trees."
- *Self-aware:* They are aware of their own biases and are quick to point them out and take them into consideration when analyzing a situation.
- *Creative:* They can break out of established patterns of thinking and approach situations from innovative directions.
- *Passionate:* They have a passion for understanding and are always striving to see issues and problems with more clarity.

The Process of Critical Thinking

A critical thinker is someone who approaches life in an informed and reflective way. This approach is one that you can use in virtually every area of your life as you work to understand your experience and make informed decisions. A critical thinking approach is also appropriate in all the various academic disciplines. Understanding history, psychology, economics, biology, or any other field of study involves much more than mastering that discipline's accumulated knowledge. Genuine understanding means using your critical thinking abilities to understand how each discipline organizes experience, provides explanations, applies concepts, and constructs knowledge. A critical thinking approach to the academic disciplines thus involves learning how to "think like a historian," "think like a psychologist," and so on.

The same is true of philosophy. "Thinking philosophically"—what we have designated as *doing philosophy*—involves thinking critically about the unique areas of experience with which philosophy is concerned, areas that include the most fundamental questions and issues in human experience. What sets philosophy apart from other academic disciplines is that they all have their roots in philosophy, the "mother" of all disciplines. The same is true for critical thinking—the abilities and attitudes that characterize a critical thinker originated for the most part in philosophical inquiry.

Let's examine this process in action by exploring how a critical thinker approaches a philosophical issue such as *free will*. It is the synthesis of critical thinking with philosophical subjects such as "free will" that leads to "thinking philosophically." The process of learning to think philosophically requires ongoing practice and reflection. The following critical thinking model will help you see philosophical thinking in operation. We will be using the model to think about an important issue that confronts every human being: "Are people capable of choosing freely?"

1. State Your Initial Point of View

Reasoning always begins with a point of view. As a critical thinker and aspiring philosopher, you need to take thoughtful positions and express your views with confidence. Using this statement as a starting point: "I believe (or don't believe) that people can choose freely because. . . ." Here is a sample response:

> *I believe that people are capable of choosing freely because when I am faced with choosing among a number of possibilities, I really have the feeling that it is up to me to make the choice that I want to.*

> **"** For every complex question there's a simple answer—and it is clever, neat, and wrong. **"**
> **H. L. MENCKEN**

> **"** Just like anything else, thinking skills require upkeep. If they aren't nourished, they'll fade away. **"**
> **DAVID PERKINS**

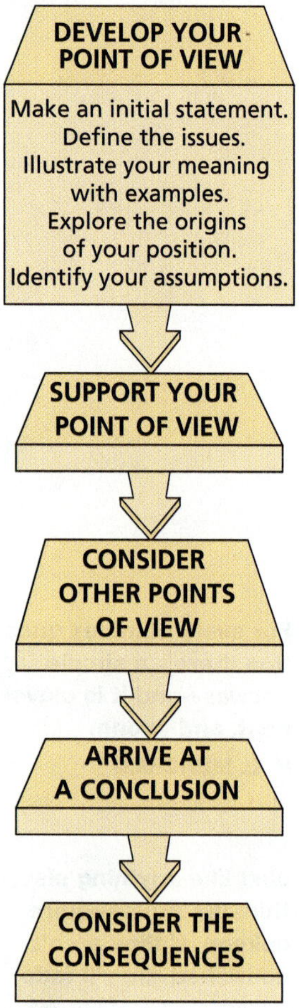

DEVELOP YOUR
POINT OF VIEW

Make an initial statement.
Define the issues.
Illustrate your meaning
with examples.
Explore the origins
of your position.
Identify your assumptions.

SUPPORT YOUR
POINT OF VIEW

CONSIDER
OTHER POINTS
OF VIEW

ARRIVE AT
A CONCLUSION

CONSIDER THE
CONSEQUENCES

Figure 1-1
Critical Thinking Model

2. Define Your Point of View More Clearly

After stating your initial point of view, define the issues more clearly and specifically. The language that we use has multiple levels of meaning, and it is often not clear precisely what meaning(s) people are expressing. To avoid misunderstandings and sharpen your own thinking, you must clarify the key concepts as early as possible. In this case, the key concept is "choosing freely." Begin by completing the following statement: "From my point of view, the concept of 'choosing freely' means...." Here is a sample response:

From my point of view, the concept of "choosing freely" means that when you are faced with a number of alternatives, you are able to make your selection based solely on what you decide, not because you are being forced by other influences.

3. Give an Example of Your Point of View

Once your point of view is clarified, you should provide an example that illustrates your meaning. The process of forming and defining concepts involves the process of *generalizing* (identifying general qualities) and the process of *interpreting* (locating specific examples). Here is a sample response:

An example of a free choice I made was deciding what area to major in. There are a number of career directions I could have chosen, but I chose my major entirely on my own, without being forced by other influences.

4. Explore the Origin of Your Point of View

To fully understand and critically evaluate your point of view, you must review its history. How did the point of view develop? Have you always held this view, or did it develop over time? This sort of analysis will help you understand how your perspective regarding this issue was formed. Here is a sample response:

I used to believe that everything happened because it had to, because it was determined. Then, when I was in high school, I got involved with the "wrong crowd" and developed some bad habits. I stopped doing schoolwork and even stopped attending most classes. I was on the brink of failing when I suddenly came to my senses and said to myself, "This isn't what I want for my life." Through sheer willpower, I turned everything around. I changed my friends, improved my habits, and ultimately graduated with flying colors. From that time on I knew that I had the power of free choice and that it was up to me to make the right choices.

5. Identify Your Assumptions

Assumptions are beliefs, often unstated, that underlie your point of view. Many disputes occur and remain unresolved because the people involved do not recognize or express their assumptions. For example, in the very emotional debate over abortion, when people who are opposed to abortion call their opponents "murderers," they are assuming the fetus, at any stage of development from the fertilized egg onward, is a "human life," because murder refers to the taking of a human life. On the other hand, when people in favor of abortion call their opponents "moral fascists," they are assuming that antiabortionists are merely interested in imposing their narrow moral views on others.

Thus all parties must identify clearly the assumptions that form the foundation of their points of view. They may still end up disagreeing, but at least they will know what they are arguing about. Thinking about the issue that we have been exploring, respond by completing the following statement: "When I say that I believe (or don't believe) in free choice, I am assuming that. . . ." Here is a sample response:

> *When I say that I believe in free choice, I am assuming that people are often presented with different alternatives to choose from, and I am also assuming that they are able to select freely any of these alternatives independent of any influences.*

6. Offer the Reasons, Evidence, and Arguments That Support Your Point of View

Everybody has beliefs. What distinguishes informed beliefs from uninformed beliefs is the quality of the reasons, evidence, and arguments that support the beliefs. In the next section, "Understanding Arguments," we will take a closer look at how to evaluate the strength of your reasons, evidence, and arguments. Here is an example of an argument supporting the writer's belief in free choice:

> *Our society is based on the possibility of free choice. Otherwise, we wouldn't be able to hold people responsible for their choices and the consequences of these choices. But we do hold people responsible, suggesting that the reality of free choice is an integral part of how humans see themselves.*

7. Consider Other Points of View

One of the hallmarks of critical thinkers—and philosophers—is that they strive to view situations from perspectives other than their own, to "think empathetically" within other viewpoints, particularly those of people who disagree with their own. If we stay entrenched in our own narrow ways of viewing the world, the development of our minds will be severely limited. Empathetic thinking is the only way to achieve a full understanding of life's complexities. In working to understand other points of view, we need to identify the reasons, evidence, and arguments that have brought people to these conclusions. Here is a sample response:

> *Another point of view on this issue might be that our choices are influenced by people around us, although we may not be fully aware of it. For example, we may go along with a group decision of our friends, mistakenly thinking that we are making an independent choice. Or in a more general way, our ways of thinking may have been conditioned by our family and culture over time, so that while we think we're making free choices, we're really not.*

Of course, simply listening and trying to understand other perspectives is not enough: We need to *respond* to other points of view, explaining why we are unconvinced by these conflicting views and the arguments that support them. Here's a possible response:

> *I agree that there may sometimes be influences on our thinking and choices of which we are not aware. Sometimes when we look back we can see that our reactions in a given situation were influenced by unconscious motivations or by*

*social conditioning. But I believe that we can escape the influence of these factors by **becoming aware** and choosing to transcend their power over us. This is where critical thinking comes in: using our thinking abilities to understand ourselves and the forces at work on us so that we can make genuinely free choices.*

8. Arrive at a Conclusion, Decision, Solution, or Prediction

The ultimate purpose of critical thinking is to reach an informed and successful conclusion, decision, solution, or prediction. With respect to the sample issue we have been considering— determining whether we can make free choices—the goal is to achieve a thoughtful conclusion. This is a complex process of analysis and synthesis in which we consider all points of view; evaluate the supporting reasons, evidence, and arguments; and then construct our most informed conclusion. We may find that our initial point of view changes as we work through the steps. The next section, "Understanding Arguments," will help you evaluate the strength of your conclusions. Here is a sample response:

After examining different points of view and critically evaluating the reasons, evidence, and arguments that support the various perspectives, my conclusion about free choice is that we are capable of making free choices but that our freedom is sometimes limited. For example, many of our actions are conditioned by our past experience, and we are often influenced by other people without being aware of it. To make free choices, we need to become aware of these influences and then decide what course of action we want to choose. As long as we are unaware of these influences, they can limit our ability to make free, independent choices.

9. Consider the Consequences

The final step in the reasoning process is to determine the consequences of our conclusion, decision, solution, or prediction. The consequences refer to what is likely to happen if our conclusion is adopted. Looking ahead in this fashion is helpful not simply for anticipating the future but for evaluating the present. Here is a sample response:

The consequences of believing in free choice involve increasing personal responsibility and showing people how to increase their freedom. The first consequence is that if people are able to make free choices, then they are responsible for the results of their choices. They can't blame other people, bad luck, or events "beyond their control." They have to accept responsibility. The second consequence is

---

thinking philosophically

APPLYING THE CRITICAL THINKING MODEL

Identify an issue that is important to you and apply the critical thinking model to analyze it:

- What is your initial point of view?
- How can you define your point of view more clearly?
- What is an example of your point of view?
- What is the origin of your point of view?
- What are your assumptions?
- What are the reasons, evidence, and arguments that support your point of view?
- What are other points of view on this issue?
- What is your conclusion, decision, solution, or prediction?
- What are the consequences?

that although our freedom can be limited by influences of which we are unaware, we can increase our freedom by becoming aware of these influences and then deciding what we want to do. On the other hand, if people are not able to make free choices, then they are not responsible for what they do, nor are they able to increase their freedom. This could lead people to adopt an attitude of resignation and apathy.

Stages in Critical Thinking

Most people in our culture are socialized to believe that knowledge and truth are absolute and unchanging. One major goal of social institutions, including family, the school system, and religion, is to transfer the knowledge that has been developed over the ages. Under this model, the role of learners is to absorb this information passively, like sponges. However, achieving knowledge and truth is a complicated process. Instead of simply relying on the testimony of authorities like parents, teachers, textbooks, and religious leaders, critical thinkers have a responsibility to engage *actively* in the learning process and participate in developing their own understanding of the world.

The need for this active approach to knowing is underscored by the fact that authorities often disagree about the true nature of a given situation or the best course of action. It is not uncommon, for example, for doctors to disagree about a diagnosis, for economists to differ on the state of the economy, for researchers to present contrasting views on the best approach to curing cancer, for psychiatrists to disagree on whether a convicted felon is a menace to society or a harmless victim of social forces, and for religions to present conflicting approaches to achieving eternal life.

What do we do when experts disagree? As a critical thinker, you must analyze and evaluate all the available information, develop your own well-reasoned beliefs, and recognize when you don't have sufficient information to arrive at well-reasoned beliefs. You must realize that these beliefs may evolve over time as you gain information or improve your insight.

Although there are compelling reasons to view knowledge and truth in this way, many people resist it. Either they take refuge in a belief in the absolute, unchanging nature of knowledge and truth, as presented by the appropriate authorities, or they conclude that there is no such thing as knowledge or truth and that trying to seek either is a futile enterprise. Some beliefs *are* better than others, not because an authority has proclaimed them so but because they can be analyzed in terms of the following criteria:

Watch the **Video** *Definition of Epistemology* on **mysearchlab.com**

- How effectively do your beliefs *fully explain what is taking place?* The purpose of our beliefs is to help us make sense of our experience, to relate and communicate clearly with others, to inform our decisions and help us reach our goals. The most effective beliefs are usually those that provide the fullest and most accurate explanations for us, and this is an essential criteria to apply when we are deciding which beliefs to adopt.

- To what extent are these beliefs *consistent with other beliefs* you have about the world? When we are evaluating the worthiness of prospective beliefs, an important consideration is to what extent these new beliefs are consistent with other beliefs of ours which we have already evaluated as being well grounded. If the new beliefs conflict with our already established beliefs, then we need to determine which set of beliefs are the most accurate.

- To what extent are your beliefs supported by *sound reasons* and *compelling evidence* derived from *reliable sources?* Everybody has beliefs; the accuracy and usefulness of our beliefs are determined by the strength and relevance of the reasons and evidence that support these beliefs. A simple test for this is to ask yourself why you have the beliefs you do. If your beliefs are well grounded, you should be able to provide a clear explanation of the reasons and evidence that led you to your beliefs. If you are not able to provide this sort of compelling justification, that's a warning sign that you need to do some more investigation.

- How effectively do your beliefs help you *predict what will happen* in the future? Beliefs that explain what happened in the past have value, but beliefs that are able to predict what will happen in the future have even more. Predicting the future provides much more compelling evidence for beliefs than simply providing an account of past events, an explanation that may be difficult to prove one way or another.

- To what extent are your beliefs *falsifiable?* Another important criterion for evaluating your beliefs is whether the beliefs are *falsifiable.* This means that you can state conditions—tests—under which the beliefs could be disproved, and the beliefs nevertheless pass those tests. For example, if you believe that you can create ice cubes by placing water-filled trays in a freezer, it is easy to see how you can conduct an experiment to determine if your belief is accurate. If you believe that your destiny is related to the positions of the planets and stars (as astrologers do), it is not clear how you can conduct an experiment to determine if your belief is accurate. Because a belief that is not falsifiable can never be proved, such a belief is of questionable accuracy.

A critical thinker sees knowledge and truth as goals that we are striving to achieve, processes that we are all actively involved in as we construct our understanding of the world. Developing accurate knowledge about the world is often a challenging process of exploration and analysis in which our understanding grows and evolves over a period of time.

The road to becoming a critical thinker is a challenging journey that involves passing through different *stages of critical thinking* in order to achieve an effective understanding of the world. These stages, ranging from simple to complex, characterize people's thinking and the way they understand their world. A critical thinker is a person who has progressed through all of the stages to achieve a sophisticated understanding of the nature of knowledge. This framework is based on the work of Harvard psychologist William Perry (*Forms of Intellectual and Ethical Development in the College Years: A Scheme*), who used in-depth research to create a developmental model of human thought. This text uses a condensed three-stage version of Perry's framework:

Stage 1: The Garden of Eden

Stage 2: Anything Goes

Stage 3: Thinking Critically

An individual may be at different stages simultaneously, depending on the subject or area of experience. For example, a person may be at an advanced stage in one area of life (academic work) but at a less sophisticated stage in another area (romantic relationships or conception of morality). In general, however, people tend to operate predominantly within one stage in most areas of their lives.

Stage 1: The Garden of Eden

People in the Garden of Eden stage of thinking tend to see the world in terms of black and white, right and wrong. How do they determine what is right, what to believe? The "authorities" *tell* them. Just like in the biblical Garden of Eden, knowledge is absolute, unchanging, and in the sole possession of authorities. Ordinary people can never determine the truth for themselves; they must rely on the experts. If someone disagrees with what they have been told by the authorities, then that person *must* be wrong. There is no possibility of compromise or negotiation.

Who are the authorities? The first authorities we encounter are usually our parents. When parents are rooted in this stage of thinking, they expect children to do as they're told. Parents are the authorities, and the role of children is to benefit from their parents' years of experience, their store of knowledge, and their position of authority. Similarly, when children enter a school system built on the foundation of Stage 1 thinking (as most school systems are), they are likely to be told, "We have the questions and the answers; your role is to learn them, not ask questions of your own"—an approach that runs counter to children's natural curiosity.

People in this Garden of Eden stage of thinking become dissatisfied when they realize that they can't simply rely on authorities to tell them what to think and believe because in almost every arena—medicine, religion, economics, psychology, education, science, law, child-rearing—authorities often disagree with each other. This phenomenon poses a mortal threat to Stage 1 thinking. If the authorities disagree with each other, then how do we figure out what (and whom) to believe? Stage 1 thinkers try to deal with this contradiction by maintaining that *my* authorities know more than *your* authorities. But if we are willing to think clearly and honestly, this explanation simply doesn't hold up: We have to explain *why* we choose to believe one authority over another. And as soon as that happens, we have transcended Stage 1 thinking. Just as Adam and Eve could not go back to blind, uncritical acceptance of authority once they had tasted the fruit of the Tree of the Knowledge of Good and Evil, so it is nearly impossible to return to Stage 1 after recognizing its oversimplifying inadequacies.

Stage 2: Anything Goes

Once one has rejected the dogmatic, authoritarian framework of Stage 1, the temptation in Stage 2 is to go to the opposite extreme and believe that anything goes. The reasoning is something like this: If authorities are not infallible and we can't trust their expertise, then no one point of view is ultimately any better than any other. In Stage 1, the authorities could resolve such disputes, but if their opinion is on the same level as yours and mine, then there is no rational way to resolve differences.

In the tradition of philosophy, such a view is known as *relativism*: the truth is relative to any individual or situation, and there is no objective, universal standard we can use to decide which beliefs make the most sense. Take the example of fashion. You may believe that an attractive presentation includes loose-fitting clothing in muted colors, a natural hairstyle, and a minimum of makeup and jewelry. Someone else might prefer tight-fitting black clothing, gelled hair, tattoos, and body piercings. In Stage 2 thinking, there's no way to evaluate these or any other fashion preferences: They are simply "matters of taste." And, in fact, if you examine past photographs of yourself and what you considered to be "attractive" years ago, this relativistic point of view probably makes some sense.

Although Stage 2 thinking may be appropriate in matters of taste, it is not appropriate in most areas of life where some beliefs are clearly more informed than others. In fact, when we think things through, it's obvious that the Stage 2 "Anything Goes" level of thinking simply doesn't work because it leads to absurd conclusions that run counter to our deeply felt conviction that some beliefs *are* better than other beliefs in most areas of life. So while Stage 2 may represent a slight advance over Stage 1 in sophistication and complexity, it's clear to a discerning thinker that a further advance to the next stage is necessary.

Stage 3: Thinking Critically

The two opposing perspectives of Stages 1 and 2 find their synthesis in Stage 3, Thinking Critically. When people achieve this level of understanding, they recognize that some viewpoints *are* better than other viewpoints, not simply because authorities say so but because there are *standards* or *criteria* we can use to evaluate the accuracy of beliefs, including those we mentioned earlier:

- How effectively do your beliefs *fully explain what is taking place?*
- To what extent are these beliefs *consistent with other beliefs* you have about the world?
- To what extent are your beliefs supported by *sound reasons* and *compelling evidence* derived from *reliable sources?*
- How effectively do your beliefs help you *predict what will happen* in the future?
- To what extent are your beliefs *falsifiable?*

These are the same standards that we will be using in this text to evaluate various philosophical theories. As a student of philosophy, your challenge is not simply to *learn* about the theories philosophers have developed to help us make sense of our human experience and the world in which we live: your responsibility is also to *evaluate* the strengths and weaknesses of these various theories, so that you can decide what philosophical positions *you* want to adopt. And by working towards this goal of developing informed perspectives on the world, you will also be in a position to explain *why* you have committed yourself to the beliefs that you have.

At the same time, people in this Critical Thinking stage are open-minded toward other viewpoints, especially those that disagree with theirs. They recognize that there are often a number of legitimate perspectives on complex issues, and they accept the validity of these perspectives to the extent that they are supported by persuasive reasons and evidence.

Consider a more complicated issue, like euthanasia. A Stage 3 thinker approaches this as she approaches all issues: trying to understand all of the different viewpoints on the issue, evaluating the reasons that support each of these viewpoints, and then coming to her own thoughtful conclusion. When asked, she can explain the rationale for her viewpoint, but she also respects differing viewpoints that are supported by legitimate reasons, even though she feels her viewpoint makes more sense. In addition, a Stage 3 thinker maintains an open mind, always willing to consider new evidence that might convince her to modify or even change her position.

But while people in the Thinking Critically stage are actively open to different perspectives, they also *commit* themselves to definite points of view and are confident in explaining the reasons and evidence that have led them to their conclusions. Being open-minded is not the same thing as being intellectually wishy-washy. In addition to having clearly defined views, Stage 3 thinkers are always willing to listen to people who disagree with them. In fact, they actively seek out opposing viewpoints because they know that this is the only way to achieve the clearest, most insightful, most firmly grounded understanding. They recognize that their views may evolve over time as they learn more.

Becoming a Stage 3 thinker is a worthy goal, and it is the only way to adequately answer Socrates' challenge to examine our lives thoughtfully and honestly. To live a life of reflection and action, of open-mindedness and commitment, of purpose and fulfillment, requires the full development of our intellectual abilities and positive traits of character.

Stages of Critical Thinking

Stage 1: The Garden of Eden

Knowledge is clear, certain, and absolute and is provided by authorities. Our role is to learn and accept information from authorities without question or criticism. Anyone who disagrees with the authorities must be wrong.

Stage 2: Anything Goes

Because authorities often disagree with each other, no one really "knows" what is true or right. All beliefs are of equal value, and there is no way to determine whether one belief makes more sense than another belief.

Stage 3: Thinking Critically

Some viewpoints *are* better than other viewpoints, not because authorities say so but because there are compelling reasons to support these viewpoints. We have a responsibility to explore every perspective, evaluate the supporting reasons for each, and develop our own informed conclusions that we are prepared to modify or change based on new information or better insight.

1.4 Understanding Arguments

Thinking philosophically requires the ability to analyze your own reasoning as well as the reasoning of others. As one of the central branches of philosophy, **logic** seeks to establish the rules of correct reasoning, clear understanding, and valid argumentation. It addresses such questions as, **What are the principles of correct reasoning** and **How do people use incorrect reasoning to reach false conclusions**? Over the centuries, philosophers working in the field of logic have systematized the study of reasoning, developing it into a powerful and rewarding system of analysis. This section presents a brief practical introduction to the more structured field of logic as represented in the way we construct and evaluate arguments.

((•⊸ **Listen** to the **Podcast**
*Finding Equality
Through Logic* on
mysearchlab.com

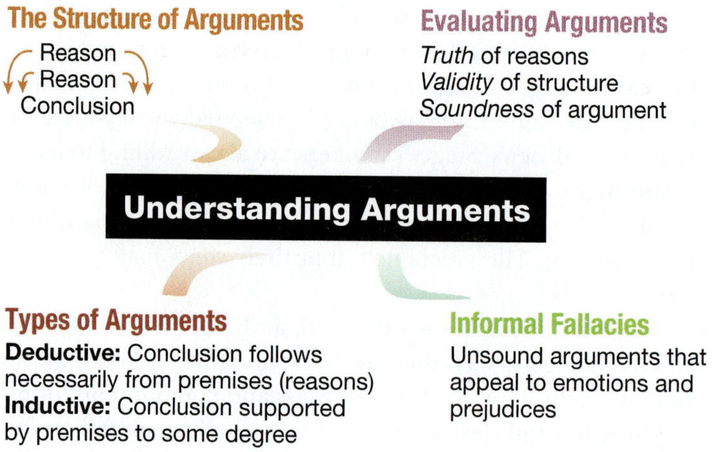

The Structure of Arguments

Reason
Reason
Conclusion

Evaluating Arguments

Truth of reasons
Validity of structure
Soundness of argument

Understanding Arguments

Types of Arguments

Deductive: Conclusion follows necessarily from premises (reasons)
Inductive: Conclusion supported by premises to some degree

Informal Fallacies

Unsound arguments that appeal to emotions and prejudices

The Structure of Arguments

Katherine: Did you hear about the group of animal-rights activists who were sentenced to two years in prison for breaking into a laboratory where they experiment on animals? All they wanted to do was rescue those unfortunate creatures—which they did. That's no reason for convicting them of breaking and entering, robbery, and malicious destruction of property. And a sentence of two years . . . you must agree that's crazy! After all, even people convicted of serious crimes often don't get punished like that. Everything I know about the case leads me to believe that they should receive a public service award for what they did, not a prison sentence. I believe that causing animals pain by experimenting on them is morally wrong, and it is for that reason I conclude that you sometimes have to act on your conscience even if it conflicts with the law.

Maria: Well, first of all, they did know the risks going in. And secondly, they did break the law and effectively destroyed many of the experiments the lab was working on. Without the animals, they're going to have to start over. As a result, I don't think two years is too harsh a sentence. After all, suppose that a group you didn't agree with broke in and caused damage to a business—would you be so sympathetic then? Doesn't that suggest that what they did was wrong and they ought to be punished? Furthermore, don't we have to set a clear example to society that illegal and destructive actions will not be tolerated, no matter what the reason?

This brief exchange is an illustration of two people engaging in *dialogue,* a systematic exchange of ideas. Participating in this sort of dialogue with others is one of the keys to thinking critically because it encourages you to see issues from various perspectives and to develop reasons to support your conclusions. It is this last quality of thinking critically—supporting conclusions with reasons—that we will be exploring in this section. When we offer reasons to support a conclusion, we are presenting an **argument**.

In common speech, "argument" usually refers to a dispute or quarrel between people, often involving intense feelings (for example: "I got into a terrible argument

Argument A form of thinking in which certain statements (**reasons**) are offered in support of another statement (a **conclusion**).

with the idiot who hit the back of my car"). In philosophy, an argument is a form of thinking in which certain statements (**reasons** or **premises**) are offered in support of another statement (a **conclusion**).

In the dialogue between Katherine and Maria, each person presents an argument about what constitutes a just punishment for the illegal actions a group of animal rights activists. Katherine's argument can be summarized as follows:

Reason: When they acted to remove the animals from the testing laboratory, the group believed they were taking an ethically correct action.

Reason: There are other more serious crimes for which the offenders don't receive such stiff sentences.

Reason: Sometimes you have to follow the dictates of your conscience even if that means disagreeing with an existing law, and my conscience tells me that causing animals unnecessary pain is wrong and should be halted.

Conclusion: Therefore, a two-year sentence is an unjust punishment for the actions they committed.

Maria's opposing argument can also be framed in terms of reasons and a conclusion:

Reason: The group did know, or should have known, the risks (and potential punishment) when they took action against the laboratory.

Reason: The group did in fact break the law and destroyed experiments that the laboratory had been conducting.

Reason: Katherine might come to a different conclusion if she did not agree with the reason or "cause" that was motivating the group.

Reason: Sometimes we have to set a clear example to society that illegal and destructive actions will not be tolerated, no matter what the reason.

Conclusion: I don't think that two years is too harsh a sentence.

Our language provides guidance in our efforts to identify reasons and conclusions. Certain key words, known as **cue words**, signal that a reason is being offered in support of a conclusion or that a conclusion is being announced on the basis of certain reasons. For example, in the brief exchange between Katherine and Maria, here are some cue words and phrases that signal a reason is being offered in support of a conclusion: *it's for that reason; after all; first of all; secondly; furthermore.* And here are some cue words and phrases that signal that a conclusion is being offered based on certain reasons: *you must agree; leads me to believe; I conclude; as a result; doesn't that suggest.* Here is a list of some other commonly used cue words for reasons and conclusions:

Reasons or **premises** Statements that support another statement (known as a **conclusion**), justify it, or make it more probable.

Conclusion A statement that explains, asserts, or predicts on the basis of statements (known as **reasons** or **premises**) that are offered as evidence for it.

Cue Words Signaling Reasons

since	in view of	for	because
as shown by	may be inferred from	as indicated by	may be deduced from
given that	may be derived from	assuming that	for the reason that
after all	first of all	secondly	furthermore

Cue Words Signaling Conclusions

therefore	then	thus	it follows that/
hence	thereby showing	demonstrates that	as a result
allows us to infer	(which) proves that	suggests strongly	(which) shows
you see that/	points to	consequently	implies that
agree that			leads me to believe

Of course, identifying reasons, conclusions, and arguments involves more than looking for cue words. The words and phrases listed here do not always signal reasons and conclusions, and in many cases arguments are made without the use of cue words. However, cue words do help alert us that an argument is being made.

Evaluating Arguments

Arguments are evaluated in terms of their effectiveness or *soundness* through a process that investigates both the truth of the reasons and the validity of the conclusion. This evaluation centers on the following questions:

1. How true are the reasons being offered to support the conclusion?
2. To what extent do the reasons support the conclusion, or to what extent does the conclusion follow from the reasons offered?
3. Does the argument pass the tests of both truth and validity?

Truth: How True are the Supporting Reasons?

The first aspect of the argument you must evaluate is the truth of the reasons that are being used to support a conclusion. Does each reason make sense? What evidence is being offered as part of each reason? Do you know each reason to be true based on your experience? Is each reason based on a source that can be trusted? You use these questions and others like them to analyze the reasons offered and to determine how true they are. Typically, evaluating the sort of beliefs usually found as reasons in arguments is a complex and ongoing challenge.

Validity: Do the Reasons Support the Conclusion?

Valid argument An argument in which the reasons support the conclusion so that the conclusion follows from the reasons offered.

Invalid argument An argument in which the reasons do *not* support the conclusion so that the conclusion does *not* follow from the reasons offered.

In addition to determining whether the reasons are true, evaluating arguments involves investigating the *relationship* between the reasons and the conclusion. When the reasons support the conclusion so that the conclusion follows from the reasons being offered, the argument is considered to be **valid**. (In formal logic, the term *validity* is reserved for deductively valid arguments in which the conclusions follow *necessarily* from the premises, which we will discuss in the next section.) If, however, the reasons do *not* support the conclusion so that the conclusion does *not* follow from the reasons being offered, the argument is considered to be **invalid**. For example, someone might make the following argument, which is invalid because the conclusion does not follow from the reasons offered.

Reason: Company X will not consider alternatives to animal testing.

Reason: Company X makes products that are inferior.

Conclusion: It is ethically wrong for this company to experiment on animals.

One way to focus on the concept of validity is to *assume* that all the reasons in the argument are true and then try to determine how probably they make the conclusion.

Soundness: Does the Argument Pass the Tests of Both Truth and Validity?

When an argument includes both true reasons and a valid structure, the argument is considered to be **sound**. When an argument has either false reasons or an invalid structure, however, the argument is considered to be **unsound**. For example, consider the following argument:

> *Reason:* For a democracy to function most effectively, its citizens should be able to think critically about the important social and political issues.
>
> *Reason:* Education plays a key role in developing critical thinking abilities.
>
> *Conclusion:* Therefore, education plays a key role in ensuring that a democracy is functioning most effectively.

A good case could be made for the soundness of this argument because the reasons are persuasive and the argument structure is valid. Of course, someone might contend that one or both of the reasons are not completely true, which illustrates an important point about the arguments we construct and evaluate. Many of the arguments we encounter in life fall somewhere between complete soundness and complete unsoundness because we are often not sure if our reasons are completely true.

Sound argument An argument that has both true reasons and a valid structure.

Unsound argument An argument that has either false reasons or an invalid structure.

Deductive Arguments

Philosophers have classified arguments into two different categories, *deductive arguments* and *inductive arguments*. We will focus first on **deductive arguments**, which are those most commonly associated with the study of logic. In a deductive argument, if the argument form is valid, and if you accept the supporting reasons (also called *premises*) as true, then you must necessarily accept the conclusion as true. For example, consider the following famous deductive argument:

> *Reason/Premise:* All men are mortal.
>
> *Reason/Premise:* Socrates is a man.
>
> *Conclusion:* Therefore, Socrates is mortal.

Deductive argument An argument form in which one reasons from premises that are known or assumed to be true to a conclusion that follows necessarily from these premises.

This argument is structured according to a valid argument form called the categorical syllogism, which we will examine next. Because the form is valid, accepting the premises of the argument as true means that the conclusion necessarily follows; it cannot be false. There are also, however, a large number of *invalid* deductive forms, one of which is illustrated in the following syllogism:

> *Reason/Premise:* All men are mortal.
>
> *Reason/Premise:* Socrates is a man.
>
> *Conclusion:* Therefore, all men are Socrates.

The following are some common valid deductive argument forms.

Categorical Syllogism

A **syllogism** is an argument form that consists of two supporting premises and a conclusion. In a *categorical syllogism*, the premises and conclusion are all categorical

Syllogism An argument form that consists of two premises and a conclusion.

statements, that is, statements about a category of things. In the example below, the categories are *men* and *things that are mortal.*

> *Premise:* All A (men) are B (mortal).
> *Premise:* S is an A (Socrates is a man).
> *Conclusion:* Therefore, S is B (Socrates is mortal).

Modus Ponens

A second valid deductive form that we commonly use in our thinking goes by the name *modus ponens*—that is, "affirming the antecedent." The *antecedent* is the first part of a hypothetical statement: "If I have prepared thoroughly." The second part of a hypothetical statement is known as the *consequent*: "then I will do well." In this kind of syllogism, a hypothetical statement is presented in the first premise, and the conditions of the antecedent are affirmed in the second premise.

> *Premise:* If A (I have prepared thoroughly), then B (I will do well).
> *Premise:* A (I have prepared thoroughly).
> *Conclusion:* Therefore, B (I will do well).

Modus Tollens

A third commonly used valid deductive form has the name *modus tollens*—that is, "denying the consequence." Again, the first premise is a hypothetical statement (*if/then*), but the second premise focuses on the consequent (the *then* part of the statement). The conditions of the consequent are denied in the second premise.

> *Premise:* If A (Janice is a really good friend), then B (She will remember my birthday).
> *Premise:* Not B (Janice did not remember my birthday).
> *Conclusion:* Therefore, not A (Janice doesn't really care about me).

Disjunctive Syllogism

A fourth common form of a valid deductive argument is known as a *disjunctive syllogism.* The term *disjunctive* means presenting alternatives, as in the first premise of our example below. The second premise denies one of the alternatives and the conclusion affirms the remaining option.

> *Premise:* Either A (I left my wallet on my dresser) or B (I must have lost it).
> *Premise:* Not A (The wallet is not on my dresser).
> *Conclusion:* Therefore B (I have lost it).

Inductive argument An argument form in which one reasons from premises that are known or assumed to be true to a conclusion that is supported by the premises but does not necessarily follow from them.

Inductive Arguments

The previous section focused on deductive reasoning, an argument form in which one reasons from premises to a conclusion that follows necessarily from the premises. In this section we will examine **inductive arguments** an argument form in which one reasons from premises to a conclusion that is supported by the premises but does not follow necessarily from them. When you reason inductively, your premises provide evidence that makes it more or less probable (but not certain) that the conclusion is true. Consider these two conclusions arrived at using inductive reasoning:

> The solar system is probably the result of an enormous explosion—a "big bang"—that occurred billions of years ago.
>
> On the average, a person with a college degree will earn over $1,340,000 more in his or her lifetime than a person with just a high school diploma.

The first statement, about the origins of the solar system, is an example of a conclusion arrived at by **causal reasoning**. In this form of induction, an event (e.g., the creation of the solar system) is claimed to be the result of the occurrence of another event (e.g., the "big bang"). The evidence used to support this conclusion is too lengthy and complex to present here, but it is based on inferences drawn from observation. As you use your thinking abilities to try to understand the world you live in, you often ask the question, "Why did that happen?" You assume that there is some factor (or factors) responsible for what is occurring, some *cause* (or causes) that results in the *effect* (or effects) you are observing. Causal reasoning is thus one of the basic patterns of thinking we use to organize and make sense of our experience.

Causal reasoning A form of inductive argument in which one event is claimed to be the result of the occurrence of another event.

The second statement, about the earning difference of two groups of people, is an example of a conclusion drawn from a type of inductive reasoning called **empirical generalization**. Empirical generalization involves reasoning from a limited sample to a general conclusion based on this sample. Ideally, researchers would interview everyone in the *target population* (in this case, wage earners), but this, of course, is hardly practical. Instead, they select a relatively small group of individuals from the target population, known as a *sample,* whom they have determined to adequately represent the group as a whole. For this type of reasoning to be valid, the sample size needs to be sufficient and the people sampled need to be truly representative of the target population. Researchers who use this method of reasoning have developed guidelines for judging the size and representativeness of samples.

Empirical generalization A form of inductive reasoning in which a general statement is made about an entire group (the "target population") based on observing some members of the group (the "sample population").

Informal Fallacies

To this point, we have been examining ways of reasoning which are logical and effective. However, there are other forms of reasoning that are not logical and, as a result, are usually not effective. These ways of pseudo-reasoning (false reasoning) are termed **fallacies**: arguments that are not sound because of various errors in reasoning. Fallacious reasoning is typically used to influence others. It seeks to persuade not on the basis of sound arguments and critical thinking but rather on the basis of emotional and illogical factors. There are many different kinds of fallacies that have been identified and catalogued over the centuries. In the next chapter, we will observe some of them being used by the opponents of Socrates, and other fallacies will come up in later chapters. For now, here is an overview of some common fallacies.

Fallacies Unsound arguments that are often persuasive because they usually appeal to our emotions and prejudices and because they often support conclusions that we want to believe are accurate.

Fallacies of False Generalization

This group of fallacies arises from errors in reaching a general conclusion from a group of particulars and in applying general ideas to specific instances:

- *Hasty generalization:* As the name implies, this type of fallacy occurs when people try to reach a general conclusion too quickly, lacking a sufficient number of instances in the sample population to legitimately justify generalization to the target population. For example:

> *My boyfriends have never shown any real concern for my feelings. My conclusion is that men are insensitive, selfish, and emotionally superficial.*

> *In my philosophy class, we have been examining some of the obstacles to discovering truth. Therefore, I conclude that it is impossible to ever discover truth.*

- *Sweeping generalization:*   Another error in making generalizations involves the failure to take into account exceptions to the rule, "sweeping" the exceptions into a larger group.

  > *Vigorous exercise contributes to overall good health. Therefore, vigorous exercise should be practiced by recent heart attack victims, people who are out of shape, and women who are about to give birth.*

  > *People should be allowed to make their own decisions, providing that their actions do not harm other people. Therefore, people who are trying to commit suicide should be left alone to do what they want.*

- *False dilemma:*   This fallacy—also known as the "either/or" fallacy or the "black-or-white" fallacy—occurs when we are asked to choose between two extreme alternatives without being able to consider additional options. For example, someone may say, "Either we are completely free to make choices or everything we do is determined by factors outside our control and we have no freedom whatsoever. There's nothing in between."

Causal Fallacies

In our attempts to make sense of the world, we are in a constant state of attributing causes to events and situations. Here are a few common fallacies that may arise when we connect cause and effect without thinking critically:

- *Questionable cause:*   The fallacy of *questionable cause* occurs when someone presents a causal relationship for which no real evidence exists. Superstitious beliefs, such as bad luck resulting from breaking mirrors, walking under ladders, or encountering black cats usually fall into this category, as does dreaming the winning lottery numbers. Many people feel that astrology, a system of beliefs tying one's personality and fortunes in life to the position of the planets at the moment of birth, also falls into this category.

- *Misidentification of the cause:*   In causal situations, we are not always certain about what is causing what—in other words, what is the cause and what is the effect? *Misidentifying the cause* is easy to do. For example, which are the causes and which are the effects in the following pairs of items? Why?

  - Drug dependency and emotional difficulties
  - Shyness and lack of confidence
  - Failure in school and personal problems

- *Post hoc ergo propter hoc:*   The translation of this Latin phrase is "After it, therefore because of it," and it refers to those situations in which, because two things occur close together in time, we assume that one caused the other. For example, if your team wins the game each time you wear your favorite shirt, you might be tempted to conclude that the one event (wearing your favorite shirt) has some influence on the other event (winning the game). As a result, you might continue to wear this shirt "for good luck."

- *Slippery slope:*   Slippery slope thinking asserts that one undesirable action will inevitably lead to a worse action, which will necessarily lead to a worse one still, all the way down the "slippery slope." Although this progression may indeed happen, there is certainly no causal guarantee that it will. This fallacy is illustrated in the following advice:

> *If you get behind on one credit card payment, it won't be long before you'll be behind on all of your bills and you'll gradually lose control of your finances. In time, your telephone and electricity will be turned off, and you'll eventually get evicted from your apartment. You'll have to drop out of school, your friends will desert you, and your life will be in shambles. You'll live out the rest of your life as a homeless person, wandering the streets.*

Fallacies of Relevance

Many fallacious arguments appeal for support to factors that have little or nothing to do with the argument being offered and so are labeled "fallacies of relevance." In these cases, false appeals substitute for sound reasoning and a critical examination of the issues.

- *Appeal to authority/tradition/bandwagon:*   Fallacies of this sort appeal to opinions outside of oneself to justify conclusions, rather than basing conclusions on critical analysis. *Appeal to authority* argues that we should agree with a point of view simply because it is endorsed by an "authority." But authorities often conflict with one another, and in the final analysis we have to weigh all of the evidence and come to our own reasoned points of view, not uncritically believe what we are being told. Analogously, the fallacy of *appeal to tradition* argues that a practice or way of thinking is "better" or right simply because it is traditional and it has "always been done that way." Although traditional beliefs often express some truth or wisdom, they are also often misguided or false, as in traditional beliefs about the inferiority of women or minority groups. Finally, the fallacy *bandwagon* relies on the uncritical acceptance of other opinions because "everyone believes it." People experience this all the time through peer pressure, when an unpopular view is squelched and modified by the group opinion. Of course, popularity is no guarantee of accuracy.

Have you experienced the appeal to authority? Many people look to Oprah Winfrey and Dr. Phil for advice on the choices they need to make in their lives. Does this make sense?

- *Appeal to emotion:*   This family of fallacies appeals to various emotions to encourage or manipulate others into agreement. It includes *appeal to pity* ("If you don't give me an A, I'll lose my scholarship"); *appeal to fear* ("If you don't support my plan, the enemy will be emboldened"); and *appeal to flattery* ("Someone as smart as you can surely see the merits of my argument").

thinking philosophically

EVALUATING ARGUMENTS

The media are fertile ground for hunting down fallacies because so many groups are interested in manipulating and influencing your thinking at any cost. Advertisers want you to buy their products; networks want you to watch their shows; politicians want you to support their careers; televangelists are hoping to gather you into their fold; and so on. Embark on a "fallacy hunt" and locate examples of five different kinds of fallacies illustrated in the media (newspapers, magazines, television, Internet). In each case, write an analysis of how the source is using fallacious reasoning to influence your thinking and behavior. After you've completed the project, pay special attention to how becoming aware of the ways fallacious reasoning is used helps us become aware of it and resist its subtle—and not so subtle—manipulation.

- *Appeal to personal attack:* This has been one of the most frequently used fallacies through the ages. Its effectiveness results from ignoring the issues of the argument and focusing instead on the personal qualities of the person making the opposing argument. This fallacy is also referred to as the *ad hominem* argument, which means "to the man" rather than "to the issue," and *poisoning the well* because the arguer tries to ensure that any water (argument) drawn from the opponent's well (mind) will be treated as undrinkable (unsound).

- *Red herring:* Also known as "smoke screen" and "wild goose chase," the red herring fallacy is committed by introducing an irrelevant topic to divert attention from the original issue being discussed. For example: "I really don't believe that grade inflation is a significant problem in education. Everybody wants to be liked, and teachers are just trying to get students to like them."

1.5 Branches of Philosophy

The investigations of philosophers over the centuries in many cultures can be classified by the questions that they explored. Described below are the traditional branches of philosophy, along with some of the central questions that they are endeavoring to answer. Of course, these divisions are somewhat artificial because philosophical issues and modes of inquiry overlap and interrelate. But there is also value to organizing them into coherent categories.

For some people, philosophy has a reputation of being removed from daily life, concerned with abstract questions to which there are no answers and about which most people don't really care. And philosophers are sometimes stereotyped as impractical dreamers, with their heads in the clouds, separated from the lives and concerns of average people. The truth is that Western philosophy began in ancient Greece as a very practical activity, designed to help people better understand the world around them and to serve as a guide in living enlightened lives. In fact, Socrates spent his days in the public marketplace (the *agora*), discussing philosophical issues with all who were willing and challenging them to live reflective, virtuous lives. And, after all these centuries, the true spirit of philosophy remains at the core of our lives, helping us make sense of our world and create purposeful lives.

The questions and issues included in the various branches of philosophy are central to how you live your life: the way you think, the choices you make, the way you relate to other people, the issues you analyze, the problems you try to solve. In this section, we'll introduce the various branches of philosophy, each of which will be explored in depth in the chapters that follow. As you learn about the subjects of philosophical inquiry, consider the ways in which philosophy might influence your daily life in practical and profound ways.

Major Branches of Philosophy

Branch of Philosophy	Major Questions
Metaphysics: the study of the ultimate characteristics of reality or existence	What is the nature of reality? What is the nature of the self? How are the mind and body related to each other? Do we have personal freedom or are our choices limited? What are the arguments for and against the existence of God? Is there life after death? Does life have meaning?
Epistemology: the study of knowledge, identifying and developing criteria and methodologies for what we know and why we know it	What is truth? Can we ever really know anything? What are the sources of knowledge? What is the relation between truth and knowledge? How can you increase your wisdom?
Ethics: the study of moral values and principles	How should we treat other people? Is there a "good life" for humans? What is the relation between moral values and religion? How do we decide on the moral rightness of social issues?
Political and Social Philosophy: the study of social values and political forms of government	What is the nature of justice? What is the most enlightened form of government?
Aesthetics: the study of beauty, art, and taste	What is the nature of beauty? What is art?
Logic: the branch of philosophy that seeks to establish the rules of correct reasoning, clear understanding and valid arguments	What are the logical principles of correct reasoning? How do people use incorrect reasoning to reach false conclusions?

Metaphysics

Metaphysics involves the study of the most general or ultimate characteristics of reality or existence. It explores issues beyond the physical world such as the meaning of life, the existence of free will, the nature of mind, the fundamental principles of the universe, and the possibility of life beyond death. The philosopher Bertrand Russell provides the following definition:

> *Metaphysics, or the attempt to conceive the world as a whole by means of thought, has been developed, from the first, by the union and conflict of two very different impulses, the one urging men towards mysticism, the other urging them toward science.*

In other words, humans are motivated to understand the world of their experience in ways that are scientifically valid and clearly delineated. However, many of the most

Watch the **Video** *Modern Philosophy* on **mysearchlab. com** compelling issues in our lives are resistant to scientific analysis and evaluation. One doesn't discover the meaning of life, the possibility of freedom, or the existence of an afterlife with microscopes and test tubes. We need to develop other means of investigation in order to discover these more elusive "mystical" dimensions of human life.

What is the nature of the "self"? This question is at the core of metaphysical inquiry. We will begin our study of metaphysics with this question in Chapter 3. Do people have souls? What is a "mind"? What essential qualities make each of us unique? Related to the nature of the "self" is the question of **How are the mind and body related to each other**? How does the mind influence the body, and vice versa? What are the implications of the recent research on the relations between mind and brain? The surprisingly elusive questions "Who am I?" and "What is the nature of my 'self'?" are the catalysts for living, and our success—or lack of success—influences every dimension of our lives. Even though we've been living with our "selves" our entire lives, we are still often strangers to our selves, as Friedrich Nietzsche observed: "We are unknown, we knowers, ourselves to ourselves; this has good reason. We have never searched for ourselves...." Just as relevant are the questions of how the self develops and what power we have to shape the person we want to become, questions that represent the intersection of personal identity, the nature of free choice, and the meaning of life.

Thus, another important question for metaphysics is one that we will explore in Chapter 4, namely, **Do we have free wills that enable us to make independent choices**? Or are all of our actions determined by causes beyond our control? In what ways is our freedom limited? Can we increase our freedom by eliminating internal and external constraints?

Many people have naïve and inaccurate beliefs regarding their personal freedom. They often lack awareness of the many ways their freedom is limited and what they can do to increase their freedom. For example, we often find ourselves in limiting situations that we assume are beyond our control. Yet we have often contributed to creating these circumstances, and we can change them by making different choices. If you find yourself dissatisfied with your financial situation, your social group, your major—or virtually any other area of your life—there are likely alternative choices available that you haven't thought about or considered. Studying philosophy can encourage you to expand your thinking, use your imagination to create new ways of viewing your current reality as well as future possibilities, and stimulate your imagination to create new ideas and alternatives.

One of the central questions metaphysics addresses is, **What is the nature of reality**? Does the world exist independent of our perception of it? Do people experience the same or different realities? Is there an "ultimate" reality in the universe? The ancient Greek philosopher Plato offered a powerful metaphor that symbolically portrays the nature of reality and the path to enlightenment. According to Plato, most people do not experience genuine reality: instead, they are restricted to seeing images created

---

thinking philosophically

ARE YOU WILLING TO QUESTION YOUR BELIEFS?

Reflect on some of your most closely held beliefs regarding "who" you are, whether you have a free will, your view of reality, and your religious beliefs. Why are beliefs in these areas often so difficult to explore deeply and critically? Have some of these beliefs been "off-limits" for questioning? Can you envision the benefits of putting these beliefs to the test in order to create a rock-solid foundation for your philosophy of life?

by others, designed to shape their minds and manipulate their thinking. We will explore this notion, embodied in Plato's Allegory of the Cave, in Chapter 5. These issues are particularly relevant in the world today, when so much of our information about the world is filtered through the media. The information presented is always biased in the sense that those in charge have selected what information to include and the particular interpretation, spin, or slant they give it. In many cases, people passively accept the information they are given, placing themselves in jeopardy of attitude manipulation. How can studying philosophy help avoid this danger? By teaching us to critically evaluate the validity and objectivity of information, explore multiple perspectives, and develop independent and well-founded beliefs that we can use to guide our choices.

The nature of religious beliefs is also a metaphysical issue, addressing such questions as, **Does God exist**? If so, what is the nature of God? Is there more than one God? Is God the same for different people? What is God's relation to human events? What is the nature of divine revelation? If there is a God, why does God allow evil? A related area concerns the question, **Is there life after death**? Is there life before birth? Is there communication between those who have died and those currently alive? Chapter 7 explores how different thinkers have addressed these questions in the philosophy of religion.

Studying philosophy is not for the fainthearted—it requires uncommon courage to be willing to question some of your most closely held beliefs, as religious beliefs often are. But acting courageously in search of the truth is also a liberating and intoxicating experience. Why? Because being willing to question your beliefs puts you in control of your own intellectual destiny. You are no longer dependent on others to tell you what to think and believe—you have taken that authority for yourself. And because you are willing to follow the logic of your own reasoning, you are assured of reaching conclusions that are thoughtful, well-founded, and, most significantly, completely your own. You will have the confidence to discuss your beliefs in the arena of public opinion because you have already scrutinized the validity of your beliefs. And because your commitment is to the truth, rather than someone else's agenda, you are open to revising your beliefs based on clearer thinking or more compelling reasons. Commitment to the truth does, in fact, "set you free," and it gives you an unshakeable sense of intellectual security. You know *what* you believe, and you know *why* you believe it. And that confidence stimulates you to continue expanding your mind through a process of courageous questioning.

> The way God has been thought of for thousands of years is no longer convincing; if anything is dead, it can only be the traditional thought of God.
> **HANNAH ARENDT**

> The nature of God is a circle whose center is everywhere and whose circumference is nowhere.
> **SAINT AUGUSTINE**

> There is no absolute knowledge. And those who claim it, whether scientists or dogmatists, open the door to tragedy. All information is imperfect, we have to treat it with humility. That is the human condition.
> **JACOB BRONOWSKI**

Epistemology

Epistemology is the theory of knowledge. It seeks to establish a framework that we can use to arrive at genuine and accurate understanding. This involves identifying and developing criteria and methodologies for determining what we know and why we know it. Metaphysics and epistemology are interdependent, and answering the questions in the one area frequently involves

thinking philosophically

HOW DO YOU KNOW WHAT IS TRUE?

Reflect on your approach to the information you receive from the sources in your life: friends, family, teachers, books, television, newspapers, the Internet, magazines, and so on. How often do you make a special effort to question, analyze, and critically evaluate the information? How often do you tend to simply accept the information in the form it's provided? In what ways would taking a more critical thinking approach to information help you arrive at well-supported knowledge?

answering the questions in the other area. For example, discovering the nature of reality, as one escaping from Plato's cave, necessarily involves addressing questions of knowledge and truth. These integrated areas of metaphysics and epistemology are explored in Chapters 5 and 6.

The most basic question that epistemology seeks to answer is, **Can we ever really know anything**? How do we know when we *don't* know something? What is the difference between "belief" and "knowledge"? Why do some people believe that we're "drowning" in information, but we're "starved" for knowledge? Many people today believe that their opinions have value, no matter how uninformed and unsubstantiated, merely because they are *their* opinions. But from the standpoint of epistemology, beliefs have no real standing until they are evaluated by rigorous criteria in order to determine if they are worth endorsing.

The question, **What is truth**? is naturally related to epistemology's quest for knowledge. What are the roles of reason and experience in constructing knowledge and determining truth? Does truth evolve or is it unchanging? Can there be different "truths" for different people?

We're bombarded with information on a daily basis, and much of that information is false, incomplete, and/or biased. Studying philosophy gives you the thinking tools needed to sift through this tangled morass of information and arrive at knowledge that is clear, insightful, and well supported with reasons and evidence. The fact is that all information is "biased" in the sense that it reflects the needs and interests of the sources providing it. To construct intelligent knowledge, we need to become aware of the "lenses" through which we and others view the world, lenses that shape and influence our points of view. Additionally, we should never be content with just one point of view. Instead, we should always strive to view situations and issues from a variety of contrasting perspectives to develop a well-rounded and balanced understanding. Unfortunately, many people tend to accept uncritically the information they encounter, lacking both the initiative and thinking tools to analyze and evaluate it.

Ethics

Ethics involves the study of moral values and principles. The study of ethics is derived from the Greek word *ethos*, which refers to moral purpose or "character"—as in "a person of upstanding character." Ethics and morals are terms that refer to the principles that govern our relationships with other people: the ways we ought to behave, the rules and standards that we should employ in the choices we make.

The question of **How should we treat other people**? is central to the study of ethics. Are there universal moral values that apply to all people? Or are moral values relative to cultural norms or personal preferences? What moral principles should we use to guide our decisions?

Ethics is also concerned with questions related to the purpose of life, such as, **Is there a "good life" for humans**? Do we have moral responsibilities to others? Are we our "brothers'" and "sisters'" keepers? What is the ultimate goal of our lives? How can we achieve our moral potential?

The question of **What is the relation between moral values and religion**? is another issue that has been a focus of ethics throughout history. What role does belief in a divine being play in moral conduct? Does one need to believe in God to be a moral

> **Unless you expect the unexpected you will never find truth, for it cannot be found by search or trail.**
> HERACLITUS

> **The truth is cruel, but it can be loved, and it makes free those who have loved it.**
> GEORGE SANTAYANA

> **There is therefore but one categorical imperative, namely, this: Act only on that maxim whereby thou canst at the same time will that it should become a universal law.**
> IMMANUEL KANT

person? Why do different religions agree about many moral values? Why do they disagree? What is the foundation for a humanistic code of ethics?

On a more practical, day-to-day level, ethics is also concerned with the question, **How do we decide on the moral rightness of social issues**? Issues include capital punishment, euthanasia, lying, human rights, abortion, cloning, pornography, and so on. Slavery was once legal and considered to be morally acceptable by many people in the United States. Were these people morally wrong, or did the moral rules change? How can we determine the right

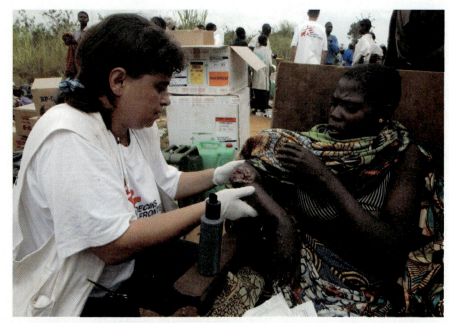

What are our moral responsibilities? The study of ethics explores our obligations to act in the interest of others as well as ourselves. Do you think we are "our brothers' keepers"? Or do you believe in "every man for himself"?

views on moral issues that we are confronted with in today's world? In Chapter 9, we will consider a social issue—do animals have rights? Does the ethical principle on which human equality rests also apply to other beings?

Creating yourself to be a wise and knowledgeable person entails developing an enlightened moral compass that will guide your decisions. People typically rely on what they "feel" is right when faced with challenging moral dilemmas. But how we "feel" is an unreliable moral guide. The only way to ensure that we are making informed and appropriate moral decisions is to develop a clear ethical code that we can use to guide us, as a student observes in the following passage:

> *Taking this class has enlightened my moral compass and provided me with a moral foundation that I will cultivate throughout my lifetime. Before I began reflecting on my moral values, I made choices based on if I "felt" they were the right things to do. I never gave much thought to my decisions or the reasons for them, only that they were right for me and that they did not impose on other people. Now that I have studied the ethical principles of several philosophers, I will approach moral dilemmas with a clearer understanding of why I make the choices I do. The teachings of Immanuel Kant have made me realize that I should not consider my actions as affecting only me; that I should also consider the consequences affecting any other people involved: "Act so that you treat humanity, whether in your*

> **An action then may be said to be conformable to the principle of utility ... when the tendency it has to augment the happiness of the community is greater than any it has to diminish it.**
> **JEREMY BENTHAM**

> **Live not as though there were a thousand years ahead of you. Fate is at your elbow; make yourself good while life and power are still yours.**
> **MARCUS AURELIUS**

thinking philosophically

DO YOU HAVE A MORAL PHILOSOPHY?

Think about some of the particularly confusing and challenging moral decisions that you've had to make in your life. What made these decisions so difficult? Do you believe that you have a clear and accurate moral compass that you can use to guide you when complicated moral dilemmas arise in the future? What are some of the moral areas of your life in which you would like to have a clearer set of values?

own person or in that of another, always as an end and never as a means only." Finally, in whatever choices I make, I am aware that I must take responsibility for the consequences, whether good or bad.

Joshua Bartlett

Political and Social Philosophy

> Politics must conform to the essence and aims of society, not to the passions of rulers.
> **PAUL HENRI THIRY, BARON D'HOLBACH**

> It is evident that the state is a creation of nature, and that man is by nature a political animal.
> **ARISTOTLE**

> The precepts of the laws are these: to live honorably, to injure no other man, to render to every man his due.
> **JUSTINIAN I**

Political and social philosophy involves the study of social values and political forms of government. It explores the various ways in which people should organize and govern themselves. This involves analyzing the values on which society should be based and the role of social justice and individual rights. Questions debated by political and social philosophers will be explored in Chapter 10, "What Is Social Justice?"

One of the core questions of this branch of philosophy is, **What is the most enlightened form of government?** Who has the right to exercise power? What are the limits of the state?

A related question but one that has more immediate relevance for most people is, **What is the nature of justice?** What individual rights are people entitled to? What is the relationship between the needs of the state and personal liberties? What are the different concepts of justice, and how should they be applied?

Philosophical study about political and social themes equips us not only to understand but to *act*. As citizens, we all have a responsibility to construct a society in which government expresses the will of an enlightened population. To ensure that we live in a just society, we have to be active participants in that society, in its institutions, and in the public discourse that shapes our nation's policies. We live in a world rife with

Are citizens entitled to universal health care?
In this mural, *The History of Medicine in Mexico, and the People Demanding Health*, Diego Rivera dramatizes the struggle of the poor for access to a health care system that favors the rich. Social and political philosophy explores questions about social justice, human rights, and government responsibilities. *Diego Rivera (1866–1957). The History of Medicine in Mexico, The People Demanding Health, 1953. [Detail] Fresco, approx. 7.4 × 10.8 m. Hospital de la Raza, Mexico City, D.F., Mexico. Schalkwijk / Art Resource, NY / © 2011 Banco de México Diego Rivera Frida Kahlo Museums Trust, Mexico, D.F. / Artists Rights Society (ARS), New York.*

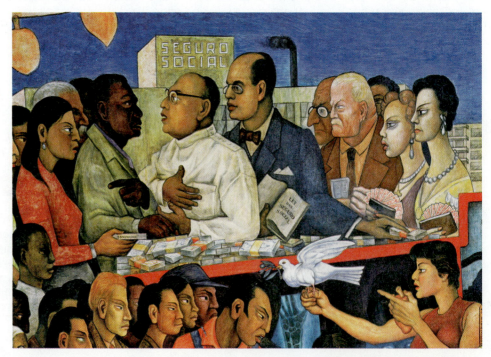

injustice, persecution, and war. Thus, thinking philosophically and acting effectively are not luxuries, they are essential to create the kind of world in which we all want to live.

Aesthetics

Aesthetics involves the study of beauty and art. It analyzes efforts to establish standards for beauty in all of its various manifestations. And it explores the nature and purpose of art in human affairs. (Because of space limitations, we are not able to devote a chapter to aesthetics.)

One of the oldest questions in the philosophy of art is, **What is the nature of beauty**? How do we identify principles of beauty and artistic value? Are there universal standards of beauty, or are they relative to cultural and individual taste? Is there one core concept of beauty or many different concepts?

Another question aesthetics deals with is, **What is art**? Modern and contemporary artists have challenged traditional notions that art should be beautiful, represent reality, or even be an object for permanent display. The philosophy of art helps us understand the conceptual issues and controversies surrounding the art of today, as well as questions such as: Should art be used for social and political purposes? Should the government be allowed to censor "artistic expression" that it considers obscene? Our world is increasingly infused with the power of visual images, which shape and influence our thinking in profound ways. We need to develop our ability to critically evaluate these images as well as ideas that are presented in written and oral form, and a significant part of understanding the meaning of images is understanding the aesthetic principles on which they are constructed.

Is it art? Twentieth-century artists began challenging audiences to consider new ideas about what constitutes art. The contemporary artist Matthew Barney uses his own body as the basis for elaborate images based on mythological stories of his own invention. *CREMASTER 3: Five Points of Fellowship, 2002 C-print in acrylic frame 54 x 44 inches Copyright Matthew Barney Courtesy Gladstone Gallery, New York and Brussels.*

> **Art is a lie which makes you realize the truth.**
> PICASSO

> **Beauty in things exists in the mind which contemplates them.**
> DAVID HUME

1.6 Reading Critically: Working with Primary Sources

In addition to developing and refining your critical thinking abilities, thinking philosophically also involves studying the ideas of great thinkers who have created coherent frameworks for understanding every dimension of human experience. There is no point in "reinventing the wheel" when brilliant minds have already made significant progress in understanding the most complex and challenging issues in life. So learning to think philosophically involves developing your critical thinking abilities while reading and analyzing the ideas of exceptional philosophers, present and past. The **Reading Critically** boxes that follow philosophical texts are designed to support you in this endeavor.

In the following selection from his book *The Problems of Philosophy*, the British philosopher Bertrand Russell addresses the core question that we have considered in this chapter—what is the value of philosophy? The excerpt provides an excellent opportunity to see a philosophical mind at work.

Bertrand Russell
(1872–1970). Russell was a British philosopher who was one of the founders of modern logic. In *The Principles of Mathematics* (1903), and with Alfred North Whitehead in *Principia Mathematica* (1910–1913), he advanced the view that all of mathematics could be derived from logical premises. He also wrote on a broad range of other subjects (education, marriage, politics, history, religion, science, ethics) and was awarded the Nobel Prize in Literature in 1950. Also known for his many spirited antiwar and antinuclear protests, Russell was a prominent and controversial public figure.

Bertrand Russell, from *The Value of Philosophy*

Having now come to the end of our brief and very incomplete review of the problems of philosophy, it will be well to consider, in conclusion, what the value of philosophy is, and why it ought to be studied. It is the more necessary to consider this question, in view of the fact that many men, under the influence of science or of practical affairs, are inclined to doubt whether philosophy is anything better than innocent but useless trifling, hair-splitting distinctions, and controversies on matters concerning which knowledge is impossible.

This view of philosophy appears to result, partly from a wrong conception of the ends of life, partly from a wrong conception of the kind of goods which philosophy strives to achieve. Physical science, through the medium of inventions, is useful to innumerable people who are wholly ignorant of it; thus the study of physical science is to be recommended, not only, or primarily, because of the effect on the student, but rather because of the effect on mankind in general. Thus utility does not belong to philosophy. If the study of philosophy has any value at all for others than students of philosophy, it must be only indirectly, through its effect upon the lives of those who study it. It is in these effects, therefore, if anywhere, that the value of philosophy must be primarily sought.

But further, if we are not to fail in our endeavour to determine the value of philosophy, we must first free our minds from the prejudices of what are wrongly called "practical" man. The "practical" man, as this word is often used, is one who recognizes only material needs, who realizes that men must have food for the body, but is oblivious of the necessity of providing food for the mind. If all men were well off, if poverty and disease had been reduced to their lowest possible point, there would still remain much to be done to produce a valuable society; and even in the existing world the goods of the mind are at least as important as the goods of the body. It is exclusively among the goods of the mind that the value of philosophy is to be found; and only those who are not indifferent to these goods can be persuaded that the study of philosophy is not a waste of time.

Philosophy, like all other studies, aims primarily at knowledge. The knowledge it aims at is the kind of knowledge which gives unity and system to the body of the sciences, and the kind which results from a critical examination of the grounds of our convictions, prejudices, and beliefs. But it cannot be maintained that philosophy has had any very great measure of success in its attempts to provide definite answers to its questions. If you ask a mathematician, a mineralogist, a historian, or any other man of learning, what definite body of truths has been ascertained by his science, his answer will last as long as you are willing to listen. But if you put the same questions to a philosopher, he will, if he is candid, have to confess that his study has not achieved positive results such as have been achieved by other sciences. It is true that this is partly accounted for by the fact that, as soon as definite knowledge concerning any subject becomes possible, this subject ceases to be called philosophy, and becomes a separate science. The whole study of the heavens, which now belongs to astronomy, was once included in philosophy; Newton's great work was called "the mathematical principles of natural philosophy." Similarly, the study of the human mind, which was a part of philosophy, has now been separated from philosophy and has become the science of psychology. Thus, to a great extent, the uncertainty of philosophy is more apparent than real: those questions which are already capable of definite answers are placed in the sciences, while those only to which, at present, no definite answer can be given, remain to form the residue which is called philosophy.

This is, however, only a part of the truth concerning the uncertainty of philosophy. There are many questions—and among them those that are of the profoundest interest to our spiritual life—which, so far as we can see, must remain insoluble to the human intellect unless its powers become of quite a different order from what they are now. Has the universe any unity of plan or purpose, or is it a fortuitous concourse of atoms? Is consciousness a permanent part of the universe, giving hope of indefinite growth in wisdom, or is it a transitory accident on a small planet on which life must ultimately become impossible? Are good and evil of importance to the universe or only to man? Such questions are asked by philosophy, and variously answered by various philosophers. But it would seem that, whether answers be otherwise discoverable or not, the answers suggested by philosophy are none of them demonstrably true. Yet, however slight may be the hope of discovering an answer, it is part of the business of philosophy to continue the consideration of such questions, to make us aware of their importance, to examine all the approaches to them, and to keep alive that speculative interest in the universe which is apt to be killed by confining ourselves to definitely ascertainable knowledge....
The value of philosophy is, in fact, to be sought largely in its very uncertainty. The man who has no tincture of philosophy goes through life imprisoned in the prejudices derived from common sense, from the habitual beliefs of his age or his nation, and from convictions which have grown up in his mind without the co-operation or consent of his deliberate reason. To such a man the world tends to become definite, finite, obvious; common objects rouse no questions, and unfamiliar possibilities are contemptuously rejected. As soon as we begin to philosophize, on the contrary, we find that even the most everyday things lead to problems to which only very incomplete answers can be given. Philosophy, though unable to tell us with certainty the true answer to the doubts which it raises, is able to suggest many possibilities which enlarge our thoughts and free them from the tyranny of custom. Thus, while diminishing our feeling of certainty as to what things are, it greatly increases our knowledge as to what they may be; it removes the somewhat arrogant dogmatism of those who have never travelled into the region of liberating doubt, and it keeps alive our sense of wonder by showing familiar things in an unfamiliar aspect.

Apart from its utility in showing unsuspected possibilities, philosophy has a value—perhaps its chief value—through the greatness of the objects which it contemplates, and the freedom from narrow and personal aims resulting from this contemplation. The life of the instinctive man is shut up within the circle of his private interests: family and friends may be included, but the other world is not regarded except as it may help or hinder what comes within the circle of instinctive wishes. In such a life there is something feverish and confined, in comparison with which the philosophic life is calm and free. The private world of instinctive interests is a small one, set in the midst of a great and powerful world which must, sooner or later, lay our private world in ruins. Unless we can so enlarge our interests so as to include the whole outer world, we remain like a garrison in a beleaguered fortress, knowing that the enemy prevents escape and that ultimate surrender is inevitable. In such a life there is no peace, but a constant strife between the insistence of desire and the powerlessness of will. In one way or another, if our life is to be great and free, we must escape this prison and this strife.

One way of escape is by philosophic contemplation. Philosophic contemplation does not, in its widest survey, divide the universe into two hostile camps—friends and foes, helpful and hostile, good and bad—it views the whole impartially. Philosophic contemplation, when it is unalloyed, does not aim at proving that the rest of the universe is akin to man.... In contemplation, on the contrary, we start from the non-Self, and through its greatness the boundaries of Self are enlarged; through the infinity of the universe the mind which contemplates it achieves some share in infinity.

> **Philosophy is to be studied, not for the sake of any definite answers to its questions since no definite answers can, as a rule, be known to be true, but rather for the sake of the questions themselves.**

Thus, to sum up our discussion of the value of philosophy: Philosophy is to be studied, not for the sake of any definite answers to its questions since no definite answers can, as a rule, be known to be true, but rather for the sake of the questions themselves; because these questions enlarge our conception of what is possible, enrich our intellectual imagination and diminish the dogmatic assurance which closes the mind against speculation; but above all because through the greatness of the universe which philosophy contemplates, the mind also is rendered great, and becomes capable of that union with the universe which constitutes its highest good.

< READING CRITICALLY >

Analyzing Russell on the Value of Philosophy

- According to Russell, the "practical" man does not understand that "the goods of the mind are at least as important as the goods of the body." Explain what you think he means by this statement.

- One reason that philosophy does not provide definite answers to its questions is that "as soon as definite knowledge concerning any subject becomes possible, this subject ceases to be called philosophy, and becomes a separate science." Explain what Russell means and how this relates to the characterization of philosophy as the "mother of all disciplines."

- A second reason that Russell believes philosophy does not provide definite answers to its questions is that many of its questions "must remain insoluble to the human intellect unless its powers become of quite a different order from what they are now." Identify five such questions and explain why the answers are likely to remain insoluble.

- "The value of philosophy is, in fact, to be sought largely in its very uncertainty. The man who has no tincture of philosophy goes through life imprisoned in the prejudices derived from common sense, from the habitual beliefs of his age or his nation, and from convictions which have grown up in his mind without the cooperation or consent of his deliberate reason. To such a man the world tends to become definite, finite, obvious; common objects rouse no questions, and unfamiliar possibilities are contemptuously rejected. As soon as we begin to philosophize, on the contrary, we find that even the most everyday things lead to problems to which only very incomplete answers can be given." Explain what Russell means in this passage and how it relates to Socrates' admonition, "The unexamined life is not worth living."

- According to Russell, "Philosophy is to be studied, not for the sake of any definite answers to its questions since no definite answers can, as a rule, be known to be true, but rather for the sake of the questions themselves; because these questions enlarge our conception of what is possible, enrich our intellectual imagination and diminish the dogmatic assurance which closes the mind against speculation; but above all because through the greatness of the universe which philosophy contemplates, the mind also is rendered great, and becomes capable of that union with the universe which constitutes its highest good." Explain in your own words what Russell means in this passage. How do his views on the ultimate aim of philosophy compare with those of Perictione, the Greek philosopher writing over 2,000 years earlier (p. 7). Can you identify additional reasons for studying philosophy based on your work in this chapter?

1.7 Making Connections: The Search for a Meaningful Life

This first chapter has been designed to introduce you to the discipline of philosophy and to suggest ways that studying philosophy can enrich your life. Studying philosophy is unique because as you develop your mind by learning how to think philosophically, you are also enlarging yourself as a person—the perspective from which you view the world, the concepts and values you use to guide your choices, and the impact you have on the world as a result of those choices. Learning to think philosophically does not mean simply gaining certain intellectual tools—it involves your personal transformation. Everybody "thinks"—*Homo sapiens* means "thinking man"—but most people don't "think" very well. By learning to think philosophically, you can develop your mind into a powerful, sophisticated resource that will enrich all dimensions of your life. It will initiate a process that transforms the way you view yourself and conduct your business in the world.

We all long to live lives that are meaningful and purposeful, as Viktor Frankl expresses so eloquently in the following passage:

> *Man's search for meaning is the primary motivation in his life. This meaning is unique and specific in that it must and can be fulfilled by him alone; only then does it achieve a significance which will satisfy his own will to meaning.*

How do we discover the meaning of life? Viktor Frankl discovered that, even under the most inhumane of conditions, it is possible to have a meaningful life, defined by the ways we choose to respond to life's challenges. Do you believe that this is true? Why?

This insight by Frankl, a psychiatrist and concentration camp survivor, penetrates to the soul of who we are. A well-known Viennese psychiatrist in the 1930s, Frankl and his family were arrested by the Nazis, and he spent three years in the Auschwitz concentration camp. Every member of his family, including his parents, his siblings, and his pregnant wife, was killed. He himself miraculously survived, enduring the most unimaginably abusive and degrading conditions. Following his liberation by Allied troops, he wrote *Man's Search for Meaning*, an enduring and influential work, which he began on scraps of paper during his internment. Since its publication in 1945, it has been read by millions of people in twenty languages. Its success reflects the hunger for meaning that people are experiencing, trying to answer a question that, in the author's words, "burns under their fingernails." This hunger expresses the pervasive meaning*lessness* of our age, the "existential vacuum," in which many people exist.

Frankl discovered that even under the most inhumane of conditions, it is possible to live a life of purpose and meaning. But, for the majority of prisoners at Auschwitz, a meaningful life did not seem possible. Immersed in a world that no longer recognized the value of human life and human dignity, which robbed them of their will and made them objects to be exterminated, most prisoners suffered a loss of their values. Prisoners who did not struggle against this spiritual destruction lost their feeling of being individuals, beings with a mind, with inner freedom and personal value. Their existence descended to the level of animal life, plunging them into a depression so deep that they became incapable of action. No entreaties, no blows, no threats would have any effect on this apathetic paralysis, underscoring the Russian novelist Fyodor Dostoevsky's observation: "Without a firm idea of himself and the purpose of his life, man cannot live, and would sooner destroy himself than remain on earth, even if he was surrounded with bread."

Dr. Frankl found that the meaning of *his* life in this situation was to try to help his fellow prisoners restore their psychological health. He had to find ways for them to look forward to the future: a loved one waiting for his return, a talent to be used, or perhaps work yet to be completed. These were the threads he tried to weave back into the patterns of meaning in these devastated lives. His efforts led him to the following epiphany:

> We had to learn ourselves, and furthermore we had to teach the despairing men, that it did not matter what we expected from life, but rather what life expected from us. We needed to stop asking about the meaning of life but instead to think of ourselves as those who were being questioned by life, daily and hourly. Our answer must consist not in talk and meditation, but in right action and in right conduct. Life ultimately means taking the responsibility to find the right answer to its problems and to fulfill the tasks which it constantly sets for each individual.

We each long for a life of significance, to feel that in some important way our life has made a unique contribution to the world and to the lives of others. We each strive to create our self as a person of unique quality, someone who is admired by others as extraordinary. We hope for lives characterized by unique accomplishments and lasting relationships that will distinguish us as memorable individuals both during and after our time on earth. Unfortunately, we often don't achieve these lofty goals. To discover the meaning of our lives, we need to understand "who" we are. And we live in an age in which many people are not sure "who" they are or whether in fact their lives have *any* significant meaning whatsoever.

When we are asked such questions as "Who are you?" or "What is the meaning of your life?" we often lack any idea how to respond. But an even more revealing symptom of our confusion and alienation is the fact that we rarely even *pose* these questions, to ourselves or to others. We are too busy "living" to wonder *why* we are living or *who* the person is that is doing the living. But can we afford to be too busy to find meaning in our lives? *Our lives depend on our answer to this question.* Not our biological lives necessarily, but the life of our *spirit.* We so often cruise along on autopilot—days slipping into weeks, weeks merging into years, years coalescing into a life—without confronting these important questions. If we are to become human in the fullest sense, achieving our distinctive potentials and living a life of significance, we must first have what the theologian Paul Tillich characterized as *the courage to be.*

There is a terrible price to pay for this loss of wonder and lack of meaning, for such a loss corrodes any life, eating it away from the inside until only a shell remains. The existentialist novelist Albert Camus expressed it this way:

> *To lose one's life is a little thing and I shall have the courage to do so if it is necessary; but to see the meaning of this life dissipated, to see our reason for existing disappear, that is what is unbearable. One cannot live without meaning.*

Many people are in fact living with a diminished sense of meaning, and they struggle to fill the void within themselves by frantically pursuing power, money, pleasure, thrills, mind-altered states, or the latest cultural fad. Yet these compulsive cravings only serve to reveal the *lack* of purpose in their lives, poor substitutes for a life built around authentic purpose and genuine meaning. Dr. Frankl provided an eloquent analysis of the desperate situation in which we find ourselves:

> *Modern men and women are caught in an existential vacuum, the total and ultimate meaninglessness of their lives. They lack the awareness of a meaning worth living for. They are haunted by the experience of their inner emptiness, a void within themselves. The existential vacuum is a widespread phenomenon of the 20th century.... No instinct tells them what they have to do, and no tradition tells them what they ought to do; soon they will not know what they want to do.*

This, then, is the real significance of Socrates' challenge, "The unexamined life is not worth living." Socrates' unambiguous message is that when we live our lives unreflectively, simply reacting to life's situations and not trying to explore its deeper meanings, then our lives have diminished value. When unreflective, we are not making use of the distinctive human capacity to think deeply about important issues and develop thoughtful conclusions about ourselves and our world.

Thinking philosophically in our current world is typically not a simple matter.

thinking philosophically

WHAT DO YOU HOPE TO LEARN?

This course in philosophy is going to provide you with a unique opportunity to respond to Socrates' challenge by prompting you to explore profound ideas and develop powerful intellectual abilities. This first chapter is designed to be a personal invitation for you to begin—or continue—your own personal philosophical journey. Think about the philosophical themes and ideas that you have examined in this chapter and then write a paper that explains your personal goals for this course. Discuss the insights and knowledge you would like to achieve and the ways you would like to develop your mind.

It's a fast-paced world in which we are bombarded by overwhelming amounts of information and incessant demands on our time. It's not unusual to feel that we are rushing from deadline to deadline, skating on the surface of life, meeting our endless responsibilities, and seeming to be in perpetual motion like hamsters on an exercise wheel. It's difficult to find the time to reflect deeply about important questions and to have in-depth discussions with others regarding significant issues of mutual concern. We're so busy caught up in the process of living that we simply don't make the time or effort to plumb the depths of ourselves, reflect on the meaning of our existence, shape the direction of our lives, and create ourselves as unique and worthy individuals. Yet if we are to take Socrates' challenge seriously, making time to think deeply is exactly what we *must* do if our lives are to have genuine significance.

((•●—[**Listen** to the **Interview**
Joking, and Learning,
About Philosophy on
mysearchlab.com

writing about philosophy: Analyzing Your Beliefs

The Assignment

As we noted earlier in the chapter, every person "*has*" a philosophy of life—a collection of beliefs that is used to guide his or her thoughts and actions. These beliefs, formed over the years of your life, influence that way you see the world and the choices that you make. You may not be aware of all your beliefs—some may be deeply buried in your consciousness—but they can still influence you. Of course, an individual's philosophy of life can also contain beliefs that are wildly inaccurate, biased, or destructive. *Doing* philosophy involves thinking critically about your beliefs to ensure that they are the most accurate and enlightened beliefs possible.

This assignment is an opportunity for you to begin thinking critically about the beliefs you have formed. The **Thinking Philosophically** activity on page 11 poses questions that relate to the various branches of philosophy. For example:

- "What moral beliefs influence your behavior towards others?" relates to **Ethics**
- "Do you believe that your choices are free?" relates to **Metaphysics**
- "How do you know when you 'know' something is true?" relates to **Epistemology**
- "Are all people entitled to basic human rights?" relates to **Social and Political Philosophy**

- "What role do religious beliefs play in your life?" relates to **Philosophy of Religion**
- "What do you consider to be 'beautiful'?" relates to **Aesthetics**

Select a number of your responses (suggested by your professor) and think critically about them by applying the Critical Thinking Model described on pages 13–17. This will involve critically examining your beliefs by responding to the following guidelines:

1. State you initial point of view.
2. Define your point of view more clearly.
3. Give an example of your point of view.
4. Explore the origin of your point of view.
5. Identify your assumptions.
6. Offer the reasons, evidence, and arguments that support your point of view.
7. Consider other points of view.
8. Arrive at a conclusion, decision, solution, or prediction.
9. Consider the consequences.

Your responses to this activity will serve as a useful point of reference. As you immerse yourself in the course, you will discover that as your abilities to *think philosophically* improve, your beliefs about the world are becoming clearer, more accurate, and better founded.

MySearchLab Connections

Watch. Listen. Explore. Read. Mysearchlab is designed just for you. Each chapter features a customized study plan to help you learn and review key concepts and terms. Dynamic visual activities, videos, and readings found in the multimedia library will enhance your learning experience.

Here are a few questions and activities to help you understand this chapter:

1. **Listen** to the **Podcast** *Alain DeBotton on Philosophy Within and Outside the Academy* on **mysearchlab.com**   Why did the academic philosophers largely reject DeBotton's work?

2. **Watch** the **Video** *Definition of Epistemology* on **mysearchlab.com**   Can you completely trust the information your senses provide you? Explain your answer.

3. **Listen** to the **Podcast** *Finding Equality Through Logic* on **mysearchlab.com**   How could you use philosophy to improve your life or the lives of those in your community?

4. **Watch** the **Video** *Modern Philosophy* on **mysearchlab.com**   Why did Kant believe that metaphysics was impossible?

5. **Listen** to the **Interview** *Joking, and Learning, About Philosophy* on **mysearchlab.com**   Do you believe that humor is an effective way to teach philosophical concepts? Why or why not?

Why Study Philosophy?

- Philosophy, or the love and pursuit of wisdom, is as much a way of living and process of thinking as it is a body of knowledge. Our responsibility as thoughtful, critical citizens is to define for ourselves our own "philosophy of life"—and then to *do* philosophy by continually testing that philosophy against new knowledge and experience.

[pp. 4–5]

Defining Philosophy

- Philosophy has its origins in the human capacity for wonder. The activity of philosophy is a rigorous, critical, and honest process of testing and discussing our beliefs. In that activity is implied a conflict, or "dialectic"; in doing philosophy, we continually test ideas and concepts against their opposites, working toward synthesis. That synthesis, or unity, is a goal of philosophy: to improve the quality of our lives by enlightening and broadening our minds.

[pp. 6–9]

Thinking Philosophically: Becoming a Critical Thinker

- To "do philosophy" effectively requires developing the attributes of *critical thinking*. These attributes include adopting different perspectives, making informed decisions, analyzing complex issues, establishing appropriate goals, communicating effectively, critically evaluating information, asking questions, and exchanging ideas with others (Socratic analysis).

[pp. 9–21]

Understanding Arguments

- The branch of philosophy known as logic seeks to establish the rules of correct reasoning, clear understanding, and valid argumentation.
- We can evaluate arguments in terms of their soundness by investigating both the truth of the reasons and the validity of the conclusion.
- In a deductive argument, if the argument form is valid and the supporting reasons are true, then it follows that the conclusion will be true. In an inductive argument, the supporting reasons make it more or less probable—but not certain—that the conclusion is true.
- Arguments that contain informal fallacies may seem persuasive but in fact are based on errors in reasoning.

[pp. 21–30]

for further reading, viewing & research

Read the Primary Source on MySearchLab

- *The Value of Philosophy*, Bertrand Russell

Films

- **American Beauty** (1999) What are the dangers of "sleepwalking through life"? Lester Burnham lives a seemingly perfect life in suburbia with his high-powered wife and adolescent daughter. But he is depressed with his mundane existence until he develops a crush on his daughter's friend. His actions in the wake of this fantasy have powerful effects on himself and all those around him.

- **It's a Wonderful Life** (1947) How do people find meaning in seemingly hopeless situations? George Bailey is a compassionate man who has devoted his life and resources to his town and family. But when his business fails, threatening the stability of the life he has created, he contemplates suicide. An angel appears to show him why his life is meaningful and valuable.
- **Life Is Beautiful** (1997) Is it possible to create meaning in desperate circumstances? A charismatic and playful Jewish bookkeeper refuses to lose hope or give up when he, his wife, and his young son are sent to a Nazi concentration camp. Instead, he finds ways to communicate with his family and, through humor and playacting, attempts to convince his son that the camp is an elaborate game.
- **Schindler's List** (1993) How does one find a purpose in life? This film is based on the true story of Oskar Schindler, a businessman who intended to exploit Jewish labor to amass a personal fortune. Witnessing the horrors of the Holocaust profoundly affects his perspective, and he then uses his business to save 1,100 Jews from extermination in the gas chambers at Auschwitz. It is a story of personal transformation, self-sacrifice, and the ability of a single person to influence the lives of many.

Branches of Philosophy

The traditional branches of philosophy are

- Metaphysics—The study of the ultimate characteristics of reality or existence *(What is the nature of reality? Does God exist?)*

- Epistemology—The study of the construction of knowledge *(What is truth? Can we ever really know anything?)*

- Ethics—The study of moral values and principles *(How should we treat other people? Is there a "good life" for humans?)*

- Political and social philosophy—The study of social values and political forms of government *(What is the nature of justice? What is the most enlightened form of government?)*

- Aesthetics—The study of beauty, art, and taste *(What is the nature of beauty? What is art?)*

- Logic and critical thinking—The study of correct reasoning, clear understanding, and valid arguments *(What are the logical principles of correct reasoning? Why do many people think ineffectively?)*

- There is considerable overlap and nuance between these different categories.

[pp. 30–37]

Reading Critically: Working with Primary Sources

- Thinking philosophically also involves studying the ideas of great thinkers. You will develop your critical thinking abilities while reading and analyzing the ideas of exceptional philosophers, present and past. Bertrand Russell's essay on the value of philosophy provides the first opportunity to practice these skills.

[pp. 37–40]

KEY TERMS

argument

reasons or premises

conclusion

valid argument

invalid argument

sound argument

unsound argument

deductive argument

syllogism

inductive argument

causal reasoning

empirical generalization

fallacies

visual summary

Literature

- ***Hamlet,*** William Shakespeare. Following his father's murder, the title character in Shakespeare's famous tragedy contemplates revenge. In doing so, he addresses profound ethical and metaphysical themes, including the nature of reality, the nature of evil, the nature of madness, the mystery of death, and the possibility or impossibility of attaining true knowledge about the world and one's self.

- ***Man's Search for Meaning,*** Viktor E. Frankl. Begun on scraps of paper during his internment in a Nazi concentration camp, Frankl's harrowing account both poses and answers the question of how one can find meaning and purpose in the most inhumane and devastating circumstances.

- ***Meditations,*** Marcus Aurelius. The reflections of this Roman emperor and warrior, written during his military campaigns, address the complexities of the human condition. Though trained in Stoic philosophy, Marcus Aurelius anticipates many of the themes of Christianity as he meditates on both life and death.

- ***Slaughterhouse Five,*** Kurt Vonnegut. An American soldier, Billy Pilgrim, travels backwards and forwards in time after being captured by Germans in World War II. Billy's journey is a philosophical one as Vonnegut raises questions about fate and free will, fiction and reality, the absurdity of war, and the effects of such a war on the human psyche.

(*Raphael*, The School of Athens. *Vatican Museums, Rome, Italy. Scala/Art Resource, NY*)

The Socratic Method
Seeking clarity and truth through penetrating questioning and astute analysis

Socrates' Ethos
The goal of life is to "know thyself" and improve our souls through virtuous living

what is the philosopher's way?

SOCRATES AND THE EXAMINED LIFE

Socrates' Trial
Using his legal defense to embody his ethical values and principles of rational inquiry

Socrates' Death
Becoming a heroic martyr to enlightened thinking and virtuous living by refusing to compromise the values that defined his life

◀ **Where does philosophy begin?** Raphael's mural, *The School of Athens*, depicts the early Greek philosophers engaged in reflection, discussion, and debate. We will start the philosophical journey with Socrates, whose life embodied the philosopher's way.

PHILOSOPHERS AND THINKERS IN THIS CHAPTER (DATES ARE APPROXIMATE)	
Thales	62?–546 B.C.E.
Anaximenes	?–528 B.C.E.
Pythagoras	570–497 B.C.E.
Heraclitus	540–480 B.C.E.
Parmenides	510–450 B.C.E.
Anaxagoras	500–428 B.C.E.
Socrates	469–399 B.C.E.
Democritus	460–370 B.C.E.
Thrasymachus	459–400 B.C.E.
Xenophon	444–357 B.C.E.
Plato	427–347 B.C.E.
Aristotle	384–322 B.C.E.

2.1 Socrates: A Model for Humanity

When you reflect on your own personal and intellectual development, you can likely identify key people in your life who stimulated your thinking, challenged your limited perspective, and inspired your spirit to soar to new and unexpected levels. Who are some of these people? How did they stimulate you and enrich your life? Do they continue to influence you, even though you may no longer be in touch with them?

For people living in Athens, Greece, 2,500 years ago, **Socrates** was such a person. Several hundred years previously, the Greek thinker Heraclitus had warned, "One ought not to talk or act as if he were asleep," cautioning against the tendency of many people to live their lives as sleepwalkers: drifting along with life's current, unreflective, unthinking. Socrates embraced Heraclitus's challenge as his life mission, characterizing himself as a *gadfly*, an annoying, biting insect, attached "to a horse that is large and well-bred but rather sluggish from its size, and needing to be aroused. It seems to me that the god has attached me like that to the state, for I am constantly alighting upon you at every point to rouse, persuade, and reproach each of you all day long."

Centuries later, Socrates is still relevant to us today with the same compelling immediacy with which he spoke to his fellow Athenians. Too often we are drowsy sleepwalkers, shuffling through life, submerged in mundane daily tasks, predictable habits, restricted visions of ourselves and who we can be. More than ever we need the gadfly of Socrates to wake us from our dozing, energize our thinking, and open our mind's eye to the depths of our souls and the wonders of the universe. Being shaken awake is not usually a pleasant experience, and Socrates noted, "You are indignant, as drowsy persons are, when they are awakened," tempted initially to "sleep on undisturbed for the rest of your lives." But if we rouse ourselves to full alertness, our minds can become catalysts of creative energy, infusing our lives with vibrant emotions, penetrating ideas, and galvanizing experiences, as expressed in the following student passage:

> *Beginning with Socrates' call to arms, this course has aided me considerably in my philosophical journey. I have learned to think more critically, to doubt, instead of accepting all that is "intravenously" fed to me through my environment. I discovered what it is to truly make a free decision and what it is to be moral. I read about many intriguing philosophers and their insightful convictions. But most of all I had the opportunity to grow as a person and create my own philosophy of life.*
>
> Danielle Malkusz

Hesiod, Homer, and the Birth of Philosophy

Here's an opportunity for you to use your imagination. Erase from your mind your entire scientific understanding of the world. Imagine that you and all of the people in your culture explain events in the natural world through superstition, fairy tales, and religion. The sun rises in the morning because it wishes to. Rain needed to grow crops is dependent on the pleasure of the gods. Issues of sickness and health, and life and death, reflect unseen spirits living among us. Your personal destiny is entirely determined by the position of the planets.

As strange as these beliefs are to our modern consciousness, this was very much the state of affairs in the ancient world. Although understanding of the world progressed in various cultures, it was invariably inhibited by nonscientific factors. The Chinese, Babylonians, Mayans, and Egyptians had developed advanced practical technology in areas such as construction (the pyramids) and astronomy (predicting solar and lunar eclipses), and they had made impressive gains in mathematics. But in every case, superstition, myths, and religion infiltrated the processes of reason and observation. For example, Babylonian knowledge of astronomy was intertwined with an unshakeable belief in astrology, and Egyptian advancements in mathematics were permeated with religious superstition.

What is the nature of reality? Pythagoras, Heraclitus, and Parmenides were three "pre-Socratic" philosophers who offered answers to this and other philosophical questions.

Although the Greeks had pervasive beliefs in religion and myths as well, theirs incorporated values and a worldview that sowed the seeds for the birth of Western philosophy. In order to fully appreciate the unique and revolutionary nature of the ancient Greek philosophers, we need to examine the historical and cultural context from which they emerged. Since the dawn of reflection, humans have posed fundamental questions about their existence. *Who am I and why do I exist? Does life have meaning or is it simply a random collection of events? Is there a way I ought to live my life and treat other people? Does life continue after death or does it end with the death of our bodies? Is there an ultimate reality and if so, can I gain knowledge of it?*

Traditionally, various cultures have attempted to provide answers to these profound questions by creating stories. These stories are typically religious in nature, involving supernatural beings (gods) or awe-inspiring forces responsible for creating the world and the human beings that inhabit it. In Greek culture, these religious stories formed a rich and colorful array of divine characters, many of whom are still familiar to us today. They include gods and goddesses like Zeus, Hera, Poseidon, Ares, Hermes, Athena, Heracles, Dionysus, Artemis, and Apollo. The early Greek poet Hesiod composed the original compendium of these gods in his poem entitled *Theogony* (meaning "origin or birth of the gods") in the eighth century B.C.E. Hesiod claimed to be inspired by "the Muses" who "taught Hesiod to sing sweet songs" (*Theogony*, 21–35):

And sending out
Unearthly music, first they celebrate
The august race of first-born gods, whom Earth
Bore to broad Heaven, then their progeny,
Givers of good things. Next they sing of Zeus
The father of gods and men, how high he is
Above the other gods, how great in strength.
Theogony, *42–48*

These gods were portrayed as having complex and dramatic lives filled with conflict, lust, betrayal, violence, love, competition, and passion. As with most societies, these religious stories became an integral part of the culture, institutionalized in temples, rituals, sacred objects, and religious priests and priestesses. More significantly, the gods became a central part of the culture's belief system, treated and taught as real beings engaged in actual events. And like other societies, these religious stories ended up profoundly shaping the way the people viewed themselves and their world.

What made the religious stories of the ancient Greek culture unique were the themes upon which they were based. It's undeniably true that the actions—and antics—of the gods often seemed like an X-rated soap opera, as the pre-Socratic philosopher Xenophanes observed:

"Homer and Hesiod have attributed to the gods all those things which in men are a matter for reproach and censure: stealing, adultery, and mutual deception" (DK Z1 B11, *IEGP* 55). It's also true that as portrayed, the Greek gods had little use for humans, viewing our tragedies and comedies as entertainment for which they are mainly spectators. Zeus observes this in a passage in *The Iliad*, in which a battle between the Greeks and the Trojans is about to rage:

> "These mortals do concern me, dying as they are.
> Still, here I stay on Olympus throned aloft,
> Here in my steep mountain cleft, to feast my eyes
> And delight my heart."
> The Iliad, *Book 20, 26–29*

Homer: In the Western classical tradition **Homer** is the author of the *Iliad* and the *Odyssey*, and is revered as the greatest ancient Greek epic poet. These epics lie at the beginning of the Western canon of literature, and have had an enormous influence on the history of literature.

Yet despite these unflattering portrayals, it's also true that in their dealings with one another, they embodied core values that helped shape the Greek culture and character, including:

- Justice is to be revered: injustice and wickedness will eventually be punished.
- Order and clarity are to be pursued: disorder and chaos rejected.
- Developing one's intellect and cunning is to be aspired to: being thoughtless and foolish avoided at all costs.
- Harmony and moderation are rewarded: excess and arrogance eschewed.
- Beauty is to be appreciated and created; ugliness in any form is unappealing.
- Courage and bold action are prized; cowardice and weakness of character despised.
- Honesty and honor should be pursued; duplicity and falseness will end badly.

Since these values were so deeply entrenched in these oft-repeated stories of the gods, they served as exemplars that members of the culture should prize and emulate, and they created a fertile garden from which philosophical thought would develop.

The shaping of the Greek culture and character around these values was reinforced and perpetuated by the profoundly influential stories attributed to a blind poet named Homer, as the philosopher Xenophanes was to observe, "from the beginning all have learnt in accordance with Homer." Homer's two great poems were *The Iliad* and *The Odyssey. The Iliad* is a mythical retelling of what were thought to be actual historical events: Greece's attack on the city of Troy, in the thirteenth century B.C.E., triggered by the seduction and theft of Helen, the wife of the Spartan king Menelaus by the son of Priam, king of Troy. *The Odyssey* tells the story of the Greek warrior Odysseus who, following the defeat of Troy, embarks on a ten-year journey to return home, an adventure filled with challenge, danger and drama, and ultimate triumph. But though these events may have been loosely based on actual events, Homer's retelling of them is on a mythic level, filled with superheroes like Achilles, Hector, and Odysseus (Ulysses in Roman lore), dramatic action and adventure on the largest scale imaginable, and the periodic intervention of the gods in these human affairs. Once again, the character-shaping values were in evidence: courage, honor, justice, wisdom, bold action, beauty, order, and harmony. Even confronted with the often mindless and destructive world of war, humans can seek to act with courage, intelligence, and integrity within that reality and try to achieve *kleos:* fame or glory; literally "your name on the lips of others." And what ultimately wins the war for the Greeks is not "brawn" but "brains." The opening lines of *The Iliad* provide a preview of the high drama that is about to unfold:

> Rage—Goddess, sing the rage of Peleus' son Achilles,
>
> Murderous, doomed, that cost the Achaeans countless losses,
>
> Hurling down to the House of Death so many sturdy souls,
>
> Great fighters' souls, but made their bodies carrion,
>
> Feasts for the dogs and birds,
>
> And the will of Zeus was moving toward its end.
>
> Begin Muse, when the two first broke and clashed,
>
> Agamemnon lord of men and brilliant Achilles,
>
> What god drove them to fight with such a fury?
>
> Apollo, the son of Zeus and Leto. Incensed at the king
>
> He swept a fatal plague through the army—men were dying
>
> And all because Agamemnon had spurned Apollo's priest.
>
> The Iliad, *Book 1, 1–12*

The Odyssey reflects in even more explicit terms the Greeks' understanding of the human condition and the value they place on the creation of order in the midst of chaos. In contrast to *the Iliad,* which is primarily an account of living in the world of war, *The Odyssey* focuses on the importance of the human world, the one that people create, the one that Odysseus had created in his home of Ithaka and fights to return to. Odysseus battles the obstacles of the universe, both external (natural obstacles—for example, the sea, embodied by Poseidon) and internal (Odysseus's own pride makes him reveal his identity to the Cyclops, which creates further trouble for him) in order to make it home and restore order. This was because, in spite of the chaos of existence, the Greeks believed that human beings were capable of (and responsible for) creating order and civilization. The universe was not going to give them the answers, so the human beings had to do it.

At the heart of the creation of order was the *polis.* The polis was more than just a "city-state" and more than just a location. It was an idea. To the ancient Greek mind, the *polis* was (roughly translated) "a place you can walk across in a single day and have a conversation with all you meet." The *polis* was a social idea—it could not exist without human conversation, and if it was too large, it would mean that people were not able to participate in the conversation that was necessary for the *polis* to function. The *polis* depends upon justice, law, etc., and these are created by humans through reason and conversation (which is why the agora became so important).

Odysseus is a "maker of order/civilization" and the creator of an ethical code in order to achieve this. For Homer, he embodies the creation of order within chaos—that he is at the story's center tells us that this creation of order is essential to the Greeks. Odysseus is known as a just ruler—when he leaves Ithaka, it falls into the hands of the suitors who become symbols of the potential of humans to create chaos; they have taken control, acting without reason or ethics, and his home is in chaos. Ithaka is not Ithaka without Odysseus there. Odysseus's own journey home is filled with chaotic elements that he guides his crew through. When the crew sees Odysseus, after thinking him lost, they exclaim with tears running down their faces, "Now Ithaka seems here, and we in Ithaka!" Odysseus represents everything they understand of their *polis*—the order, the justice, etc. The full passage:

"My crew poured round me when they saw me come—

their faces wet with tears as if they saw

their homeland, and the crags of Ithaka,

even the very town where they were born.

And weeping still they all cried out in greeting:

'Prince, what joy this is, your safe return!

Now Ithaka seems here, and we in Ithaka!'"

The Odyssey, *Book X, 461–467*

Odysseus returns home, and as he has done with the challenges on his journey, restores order out of the chaos. For Greeks, this is the goal—to create our own

Odyssey

ordered *polis* in the midst of an absurd and amoral universe. How do they create order by determining what is just in order to create this *polis*? Ultimately the answer is "philosophy."

Yet as compelling and inspiring as these stories of gods and heroes are, they are not philosophy. As with most cultures, these stories and the values they represented were considered to be settled wisdom, and thus accepted and emulated without question or reflection. Philosophy—"love of wisdom"—enters the scene when the human mind begins asking the question "Why?" Why ought these stories be accepted as true? Why should we seek to conform to the values and ideals that they espouse? What are the reasons that legitimize these values? Are there other, potentially more enlightened values and principles of living that we ought to investigate? How can we best use our thinking abilities to pursue truth and knowledge of reality?

Because the essence of philosophy is to question the authenticity and truth of these cultural stories and myths, philosophy often finds itself at odds with the prevailing culture. What is remarkable about ancient Greece was that philosophy was permitted and even encouraged to thrive, relying on the clarifying power of human reason to explore and seek to understand every meaningful dimension of human experience and the cosmos. One reason for this was that the values that were promulgated in the stories and myths often championed qualities consistent with philosophical wonder: independence of thought, strength of character, development of the intellect, living life honorably and courageously, seeking order and clarity. Of course, as we will see in the case of Socrates, there were times when even in the intellectually open and creative culture of ancient Greece, the underlying tension between established religion and archetypal myths exploded into open conflict with devastating results.

The unique values and worldview embodied in Greek religion and myths helped create the conditions for the birth of philosophy in Greece, embodied in a group of individuals collectively called the "pre-Socratic" philosophers (i.e., "before" Socrates) who surfaced between 600 and 500 B.C.E. These pre-Socratic philosophers served as intellectual catalysts and laid the foundation for Socrates, Plato, Aristotle, and the formal birth of Western philosophy. These early thinkers were able to take a progressively fresh view of the human experience, approaching the natural world using the powerful lenses of *reason* and *observation* to create an intelligible picture of the universe. In so doing, they avoided the limiting effects of superstition, myth, and religion that had influenced Greece and other cultures. In a strictly chronological sense, several of these thinkers were actually contemporaneous with Socrates and even his student Plato. However, we can still refer to all of these early Greek thinkers as "pre-Socratic" in the sense that they were not directly influenced by the views of Socrates. These pre-Socratic thinkers were particularly interested in identifying the underlying essence of the universe, and they wrestled with the apparent contradictions between the eternal and the finite, the immutable and the changing, appearance and reality. However, several of these early thinkers were also concerned about questions that were to be the primary focus of Socrates: the best way to live a human life, and the ethical issues that are integral to this project.

Watch the **Video** *Carl Sagan—Cosmos— Democritus* on **mysearchlab.com**

Thales proposed that the primal element of the universe was water; **Anaximenes** suggested it was air; and **Heraclitus** contended that it was fire because "All is change." **Democritus** advanced the prescient view that all matter in the universe was composed of indivisible atoms, and **Anaxagoras** anticipated modern cosmology in proposing that the entire universe is composed of matter in motion, though he also maintained that what he called Mind (*nous*) was the cause of the ordered universe. **Pythagoras** was convinced that the fundamental principles of the universe were mathematical relations (a view that fore-shadowed the thinking of Albert Einstein a few thousand years later). **Parmenides** was an accomplished mathematician who believed that there was a necessary, static, unchanging unity running throughout all of what is in flux in the world of experience. Although these early efforts were somewhat off the mark, the approach they used, based fundamentally on reason and observation, played an essential role in creating the evolution of Greek philosophy and Western civilization as a whole. We will examine these early pre-Socratic philosophers, several of whom are depicted on page 51, in more depth in Chapter 5, "How Can We Know the Nature of Reality?"

Although the pre-Socratics are the first group of thinkers to be thought of as "philosophers," if we use a wider lens, we can see that at approximately the same time period, at about 500 B.C.E., there were occurring in many other parts of the world astonishing advances in human consciousness, humans seeking a more profound understanding of themselves and of the reality of the world in which they lived. The twentieth-century philosopher **Karl Jaspers** describes this era as the "Axial Period"—the "turning point of civilization."

Karl Jaspers from *The Axial Period*

It would seem that this axis of history is to be found in the period of about 500 B.C., in the spiritual process that occurred between 800 and 200 B.C. It is there that we meet with the most deeply cut dividing line in history. Man, as we know him today, came into being. For short, we may style this the "Axial Period."

The most extraordinary events are concentrated in this period. Confucius and Lao-tse were living in China, and all the directions of Chinese philosophy came into being, including those of Mo-ti, Chuang-tse, Lieh-tsu, and a host of others; India produced the Upanishads and Buddha, and, like China, ran the whole gamut of philosophical possibilities down to skepticism, to materialism, sophism and nihilism; in Iran, Zarathustra taught the challenging view of the world as a struggle between good and evil; in Palestine, the prophets made their appearance, from Elijah, by way of Isaiah and Jeremiah, to Deutero-Isaiah; Greece witnessed the appearance of Homer, of the philosophers—Parmenides, Heraclitus, and Plato—of the tragedians, of Thucydides and of Archimedes. Everything that is merely intimated by these names developed during these few centuries almost simultaneously in China, India, and the Occident without any one of these knowing of the others.

What is new about this age, in all three of these worlds, is that man becomes aware of Being as a whole, of himself and his limitations. He experiences the terrible nature of the world and his own impotence. He asks radical questions. Face to face with the void, he strives for liberation and redemption. By consciously recognizing his limits, he sets himself the highest goals. He experiences unconditionality in the depth of selfhood and in the clarity of transcendence. This took place in reflection...

In this age were born the fundamental categories within which we still think today, and the beginnings of the world religions, by which human beings still live, were created. The step into universality was taken in every sense.

As a result of this process, hitherto unconsciously accepted ideas, customs, and conditions were subjected to examination, questioned, and liquidated. Everything was swept into the vortex. Insofar as the traditional substance still possessed vitality and actuality, its manifestations were illuminated and thereby transmuted.

The *Mythical Age,* with its tranquility and self-evidence, was at an end.... For the first time *philosophers* appeared. Human beings dared to rely on themselves as individuals. Hermits and wandering thinkers in China, ascetics in India, philosophers in Greece, and prophets in Israel all belong together, however much they may differ from each other in their beliefs, the contents of their thought, and their inner dispositions. Man proved capable of confronting inwardly the entire universe. He discovered within himself the origin from which to raise himself above his own self and the world. In *speculative thought,* he lifts himself up toward Being itself.

From Karl Jaspers, *Basic Philosophical Writings—Selections.* Ed., trans., and with introductions by Edith Ehrlich, Leonard H. Ehrlich, and George B. Pepper. (Athens, OH: Ohio University Press), pp. 382–387.

A Man from Greece

Socrates was the son of Sophroniscus, a sculptor, and Phaenarete, a midwife, whose careers were to serve as rich metaphors for Socrates throughout his life, as he used the skills of practical wisdom to "shape" the mind and help others "give birth" to new understanding. Socrates was mentored by some of the great philosophers of his time, learning cosmology from Anaxagoras, rhetoric from Aspasia (who had taught Pericles), and a question-and-answer approach to knowledge from Parmenides. Unlike the great pre-Socratic thinkers, Socrates was not as concerned with the physics of the natural world as he was with the psychology of the mind, and, as he describes in Plato's dialogue *Phaedo,* he decided to develop his own methods of searching for knowledge based on the underlying intuition that all things have an intelligent cause directed toward what is best. In the words of the Roman philosopher Cicero (106–43 B.C.E.), Socrates brought philosophy "out of the clouds and into the market place," into the cities and houses of people. He loved the exploration and interplay of ideas in discussions with others, and it was through these experiences that he developed what has come to be known as the **Socratic Method**. This method used a dynamic approach of questioning and intellectual analysis to draw answers out of people rather than lecture them.

Socrates left no writing of his own, so all of what we know about him comes through other sources. The richest source of his ideas comes from the *Dialogues*, short dramas written by Socrates' student and disciple, **Plato**. Although Plato wrote these masterful and enduring *Dialogues* years after Socrates' death, most experts agree that at least the initial *Dialogues* (*Euthyphro, The Apology, Crito*) are faithful portrayals of Socrates' ideas. As far as Plato's later *Dialogues* are concerned, there are varying opinions regarding the extent to which they express Socrates' or Plato's views, though there was undoubtedly a great deal of agreement between the two.

The other major source of our knowledge of Socrates comes from another of his students, **Xenophon**, a soldier and writer whose best-known work is his *Memorabilia*. In one of his writings, he records Socrates asking him, "Where does one go to learn to become an honest man?" When Xenophon is at a loss for words, Socrates responds, "Come with me and I'll show you."

A Midwife of Ideas

Imagine again: It's a beautiful morning, and you decide to take a stroll in the **agora**, the bustling, noisy marketplace of your native Athens. It's a large area on the north side of the hill of the Acropolis, and the agora is clearly where the action is. Vendors

Socratic Method
Investigation of complex issues through a question-and-answer format.

Agora Open marketplace in Athens, a place where crowds would gather for political speech and discussion.

👁 **Watch** the **Video**
The Socratic Method
on **mysearchlab.com**

Plato (427–347 B.C.E.) Ancient Greek philosopher of extraordinary significance in the history of ideas. Plato not only preserved Socrates' teachings for future generations but also contributed original ideas on a wide range of issues such as morality, politics, metaphysics, and epistemology.

Xenophon (c. 444–c.357 B.C.E.) Biographer of Socrates and his student as a youth. In addition to four works on Socrates, Xenophon wrote histories and practical treatises on leadership, horsemanship, hunting, and economics. Also a warrior, he fought for the Greeks and then for their enemies, the Spartans.

have set up their stalls and are selling everything you might imagine, and then some, as the comic poet Eubulus explains:

> *You will find everything sold together in the same place in Athens: figs, witnesses to summonses, bunches of grapes, turnips, pears, apples, givers of evidence, roses, medlars, porridge, honeycombs, chickpeas, lawsuits, beestings-puddings, myrtle, allotment machines, lambs, water clocks, laws, indictments.*

What draws you to the agora is not the fruits, vegetables, or water clocks, however—it's the spirited conversations that are taking place among the citizens. In fact, the word *agora* is derived from the Greek verb *agoreuein*, which means "to speak," "to address," and "to harangue," and that's exactly what you're looking for—food for thought. You make your way to the Stoa of Zeus Eleutherios, a shady, colonnaded stretch of the agora, and there, as expected, you see a crowd of people clustered around several men engaged in an animated discussion. Even above the general din of the market you can hear the audience laughing and offering comments as they listen intently to the conversation. As you move closer, you see that one of the discussants is a handsome youth, beautifully proportioned and very well dressed, like many of the men and women at the agora. The other man is striking because of his physical unattractiveness: His heavily bearded face frames a balding, knobby head; broad, snubbed nose; bulging eyes; and protruding lips. This arresting head is set atop a powerfully built, stocky torso; bowed legs; and a paunch that he himself described as "a stomach rather too large for convenience," that he perennially announces he intends to "dance off." He is clothed in a worn and somewhat tattered cloak, in stark contrast to the exquisite fabric adorning many of those at the market.

This remarkable figure is Socrates, known to all in Athens and widely considered to be the wisest man in Greece. You move closer. As soon as you begin hearing his resonant voice, experiencing the charismatic influence of his persona, and considering the clarity and insight of his ideas, all thoughts of his physical appearance disappear. As Socrates' friend Alcibiades (a man whose life Socrates had saved with uncommon valor during a horrific battle with Sparta) once noted, Socrates was like the little statues of the Silens that were sold at the stone carvers' booths—physically ugly in superficial appearance but "on being opened, are found to have images of the gods inside them." It is clear to you why Socrates is so idolized and respected by so many in Athens, particularly the spirited and intellectual young men. Socrates is a crown jewel in your native city, and you have come to learn and be entertained as he wields his brilliant intellect to, as he explained, "find who is wise and who pretends to be wise but isn't," a quest that he vowed to continue into the afterlife.

The agora was Socrates' true home—intellectually, emotionally, spiritually—and he loved the crowds and human energy of this social core, as Xenophon explains: "For early in the morning he used to go to the walkways and gymnasia, to appear in the agora as it filled up, and to be present wherever he would meet with the most people." Once teased by his friend Phaedrus for "never setting foot in the country or going outside the city walls," Socrates rejoined, "Look at it my way, my good friend. It is because I love knowledge, and it is the people in the city who teach me, not the country or the trees."

Socrates' claim that it was "the people in the city who teach me" seems genuine, as one of his recurring themes was his role as an intellectual "midwife," assisting others

in the birth of their ideas. The metaphor of "midwife" is particularly appropriate for Socrates, as this was his mother's profession:

> *The obstetrics which I practice is the same as that of all midwives, except that they practice on women, while I do so on men. They deal with the body, and I deal with the mind. . . . I myself am empty of wisdom, which is why the god Apollo makes me attend to the wisdom of others, and prevents me from giving birth myself.*

Socrates believed that his special wisdom consisted in his ability to stimulate and guide others in the philosophical exploration of profound questions, enabling them to "give birth" to their own understanding.

The Wisest of Men?

> *You remember Chaerephon. From youth upwards he was my comrade. . . . Once he went to Delphi and ventured to put this question to the oracle—he asked if there was any man who was wiser than I. The priestess answered that there was no one.*
>
> Socrates *in The Apology*

In ancient Greece, an oracle was a religious shrine where a specially designated priestess would provide answers on behalf of the gods to questions asked by visitors. The most famous oracle was the oracle at Delphi, which was housed in the great temple to the god Apollo. This temple was the most sacred sanctuary for the ancient Greeks, and they considered it the center of the world, marking the site with a large conical stone, the *omphalos*, meaning navel or center.

For at least twelve centuries, the Oracle at Delphi spoke on behalf of the gods, advising rulers, citizens, and philosophers on everything from their sex lives to affairs of state. The oracle was always a woman, her divine utterances made in response to a

The Oracle at Delphi. According to the revered Oracle at Delphi, no man was wiser than Socrates. What does the use of oracles suggest about the culture of ancient Greece? How does Socrates apply reason within that culture? (© *Bildarchiv Pressischer Kulturbestiz/Art Resource*)

petitioner's request. Before a prophetic session, the oracle would descend into a basement cell and breathe in the sacred fumes. Then, in a trance, at times in a frenzy, she would answer questions, give orders, and make prophecies. In a fascinating epilogue, archeologists have recently determined that the oracle probably came under the influence of ethylene—a sweet-smelling gas once used as an anesthetic. In light doses, it produces feelings of aloof euphoria and inspirational visions.

The oracle's announcements exerted wide influence, and one of the most famous and admired was that no man was wiser than Socrates, a pronouncement delivered when he was only thirty years old. Yet as the following passage from Plato's dialogue *The Apology* reveals, Socrates did not accept this authoritative statement at face value. Consistent with his commitment to rational investigation, he set out to gather evidence to prove or disprove its truth.

> ### Plato, from *The Apology*
>
> When I [Socrates] heard of the oracle I began to reflect: What can the god mean by this riddle? I know very well that I am not wise, even the smallest degree. Then what can she mean by saying that I am the wisest of men? It cannot be that she is speaking falsely, for she is a god and cannot lie. For a long time I was at a loss to understand her meaning.
>
> Then, very reluctantly, I turned to seek for it in this manner: I went to a man who was reputed to be wise, thinking that there, if anywhere, I should prove the answer wrong, and meaning to point out to the oracle its mistake, and to say, "You said that I was the wisest of men, but this man is wiser than I am." So I examined the man—I need not tell you his name, he was a politician—but this was the result, Athenians. When I conversed with him I came to see that, though a great many persons, and most of all he himself, thought that he was wise, yet he was not wise. Then I tried to prove to him that he was not wise, though he fancied that he was; and by so doing I made him indignant, and many of the bystanders. So when I went away, I thought to myself, I am wiser than this man: neither of us knows anything that is really worthwhile, but he thinks that he has knowledge when he has not, while I, having no knowledge, do not think that I have. I seem, at any rate, to be a little wiser than he is on this point: I do not think that I know what I do not know. Next I went to another man who was reputed to be still wiser than the last, with exactly the same result. And there again I made him, and many other men, indignant. . . .
>
> Athenians, I must tell you the truth: by the god, this was the result of the investigation which I made at the god's bidding: I found that the men whose reputation for wisdom stood highest were nearly the most lacking in it, while others who were looked down on as common people were much more intelligent. . . .
>
> But, my friends, I believe that the god is really wise, and that by this oracle he meant that human wisdom is worth little or nothing. I do not think that he meant that Socrates was wise. He only made use of my name and took me as an example, as though he would say to men; He among you is the wisest who, like Socrates, knows that in truth his wisdom is worth nothing at all.

He among you is the wisest who, like Socrates, knows that in truth his wisdom is worth nothing at all.

This passage articulates Socrates' character and philosophy of life in a fashion consistent with all that we know of him. Rather than basking in the glow of the oracle's pronouncement that there is no wiser man than he, Socrates immediately begins thinking critically:

- What does it mean to say "no one is wiser?"
- Is the statement true, particularly because I don't *believe* that I am so wise?
- How can I go about determining the accuracy of the statement?

For Socrates, everything in human experience should be open to critical scrutiny, not in a negative *destructive* way, but in the *constructive* effort to achieve clearer understanding. Socrates is convinced that *reason* is the path to the truth, not opinion or conjecture, and he is willing to follow rational inquiry wherever it might lead—even if it means demonstrating that he is *not* the wisest man! So he embarks on his own experimental exploration, interviewing the people thought to be the wisest in Athens, using his Socratic Method, which we will analyze in the next section.

The results? Under the penetrating analysis of his questioning inquiry, Socrates discovers that those people thought to be wise are unable to articulate their ideas with clarity, logical soundness, and compelling rationale. In fact, it is their smug self-certainty that has inhibited their search for wisdom—they think they've already achieved it! Socrates' search reveals another element of his character: his obvious delight in unmasking pretension, deflating oversized egos, and revealing the emptiness and illogic of unexamined beliefs.

Characteristically, Socrates concludes that his investigations have not "proven" that he is the wisest man—only that he is "a little wiser" than others because he recognizes his lack of *true wisdom*. This echoes the memorable statement by the Chinese philosopher Confucius (sixth to fifth century B.C.E.): "He who knows he is a fool is not a great fool."

< READING CRITICALLY >

Analyzing Socrates on Wisdom and Humility

- How do you think most people would respond to being told that they are the most intelligent person in their community? Why do you think Socrates reacts as he does?

- In another part of the *Apology*, Socrates explains how he interviewed people who were exceptionally talented in one particular area, such as poetry or the arts. He found that these people believed that "because of their poetry (or other talent), they thought that they were the wisest of men in other matters too, which they were not." Describe several examples of people you know who are talented in one area and who believe that they are exceptionally wise in other areas as well.

- Socrates is a very complex individual; and, when we read Plato's dialogues, in which he appears as the main character, we need to be attentive to the many layers of meaning, intricate logic, and subtlety in his nuanced use of language. Do you think that he really believes that he is only a "little wiser" than others, and that his advantage is solely due to his acceptance of the fact that he is *not* wise? Why or why not? Why is the admission of ignorance the beginning of wisdom?

2.2 The Socratic Method

Socrates: Tell me, Euthydemus, have you ever gone to Delphi?

Euthydemus: Yes, twice.

Socrates: And did you observe what is written on the temple wall—"Know thyself"?

Euthydemus: I did.

Socrates: And did you take no thought of that inscription, or did you attend to it, and try to examine yourself, and ascertain what sort of character you are?

((••— **Listen** to the **Podcast**
*M.M. McCabe on the
Socratic Method* on
mysearchlab.com

This excerpt from Xenophon's autobiography *Memorabilia* expresses one of Socrates' central themes, as well as the approach he preferred to communicate his ideas to others. As we discovered in the first chapter, the keystone to Socrates' philosophy was his conviction that "The unexamined life is not worth living." This is the insight that Socrates wants Euthydemus to understand and embrace; but, instead of exhorting or "preaching" to him, Socrates uses a sequence of carefully crafted questions to help Euthydemus achieve this understanding by means of his own efforts. "Have you ever gone to Delphi?" An innocent enough question. "Did you observe the inscription written on the wall—'Know thyself?'" Socrates begins to focus in on his central point. "Did you take no thought of that inscription, or did you attend to it...?" In other words, Socrates is asking, did you ignore the inscription so as to continue your life as a sleepwalker, or did you use the message as a catalyst to examine who you are and whom you want to become? With three brief questions, Socrates has challenged Euthydemus to think about his life in profound terms. In his role as an educational midwife, Socrates is striving to draw out from Euthydemus a reflective insight that he will take seriously and act on. For Socrates, philosophy was best practiced in conversation with others, and this was an activity that he engaged in with great enthusiasm. "Conversation" did not simply mean "talking"—it was instead a disciplined and investigative give-and-take, probing complex issues in a question-and-answer format. This dynamic exchange of ideas was characterized by Plato as a **dialectic**, which is derived from a Greek word for conversation, and its goal was to achieve a deep, clear, rationally founded understanding of the most significant areas of human experience: knowledge, justice, morality, religion, beauty, goodness, and the traits of good character such as courage and piety.

Dialectic From the Greek word for "to argue" or "converse," a dynamic exchange or method involving contradiction or a technique for establishing an informed conclusion.

In most instances, Socrates would begin with a general definition of an important concept, such as justice, and then use his dialectical method to seek an understanding of the *essential nature* of the central concept. To arrive at this point of clarity, Socrates first worked to clear away the debris of inadequate and inconsistent definitions, typically at the expense of his dialogue partner.

In the following passage from Plato's most famous dialogue, *Republic*, Socrates engages with a formidable opponent, Thrasymachus (c. 459–c. 400 B.C.E.), a leading Sophist of the day. The **Sophists** were an influential group of traveling educators who, for a fee, would teach people how to argue persuasively. They were, in general, interested in teaching the rhetorical techniques and tricks needed to win an argument at all costs, rather than determining what was "true" or "right" through collaborative investigation. In this sense, they were diametrically opposed to Socrates' quest for genuine knowledge and universal truth. In fact, many Sophists were "relativists" and "skeptics," philosophical views that contend that knowledge is only a matter of opinion and truth is always relative to a particular context. From this vantage point, universal truth and genuine knowledge simply don't exist: Each person and culture determine their own version of "truth" and "knowledge." Relativism and skepticism are philosophical theories that we will explore in great depth in later chapters.

Sophists Influential group of traveling educators who would teach rhetoric and oration for a fee. Many Sophists believed truth to be relative.

Before the aggressive Thrasymachus bursts onto the scene in the following passage, Socrates has been having a relatively calm and civilized discussion with a number of participants, considering and discarding a variety of efforts to define the essential nature of "justice."

Plato, from *The Republic*

Listen to the **News**
*Plato's Republic Still
Influential Author Says*
on **mysearchlab.com**

While we had been talking Thrasymachus had often tried to interrupt, but had been prevented by those sitting near him, who wanted to hear the argument concluded; but when we paused … he was no longer able to contain himself and gathered himself together and sprang on us like a wild beast, as if he wanted to tear us in pieces. Polemarchus and I [Socrates] were scared stiff, as Thrasymachus burst out and said, "What is all this nonsense, Socrates? Why do you go on in this childish way being so polite about each other's opinions? If you really want to know what justice is, stop asking questions and then playing to the gallery by refuting anyone who answers you. You know perfectly well that it is easier to ask questions than to answer them. Give us an answer yourself, and tell us what you think justice is. And don't tell me that it's duty, or expediency, or advantage, or profit, or interest. I won't put up with nonsense of that sort; give me a clear and precise definition."

In stark contrast to the preceding atmosphere of thoughtful exchanges and mutual respect, Plato portrays Thrasymachus as loud, sarcastic, and insulting, often on the verge of physical violence. This should be interesting!

I [Socrates] was staggered by his attack and looked at him in dismay. If I had not seen him first I believe I should have been struck dumb; but I had noticed him when our argument first began to annoy him, and so managed to answer him, saying diffidently: "Don't be hard on us, Thrasymachus. If we have made any mistake in the course of our argument, I assure you we have not done so on purpose. For if we were looking for gold, you can't suppose that we would willingly let mutual politeness hinder our search and prevent our finding it. Justice is much more valuable than gold, and we aren't likely to cramp our efforts to find it by any idiotic deference to each other. I assure you we are doing our best. It's the ability that we lack, and clever chaps like you ought to be sorry for us and not get annoyed with us."

Plato, from *The Republic*

Notice how clever Socrates is in handling this aggressive assault. Thrasymachus charges like an angry bull, and Socrates deftly steps aside and lets him go galloping past. It's a form of verbal judo that Socrates perfected: Instead of meeting aggression with aggression, or backing down in the face of the onslaught, Socrates turns the aggressive energy of his opponent *against* him, leaving Thrasymachus (in this case) looking foolish when Socrates explains, "If we have made any mistake in the course of our argument, I assure you we have not done so on purpose."

Another thing to note is Socrates' exquisite use of **irony**, a form of rhetoric that has at least two conflicting levels of meaning—a literal or obvious level and a hidden or real level. So when Socrates says, "It's the ability that we lack, and clever chaps like you ought to be sorry for us and not get annoyed with us," there are two messages:

- *Literal, obvious meaning:* You are much more intelligent than we are, so please be patient with us.
- *Hidden, real meaning:* You *think* you're more intelligent, but you're really a pretentious buffoon, which I intend to demonstrate to everyone here.

Socrates was a master of irony and used it to expertly create a false sense of security in his dialogue partners and create the conditions for unmasking their foolishness and ignorance.

Irony A form of rhetoric that has at least two conflicting levels of meaning—an obvious one and a hidden one.

Plato, from *The Republic*

Thrasymachus laughed sarcastically, and replied, "There you go with your old affectation, Socrates. I knew it, and I told the others that you would never let yourself be questioned, but go on shamming ignorance and do anything rather than give a straight answer."

"That's because you're so clever, Thrasymachus," I [Socrates] replied, "and you know it. You ask someone for a definition of twelve and add, 'I don't want to be told that it's twice six, or three times four, or six times two, or four times three; that sort of nonsense won't do.' You know perfectly well that no one would answer you on those terms. (This person) would reply, 'What do you mean, Thrasymachus; am I to give none of the answers you mention? If one of them happens to be true, do you want me to give a false one?' And how would you answer him?"

"That's not a fair parallel," he replied.

"I don't see why not," I said: "but even if it is not, we shan't stop anyone else answering like that if he thinks it fair, whether we like it or not."

"So I suppose that is what you are going to do," he said; "you're going to give one of the answers I barred."

"I would not be surprised," said I, "if it seemed to me on reflection to be the right one."

"What if I give you a quite different and far better definition of justice? What plea will you enter then?"

"The plea of ignorance: for those who don't know must learn from those who do."

"You must have your joke," said he, "but you must pay your costs as well." [Thrasymachus is having his own "joke" by suggesting that Socrates pay him his customary fee for "instructing" him.]

"I will when I have any cash."

"The money's all right," said Glaucon; "we'll pay up for Socrates. So let us have your definition, Thrasymachus."

"I know," he replied, "so that Socrates can play his usual tricks, never giving us his own views but always asking others to explain theirs and refuting them."

"But what am I to do?" I asked. "I neither know nor profess to know anything about the subject, and even if I did I've been forbidden to say what I think by no mean (insignificant) antagonist. It's much more reasonable for you to say something, because you say you know, and really have something to say. Do please do me a favour and give me an answer, and don't grudge your instruction to Glaucon and the others here."

Glaucon and the others backed up what I had said, and it was obvious that Thrasymachus was anxious to get the credit for the striking answer he thought he could give: but he went on pretending he wanted to win his point and make me reply. In the end, however, he gave in, remarking, "So this is the wisdom of Socrates: he won't teach anyone anything, but goes round learning from others and is not even grateful."

To which I replied, "It's quite true, Thrasymachus, to say I learn from others, but it's not true to say I'm not grateful. I am generous with my praise—the only return I can give, as I have no money. You'll see in a moment how ready I am to praise any view I think well founded, for I'm sure the answer you're going to give will be that."

Thrasymachus *is* clever enough to recognize Socrates' preference for having others propose ideas and definitions, which he would then critically analyze through relentless, incisive questioning. Socrates' goal was to achieve a deep understanding of essential truths through the process of uncovering unjustified claims to knowledge, exposing logical inconsistencies, and gradually making his discussion partners aware of their *lack* of rational understanding of things they thought they knew. This dialectical analysis of concepts is unique in recorded history, because it is the first systematic use of reason for its own sake in philosophy. And as Thrasymachus rightly notes, it is very difficult to propose and defend a definition of a complex idea like "justice," particularly when faced with the prospect of being carved up by the surgical blade of Socrates' formidable intelligence. Yet despite his wariness and insistence that Socrates be the one to offer a definition of justice, Thrasymachus can't help taking center stage with what he believes to be the truthful definition of justice.

> "Listen then," [Thrasymachus] replied. "I define justice or right as what is in the interest of the stronger party. Now where is your praise? I can see you're going to refuse it."
>
> "You shall have it when I [Socrates] understand what you mean, which at present I don't. You say that what is in the interest of the stronger party is right; but what do you mean by interest? For instance, Polydamas the athlete is stronger than us, and it's in his interest to eat beef to keep it; we are weaker than he, but you can't mean that the same diet is in our interest and so right for us."
>
> "You're being tiresome, Socrates," he returned, "and taking my definition in the sense most likely to damage it."
>
> "I assure you I'm not," I said: "you must explain your meaning more clearly."
>
> "Well then, you know that some states are tyrannies, some democracies, some aristocracies? And that in each city power is the hands of the ruling class?"
>
> "Yes."
>
> "Each ruling class makes laws that are in its own interest, a democracy democratic laws, a tyranny tyrannical ones and so on; and in making these laws they define as 'right' for their subjects what is in the interest of themselves, the rulers, and if anyone breaks their laws he is punished as a 'wrongdoer.' That is what I mean when I say that 'right' is the same thing in all states, namely the interest of the established ruling class; and this ruling class is the 'strongest' element in each state, and so if we argue correctly we see that 'right' is always the same, the interest of the stronger party.... Consider how the just man always comes off worse than the unjust. For instance, in any business relations between them, you won't find the just man better off at the end of the deal than the unjust. Again, in their relations with the state, when there are taxes to be paid the unjust man will pay less on the same income, and when there's anything to be got he'll get it all. Thus if it's a question of office, if the just man loses nothing else he will suffer from neglecting his private affairs; his honesty will prevent him appropriating public funds, and his relations and friends will detest him because his principles will not allow him to push their interests. But quite the reverse is true of the unjust man ... the man ... who can make profits in a big way: he's the man to study if you want to find how much more private profit there is in wrong than in right.... So we see that injustice, given scope, has greater strength and freedom and power than justice; which proves what I started by saying, that justice is the interest of the stronger party, injustice the interest and profit of oneself."

Plato, from *The Republic*

Thrasymachus has presented a forceful definition of "justice" that is consistent with the Sophist's penchant for skepticism regarding universal truths—namely, there *is* no universal definition of justice. Justice is simply what is in the interest of the stronger party, the person (or people) who have the authority to *command* what they think is "just" and "right." We can sum up this view with the aphorism, *Might makes right.* And Thrasymachus provides a rationale that on the surface seems to have some intuitive credibility.

When we examine various cultures around the world and throughout history, it is often the case that the most powerful individuals create a form of government that serves their interests, and make laws to ensure that the general populations act in ways that also contribute to their interests. But the real question that Thrasymachus is not addressing is whether we would consider all of these forms of government equally just. In other words, if we compare a tyrannical form of government, such as Nazi Germany under Adolf Hitler or the Soviet Union under Joseph Stalin, with democratic forms of government such as Germany today or the United States, would we consider the tyrannies to be as "just" as the democracies? Although it's true that

Hitler and Stalin defined what was "right" in their eyes, does that mean that it was *really* "right"? Or was it a *perversion* of what is truly "right" and "just"?

The same logic applies to the other examples Thrasymachus uses: comparing a "just" (honest) person with an "unjust" (dishonest) person in doing business, paying taxes, and going into politics. Thrasymachus's argument is that a dishonest person will come out on top in business deals, cheat on his taxes, and corruptly use his political position to steal for himself and help his friends. But even if all of this is true, does it prove that the dishonest man is a genuine example of a "just" man, simply because he has accumulated more money through dishonest and corrupt behavior? Just the fact that Thrasymachus uses such terms as *just* and *unjust, honest* and *dishonest,* suggests that these concepts have meaning that goes beyond simply exploiting others and stealing money. The question is, how is Socrates going to reveal the problems inherent in the *might makes right* point of view?

Plato, from *The Republic*

"Now," I [Socrates] said, "I understand your meaning, and we must try to find out whether you are right or not. Your answer defines 'right' and 'interest' but adds the qualification 'of the stronger party.'"

"An insignificant qualification, I suppose you will say."

"Its significance is not yet clear; what is clear is that we must consider whether your definition is true. For I quite agree that what is right is an 'interest'; but you add that it is the interest 'of the stronger party,' and that's what I don't know about and want you to consider."

"Let us hear you."

"You shall," said I. "You say that obedience to the ruling power is right and just?"

"I do."

"And are those in power in the various states infallible or not?"

"They are, of course, liable to make mistakes," he replied.

"When they proceed to make laws, then, they may do the job well or badly."

"I suppose so."

"And if they do it well the laws will be in their interest, and if they do it badly they won't, I take it."

"I agree."

"But their subjects must obey the laws they make, for to do so is right."

"Of course."

"Then according to your argument it is *right* not only to do what is in the interest of the stronger party but also the opposite."

"What do you mean?"

"My meaning is the same as yours, I think. Let us look at it more closely. Did we not agree that when the ruling powers order their subjects to do something they are sometimes mistaken about their own best interest, and yet that it is *right* for the subject to do what his ruler enjoins?"

"I suppose we did."

"Then you must admit that it is *right* to do things that are *not* in the interest of the rulers, who are the *stronger* party; that is, when the rulers mistakenly give orders that will harm them and yet (so you say) it is right for their subjects to obey those orders. For surely, my dear Thrasymachus, in those circumstances it follows that it is 'right' to do the opposite of what you say is right, in that the weaker are *ordered* to do what is against the interest of the stronger."

In like a bull, out like a lamb. Socrates has clearly dismantled Thrasymachus's position by reducing it to a contradiction. In logical terms, this form of argument is known by the Latin phrase *reductio ad absurdum,* which means "reducing to absurdity," achieved in this case by forcing Thrasymachus to acknowledge that his view of justice results in believing two contradictory definitions:

- Justice, or the right action, is doing what is in the interest of the stronger.
- Justice, or the right action, is doing what is *not* in the interest of the stronger.

How does Socrates put a clever debater like Thrasymachus in such a logically untenable position? He has led Thrasymachus to state the following:

A. Right actions are what is in the interest of the stronger.

B. Obedience to the ruling power is right.

C. Rulers are liable to make mistakes, issuing laws that are not in their interest.

These three claims can lead to a conflict: a ruler could issue a law against his interest (C), and then by B it is right to follow the law, but by A it is not right to follow the law. Thus, Thrasymachus must give up one of the three statements.

Of course, the real problem for Thrasymachus is what we noted earlier: Defining "right" as whatever the powers that be say "right" is does not address the question of whether what they say is "right" and "just" is *really* "right" and "just." That's why Socrates is able to force Thrasymachus to acknowledge the self-contradictory nature of his position—because his definition of "right" and "justice" is not based on a clearly defined standard but instead is "relative" to human desire, which is notoriously inconsistent.

This brief excerpt reveals the intellectual power of the Socratic Method, as well as the formidable logical and interpersonal skills that Socrates brought to each encounter. Based on all we know, he could be an intimidating and infuriating discussion partner—brilliant, devious, capable of biting sarcasm and irony. It's no wonder that people were drawn to him and his conversational performances, and it is also no surprise that those he had made to look foolish often developed an abiding anger toward him, an accumulated enmity that would end up contributing to his death.

< READING CRITICALLY >

Analyzing a Socratic Dialogue

- Review the central argument proposed by Thrasymachus carefully: How might you go about strengthening the argument to better withstand the critique by Socrates?

- Describe an incident in which you got into an argument with someone with an aggressive discussion style (à la Thrasymachus). What was the outcome? Then describe how you might have adopted Socrates' "bull fighter" or "jujitsu" style in deflecting the aggression and moving the discussion in a more productive direction. How might the outcome have been different?

- There are many instances in everyday experience when people use a *might makes right* philosophy. For example:

    "Why should you go to bed now? Because I'm your parent, and I said so."

    "I don't want to hear any more questions about my policy—that is, if you want to keep your job. The right thing for you to do is to follow the procedure I gave you."

    "I gave you a low grade on your Shakespeare paper because your interpretation simply isn't right: It's too far out of what I consider to be the mainstream of scholarly critique."

    Describe an incident in which someone has presented you with a *might makes right* philosophy of justice. Then compose a brief dialogue that demonstrates how Socrates might have handled the situation.

Psyche The true self or "soul," which is immortal and imperishable.

2.3 Socrates' Central Concern: The Soul

For Socrates, the central concern of philosophy is the **psyche**, the "true self" or "soul." What is the soul? It is your core identity, your unique spirit that makes you distinctively *you*. This is your authentic personality, your distinctive character. Your soul is the source of your deepest thoughts and highest aspirations, the unique life force that shapes and defines itself through choices made on a daily basis. According to Socrates, your soul is "immortal and imperishable, and after death should continue to exist in another world."

Every soul seeks happiness, Socrates believes, and there is a clearly defined path to achieving happiness, though many don't choose to take it. The only people who are truly happy are those who are virtuous and wise, who live reflective, "examined" lives and strive to behave rightly and justly in every area of their lives. These people create souls that are good, wise, and courageous and as a result they achieve genuine and lasting happiness.

But many people are not happy because they have not pursued virtue and wisdom. Out of ignorance, they have devoted their lives to accumulating material possessions, indulging themselves in mindless pleasure, enlarging their reputations and inflating their egos, and using their relationships with others to further their own interests. These are the "sleepwalking" individuals in life, the people who are only going through the motions of living. Rather than creating souls of shimmering virtue and dazzling insight, their souls are diseased and corrupted, their lives lacking significance and happiness.

It is for this reason that Socrates saw himself as a "physician of the soul," seeking to help cure people of the disease of their spirits. Socrates believed that people were not inherently evil, they were simply unaware of how they *ought* to live to achieve what they most desire—happiness and fulfillment. In the following passage, taken from the *Apology*, Socrates explains his life mission to the people sitting in judgment of him.

Plato, from *The Apology*

Men of Athens, I honour and love you; but I shall obey God rather than you, and while I have strength I shall never cease from the practice and teaching of philosophy, exhorting anyone whom I meet and saying to him after my manner: You, my friend—a citizen of the great and mighty and wise city of Athens—are you not ashamed of heaping up the greatest amount of money and honour and reputation, and caring so little about wisdom and truth and the greatest improvement of the soul, which you never regard or heed at all? And if the person with whom I am arguing, says: Yes, but I do care; then I do not leave him or let him go at once; but I proceed to interrogate and examine and cross-examine him, and if I think that he has no virtue in him, but only says that he has, I reproach him with undervaluing the greater, and overvaluing the less. And I shall repeat the same words to everyone I meet, young and old, citizen and alien, but especially to the citizens. . . .

For know that this is the command of the god; and I believe no greater good has happened to this state than my service to the god. For I do nothing but go about persuading you all, old and young alike, not to take thought for your persons or your properties, but first and chiefly to care about the greatest improvement of your soul. I tell you that virtue is not given by money, but that from virtue comes money and every other good of man, public as well as private. This is my teaching.

Socrates' conviction that the improvement of the soul is the central project of philosophy and indeed, the preeminent life project for each one of us, is the foundation of his core teachings:

- *The unexamined life is not worth living.* Socrates was convinced that we have a moral obligation to achieve our full human potential, "actively exercising our soul's powers," which is the Greek definition of happiness (*eudaemonia*). When we live our lives unreflectively, not actively exploring deeper questions such as "Who am I?" and "What is the meaning of my life?" then our lives have diminished value. Yet most disturbing to Socrates was the fact that his fellow citizens so rarely even *posed* these questions, to themselves or to others. They were too busy "living" to wonder *why* they were living or developing a profound understanding of *who* was doing the living. And if Socrates was alive today, it is likely that he would be at least as concerned regarding the "sleepwalking" of people in our culture and world as he was then. The gift of human reason provides us with the extraordinary ability not just to live but to critically examine our lives to make them as productive and worthwhile as possible. If we are to become human in the fullest sense, achieving our distinctive potential and genuine happiness, then we must live "an examined life."

- *The truth lies within each of us.* By living an examined life, we can discover the principles of right thinking and action within us. In our effort to improve our souls and make them more godlike, we need only to apply the divine gift of reason to look deep within ourselves and discover immutable, universal truths. Of course, this process is aided tremendously by engaging in shared explorations with others through dialectical conversations. But the ultimate answers lie within us. Socrates also extends this concept of implicit knowledge to other insights regarding the nature of reality, such as mathematics. In the dialogue

Are we a society of sleepwalkers? Socrates warned the citizens of Athens against "sleepwalking through life." Do you think citizens of our culture run a similar risk of "rushing through life" without taking the time to reflect deeply on the meaning of life and the state of their souls?

Meno, he offers a compelling demonstration to his friend Menon to prove that "there is no such thing as teaching, only remembering." He interviews an uneducated Greek slave boy, beginning with the concept of a $2' \times 2'$ square, and then uses a series of skillful questions to successfully elicit some of the basic rules of geometry (for example, if a $2' \times 2'$ space is 4 square feet, what must be the dimensions of an $8'$ space?) Socrates concludes, "Now then, Menon, what do you think? Was there one single opinion which the boy did not give as his own? ... Then if he did not get them in this life, is it not clear now that he had them and had learnt at some other time?" (*Meno*). Socrates' belief that we each possess implicit knowledge that we can discover through reflective critical analysis of our own minds fits well with his belief in the immortality of the soul: We brought this knowledge with us when our souls entered this life on Earth.

- *We should strive for excellence in all areas of life.* As previously mentioned, the Greeks in general and Socrates in particular believed that happiness was a consequence of actively exercising *all* of our soul's powers, and Socrates was a living example of this commitment. History emphasizes the excellence he achieved in developing his intellect and his extraordinary skills as an educator through his ongoing discussions. But he was fully committed to achievement in other areas as well. As a youth Socrates was apprenticed to his father, a sculptor, and according to one tradition, he worked on the masterful *The Three Muses in Their Habits*, which adorned the Acropolis. When the Peloponnesian War broke out with neighboring Sparta, Socrates was drafted into service as a foot soldier (*hoplite*), armed with a shield and a sword. Despite his lowly rank, he distinguished himself with uncommon valor. In the midst of one battle he spied his friend, Alcibiades, lying wounded on the ground. He fought his way to him, slung him over his shoulder, and carried him to safety through a mass of armed enemy soldiers. During

Who exemplifies Socrates' teachings? Socrates believed that we should live examined lives and have the courage to act on our principles despite the challenges we encounter, qualities exhibited by Mohandas Gandhi in leading India to independence in the first half of the twentieth century, and by Nelson Mandela in helping to liberate South Africa from the oppression of apartheid. What individuals would you include as exemplars of Socrates' ideals?

the battle of Delium, his army broke ranks and retreated before the advancing Spartans. Socrates stood his ground and was the last Athenian soldier to join his comrades. For Socrates, a good and honorable life entailed making full use of all of one's gifts: intellectually, creatively, courageously. And as we shall see, his intellectual and physical courage dominated the final chapter of his life, his trial and execution.

- *No one knowingly does evil.* For Socrates, goodness and wisdom were partners, inextricably connected at their roots. He believed that virtue and excellence (**arete**) of the soul is the consequence of knowledge (**epistêmê**) and wisdom (**sophia**). It is by determined and clearheaded thinking that we develop an understanding of the rigorous standards of conduct that humans should follow, individually and socially. By training our minds to explore the central questions in life regarding justice, morality, and goodness, we cannot help but become good persons ourselves. Because all people want to be happy, and genuine happiness is the result of living an enlightened, examined life, then people will naturally live morally upright lives so that they can achieve authentic happiness. So why doesn't everyone choose to emulate Socrates' model of virtue and wisdom? Because they are ignorant. They want to be happy, but they are misguided in how to go about achieving this. They believe, like Thrasymachus, that they will become happy by accumulating money, becoming powerful, indulging their senses, or controlling other people. They don't realize that these venal pursuits will not only inhibit their quest for happiness but also corrupt their souls. Their only hope is to recognize that they need to pursue virtue and wisdom to be genuinely happy, and once they achieve this profound insight, this is the life path that they will choose.

> **Arete** Virtue and excellence.
>
> **Epistêmê** The Greek word most often translated as knowledge, while *technê* is translated as either craft or art.
>
> **Sophia** Wisdom.

- *"It is better to suffer wickedness than to commit it."* Why be moral? As just noted, Socrates' response is that becoming a moral person is the only way to become a truly happy, psychologically healthy person. Often adages are clichéd and empty of meaning, but for Socrates, the idea that "virtue is its own reward" contains a substantial measure of truth, a point he expresses in his observation that doing wrong "will harm and corrupt that part of ourselves that is improved by just actions and destroyed by unjust actions." As a thinking individual, you create yourself through the choices that you make much as a sculptor gradually forms a figure through countless cuts of the chisel. If you create yourself as a moral person, you create a person of character and worth, with an acute sense of right and wrong and the power to choose appropriately. But if, out of ignorance, you don't choose to create yourself as a moral person, your soul gradually becomes corrupted. You lose your moral sensitivity, developing a moral blindness that handicaps your ability to see yourself or the world clearly. It is no wonder that Socrates believed that "it is better to suffer wickedness than to commit it." Choosing immorality binds your hands, one loop of thread at a time, until your freedom of movement disappears. Although virtuous people enjoy healthy personalities and spiritual wholeness, immoral people are corrupted at their core, progressively ravaged by a disease of the spirit. And because our soul is immutable and eternal, it is impossible for a virtuous person to ever be harmed by others in any meaningful, lasting sense, and it is for this reason also that, Socrates believes, a virtuous person should have no fear of death.

> **< READING CRITICALLY >**
>
> ### Analyzing the Core Teachings of Socrates
>
> - When you think about your "self," what image comes to mind? Describe, as best you can, the entity that Socrates refers to as your "soul": that core identity that distinguishes you from every other living creature. Do you think this identity is immortal? Why or why not?
>
> - Socrates posed the following challenge to his fellow citizens: "... are you not ashamed of heaping up the greatest amount of money and honour and reputation, and caring so little about wisdom and truth and the greatest improvement of the soul?" Do you think that this challenge is still relevant today? Explain your reasoning.
>
> - Socrates believes that the most important truths already exist within our minds—we need only develop our powers of reflective analysis to discover them. Do you agree with this view? What might be examples of "truths" that exist within every person's mind?
>
> - According to Socrates, no one knowingly does evil. Immoral conduct is always the result of ignorance, and if people are educated regarding the "right" way to act, they will necessarily do it. Do you agree with this view? Have you ever known the "right" thing to do but suffered from a "failure of will" and ended up doing the wrong thing? If so, how would Socrates analyze your experience?

2.4 The Trial and Death of Socrates

Although Socrates lived an exemplary and influential life, if it hadn't been for his trial and ultimate execution, it is very possible that we would not be studying him today. These events were so dramatic and the principles they embodied so profound and timeless that they elevated Socrates to a near mythic level.

These final extraordinary days in Socrates' life are captured in Plato's dialogue *Apology*, a term that refers to a philosophical defense of an action or viewpoint. At the age of seventy, Socrates finds himself at the court of Athens on trial for his life due to allegations that he has "corrupted the youth" of Athens and that he "does not believe in the gods whom the state believes in, but in other new divinities." As in the case of many political trials of this sort throughout history, these charges were merely a cover for more sinister forces at work. Socrates was indeed unpopular with many influential citizens and political leaders because he had encouraged people throughout his life *not* to blindly accept authority or the pronouncements of self-appointed "wise" people. Instead, in his countless discussions in the agora, he insisted by word and example that people think for themselves and that all ideas be held up to the scrutiny of critical analysis to determine their value and truth.

Socrates had also developed enemies because of his political views, especially during the two greatest political convulsions in Athens's history. In 411 and again in 404, the Athenian democracy was overthrown by a group led by antidemocratic aristocrats. In both cases forces committed to democracy were able to overcome the dictators. The rebellion in 411 ("The rule of the 400") was initiated by one of Socrates' star students, Alcibiades, who oversaw a four-month reign of terror. The rebellion in 404 was initiated by two students of Socrates who are featured in a number of Plato's dialogues—Critias and Cheredon. Their savage rule lasted eight months. Never in the history of Athens were basic rights and property as threatened as in those two aristocratic dictatorships. Yet there is no evidence that Socrates, during those fateful conflicts and their humane resolution, took part in either the overthrow or the restoration of democracy. He sided neither with the disaffected aristocrats who seized power nor with the democrats they killed or expelled from the city. Nor are these crucial events in Greek history addressed in any of Plato's dialogues. Socrates was aware of the criticism he had provoked by his abstention from politics, and he explained at his trial that his famous *daimonion*—the inner voice, or guiding spirit he claimed to possess—had warned him against engaging in politics. "A man who really fights for the right, if he is to preserve his life for even a little while, must be a private citizen, not a public man." Socrates may have believed that his mission was outside of the political process, acting as an independent "gadfly" to rouse and inspire people to follow an enlightened path in life. Whatever the reason, his lack of political involvement engendered real-world political consequences.

Finally, Socrates was also the target of a vindictive father, Anytus, who was the man behind the charges against him. Several years earlier, the son of Anytus had come to study with Socrates and was so inspired that he decided to pursue philosophy instead of working in the family leather-tanning business. Enraged by his son's decision, Anytus arranged for Meletus, a young, unsuccessful poet with a sarcastic streak, to bring the obviously concocted charges against Socrates. Under Athenian law, Socrates' jury was 501 citizens, a cross-section of the 45,000 free citizens living in Athens.

Let's explore this last and most dramatic chapter in Socrates' life and examine how he applied his philosophical convictions to the greatest challenge he had ever faced. Plato's account of the trial begins at the Court of Justice with an opening statement by Socrates, which is following a statement of the charges against him by his accusers.

Plato, from *The Apology*

I cannot tell what impression my accusers have made upon you, Athenians. For my own part, I know that they nearly made me forget who I was, so believable were they; and yet they have scarcely uttered one single word of truth. But of all their many falsehoods, the one which astonished me most was when they said that I was a clever speaker, and that you must be careful not to let me mislead you. I thought that it was most impudent of them not to be ashamed to talk in that way; for as soon as I open my mouth they will be refuted, and I shall prove that I am not a clever speaker in any way at all—unless, indeed, by a clever speaker they mean a man who speaks the truth. If that is their meaning, I agree with them that I am a much greater orator than they. My accusers, then I repeat, have said little or nothing that is true; but from me you shall hear the whole truth. Certainly you will not hear an elaborate speech, Athenians, dressed up, like theirs, with words and phrases. I will say to you what I have to say, without preparation, and in the words which come first, for I believe that my cause is just; so let none of you expect anything else. Indeed, my friends, it would hardly be seemingly for me, at my age, to come before you like a young man with his specious phrases. But there is one thing, Athenians, which I do most earnestly beg and entreat of you. Do not be surprised and do not interrupt with shouts if in my defense I speak in the same way that I accustomed to speak in the market place, at the tables of the moneychangers, where many of you have heard me, and elsewhere. The truth is this. I am more than seventy years old, and this is the first time that I have ever come before a law court; so your manner of speech here is quite strange to me. If I had been really a stranger, you would have forgiven me for speaking in the language and the fashion of my native country; and so now I ask you

> to grant me what I think I have a right to claim. Never mind the style of my speech—it may be better or it may be worse—give your whole attention to the question, Is what I say just, or is it not? That is what makes a good judge, as speaking the truth makes a good advocate.

These initial remarks reveal a vintage Socrates. Fully aware of Socrates' effectiveness in thinking, reasoning, and persuading, his accusers have attempted to undermine his effectiveness by "warning" the jury not to be misled by his cleverness as a speaker. In logical terms, this is a fallacy known as "poisoning the well," in which the attempt is made to discredit someone's point of view before they even have an opportunity to speak. Socrates recognizes this threat to his credibility and immediately turns the threat back against his accusers by asserting that his only cleverness is "speaking the truth," and if this is what they mean, then he is indeed "clever." One of the many fascinating qualities of Socrates was the fact that, despite the power of his intellect, his language was plainspoken and direct. He avoided the elaborate and ornate language that the Sophists were prone to use, instead choosing to express himself as clearly as possible. It is for this reason that he asks the court not to object or interrupt him for using his familiar, vernacular form of expression rather than the more formal language customary in the court. Instead, he requests that the court focus solely on the content of what he is saying—is it just or not? After all of those years of conversing with and educating people in every imaginable situation, Socrates cannot resist educating the jury as well, advising them that focusing on the justice of the ideas "is what makes a good judge, as speaking the truth makes a good advocate." In other words, he will speak the truth; they need only concentrate on understanding the justice of his case. "Be careful of Socrates' cleverness." Once again, he has outmaneuvered his opponents with a clearly articulated display of rhetorical artistry.

Socrates then goes on to say:

Plato, from *The Apology*

> I have to defend myself, Athenians, first against the old false accusations of my old accusers, and then against the later ones of my present accusers. For many men have been accusing me to you, and for very many years, who have not uttered a word of truth; and I fear them more than I fear Anytus and his associates, formidable as they are. But, my friends, those others are still more formidable for they got hold of most of you when you were children, and they have been more persistent in accusing me untruthfully and have persuaded you that there is a certain Socrates, a wise man, who speculates about the heavens, and who investigates things that are beneath the earth, and who can make the weaker reasons appear the stronger. These men, Athenians, who spread abroad this report are the accusers whom I fear; for their hearers think that persons who pursue such inquiries never believe in the gods. Then they are many, and their attacks have been going on for a long time, and they spoke to you when you were at the age most readily to believe them, for you were all young, and many of you were children, and there was no one to answer them when they attacked me. And the most unreasonable thing of all is that I do not even know their names; I cannot tell you who they are except when one happens to be a comic poet. But all the rest who have persuaded you, from motives of resentment and prejudice, and sometimes it may be, from conviction, are hardest to cope with. For I cannot call any one of them forward in court to cross-examine him. I have, as it were, simply to spar with shadows in my defense, and to put questions which there is no one to answer. I ask you, therefore, to believe that, as I say, I have been attacked by two kinds of accusers—first, by Meletus and his associates, and, then, by those older

ones of whom I have spoken. And, with your leave, I will defend myself first against my old accusers; for you heard their accusations first, and they were much more forceful than my present accusers are.

Well, I must make my defense, Athenians, and try in the short time allowed me to remove the prejudice which you have been so long a time acquiring. I hope that I may manage to do this, if it be good for you and for me, and that my defense may be successful; but I am quite aware of the nature of my task, and I know that it is a difficult one. Be the outcome, however, as is pleasing to God, I must obey the law and make my defense.

In this passage, Socrates is acknowledging the difficulty of overcoming deeply ingrained prejudice. Throughout his life, he contends, there have been those who have spread malicious lies about him, constructing an untrue portrayal of him as one "who speculates about the heavens," "who can make the weaker reasons appear the stronger," and who doesn't "believe in the gods." This prolonged character assassination has been particularly insidious because the young men comprising the jury began hearing these lies as children, when their minds were still malleable and their views of the world still being formed. So to judge him fairly, Socrates is warning, they're going to have to think critically by becoming aware of and setting aside their prejudices against him.

One of the most frustrating elements about personal attacks is that the originators tend to create their mischief behind your back rather than confronting you directly, forcing you to "spar with shadows." But Socrates does name one person who, for some reason, conducted a long-running public campaign to ridicule and discredit him: the "comic poet" Aristophanes (c. 448–380 B.C.E.), the Greek dramatist who authored such classic plays as *The Birds* and *The Clouds*. For example, in response to Socrates' metaphoric characterization of himself as a "midwife" to men's understanding, Aristophanes contended that too often Socrates produced only a "miscarriage of ideas." In his play *The Clouds* he even—sarcastically—features Socrates as a major airhead with his head "in the clouds."

Socrates continues his defense in the following passage:

thinking philosophically

COUNTERING PERSONAL ATTACKS

- One of the attacks against Socrates was an example of "poisoning the well," attempting to undermine his credibility before he even had an opportunity to make his case. Has this technique ever been used against you? Can you describe it? What do you think is the best way to counter this sort of attack?

- Socrates was also the victim of people spreading false and damaging rumors about him. Can you describe a situation in which this has happened to you? Did these rumors influence the opinions of other people toward you? How did you respond to these attacks? How would you respond if they occur in the future?

Let us begin from the beginning, then, and ask what is the accusation which has given rise to the prejudice against me, which was what Meletus relied on when he brought his indictment. What is the prejudice which my enemies have been spreading about me? I must assume that they are formally accusing me, and read their indictment. It would run somewhat in this fashion: Socrates is a wrongdoer who meddles with inquiries into things beneath the earth and in the heavens and who makes the weaker reason appear the stronger, and who teaches others these same things. That is what they say; and in the comedy of Aristophanes (*Clouds*) you yourselves saw a man called Socrates swinging round in a

Plato, from *The Apology*

basket and saying that he walked on the air, and prattling a great deal of nonsense about matters of which I understand nothing, either more or less. I do not mean to disparage that kind of knowledge if there is anyone who is wise about these matters. I trust Meletus may never be able to prosecute me for that. But the truth is, Athenians, I have nothing to do with these matters, and almost all of you are yourselves my witnesses of this. I beg all of you who have heard me discussing, and they are many, to inform your neighbors and tell them if any of you have ever heard me discussing such matters, either more or less. That will show you that the other common stories about me are as false as this one.

But the fact is that not one of these is true. And if you have heard that I undertake to educate men, and make money by so doing, that is not true either, though I think that it would be a fine thing to be able to educate men....

Perhaps some of you may reply: But, Socrates, what is the trouble with you? What has given rise to these prejudices against you? You must have been doing something out of the ordinary. All these stories and reports of you would never have arisen if you had not been doing something different from other men. So tell us what it is, that we may not give our verdict in the dark. I think that that is a fair question, and I will try to explain to you what it is that has raised these prejudices against me and given me this reputation. Listen, then: some of you, perhaps, will think that I am joking, but I assure you that I will tell you the whole truth. I have gained this reputation, Athenians, simply by reason of a certain wisdom. But by what kind of wisdom? It is by just that wisdom which is perhaps human wisdom. In that, it may be, I am really wise...

You remember Chaerephon. From youth upwards he was my comrade; and also a partisan of your democracy, sharing your recent exile and returning with you. You remember, too, Chaerephon's character—how vehement he was in carrying through whatever he took in hand. Once he went to Delphi and ventured to put this question to the oracle—I entreat you again, my friends, not to interrupt me with your shouts—he asked if there was any man who was wiser than I. The priestess answered that there was no one. Chaerephon himself is dead, but his brother here will confirm what I say.

Astutely, Socrates addresses the common belief that "where there's smoke, there's fire" by undertaking to explain how the campaign to ridicule and discredit him came about. In doing so, he's making use of a very effective discussion strategy, namely, anticipating a potential criticism or counterargument against your position and then providing an explanation to counter it.

His explanation is explored earlier in this chapter (pages 59–61). Not convinced of the accuracy of the oracle's pronouncement that there was no man wiser than he, Socrates sets out to investigate this claim by interviewing men reputed to be wise. Under the scrutiny of his penetrating questions, he discovers, of course, that these supposed "wise men" are not wise at all. The result of his tenacious questioning and stripping away of arrogance and pretension? His victims and their friends became angry and resentful of Socrates, creating over the years a growing number of people interested in destroying his reputation and ultimately destroying him.

In addition, Socrates had over the years attracted a large number of mainly young disciples who considered him to be "the bravest, most wise and most upright man of our times." Like the son of his chief accuser, Anytus, they sought to emulate him and his questioning techniques, performing the same debunking of false knowledge that their teacher was so fond of. The predictable result was the allegation by those unsympathetic to Socrates that he was "corrupting the young."

From this examination, Athenians, has arisen much fierce and bitter indignation, and from this a great many prejudices about me, and people say that I am "a wise man." For the bystanders always think that I am wise myself in any matter wherein I refute another. But, my friends, I believe that the god is really wise and that by this oracle he meant that human wisdom is worth little or nothing. I do not think that he meant that Socrates was wise. He only made use of my name, and took me as an example, as though he would say to men: He among you is the wisest who, like Socrates, knows that in truth his wisdom is worth nothing at all.

Besides this, the young men who follow me about, who are the sons of wealthy persons and have the most leisure, take pleasure in hearing men cross-examined. They often imitate me among themselves; they try their hands at cross-examining other people. And, I imagine, they find plenty of men who think that they know a great deal when in fact they know little or nothing. Then the persons who are cross-examined get angry with me instead of with themselves, and say that Socrates is an abomination and corrupts the young. When they are asked, Why, what does he do? what does he teach? They do not know what to say...

What I have told you, Athenians, is the truth: I neither conceal nor do I suppress anything, small or great. Yet I know that it is just this plainness of speech which rouses indignation. But that is only a proof that my words are true, and that the prejudice against me, and the causes of it, are what I have said. And whether you look for them now or hereafter, you will find that they are so.

Plato, from *The Apology*

Having illuminated the accumulated prejudice against him by people whom he has publicly revealed to be "ignorant pretenders to knowledge they don't possess" or those who resent him because of his unvarnished critique of the decadent morals and corrupt political values of many of his fellow citizens, Socrates turns his attention to the matter at hand: the specific charges brought against him by Meletus, the front man for the angry and vindictive tanner, Anytus. It's time for Socrates to demonstrate his Socratic Method to the court, at the expense of Meletus.

What I have said must suffice as my defense against the charges of my first accusers. I will try next to defend myself against Meletus, that "good patriot," as he calls himself, and my later accusers. Let us assume that they are a new set of accusers, and read their indictment, as we did in the case of the others. It runs thus. He says that Socrates is a wrongdoer who corrupts the youth, and who does not believe in the gods whom the state believes in, but in other new divinities. Such is the accusation. Let us examine each point in it separately. Meletus says that I do wrong by corrupting the youth. But I say, Athenians, that he is doing wrong, for he is playing a solemn joke by lightly bringing men to trial, and pretending to have zealous interest in matters to which he has never given a moment's thought. Now I will try to prove to you that it is so.

Come here, Meletus. Is it not a fact that you think it very important that the young should be as excellent as possible?

Meletus: It is.

Socrates: Come then, tell the judges who is it who improves them? You care so much, you must know. You are accusing me, and bringing me to trial, because, as you say, you have discovered that I am the corrupter of the youth. Come now, reveal to the gentlemen who improves them. You see, Meletus, you have nothing to say; you are silent. But don't you think that this is shameful? Is not your silence a conclusive proof of what I say—that you have never cared? Come, tell us, my good sir, who makes the young better citizens?

Meletus: The laws.

Plato, from *The Apology*

Socrates: That, my friend, is not my question. What man improves the young, who starts with the knowledge of the laws?

Meletus: The judges here, Socrates.

Socrates: What do you mean, Meletus? Can they educate the young and improve them?

Meletus: Certainly.

Socrates: All of them? Or only some of them?

Meletus: All of them.

Socrates: By Hera, that is good news! Such a large supply of benefactors! And do the listeners here improve them, or not?

Meletus: They do.

Socrates: And do the senators?

Meletus: Yes.

Socrates: Well then, Meletus, do the members of the assembly corrupt the young or do they again all improve them?

Meletus: They, too, improve them.

Socrates: Then all the Athenians, apparently, make the young into good men except me, and I alone corrupt them. Is that your meaning?

Meletus: Most certainly; that is my meaning.

Socrates: You have discovered me to be most unfortunate. Now tell me: do you think that the same holds good in the case of horses? Does one man do them harm and everyone else improve them? On the contrary, is it not one man only, or a very few—namely, those who are skilled with horses—who can improve them, while the majority of men harm them if they use them and have anything to do with them? Is it not so, Meletus, both with horses and with every other animal? Of course it is, whether you and Anytus say yes or no. The young would certainly be very fortunate if only one man corrupted them, and everyone else did them good. The truth is, Meletus, you prove conclusively that you have never thought about the youth in your life. You exhibit your carelessness in not caring for the very matters about which you are prosecuting me.

Now be so good as to tell us, Meletus, is it better to live among good citizens or bad ones? Answer, my friend. I am not asking you at all a difficult question. Do not the bad harm their associates and the good do them good?

Meletus: Yes.

Socrates: Is there any man who would rather be injured than benefited by his companions? Answer, my good sir; you are obliged by the law to answer. Does nary one like to be injured?

Meletus: Certainly not.

Socrates: Well then, are you prosecuting me for corrupting the young and making them worse, intentionally or unintentionally?

Meletus: For doing it intentionally.

Socrates: What, Meletus? Do you mean to say that you, who are so much younger than I, are yet so much wiser than I that you know that bad citizens always do evil, and that good citizens do good, to those with whom they come in contact, while I am so extraordinarily stupid as not to know that, if I make any of my companions evil, he will probably injure me in some way, and as to commit this great evil, as you allege, intentionally? You will not make me believe that, nor anyone else either, I should think. Either I do not corrupt the young at all or, if I do, I do so unintentionally: so that you are lying in either case. And if I corrupt them unintentionally, the law does not call upon you to prosecute me for an error which is unintentional, but to take me aside privately and reprove and instruct me. For, of course, I shall cease from doing wrong involuntarily, as soon as I know that I have been doing wrong. But you avoided associating with me and educating me; instead you bring me up before the court, where the law sends persons, not for instruction, but for punishment.

What an excellent example of Socrates' ability to slice through confused thinking and emotionally charged generalities to arrive at a clear delineation of the truth! And to do so in such an entertaining way, in a form combining persuasive logic with subtle irony. Socrates begins by engaging Meletus's services in deconstructing the emotionally laden charge that Socrates has been "corrupting the young." Drawing on his years as an educator, Socrates explores the question, "What is the process of shaping a people's thinking and characters?" Meletus quite rightly acknowledges that numerous people influence our development over a long period of time, echoing the African proverb, "It takes a village to raise a child." But if that's the case, Socrates wonders, then how is it possible that he, as a solitary individual, could possibly nullify the influence of all the people the youth of Athens have been taught and influenced by? It's irrational and defies belief. As Socrates notes: "The young would certainly be very fortunate if only one man corrupted them, and everyone else did them good."

What are the influences on character? Do you agree with Socrates that the formation of a person's thinking and character is typically the result of many influences throughout their lives? What about cases where a cult leader is able to exert control over others' thinking? Contrast that type of mind control with the Socratic Method of questioning and dialectical exploration.

Further, Socrates presses Meletus, what incentive would Socrates have to influence the youth of Athens to be evil rather than good? Creating evil disciples would only end up hurting himself, so it only makes sense to believe that he has been trying to influence people to be good. If he has made mistakes in this quest, they have obviously been unintentional, in which case he should be educated, not punished. But of course the truth is that these are not real charges, they are simply excuses to attempt to hurt Socrates, genuinely "impious" efforts for which he has only contempt:

> Meletus says that I do wrong by corrupting the youth. But I say, Athenians, that he is doing wrong, for he is playing a solemn joke by lightly bringing men to trial, and pretending to have zealous interest in matters to which he has never given a moment thought.... The truth is, Meletus, you prove conclusively that you have never thought about the youth in your life. You exhibit your carelessness in not caring for the very matters about which you are prosecuting me.

Plato, from *The Apology*

Having demolished the charge of "corrupting the youth," Socrates now addresses the allegation that he "does not believe in the gods whom the state believes in, but in other new divinities":

> ... now tell us, Meletus, how do you say that I corrupt the young? Clearly, according to your indictment, by teaching them not to believe in the gods the state believes in, but other new divinities instead. You mean that I corrupt the young by that teaching, do you not?
>
> **Meletus:** Yes, most certainly I mean that.
>
> **Socrates:** Then in the name of these gods of whom we are speaking, explain yourself a little more clearly to me and to these gentlemen here. I cannot understand what you mean. Do you mean that I teach the young to believe in some gods, but not in the gods of the state? Do you accuse me of teaching them to believe in strange gods? If that is your

Plato, from *The Apology*

meaning, I myself believe in some gods, and my crime is not that of absolute atheism. Or do you mean that I do not believe in the gods at all myself, and I teach other people not to believe in them either?

Meletus: I mean that you do not believe in the gods in any way whatever.

Socrates: You amaze me, Meletus! Why do you say that? Do you mean that I believe neither the sun nor the moon to be gods, like other men?

Meletus: I swear he does not, judges; he says that the sun is a stone, and the moon earth.

Socrates: My dear Meletus, do you think that you are prosecuting Anaxagoras [a pre-Socratic philosopher who believed that the entire universe is composed of matter in motion governed by the principle of mind *(nous)*]? You must have a very poor opinion of these men, and think them illiterate, if you imagine that they do not know that the works of Anaxagoras of Clazomenae are full of these doctrines. And so young men learn these things from me, when they can often buy places in the theater for a drachma at most, and laugh at Socrates were he to pretend that these doctrines, which are very peculiar doctrines, too, were his own. But please tell me, do you really think that I do not believe in the gods at all?

Meletus: Most certainly I do. You are a complete atheist.

Socrates: No one believes that, Meletus, not even you yourself. It seems to me, Athenians, that Meletus is very insolent and reckless, and that he is prosecuting me simply out of insolence, recklessness and youthful bravado. For he seems to be testing me, by asking me a riddle that has no answer. Will this wise Socrates, he says to himself, see that I am joking and contradicting myself? Or shall I outwit him and everyone else who hears me? Meletus seems to me to contradict himself in his indictment: it is as if he were to say, Socrates is a wrongdoer who does not believe in the gods, but who believes in the gods. But that is mere joking.

Now, my friends, let us see why I think that this is his meaning. Do you answer me, Meletus; and do you, Athenians, remember the request which I made to you at the start, and do not interrupt me with shouts if I talk in my usual way.

Is there any man, Meletus, who believes in the existence of things pertaining to men and not in the existence of men? Make him answer the question, my friends, without these interruptions. Is there any man who believes in the existence of horsemanship and not in the existence of horses? Or in flute-playing and not in flute-players? There is not, my friend. If you will not answer, I will tell both you and the judges. But you must answer my next question. Is there any man who believes in the existence of divine things and not in the existence of divinities?

Meletus: There is not.

Socrates: I am very glad that these gentlemen have managed to extract an answer from you. Well then, you say that I believe in divine beings, whether they be old or new ones, and that I teach others to believe in them; at any rate, according to your statement, I believe in divine beings. That you have sworn in your indictment. But if I believe in divine beings, I suppose it follows necessarily that I believe in divinities. Is it not so? It is. I assume that you grant that, as you do not answer. But do we not believe that divinities are either gods themselves or the children of gods? Do you admit that?

Meletus: I do.

Socrates: Then you admit that I believe in divinities. Now, if these divinities are gods, then, as I say, you are joking and asking a riddle, and asserting that I do not believe in the gods, and at the same time that I do, since I believe in divinities.... You must have indicted me in this manner, Meletus, either to test me or because you could not find any crime that you could accuse me of with truth. But you will never contrive to persuade any man with any sense at all that a belief in divine things and things of the gods does not necessarily involve a belief in divinities, and in the gods, and in heroes.

But in truth, Athenians, I do not think that I need say very much to prove that I have not committed the crime for which Meletus is prosecuting me. What I have said is enough to prove that. But I repeat it is certainly true, as I have already told you, that I have aroused much indignation. That is what will cause my condemnation if I am condemned; not Meletus nor Anytus either, but that prejudice and suspicion of the multitude which have been the destruction of many good men before me, and I think will be so again. There is no fear that I shall be the last victim.

Socrates wastes no time in demolishing the remaining accusations Meletus has brought against him at the behest of Anytus. He begins by demanding a clear definition of the key concepts under discussion—in this case, the accusation that Socrates is corrupting the young "by teaching them not to believe in the gods the state believes in, but other new divinities instead." In fact, the insistence on "defining your terms" has been a core strategy of philosophy ever since Socrates introduced it. Why is it so important to begin discussions with a clear and precise definition of key terms and concepts? It's because those definitions form the bedrock of analysis. If the concepts are permitted to remain vague and ambiguous, it's impossible to make meaningful progress in the analysis and exploration of those terms. That's exactly why so many discussions and debates go awry, because vague, imprecise definitions encourage each party to "fill in" their own meanings, encouraging miscommunication and conceptual confusion. So Socrates presses Meletus:

I cannot understand what you mean. Do you mean that I teach the young to believe in some gods, but not in the gods of the state? Do you accuse me of teaching them to believe in strange gods? If that is your meaning, I myself believe in some gods, and my crime is not that of absolute atheism. Or do you mean that I do not believe in the gods at all myself, and I teach other people not to believe in them either?

Plato, from *The Apology*

Meletus, forced to commit himself to a precise definition of what he means, rather than hiding behind the vague characterization of "corrupting the young by teaching them new divinities," wastes no time in fashioning a semantic noose and hanging himself: "I mean that you do not believe in the gods in any way whatever . . . you are a complete atheist." But Meletus has already acknowledged in his indictment that Socrates believes in some gods—just not the "state-approved" gods. In the same way that Thrasymachus ends up contradicting himself as he struggles to define and redefine "might makes right," so Meletus now finds himself in the position of maintaining that Socrates is a wrongdoer who does not believe in gods, but who believes in the gods. *Reductio ad absurdum!*

Despite administering the coup de grâce to Meletus's feeble argument, Socrates goes on to pursue an intriguing line of reasoning that will foreshadow one of the strongest arguments for the existence of God—the argument by design—used consistently during the past several thousand years. The "argument by design" reasons that

- every dimension of the universe displays design and purpose.
- design and purpose implies a designer who is responsible for creating the design and purpose.
- therefore, God—the supernatural designer—must exist.

Notice how Socrates' line of reasoning echoes the fundamental structure of this argument:

Plato, from *The Apology*

> Is there any man, Meletus, who believes in the existence of things pertaining to men and not in the existence of men? . . . Is there any man who believes in the existence of horsemanship and not in the existence of horses? Or in flute-playing and not in flute-players? . . . Is there any man who believes in the existence of divine things and not in the existence of divinities?

Socrates concludes this section by noting that although he has conclusively demonstrated his innocence with respect to the charges brought against him, he recognizes those charges are masquerading more sinister forces attempting to destroy him: the anger he has aroused by a lifetime of critically examining the beliefs and values of his fellow citizens, as well as the "prejudice and suspicion of the multitude which have been the destruction of many good men before me, and I think will be so again." This last phrase is a chilling prediction of his soon-to-be-decided fate, a concern underscored by his next sentence, "There is no fear that I shall be the last victim."

Yet despite his belief that he is likely to be found guilty for reasons that had nothing to do with the "official" charges against him, Socrates had no intention of providing the court with an easy way out of the situation they had constructed. He realized that if he promised to cease the philosophical activity that he had practiced for his entire adult life, the court would likely forgo any serious punishment. But he wanted to make clear to them that discontinuing his life work was not an option that he would ever consider. If they were intent on finding him guilty, then they would have to take the responsibility of sentencing him to death.

Plato, from *The Apology*

> I will never do what I know to be evil, and shrink in fear from what I do not know to be good or evil. Even if you acquit me now, and do not listen to Anytus's argument that, if I am to be acquitted, I ought never to have been brought to trial at all, and that, as it is, you are bound to put me to death because, as he said, if I escape all your sons will be utterly corrupted by practicing what Socrates teaches. If you were therefore to say to me: Socrates, this time we will not listen to Anytus; we will let you go, but on this condition, that you give up this investigation of yours, and philosophy; if you are found following those pursuits again, you shall die. I say, if you offered to let me go on these terms, I should reply: Athenians, I hold you in the highest regard and affection, but I will be persuaded by the god rather than by you; and as long as I have breath and strength I will not give up philosophy and exhorting you and declaring the truth to every one of you whom I meet, saying, as I am accustomed, "My good friend, you are a citizen of Athens, a city which is very great and very famous for its wisdom and strength—are you not ashamed of caring so much for the making of money and for fame and prestige, when you neither think nor care about wisdom and truth and the improvement of your soul?" . . . For know that the god has commanded me to do so. And I think that no greater good has ever befallen you in Athens than my service to the god. For I spend my whole life in going about and persuading you all to give your first and greatest care to the improvement of your souls, and not till you have done that to think of your bodies or your wealth; and telling you that virtue does not come from wealth, but that wealth, and every other good thing which men have, whether in public or in private, comes from virtue. If then I corrupt the youth by this teaching, these things must be harmful; but if any man says that I teach

> **[W]ealth, and every other good thing which men have, whether in public or in private, comes from virtue . . .**

anything else, there is nothing in what he says. And therefore, Athenians, I say, whether you are persuaded by Anytus or not, whether you acquit me or not, be sure I shall not change my way of life; no, not if I have to die for it many times....

Do not interrupt me, Athenians, with your shouts. Remember the request which I made to you, and do not interrupt my words. I think that it will profit you to hear them. I am going to say something more to you, at which you may be inclined to protest, but do not do that. Be sure that if you put me to death, who am what I have told you that I am, you will do yourselves more harm than me. Meletus and Anytus can do me no harm: that is impossible, for I am sure it is not allowed that a good man be injured by a worse. They may indeed kill me, or drive me into exile, or deprive me of my civil rights; and perhaps Meletus and others think those things great evils. But I do not think so. I think it is a much greater evil to do what he is doing now, and to try to put a man to death unjustly. And now, Athenians, I am not arguing in my own defense at all, as you might expect me to do, but rather in yours in order (that) you may not make a mistake about the gift of the god to you by condemning me. For if you put me to death, you will not easily find another who, if I may use a ludicrous comparison, clings to the state as a sort of gadfly to a horse that is large and well-bred but rather sluggish from its size, and needing to be aroused. It seems to me that the god has attached me like that to the state, for I am constantly alighting upon you at every point to rouse, persuade, and reproach each of you all day long. You will not easily find anyone else my friends, to fill my place; and if you are persuaded by me, you will spare my life. You are indignant, as drowsy persons are, when they are awakened, and, of course, if you are persuaded by Anytus, you could easily kill me with a single blow, and then sleep on undisturbed for the rest of your lives, unless the god in his care for you sends another to rouse you.

< READING CRITICALLY >

Analyzing Socrates on Trial

- Explain what Socrates means when he says, "that virtue does not come from wealth, but that wealth, and every other good thing which men have, whether in public or in private, comes from virtue." Do you agree with this statement? Why or why not?
- Explain what Socrates means when he says, "Be sure that if you put me to death, who am what I have told you that I am, you will do yourselves more harm than me." Do you agree with this statement? Why or why not?
- Explain why Socrates compares himself to a "gadfly." Identify a person in your life who acts as your own personal Socratic "gadfly" and explain why.
- Identify people in our culture who function as Socratic "gadflies." Select one such person and conduct research to develop more information about him or her that you can share with your classmates.

Socrates is now ready to make his final statement—his summation—to the court before they pass judgment on him. Although it was common for the accused to plead for mercy and even bring friends and relatives in to induce the sympathy of the judges and jury, Socrates found this sort of conduct distasteful and inappropriate. He felt strongly that the court should render its decision based on a fair and just interpretation of the case against him, a case that he feels was transparently false and laughable.

Plato, from *The Apology*

Well, my friends, this, and perhaps more like this, is pretty much what I have to say in my defense. There may be some one among you who will be indignant when he remembers how, even in a less important trial than this, he begged and entreated the judges, with many tears, to acquit him, and brought forward his children and many of his friends and relatives in Court in order to appeal to your feelings; and then finds that I shall do none of these things, though I am in what he would think the supreme danger. Perhaps he will harden himself against me when he notices this: it may make him angry, and he may cast his vote in anger. If it is so with any of you—I do not suppose that it is, but in case it should be so—I think that I should answer him reasonably if I said: My friend, I have relatives too, for, in the words of Homer, "I am not born of an oak or a rock" but of flesh and blood; and so, Athenians, I have relatives, and I have three sons, one of them a lad, and the other two still children. Yet I will not bring any of them forward before you and implore you to acquit me. And why will I do none of these things? It is not from arrogance, Athenians, nor because I lack respect for you—whether or not I can face death bravely is another questions—but for my own good name, and for your good name, and for the good name of the whole state. I do not think it right, at my age and with my reputation, to do anything of that kind. Rightly or wrongly, men have made up their minds that in some way Socrates is different from the mass of mankind. And it will be shameful if those of you who are thought to excel in wisdom, or in bravery, or in any other virtue, are going to act in this fashion. I have often seen men of reputation behaving in an extraordinary way at their trial, as if they thought it a terrible fate to be killed, and as though they expected to live forever if you did not put them to death. Such men seem to me to bring shame upon the state.... Those of you, Athenians, who have any reputation at all ought not to do these things, and you ought not to allow us to do them; you should show that you will be much more ready to condemn men who make the state ridiculous by these pitiful pieces of acting, than men who remain quiet.

But apart from the question of reputation, my friends, I do not think that it is right to entreat the judge to acquit us, or to escape condemnation in that way. It is our duty to convince him by reason. He does not sit to give away justice as a favor, but to pronounce judgment; and he has sworn, not to favor any man whom he would like to favor, but to judge according to law. And, therefore, we ought not to encourage you in the habit of breaking your oaths; and you ought not to allow yourselves to fall into this habit, for then neither you nor we would be acting piously. Therefore, Athenians, do not require me to do these things, for I believe them to be neither good nor just nor pious; and, more especially, do not ask me to do them today when Meletus is prosecuting me for impiety. For were I to be successful and persuade you by my entreaties to break your oaths, I should be clearly teaching you to believe that there are no gods, and I should be simply accusing myself by my defense of not believing in them. But, Athenians, that is very far from the truth. I do believe in the gods as no one of my accusers believes in them: and to you and to God I commit my cause to be decided as is best for you and for me.

He is found guilty by 281 votes to 220.

281 to 220! Looking at this event through our lenses over 2,500 years later, it seems incredible that Socrates could have been found guilty, based on such flimsy, unsubstantiated charges. But the truth is, every culture is vulnerable to powerful emotions that can skew rational judgment. For example, during World War II, irrational fear and ethnic prejudice influenced President Franklin Roosevelt and the U.S. Congress to imprison Japanese American citizens in internment camps for the duration of the war. And several years later, Senator Joseph McCarthy used a widespread fear of communism to conduct "hearings" that ruined the lives of many innocent citizens, based on unsubstantiated allegations.

When Socrates says, "Rightly or wrongly, many have made up their minds that in some way Socrates is different from the mass of mankind," he is surely speaking the truth. Even in his closing statement, his concern is for the souls of his judges and for Athens in general, for he knows that they will soon regret such an unjust persecution: "And it will be shameful if those of you who are thought to excel in wisdom, or in bravery, or in any other virtue, are going to act in this fashion." He was a person for whom his principles were more important than anything, even his own life.

It is for this reason that Socrates refused to make emotional appeals to the court. Such false appeals have a long and infamous history in human affairs, and they are one of the more popular "fallacies." As we saw in Chapter 1, fallacies are unsound arguments that are often persuasive because they can appear to be logical and because they usually appeal to our emotions and prejudices. As Socrates points out, appealing to the court for pity or sympathy to influence them to find him innocent or lessen his punishment is illogical, and it would be a violation of their oaths to decide the case based on justice. Although Socrates is convinced that he has proven conclusively that the charges against him are false, he does not want to be found innocent for the wrong—illogical—reasons. For him, a commitment to the principles of clear thinking, logical soundness, and honesty are absolute and unwavering.

In the Athenian legal system, once a person was found guilty and a punishment proposed, the convicted person was entitled to propose a lesser punishment. In Socrates case, Meletus and Anytus have asked for the death penalty: An appropriate counterproposal would be on the order of agreeing to exile or paying a substantial fine. Once again, Socrates departs from the norm, and in this instance, it seals his fate.

How is it possible that a revered figure like Socrates could have been convicted in the Athenian court of a capital crime based on such flimsy, unsubstantiated charges? The truth is that every culture is vulnerable to powerful emotions that can skew rational judgment and destroy innocent lives, like the national anticommunist hysteria created by Senator Joseph McCarthy and his witch hunt "hearings."

I am not indignant at the verdict which you have given, Athenians, for many reasons. I expected that you would find me guilty; and I am not so much surprised at that as at the numbers of the votes. I certainly never thought that the majority against me would have been so narrow. But now it seems that if only thirty votes had changed sides, I should have escaped. So I think that I have escaped Meletus, as it is; and not only have I escaped him, for it is perfectly clear that if Anytus and Lycon had not come forward to accuse me, too, he would not have obtained the fifth part of the votes, and would have had to pay a fine of a thousand drachmae.

So he proposes death as the penalty. Be it so. And what alternative penalty shall I propose to you, Athenians? What I deserve, of course, must I not? What then do I deserve to pay or to suffer for having determined not to spend my life in ease? I neglected the things which most men value, such as wealth, and family interests, and military commands, and popular oratory, and all the political appointments, and clubs, and factions,

Plato, from *The Apology*

that there are in Athens; for I thought that I was really too honest a man to preserve my life if I engaged in these matters. So I did not go where I should have done no good either to you or to myself. I went, instead, to each one of you privately to do him, as I say, the greatest of services, and tried to persuade him not to think of his affairs until he had thought of himself and tried to make himself as good and wise as possible, nor to think of the affairs of Athens until he had thought of Athens herself; and to care for other things in the same manner. Then what do I deserve for such a life? Something good, Athenians, if I am really to propose what I deserve; and something good which it would be suitable to me to receive. Then what is a suitable reward to be given to a poor benefactor who requires leisure to exhort you? There is no reward, Athenians, so suitable for him as a public maintenance in the Prytaneum. It is a much more suitable reward for him than for any of you who has won a victory at the Olympic games with his horse or his chariots. Such a man only makes you seem happy, but I make you really happy; and he is not in want, and I am. So if I am to propose the penalty which I really deserve, I propose this—a public maintenance in the Prytaneum.

Perhaps you think me stubborn and arrogant in what I am saying now, as in what I said about the entreaties and tears. It is not so, Athenians; it is rather that I am convinced that I never wronged any man intentionally, though I cannot persuade you of that, for we have discussed together only a little time. If there were a law at Athens, as there is elsewhere, not to finish a trial of life and death in a single day, I think that I could have persuaded you; but now it is not easy in so short a time to clear myself of great prejudices. But when I am persuaded that I have never wronged any man, I shall certainly not wrong myself, or admit that I deserve to suffer any evil, or propose any evil for myself as a penalty. Why should I? Lest I should suffer the penalty which Meletus proposes when I say that I do not know whether it is a good or an evil? Shall I choose instead of it something which I know to be an evil, and propose that as a penalty? Shall I propose imprisonment? And why should I pass the rest of my days in prison, the slave of successive officials? Or shall I propose a fine, with imprisonment until it is paid? I have told you why I will not do that. I should have to remain in prison, for I have no money to pay a fine with. Shall I then propose exile? Perhaps you would agree to that. Life would indeed be very dear to me if I were unreasonable enough to expect that strangers would cheerfully tolerate my discussions and reasonings when you who are my fellow citizens cannot endure them, and have found them so irksome and odious to you that you are seeking now to be relieved of them. No, indeed, Athenians, that is not likely. A fine life I should lead for an old man if I were to withdraw from Athens and pass the rest of my days in wandering from city to city, and continually being expelled. For I know very well that the young men will listen to me wherever I go, as they do here; and if I drive them away, they will persuade their elders to expel me, and if I do not drive them away, their fathers and kinsmen will expel me for their sakes.

Perhaps someone will say, "Why cannot you withdraw from Athens, Socrates, and hold your peace?" It is the most difficult thing in the world to make you understand why I cannot do that. If I say that I cannot hold my peace because that would be to disobey the god, you will think that I am not in earnest and will not believe me. And if I tell you that no better thing can happen to a man than to discuss virtue every day and the other matters about which you have heard me arguing and examining myself and others, and that an unexamined life is not worth living, then you will believe me still less. But that is so, my friends, though it is not easy to persuade you. And, what is more, I am not accustomed to think that I deserve any punishment. If I had been rich, I would have proposed as large a fine as I could pay: that would have done me no harm. But I am not rich enough to pay a fine unless you are willing to fix it at a sum within my means. Perhaps I could pay you a mina, so I propose that. Plato here, Athenians, and Crito, and Critobulus, and Apollodorus bid me propose thirty minae, and they will be sureties for me. So I propose thirty minae. They will be sufficient sureties to you for the money.

He is condemned to death by a vote of 361 to 140.

It's something of an understatement to observe that Socrates' remarks regarding his proposed punishment of death were not well received—eighty men who had voted to find him innocent switched sides to recommend the death penalty! Why? Because Socrates had failed to demonstrate either remorse or respect for the power of the court. It was customary for men facing the death penalty to take extreme measures, pleading for mercy, covering themselves with dirt and tearing their clothes to symbolize their remorse, rolling on the ground while wailing in anguish. Further, they were expected to acknowledge the authority of the court, speaking deferentially and demonstrating their utmost respect. Socrates did none of this. Instead, consistent with his self-proclaimed role as a "gadfly," he revealed the errors of their thinking in convicting him and warned them against corrupting their souls if they didn't act justly. Rather than propose serious counterpenalties, he recommended that the court award him a special honor for his years of service to Athens and provide him with a pension! Instead of offering to pay a hefty fine, he suggested paying a comparatively miniscule amount (a *mina*), which he asked his friends to increase to 30 minae. In short, Socrates displayed clearly and entertainingly his total contempt for the bogus case that had been brought against him and his moral disapproval of the role that the judges and jury were playing in the personal vendetta against him. Not surprisingly, the court was not amused, preferring to extinguish the gadfly rather than enduring its ongoing bites.

Despite his unwillingness to adhere to court custom, Socrates does make a compelling case for himself. Why should he be punished if he has "never wronged any man intentionally"? If he has only sought to elevate and enlighten all he came into contact with by having them understand that "an unexamined life is not worth living," why should he propose exile as a punishment, when it would mean, as an old man, wandering strange lands and annoying people who don't know him with his philosophical inquiries? Or why should he propose paying a hefty fine, when it would mean going to prison indefinitely because he did not have the resources to pay for it? And why should he agree to terminate his teaching and philosophical inquiries, because this would

The Death of Socrates, **by Jacques Louis David.** The 18th-century French painter David portrayed Socrates as undaunted at the prospect of death, philosophically engaged while reaching for the cup of poison. Plato is seated on the far left, his writing beside him on the floor. Crito grasps Socrates' robes. Do you think Socrates should have tried to escape death, or did his decision show wisdom?

mean abandoning his life work and disobeying the gods he believes have given him a mandate to wake people from their unthinking slumbers? But the judges and jury were in no mood to even hear these questions, much less provide thoughtful responses before passing judgment. Their anger spoke, not their reason, condemning Socrates to death and, ironically, immortality as a martyr to reason and moral principle.

Although many people react to a murder verdict against them with stunned silence, for Socrates it was simply another opportunity to reflect deeply on the human issues that the trial and its outcome provoked.

Plato, from *The Apology*

> You have not gained very much time, Athenians, and, as the price of it, you will have an evil name for all who wish to revile the state, and they will say that you put Socrates, a wise man, to death. For they will certainly call me wise, whether I am wise or not, when they want to reproach you. If you would have waited for a little while, your wishes would have been fulfilled in the course of nature; for you see that I am an old man, far advanced in years, and near to death. I am saying this not to all of you, only to those who have voted for my death. And to them I have something else to say. Perhaps, my friends, you think that I have been convicted because I was wanting in the arguments by which I could have persuaded you to acquit me, if, that is, I had thought it right to do or to say anything not in arguments, but in impudence and shamelessness—because I would not plead before you as you would have liked to hear me plead, or appeal to you with weeping and wailing, or say and do many other things which I maintain are unworthy of me, but which you have been accustomed to from other men. But when I was defending myself, I thought that I ought not to do anything unworthy of a free man because of the danger which I ran, and I have not changed my mind now. I would very much rather defend myself as I did, and die, than as you would have had me do, and live. Both in a lawsuit and in war, there are some things which neither I nor any other man may do in order to escape from death. In battle, a man often sees that he may at least escape from death by throwing down his arms and falling on his knees before the pursuer to beg for his life. And there are many other ways of avoiding death in every danger if a man is willing to say and to do anything. But, my friends, I think that it is a much harder thing to escape from wickedness than from death, for wickedness is swifter than death. And now I, who am old and slow, have been overtaken by the slower pursuer: and my accusers, who are clever and swift, have been overtaken by the swifter pursuer—wickedness. And now I shall go away, sentenced by you to death; and they will go away, sentenced by truth to wickedness and injustice. And I abide by this award as well as they. Perhaps it was right for these things to be so; and I think that they are fairly measured.
>
> And now I wish to prophesy to you, Athenians, who have condemned me. For I am going to die, and that is the time when men have most prophetic power. And I prophesy to you who have sentenced me to death that a far more severe punishment than you have inflicted on me will surely overtake you as soon as I am dead. You have done this thing, thinking that you will be relieved from having to give an account of your lives. But I say that the result will be very different. There will be more men who will call you to account, whom I have held back, though you did not recognize it. And they will be harsher toward you than I have been, for they will be younger, and you will be more indignant with them. For if you think that you will restrain men from reproaching you for not living as you should, by putting them to death, you are very much mistaken. That way of escape is neither possible nor honorable. It is much more honorable and much easier not to suppress others, but to make yourselves as good as you can. This is my parting prophecy to you who have condemned me.

" **But, my friends, I think that it is a much harder thing to escape from wickedness than from death, for wickedness is swifter than death.** "

For those who voted to condemn Socrates to death, his powerful and ominous response must have been disturbing, sowing the first seeds of doubt into what they had just done. Socrates' profound insight into human nature gave him the talent to be an uncanny prognosticator of future events.

Plato, from *The Apology*

You have not gained very much time, Athenians, and, as the price of it, you will have an evil name for all who wish to revile the state, and they will say that you put Socrates, a wise man, to death. For they will certainly call me wise, whether I am wise or not, when they want to reproach you.

Socrates seems to understand that, despite the people he has annoyed and the enemies he has made, his reputation as a wise and honest man seeking to discover the truth and elevate those around him is secure and that once the hysteria surrounding his trial has been punctured by his death, the majority of people will come to their senses and recognize the enormous folly—and injustice—of what they have done. This is precisely what happened. Within days following his execution, the city of Athens declared a period of mourning, closing the schools and businesses in honor of their finest citizen. And, in an ironic reversal of fortune, his chief accuser, Meletus, was condemned to death, and the chief orchestrator of the trial against him, Anytus the tanner, was banished from Athens. As a crowning tribute, the sculptor Lysippus was commissioned to create a bronze statue that was placed on the Sacred Way.

But Socrates' prescience seems to go far beyond the events immediately following his death when he states:

Plato, from *The Apology*

But, my friends, I think that it is a much harder thing to escape from wickedness than from death, for wickedness is swifter than death. And now I, who am old and slow, have been overtaken by the slower pursuer: and my accusers, who are clever and swift, have been overtaken by the swifter pursuer—wickedness. And now I shall go away, sentenced by you to death; and they will go away, sentenced by truth to wickedness and injustice. And I abide by this award as well as they. Perhaps it was right for these things to be so; and I think that they are fairly measured.

This last sentence suggests that he understands that his death is necessary in order for his revolutionary beliefs to have their fullest impact on future generations, etching wickedness and righteousness indelibly on the consciousness of mankind. Through death, Socrates rose to archetypal status, his life and death embodying a compelling model for all people to emulate.

Confronting death, Socrates is unwavering in his certainty that he has lived a life that is just and true, and he is secure in his confidence that no harm can come to one who has lived such a life. For a just and true individual, death cannot be something to be feared.

Plato, from *The Apology*

And if we reflect in another way, we shall see that we may well hope that death is a good. For the state of death is one of two things: either the dead man wholly ceases to be and loses all consciousness or, as we are told, it is a change and migration of the soul to another place. And if death is the absence of all consciousness, and like the sleep of one whose slumbers are unbroken by any dreams, it will be a wonderful gain. For if a man had to select that night in which he slept so soundly that he did not even dream, and had to compare with it all the other nights and days of his life, and then had to say how many days and nights in his life he had spent better and more pleasantly than this night, I think that a private person, nay, even the great King himself, would find them easy to count, compared with the others. If that is the nature of death, I for one count it a gain. For then it appears that all time is nothing more than a single night. But if death is a journey to another place, and what we are told is true—that there are all who have died—what good could be greater than this, my judges? Would a journey not be worth taking, at the end of which, in the other world, we should be released from the self-styled judges here and should find the true judges who are said to sit in judgment below.... And above all, I could spend my time in examining those who are there, as I examine men here, and in

> finding out which of them is wise, and which of them thinks himself wise when he is not wise. What would we not give, my judges, to be able to examine the leader of the great expedition against Troy, or Odysseus, or Sisyphus, or countless other men and women whom we could name? It would be an infinite happiness to discuss with them and to live with them and to examine them. Assuredly there they do not put men to death for doing that. For besides the other ways in which they are happier than we are, they are immortal, at least if what we are told is true.

And then in an extraordinary moment of personal transcendence, Socrates looks beyond himself and his imminent death to reassure and comfort those close to him. This moment, he explains, was destined by fate and serves a higher purpose than the end of his life. Far from being a tragedy, his death at this moment is the right thing to happen, ordained by the gods and releasing him from the difficulties that are an inescapable part of life. All he asks, as he prepares to drink the hemlock, is that they nurture his sons, treating them in the same way Socrates has treated his friends. And then with calm determination, Socrates embraces his fate, making a final statement that expresses the mystery that each one of us must ultimately confront.

Plato, from *The Apology*

> And you, too, judges, must face death hopefully, and believe this as a truth that no evil can happen to a good man, either in life or after death. His fortunes are not neglected by the gods; and what has happened to me today has not happened by chance. I am persuaded that it was better for me to die now, and to be released from trouble; and that was the reason why the sign never turned me back. And so I am not at all angry with my accusers or with those who have condemned me to die. Yet it was not with this in mind that they accused me and condemned me, but meaning to do me an injury. So far I may blame them.
>
> Yet I have one request to make of them. When my sons grow up, punish them, my friends, and harass them in the same way that I have harassed you, if they seem to you to care for riches or for any other thing more than virtue; and if they think that they are something when they are really nothing, reproach them, as I have reproached you, for not caring for what they should, and for thinking that they are great men when really they are worthless. And if you will do this, I myself and my sons will have received justice from you.
>
> But now the time has come, and we must go away—I to die, and you to live. Whether life or death is better is known to God, and to God only.

2.5 Making Connections: Socrates' Legacy

This is the only chapter in this book that is devoted to just one philosopher. Why does Socrates merit that distinction and the careful analysis we have given his life and ideas? Why is he often termed "the father of Western philosophy"? Does he deserve this exalted title? Let's examine the evidence so that you can judge for yourself:

((•— **Listen** to the
Interview *Socrates* on
mysearchlab.com

- *Socrates was the catalyst for a significant advancement in human consciousness.* Prior to Socrates, thinkers and writers had focused their attention on past events and the physical universe. Taking as his cue the inscription at Delphi, "Know thyself," Socrates was the first important Western thinker to focus the light of human reason and intelligence on human beings themselves. For the first time in recorded history, humans became the subjects of systematic study—our psyches, our moral aspirations, our relationships with one another, our quest for self-understanding and meaningful lives, our souls. Socrates was in deadly earnest when he announced, "The unexamined life is not worth living."

- *Socrates was an archetypal thinker, a quintessential model of rational inquiry.* Socrates believed in the supreme importance of thinking as well as possible, and for him, everything in human experience was an appropriate subject for exploration and critical analysis. He developed a method of dialectical inquiry that was qualitatively different than anything the world had seen, and which continues to be the bedrock of philosophical thought. Using penetrating questions, Socrates' method insisted on the criteria of logical soundness, clear definitions, consistency, and freedom from self-contradiction. He insisted on:

  - establishing clear starting points.
  - viewing issues from multiple perspectives.
  - exploring logical connections and the consequences of beliefs.
  - expressing publicly one's own thinking process and inviting others to respond.
  - being willing to follow the argument wherever it might lead.
  - being open to revising one's opinions based on new insight.

All of these higher-order intellectual operations have come to be woven into human culture since he taught them over 2,500 years ago.

- *Socrates was committed to making our actions reflect our convictions.* For Socrates, striving to think well meant striving to live well, developing consistent and rigorous standards of conduct and then following through with the choices that we make. For Socrates, there was no distinction between theory and practice, thought and action—in the virtuous person, they are the same. There is an intimate connection between knowledge and virtue, and as we gain intellectual understanding, we should naturally live more enlightened lives.

- Socrates believed that philosophical inquiry was a social activity. In contrast to the "ivory tower" dreamer, Socrates found his greatest pleasure engaging in passionate and energetic discussions with others. Socrates was certainly capable of deep, introspective thought.

  Alcibiades records an incident that occurred when Socrates was in the military. Socrates had arisen early to ponder a particularly difficult problem. He struck a contemplative pose and remained there, oblivious to the world, throughout the day and the following night, to the amazement of his fellow soldiers. But for Socrates, the real testing of one's ideas came through the rough-and-tumble exchanges with others, creating that extraordinary chemistry that results when human minds come into contact with one another.

- *Socrates was a heroic martyr to enlightened thinking and virtuous living.* It wasn't just that he died but rather that he died *willingly* for the moral principles and values on which his life was constructed. There were numerous ways he could have avoided death, but all of them would have meant betraying his principles and violating his character in some significant way. Not that all great thinkers made the same courageous choice that he did. Some years later, Aristotle, when faced with a similar

What is Socrates' legacy? Socrates' commitment to rational inquiry lived on through his disciples and became the standard for Western culture. This picture depicts Plato's disciple Aristotle (384–322 B.C.E.) teaching a youthful Alexander the Great of Macedonia. Alexander would eventually conquer the Persian Empire, bringing Socratic ideas with him. What Socratic ideas do you recognize as being an integral part of our culture?

thinking philosophically

IS SOCRATES RELEVANT TODAY?

Consider the following quote of Socrates: "My good friend, you are a citizen of Athens, a city which is very great and very famous for its wisdom and strength—are you not ashamed of caring so much for the making of money and for fame and prestige, when you neither think nor care about wisdom and truth and the improvement of your soul?" Do you think it would be accurate to substitute "the United States" for "Athens"? Identify some examples from our culture that suggest that people care more about making money and achieving fame and prestige than they do about pursuing wisdom, truth, and the improvement of their souls. How would you evaluate your values in relation to Socrates' exhortation?

decision, chose to be exiled from Athens rather than put to death. Galileo, under threat of death from the Catholic Inquisition, recanted his belief that Earth orbits around the sun and then spent twenty years under house arrest, supposedly doing penance for his "blasphemous" beliefs. But for Socrates, his choice was never in doubt, and he confronted it with stirring courage and heartrending eloquence. Socrates' trial, and Plato's literary genius in recreating it with such eloquence and power, epitomizes the eternal struggle between reason and chaos, enlightenment and ignorance, integrity and corruption. The writer I. F. Stone observed:

> … *His martyrdom, and the genius of Plato, made him a secular saint, the superior man confronting the ignorant mob with serenity and humor. This was Socrates' triumph and Plato's masterpiece. Socrates needed the hemlock, as Jesus needed the Crucifixion, to fulfill a mission.*

Socrates seemed to sense that fulfilling his mission on Earth meant dying for the beliefs that he had lived for. And it is both his extraordinary life and his memorable death that securely fixes Socrates as an archetypal figure worthy of our thoughtful study and personal emulation.

writing about philosophy: A Socratic Dialogue

The Assignment

Throughout history, people of high moral character have faced punishment, imprisonment, and even death rather than forsake their guiding principles. In Socrates' case, he was unwilling to renounce his commitment to searching for wisdom, examining himself and others, and exhorting others to live virtuously and attend to their souls. Other people have been unwilling to renounce their religious beliefs, surrender their commitment to personal and political freedom, or behave in a way that they considered to be immoral.

Think about your deepest convictions for which you would be willing to face imprisonment or death. Imagine yourself in a court setting, similar to Socrates, in which you have one final chance to persuade your accusers that you do not deserve to die, even though you are unwilling to renounce your beliefs. Then compose a Socratic dialogue between yourself and your accusers in which you use penetrating questioning and compelling

logic to make your case. Members of the class will act as your jury, deciding whether you have made a strong enough case to survive or whether you will be condemned. Your dialogue should embody the qualities of Socratic analysis. Begin generating ideas for this assignment by listing all the reasons, evidence, and arguments that support your position and then listing the arguments that oppose it. Refer to the list of fallacies on pages 27–30 to see if your accusers' arguments contain any errors that you can expose in your questioning. Try to find a contradiction in your opponent's position so that you can dismantle his or her argument, as Socrates did with Thrasymachus (pages 62–67). Then draft the exchange of ideas, perhaps even giving your accuser a personality, like the aggressive Thrasymachus, while you remain calm and reasonable, like Socrates. Introduce your dialogue with a short description of the situation that has led to your trial and the charges against you. Conclude with a concise summary of your convictions and your commitment to that ideal.

■ ■ ■   **Student Essay**

SOCRATIC DIALOGUE
by Gina Szeto

(This sample paper was written by a student who imaginatively recreates her father's experience as a victim of the Great Proletarian Cultural Revolution in China in 1968.) The Great Proletarian Cultural Revolution was a radical political movement in China that closed schools, slowed production, and virtually severed China's relations with the outside world. Mao Zedong's goals were to rid the schools, the Communist party, the bureaucracy, the army, and the intellectual community of those who opposed him—all of whom he considered "revisionists" determined to lead China back toward middle class capitalism and free enterprise.

Although it was difficult to enter universities before the revolution, I was doing well in school and preparing to take my entrance examination. I was nineteen years old when, in June of 1966, the system of university entrance examinations was halted and the Cultural Revolution closed the doors of learning, jailing the educated and forbidding schooling. The daughter of intellectual parents, I was forced to the countryside— my days filled with a dangerous, relentless pursuit of an education for myself. Although I could not return to school, I began reading books and studying on my own. Most of the books in China were prohibited at the time, so I formed associations with people who smuggled books in and out of closed libraries. As a result of these actions, I am accused of being an antirevolutionary, a capitalist, a traitor to Red China. These crimes are punishable by death. The year is 1968, the height of the Revolution, and I have been brought before The Court of Justice for trial.

Gina: Two years ago, before the Cultural Revolution began, I was preparing to take my entrance exams. I, like the Red Guards, devoted myself to Mao, never questioning his policies or authority. Since then, my days have been filled with public humiliations and Red Guard raids. My father, like many of yours, has been stoned, beaten, and purged, though I have never seen him act in a way that was disloyal to Mao or China. So why does this country that my father loves so much treat him this way? Why, now that I am at the top of my class, would Mao force me to the countryside and forbid me from learning, from reading, from thinking? I began to question whether my blind devotion to Mao Zedong was more foolish than following the intuitive belief that I, and all Chinese people, had a right to do these things.

I have lived through the failure of the Great Leap Forward, a movement in which millions of our countrymen died because the policies of the party were never questioned. Today, I am living through another movement, larger, more destructive. I will not convince you that I am not guilty of smuggling books out of closed libraries or questioning Mao's policies. I am here today to convince you that I am not a traitor to China. But even more significantly, I am here to ask whether a blind adherence to party policies could be more detrimental to China than cultivating a generation to read, think, imagine, and question; to pose questions like What is freedom? What is

■ ■ ■ **Student Essay** (continued)

truth?; and to question how just it is to be incarcerated and put to death for thinking, reading, and learning. I am here today to convince you of our basic right to do these things.

Court: These are questions of a Western mind.

Gina: Too much attention is spent discarding ideas based on criteria that has no relationship to the idea's content. More time needs to be devoted to determining whether the idea is true, if is applicable, and if it is, how it can be put to use. Don't you agree?

Court: In conceiving a Western idea, the assumption is that it will be applied in a Western society, a society that is politically and culturally very different than ours.

Gina: I am in no way implying that we should adopt all political, economic, and social policies endorsed by the West. I am asking if an idea that happens to be Western in origin should be discarded simply because it is Western. What criteria is used to determine the value of an idea?

Court: Mao is the leader of China. His policies and authority should never be questioned, when his authority is questioned, China is questioned, and our society will fall into chaos. This is done for the well being of everyone.

Gina: Is it somewhat naïve to assume that despite countless failed attempts over man's history to resolve the questions of right and wrong, relative and absolute, that only Mao has the answer? The evolution of social and political policies, the constant revision of scientific theories, and the regret, in hindsight, of religious and political actions committed in the name of truth attest to man's, not to mention Mao's, fallibility. Is Mao not also a human, like you and me? Has he, despite his ostensibly good intentions, failed nonetheless? Would he too not suffer if he were tortured, humiliated, and purged in front of his colleagues, family, and friends?

Court: Yes.

Gina: Is it therefore more productive to acknowledge the frailty of the human condition, our uncertainty of our notion of truth, and in so doing, keep our minds, and therefore theories and policies in the public sector, open to progress, flexible in the face of adversity and change? Or is it more productive to construct absolute policies, which are themselves a product of the political and social climate of the time, at the expense of truth, at the expense of our people?

You do not answer because you too have been silently struggling with these questions. Answer: Did the Great Leap Forward fail due to a lack of better ideas, because it was impossible to predict the outcome of such ill-conceived policies?

Court: We were not able to question him.

Gina: We were not then, and we cannot now. What are we if we cannot think, rationalize, or question? At the most, animals; at the least, puppets.

Ideas should be judged for the content and efficacy with little regard to its source. New ideas cannot threaten the principles upon which a culture is based if those philosophies are fundamentally true. In science, proof of natural laws, contrary to popular belief, is nearly impossible. Experiments are devised to disprove or rule out theories—it only takes one instance of inconsistent date to invalidate a theory, regardless of its longevity in past investigations. At the same time, numerous instances of data consistent to a hypothesis is not conclusive enough evidence of its truth. If theories in scientific investigations are constantly open to refutation, how can policies that regulate human values, a concept intuitively more subjective and obscure than science, ever be absolute?

Court: Mao has examined all these things for us already. He has taken all the necessary and logical steps to ensure his policies are accurate.

Gina: If we agree that we are a part of and subject to the same complex, covert laws of science, how can an examination of the human condition, our needs, wants, and values, be determined without a thorough, systematic and acute analysis of it? How can we think critically about right from wrong if we are deprived of our ability to read and think? How can we reason for ourselves that Mao is just in depriving us of these intuitively basic rights? How do we know Mao's policies are in fact true? Or more generally, how is any truth found?

Court: It depends.

Gina: Do plants need sunlight to survive?

Court: Yes, plants need the sun to survive.

Gina: How do you know?

Court: From what I see. Plants don't grow well in the dark.

Gina: So, you reason, from your observation and experience, that plants need sunlight to survive. Observation, experience, and analysis therefore characterize a seemingly mundane inquiry regarding the world we live in. Would you agree that a question concerning a more meaningful aspect of existence, such as "What are fundamental human rights?," might require similar, if not more complex logic to determine? If Mao told us that plants grow best in the dark, don't we have an obligation to investigate that theory? Don't we all have a right to determine truth, however mundane, for ourselves?

Court: Ideally, yes. If everyone sought out to find their "truth" nothing would be accomplished. Immorality would be rampant.

Gina: If one believes that by nature we are corrupt and immoral. A closer and more thoughtful inspection of human nature reveals a universal desire to coexist freely, peacefully, and responsibly. Legislation that takes into consideration these natural inclinations can only produce a community willing to live by those laws. When policies deprive that same community of intuitively basic human rights, like freedom, the community suffers.

Court: How are we depriving them of "intuitively basic human rights?"

Gina: Why were prisons created? As a form of compensation or punishment?

Court: Of course for punishment.

Gina: Why of course?

Court: One's freedom is restricted, one is no longer his own person. He becomes the property of the state, with no voice in society, he no longer exists.

Gina: *"With no voice in society."* So incarceration is not only a physical bondage, but an intellectual one; existence is dependent on a person's ability to not only physically interact with others, but to validate himself intellectually among them.

■ ■ ■   **Student Essay** *(continued)*

If a restriction of one's freedom both mentally and physically is considered punishment, freedom, then, in these respects, is considered a good. Is it the natural inclination of all men to exist in this way?

Court: Yes, I suppose.

Gina: Prohibiting books and learning curtailing education, and forcing youth to the countryside, is a deprivation of freedom both mentally and physically. What have the Chinese people done to warrant such punishment?

Court: They do not know any better.

Gina: If freedom is considered an intuitive good, doesn't going against one's natural inclination produce suffering? Does invoking suffering in others foster loyalty? If a foreign party were capable of overthrowing the existing government, would people who are suffering defend the very government that produces their suffering? Does it seem compassionate to deprive one of an intuitively basic human right?

Court: Survival is not based on compassion.

Gina: True. Then let me ask another question, if the question of compassion is moot, does it seem practical, in terms of survival, to deprive one of their freedom? Meaning, if something similar to the Great Leap Forward were to be proposed today, how could the results, as disastrous as they were, be avoided without the freedom to think or question its effectiveness? In a similar way, how are better policies proposed if one's freedom to think, or freedom to learn, is suppressed?

Court: I don't know.

Gina: Is it more likely that a generation of thinkers educated in history, science, and logic will detect and ultimately rectify unsound economic and social policies, or a generation of illiterate farmers? What is the best defense if and when our country comes under foreign invasion? Is brute force enough or is strategy a necessary component?

Court: Of course strategy is necessary, and Mao will devise those plans.

Gina: And all other proposals are useless. Mao is the brain, and we are his limbs.

Court: It is for the welfare of all.

Gina: If my purpose is simply to exist, to breathe, and not utilize my inherent ability to think, rationalize, or question, then I would rather not live. A sentiment, as you know, shared by the thousands that have committed suicide over the past decade. If this is Mao's purpose for the People's Republic, he would do no worse if more resources were allocated toward building machines and robots, because they will not rebel, they will not fight for the right to be free, because they, unlike us, inherently are not capable of freedom.

Court: How do you know we are free?

Gina: I cannot be certain, philosophically. I can be certain, however, that if I am not free, it is not because Mao Zedong, a man made of flesh and bone, tells me I am not. As much as anyone else tries to repress or contain me by physical means, killing or incarcerating me, they will never defeat me. Defeat only exists when I relinquish my intellectual and emotional judgment to the man you hail the Savior of the People's Republic.

MySearchLab Connections

Watch. Listen. Explore. Read. Mysearchlab is designed just for you. Each chapter features a customized study plan to help you learn and review key concepts and terms. Dynamic visual activities, videos, and readings found in the multimedia library will enhance your learning experience.

Here are a few questions and activities to help you understand this chapter:

1. **Watch** the **Video** *Carl Sagan — Cosmos — Democritus* on **mysearchlab.com**   Explain the ways in which Democritus' beliefs put him at odds with the prevailing culture of his time.

2. **Watch** the **Video** *The Socratic Method* on **mysearchlab.com**   Explain how the Socratic Method leads an individual to the truth.

3. **Listen** to the **Podcast** *M.M. McCabe on the Socratic Method* on **mysearchlab.com**   Explain what McCabe means when she states that "Socrates was the original consequentialist."

4. **Listen** to the **News** *Plato's Republic Still Influential, Author Says* on **mysearchlab.com**   Why does Blackburn believe that today's neo-conservative movement was influenced by *The Republic*?

5. **Listen** to the **Interview** *Socrates* on **mysearchlab.com**   Why was Socrates such an influential figure in Western philosophy?

Socrates: A Model for Humanity

- Socrates, a Greek philosopher who lived 2,500 years ago, created the conceptual framework and method of inquiry for Western consciousness and culture. Among his revolutionary approaches to understanding the social and natural world was to bring philosophy into the marketplace, or *agora*, provoking discussion and debate among people and setting the foundations for academic and political discourse as practiced throughout much of the world today. Socrates did not leave any writing of his own. What we know of his rhetoric, his style, and his thought has come down to us through the *Dialogues*, a series of dialectical conversations written by Socrates' student Plato. [pp. 49–61]

KEY TERMS
Socratic Method
agora

The Socratic Method

- The Socratic Method uses questions and analysis to draw people into an exchange of ideas regarding a central concept, in an attempt to get at the essential nature of that concept. Sometimes coaxing, occasionally sarcastic, and frequently combative, the Socratic Method as practiced by Socrates sought to strip away pretensions, inconsistencies, and false ideas to get at a universal truth.
- Among the opponents of Socrates were the Sophists, educators who believed that "truth" was relative (that is, dependent on context) and "knowledge" merely a matter of opinion. [pp. 61–67]

KEY TERMS
dialectic
Sophists
irony

for further reading, viewing & research

Read the Primary Source on MySearchLab

- *The Apology*, Plato
- *The Republic*, Plato

Films

- *12 Angry Men* (1957) What are the primary causes of prejudice, and how do they affect justice? A jury decides the fate of a young man accused of murdering his father. A guilty verdict will result in a mandatory death sentence. The case appears to be open and shut until one juror challenges the others to move beyond their prejudices and presumptions to address the facts before arriving at a decision.
- *Cool Hand Luke* (1967) How can the spirit be free while the body is imprisoned? When Luke Jackson is sent to prison camp, he refuses to submit to the tyrannical authority of the camp's captain. His repeated escapes and attempts to bring meaning and fraternity to the other prisoners only provoke the anger of the captain, who makes it his mission to break Luke's spirit.
- *Good Night, and Good Luck* (2005) What methods are appropriate for protesting injustice? Based on a true story, this film depicts the conflict between journalist Edward R. Murrow and Senator Joseph McCarthy

during the anticommunist committee hearings of the 1950s—hearings that destroyed the careers of many and created hysteria in the country. In spite of pressure from his television station to remain silent, as well as threats that he would be the next target of government investigation, Murrow openly criticized and exposed the scare tactics employed by the committee.

- *Malcolm X* (1992) How can one find meaning in an unjust world? Based on the autobiography, this film follows the life of the famous African American leader. After his father is killed by the Ku Klux Klan, Malcolm Little becomes a gangster before discovering the Nation of Islam while in prison. He subsequently becomes a militant political activist fighting against racism for the rights of African Americans, who advocated black pride, black power, identity politics, and economic self-reliance. When he is assassinated, he becomes a martyr for human rights and equality.

Socrates' Central Concern: The Soul

Fundamental to Socrates' philosophy is the conviction that every human being has a soul, and that soul is in search of happiness *(eudaemonia)*, which is achieved through a life of enlightened thinking and virtuous actions. His core teachings, which speak to this conviction, are

- "The unexamined life is not worth living."
- The truth lies within each of us.
- We should strive for excellence in all areas of life.
- No one knowingly does evil.
- "It is better to suffer wickedness than to commit it."

[pp. 68–72]

The Trial and Death of Socrates

- Socrates died willingly for the moral principles and values on which his life was constructed. Socrates' trial epitomizes the eternal struggle between reason and chaos, enlightenment and ignorance, integrity and corruption.

[pp. 72–90]

KEY TERMS

psyche
arete
epistêmê
sophia

visual summary

- *On the Waterfront* **(1954)** What does it mean to have the courage of your convictions? A former prizefighter turned longshoreman, Terry Malloy (portrayed by Marlon Brando) is faced with the decision of whether to stand up to corrupt union bosses after the murder of one of his colleagues is covered up. Over the course of the film, Malloy assesses his past, struggles to take responsibility for his present, and considers the person he wants to become.

- *One Flew over the Cuckoo's Nest* **(1975)** What does it mean to be sane? A criminal, Randle Patrick McMurphy, pretends to be insane to avoid a prison sentence. He is sent to a mental institution, where a tyrannical nurse uses any means necessary to force the patients into numbed submission. Based on the book of the same name, the film follows McMurphy's attempts to save himself and his fellow inmates from the oppressive authority of the mental hospital.

Literature

- *An Enemy of the People,* Henrik Ibsen. A doctor discovers that the industry that supports his town's economy is also contaminating the water system. As he tries to reveal the truth and protect the health of innocent people, the doctor is met with resistance on the part of the town's politicians, members of the media, and eventually his fellow citizens who come to view him as the "enemy." In spite of this, the doctor remains committed to speaking out against a corrupt system and the majority who blindly follow and support it.

- *To Kill a Mockingbird,* Harper Lee. Atticus Finch, a prominent lawyer in a racist Southern town, refuses to bow under the weight of societal pressure when he defends a black man accused of raping a white woman, in spite of the risk this poses to his own life and livelihood. Atticus's adamant sense of justice has a profound effect on his young daughter, Scout, and inspires her to reach out to and eventually empathize with a man who has been ostracized by the community.

- *The Trial,* Franz Kafka. An ordinary man, Josef K., is arrested and tried for a crime he did not commit, the nature of which is never explained to him. He finds himself at the mercy of an irrational and arbitrary court system, and his attempts to obtain information about both the crime and his fate lead nowhere. The protagonist's maddening journey undermines his sense of life's order and predictability, and raises existential questions about justice, alienation, and the possibility of meaning in the modern world.

- *The Trial of Socrates,* I. F. Stone. Stone provides a social and political portrait of Athens during the time of Socrates' trial, and offers an alternative perspective on the philosopher and the reasons for his being tried.

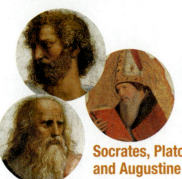

Socrates, Plato, and Augustine
The self is an immortal soul that exists over time.

Descartes
The self is a thinking thing, distinct from the body

John Locke
Personal identity is made possible by self-consciousness.

David Hume
There is no "self," only a bundle of constantly changing perceptions passing through the theatre of our minds.

who are you?

CONSCIOUSNESS, IDENTITY, AND THE SELF

Immanuel Kant
The self is a unifying subject, an organizing consciousness that makes intelligible experience possible.

Sigmund Freud
The self is multi-layered.

Gilbert Ryle
The self is the way people behave.

Paul Churchland
The self is the brain. Mental states will be superseded by brain states.

Maurice Merleau-Ponty
The self is embodied subjectivity.

◀ **What is the self?** In Chuck Close's portrait, *Maggie*, the face is quite recognizable when viewed from a distance. Close up, it takes on an entirely different appearance. Your concept of the self may also shift as you read this chapter.

3

chapter

PHILOSOPHERS AND THINKERS IN THIS CHAPTER	
Socrates	469–399 B.C.E.
Plato	427–347 B.C.E.
St. Augustine	354–430
René Descartes	1596–1650
John Locke	1632–1704
David Hume	1711–1776
Immanuel Kant	1724–1804
Sigmund Freud	1856–1939
Edmund Husserl	1859–1938
Marcel Proust	1871–1922
Gilbert Ryle	1900–1976
Maurice Merleau-Ponty	1908–1961
Paul Churchland	B. 1942

3.1 Know Thyself?

The cornerstone of Socrates' philosophy was the Delphic Oracle's command to "Know thyself." But what exactly does that mean? Who exactly *is* your "self"? What are the qualities that define it? What differentiates your particular "self" from all others? What is the relation of the "self" you were as a child to the "self" you are now? What is the relation of your "self" to your "body"? How does your "self" relate to other "selves"? What happens to a "self" when the body dies? In what ways is it possible for you to "know" your "self"? In what ways might you never fully know your "self"? What do you mean when you say, "I don't feel like myself today" or when you encourage someone else to "Just be yourself!"

As with many themes and issues in philosophy, the nature of the self is a subject that most people take for granted. Many people simply *live*, assuming the existence of their personal self-identity. And when they do think about their self, their concerns are typically practical rather than philosophical: How can I make myself happy? How can "I" (shorthand for my "self") develop fulfilling relationships with other selves? How can I improve myself? And so on. Yet when we go searching for our self with a philosophical lens, we soon discover that what we thought was a straightforward and familiar presence is in fact elusive, enigmatic, and extraordinarily complex.

Developing insight into the nature of the human self in general and into your self in particular is a daunting task, underscored by the less-than-successful efforts of the best human thinkers for nearly 3,000 years. Yet if we are to fulfill Socrates' exhortation to live an examined life, a life of purpose and value, we must begin at the source of all knowledge and significance—our self.

> **We are unknown, we knowers, ourselves to ourselves; this has good reason. We have never searched for ourselves—how should it then come to pass, that we should ever find ourselves?**
> **FRIEDRICH NIETZSCHE**

Begin your exploration of your self by responding to the questions in the Thinking Philosophically box on the next page. The difficulties that you may encounter when completing those questions are an indication of the philosophical challenges posed by the concept of self. As your philosophical understanding becomes deeper and more sophisticated, your appreciation for the profound nature of these questions will grow as well. Those people who provide simple, ready-made answers to questions like these are likely revealing a *lack* of philosophical understanding. ("Of course I know myself…I'm *me!*") So don't be concerned if you find that you are beginning to get confused about subjects like the self that you thought you understood—such confusion is the sign of a lively, inquiring mind. As the newspaperman and writer H. L. Mencken noted: "To every complex question there's a simple answer—and it is clever, neat, and wrong!"

Your responses also likely reflected the cultural and religious environment in which you were raised. Cultures that originated in Europe have tended to use a common religious and philosophical framework for understanding the self that was first introduced by Socrates and Plato in ancient Greece. For example, did your responses reflect the belief that your self

- is a unique personal identity that remains the same over time?
- is synonymous with your "soul"?

- is a very different sort of thing from your "body"?
- can be understood by using your reasoning abilities?
- will continue to exist in some form after your body dies?
- is able to connect with other selves in some personal way?

If you found that your responses reflected some (or all) of these beliefs, don't be surprised. These beliefs form the basic conceptual framework for understanding the self that has shaped much of Western religious and philosophical thought. So to fully appreciate the way our most fundamental views regarding ourselves have been formed, it makes sense for us to return to the birthplace of those views twenty-five hundred years ago and then to trace the development of these perspectives up to the current century. As we journey on this quest for the self, we will also encounter some non-Western perspectives as well, such as the Buddhist concept of *anatta* or "no-self," which is covered in this chapter. Buddhist doctrine believes that the notion of a permanent self that exists as a unified identity through time is an illusion. For Buddhists, every aspect of life is impermanent, and all elements of the universe are in a continual process of change and transition, a process that includes each self as well. The self can best be thought of as a flame that is continually passed from candle to candle, retaining a certain continuity but no real personal identity—a concept very different from the self of Western consciousness.

thinking philosophically

DO YOU KNOW YOURSELF?

Answer the following questions regarding your self as fully and specifically as you can.

- How would you describe your self?
- What are the qualities that differentiate you from all other selves?
- In what ways has your self changed during the course of your life? In what ways has it remained the same?
- How would you describe the relation of your self to your body?
- How are you able to come to know other selves? Do you think they are similar to or different from you?
- What do you think will happen to your self after you die? If you believe that your self will continue to exist in some form, will you be able to recognize other selves who have died? How?

3.2 The Soul Is Immortal: Socrates and Plato

Socrates was the first thinker in Western history to focus the full power of reason on the human self: who we are, who we should be, and who we will become. Socrates was convinced that, in addition to our physical bodies, each person possesses an immortal soul that survives beyond the death of the body. He explored this subject with his friends in the days following his trial and before his sentence of death was executed, a time in his life when the question of immortality no doubt had a special immediacy and significance. The following passage is from **Plato**'s dialogue, *Phaedo*.

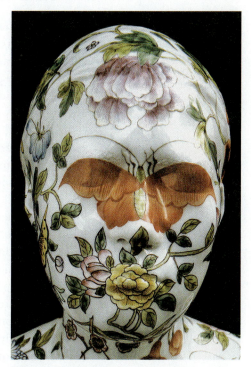

Who are you? In *China, China*, artist Ah Xian has layered images from traditional Chinese porcelains onto the bust of a contemporary Chinese woman. The work vividly communicates an idea about the relationship between culture and the self. How is your culture reflected in the person you are?

Socrates (469–399 B.C.E.). Ancient Greek philosopher often called "the father of Western philosophy." Socrates created the conceptual framework and method of inquiry for much of Western thought. His teachings are known to us primarily through the writing of his student, Plato.

Dualistic Twofold. Related to dualism, the view that material substance (physical body) and immaterial substance (mind or soul) are two separate aspects of the self.

Plato, from *Phaedo*

Socrates: And were we not saying long ago that the soul when using the body as an instrument of perception, that is to say, when using the sense of sight or hearing or some other sense (for the meaning of perceiving through the body is perceiving through the senses)—were we not saying that the soul too is then dragged by the body into the region of the changeable, and wanders and is confused; the world spins round her, and she is like a drunkard, when she touches change?

Cebes: Very true.

Socrates: But when returning into herself she reflects, then she passes into the other world, the region of purity, and eternity, and immortality, and unchangeableness, which are her kindred, and with them she ever lives, when she is by herself and is not let or hindered; then she ceases from her erring ways, and being in communion with the unchanging is unchanging. And this state of the soul is called wisdom?

Cebes: That is well and truly said, Socrates.

Socrates: And to which class is the soul more nearly alike and akin, as far as may be inferred from this argument, as well as from the preceding one?

Cebes: I think, Socrates, that, in the opinion of everyone who follows the argument, the soul will be infinitely more like the unchangeable—even the most stupid person will not deny that.

Socrates: And the body is more like the changing?

Cebes: Yes.

This brief exchange provides a cogent summary of Socrates' metaphysical framework. For Socrates, reality is **dualistic**, made up of two dichotomous realms. One realm is changeable, transient, and imperfect, whereas the other realm is unchanging, eternal, immortal. The physical world in which we live—comprising all that we can see, hear, taste, smell, and feel—belongs to the former realm. All aspects of our physical world are continually changing, transforming, disappearing.

In contrast, the unchanging, eternal, perfect realm includes the intellectual essences of the universe, concepts such as *truth, goodness,* and *beauty.* We find examples of these ideal forms in the physical world—for example, we might describe someone as truthful, good, or beautiful. But these examples are always imperfect and limited: It is only the ideal forms themselves that are perfect, unchanging, and eternal.

Socrates' metaphysical scheme may, at first glance, seem abstract and impractical, but it has a profound impact on the way the self is understood. For Socrates, our bodies belong to the physical realm: They change, they're imperfect, they die. Our souls, however, belong to the ideal realm: They are unchanging and immortal, surviving the death of the body. And although a close relationship exists between our souls and our bodies, they are radically different entities. Our souls strive for wisdom and perfection, and reason is the soul's tool to achieve this exalted state. But as long as the soul is tied to the body, this quest for wisdom is inhibited by the imperfection of the physical realm, as the soul is "dragged by the body into the region of the changeable," where it "wanders and is confused" in a world that "spins round her, and she is like a drunkard." But reason is a powerful tool, enabling the soul to free itself from the corrupting imperfection of the physical realm and achieve "communion with the unchanging."

What is truly remarkable about these ideas is how closely they parallel modern Western consciousness. A finite body; an immortal soul; a perfect, eternal realm with which the soul seeks communion and eternal bliss: All of the basic elements of Western (and some Eastern) religions are present. Even on a secular level, the ideas resonate with modern concepts of the self: the notion that the thinking, reasoning self and the physical body are radically distinct entities that have a complicated and problematic relationship with one another.

Having described his overall metaphysical vision, Socrates goes on to elaborate his ideas and argue for their plausibility.

Plato, from *Phaedo*

> **Socrates:** Yet once more consider the matter in another light: When the soul and the body are united, then nature orders the soul to rule and govern, and the body to obey and serve. Now which of these two functions is akin to the divine? And which to the mortal? Does not the divine appear to you to be that which naturally orders and rules, and the mortal to be that which is subject and servant?
>
> **Cebes:** True.
>
> **Socrates:** And which does the soul resemble?
>
> **Cebes:** The soul resembles the divine, and the body the mortal—there can be no doubt of that, Socrates.
>
> **Socrates:** Then reflect, Cebes: of all which has been said is not this the conclusion?—that the soul is in the very likeness of the divine, and immortal, and intellectual, and uniform, and indissoluble, and unchangeable; and that the body is in the very likeness of the human, and mortal, and unintellectual, and multiform, and dissoluble, and changeable. Can this, my dear Cebes, be denied?
>
> **Cebes:** It cannot.

Although Plato was for the most part committed to Socrates' view of the essence of the self—the soul—as a unified, indissoluble, immortal entity that remains the same over time, he also recognizes the inherent difficulties with this view. In his dialogue *The Symposium*, Plato cites the views of the female philosopher Diotima, who presents a very different perspective on the nature of the self:

> *Although we speak of an individual as being the same so long as he continues to exist in the same form, and therefore assume that a man is the same person in his old age as in his infancy, yet although we call him the same, every bit of him is different, and every day he is becoming a new man, while the old man is ceasing to exist, as you can see from his hair, his flesh, his bones, his blood, and all the rest of his body. And not only his body, for the same thing happens to his soul. And neither his manners, nor his dispositions, nor his thoughts, nor his desires, nor his pleasures, nor his sufferings, nor his fears are the same throughout his life, for some of them grow, while others disappear.... Thus, unlike the gods, a mortal creature cannot remain the same throughout eternity; it can only leave behind new life to fill the vacancy that is left as it passes away.... And so it is no wonder that every creature prizes its own offspring, since everything is inspired by this love, this passion for immortality.*

Plato (427–347 B.C.E.). Ancient Greek philosopher of extraordinary significance in the history of ideas. Plato not only preserved Socrates' teachings for future generations but contributed original ideas on a wide range of issues such as morality, politics, metaphysics, and epistemology.

Plato's description of Diotima's position penetrates to the core of the problem of personal identity. How is it possible to say that a self remains the same when it is obvious that every self is defined by a process of continual change and evolution? This is visibly apparent in our physical bodies, and contemporary science has revealed that, even on the cellular level, old cells are dying and being replaced by new cells on an ongoing basis. In what sense can we say that an infant at the age of six months is the same person at the age of sixty years, when so much of his or her physical body has changed? And Diotima astutely points out that this same process of continual growth and evolution also defines your "soul." It is analogous to completely renovating an old house,

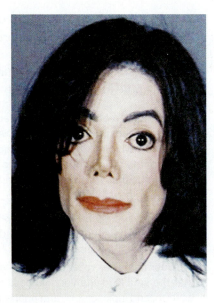

Who Was Michael Jackson? All of us experience changes to our bodies as we age, but Michael Jackson's transformations dramatize philosophical questions about identity. In what sense does the self change as the body changes? In what sense does the self remain the same?

gradually replacing every part of it over time: At what point does it lose its "original" identity and become a "new" house? For Diotima, this dynamic, changing quality of the soul leads her to a very different conclusion than Plato's: Unlike the gods, the human soul is not immortal, though we fervently want it to be. And it is this doomed passion for immortality that inspires the "prizing" of our children. They will become our living legacy as we "leave behind new life to fill the vacancy that is left as it passes away."

< READING CRITICALLY >

Analyzing Socrates on the Self

- Compare Socrates' concept of the "soul" with your concept of the self which you described in the "Thinking Philosophically" activity on page 103. Did you view your self as a unified identity that remains the same over time? An indissoluble entity that is immortal and will survive death? An entity that is very different in kind from your physical body? An entity that strives to achieve communion with some ultimate reality?

- In characterizing the relationship between the soul and the body, Socrates explains that the soul uses the body as "an instrument of perception," and that the soul "rules" the body in the same way that the divine rules the mortals. Do you agree with this analysis? Why or why not? How would you characterize the relationship between your soul/self and your body?

- Socrates argues that because the soul is of a unified, indissoluble form we should not be concerned about death because the soul is incapable of being dispersed into nonexistence—it must be eternal. Does this argument address your fears about the potential death of your soul/self? Why or why not?

- For Socrates, our physical existence on Earth is merely an imperfect reflection of ultimate and eternal reality, and our purpose in life is to achieve communion with this ultimate reality. How do his views compare with your perspective on the purpose of life? Do you believe that our goal in life is to achieve spiritual transcendence and/or intellectual enlightenment? If not, what do you believe is the purpose of your life?

Plato elaborates his concept of the soul (the Greek word is *psyche*) in his later dialogues such as the monumental *Republic* and *Phaedrus.* In particular, he introduces the idea of a three-part soul/self constituted by

Reason—Our divine essence that enables us to think deeply, make wise choices, and achieve a true understanding of eternal truths.

Physical Appetite—Our basic biological needs such as hunger, thirst, and sexual desire.

Spirit or Passion—Our basic emotions such as love, anger, ambition, aggressiveness, empathy.

These three elements of our selves are in a dynamic relationship with one another, sometimes working in concert, sometimes in bitter conflict. For example, we may develop a romantic relationship with someone who is an intellectual companion (Reason), with whom we are passionately in love (Spirit), and whom we find sexually attractive, igniting our lustful desires (Appetite). Or we may find ourselves in personal conflict, torn between three different relationships, each of which appeals to a different part of our self: Reason, Spirit, Appetite. When conflict occurs, Plato believes it is the responsibility of our Reason to sort things out and exert control, reestablishing a harmonious relationship among the three elements of our selves.

Plato illustrates his view of the soul/self in *Phaedrus* with a vivid metaphor: The soul is likened to a chariot drawn by two powerful winged horses—a noble horse, representing Spirit, and a wild horse, embodying Appetite. The charioteer is Reason, whose task is to guide the chariot to the eternal realm by controlling the two independent-minded horses. Those charioteers who are successful in setting a true course and ensuring that the two steeds work together in harmonious unity achieve true wisdom and banquet with the gods. However, those charioteers who are unable to control their horses and keep their chariot on track are destined to experience personal,

The chariot analogy.
Plato says, "We will liken the soul to the composite nature of a pair of winged horses and a charioteer." One horse represents Passion, the other Appetite, and the charioteer who tries to control them is Reason. Do you find this to be a useful metaphor for understanding your self? Why or why not?

intellectual, and spiritual failure. The fact that the horses are "winged" suggests the capacity of the soul to soar to the elevated realm of wisdom and intellectual enlightenment. These are themes that we will explore more fully in Chapter 4 when we deal with the subjects of human nature and personal freedom and in Chapter 5 when we explore the nature of truth and reality.

Plato, from *Phaedrus, The Chariot Analogy*

We will liken the soul to the composite nature of a pair of winged horses and a charioteer. Now the horses and charioteers of the gods are all good and of good descent, but those of other races are mixed; and first the charioteer of the human soul drives a pair, and secondly one of the horses is noble and of noble breed, but the other quite the opposite in breed and character. Therefore in our case the driving is necessarily difficult and troublesome. Now we must try to tell why a living being is called mortal or immortal. Soul, considered collectively, has the care of all that which is soulless, and it traverses the whole heaven, appearing sometimes in one form and sometimes in another; now when it is perfect and fully winged, it mounts upward and governs the whole world; but the soul which has lost its wings is borne along until it gets hold of something solid, when it settles down, taking upon itself an earthly body, which seems to be self-moving, because of the power of the soul within it; and the whole, compounded of soul and body, is called a living being, and is further designated as mortal. It is not immortal by any reasonable supposition, but we, though we have never seen or rightly conceived a god, imagine an immortal being which has both a soul and a body which are united for all time. Let that, however, and our words concerning it, be as is pleasing to God; we will now consider the reason why the soul loses its wings. It is something like this.

The natural function of the wing is to soar upwards and carry that which is heavy up to the place where dwells the race of the gods. More than any other thing that pertains to the body it partakes of the nature of the divine. But the divine is beauty, wisdom, goodness, and all such qualities; by these then the wings of the soul are nourished and grow, but by the opposite qualities, such as vileness and evil, they are wasted away and destroyed. Now the great leader in heaven, Zeus, driving a winged chariot, goes first, arranging all things and caring for all things. He is followed by an army of gods and spirits, arrayed in eleven squadrons; Hestia alone remains in the house of the gods. Of the rest, those who are included among the twelve great gods and are accounted leaders, are assigned each to his place in the army. There are many blessed sights and many ways hither and thither within the heaven, along which the blessed gods go to and fro attending each to his own duties; and whoever wishes, and is able, follows, for jealousy is excluded from the celestial band. But when they go to a feast and a banquet, they proceed steeply upward to the top of the vault of heaven, where the chariots of the gods, whose well matched horses obey the rein, advance easily, but the others with difficulty; for the horse of evil nature weighs the chariot down, making it heavy and pulling toward the earth the charioteer whose horse is not well trained. There the utmost toil and struggle await the soul. For those that are called immortal, when they reach the top, pass outside and take their place on the outer surface of the heaven, and when they have taken their stand, the revolution carries them round and they behold the things outside of the heaven.

But the region above the heaven was never worthily sung by any earthly poet, nor will it ever be. It is, however, as I shall tell; for I must dare to speak the truth, especially as truth is my theme. For the colorless, formless, and intangible truly existing essence, with which all true knowledge is concerned, holds this region and is visible only to the mind, the pilot of the soul. Now the divine intelligence, since it is nurtured on mind and pure knowledge, and the intelligence of every soul which is capable of receiving that which befits it, rejoices in seeing reality for a space of time and by gazing upon truth is nourished and made happy until the revolution brings it again to the same place. In the revolution it beholds absolute justice, temperance, and knowledge, not such knowledge

> "[T]he divine is beauty, wisdom, goodness, and all such qualities; by these then the wings of the soul are nourished and grow..."

as has a beginning and varies as it is associated with one or another of the things we call realities, but that which abides in the real eternal absolute; and in the same way it beholds and feeds upon the other eternal verities, after which, passing down again within the heaven, it goes home, and there the charioteer puts up the horses at the manger and feeds them with ambrosia and then gives them nectar to drink.

Such is the life of the gods; but of the other souls, that which best follows after God and is most like him, raises the head of the charioteer up into the outer region and is carried round in the revolution, troubled by the horses and hardly beholding the realities; and another sometimes rises and sometimes sinks, and, because its horses are unruly, it sees some things and fails to see others. The other souls follow after, all yearning for the upper region but unable to reach it, and are carried round beneath, trampling upon and colliding with one another, each striving to pass its neighbor. So there is the greatest confusion and sweat of rivalry, wherein many are lamed, and many wings are broken through the incompetence of the drivers; and after much toil they all go away without gaining a view of reality, and when they have gone away they feed upon opinion. But the reason of the great eagerness to see where the plain of truth is, lies in the fact that the fitting pasturage for the best part of the soul is in the meadow there, and the wing on which the soul is raised up is nourished by this. And this is a law of Destiny, that the soul which follows after God and obtains a view of any of the truths is free from harm until the next period, and if it can always attain this, is always unharmed; but when, through inability to follow, it fails to see, and through some mischance is filled with forgetfulness and evil and grows heavy, and when it has grown heavy, loses its wings and falls to the earth.

Plato believed that genuine happiness can only be achieved by people who consistently make sure that their Reason is in control of their Spirits and Appetites. This harmonious integration under the control of Reason is the essence of Plato's concept of justice, both at the individual level and, as we shall see in Chapter 10, at the social and political level as well.

< READING CRITICALLY >

Analyzing the Chariot Analogy

- Describe an experience in your life in which you experienced a vigorous conflict between the three dimensions of your *self* identified by Plato: Reason, Appetite, and Spirit. What was the nature of the conflict? How was it resolved?
- Describe an experience in your life in which Reason prevailed over Passion and Appetite. How was Reason able to prevail? Did you gain increased wisdom from the experience?
- Describe an experience in your life in which the three elements of your *self* identified by Plato worked together in a productive and harmonious fashion, enabling you to achieve a great success.

3.3 St. Augustine's Synthesis of Plato and Christianity

Plato's (and Socrates') metaphysical views were revolutionary and included:

- The existence of an immaterial reality separate from the physical world.
- The radical distinction between an immaterial soul and physical body.
- The existence of an immortal soul that finds its ultimate fulfillment in union with the eternal, transcendent realm.

St. Augustine (354–430) Christian philosopher and Bishop of Hippo in North Africa. Augustine's synthesis of Platonic and Christian concepts was a major influence in the development of medieval Christian doctrine and western philosophy. His writing includes a spiritual autobiography, *The Confessions* and a discussion of the spiritual path, *The City of God*. Augustine was canonized by the Catholic church in the fourteenth century.

However, these ideas would have died had they not been adopted and perpetuated by subsequent cultures. The Roman Empire both conquered and absorbed Greek culture, preserving much of its extraordinary accomplishments in the arts, philosophy, and politics. Plato died in 347 B.C.E., and more than 500 years, later a Roman philosopher named Plotinus (205–270 C.E.) breathed new life into Plato's ideas, spearheading an intellectual movement that came to be known as **neoplatonism**. Plotinus based his views on Plato's core concepts believing, for example, that "the soul, since it is a spiritual substance in its own right and can exist independently of the body, possesses a categorical superiority over the body." Plotinus was so fervently committed to his Platonic ideas regarding the imperfection of his physical body, in contrast to the perfection of his eternal soul that he refused to celebrate his birthday. His reasoning was that he was ashamed that his immortal soul had to be contained in such an imperfect vessel as his body, and that celebrating its birth was a cause for regret, not celebration. Similarly, he refused to have his physical likeness painted or sculpted, as he wanted no permanent record of his physical self. His disdain for his body led to his neglect of his physical health, resulting in the loss of his voice and pus-laden sores and abscesses that covered his hands and feet. Because he was a teacher with his own school and had a penchant for embracing his students, his physical deterioration ended up driving his students away.

In any case, Plotinus's ideas had a profound influence on the last of the great ancient philosophers, **St. Augustine**, and through him on all of Western consciousness. This extraordinary and far-reaching influence was the result of Augustine integrating the philosophical concepts of Plato with the tenets of Christianity. Augustine was convinced that Platonism and Christianity were natural partners, going so far as to contend, "If (the Platonists) could have had this life over again with us . . . they would have become Christians, with the change of a few words and statements." He enthusiastically adopted Plato's vision of a bifurcated universe in which "there are two realms, an intelligible realm where truth itself dwells, and this sensible world which we perceive by sight and touch," but then adapted this metaphysic to Christian beliefs. Thus, Plato's ultimate reality, the eternal realm of the Forms, became in Augustine's philosophy a transcendent God. In the same way, Plato's vision of immortal souls striving to achieve union with this eternal realm through intellectual enlightenment became transformed by Augustine into immortal souls striving to achieve union with God through faith and reason. The transient, finite nature of the physical world described by Plato became in Christianity a proving ground for our eternal destinies. Plato's metaphysical framework thus provided philosophical justification for Christian beliefs that might otherwise have been considered farfetched.

Augustine was a complex and fascinating figure. Born to successful parents in northern Africa, he spent much of his youth and young adulthood carousing with friends, indulging in numerous love affairs, and even fathering an illegitimate child. But he also had a powerful and curious intellect, and his explorations ultimately led him to conversion to Christianity when he was thirty-three years old. His personal odyssey is recorded in one of the most extraordinary and compelling books of its kind, his *Confessions*. He spent the remainder of his life in his home country, serving as bishop of Hippo and writing books and letters that helped shape the theology of Christianity for subsequent centuries.

Like Plato and Plotinus, Augustine believed that the physical body was both radically different from and inferior to its inhabitant, the immortal soul. Early in his philosophical development, he describes the body as a "snare" and a "cage" for the soul. He considers the body a "slave" to the soul, and sees their relation as contentious: "The soul makes war with the body." As his thinking matured, Augustine sought to develop a more unified perspective on body and soul. He ultimately came to view the body as the "spouse" of the soul, with both attached to one another by a "natural appetite." He concludes, "That the body is united with the soul, so that man may be entire and complete, is a fact we recognize on the evidence of our own nature." Nevertheless, as for Plato, Plotinus, and all the other neoplatonists, body and soul remain irreconcilably divided, two radically different entities with diverging fates: the body to die, the soul to live eternally in a transcendent realm of Truth and Beauty.

In melding philosophy and religious beliefs together, Augustine has been characterized as Christianity's first **theologian,** a term derived from the Greek *theos* (God) and *logos* (study of)—the study of God. His ideas influenced the structure of Christianity for the next 1,500 years, but by serving as a conduit for Plato's fundamental ideas, Augustine's influence extended beyond Christianity to the cultural consciousness of Western civilization as a whole. We will

> ### thinking philosophically
>
> ### DO YOU BELIEVE IN AN IMMORTAL SOUL?
>
> Though you may not have realized it, many of your fundamental ideas about your self probably reflect the influence of Plato and Augustine. Consider your views on the following Platonic concepts:
>
> - There is an immaterial reality that exists separate from the physical world.
> - There is a radical distinction between an immaterial soul and physical body.
> - There are immortal souls that find their ultimate fulfillment in union with the eternal, transcendent realm (for Augustine, this is God).
>
> In each case, compare and contrast your beliefs with those of Plato and Augustine.

see Augustine's direct impact on the thinking of the next individual we consider, the French philosopher René Descartes. In addition to establishing the groundwork for Descartes' thinking regarding the soul and the body, Augustine also foreshadowed Descartes' theory of knowledge. Engaging in a similar quest for certainty that was to consume Descartes 1,200 years later, Augustine identified as a first principle, "I am doubting, therefore I am," a statement eerily prescient of Descartes' famous pronouncement, *cogito, ergo sum*—"I think, therefore I am."

3.4 Descartes' Modern Perspective on the Self

Although Socrates is often described as the "father of Western philosophy," the French philosopher **René Descartes** is widely considered the "founder of modern philosophy." As profoundly insightful as such thinkers as Socrates and Plato were regarding the nature of the self, their understanding was also influenced and constrained by the consciousness of their time periods. Descartes brought an entirely new—and thoroughly modern—perspective to philosophy in general and the self in particular. Earlier philosophers had focused on exploring the fundamental questions of human existence, such as:

- What is the nature of reality?
- What is the "good life" and how ought we to behave?
- Does God exist? If so, what is God's nature and relation to humankind?
- What is the nature of the soul?
- What is the ideal society?

René Descartes (1596–1650). French philosopher considered the founder of modern philosophy. A mathematician and scientist as well, Descartes was a leader in the seventeenth-century scientific revolution. In his major work, *Meditations on First Philosophy* (1641), he rigorously analyzed the established knowledge of the time.

Although Descartes recognized these as significant questions, he was more concerned with understanding the *thinking process* we use to answer questions such as these. He agreed with the great thinkers before him that the human ability to *reason* constitutes the extraordinary instrument we have to achieve truth and knowledge. But instead of simply *using* reason to try to answer questions, Descartes wanted to penetrate the nature of our *reasoning process* and understand its relation to the human self. He was convinced that to develop the most informed and well-grounded beliefs about human existence, we need to be clear about the thinking instrument we are employing. For if our thinking instrument is flawed, then it is likely that our conclusions will be flawed as well.

As an accomplished mathematician (he invented analytic geometry) and an aspiring scientist, Descartes was an integral part of the scientific revolution that was just beginning. (His major philosophical work, *Meditations on First Philosophy*, was published in 1641, the year before Galileo died and Isaac Newton was born.) The foundation of this scientific revolution was the belief that genuine knowledge needed to be based on independent rational inquiry and real-world experimentation. It was no longer appropriate to accept without question the "knowledge" handed down by authorities—as was prevalent during the religion-dominated Middle Ages. Instead, Descartes and others were convinced that we need to use our own thinking abilities to investigate, analyze, experiment, and develop our own well-reasoned conclusions, supported with compelling proof. In a passage from his *Discourse on Method*, Descartes contrasts the process of learning to construct knowledge by thinking independently with simply absorbing information from authorities:

> For we shall not, e.g., turn out to be mathematicians though we know by heart all the proofs others have elaborated, unless we have an intellectual talent that fits us to resolve difficulties of any kind. Neither, though we may have mastered all the arguments of Plato and Aristotle, if yet we have not the capacity for passing solid judgment on these matters, shall we become Philosophers; we should have acquired the knowledge not of a science, but of history.

But reasoning effectively does not mean simply thinking in our own personal, idiosyncratic ways: That type of commonsense thinking is likely to be seriously flawed. Instead, effective use of "the natural light of reason" entails applying scientific discipline and analytic rigor to our explorations to ensure that the conclusions that we reach have genuine merit:

> So blind is the curiosity by which mortals are possessed, that they often conduct their minds along unexplored routes, having no reason to hope for success . . . it were far better never to think of investigating truth at all, than to do so without a method. For it is very certain that unregulated inquiries and confused reflections of this kind only confound the natural light and blind our mental powers. . . . In (method) alone lies the sum of all human endeavor, and he who would approach the investigation of truth must hold to this rule. For to be possessed of good mental powers is not sufficient; the principal matter is to apply them well. The greatest minds are capable of the greatest vices as well as of the greatest virtues, and those who proceed very slowly may, provided they always follow the straight road, really advance much faster than those who, though they run, forsake it.

One of the reasons Descartes is such an influential and enduring figure in philosophy is his willingness to test his reasoning powers to their limit and to record with absolute candor the results of his explorations. To this end, Descartes typically writes in the first person, inviting us to participate in his reasoning process and compare it with our own. He's saying, in effect: "This is what makes sense to me—do you agree?" In his best known work, *Meditations on First Philosophy*, Descartes shares with us his own philosophical journal, analogous to the philosopher's journal that you have been encouraged to keep as an integral part of this course. In an opening passage that virtually every young adult can appreciate, Descartes confesses that he has come to the conclusion that virtually everything he has been taught from authorities and other adults is questionable and likely false. His radical solution? To establish a fresh start on gaining true, well-supported beliefs by simply erasing his endorsement of anything he has previously been taught. What a bold and extraordinary project!

René Descartes, from *Meditations on First Philosophy*

1. Several years have now elapsed since I first became aware that I had accepted, even from my youth, many false opinions for true, and that consequently what I afterward based on such principles was highly doubtful; and from that time I was convinced of the necessity of undertaking once in my life to rid myself of all the opinions I had adopted, and of commencing anew the work of building from the foundation, if I desired to establish a firm and abiding superstructure in the sciences. But as this enterprise appeared to me to be one of great magnitude, I waited until I had attained an age so mature as to leave me no hope that at any stage of life more advanced I should be better able to execute my design. On this account, I have delayed so long that I should henceforth consider I was doing wrong were I still to consume in deliberation any of the time that now remains for action. Today, then, since I have opportunely freed my mind from all cares [and am happily disturbed by no passions], and since I am in the secure possession of leisure in a peaceable retirement, I will at length apply myself earnestly and freely to the general overthrow of all my former opinions.

2. But, to this end, it will not be necessary for me to show that the whole of these are false—a point, perhaps, which I shall never reach; but as even now my reason convinces me that I ought not the less carefully to withhold belief from what is not entirely certain and indubitable, than from what is manifestly false, it will be sufficient to justify the rejection of the whole if I shall find in each some ground for doubt. Nor for this purpose will it be necessary even to deal with each belief individually, which would be truly an endless labor; but, as the removal from below of the foundation necessarily involves the downfall of the whole edifice, I will at once approach the criticism of the principles on which all my former beliefs rested.

Descartes is convinced that committing yourself to a wholesale and systematic doubting of all things you have been taught to simply accept without question is the only way to achieve clear and well-reasoned conclusions. More important, it is the only way for you to develop beliefs that are truly *yours* and not someone else's. He explains, "If you would be a real seeker after truth, it is necessary that at least once in your life you doubt, as far as possible, all things." This sort of thoroughgoing doubting of all that you have been taught requires great personal courage, for calling into question things like your religious beliefs, cultural values, and even beliefs about your self can be, in the short term, a very disruptive enterprise. It may mean shaking up your world, questioning the beliefs of important people in your life, perhaps challenging your image of yourself. Yet there is a compelling logic to Descartes' pronouncement: For, if you are *not* willing to question all that you have been asked to accept "on faith," then you will never have the opportunity to construct a rock-solid

Questioning common assumptions. Do you agree with Descartes that "If you would be a real seeker after truth, it is necessary that at least once in your life you doubt, as far as possible, all things?"

foundation for your beliefs about the world and your personal philosophy of life. What's more, you will never have the experience to develop the intellectual abilities and personal courage required to achieve your full potential in the future.

This, then, is the beginning of Descartes' quest for true knowledge that leads to his famous first principle: *Cogito, ergo sum*—"I think, therefore I am." We will be exploring his epistemological odyssey in some detail in the sections on Knowledge and Truth (Chapters 5 and 6). For now, we're going to focus on Descartes' analysis of the self, the theme of this chapter.

Cogito, ergo sum is the first principle of Descartes' theory of knowledge because he is confident that no rational person will doubt his or her own existence as a conscious, thinking entity—*while we are aware of thinking about our self.* Even if we are dreaming or hallucinating, even if our consciousness is being manipulated by some external entity, it is still my *self-aware self* that is dreaming, hallucinating, or being manipulated. Thus, in addition to being the first principle of his epistemology, *cogito ergo, sum* is also the keystone of Descartes' concept of self. The essence of existing as a human identity is the possibility of *being aware of our selves*. Being self-conscious in this way is integral to having a personal identity. Conversely, it would be impossible to be self-conscious if we didn't have a personal identity of which to be conscious. In other words, having a *self-identity* and being *self-conscious* are mutually dependent on one another. Here's how Descartes explains this phenomenon in his *Meditation II*.

René Descartes,
from *Meditations on First Philosophy*

> Thinking is another attribute of the soul; and here I discover what properly belongs to myself. This alone is inseparable from me. I am—I exist: this is certain; but how often? As often as I think; for perhaps it would even happen, if I should wholly cease to think, that I should at the same time altogether cease to be. I now admit nothing that is not necessarily true. I am therefore, precisely speaking, only a thinking thing, that is, a mind, understanding, or reason, terms whose signification was before unknown to me. I am, however, a real thing, and really existent; but what thing? The answer was, a thinking thing....
>
> But what, then, am I? A thinking thing, it has been said. But what is a thinking thing? It is a thing that doubts, understands [conceives], affirms, denies, wills, refuses; that imagines also, and perceives.

❝ *Cogito ergo sum* **I think, therefore I am.** **DESCARTES** **❞**

For Descartes, then, this is the essence of your self—you are a "thinking thing," a dynamic identity that engages in all of those mental operations we associate with being a human self. For example,

- You *understand* situations in which you find yourself.
- You *doubt* the accuracy of ideas presented to you.
- You *affirm* the truth of a statement made about you.
- You *deny* an accusation that someone has made.
- You *will* yourself to complete a task you have begun.
- You *refuse* to follow a command that you consider to be unethical.
- You *imagine* a fulfilling career for yourself.
- You *feel* passionate emotions toward another person.

But in addition to engaging in all of these mental operations—and many other besides—your self-identity is dependent on the fact that *you are capable of being aware you are engaging in these mental operations while you are engaged in them.* If you were consistently *not* conscious of your mental operations, consistently *unaware* of your thinking, reasoning, and perceiving processes, then it would not be possible for you to have a self-identity, a unique essence, a *you.*

But what about your body? After all, a great deal of our self-concept and self-identity is tied up with our physical existence: our physical qualities, appearance, gender, race, age, height, weight, hair style, and so on. Despite this, Descartes believes that your physical body is secondary to your personal identity. One reason for this is that he believes you can conceive of yourself existing independently of your body.

thinking philosophically

ARE YOU A SEEKER AFTER TRUTH?

- Explain your reaction to Descartes' challenge, "If you would be a real seeker after truth, it is necessary that at least once in your life you doubt, as far as possible, all things." Do you agree with this statement? Why or why not? If so, how?

- Describe some important areas of your life in which you would consider yourself to be a "real seeker after truth." Identify several examples of beliefs you had been taught or raised with which you questioned for the purpose of developing your own independent conclusions.

- Describe some important areas of your life in which, in your opinion, you *fell short* of being a "real seeker after truth." Identify several examples of beliefs you have been raised with that you have been reluctant to question. What factors have made it difficult for you to doubt these beliefs? Do you think you will critically analyze them at some point in the future?

The question now arises, am I anything else besides? I will stimulate my imagination with a view to discover whether I am not still something more than a thinking being. Now it is plain I am not the assemblage of members called the human body; I am not a thin and penetrating air diffused through all these members, or wind, or flame, or vapor, or breath, or any of all the things I can imagine; for I supposed that all these were not, and, without changing the supposition, I find that I still feel assured of my existence. But it is true, perhaps, that those very things which I suppose to be non-existent, because they are unknown to me, are not in truth different from myself whom I know. This is a point I cannot determine, and do not now enter into any dispute regarding it. I can only judge of things that are known to me: I am conscious that I exist, and I who know that I exist inquire into what I am. It is, however, perfectly certain that the knowledge of my existence, thus precisely taken, is not dependent on things, the existence of which is as yet unknown to me: and consequently it is not dependent on any of the things I can feign in imagination.

René Descartes, from *Meditations on First Philosophy*

Nevertheless, even though your body is not as central to your self as is your capacity to think and reflect, it clearly plays a role in your self-identity. In fact, Descartes contends, if you reflect thoughtfully, you can see that you have clear ideas of both your *self as a thinking entity* and your *self as a physical body.* And these two dimensions of your self are quite distinct.

And, firstly, because I know that all which I clearly and distinctly conceive can be produced by God exactly as I conceive it, it is sufficient that I am able clearly and distinctly to conceive one thing apart from another, in order to be certain that the one is different from the other, seeing they may at least be made to exist separately, by the omnipotence of God; and it matters not by what power this separation is made, in order to be compelled to judge them different; and, therefore, merely because I know with certitude that I exist, and because, in the meantime, I do not observe that anything else necessarily

René Descartes, from *Meditations on First Philosophy*

belongs to my nature or essence beyond my being a thinking thing, I rightly conclude that my essence consists only in my being a thinking thing [or a substance whose whole essence or nature is merely thinking]. And although I may, or rather, as I will shortly say, although I certainly do possess a body with which I am very closely conjoined; nevertheless, because, on the one hand, I have a clear and distinct idea of myself, in as far as I am only a thinking and unextended thing, and as, on the other hand, I possess a distinct idea of body, in as far as it is only an extended and unthinking thing, it is certain that I, [that is, my mind, by which I am what I am], is entirely and truly distinct from my body, and may exist without it.

It is at this point that we can see the pervasive influence of the metaphysical framework created by Socrates and Plato and perpetuated through the centuries by such thinkers as Plotinus and Saint Augustine. Following directly in their footsteps, Descartes declares that the *essential self*—the *self as thinking entity*—is radically different than the *self as physical body*. The *thinking self*—or soul—is a nonmaterial, immortal, conscious being, independent of the physical laws of the universe. The *physical body* is a material, mortal, nonthinking entity, fully governed by the physical laws of nature. What's more, your soul and your body are independent of one another, and each can exist and function without the other. How is that possible? For example, in the case of physical death, Descartes believes (as did Plato) that your soul continues to exist, seeking union with the spiritual realm and God's infinite and eternal mind. On the other hand, in cases in which people are sleeping or comatose, their bodies continue to function even though their minds are not thinking, much like the mechanisms of a clock.

René Descartes,
from *Meditations on First Philosophy*

And as a clock, composed of wheels and counter weights, observes not the less accurately all the laws of nature when it is ill made, and points out the hours incorrectly, than when it satisfies the desire of the maker in every respect; so likewise if the body of man be considered as a kind of machine, so made up and composed of bones, nerves, muscles, veins, blood, and skin, that although there were in it no mind, it would still exhibit the same motions which it at present manifests involuntarily, and therefore without the aid of the mind, and simply by the dispositions of its organs....

Thus Descartes ends up with Plato's metaphysic, a dualistic view of reality, bifurcated into

- a spiritual, nonmaterial, immortal realm that includes conscious, thinking beings, *and*
- a physical, material, finite realm that includes human bodies and the rest of the physical universe.

In the case of the human self, the soul (or mind) and the physical body could not be more different. For example, you can easily imagine the body being divided into various parts, whereas it is impossible to imagine your soul as anything other than an indivisible unity (precisely the point that Socrates makes when he's arguing for the immortality of the soul):

René Descartes,
from *Meditations on First Philosophy*

To commence this examination accordingly, I here remark, in the first place, that there is a vast difference between mind and body, in respect that body, from its nature, is always divisible, and that mind is entirely indivisible. For in truth, when I consider the mind, that is, when I consider myself in so far only as I am a thinking thing, I can distinguish in myself no parts, but I very clearly discern that I am somewhat absolutely one and entire; and although the whole mind seems to be united to the whole body, yet, when a foot, an arm, or any other part is cut off, I am conscious that nothing has been taken from my mind; nor can the faculties of willing, perceiving, conceiving, etc., properly be called its parts, for it is the same mind that is exercised [all entire] in willing, in perceiving, and in conceiving, etc. But quite the opposite holds in corporeal or extended things; for I cannot imagine any one of them [how small soever it may be], which I cannot easily sunder in thought, and which, therefore, I do not know to be divisible. This would be sufficient to teach me that the mind or soul of man is entirely different from the body, if I had not already been apprised of it on other grounds.

This dualistic view of the self is particularly useful for Descartes, who was faced with a serious conflict in his personal and professional life. As previously noted, Descartes was first and foremost a scientist in his professional life, committed to establishing true knowledge through rigorous reasoning, experimentation, and analysis. Many scientists of the time—physicists, astronomers, biologists—were inclined to view the human self in terms of the physical body, governed by the same laws of physics that defined the operation of the rest of the physical universe. However, if the self is seen exclusively in terms of the physical body, the self is terminated when the body dies.

As a devout Catholic who believed in God, immortal souls, and eternal life, this view of the world was completely unacceptable to Descartes. However, by advocating a dualistic metaphysic, Descartes was able to maintain both his scientific integrity and his religious convictions. The *physical self* is a part of nature, governed by the physical laws of the universe, and available to scientific analysis and experimentation. At the same time, the *conscious self (mind, soul)* is a part of the spiritual realm, independent of the physical laws of the universe, governed only by the laws of reason and God's will.

Although a bifurcated view of the universe solves some immediate problems for Descartes, it creates other philosophical difficulties, most notably the vexing question, "What is the relationship between the mind and the body?" In our everyday experience, our minds and bodies appear to be very closely related to one another. Our thinking and emotions have a profound effect on many aspects of our physical bodies, and physical events with our bodies have a significant impact on our mental lives. For the most part, we experience our minds and bodies as a unified entity, very different from the two different and completely independent substances that Descartes proposes. As the writer and humorist Mark Twain noted, "How come the mind gets drunk when the body does the drinking?" Even Descartes recognized the need to acknowledge the close, intimate relationship between mind and body, as the following passage reveals:

Listen to the **Interview** *Mind/Body Problem* on **mysearchlab.com**

Nature likewise teaches me by these sensations of pain, hunger, thirst, etc., that I am not only lodged in my body as a pilot in a vessel, but that I am besides so intimately conjoined, and as it were intermixed with it, that my mind and body compose a certain unity. For if this were not the case, I should not feel pain when my body is hurt, seeing I am merely a thinking thing, but should perceive the wound by the understanding alone, just as a pilot perceives by sight when any part of his vessel is damaged; and when my body has need of food or drink, I should have a clear knowledge of this, and not be made aware of it by the confused sensations of hunger and thirst: for, in truth, all these sensations of hunger, thirst, pain, etc., are nothing more than certain confused modes of thinking, arising from the union and apparent fusion of mind and body.

René Descartes,
from *Meditations on First Philosophy*

Descartes believed that the "intermingling" point of contact was through the pineal gland, a small gland located at the base of the skull. It was here that he believed that the thinking self connected to the physical brain. Why the pineal gland? Descartes found its physical location appropriate, and it had no known biological function in Descartes' time. Ever the scientist, Descartes dissected a variety of animals to learn more about this mysterious gland.

Recognizing the problem of the mind/body relationship in a dualistic system and solving the problem in a satisfactory way are two very different things. Most philosophers agree that Descartes' efforts to provide an integrated model of his concepts of the mind and body were not successful, and it's a problem that has challenged thinkers in every discipline ever since. We will continue our exploration of the mind/body "problem" later in this chapter.

How did Descartes' views regarding the self relate to his personal life? In a fascinating way: Descartes was plagued by frail health, a condition that caused him throughout his life to sleep late into the morning. A financial inheritance from his parents meant he didn't have to work. Instead, he devoted his life to study and experimentation, spending much of his time alone, and moving from place to place on a regular basis (he lived in twenty different houses in one twenty-year period). Descartes preferred the company of himself because it provided him the opportunity to fully devote himself to his scientific, mathematical, and philosophical activities, without the distraction of social relationships (although he did find time to father an illegitimate child with a servant). Ironically, it was an error in judgment that hastened the death of his body. Against his better judgment, he accepted the invitation of Queen Christina of Sweden to come to Stockholm and tutor her. Unfortunately, the queen turned out to be an early riser, depriving Descartes of his beloved sleep. That, combined with the cold and damp climate of Stockholm, led to pneumonia and his premature death at the age of fifty-three, providing him with a first-hand opportunity to test his theory of an immortal soul.

((⦿— **Listen** to the **Interview** The *Mind/Body Problem* with *Melvyn Bragg* on **mysearchlab.com**

< READING CRITICALLY >

Analyzing Descartes on the Mind/Body Problem

- Describe some of the ways your mind significantly affects your body: for example, when you are anxious, elated, depressed, in love (or lust), and so on.
- Describe some of the ways your body significantly affects your mind: for example, when you are feeling sick, deprived of sleep, taking medications, or finding yourself in a physically dangerous/threatening situation.
- Create your own metaphysical framework for the "*self*" by describing
  - your *self as thinking subject*.
  - your *self as physical body*.
  - your analysis of how these two aspects of your *self* relate to one another.
- Reconsider your views on human souls—what do you believe happens to the *self* after the death of the body? Why do you believe it? What would Descartes think of your views and your justification for them?

3.5 The Self Is Consciousness: Locke

The English philosopher—and physician—**John Locke** continued exploring the themes Descartes had initiated, both in terms of the nature of knowledge (epistemology) and the nature of the self. He shared with Descartes a scientist's perspective, seeking to develop knowledge based on clear thinking, rigorous analysis, and real-world observation and experimentation. However, Locke brought a very different approach to this epistemological enterprise. Descartes believed that we could use the power of reason to achieve absolutely certain knowledge of the world and then use this rationally based knowledge to understand our world of experience. His extensive work in mathematics served as a model, convincing him that there were absolute truths and knowledge waiting to be discovered by reasoned, disciplined reflection.

Locke's work as a physician, rather than a mathematician, provided him with a very different perspective. The physician's challenge is to gather information regarding the symptoms a patient is experiencing, and then relate these symptoms to his (the physician's) accumulated knowledge of disease. Although a successful doctor uses sophisticated reasoning abilities in identifying patterns and making inferences, his conclusions are grounded in experience. Knowledge, in other words, is based on the careful observation of sense experience and/or memories of previous experiences. Reason plays a subsequent role in helping to figure out the significance of our sense experience and to reach intelligent conclusions.

To sum up: For Descartes, our *reasoning ability* provides the origin of knowledge and final court of judgment in evaluating the accuracy and value of the ideas produced. For Locke, all knowledge originates in our direct *sense experience*, which acts as the final court of judgment in evaluating the accuracy and value of ideas. As a result, Descartes is considered an archetypal proponent of the **rationalist** view of knowledge, whereas Locke is considered an archetypal advocate of the **empiricist** view of knowledge.

These are themes that we will be exploring in depth in Chapters 5 and 6. For now, we will focus on the way in which these contrasting approaches to the world influence their views on the nature of the self.

True to his philosophical commitment to grounding his ideas in sense experience, Locke, in his essay entitled "On Personal Identity" (from his most famous work, *An Essay Concerning Human Understanding*) engages in a reflective analysis of how we experience our self in our everyday lives.

John Locke (1632–1704). British philosopher and physician who laid the groundwork for an empiricist approach to philosophical questions. Locke's revolutionary theory that the mind is a tabula rasa, a blank slate on which experience writes, is detailed in his *Essay Concerning Human Understanding* (1690).

Rationalism The view that reason is the primary source of all knowledge and that only our reasoning abilities can enable us to understand sense experience and reach accurate conclusions.

Empiricism The view that sense experience is the primary source of all knowledge and that only a careful attention to sense experience can enable us to understand the world and achieve accurate conclusions.

John Locke, from *On Personal Identity*

To find wherein personal identity consists, we must consider what *person* stands for;—which, I think, is a thinking intelligent being, that has reason and reflection, and can consider itself as itself, the same thinking thing, in different times and places; which it does only by that consciousness which is inseparable from thinking, and as it seems to me, essential to it: it being impossible for any one to perceive without *perceiving* that he does perceive. When we see, hear, smell, taste, feel, meditate, or will anything, we know that we do so. Thus it is always as to our present sensations and perceptions: and by this every one is to himself that which he calls self:—it not being considered, in this case, whether the same self be continued in the same or divers substances. For, since consciousness always accompanies thinking, and it is that which makes everyone to be what he calls self, and thereby distinguishes himself from

> all other thinking things, in this alone consists personal identity, i.e., the sameness of a rational being: and as far as this consciousness can be extended backwards to any past action or thing, so far reaches the identity of that person; it is the same self now it was then; and it is by the same self with this present one that now reflects on it, that that action was done.

In this initial passage, Locke makes the following points, implicitly asking the question of his readers, "Aren't these conclusions confirmed by examining your own experiences?"

1. To discover the nature of *personal identity*, we're going to have to find out what it means to be a *person.*
2. A *person* is a thinking, intelligent being who has the abilities to reason and to reflect.
3. A *person* is also someone who considers itself to be the *same* thing in different times and different places.
4. *Consciousness*—being aware that we are thinking—always accompanies thinking and is an essential part of the thinking process.
5. *Consciousness* is what makes possible our belief that we are the same identity in different times and different places.

Reflect carefully on Locke's points—do you find that his conclusions match your own personal experience? Certainly his first three points seem plausible. What about points 4 and 5? Does *consciousness* always accompany the thinking process? Locke explains: "When we see, hear, smell, taste, feel, meditate, or will anything, we know that we do so. Thus it is always as to our present sensations and perceptions: and by this every one is to himself that which he calls self." Consider what you are doing at this moment: You are thinking about the words on the page, the ideas that are being expressed—are you also aware of yourself as you are reading and thinking? Certainly once the question is posed to you, you're aware of your self. Perhaps it's more accurate to say that when you think, you are either conscious of your self—or *potentially* conscious of your self. In other words, are there times in which you are fully immersed in an activity—such as dancing, driving a car, or playing a sport—and not consciously aware that you are doing so? Analogously, are there times in which you are fully engaged in deep thought—wrestling with a difficult idea, for example—and not aware that you are doing so? But even if there are times in which you are unreflectively submerged in an activity or thought process, you always have the potential to *become* aware of your self engaged in the activity or thought process.

What about Locke's fifth point, that consciousness is necessary for us to have a unified self-identity in different times and places? This seems like a point well taken. You consider your self to be the same self who was studying last night, attending a party at a friend's house two weeks ago, and taking a vacation last summer. How can you be sure it's the same self in all of these situations? Because of your *consciousness* of being the same self in all of these different contexts.

These points become clearer when we contrast human thinking with animal thinking. It's reasonable to believe that mammals such as chipmunks, dogs, and dolphins are able to see, hear, smell, taste, and feel, just like humans. But are they *conscious* of the fact that they are performing these activities as they are performing them? Most people would say "no." And because they are not conscious that they are performing these activities, it's difficult to see how they would have a concept of self-identity that remains the same over time and place. So consciousness—or more specifically, self-consciousness—does seem to be a necessary part of having a coherent self-identity. (Some people believe that higher-order mammals such as chimpanzees and gorillas present more complicated cases.)

Descartes would agree with Locke's view that a person—or self—is a thinking, intelligent being that has the abilities to reason and to reflect. And he likely would be sympathetic to Locke's contention that consciousness accompanies thinking and makes possible the concept we have of a self that remains the same at different times and in different places. But in the following passage, Locke expresses a belief that many people—including Descartes—would likely disagree with. Let's examine his unusual belief regarding the self.

Consciousness Makes Personal Identity

John Locke, from *On Personal Identity*

But it is further inquired, whether it [*personal identity*] be the same identical substance. This few [*Locke refers here to Descartes*] would think they had reason to doubt of, if these perceptions, with their consciousness, always remained present in the mind, whereby the same thinking thing would be always consciously present, and, as would be thought, evidently the same to itself. But that which seems to make the difficulty is this, that this consciousness being interrupted always by forgetfulness, there being no moment of our lives wherein we have the whole train of all our past actions before our eyes in one view, but even the best memories losing the sight of one part whilst they are viewing another; and we sometimes, and that the greatest part of our lives, not reflecting on our past selves, being intent on our present thoughts, and in sound sleep having no thoughts at all, or at least none with that consciousness which remarks our waking thoughts,—I say, in all these cases, our consciousness being interrupted, and we losing the sight of our past selves, doubts are raised whether we are the same thinking thing, i.e., the same *substance* or no. Which, however reasonable or unreasonable, concerns not *personal* identity at all. The question being what makes the same person; and not whether it be the same identical substance, which always thinks in the same person, which, in this case, matters not at all: different substances, by the same consciousness (where they do partake in it) being united into one person, as well as different bodies by the same life are united into one animal, whose identity is preserved in that change of substances by the unity of one continued life. For, it being the same consciousness that makes a man be himself to himself, personal identity depends on that only, whether it be annexed solely to one individual substance, or can be continued in a succession of several substances. For as far as any intelligent being *can* repeat the idea of any past action with the same consciousness it had of it at first, and with the same consciousness it has of any present action; so far it is the same personal self. For it is by the consciousness it has of its present thoughts and actions, that it is *self to itself* now, and so will be the same self, as far as the same consciousness can extend to actions past or to come; and would be by distance of time, or change of substance, no more two persons, than a man be two men by wearing other clothes to-day than he did yesterday, with a long or short sleep between: the same consciousness uniting those distant actions into the same person, whatever substances contributed to their production.

As this passage makes clear, Locke is proposing a radically different version of the self than the philosophical tradition before him. Plato and Descartes had agreed that the self existed in the form of an immortal, nonmaterial soul that continues to exist following the death of the body. In a fascinating twist, Locke denies that the individual self necessarily exists in a single soul or substance. For Locke, the essence of the self is its conscious awareness of itself as a thinking, reasoning, reflecting identity. But this in no way means that this self is necessarily embedded in a single substance or soul—it might very well take up residence in any number of substances or souls.

In Locke's mind, conscious awareness and memory of previous experiences are the keys to understanding the self. In other words, you have a coherent concept of your self as a personal identity because you are *aware* of your self when you are thinking, feeling, and willing. *And* you have memories of times when you were aware of your self in the past, in other situations—for example, at the party two weeks ago, or your high school graduation several years ago. *But,* as we noted earlier, there are many moments when we are *not* consciously aware of our self when we are thinking, feeling, and willing—we are simply, unreflectively, *existing.* What's more, there are many past experiences that we have forgotten or have faulty recollections of. All of which means that during those lapses, when we were not aware of our self, or don't remember being aware of our self, we can't be sure if we were the same person, the same substance, the same soul! Our personal identity is not in doubt or jeopardy because we are aware of our self (or remember being aware of it). But we have no way of knowing if our personal identity has been existing in one substance (soul) or a number of substances (souls). For Locke, personal identity and the soul or substance in which the personal identity is situated are two very different things. Although the idea seems rather strange at first glance, Locke provides a very concrete example to further illustrate what he means.

John Locke, from *On Personal Identity*

Personal Identity in Change of Substance

That this is so, we have some kind of evidence in our very bodies, all whose particles, whilst vitally united to this same thinking conscious self, so that we feel when they are touched, and are affected by, and conscious of good or harm that happens to them, are a part of ourselves; i.e., of our thinking conscious self. Thus, the limbs of his body are to every one a part of himself; he sympathizes and is concerned for them. Cut off a hand, and thereby separate it from that consciousness he had of its heat, cold, and other affections, and it is then no longer a part of that which is himself, any more than the remotest part of matter. Thus, we see the *substance* whereof personal self consisted at one time may be varied at another, without the change of personal identity; there being no question about the same person, though the limbs which but now were a part of it, be cut off.

It's a rather gruesome example Locke provides, but it makes his point. Every aspect of your physical body (substance) is integrated with your *personal identity*—hit your finger with a hammer, and it's *you* that is experiencing the painful sensation. But if your hand is cut off in an industrial accident, your *personal identity* remains intact, although the substance associated with it has changed (you now only have one hand). Or to take another example: The cells of our body are continually being replaced, added to, subtracted from. So it's accurate to say that in many ways you are not the same *physical person* you were five years ago, ten years ago, fifteen years ago, and so on.

What if consciousness could be transferred?
In the movie, *The Curious Case of Benjamin Button,* the character played by Brad Pitt finds that his twelve-year-old personal identity is installed in the body of an adult version of himself—the kind of self mobility that Locke suggests might be possible.

Nevertheless, you are likely convinced that your *personal identity* has remained the same despite these changes in physical substance to your body. This leads Locke to conclude that our *personal identity* is distinct from whatever substance it finds itself associated with.

< READING CRITICALLY >

Analyzing Locke on the Conscious Self

- Evaluate Locke's claim that your *conscious self* is not permanently attached to any particular body or substance. Does this view make sense? Why or why not?
- Locke believes that it is our memory that serves to link our *self* at this moment with our *self* in previous circumstances. But people's memories are often faulty. How can we distinguish between accurate memories of our *self* and inaccurate memories? To do so, don't we have to assume that we have a continuous *self* that is performing the evaluation? But because memory is supposed to explain the existence of our *self*, doesn't this mean that Locke's reasoning is circular? Explain your analysis of this dilemma.

3.6 There Is No Self: Hume

David Hume continued in the empiricist tradition of John Locke, believing that the source of all genuine knowledge is our direct sense experience. As we have seen, this empiricist approach had led Locke to a number of surprising conclusions regarding the self, including the belief that the self's existence is dependent on our consciousness of it. In Locke's view, your self is not tied to any particular body or substance, and it only exists in other times and places because of our *memory* of those experiences. Using the same empiricist principles as Locke, Hume ends up with an even more startling conclusion—if we carefully examine our sense experience through the process of introspection, we discover that *there is no self!* How is this possible? From Hume's perspective, this astonishing belief is the only possible conclusion consistent with an honest and objective examination of our experience. The following passages are from Hume's essay "On Personal Identity."

David Hume (1711–1776). Scottish philosopher whose skeptical examinations of religion, ethics, and history were to make him a controversial eighteenth-century figure. A prolific writer, his works include *Enquiry Concerning Human Understanding* (1748) and *Dialogue Concerning Natural Religion* (1779), held for publication until after his death. *(Allen Ramsay/Library of Congress)*

David Hume, from *On Personal Identity*

There are some philosophers, who imagine we are every moment intimately conscious of what we call our SELF [*Hume is referring to Descartes and Locke, among others*], that we feel its existence and its continuance in existence and are certain, beyond the evidence of a demonstration, both of its perfect identity and simplicity. The strongest sensation, the most violent passion, say they, instead of distracting us from this view, only fix it the more intensely, and make us consider their influence on self either by their pain or pleasure. To attempt a farther proof of this were to weaken its evidence; since no proof can be derived from any fact, of which we are so intimately conscious; nor is there any thing of which we can be certain, if we doubt of this.

Unluckily all these positive assertions are contrary to that very experience, which is pleaded for them, nor have we any idea of self, after the manner it is here explained. For from what impression could this idea be derived? This question is impossible to answer with out a manifest contradiction, and absurdity; and yet it is a question, which must necessarily be answered, if we would have the idea of self pass for clear and intelligible. It must be some one impression, that gives rise to every real idea. But self or person is not any one impression but that to which our several impressions and ideas are supposed to have a reference. If any impression gives rise to the idea of self, that impression must continue invariably the same, through the whole course of our lives; since self is supposed to exist after that manner. But there is no impression constant and invariable. Pain and pleasure, grief and joy, passions and sensations succeed each other, and never all exist at the same time. It cannot, therefore, be from any of these impressions, or from any other, that the idea of self is derived; and consequently there is no such idea.

Read the **Document**
My Own Life (1776)
on **mysearchlab.com**

According to Hume, if we carefully examine the contents of our experience, we find that there are only two distinct entities, "impressions" and "ideas":

Impressions—Impressions are the basic sensations of our experience, the elemental data of our minds: pain, pleasure, heat, cold, happiness, grief, fear, exhilaration, and so on. These impressions are "lively" and "vivid."

Ideas—Ideas are *copies* of impressions, and as a result they are less "lively" and "vivid." Ideas include thoughts and images that are built up from our primary impressions through a variety of relationships, but because they are derivative copies of impressions they are once removed from reality.

If we examine these basic data of our experience, we see that they form a fleeting stream of sensations in our mind and that nowhere among them is the sensation of a "constant and invariable" self that exists as a unified identity over the course of our lives. And because the self is not to be found among these continually changing sensations, we can only conclude that there is no good reason for believing that the self exists. Hume goes on to explain:

David Hume, from
On Personal Identity

But farther, what must become of all our particular perceptions upon this hypothesis? All these are different, and distinguishable, and separable from each other and may be separately considered, and may exist separately, and have no need of any thing to support their existence. After what manner, therefore, do they belong to self and how are they connected with it? For my part, when I enter most intimately into what I call *myself*, I always stumble on some particular perception or other, of heat or cold, light or shade, love or hatred, pain or pleasure. I never can catch *myself* at any time without a perception, and never can observe any thing but the perception. When my perceptions are removed for any time, as by sound sleep; so long am I insensible of myself, and may truly be said not to exist. And were all my perceptions removed by death, and could I neither think, nor feel, nor see, nor love, nor hate after the dissolution of my body, I should be entirely annihilated, nor do I conceive what is further requisite to make me a perfect nonentity. If any one upon serious and unprejudiced reflection, thinks he has a different notion of *himself*, I must confess I can reason no longer with him. All I can allow him is, that he may be in the right as well as I, and that we are essentially different in this particular. He may, perhaps, perceive something simple and continued, which he calls *himself*; though I am certain there is no such principle in me.

"I can never catch *myself* at any time without a perception, and never can observe any thing but the perception." Even when we actively look for the self, Hume contends, we simply can't find it! All of our experiences are perceptions, and none of these perceptions resemble a unified and permanent self-identity that exists over time. Furthermore, when we are not experiencing our perceptions—as when we sleep—there is no reason to suppose that our self exists in any form. Similarly, when our body dies and all empirical sensations cease, it makes no sense to believe that our self continues to exist in some form. Death is final. And what of people who claim that they *do* experience a self in their stream of perceptions? Hume announces that "I must confess I can reason no longer with him. . . . He may, perhaps, perceive something simple and continued, which he calls *himself*; though I am certain there is no such principle in me." In other words, as an empiricist, Hume cannot do more than provide an honest description and analysis of his own experience, within which there is no self to be found. But if Hume is right, then why does virtually everybody but Hume believe with certainty that they *do* have a self-identity that persists through time and serves to unify their life and give it meaning? After all, it's not enough to say to the rest of the world: You're wrong, and I'm right, and I'm not going to discuss the issue if you insist on disagreeing with me. Let's examine Hume's explanation of the self that most people would claim they experience.

But setting aside some metaphysicians of this kind, I may venture to affirm of the rest of mankind, that they are nothing but a bundle or collection of different perceptions, which succeed each other with an inconceivable rapidity, and are in a perpetual flux and movement. Our eyes cannot turn in their sockets without varying our perceptions. Our thought is still more variable than our sight; and all our other senses and faculties contribute to this change; nor is there any single power of the soul, which remains unalterably the same, perhaps for one moment. The mind is a kind of theatre, where several perceptions successively make their appearance; pass, repass, glide away, and mingle in an infinite variety of postures and situations.

There is properly no *simplicity* in it at one time, nor *identity* in different; whatever natural propension we may have to imagine that simplicity and identity. The comparison of the theatre must not mislead us. They are the successive perceptions only, that constitute the mind: nor have we the most distant notion of the place, where these scenes are represented, or of the materials, of which it is composed.

The identity, which we ascribe to the mind of man, is only a fictitious one, and of a like kind with that which we ascribe to vegetables and animal bodies. It cannot, therefore, have a different origin, but must proceed from a like operation of the imagination upon his objects.

Our last resource is to . . . boldly assert that these different related objects are in effect the same, however interrupted and variable. In order to justify to ourselves this absurdity, we often feign some new and unintelligible principle, that connects the objects together, and prevents their interruption or variation. Thus we feign the continued existence of

David Hume, from
On Personal Identity

"
**The mind is a kind
of theatre, where
several perceptions
successively make their
appearance . . .**
"

the perceptions of our senses, to remove the interruption; and run into the notion of a *soul*, and *self*, and *substance*, to disguise the variation. But we may farther observe, that where we do not give rise to such a fiction, our propension to confound identity with relation is so great, that we are apt to imagine something unknown and mysterious connecting the parts, beside their relation; and this I take to be the case with regard to the identity we ascribe to plants and vegetables. And even when this does not take place, we still feel a propensity to confound these ideas, though we are not able fully to satisfy ourselves in that particular, nor find any thing invariable and uninterrupted to justify our notion of identity.

What is the self we experience according to Hume? A "bundle or collection of different perceptions, which succeed each other with an inconceivable rapidity, and are in a perpetual flux and movement." Humans so desperately *want* to believe that they have a unified and continuous self or soul that they use their imaginations to construct a fictional self. But this fictional self is not real; what we call the self is an imaginary creature, derived from a succession of impermanent states and events. What is our mind? According to Hume, it's "a kind of theatre, where several perceptions successively make their appearance, pass, repass, glide away, and mingle in an infinite variety of postures and situations."

< READING CRITICALLY >

Analyzing Hume on the Absence of Self

- Perform your own empiricist investigation by examining the contents of your consciousness. What do you find there? Fleeting and temporary sensations, perceptions, and ideas, as Hume describes? Is your *self* anywhere to be found?

- Hume uses the terms *I* and *myself* throughout his writings, words that seem to suggest a continually existing *self-identity* that he is denying. Does Hume contradict himself? Why or why not?

- Descartes' key point was that even if we are dreaming, fantasizing, or being deceived, the *act of doubting* proves that I have a *self* that is engaged in the activity of doubting. Is the same true for Hume? By denying the existence of a *self*, is he at the same time *proving* that his *self* exists, the *self* that is engaged in the act of denying? Why or why not?

- If you believe that you have a unifying and conscious *self* that exists through time but you can't "catch yourself" when you examine your immediate experience, then where does your *self* exist? What is the nature of your *self* if you can't perceive it? (This is precisely the challenge taken up by our next philosopher, Immanuel Kant.)

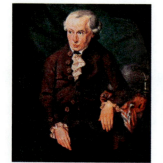

Immanuel Kant
(1724–1804). German philosopher considered by many to be the greatest thinker of the eighteenth century. Kant attempted to synthesize the two competing schools of the modern period, rationalism and empiricism, by showing the important role both experience and reason play in constructing our knowledge of the world. His works include the *Critique of Pure Reason* (1781; 1787) and *Prolegomena to Any Future Metaphysics* (1783).

3.7 We Construct the Self: Kant

Brilliant and idiosyncratic, the German philosopher **Immanuel Kant** helped create the conceptual scaffolding of modern consciousness in the areas of metaphysics, epistemology, and ethics. Kant was alarmed by David Hume's notion that the mind is simply a container for fleeting sensations and disconnected ideas, and our reasoning ability is merely "a slave to the passions." If Hume's views proved true, then humans would never be able to achieve genuine knowledge in any area of experience: scientific, ethical, religious, or metaphysical, including questions such as the nature of our selves.

For Kant, Hume's devastating conclusions served as a Socratic "gadfly" to his spirit of inquiry, awakening him from his intellectual sleep and galvanizing him to action:

> I admit it was David Hume's remark that first, many years ago, interrupted my dogmatic slumber and gave a completely different direction to my inquiries in the field of speculative philosophy.

Kant was convinced that philosophers and scientists of the time did not fully appreciate the potential destructiveness of Hume's views, and that it was up to him (Kant) to meet and dismantle this threat to human knowledge.

Immanuel Kant, from *Prolegomena to Any Future Metaphysics*

Since the origin of metaphysics so far as we know its history, nothing has ever happened which could have been more decisive to its fate than the attack made upon it by David Hume. He threw no light on this species of knowledge, but he certainly struck a spark by which light might have been kindled had it caught some inflammable substance and had its smouldering fire been carefully nursed and developed.... However hasty and mistaken Hume's inference may appear, it was at least founded upon investigation, and this investigation deserved the concentration of the brighter spirits of his day as well as determined efforts on their part to discover, if possible, a happier solution of the problem in the sense proposed by him....

But Hume suffered the usual misfortune of metaphysicians, of not being understood. It is positively painful to see how utterly his opponents...missed the point of the problem; for while they were ever taking for granted that which he doubted, and demonstrating with zeal and often with impudence that which he never thought of doubting, they so misconstrued his valuable suggestion that everything remained in its old condition, as if nothing happened.

How did Hume's empirical investigations lead him to the unsatisfying conclusion that genuine knowledge—and the self—do not exist? Kant begins his analysis at Hume's starting point—examining immediate sense experience—and he acknowledges Hume's point that all knowledge of the world begins with sensations: sounds, shapes, colors, tastes, feels, smells. For Hume, these sensations are the basic data of experience, and they flow through our consciousness in a torrential rushing stream:

> (The sensations in our senses) succeed each other with an inconceivable rapidity and are in a perpetual flux and movement.... The mind is a kind of theatre where several perceptions successively make their appearance, pass, repass, glide away, and mingle in an infinite variety of postures and situations.

But in reflecting on his experience, Kant observes an obvious fact that Hume seems to have overlooked, namely, that *our primary experience of the world is not in terms of a disconnected stream of sensations.* Instead, we perceive and experience an organized world of objects, relationships, and ideas, all existing within a fairly stable framework of space and time. True, at times discreet and randomly related sensations dominate our experience: for example, when we are startled out of a deep sleep and "don't know where we are," or when a high fever creates bizarre hallucinations, or the instant when an unexpected thunderous noise or blinding light suddenly dominates our awareness. But in general, we live in a fairly stable and orderly world in which sensations are woven together into a fabric that is familiar to us. And integrated throughout this fabric is our conscious self who is the knowing subject at the center of our universe. Hume's problem wasn't his starting point—empirical experience—it was the fact that he remained fixated on the starting point, refusing to move to the next, intelligible level of experience. Here's how Kant explains the situation:

Immanuel Kant, from *The Critique of Pure Reason*

There can be no doubt that all our knowledge begins with experience. For how should our faculty of knowledge be awakened into action did not objects affecting our sense partly of themselves produce representations, partly arouse the activity of our understanding to compare these representations, and, by combining or separating them, work up the raw material for the sensible impressions into that knowledge of objects which is entitled experience? In the order of time, therefore, we have no knowledge antecedent to experience, and with experience all our knowledge begins.

But though all our knowledge begins with experience, *it does not follow that it all arises out of experience.* [italics added] For it may well be that even our empirical knowledge is made up of what we receive through impressions and of what our own faculty of knowledge (sensible impressions, serving merely as the occasion) supplies from itself. If our faculty of knowledge makes any such addition, it may be that we are not in a position to distinguish it from the raw material, until with long practice of attention we have become skilled in separating it.

This, then is a question which at least calls for closer examination, and does not allow of any off-hand answer:—whether there is any knowledge that is thus independent of experience and even of all impressions of the senses. Such knowledge is entitled *a priori*, and distinguished from the *empirical*, which has its sources *a posteriori*, that is, in experience.

Where does the order and organization of our world come from? According to Kant, it comes in large measure from *us.* Our minds actively sort, organize, relate, and synthesize the fragmented, fluctuating collection of sense data that our sense organs take in. For example, imagine that someone dumped a pile of puzzle pieces on the table in front of you. They would initially appear to be a random collection of items, unrelated to one another and containing no meaning for you, much like the basic sensations of immediate unreflective experience. However, as you began to assemble the pieces, these fragmentary items would gradually begin to form a coherent image that would have significance for you. According to Kant this meaning-constructing activity is precisely what our minds are doing all of the time: taking the raw data of experience and actively synthesizing it into the familiar, orderly, meaningful world in which we live. As you might imagine, this mental process is astonishing in its power and complexity, and it is going on all of the time.

How do our minds know the best way to construct an intelligible world out of a never-ending avalanche of sensations? We each have fundamental organizing *rules* or *principles* built into the architecture of our minds. These dynamic principles naturally order, categorize, organize, and synthesize sense data into the familiar fabric of our lives, bounded by space and time. These organizing rules are a priori in the sense that they precede the sensations of experience and they exist independently of these sensations. We didn't have to "learn" these *a priori* ways of organizing and relating the world—they came as software already installed in our intellectual operating systems.

Kant referred to his approach to perception and knowledge as representing a "Copernican revolution" in metaphysics and epistemology, derived from the breakthrough of the Polish astronomer Copernicus (1473–1543), who was one of the first and most definitive voices asserting that instead of the sun orbiting around Earth, it's actually the reverse—Earth orbits the sun.

In a similar fashion, empiricists like Hume had assumed that the mind was a passive receptacle of sensations, a "theatre" in which the raw data of experience moved across without our influence. According to Hume, our minds conform to the world of which we are merely passive observers. Kant, playing the role of Copernicus, asserted that this is a wrongheaded perspective. The sensations of experience are necessary for knowledge, but they are in reality the "grist" for our mental "mills." Our minds *actively* synthesize and relate these sensations in the process of creating an intelligible world. As a result, the sensations of immediate experience conform to our minds, rather than the reverse. We *construct* our world through these conceptual operations; and, as a result, this is a world of which we can gain insight and knowledge.

Hitherto it has been assumed that all our knowledge must conform to objects. But all attempts to extend our knowledge of objects by establishing something in regard to them by means of concepts have, on this assumption, ended in failure. We must, therefore, make trial whether we may not have more success if we suppose that objects must conform to our knowledge.

Immanuel Kant,
from *The Critique of Pure Reason*

This is a brief overview of Kant's epistemological framework, which we will examine in more depth in Chapter 6. For now we are interested in how this framework influences Kant's conception of the self. Actually, from Kant's standpoint, it's our self that makes experiencing an intelligible world possible because it's the self that is responsible for synthesizing the discreet data of sense experience into a meaningful whole. Metaphorically, our self is the weaver who, using the loom of the mind, weaves together the fabric of experience into a unified whole so that it becomes *my* experience, *my* world, *my* universe. Without our self to perform this synthesizing function, our experience would be unknowable, a chaotic collection of sensations without coherence or significance.

Sensations would be nothing to us, and would not concern us in the least, if they were not received into our (orderly) consciousness. Knowledge is impossible in any other way....For perceptions could not be perceptions of anything for me unless they could at least be connected together into (my) one consciousness. This principle stands firm *a priori*, and may be called the "transcendental principle of unity" for all the multiplicity of our perceptions and sensations.

Immanuel Kant,
from *The Critique of Pure Reason*

The *unity of consciousness* is a phrase invented by Kant to describe the fact that the thoughts and perceptions of any given mind are bound together in a unity by being all contained in *one* consciousness—*my* consciousness. That's precisely what makes your world intelligible to you: It's your self that is actively organizing all of your sensations and thoughts into a picture that makes sense to you. This picture is uniquely *your* picture. You are at the center of your world, and you view everything in the world from your perspective. For example, think about a time in which you shared an experience with someone but you each

thinking philosophically

SENSE, PERCEPTION, AND YOUR SELF

- Reflect on your mind and identify the contents that you are experiencing as Hume would describe them: isolated and fleeting sounds, images, tastes, smells, and so on. Did this require a special effort on your part? Why or why not?

- Now reflect on the contents of your mind and identify the contents that you are experiencing as Kant would describe them: an integrated world of objects, relationships, space, and time. How did this mental "experiment" compare with the previous one?

- Describe a time in your life in which your experience was very much as Hume describes it and then how it changed into an experience that was more Kantian.

had radically different experiences: attending a party, viewing a movie, having a communication misunderstanding. Reflect on the way each person instinctively describes the entire situation from *his* or *her* perspective. *That's* the unity of consciousness that Kant is describing.

Your self is able to perform this synthesizing, unifying function because it *transcends* sense experience. Your self isn't an object located in your consciousness with other objects—your self is a *subject*, an *organizing principle* that makes a unified and intelligible experience possible. It is, metaphorically, "above" or "behind" sense experience, and it uses the categories of your mind to filter, order, relate, organize, and synthesize sensations into a unified whole. That's why Kant accords the self "transcendental" status: It exists independently of experience. The self is the product of reason, a *regulative principle* because the self "regulates" experience by making unified experience possible. Other such "transcendental regulative ideas" include the ideas of *cosmos* and *God*.

Immanuel Kant,
from *Critique of Pure Reason*

Everything that has its basis in the nature of our powers must be appropriate to, and consistent with, their right employment—if we can only guard against a certain misunderstanding and so discover the proper direction of these powers. We are entitled, therefore, to suppose that transcendental ideas...have an excellent, and indeed indispensably necessary, regulative employment, namely, that of directing the understanding towards a certain goal upon which the routes marked out by all its rules converge.

The first (regulative) idea is the "I" itself, viewed simply as thinking nature or soul...: in a word, the idea of a simple self-sustaining intelligence. [Reason operates] to represent all determinations as existing in a single subject, all powers, so far as possible, as derived from a single fundamental power, all change as belonging to the states of one and the same permanent being.

So where did Hume go wrong, from Kant's standpoint? How could Hume examine his mind's contents and not find his self, particularly because, in Kant's view, the self is required to *have* intelligible experience? Hume's problem (according to Kant) was that he looked for his self in the wrong place! Contrary to what Hume assumed, the self is not an object of consciousness, one of the contents of the mind. Instead, the self is the transcendental activity that synthesizes the contents of consciousness into an intelligible whole. Because the self is not a "content" of consciousness but rather the invisible "thread" that ties the contents of consciousness together, it's no wonder that Hume couldn't find it. It would be analogous to you going to a sporting event and looking in vain to see the "team," when all you see are a collection of players. The "team" is the network of relationships between the individuals that is not visible to simple perception. The "team" is the synthesizing activity that creates a unity among the individuals, much like the self creates a unity in experience by synthesizing its contents into an intelligible whole. And because experience is continually changing, this intelligible picture of the world is being updated on an instantaneous basis.

We can also see Kant's refinement of Descartes' concept of the self, which he interprets as a simple, self-evident fact: "I think, therefore I am." Kant was interested in developing a more complex, analytical, and sophisticated understanding of the self as a thinking identity. To begin with, Descartes was focusing on one dimension of the thinking process: our ability to reflect, to become aware of our self, to be *self-conscious*. But from Kant's standpoint, the thinking self—consciousness—has a more complex structure than simple self-reflection. The self is a dynamic entity/activity, continually synthesizing sensations and ideas into an integrated, meaningful whole. The self, in the form of consciousness, utilizes conceptual categories (or "transcendental rules") such as *substance, cause and effect, unity, plurality, possibility, necessity,* and *reality* to construct an orderly and "objective" world that is stable and can be investigated scientifically. It is in this sense that the self constructs its own reality, actively creating a world that is familiar, predictable, and, most significantly, *mine.*

Kant's "Copernican Revolution" accompanied by his comprehensive and penetrating analysis of the central themes of philosophy helped usher in a modern consciousness. In fact, many of his foundational premises have been supported by research in the sciences and social sciences. For example, the renowned developmental psychologist Jean Piaget (1896–1980) conducted painstaking empirical research on the way the human mind develops, an interactive process involving both sensory experience and innate cognitive structures. His seminal book *Construction of Reality in the Child* (1950) (published almost 150 years after Kant's death) could very easily have been written by Kant had he been a modern developmental psychologist. Similarly, work in language development by linguists such as Noam Chomsky (1928–) have also supported the Kantian idea that human experience—such as language abilities—are the product of both exposure to a specific language and innate, a priori intellectual rules or categories that are "hardwired" into each human being.

Kant's dominant influence on Western philosophy and the intellectual framework of modern consciousness was in sharp contrast to his quiet, limited life. Never traveling more than sixty miles from his birthplace in Germany, Kant never married and lived a life of such precise habits that it was said the citizens of his hometown could set their watches based on his daily walks. He was a popular university professor, and his passion for understanding both the universe and human nature is reflected in the inscription he wrote for his tombstone: "The starry heavens above me; the moral law within me."

< READING CRITICALLY >

Analyzing Kant's Unity of Consciousness

Here's an opportunity for you to be a philosophy detective engaged in a "missing person" investigation—looking for your *self*. If Kant is right, you should not be able to find your *self* among the contents of your consciousness. Instead, your *self* should be revealed as the synthesizing principle that unites your experience. Launch a reflective investigation into your *self* and then describe as clearly as you can what you find. Did you discover your *self*? How would you describe the qualities of your *self*? In what ways is your *self* similar to all other selves? In what ways is your *self* different from all other selves?

3.8 The Self Is Multilayered: Freud

Our explorations of the self have, until this point, focused almost exclusively on the conscious self. Of course, Kant's idea of the self as a "transcendental unifying principle of consciousness" is certainly not "conscious" in the traditional sense. But neither is it hidden from reflective awareness, if we know where to look for it. This *transcendental self* (or *ego*) is not to be found as an entity *in* consciousness—it is the dynamic organizing principle that makes consciousness possible. One problem with this view of the self is that there is nothing *personal* about it.

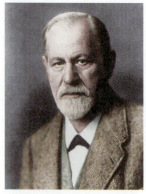

Sigmund Freud
(1956–1939) Austrian doctor who founded the psychoanalytic school of psychology. Freud's theories of the unconscious and his "talking cure" approach to treatment of certain mental illnesses had a profound influence on twentieth century culture. Among his works are *The Interpretation of Dreams* (1899) and *An Outline of Psycho-Analysis* (1940).

As an abstract organizing principle, it appears to be difficult to distinguish one *transcendental self* from another. As a result, Kant identifies *another self* the *empirical self* (or *ego*), which includes all of those particular aspects of our selves that make us uniquely different people: bodies, memories, personalities, ways of thinking, emotional patterns, and so on. The obvious problem is that this model of consciousness leaves us with *two selves*, leading to some disquieting questions: How do these two selves relate to one another? Is one self more primary or fundamental than the other? Which self is our "true" self, our identity, our soul? Are we condemned to be metaphysical schizophrenics? Kant tries mightily to answer these troubling and enigmatic questions, but it's a very difficult challenge.

Sigmund Freud's view of the self leads to an analogous dualistic view of the self, though the contours and content of his ideas are very different from Kant's. Freud is not, strictly speaking, a philosopher, but his views on the nature of the self have had a far-reaching impact on philosophical thinking, as well as virtually every other discipline in the humanities and social sciences. Naturally, his most dominant influence has been in the fields of psychology and psychoanalysis. Freud's view of the self was multitiered, divided among the conscious, preconscious, and unconscious. He explains his psychological model in the following passage from his *An Outline of Psychoanalysis*.

Sigmund Freud, from *An Outline of Psychoanalysis*

There is no need to characterize what we call *conscious*: it is the same as the consciousness of philosophers and of everyday opinion. Everything else that is mental is in our view *unconscious*. We are soon led to make an important division in this unconscious. Some processes become conscious easily; they may then cease to be conscious, but can become conscious once more without any trouble: as people say they can be reproduced or remembered. This reminds us that consciousness is in general a very highly fugitive condition. What is conscious is conscious only for a moment. . . . Everything unconscious that can easily exchange the unconscious condition for the conscious one, is therefor better described as "capable of entering consciousness," or as *preconscious*. Experience has taught us that there are hardly any mental processes, even of the most complicated kind, which cannot on occasion remain preconscious, although as a rule they press forward, as we say, into consciousness. There are other mental processes or mental material which have no such easy access to consciousness, but which must be inferred, discovered, and translated into conscious form in the manner that has been described. It is for such material that we reserve the name of the unconscious proper. Thus we have attributed three qualities to mental processes: they are either conscious, preconscious, or unconscious. The division between the three classes is neither absolute nor permanent. What is preconscious becomes conscious, as we have seen, without any activity on our part; what is unconscious can, as a result of our efforts, be made conscious, though in the process we may have an impression that we are overcoming what are often very strong resistances. . . . A lowering of resistances of this sort, with a consequent pressing forward of unconscious material, takes place regularly in the state of sleep and thus brings about a necessary precondition for the formation of dreams.

It is by no means an exaggeration to assert that the concept of the **unconscious** forms the central core in Freud's theory of the structure and dynamics of the human personality. And though the **conscious** self has an important role to play in our lives, it is the unconscious self that holds the greatest fascination for Freud, and which has the dominant influence in our personalities. Freud's focus on the unconscious self marks a significant departure from previous efforts in philosophy to understand the nature of the self, and in so doing, it challenges the traditional philosophical assumption that the self can be explored and understood primarily through rational reflection and analysis.

According to Freud, these two levels of human functioning—the *conscious* and the *unconscious*—differ radically both in their content and in the rules and logic that govern them. The unconscious contains basic instinctual drives including sexuality, aggressiveness, and self-destruction; traumatic memories; unfulfilled wishes and child-hood fantasies; thoughts and feelings that would be considered socially taboo. The unconscious level is characterized by the most primitive level of human motivation and human functioning. At this level, the most basic instinctual drives seek immediate gratification or discharge. Unheedful of the demands and restrictions of reality, the naked impulses at this level are governed solely by the "pleasure principle."

Our unconscious self embodies a mode of operation that precedes the development of all other forms of our mental functioning. It includes throughout our lives the primitive rock-bottom activities, the primal strivings on which all human functioning is ultimately based. Our unconscious self operates at a prelogical and pre-rational level. And though it exists and influences us throughout our lives, it is not directly observable and its existence can only be inferred from such phenomena as neurotic symptoms, dreams, and "slips of the tongue."

In contrast, the conscious self is governed by the "reality principle" (rather than the "pleasure principle"), and at this level of functioning, behavior and experience are organized in ways that are rational, practical, and appropriate to the social environment. Although the ultimate goals of the conscious self are the same as the unconscious self—the gratification of needs and the reduction of tensions to optimal levels—the means of achieving these goals are entirely different. Instead of seeking these goals by means that are direct, impulsive, and irrational, the conscious self usually takes into account the realistic demands of the situation, the consequences of various actions, and the overriding need to preserve the equilibrium of the entire psychodynamic system. To this end, the conscious self has the task of controlling the constant pressures of the unconscious self, as its primitive impulses continually seek for immediate discharge.

What do our dreams mean? Rousseau's painting suggests the symbolic import of the dream world. What have you learned about yourself by reflecting on your dreams?

What is the evidence for this split-level, "two-self" model of functioning? Freud believes that evidence of a powerful unconscious self can be found in the content of our dreams, inadvertent "slips of tongue," and techniques—such as free association—used by Freudian psychoanalysts in clinical treatment. However, the most compelling evidence for an unconscious self is to be found in pathological, neurotic behavior. From Freud's standpoint, the neurotic symptom has three essential aspects: it is a sign that the balance of forces within the personality system is disturbed; it is a sign that infantile conflicts have been reactivated; and it is itself an attempt at a spontaneous cure, an attempt at adaptation, although the individual may be worse off with his or her neurotic adaptation than without it. For example, an individual who experienced traumatic frustration, conflict, and guilt centering on his toilet training may "adapt" to this potentially threatening situation by compulsively washing his hands several hundred times a day in an effort to assuage his guilt and resolve his emotionally charged conflicts. Although such an adaptation may forestall the disruption of his conscious level of functioning by the anxiety generated by his unconscious conflicts and painful emotions, from the standpoint of normal overall functioning, it could not be considered to be a particularly successful one.

People whose psychological defenses are defective will react to many situations simultaneously at two levels: an adult conscious level, and an infantile unconscious level. Any situation that resembles a traumatic emotional situation of early childhood will call out a repetition of the childhood response at the same time that it calls out the adult response. The adult response is likely to be direct and overt; the childhood response is likely to be covert and derivative. This mingling of different levels of experience may be accomplished without undue stress or trouble, as in the case with normal, well-adjusted behavior and experience. However, it may lead to an exaggerated reaction that is otherwise appropriate, to ambivalent feelings and ambiguous behavior, or to neurotic symptom formation. When this last reaction is the case, the specific form of the symptom will depend both on the person's particular vulnerability and on the situation that disturbs his internal equilibrium. Because the unconscious self plays such an important role in our daily lives (according to Freud), why does it remain inaccessible to conscious awareness? Freud's explanation for this is the psychological activity of "repression," which serves as the theoretical keystone of defensive organizations in both normal and neurotic persons. Although it is thought to be related to the conscious "suppression," repression is assumed to operate at

thinking philosophically

LOOKING FOR EVIDENCE OF YOUR UNCONSCIOUS

Although the contents of the unconscious cannot be observed directly (according to Freud), we can observe them indirectly, like seeing footprints in the sand or dusting for fingerprints. There are several areas in which unconscious influences are evident. This is an opportunity for you to look for evidence of unconscious functioning in each of these areas.

- *Slips of the tongue:* Think about a time in which you unexpectedly said what you *really* thought rather than what you intended to say: for example, "I think your new haircut looks *atrocious*" instead of your intended "I think your new haircut looks *attractive*." Do you think this is persuasive evidence for Freud's concept of the unconscious?

- *Dreams:* Describe a particularly disturbing dream, or a recurring dream, that expressed surprising or disturbing themes. What do you think the dream really meant? Do you think the dream is persuasive evidence for Freud's concept of the unconscious?

- *Neurosis:* Describe one sort of neurotic behavior in which you engage. (Don't worry, everyone has at least *one* neurosis!) For example, do you have a compulsion to check and recheck locks? To eat too much or too little? To perform superstitious rituals? To be overly suspicious ("paranoid") about others' intentions? To feel excessively guilty about something? To be chronically depressed? What do you think is the origin of this neurosis? Do you think this syndrome is persuasive evidence for Freud's concept of the unconscious?

unconscious levels, like most of the psychological defenses. Repression is used to help contain the potentially disruptive aspects of unconscious functioning, and as a consequence it is usually the main defense mechanism for maintaining the ego boundaries necessary for normal conscious functioning. If a deep and inclusive regression to unconscious levels does occur while a person is awake—a situation often referred to as "the return of the repressed"—the effects can be devastating.

The purpose of psychotherapy (the therapeutic method created by Freud) is to enable the patient to acknowledge the conflicts, emotions, and memories at the root cause of his or her disorder. By acknowledging and understanding the traumatized memories, emotions, and conflicts, most of which date back to infancy and early childhood, the individual not only attains a cathartic emotional release, but also is able to resolve basic emotional conflicts that have festered unconsciously and caused abnormal maladaptive behavior. As the individual begins to see the reason for the particular symptom or cluster of symptoms that has formed, these symptoms will (in theory) tend to lose their efficacy, as their success lay precisely in the fact that they were unconscious attempts to deal with the specific traumatic contents existing unconsciously. When they and their purpose are disclosed to the individual, they will tend to be discarded as maladaptive forms of behavior, and a normal resolution and adaptation to the repressed and unconscious material will be attained. However, the acknowledgment and affirmation of the patient is not simply an intellectual understanding. Instead, he or she must recall the original memories, with all of their emotional charge and trauma, and work through the emotions involved until he or she is able to adopt a new and more adaptive attitude both toward the past of childhood and a present and future adult life.

Freud's Topographical model of the mind divided it into systems on the basis of their relationship to consciousness: conscious, preconscious, and unconscious. Freud later developed a Structural model of the mind that divided it according to mental functions: the id, the ego, and the superego. Freud emphasizes the fact that although the Structural model has certain similarities with the earlier Topographical model, the two are not the same. Although the id has virtually the same place as the unconscious in the sense of being the reservoir for the primal instinctual forces responsible for all human motivation, the ego and superego systems consist of aspects that are both conscious and unconscious in the psychoanalytic sense—in other words, they are inaccessible to consciousness except under unusual circumstances. Freud believed that the strength of the Structural model was its ability to analyze situations of mental conflict in terms of which functions are allied with one another and which are in conflict (analogous to the conflicting elements in Plato's division of the soul into Reason, Spirit, and Appetite).

Freud's penetrating and systematic analysis of the complexity of the human mind had a far-reaching impact on modern understanding of our *selves*. However, from a philosophical perspective, there are significant problems with the models of the mind that he developed. Freud's concept of the unconscious is of a "place"—a timeless, unknowable realm—or "entity" that exerts a profound and continual influence on our conscious thoughts, emotions, and behavior. But "where" exactly does this realm exist? "Who" exactly is this entity, and what is its relation to our conscious *self*? Doesn't Freud's model fragment the human mind into a collection of parts, multiple *selves* with enigmatic relationships to one another? Don't we end up with two "I thinks," one conscious and one unconscious?

Alasdair MacIntyre

Seen from another perspective, it's one thing to say that someone is "unconscious" of the true purpose, motive, or intention of their behavior; it's quite another to say that the behavior is "caused" by influences from "the unconscious." According to the philosopher **Alasdair MacIntyre** in his book *The Unconscious*, Freud was not merely offering us an instructive model in terms of which conscious thought and behavior could be envisaged. Instead, he was making an existential claim, propounding a hypothesis, asserting that "the world includes an entity hitherto undiscovered," a claim that is unwarranted and conceptually confused.

To put the same point into linguistic terms, the use of "unconscious" as an adjective or as an adverb is quite normal and acceptable in ordinary language. The problem for Freud is that he uses the concept of "unconscious" not only as an adverb and an adjective, but also as a *noun*. As MacIntyre explains it:

> *For where Freud uses "unconscious" and "unconsciously" he extends earlier uses of these words; but when he speaks of "**the** unconscious" he invents a new term for which he has to prescribe a meaning and a use. And in this innovation he is curiously dominated by a picture of the mind which he at many points explicitly rejected.*[i]

This "picture of the mind" that Freud embraces by his use of "the unconscious" as a noun is that derived from Descartes, who considered the subject as a rational spiritual entity, an entity quite different and distinct from the physical substance of the body. It is this view of the mind that has been described by the philosopher Gilbert Ryle as "the ghost in the machine," and by Jacques Maritain as "the angel in the machine." The new twist that Freud gave it, according to MacIntyre, is that of transferring the notion of the separate substance of the mind from the rational consciousness of Descartes to the irrational unconscious.

> *Now Freud clearly does not think of man as possessing this kind of rational self-knowledge in his ordinary consciousness, and in so far as he does not do this he rejects the Cartesian picture of the mind. But Freud retains from the Cartesian picture the idea of the mind as something distinct and apart, a place or a realm which can be inhabited by such entities as ideas. Only he makes dominant not "the conscious" mind but "the unconscious." He introduces "unconscious" as an adjective to describe what we may have hitherto observed but have not hitherto recognized or classified. He introduces "the unconscious" as a noun not to describe, but to explain.*

Freud's idea of an existent, spatially located "unconscious" leads to other difficulties as well, including those associated with the Freudian concept of "repression." Repression for Freud clearly refers to a datable event, an occurrence that actually happens when the memory of an experience is denied a place in consciousness and instead relegated to the unconscious. Yet by definition, repression is something of which we are unconscious, and as such is inaccessible to direct observation. As a consequence, we can only infer that something has been "repressed" from subsequent behavior and feelings: for example, neurotic behavior. But the claim that repression has occurred is logically dependent on the fact that certain alleged childhood experiences did in fact take place; yet simply to show that they did take place is not enough to show that

---

[i]Alasdair MacIntyre, *The Unconscious* (London: Routledge & Kegan Paul Ltds., 1958).

repression occurred, and it is indeed difficult to see what would be enough proof. It would therefore appear that no direct empirical evidence can be brought directly to bear on the situation to either validate or falsify the theoretical notions of "repression" and "the unconscious." And if such is the case, then it is indeed untenable to contend that repression is a datable event and that the unconscious is a place in which repressed events exist timelessly, exerting causal influence on our conscious functioning. Because such claims are in principle neither verifiable nor falsifiable, they are therefore empty. Hence any attempt to treat the unconscious as an actual existent realm containing actual repressed mental events, emotions, ideas, and so on will not only run into the traditional problems plaguing any such dualistic conception of human functioning, but also be hard put to produce any empirical evidence in its favor.

< READING CRITICALLY >

Analyzing Freud's Ideas about Mind

- What do you think Freud means when he says, "The poets and philosophers before me discovered the unconscious. What I discovered was the scientific method by which the unconscious can be studied." Can you identify some examples from poets or philosophers that suggest the existence of an "unconscious"?

- Freud uses the term "the unconscious" as if it had an identity separate from that of "the conscious." In thinking about the self, what sort of difficulties and challenges might this dualistic characterization of the human mind entail? For example, if "the unconscious" is a realm or a place, then where is it located? If "the unconscious" is a separate self, how would it relate to our conscious self?

- In describing Freud's model of the self, the psychoanalyst Norman Cameron observes:

    We are all so organized that we have active infantile and magical processes going on within us, at the same time that we are behaving adequately as mature adults. There is not the slightest possibility of eliminating all these irrational unconscious components. We all operate simultaneously at different levels of maturity and rationality: irrational and often infantile unconscious processes are normal components of everyday behavior and experience.

    According to Freud, we can never simply accept our conscious thoughts and overt behavior at face value—there is always the possibility that there are hidden unconscious meanings and motivations causing and influencing them. What sort of problems might this view pose for our achieving understanding of ourselves and others?

3.9 The Self Is How You Behave: Ryle

The dualistic metaphysic of mind and body initiated by Plato, perpetuated by Descartes, and given an "unconscious twist" by Freud leads, as we have seen, to challenging conceptual questions and vexing enigmas. Some philosophers and psychologists, in an effort to avoid the difficulties of viewing the mind and body as two radically different aspects of the *self*, have decided to simply focus on observable behavior in defining the *self*. Their solution to the mind/body "problem" is to simply deny—or ignore—the existence of an internal, nonphysical *self*, and instead focus on the dimensions of the

Gilbert Ryle (1900–1976)
Analytic Philosopher. An
important figure in the
field known as "Linguistic
Analysis" which focused on
the solving of philosophical
puzzles through an analysis
of language. He mounted
an attack against Cartesian
mind/body dualism and
supported a behaviorist
theory of mind.

self that we *can* observe. No more inner selves, immortal souls, states of consciousness, or unconscious entities: instead, the *self* is defined in terms of the behavior that is presented to the world, a view that is known in psychology as **behaviorism**.

In philosophy one of the chief advocates of this view is **Gilbert Ryle**, a British philosopher whose book, *The Concept of Mind*, had a dramatic impact on Western thought. Ryle's behaviorism was a different sort from that of psychology. He thought of his approach as a *logical* behaviorism, focused on creating conceptual clarity, not on developing techniques to condition and manipulate human behavior.

Ryle begins his book by launching a devastating attack on "Descartes' myth," characterizing it as the "official doctrine" that has insidiously penetrated the consciousness of academics, professionals, and average citizens alike. According to Ryle, it's high time that this destructive myth of dualism is debunked once and for all, and replaced with a clearer conceptual and linguistic understanding of the true nature of the *self.*

Gilbert Ryle, from *The Concept of Mind*[ii]

There is a doctrine about the nature and place of minds which is so prevalent among theorists and even among laymen that it deserves to be described as the official theory. Most philosophers, psychologists and religious teachers subscribe, with minor reservations, to its main articles and, although they admit certain theoretical difficulties in it, they tend to assume that these can be overcome without serious modifications being made to the architecture of the theory. It will be argued here that the central principles of the doctrine are unsound and conflict with the whole body of what we know about minds when we are not speculating about them.

The official doctrine, which hails chiefly from Descartes, is something like this. With the doubtful exceptions of idiots and infants in arms every human being has both a body and a mind. Some would prefer to say that every human being has both a body and a mind. His body and his mind are ordinarily harnessed together, but after the death of the body his mind may continue to exist and function.

Human bodies are in space and are subject to the mechanical laws which govern all other bodies in space. Bodily processes and states can be inspected by external observers. So a man's bodily life is as much a public affair as are the lives of animals and reptiles and even as the careers of trees, crystals and plants.

But minds are not in space, nor are their operations subject to mechanical laws. The workings of one mind are not witnessable by other observers; its career is private. Only I can take direct cognizance of the states and processes of my own mind. A person therefore lives through two collateral histories, one consisting of what happens in and to his body, and other consisting of what happens in and to his mind. The first is public, the second private. The events in the first history are events in the physical world, those in the second are events in the mental world.

Analyzed in this fashion, the dualistic division of mind and body seems rather odd, and this is precisely Ryle's point: "It will be argued here that the central principles of the doctrine are unsound and conflict with the whole body of what we know about minds when we are not speculating about them." In other words, although the majority of people assume a mind/body dualism as a general theory, on a practical level

---

[ii]Gilbert Ryle, *The Concept of Mind* (London: Taylor and Francis, 1949).

Our experience of our "selves"—and other selves—involves both change and continuity. How do the thinkers we have explored thus far explain this paradox of change and continuity of the "self"? Plato, Diotima, St. Augustine, Descartes, Locke, Hume, Kant, Freud, Ryle.

we act and speak in a much different fashion. This "ghost in the machine" dualism (Ryle's central metaphor) in which the "self" is thought to be a spiritual, immaterial ghost rattling around inside the physical body) conflicts directly with our everyday experience, revealing itself to be a conceptually flawed and confused notion that needs to be revised. Ryle continues his argument in the following passages.

Gilbert Ryle, from *The Concept of Mind*

It is customary to express this bifurcation of his two lives and of his two worlds by saying that the things and events which belong to the physical world, including his own body, are external, while the workings of his own mind are internal. This antithesis of outer and inner is of course meant to be construed as a metaphor, since minds, not being in space, could not be described as being spatially inside anything else, or as having things going on spatially inside themselves. But relapses from this good intention are common and theorists are found speculating how stimuli, the physical sources of which are yards or miles outside of a person's skin, can generate mental responses inside his skull, or how decisions framed inside his cranium can set going movements of his extremities.

Even when "inner" and "outer" are construed as metaphors, the problem of how a person's mind and body influence one another is notoriously charged with theoretical difficulties. What the mind wills, the legs, arms and the tongue execute; what affects the ear and the eye has something to do with what the mind perceives; grimaces and smiles betray the mind's moods and bodily castigations lead, it is hoped, to moral improvement.

But the actual transactions between the episodes of the private history and those of the public history remain mysterious, since by definition they can belong to neither series. They could not be reported among the happenings described in a person's autobiography of his inner life, but nor could they be reported among those described in someone else's biography of that person's overt career. They can be inspected neither by introspection nor by laboratory experiment. They are theoretical shuttlecocks which are forever bandied from the physiologist back to the psychologist and from the psychologist back to the physiologist.

How do we know other minds? For Ryle, our knowledge of other persons' minds can only be inferential at best.

"Where" precisely is the mind located in Cartesian dualism? Because the mind is conceived to be a nonmaterial entity, this question is problematic. People often use spatial metaphors or images to characterize the mind/soul/spirit: it's the "inner person" somehow contained "within" the body. But as Ryle points out, this way of thinking doesn't make a great deal of conceptual sense. The mind and the body seem connected in complex and intimate ways that spatial metaphors simply don't capture.

And to make matters worse, people tend to "forget" that these are metaphors and instead assume that they are providing an accurate description of the way things are. But this *really* doesn't make conceptual sense. If the mind and body are in reality two radically different substances, then how precisely do they connect to one another? And how could we ever discover such a connection? Neither the personal history of the mind's experiences nor the public history of the body and its movements can describe the moment of their intersection. Each realm—mental and physical—is locked within its own universe, lacking the vocabulary to observe and describe the convergence of these alien worlds with clarity and precision. As Ryle observes, these transactional events "can be inspected neither by introspection nor by laboratory experiment. They are theoretical shuttlecocks which are forever bandied from the physiologist back to the psychologist and from the psychologist back to the physiologist." And in Ryle's mind (note the commonly used spatial metaphor!) there are even more serious implications of a dualistic perspective regarding our knowledge of others.

The privileged knowledge that we have of our own mental *self* means that others are necessarily excluded from any direct understanding of what we're thinking or who we are. Unfortunately the same logic applies to us: we are prevented from having any direct knowledge of other minds/selves/spirits. Although we can observe the bodies and actions of others, we can only make *inferences* regarding the mind that is producing these actions. In fact, there is no way we can be ensured that there even *are* other minds functioning in ways similar to ours. We observe someone waving and smiling at us and we say to ourselves: "When I wave and smile, that means I'm happy to see someone, so that's what this waving and smiling must mean: the mind inside that body is happy to see me. And I'm assuming that there *is* a mind inside that body because the body is acting like I do, and I'm a mind." Of course, we can't really be sure that other minds exist, or that the movement of their bodies really expresses the meaning that we are projecting on to it.

Once again: if you're thinking that this description sounds rather peculiar, this is exactly Ryle's point. In our everyday experience, we act and speak as if we have much more direct knowledge of other minds and what they're thinking without having to go through this tortured and artificial reasoning process. We encounter others, experience the totality of their behavior, and believe that this behavior reveals directly "who" they are and what they're thinking. Ryle goes on to analyze how this apparent conflict between the theory of Cartesian dualism ("the ghost in the machine") and our everyday experience of others is actually the result of confused conceptual thinking, a logical error that he terms a "**category mistake**."

> Such in outline is the official theory. I shall often speak of it with deliberate abusiveness, as "the dogma of the Ghost in the Machine." I hope to prove that it is entirely false, and false not in detail but in principle. It is not merely an assemblage of particular mistakes. It is one big mistake and a mistake of a special kind. It is, namely, a category-mistake. It represents the facts of mental life as if they belonged to one logical type of category (or range of types or categories), when they actually belong to another. The dogma is therefore a philosopher's myth.
>
> I must first indicate what is meant by the phrase "Category-mistake." This I do in a series of illustrations.
>
> A foreigner visiting Oxford or Cambridge for the first time is shown a number of colleges, libraries, playing fields, museums, scientific departments and administrative offices. He then asks "But where is the university? I have seen where the members of the Colleges live, where the Registrar works, where the scientists experiment and the rest. But I have not yet seen the University in which reside and work the members of your University." It has then to be explained to him that the University is not another collateral institution, some ulterior counterpart to the colleges, laboratories and offices which he has seen. The University is just the way in which all that he has already seen is organized. When they are seen and when their coordination is understood, the University has been seen. His mistake lay in his innocent assumption that it was correct to speak of Christ Church, the Bodleian Library, the Ashmolean Museum *and* the University, to speak, that is, as if "the University" stood for an extra member of the class of which these others units are members. He was mistakenly allocating the University to the same category as that to which the other institutions belong. . . .

Gilbert Ryle, from *The Concept of Mind*

In the same way that the *university* is a concept expressing the entire system of buildings, curricula, faculty, administrators, and so on, Ryle believes that the *mind* is a concept that expresses the entire system of thoughts, emotions, actions, and so on that make up the human *self.* The *category mistake* happens when we think of the *self* as existing apart from certain observable behaviors, a purely mental entity existing in time but not space. According to Ryle, this "self" does not really exist, anymore than the "university" or "team-spirit" exist in some special, nonphysical universe.

This is certainly a compelling argument against Cartesian dualism. However, having made the case for an integrated mind/body perspective on the human *self,* Ryle then focuses his attention primarily on human behavior. From his perspective, the *self* is best understood as a *pattern of behavior,* the *tendency* or *disposition* for a person to behave in a certain way in certain circumstances. And this inevitably leads him to the same difficulties faced by psychologist behaviorists such as John Watson and B. F. Skinner.

> To say that a person knows something, or aspires to be something, is not to say that he is at a particular moment in process of doing or undergoing anything, but that he is able to do certain things, when the need arises, or that he is prone to do and feel certain things in situations of certain sorts. . . . Abandonment of the two-world legend involves the abandonment of the idea that there is a locked door and a still to be discovered key. Those human actions and reactions, those spoken and unspoken utterances, those tones of voice, facial expressions and gestures, which have always been the data of all the other students of men, have, after all, been the right and the only manifestations to study. They and they alone have merited but fortunately not received, the grandiose title "mental phenomena."

Gilbert Ryle, from *The Concept of Mind*

Like the behaviorists before him, Ryle has ended up solving one problem—the conceptual difficulties of Cartesian dualism—but creating another problem just as serious. For example, is the experience of "love" equivalent to the tendency to act in a certain way under certain circumstances? When you say "I am deeply in love with you," is that reducible to a series of behavioral tendencies or dispositions: I will share experiences with you, procreate children, attend you when you are sick, give thoughtful cards and gifts on your birthday, say on a regular basis "I love you," and so on? Although your proposed partner may appreciate your detailed commitments, he or she is unlikely to respond in the passionate, intimate way that you likely hope for. Reducing the complex richness of our inner life and consciousness to a list of behaviors and potential behaviors simply doesn't do the job conceptually for most people.

Ironically, Ryle ends up being his own most incisive critic. He bases his criticism of Cartesian dualism on the premise that "the central principles of the doctrine are unsound and conflict with the whole body of what we know about minds when we are not speculating about them." But exactly the same criticism can be made of Ryle's logical behaviorism: it attempts to define and translate the *self* and the complex mental/emotional richness of the life of the mind into a listing of behaviors (and potential behaviors) that "conflicts with the whole body of what we know about minds when we are not speculating about them." As the Australian philosopher J. J. C. Smart notes, "There does seem to be, so far as science is concerned, nothing in the world but complex arrangements of physical constituents. All except for one place: consciousness." In the final analysis, despite his devastating critique of Descartes' dualism, Ryle hasn't been able to provide a compelling philosophical explanation of Descartes' "I think."

Ryle's denial of inner *selves* causes a difficulty analogous to that engendered by Hume's denial of a similar entity—namely, that Ryle writes, speaks, and acts as if the existence of *their inner selves* is not in doubt. In fact, it's not clear how a person who truly believed what behaviorists say they believe would actually function in life. The philosopher Brand Blanshard (1892–1987) provides a biting analysis of the behaviorists' denial of consciousness along with their stated belief that the *self* is the same as bodily behavior.

> *Consider the behaviorist who has a headache and takes aspirin. What he means by his "headache" is the grimaces or claspings of the head that an observer might behold. Since these **are** the headache, it must be these he finds objectionable. But it is absurd to say a set of motions . . . is objectionable . . . except as they are associated with the conscious pain. Suppose again, that he identifies the pain with the grimaces and outward movements then all he would have to do to banish the pain would be to stop these movements and behave in a normal fashion. But he knows perfectly well that this is not enough; that is why he falls back on aspirin. In short, his action implies a disbelief in his own theory.[iii]*

[iii]Brand Blanchard, "The Limits of Naturalism," in *Contemporary American Philosophy*, ed. J. Smith (London: Allen and Unwin, 1970).

> **< READING CRITICALLY >**
>
> **Analyzing Ryle's View of Self as Behavior**
>
> - Think of someone you know and try to describe her solely in terms of her observable behavior. Then analyze your portrait: What aspects of her *self* does your description capture? What aspects of her *self* does your description omit?
> - Now think about yourself. Assume the perspective of someone who knows you well and describe your *self* as he might see you, *based solely on your observable behavior*. What aspects of your *self* do you think his description would capture? What aspects of your *self* do you think his portrait of you would omit?
> - Identify several of the defining qualities of your *self*: for example, empathetic, gregarious, reflective, fun-loving, curious, and so on. Then, using Ryle's approach, describe the qualities in terms of "a tendency to act a certain way in certain circumstances."
> - Analyze your characterizations. Do your descriptions communicate fully the personal qualities of your *self* that you identified? If not, what's missing?

3.10 The Self Is the Brain: Physicalism

Physicalism is the philosophical view that all aspects of the universe are composed of matter and energy and can be fully explained by physical laws.[*]

Philosophers and psychologists who are physicalists believe that in the final analysis, mental states are identical with, reducible to, or explainable in terms of physical brain states. From a physicalist perspective, there is no immaterial "self" that exists independently from the brain or the body, a view articulated by the philosopher Thomas Hobbes in his memorable statement, "The Universe, that is the whole mass of things that are, is corporeal, that is to say body; and has the dimensions of magnitude, namely length, breadth, and depth…and that which is not body is no part of the universe." There are a wide variety of theoretical perspectives within the general category of physicalism. In this section, we are going to explore two such perspectives:

- **Functionalism** This view, held by philosophers like Jerry Fodor, Daniel Dennett, and D. M. Armstrong, contends that the mind can be explained in terms of patterns of sensory inputs and behavior outputs mediated by functionally defined mental states.

- **Eliminative Materialism** This view is embodied in the work of philosophers like Paul Churchland, who believes that the mind *is* the brain and that over time a mature neuroscience vocabulary will replace the "folk psychology" that we currently use to think about our selves and our minds.

In addition to these two physicalistic theories, we will be examining the article "Contemporary Issues in Philosophy of Mind" by the philosopher Richard Brown. The article provides an overview of the current state of the argumentative landscape between dualists and physicalists, with particular attention to the nature of consciousness and its relation to the brain.

---

[*]Some philosophers use the term "materialism" to denote historical versions of this view, and "physicalism" to denote modern versions of it which include developments in mathematical physics. We will be using the terms interchangeably.

Functionalism

Gilbert Ryle's logical behaviorism that we explored in the previous section is actually a form of physicalism, since the theory holds that there is no immaterial self that exists independently of one's body or visible behavior. But, as we saw, there are serious problems with this particular view. Brand Blanshard's devastating critique of behaviorism's equating of the *self* with bodily behavior is punctuated with the indelible image of a behaviorist whose headache is defined in terms of a set of behaviors: grimacing, clutching one's head, and so on. Although Behaviorism remained an influential movement in modern psychology for much of the twentieth century, most philosophers abandoned it as a viable model of the *self*. However, with the advent of computers, some philosophers saw an opportunity to recast the behaviorist model in a new form that would avoid the conceptual inadequacy of defining the self solely in terms of a person's observable behavior, while at the same time retaining some of behaviorism's advantages. What advantages? First and foremost, as a form of physicalism, behaviorism made it possible to avoid the dualism of Plato, Augustine, Descartes, and others, the "ghost in the machine" that leaves us wondering exactly how our nonphysical, immaterial self is related to our physical, material self. As the philosopher Jerry Fodor notes in an essay entitled "The Mind–Body Problem,"

Jerry Fodor, from *The Mind/Body Problem*

The chief drawback of dualism is its failure to account adequately for mental causation. If the mind is nonphysical, it has no position in physical space. How, then, can a mental cause give rise to a behavioral effect that has a position in space? To put it another way, how can the nonphysical give rise to the physical without violating the laws of the conservation of mass, of energy and of momentum? The dualist might respond that the problem of how an immaterial substance can cause physical events is not much obscurer than the problem of how one physical event can cause another. Yet there is an important difference: there are many clear cases of physical causation but not one clear case of nonphysical causation. *Scientific American,* 1981

In other words, a dualistic perspective on the mind–body situation leaves us with a profoundly unscientific view of the self. In contrast, behaviorism's approach, denying the immaterial, unobservable self, makes it possible for scientists to observe and experiment with the behavior that is thought to define the self and the sensory stimulants that give rise to the behavior.

Jerry Fodor, *from The Mind/Body Problem*

In the past 15 years, a philosophy of the mind called functionalism that is neither dualist nor materialist has emerged from philosophical reflection on developments in artificial intelligence, computational theory, linguistics, cybernetics and psychology. All these fields, which are collectively known as the cognitive sciences, have in common a certain level of abstraction and a concern with systems that process information. Functionalism, which seeks to provide a philosophical account of this level of abstractions, recognizes the possibility that systems as diverse as human beings, calculating machines and disembodied spirits could all have mental states. In the functionalist view, the psychology of a system depends not on the stuff it is made of (living cells, metal or spiritual energy) but on how the stuff is put together.

Using computers as a model of human functioning, a new school of thought—"functionalism"—developed. It was a perspective that, like behaviorism, still maintained that the model for the human mind was the connection between sensory stimulation and observable behavior. The difference was that functionalists also acknowledged that there were "mental states" that served to "connect" the sensory stimulation and observable behavior. For functionalism, what makes something a mental state does not depend on its internal constitution, but rather the way it functions, or the role it plays, in the system of which it is a part. Jerry Fodor explains:

Computers serve functionalists as a model of human mental functioning in several ways. To begin with, computers initially operated on an input/output model: certain instructions or tasks are given to the computer, such as a mathematical problem (input), and the computer responds by solving the problem through internal operations and presenting the answer to us (output). Functionalists contend that this is the same basic model for humans: we receive a complex variety of stimuli through our senses (seeing, hearing, smelling, tasting, touching)—"input"—that activate various mental states that ultimately result in observable behavior—"output." Jerry Fodor provides an example to illustrate this point: ironically, the same "headache" example cited by the behaviorist critic Brand Blanchand:

> The intuition underlying functionalism is that what determines the psychological type to which a mental particular belongs is the causal role of the particular in the mental life of the organism. Functional individuation is differentiation with respect to causal role. A headache, for example, is identified with the type of mental state that among other things causes a disposition for taking aspirin in people who believe aspirin relieves a headache, causes a desire to rid oneself of the pain one is feeling, often causes someone who speaks English to say such things as "I have a headache" and is brought on by overwork, eyestrain and tension. This list is presumably not complete. More will be known about the nature of a headache as psychological and physiological research discovers more about its causal role.
>
> Functionalism construes the concept of causal role in such a way that a mental state can be defined by its causal relations to other mental states. In this respect, functionalism is completely different from logical behaviorism. Another major difference is that functionalism is not a reductionist thesis. It does not foresee, even in principle, the elimination of mentalistic concepts from the explanatory apparatus of psychological theories.

Jerry Fodor, *from The Mind/Body Problem*

Analyzing the example of experiencing a headache makes clear the contrast between behaviorism and functionalism. For the behaviorist, the experience is triggered by certain *sensory stimuli* that lead to *behavioral responses* associated with a headache: grimacing, clutching one's head, and so on. In describing this experience, the behaviorist does not make any reference to internal mental states or private conscious experience. The connection between the head-hurting stimulus and the observable responses are entirely public, available for all to see, not just the victim of the headache.

Functionalism provides a more complex analysis of the headache experience. Functionalists still agree with behaviorists that the core thinking connection is between the *sensory stimuli* and the *behavioral responses* associated with a headache. What's different is that the functionalist believes that there are certain *mental events, mental activities or mental processes* that form the full connection between the sensory stimulus and the observable behavioral response such as:

- the *internal head pain* that one is experiencing
- the *belief* that taking aspirin may help reduce this pain
- the *intention* to take an aspirin in order to relieve the pain

These mental events, activities, and processes then lead the individual to behave in certainly observable ways by doing things like taking an aspirin, stating "I have a headache," and so on. So for the functionalist, providing a complete analysis of the self means not only identifying the fundamental stimulus/behavioral response connection, but also describing the network of mental states, activities, and processes that are an integral part of the causal connection between the original stimulus and behavioral response.

It's reasonable to ask the functionalist, "How are the mental states, activities and processes different from the immaterial dimensions of the mind and self that traditional mind/body dualism advocates? The functionalist response is that these mental states, activities, and processes are not thought to have an independent existence apart from the *function* they serve to connect the original stimulus and observable behaviorable response. Using computers again as a model, functionalists contend that while the actual brain is analogous to "computer hardware," the mental states, activities, and processes are analogous to "computer software." As with computers, our mental "software" functions as instructions, patterns, logical sequences, that enables the original stimulus "input" to be causally connected to the behavioral "output." Just like computer software is not thought to have an independent nonmaterial "existence" apart from the function that it has within the entire system.

As Fodor notes, one intriguing implication of this view of the human mind as analogous to computer software is that it "recognizes the possibility that systems as diverse as human beings, calculating machines and disembodied spirits could all have mental states. In the functionalist view, the psychology of a system depends not on the stuff it is made of (living cells, metal or spiritual energy) but on how the stuff is put together."

So is functionalism successful in avoiding the conceptual pitfalls of mind/body dualism while still giving a compelling account of our mental, conscious existence? It's likely that philosophers on both sides of the mind/body divide will find the functionalist "solution" less than satisfying. On the one hand, for those dualists (and nonreductive physicalists) who believe human consciousness and inner conscious states can *not* be reduced to and fully explainable in terms of physical processes, the functional existence awarded to mental states, activities and processes will likely appear weak and limited—not really doing justice to the rich, robust, and very personal life of the mind and consciousness that we experience in such a compelling way.

On the other hand, hard-core physicalists who are convinced that the mind *is* reducible to or fully explainable in terms of physical brain processes may feel philosophically queasy regarding the quasi-existence accorded by the functionalists to mental states, activities, and processes. One way this critique has been expressed concerns whether functionalism can account for what we take to be the causal efficacy of our mental states. For example, if I am experiencing a headache, the pain of which is the result of a neural state, then why do I need functional mental states (like the pain itself specified in functional terms) to connect the pain stimulus (identified as a brain state) to the response of pain behaviors (such as holding my head and saying "I have a headache")? Such mental states seem to be causally irrelevant to the entire process, since we can give a complete causal explanation of my behavior without referring to functional mental states. Of course, this is a similar "mental causation" criticism that functionalists have directed towards dualism, as Fodor observes: "If the mind is non-physical it has no position in physical space. How, then, can a mental cause give rise to a behavioral effect that has a position in space?...how can the non-physical give rise to the physical without violating the laws of the conservation of mass, of energy and of momentum?" In trying to please both the mind/body dualists and the physicalists, it's possible that functionalism ends up pleasing neither.

Eliminative Materialism: Paul Churchland

Humans have known since recorded history of the close, intimate relationship between the mind and the body. The health of our bodies, the things we ingest, the experiences we endure—all of these dimensions of our physical self have a profound effect on our mental and emotional functioning. Similarly, our emotional states, the way we think about things, our levels of stress, the optimism (or pessimism) we feel—all of these dimensions of our mental self have a dramatic impact on our physical condition. As an example, just consider how the single word *heart* is used to display this intimate connection between the emotional and the physical: heartfelt, heartache, heartsick, heartened, large-hearted, heartless, lighthearted, hard-hearted, faint-hearted, heartbroken.

Paul Churchland (b. 1942) Contemporary American philosopher and professor at the University of California, San Diego. Churchland's interests are the philosophy of science, the philosophy of mind, artificial intelligence and cognitive neurobiology, epistemology, and perception. His writing includes *The Engine of Reason, The Seat of the Soul: A Philosophical Journey into the Brain* (1995).

Modern science is now able to use advanced equipment and sophisticated techniques to unravel and articulate the complex web of connections that binds consciousness and body together into an integrated self. In fact, one of the most dynamic areas of scientific research currently is that devoted to exploring the mind/brain relationship, and the information being developed is fascinating. Scientists are increasingly able to correlate specific areas in the brain with areas of mental functioning, both cognitively and emotionally. Psychotropic drugs are being developed that can influence emotional states such as depression or extreme social anxiety. Brain scans can reveal physical abnormalities that are related to personality disorders. And discoveries are being made in the reverse direction as well, detailing the physical effects of emotional states such as anxiety, depression, anger, pessimism, and optimism on the health and well-being of the body. The assumption of this approach is that to fully understand the nature of the mind we have to fully understand the nature of the brain.

The impressive success of such scientific mind/brain research has encouraged many to conclude that it is only a matter of time before the mental life of consciousness is fully explainable in terms of the neurophysiology of the brain. The ultimate goal of such explorations is to link the self—including all of our thoughts, passions, personality traits—to the physical wiring and physiological functioning of the brain. Although such thinkers recognize that achieving such a goal will take time, they are confident that we will progressively develop ways of describing the mind, consciousness, and human experience that are physiologically based. The contemporary philosopher **Paul Churchland** articulates such a vision in the following essay. He begins by acknowledging that a simple identity formula—mental states = brain states—is a flawed way in which to conceptualize the relationship between the mind and the

Eliminative materialism
The radical claim that our ordinary, commonsense understanding of the mind is deeply wrong and that some or all of the mental states posited by common sense do not actually exist.

brain. Instead, we need to develop a new, neuroscience-based vocabulary that will enable us to think and communicate clearly about the mind, consciousness, and human experience. He refers to this view as **eliminative materialism**.

Paul Churchland, from *On Eliminative Materialism*

The identity theory was called into doubt not because the prospects for a materialist account of our mental capacities were thought to be poor, but because it seemed unlikely that the arrival of an adequate materialist theory would bring with it the nice one-to-one match-ups, between the concepts of folk psychology and the concepts of theoretical neuroscience, that intertheoretic reduction requires. The reason for that doubt was the great variety of quite different physical systems that could instantiate the required functional organization. *Eliminative materialism* also doubts that the correct neuroscientific account of human capacities will produce a neat reduction of our common-sense framework, but here the doubts arise from a quite different source.

As the eliminative materialists see it, the one-to-one match-ups will not be found, and our common-sense psychological framework will not enjoy an intertheoretic reduction, *because our common-sense psychological framework is a false and radically misleading conception of the causes of human behavior and the nature of cognitive activity*. On this view, folk psychology is not just an incomplete representation of our inner natures; it is an outright *mis*-representation of our internal states and activities. Consequently, we cannot expect a truly adequate neuroscientific account of our inner lives to provide theoretical categories that match up nicely with the categories of our common-sense framework. Accordingly, we must expect that the older framework will simply be eliminated, rather than be reduced, by a mature neuroscience.

It used to be thought that when a piece of wood burns, or a piece of metal rusts, a spiritlike substance called "phlogiston" was being released: briskly, in the former case, slowly in the latter. Once gone, that "noble" substance left only a base pile of ash or rust. It later came to be appreciated that both processes involve, not the loss of something, but the gaining of a substance taken from the atmosphere: oxygen. Phlogiston emerged, not as an incomplete description of what was going on, but as a radical misdescription. Phlogiston was therefore not suitable for reduction to or identification with some notion from within the new oxygen chemistry, and it was simply eliminated from science....

The concepts of folk psychology—belief, desire, fear, sensation, pain, joy, and so on—await a similar fate, according to the view at issue. And when neuroscience has matured to the point where the poverty of our current conceptions is apparent to everyone, the superiority of the new framework is established, we shall then be able to set about reconceiving our internal states and activities, within a truly adequate conceptual framework at last. Our explanations of one another's behavior will appeal to such things as our neuropharmacological states, the neural activity in specialized anatomical areas, and whatever other states are deemed relevant by the new theory. Our private introspection will also be transformed, and may be profoundly enhanced by reason of the more accurate and penetrating framework it will have to work with—just as the astronomer's perception of the night sky is much enhanced by the detailed knowledge of modern astronomical theory that he or she possesses.

The magnitude of the conceptual revolution here suggested should not be minimized: it would be enormous. And the benefits to humanity might be equally great. If each of us possessed an accurate neuroscientific understanding of (what we now conceive dimly as) the varieties and causes of mental illness, the factors involved in learning, the neural basis of emotions, intelligence, and socialization, then the sum total of human misery might be much reduced. The simple increase in mutual understanding that the new framework made possible could contribute substantially toward a more peaceful and humane society. Of course, there would be dangers as well: increased knowledge means increased power, and power can always be misused.

Churchland's central argument is that the concepts and theoretical vocabulary we use to think about our selves—using such terms as *belief, desire, fear, sensation, pain, joy*—actually misrepresent the reality of minds and selves. All of these concepts are part of a commonsense "folk psychology" that obscures rather than clarifies the nature of human experience. Eliminative materialists believe that we need to develop a new vocabulary and conceptual framework that is grounded in neuroscience and that will be a more accurate reflection of the human mind and self. Churchland proceeds to state the arguments that he believes support his position.

Paul Churchland,
from *On Eliminative Materialism*

The arguments for eliminative materialism are diffuse and less than decisive, but they are stronger than is widely supposed. The distinguishing feature of this position is its denial that a smooth intertheoretic reduction is to be expected—even a species-specific reduction—of the framework of folk psychology to the framework of a matured neuroscience. The reason for this denial is the eliminative materialist's conviction that folk psychology is a hopelessly primitive and deeply confused conception of our internal activities. But why this low opinion of our common-sense conceptions?

There are at least three reasons. First, the eliminative materialist will point to the widespread explanatory, predictive, and manipulative failures of folk psychology. So much of what is central and familiar to us remains a complete mystery from within folk psychology. We do not know what sleep is, or why we have to have it, despite spending a full third of our lives in that condition. (The answer, "For rest," is mistaken. Even if people are allowed to rest continuously, their need for sleep is undiminished. Apparently, sleep serves some deeper functions, but we do not yet know what they are.) We do not understand how learning transforms each of us from a gaping infant to a cunning adult, or how differences in intelligence are grounded. We have not the slightest idea how memory works, or how we manage to retrieve relevant bits of information instantly from the awesome mass we have stored. We do not know what mental illness is, nor how to cure it.

In sum, the most central things about us remain almost entirely mysterious from within folk psychology....

This argument from explanatory poverty has a further aspect. So long as one sticks to normal brains, the poverty of folk psychology is perhaps not strikingly evident. But as soon as one examines the many perplexing behavioral and cognitive deficits suffered by people with damaged brains, one's descriptive and explanatory resources start to claw the air.... As with other humble theories asked to operate successfully in unexplored extensions of their old domain (for example, Newtonian mechanics in the domain of velocities close to the velocity of light, and the classical gas law in the domain of high pressures or temperatures), the descriptive and explanatory inadequacies of folk psychology become starkly evident.

The second argument tries to draw an inductive lesson from our conceptual history. Our early folk theories of motion were profoundly confused, and were eventually displaced entirely by more sophisticated theories. Our early folk theories of the structure and activity of the heavens were wildly off the mark, and survive only as historical lessons in how wrong we can be. Our folk theories of the nature of fire, and the nature of life, were similarly cockeyed. And one could go on, since the vast majority of our past folk conceptions have been similarly exploded. All except folk psychology, which survives to this day and has only recently begun to feel pressure. But the phenomenon of conscious intelligence is surely a more complex and difficult phenomenon than any of those just listed. So far as accurate understanding is concerned, it would be a miracle if we had got that one right the very first time, when we fell down so badly on all the others. Folk psychology has survived for so very long, presumably, not because it is basically correct in its representations, but because the phenomena addressed are so surprisingly difficult that any useful handle on them, no matter how feeble, is unlikely to be displaced in a hurry....

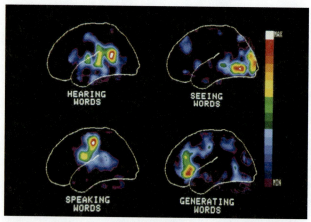

Is the self the same as the brain? Materialists contend that in the final analysis mental states are identical with, reducible to, or explainable in terms of physical brain states. What are the practical implications of such a view? If you were convinced that materialists are correct, how would this influence the way you see yourself and the choices that you make?

Churchland's point is that the most compelling argument for developing a new conceptual framework and vocabulary founded on neuroscience is the simple fact that the current "folk psychology" has done a poor job in accomplishing the main reason for its existence—explaining and predicting the commonplace phenomena of the human mind and experience. And in the same way that science replaces outmoded, ineffective, and limited conceptual frameworks with ones that can explain and predict more effectively, so the same thing needs to be done in psychology and philosophy of mind. This new conceptual framework will be based on and will integrate all that we are learning about how the brain works on a neurological level.

Although he believes strongly in the logic of his position, Churchland recognizes that many people will resist the argument he is making for a variety of reasons.

Paul Churchland, from *On Eliminative Materialism*

The initial plausibility of this rather radical view is low for almost everyone, since it denies deeply entrenched assumptions. That is at best a question-begging complaint, of course, since those assumptions are precisely what is at issue. But the following line of thought does attempt to mount a real argument.

Eliminative materialism is false, runs the argument, because one's introspection reveals directly the existence of pains, beliefs, desires, fears, and so forth. Their existence is as obvious as anything could be.

The eliminative materialist will reply that this argument makes the same mistake that an ancient or medieval person would be making if he insisted that he could just see with his own eyes that the heavens form a turning sphere, or that witches exist. The fact is, all observation occurs within some system of concepts, and our observation judgments are only as good as the conceptual framework in which they are expressed. In all three cases—the starry sphere, witches, and the familiar mental states—precisely what is challenged is the integrity of the background conceptual frameworks in which the observation judgments are expressed. To insist on the validity of one's experiences, traditionally interpreted, is therefore to beg the very question at issue. For in all three cases, the question is whether we should reconceive the nature of some familiar observational domain.

* * *

A final criticism draws a much weaker conclusion but makes a rather stronger case. Eliminative materialism, it has been said, is making mountains out of molehills. It exaggerates the defects in folk psychology, and underplays its real successes. Perhaps the arrival of a matured neuroscience will require the elimination of the occasional folk-psychological concept, continues the criticism, and a minor adjustment in certain folk-psychological principles may have to be endured. But the large-scale elimination forecast by the eliminative materialist is just an alarmist worry or a romantic enthusiasm.

Perhaps this complaint is correct. And perhaps it is merely complacent. Whichever, it does bring out the important point that we do not confront two simple and mutually exclusive possibilities here: pure reduction versus pure elimination. Rather, these are the end points of a smooth spectrum of possible outcomes, between which there are mixed cases of partial elimination and partial reduction. Only empirical research...can tell us where on that spectrum our own case will fall. Perhaps we should speak here, more liberally, of "revisionary materialism" instead of concentrating on the more radical possibility of an across-the-board elimination.

Churchland's ultimate concession that the psychology-based conceptual framework currently used by most academic disciplines and popular culture may not end up being completely eradicated and replaced by a neuroscience framework still operates within his physicalist framework: for those "folk psychology" terms not eliminated will nevertheless be reducible to neurophysical statements of brain states.

Of courses, there are many people who believe that there are fundamental differences between the life of the mind and neuroscientific descriptions of the brain's operation. Many people believe that, no matter how exhaustively scientists are able to describe the physical conditions for consciousness, this does not mean that the mental dimensions of the self will ever be *reducible* to these physical states. Why? Because in the final analysis, the physical and mental dimensions of the self are qualitatively different realms, each with its own distinctive vocabulary, logic, and organizing principles. According to this view, even if scientists were able to map out your complete brain activity at the moment you were having an original idea or experiencing an emotional epiphany, that neurobiological description of your brain would provide no clue as to the nature of your personal experience at that moment. Articulating and communicating the rich texture of those experiences would take a very different language and logic.

Fascinatingly, it was Socrates who first articulated a coherent critique of the materialist position in Plato's dialogue *Phaedo*, during the period following his trial and conviction. Socrates ridicules the materialist position, which he attributes to the philosopher Anaxagoras, which, he says, would explain his decision to remain in Athens by reference to his "bones and sinews," rather than the result of the conscious choice of his mind. With surprisingly good humor he explains that if it was up to his body he would not have remained in Athens to be executed, but rather *"I fancy that these sinews and bones would have been in the neighborhood of Megara or Boeotia long ago—impelled by a conviction of what is best!—if I did not think that it was more right and honorable to submit to whatever my country orders rather than to take to my heels and run away."* In other words, Socrates is arguing that it is his conscious, rational mind that has determined his fate, and attempting to use a materialistic framework to explain his actions makes no sense. *"If it were said that without such bones and sinews and all the rest of them I should not be able to do what I think is right, it would be true. But to say that it is because of them that I do what I am doing, and not through choice of what is best—although my actions are controlled by mind—would be a very lax and inaccurate form of expression."* For Socrates, even if we had a complete description of how the body (and by extension the brain) worked, we would still be unable to dispense with folk psychological terms like *choice* and *belief*.

< READING CRITICALLY >

Analyzing Churchland's Materialism

- Explain the reasons why materialists believe that to fully understand the nature of the mind we have to fully understand the nature of the brain.
- Based on your own experience, describe some examples of the close, interactive relationship between the physical dimensions of your *self* and the psychological aspects of your mind and experience.
- Explain why Paul Churchland believes that a close examination of the history of science suggests that we are at the beginning of a conceptual revolution in understanding the nature of the mind.
- Explain the arguments against eliminative materialism. Which arguments do you find most persuasive? Why?

Contemporary Philosophy of Mind

Logical behaviorism, functionalism, eliminative materialism…these are all contrasting physicalistic theories of the human self and mind. They all share the fundamental belief that the human mind can be fully understood by understanding and describing the human brain. The philosopher Richard Brown, of the City University of New York, publishes widely in the philosophy of mind and hosts an annual online conference that centers on the nature of consciousness. In the following essay, Brown provides a brief overview of several theoretical perspectives regarding consciousness, and he describes a number of fascinating "thought experiments" that philosophers sometimes use as vehicles for analysis.

Richard Brown, from *Contemporary Issues in Philosophy of Mind*

The philosophical study of the mind in alive and well in the twenty-first century. Broadly speaking, one might say that there are three overarching concerns in this debate. The first concerns whether consciousness ultimately depends on something computational/functional or whether it depends on something biological. The second concerns whether consciousness is ultimately physical or nonphysical, and the third concerns what role empirical results play in philosophical theories of consciousness.

Consider the first question. Some philosophers, like John Searle at UC Berkeley and Ned Block at New York University, think that consciousness is distinctly biological. To see what is at issue here we can employ a commonly used thought experiment. Neurons no doubt perform functions. Ask any psychologist or neuroscientist and they will tell you about sodium ions and potassium ions and cell membranes and neurotransmitters, action potentials and the rest. That is, we can think of a neuron as something that takes a certain kind of input (the neurotransmitters from other neurons, ions) and delivers a certain kind of output (an action potential or a graded potential). In principle it seems possible that we could use a nano machine to mimic a neuron's functional profile. This nano machine would be able to take all of the same input and deliver all of the same output. One might think of it as an artificial neuron in the sense that we have artificial hearts. It is a bit of metal and plastic but it is designed to do the exact same job that the original was meant to do. Suppose now that this nano machine zaps the neuron and quickly takes its place. Now you have all of your regular neurons and one artificial neuron. But it does everything the original neuron did, so we have no reason to think that this should change your conscious experience overly much. But now we do it with another neuron, and another, and another. The question then, is what happens to consciousness when we replace all of the neurons?

David Chalmers, a philosopher at the Australian National University and New York University, has argued that as a person moves through this process of having his or her neurons replaced with artificial ones, we have a few options. We might say that as the neurons are being replaced, that person's conscious experience is slowly fading like a light on a dimmer switch, or we might say that the conscious experience was just cut off at some point when some number of neurons were replaced, maybe even the first one! But each of these has a very strange consequence. Suppose that I am having a headache during the hour that my brain is being "fitted" with nanobots. Now suppose that my conscious experience is fading as the process progresses, with it being absent at the end. Well, okay, but the first thing to notice is that there can be no difference in your behavior as we go through the process. Each nanobot performs exactly the same function as the neuron, and we can think of the nanobot as instantaneously zapping and replacing the neuron, so that you could be driving a car or reading a book while this was happening. But then we end up with the very strange result that we are radically out of touch with our conscious experience! How do I know that I have a conscious pain? Well, I feel it! But if we were right that it can fade out, or even pop into and out of existence, without my noticing, then how do I know it isn't happening to me right now? Since we take it for granted that we are not radically out of touch with our conscious experience in normal cases Chalmers concludes that it is safer to think that the conscious experience would be the same at the end of the process. But if this is right, then consciousness depends on functional organization and not on the biology, or nonbiology, of the hardware. Those like Searle and Block hold that real neurons with their biological properties are needed in order to have consciousness and that the neural net at the end of the process would no longer be you or have thoughts or pains, but would only simulate those things. It is important to note that this dispute is independent of the dispute between physicalists and dualists. A dualist may hold that functional organization is what gives rise to the non-physical mind just as much as they may hold that it is the biology of the brain that gives rise to it. And likewise, a physicalist can be a functionalist or endorse a biology-based view. Whatever your intuitions are, this may not be science fiction for long. Neuroscience is already well along in its investigation of ways to design brain–machine interfaces (for instance, as a way of helping amputees with prosthetic limbs that are controlled just like one's own limbs), and enhancement of the human mind by prosthetic neurology is perhaps not far off.

Notice that in thinking about the question of whether the mind ultimately depends on biological or functional properties, we appealed to a thought experiment. We did not go out and do an actual experiment. We consulted what we intuitively thought about a piece of science fiction. In contemporary philosophy of mind, there are those who think that these kinds of intuitions carry great weight and those who think that they do not. Those who think that they carry water think that we can know some deep fact about the nature of consciousness on the basis of reason alone. For instance, take Frank Jackson's Mary thought experiment (Jackson is also a philosopher at the Australian National University). Imagine a brilliant scientist who is locked in a black and white room but who is able to communicate with the outside world via a black and white television screen. Mary is able to learn all of the science that we will ever be able to know. So, imagine that she knows the *truth* about physics, whatever it is. Now suppose that she is released from her room and shown a red ripe tomato. It seems natural to think that she would learn something that she might express by, "Oh, *that's* what it's like to see red! Everyone out here kept talking about red, but now that I have seen it, I know what they mean." But since she knew all of the physical facts, and yet did not know at least one fact, what it is like for her to see red, it seems like that fact must not be a physical fact. If this and related thought experiments are right. then it seems that we do not need empirical evidence of any kind to know that consciousness cannot be physical. (Note, that David Chalmers talked about above, has advocated a thought-experiment based approach against physicalism as well. He has introduced philosophical zombies, creatures that are physical duplicates of us but that lack consciousness. If these are possible, then consciousness is not a consequence of physics alone.)

These arguments, and the knowledge argument of Jackson in particular, have spawned a huge amount of responses. One very natural response is to question the inattention to scientific discoveries. Daniel Dennett, a philosopher at Tufts University, argues that this whole strategy is thoroughly misguided. We seem to think that there are these magical conscious properties—the experience of having a pain—that just aren't there. What is there is the seeming that it is so. Dennett often makes a comparison to magic. Take some professional magician, say David Copperfield. What Copperfield does is to make it seem as though he has done something else. If you wanted to know how Copperfield performed some trick, you would need to explain how he made it seem that the statue was gone, or how he made it seem that the person was levitating. You don't try to show that he really did it, but how he made it seem as though he really did. Now, is what he does real magic? There is some temptation to say no. Real magic is not just a trick. But sadly, the only magic that is in fact real is the kind that is fake. Dennett thinks the same is true of consciousness. When the functionalist explains what a pain is and someone says that this is not magic enough (Mary wouldn't know it, or a zombie would lack it), the functionalist should respond that there is no such thing as that kind of magic. What is true is that the brain makes it seem to us as though we have all of this magical stuff going on, but it only seems to be going on. Why think this? Dennett's main argument is that this has been shown to us by the empirical sciences. Take just one example, the case of so-called change blindness. (Go online and search for "the amazing color-changing card trick" to see a cool example.) In these kinds of cases, people are presented with a scene in which there is a very large central thing that changes. People are usually very bad at spotting the change. Yet when they see the difference, they cannot believe that they did not notice it before. That is, from the first-person point of view, it really seems as though one has access to a very rich and detailed scene, but actually one is mostly unaware of very large and salient changes in one's environment. If this is right, then our intuitions about science fiction cases may not be that reliable. And this is what Dennett and those like him think.

So where are we with respect to dualism versus physicalism? I think it is safe to say that at this time in history, most philosophers and scientists are physicalists of one sort or another and think that we will ultimately come to believe that the mind is just physical. Most agree that we need to pay close attention to the empirical sciences. But of course we also need to pay close attention to our own phenomenological experiences, as we will need to fully understand both if we are ever to see the relation between the two.

< READING CRITICALLY >

Analyzing Issues in Contemporary Philosophy of Mind

1. What is your own reaction to the thought experiments? Is the neural net conscious? Could Mary know what it is like to see red on the basis of physics, etc.?

2. Describe one belief that you, or someone you know, held that turned out to be falsified by some scientific fact.

3. Is an artificial heart a real heart? Why or why not?

4. Functionalists deny that we will ever eliminate psychological concepts from our talk about minds. Do you find their position convincing? Can you think of any time where some explanation of a friend's behavior seemed impossible without appealing to what they believed or desired? What about some bit of behavior that you find yourself explaining in terms of some neurological condition?

3.11 The Self Is Embodied Subjectivity: Husserl and Merleau-Ponty

In a radical break from traditional theories of the mind, the German thinker **Edmund Husserl** introduced a very different approach that came to be known as **phenomenology**. Phenomenology refers to the conviction that all knowledge of our selves and our world is based on the "phenomena" of experience. From Husserl's standpoint, the division between the "mind" and the "body" is a product of confused thinking. The simple fact is, we experience our self as a unity in which the mental and physical are seamlessly woven together. This idea of the self as a unity thus fully rejects the dualist ideas of Plato and Descartes.

A generation after Husserl, the philosopher **Maurice Merleau-Ponty** articulated the phenomenologist position in a simple declaration: "I live in my body." By the "lived body," Merleau-Ponty means an entity that can never be objectified or known in a completely objective sort of way, as opposed to the "body as object" of the dualists. For example, when you first wake up in the morning and experience your gradually expanding awareness of where you are and how you feel, what are your first thoughts of the day? Perhaps something along the lines of "Oh no, it's time to get up, but I'm still sleepy, but I have an important appointment that I can't be late for" and so on. Note that at no point do you doubt that the "I" you refer to is a single integrated entity, a blending of mental, physical, and emotional structured around a core identity: your self. It's only later, when you're reading Descartes or discussing the possibility of reincarnation with a friend that you begin creating ideas such as independent "minds," "bodies," "souls," or, in the case of Freud, an "unconscious."

According to Husserl and Merleau-Ponty, if we honestly and accurately examine our direct and immediate experience of our selves, these mind/body "problems" fall away. As Merleau-Ponty explains, "There is not a duality of substances but only the dialectic of living being in its biological milieu." In other words, our "living body" is a natural synthesis of mind and biology, and any attempts to divide them into separate entities are artificial and nonsensical.

The underlying question is "What aspect of our experience is the most 'real'?" From Husserl's and Merleau-Ponty's vantage point, it's the moments of immediate, prereflective experience that are the most real. It is the Lebenswelt or "lived world," which is the fundamental ground of our being and consciousness. To take another example, consider your experience when you are in the midst of activities such as dancing, playing a sport, or performing musically—what is your experience of your self? Most likely, you're completely absorbed in the moment, your mind and body functioning as one integrated entity. For Merleau-Ponty, this unified experience of your self is the paradigm or model you should use to understand your nature.

Phenomenologists do not assume that there are more "fundamental" levels of reality beyond that of conscious human experience. Consistent with this ontological (having to do with the nature of *being* or *existence*) commitment is the belief that explanations for human behavior and experience are not to be sought by appeal to phenomena that are somehow behind, beneath, or beyond the phenomena of lived human experience but instead are to be sought within the field of human experience itself, using terminology and concepts appropriate to this field. And when we examine our selves at this fundamental level of direct human experience, we discover

Phenomenology
A philosophical approach that attempts to give a direct description of our experience as it is in itself, without taking into account its psychological origins or causal explanations.

Edmund Husserl
(1859–1938). German philosopher who founded the field of phenomenology. In his *Logical Investigations* (1900–1901), he advocated getting back to things in themselves, that is, objects as they are presented in actual perception.

Maurice Merleau-Ponty
(1908–1961). French philosopher whose thinking was influenced by Husserl. Merleau-Ponty objected to philosophies that underestimated the significance of the body and argued that perception is fundamental to our knowledge of the world. In *The Phenomenology of Perception* (1945), he argued that consciousness is a dynamic form that actively structures our experience.

***Breathing Head* (2002), by Fred Tomaselli.** This painting evokes the idea of the self as a perceiving being. This image teems with life and energy. Might this view of the self suggest how you could feel more fully alive? *(Fred Tomaselli, Breathing Head. 2002. Leaves, photocollage, acrylic, gouache, resin on wood panel. 60 × 60 inches. Image courtesy of James Cohan Gallery, New York.)*

Watch the **Video**
Hubert Dreyfus on Husserl and Heidegger on **mysearchlab.com**

that our mind and body are unified, not separate. It is this primal consciousness, Merleau-Ponty notes in his book *Phenomenology of Perception*, that is the foundation for our perception of the world and our knowledge about it:

> *Consciousness must be reckoned as a **self-contained system of Being**, as a system of **Absolute being**, into which nothing can penetrate and from which nothing can escape. On the other side, the whole spatio-temporal world, to which man and the human ego claim to belong as subordinate singular realities, is **according to its own meaning mere intentional Being**, a Being, therefore, which has the merely secondary, relative sense of a Being for a consciousness.*

For Merleau-Ponty, everything that we are aware of—and can possibly know—is contained within our own consciousness. It's impossible for us to get "outside" of our consciousness because it defines the boundaries of our personal universe. The so-called real world of objects existing in space and time initially exists only as objects of my consciousness. Yet in a cognitive sleight-of-hand, we act as if the space/time world is primary and our immediate consciousness is secondary. This is an inversion of the way things actually are: It is our consciousness that is primary and the space/time world that is secondary, existing fundamentally as the object of our consciousness.

Nor is science exempt from condemnation, according to the phenomenologists, for scientists are guilty of the same flawed thinking as expressed in abstract philosophical and religious theories. Too often scientists treat their abstract theories as if they take precedence over the rich and intuitive reality of immediate lived experience. In cases when the two worlds conflict, scientists automatically assume that the scientific perspective is correct, and the direct experience of the individual wrong. This is the difficulty we pointed out with the concept of the unconscious: It was considered by Freud and many of his followers to be of such supreme authority that no individual's contrasting point of view can measure up to the ultimate truth of the unconscious interpretation. In his *Phenomenology of Perception*, Merleau-Ponty makes the crucial point that these theories couldn't even exist without the primal reality of lived experience to serve as their foundation. And *then* these theories have the arrogance to dismiss this fundamental reality as somehow secondary or derivative:

> *Scientific points of view are always both naïve and at the same time dishonest, because they take for granted without explicitly mentioning it, that other point of view, namely that of the consciousness, through which from the outset a world forms itself around me and begins to exist for me.*

As a philosophical theory of knowledge, phenomenology is distinctive in the sense that its goal is not to *explain* experience but rather to *clarify our understanding* of it. A phenomenologist like Merleau-Ponty sees his aim of describing what he sees and then assuming that his description will strike a familiar chord with us, stimulating us to say, "I understand what you're saying—that makes sense to me!" From this perspective, the responsibility of philosophy is not to provide explanations but to seek the root and genesis of meaning, "to reveal the mystery of the world and of reason," to help us think and see things more clearly. For example, to develop a clear understanding of your "being in love," you need to delay using elaborate psychological theories and instead begin by describing the phenomena of the experience in a clear, vivid fashion, trying to uncover the meaning of what you are experiencing. *Then* you can begin developing concepts and theories to help you make sense of the phenomena of "being in love." The danger of using theories prematurely is that you may very well distort your actual experience, forcing it to conform to someone else's idea of what "being in love" means instead of clearly understanding *your* unique experience. Concepts and theories are essential for understanding our selves and our world. It's simply a question of which comes first—the concepts/theories or the phenomena of experience that the concepts/theories are designed to explain. For phenomenologists, it's essential that we always begin (and return regularly to) the phenomena of our lived experience. Otherwise, we run the risk of viewing our experience through conceptual or theoretical "lenses" that distort rather than clarify. For instance, in providing a phenomenological analysis of "being in love," you might begin by describing precisely what your immediate responses are: physically, emotionally, cognitively. I'm currently in love and,

- I feel...
- I think...
- My physical response...
- I spontaneously...

By recording the direct phenomena of our experience, we have the basic data needed to reveal the complex meaning of this experience and begin to develop a clearer understanding of what "being in love" is all about, by using concepts and theories appropriate to the reality of our lived experience.

What exactly is "consciousness"? For Merleau-Ponty it is a *dynamic form* responsible for actively structuring our conscious ideas and physical behavior. In this sense, it is fundamentally different from Hume's and Locke's concept of the mind as a repository for sensations or the behaviorists' notion of the mind as the sum total of the reactions to the physical stimuli that an organism receives. Consciousness, for

Marcel Proust (1871–1922). French intellectual and writer. Satirical and introspective in his work, Proust's central theme involved the affirmation of life. His most ambitious work, *In Search of Time Lost* (1913–1922), runs over 3,000 pages and includes more than 2,000 characters. It is a classic of modern literature.

Merleau-Ponty, is a dimension of our *lived body*, which is not an *object* in the world, distinct from the knowing subject (as in Descartes), but is the subjects' *own point of view on the world:* The body is itself the original knowing *subject* from which all other forms of knowledge derive.

Accomplished writers often have a special talent for representing human experience in a rich, vibrant, and textured way. The French novelist **Marcel Proust** is renowned for articulating the phenomena of consciousness in a very phenomenological way. Consider the following descriptions of experiences and analyze their effectiveness from a phenomenological perspective on the self.

Marcel Proust, from *In Search of Time Lost*

Waking from Sleep

When a man is asleep, he has in a circle round him the chain of the hours, the sequence of the years, the order of the heavenly host. Instinctively, when he awakes, he looks to these, and in an instant reads off his own position on the earth's surface the time that has elapsed during his slumbers; but this ordered procession is apt to grow confused, and to break its ranks...suppose that he dozes off in an armchair, for instance, after dinner: then the world will go hurtling out of orbit, the magic chair will carry him at full speed through time and space, and when he opens his eyes again he will imagine that he went to sleep months earlier in another place...for me it was enough if, in my own bed, my sleep was so heavy as completely to relax my consciousness; for then I lost all sense of the place in which I had gone to sleep, and when I awoke in the middle of the night, not knowing where I was, I could not even be sure at first who I was; I had only the most rudimentary sense of existence, such as may lurk and flicker in the depths of an animal's consciousness: I was more destitute than a cave dweller; but then the memory—not yet of the place in which I was, but of the various other places where I had lived and might now possibly be—would come like a rope let down from heaven to draw me up out of the abyss of non-being, from which I could never have escaped by myself: but in a flash I would traverse centuries of civilization, and out of a blurred glimpse of oil-lamps, then of shirts with turned-down collars, would gradually piece together the original components of my ego. (*20*)

Marcel Proust, from *Within a Budding Grove*

Describing a Previous Relationship

I have said that Albertine had not seemed to me that day to be the same as on previous days, and that each time I saw her she was to appear different. But I felt at that moment that certain modifications in the appearance, the importance, the stature of a person may also be due to the variability of certain states of consciousness interposed between that person and ourselves...and each of those Albertines was different, as is each appearance of the dancer whose colours, form, character, are transmuted according to the endlessly varied play of a projected limelight...I ought to give a different name to each of the selves who subsequently thought about Albertine; I ought still more to give a different name to each of the Albertines who appeared before me, never the same, like those seas—called by me simply and for the sake of convenience "the sea"—that succeeded one another. (*1010*)

3.12 Buddhist Concepts of the Self

Western culture's concept of the self, initiated by Plato and continued through the centuries by thinkers like Saint Augustine and Descartes, is so woven into the philosophical frameworks of many of us that it's difficult to conceive of radically different concepts of the self if we haven't been exposed to them. Yet the fact is that these different concepts of the self do in fact exist, and they are assumed to be true by people immersed in different cultures and religions.

One of the most influential of these alternate views is the Buddhist conception of the self, and comparisons are often made between Hume's concept of the self as a unified bundle of thoughts, feelings, and sensations and Buddhism's concept of *anatta* or "no-self." Although there are surface similarities between the two views of the self, a deeper analysis reveals significant differences. For Hume, a close examination of our stream of consciousness reveals no self, soul, or "I" that exists continually through time. We each create a "fictional self" to unify these transient mental events and introduce order into our lives, but this self has no real existence.

Buddhist doctrine agrees with Hume that the notion of a permanent self that exists as a unified identity through time is an illusion. For Buddhists, every aspect of life is impermanent and all elements of the universe are in a continual process of change and transition, a process that includes each self as well. The self can best be thought of as a flame that is continually passed from candle to candle, retaining a certain continuity but no real personal identity. But if the self or "I" doesn't refer to a continuous identity, then what does it signify? According to Buddhist philosophy, the self is composed of *five aggregates*: physical form, sensation, conceptualization, dispositions to act, and consciousness. Each self is comprised of the continual interplay of these five elements, but there is no substance or identity beyond the dynamic interaction of these five elements.

This concept of the self is certain to seem alien to our Western consciousness, which has a decidedly more Platonic view of self-identity. And, in fact, there was a famous debate regarding these two points of view that occurred in the second century B.C.E., between King Menander, a Greek who ruled northwestern India, and a Buddhist monk Nagasena. Witnessed by 500 Greeks and thousands of monks, the argument hinged on a chariot simile, though in a much different fashion than that employed by Plato!

What would reincarnation mean for the self? Buddhist philosophy allows for the idea of reincarnation, as the self passes from body to body. The Buddha uses the mudra (a sacred gesture) to represent the Karmic wheel of birth, death, and rebirth. Do you believe that your actions in this life affect your self in a next life or afterlife?

Milindapanha, *The Simile of the Chariot*

Then King Menander went up to the Venerable Nagasena, greeted him respectfully, and sat down. Nagasena replied to the greeting, and the King was pleased at heart. Then King Menander asked: "How is your reverence known, and what is your name?"

"I'm known as Nagasena, your Majesty, that's what my fellow monks call me. But though my parents may have given me such a name...it's only a generally understood term, a practical designation. There is no question of a permanent individual implied in the use of the word."

"Listen, you five hundred Greeks and eighty thousand monks!" said King Menander. "This Nagasena has just declared that there's no permanent individuality implied in his name!" Then, turning to Nagasena, "If, Reverend Nagasena, there is no permanent individuality, who gives you monks your robes and food, lodging and medicines? And who makes use of them? Who lives a life of righteousness, meditates, and reaches Nirvana? Who destroys living beings, steals, fornicates, tells lies, or drinks spirits?...If what you say is true there's neither merit nor demerit, and no fruit or result of good or evil deeds. If someone were to kill you there would be no question of murder. And there would be no masters or teachers in the (Buddhist) Order and no ordinations. If your fellow monks call you Nagasena, what then is Nagasena? Would you say that your hair is Nagasena?" "No, your Majesty."

"Or your nails, teeth, skin, or other parts of your body, or the outward form, or sensation, or perception, or the psychic constructions, or consciousness? Are any of these Nagasena?" "No, your Majesty."

"Then are all these taken together Nagasena?" "No, your Majesty."

"Or anything other than they?" "No, your Majesty."

"Then for all my asking I find no Nagasena. Nagasena is a mere sound! Surely what your Reverence has said is false!"

Then the Venerable Nagasena addressed the King.

"Your Majesty, how did you come here—on foot, or in a vehicle?"

"In a chariot."

"Then tell me what is the chariot? Is the pole the chariot?" "No, your Reverence."

"Or the axle, wheels, frame, reins, yoke, spokes, or goad?" "None of these things is the chariot."

"Then all these separate parts taken together are the chariot?" "No, your Reverence."

"Then is the chariot something other than the separate parts?" "No, your Reverence."

"Then for all my asking, your Majesty, I can find no chariot. The chariot is a mere sound. What then is the chariot? Surely what your Majesty has said is false! There is no chariot!...

When he had spoken the five hundred Greeks cried "Well done!" and said to the King, "Now, your Majesty, get out of that dilemma if you can!" "What I said was not false," replied the King. "It's on account of all these various components, the pole, axle, wheels, and so on, that the vehicle is called a chariot. It's just a generally understood term, a practical designation."

"Well said, your Majesty! You know what the word 'chariot' means! And it's just the same with me. It's on account of the various components of my being that I'm known by the generally understood term, the practical designation Nagasena."

<   R E A D I N G   C R I T I C A L L Y   >

Analyzing the Buddhist Chariot Analogy

- Imagine that you were present at the debate between King Menander and the monk Nagasena. How would you critically evaluate the arguments being made by both men? Do you think a chariot is an appropriate simile to the human self? Why or why not? How would you have responded to Nagasena's argument?

- Compare how Plato (see pages 107–108) and Nagasena use the analogy of a chariot to explain the nature of the *self*. What are the similarities? What are the differences?

3.13 Making Connections: In Search of the Self

What is the self? We have seen in this chapter that this seemingly innocent question is anything but simple. It's certainly curious that this entity that is so personal and always present to us turns out to be so elusive and enigmatic. It should be some comfort to realize that the greatest minds in history have wrestled with this question without reaching conclusive answers. Is the self an immortal soul, distinct from the physical body? Is the self simply a receptacle for the stream of sensations moving through our consciousness? Is the self defined by its ability to think and reflect? Is the self an organizing principle that integrates all of the elements of experience into a personal unity? Is the self defined by its observable behavior? What is the relationship of consciousness and the physical body? Is the mind/body "problem" the result of confused thinking? Is the self identical with the brain or some part of the brain?

You may be asking yourself at this point, Do I really need to *have* a philosophy of the self? What difference does having such a philosophy make in my life? Paul Churchland mentions that a better understanding of our selves will contribute toward a more peaceful and humane society. How so? Do you agree? Your personal reflections as you have thought your way through the issues in this chapter have likely suggested some responses to these questions. Why is it important to have a philosophy of the self? In part, because we cannot influence or control what we do not understand. Achieving your goals in life, both in terms of personal growth and real-world success, is directly related to your insight into the nature of your self. The key to determining your authentic life goals, overcoming obstacles that may be inhibiting your success, and taking the most productive path to achieving your aspirations, is grounded in self-understanding. As we will see in the next chapter, "Are You Free? Freedom and Determinism," your philosophy of your self relates directly to your belief in whether free choices are possible, and if they are, how you can maximize your personal freedom.

But you do not exist in isolation: Your self is bound up in a network of relationships with other selves. The person that you are is in large measure shaped by your

Does the soul transcend death? Funeral ceremonies embody beliefs about the connection between the self and body. In this picture of a Buddhist funeral, the body of the deceased is to be cremated so that the soul can be released to the next incarnation. What beliefs are embodied in the funeral practices of your culture?

social experiences in life: your family, your culture, your religion, your community, your friends, and so on. In fact, many thinkers believe that it is a mistake to try to understand the self in isolation from others. Instead, they reason, we can only be understood in the context of the complex web of social relations that constitute and define us. This was the view of Aristotle, who observed:

> *If there were a being who could not live in society or who did not need to live in society because he was self-sufficient, then he would have to either be animal or a god. He could not be a real part of the state. A social instinct is implanted in all people by their nature.*

Developing productive and healthy relationships with others is clearly related to developing an enlightened philosophy of the self: Otherwise we're flying blind as we try to negotiate our way in the world and build relationships with others. And on a social level, developing an informed understanding of the self is certainly connected to the larger social challenges that face us. One cannot help but be concerned with all of the destructive events occurring in the world today, fueled in large measure by ignorance of the self in both its individual and social incarnations. There is a strong case that can be made for Churchland's point that creating a more peaceful and humane society—and world—is contingent on understanding ourselves. It is only through self-examination and insight that we will be able to diminish the destructive impulses that humans seem to be prone to and promote the constructive, empathetic, and creative dimensions of our selves that will help construct the sort of world in which we all yearn for.

These are some of the themes that we have explored in this chapter and that we will continue to examine throughout this text. But in a larger sense, these are questions that you will continue to explore throughout your life. Your self is a wonder, a miracle, an extraordinary creation. When Socrates urged each of us to "Know thyself" and warned that "The unexamined life is not worth living," he was issuing a challenge that requires a lifetime commitment and our mind's best work. But it is in the process of striving to understand our self that we may also discover the purpose of our existence and the path to living a productive and fulfilling life.

---

thinking philosophically

WHAT IS YOUR CONCEPT OF THE SELF?

This is your opportunity to formulate and express your own philosophy of self. You have explored many themes and issues related to the self: Now try to synthesize these ideas into your perspective on the nature of the self. What is a self? Who are you? Who do you want to become and why? What is the meaning of your life? How have the views of the thinkers we have studied influenced your understanding of your self?

This box is the basis of the "Writing about Philosophy" assignment on the next page.

writing about philosophy: Defining the Self

The Assignment

This chapter has explored the deceptively complex question, "Who Am I?" One of the great ironies of life is that though we have spent our entire waking lives with ourselves, the precise nature of our self remains elusive and enigmatic. The philosophers and psychologists we have studied in this chapter have endeavored to unravel the mysteries of consciousness, personal identity, and the soul. It is likely you have found that in studying them you have gained both insight and confusion as your understanding of these issues has deepened and your questions have become more intellectually sophisticated.

This essay assignment is an opportunity to express your own views on the nature of the self in a form that is thoughtful and coherent. Begin by reflecting on the various perspectives regarding the self that you read about and discussed in this chapter. Make notes about which theories you strongly agreed and disagreed with, and do some prewriting by drafting a paragraph on each of these theories, bringing in your own experiences to support your positions. Then use these drafts to compose a paper that reflects your own synthesis of the theories. You may find that your ideas on this complex subject become clearer as you think them through in writing. By the end of the essay, the reader should have an understanding of your concept of the self and its connection to the philosophical ideas we have been examining.

 **Student Essay**

PERCEPTIONS OF SELF
by Jessie Lange

Years ago my parents met in an elevator in Manhattan, and in an instant my existence was made possible. Had my father missed that elevator, had his dentist been running late, he might never have stepped on and seen my mother in her rainbow-striped socks and miniskirt, struggling with a stack of boxes. If she had not smiled, or he had not held the lobby door or gotten up the guts to suggest coffee sometime, or if my mother had not said, "How about right now?"—if not for everything falling into place: no love, no marriage, no me. When I was two years old at a garden party, I made my way precariously across the lawn towards the sparkling rectangle of swimming pool and toppled in. All backs were turned, and only one woman saw me. She leapt in with all of her clothing on to pull me free: again, no woman, no rescue, no me. These are the stories of how I was created that circle my consciousness and that have shaped who I am today, my "self." But where do I find this "me"? Where is the self contained? And where does it come from? From my experience, it comes partially from our history. From the stories that we have been told that shape what we believe and how we see the world. A chance meeting, a near drowning. There are so many reasons that none of us should be here, but here we all are, all of these free-floating entities miraculously arrived at this place, what the author Kurt Vonnegut calls "beams of light." Our inner self, our core: invisible and fluctuating and strong. But where do we find this self? Where is it contained? And where does it come from?

David Hume contends that the self is merely a convenient term we use to designate the fleeting perceptions that pass through our minds and that in the end *all* we are is just a collection of these perceptions: nothing more and nothing less than what we see, smell, taste, touch, and hear. There are moments when this seems valid. In Marcel Proust's *In Search of Time Lost,* the protagonist tastes a madeleine cookie dipped in tea and suddenly is transported, through the taste and texture, to his childhood and everything contained within it. As B. F. Skinner claims, to a certain extent our perspectives on the world are at the mercy of our conditioned responses to our experiences. I walked in a garden one day under trees that came together over the path like a small wooden racing boat overturned on a shelf. I had taken up rowing months before, and images from my new pastime had begun to shape my perceptions. What would that arch of trees have been before I learned what rowing meant? Perhaps at the age of four or five, I would have looked up on that garden walk and seen an empty tunnel awaiting the subway train in New York City. But once I knew the weight of the wooden edge of a boat overturned on my shoulder as I carried it dripping back inside and slid it carefully into its slot, once I had seen the wooden boat shells all stacked, all in rows, those trees became the enormous ghosts of those overturned boats. My perception, the world as only I see it, myself.

■ ■ ■ **Student Essay** (continued)

As much as stories, memories of my past, and my sensory perceptions of the world have shaped who I am, I believe that ourselves must be more than *only* our memories and our perceptions, the stories that we have heard and things we have seen. Who we are is also defined by our ability to take these things in, to observe them and to understand where these beliefs and perceptions came from. We are not helpless victims of conditioning because we have the ability to *reason* and to *challenge* our life experience. Only then can we arrive at our true self, a self that is, to use Kant's term, "created" through contemplation and analysis. For example, many people might see coincidences in life as nothing more than coincidence and near accidents as nothing more than chance. I have thought about my parents' meeting, about the things in my own life that have fallen into place, and come to the conclusion that there is some order to things. This belief is not solely rational and not solely empirical but rather a combination of Descartes' *rationalism* and Locke's *empiricism*. As humans, we experience life, we think through what we have experienced *because we can*, and we arrive at a conclusion, a belief. It is this belief that is our own and that defines us. Are we always conscious of ourselves? Are we always aware of where our beliefs come from? No, of course not. Often we are caught up entirely in *doing* or we see an arch of trees and the pattern becomes something that we cannot define or put a finger on. However, the potential for examination, consciousness and understanding is always there. The potential to bring to light the forces that have shaped our lives and to examine them critically is what makes us conscious beings.

Making the unconscious conscious, however, is not where self-understanding and growth ends. Once we are able to recognize where our impressions have come from, once we step outside of our selves and become aware of *how* we are seeing the world and *why* we are seeing it as we do, we then have the opportunity to act on this analysis and to make choices that shape and form the selves that we most want to become. Jean-Paul Sartre's view of the self is as an entity that is being always projected towards the future, creating and recreating itself as it goes through reflection and choices. When we have acknowledged what has been conditioned, it is this self-consciousness that gives us the freedom to reshape our lives, to envision our ideal future self and to make the choices that will launch us in that direction. Sartre's theory of the human experience is self-perpetuating: The more insight you have into your self the more freedom you have to create who you want to become, and the more freedom you have, the deeper your insights into what it means to create and live a meaningful and fulfilling life.

For me, the issue of how our selves continue to exist after death is best understood by a belief of the ancient Romans. On a trip to the Vatican Museum in Rome, a guide explained why the Romans created so many tombs, monuments, and carvings dedicated to a single life. The ancients, he said, did not believe in a conventional afterlife, so all that remained after death was non-existence. But if you could capture even a single part of an individual—in art, in writing, in stone—so that years later, centuries later, one person would see that little bit of lost soul, then in that moment of recognition, the person who had died would continue to exist like a flash of light in the settled dust of the universe; a nonentity that flickers on like a light in the dark void of nothingness. Similarly, the Greek Olympians competed not only for a crown, for money, and for fame in the their lifetime, but for something far more pressing—immortality: for a way in which to be remembered and so "conquer" death.

John Locke goes further than many philosophers in the soul/body issue to make the claim that the self is not even tied to a single being, a single soul, but is rather a consciousness that passes from person to person—from a prince to a cobbler, from one being to another over the centuries. This makes sense in that it is the evolution of humankind, the consciousness and understanding of self that has grown and changed and evolved over thousands of years through interactions, experiences, and the questioning of life's purpose. It is a growth of self-awareness that is the product of philosophic study as ideas pass from one mind to the next.

How do our selves fit into a social context? Are we defined by our social selves? What is a more accurate measure of self—who we think we are, or whom others see us as? I believe that our self is not only defined by those around us, but the people in our lives certainly impact who we are becoming and how we see ourselves. These are the people who recognize us not simply for what we believe we are, but also for what we value about ourselves—they see us for what we can become. Like holding up a mirror, these people who take the time and have the insight and empathy to understand enough of the many facets that make up our personalities to allow us to see ourselves more clearly. I can recall vividly an evening in which a friend said to me, "You know, it's funny: You're so much different than what I first thought. You were so quiet. I thought you were just this nice quiet person, but you turned out to be not that at all. All of a sudden you just popped out. You're so crazy!" In that instant, I had the bizarre sensation of myself "popping out," springing forth. It is odd to think of it that way, but she was right—that is exactly how it felt. People have images of self: who they want to be; who they want people to think they are; what they think they truly are underneath—hidden away, trapped and unrecognized. But once that "hidden person" emerges, "pops out," it is often not what you might have thought it was. Not as serious, not as profound, but *you*.

Somehow this friend saw me, recognized me, and held up the mirror. And for the first time, perhaps, I had an almost physical sensation of myself—as though I could see it and feel it, a glowing beam of light before me. Not perfect, not profound, not all that I aspired to be and was moving towards, but me nonetheless. And at the same time, I had a sense of all the other selves around me and thus the smallness and inconsequence of my existence. It was a glimmer of me emerging as something different than what I'd once imagined: a wavering dot on the map, a flash of light somewhere in time, and one of the millions of beams of light being projected toward the future that really shouldn't be here but are here simply because an elevator arrives just when it should or a pair of hands pulls us from the suffocating waters of nonexistence.

MySearchLab Connections

Watch. Listen. Explore. Read. Mysearchlab is designed just for you. Each chapter features a customized study plan to help you learn and review key concepts and terms. Dynamic visual activities, videos, and readings found in the multimedia library will enhance your learning experience.

Here are a few questions and activities to help you understand this chapter:

1. Listen to the Interview *Mind/Body Problem* on **mysearchlab.com**   How did Descartes explain the interaction of the mind and the body?

2. Listen to the Interview *The Mind/Body Problem* with *Melvyn Bragg* on **mysearchlab.com**   Compare and contrast Plato's view of the mind and body with Cartesian dualism.

3. Read the Document *My Own Life (1776)* on **mysearchlab.com**   How did Hume's description of himself and his work impact your understanding of his beliefs about self-consciousness and self-identity?

4. Watch the Video *Hubert Dreyfus on Husserl and Heidegger* on **mysearchlab.com**   Explain what Husserl means when he claims that "the essence of the mind is its directedness."

visual summary

Know Thyself?

- The concept and nature of the "self" has been an ongoing, and evolving, subject of inquiry among philosophers since the time of Socrates. To grapple with the concept of self is to begin to explore what it is to know, to believe, to think, to be conscious.

[pp. 102–103]

The Soul Is Immortal: Socrates and Plato

- For Socrates and Plato, the self was synonymous with the soul. Every human being, they believed, possessed an immortal soul that survived the physical body.
- Plato further defines the soul or self as having three components: Reason, Physical Appetite, and Spirit (or passion). These three components may work in concert, or in opposition.

[pp. 103–109]

KEY TERM
dualistic

Descartes' Modern Perspective on the Self

- Early modern European philosophers, including René Descartes, expanded the concept of the self to include the thinking, reasoning mind. For Descartes, the act of thinking about the self—of being *self-conscious*—is in itself proof that there is a self. Descartes still demonstrates the powerful influence of Platonic thought in his distinction between the physical body (which he believes is material, mortal, and nonthinking) and an immortal, nonmaterial thinking self, governed by God's will and the laws of reason.

[pp. 111–119]

The Self Is Consciousness: Locke

- John Locke argued that consciousness—or, more specifically, self-consciousness—of our constantly perceiving self is necessary to "personal identity," or knowledge of the self as a person.
- Instead of positing that the self is immortal and separate from the body, Locke argues that our personal identity and the immortal soul in which that identity is located are very different entities.

[pp. 119–123]

KEY TERMS
rationalism
empiricism

for further reading, viewing & research

Read the Primary Source on MySearchLab

- *Phaedo,* Plato
- *Phaedrus,* Plato
- *Discourse on Method,* René Descartes
- *Meditations on First Philosophy,* René Descartes
- *An Essay Concerning Human Understanding,* John Locke
- *Prolegomena to Any Future Metaphysics,* Immanuel Kant
- *Critique of Pure Reason,* Immanuel Kant
- *Doctrine of Not-Self,* Milindapanha

Films

- *2001: A Space Odyssey* (1968) What distinguishes human beings from other animals? Humans from machines? In this science fiction film, a crew on a mission to uncover a mystery in space runs into complications when the machine they are using begins to make decisions for them.
- *Blade Runner* (1982) What does it mean to be human? In the future as depicted in this classic science fiction film, humans have developed the technology to create replicants, clones with fixed life spans that serve

people in the colonies outside Earth. When the technology backfires and the clones rebel, a blade runner, Rick Deckard (Harrison Ford) is hired to search out and terminate replicants in Los Angeles.

- ***The Diving Bell and the Butterfly*** (2007) Who does one become when one is no longer physically oneself? Based on the memoir of the same name, this film recounts the life of Jean-Dominique Bauby, a French journalist and author who was almost entirely paralyzed after suffering a stroke at age 42. The author was only able only to blink his left eyelid, and used this to communicate and write his memoir.

- ***Memento*** (2000) How is memory connected to identity? In this neo-noir psychological thriller, a man who has lost the ability to create new memories and cannot recall his most recent memories attempts to reconstruct his identity and solve the murder of his wife. The film is

There Is No Self: Hume

- David Hume went radically further than Locke to speculate that there is no self or immortal soul in the traditional sense. Our memories and experiences, Hume argued, are made up of *impressions* and *ideas* with no one "constant and invariable," unified identity. When we are not actively perceiving, or conscious of ourselves perceiving, Hume notes, there is no basis for the belief that there is any self.

[pp. 123–126]

We Construct the Self: Kant

- If Hume's view of the mind was a kind of passive "theatre" across which random experiences flitted, Kant proposed an actively engaged and synthesizing intelligence that constructs knowledge based on its experiences. This synthesizing faculty—Kant's version of the self—transcends the senses and unifies experience.

- In addition, Kant proposed a second self, the empirical self or *ego*, which consists of those traits that make us each a unique personality.

[pp. 126–131]

KEY TERM
phenomenology

The Self Is Embodied Subjectivity: Husserl and Merleau-Ponty

- Phenomenologists Edmund Husserl and Maurice Merleau-Ponty simply dismiss Cartesian dualism as a product of philosophical misunderstanding. The living, physical body and its experiences are all one, a natural synthesis, what Husserl and Merleau-Ponty called the *Lebenswelt* (a German word meaning "lived world").

[pp. 155–158]

The Self Is the Brain: Physicalism

- Materialism holds that the self is inseparable from the substance of the brain and the physiology of the body. Contemporary advances in neurophysiology allow scientists to observe the living brain as it works to process information, create ideas, and move through dream states. Philosopher Paul Churchland argues that a new, accurate, objective, and scientifically based understanding of our "selves" will "contribute substantially toward a more peaceful and humane society."

[pp. 143–154]

KEY TERMS
materialism
eliminative materialism

---

divided into two narratives—one follows his attempts to uncover the murderer, while the second moves backwards in time through a series of flashbacks.

Literature

- **The Catcher in the Rye,** J. D. Salinger. After being expelled from prep school, Holden Caulfield finds himself wandering the streets of New York City. This coming-of-age story traces the attempts of this alienated adolescent to find meaning in a world that seems empty and superficial, and to come to terms with tragedy, injustice, abuse of power, and hypocrisy.

- **Invisible Man,** Ralph Ellison. A talented young African American from a small southern town leaves home to attend college and finds himself becoming increasingly socially invisible. As he encounters racism both at school and in New York City, he addresses vital questions about his own identity as well as the identity of African Americans in the early twentieth century.

- **Life on the Color Line,** Gregory Williams. Gregory Williams was raised as white until the age of eight, when his father told him that he was of African American heritage as they were on their way to live in a predominantly black community in Muncie, Indiana. There, he found himself to be the victim of racism and prejudice. This powerful memoir raises profound questions about one's identity in the face of social constructs as the young Williams navigates his existence on the "color line" and attempts to, and ultimately succeeds in, developing a strong sense of self and thriving without dismissing either heritage.

- **Persepolis: The Story of a Childhood,** Marjane Satrapi. In this graphic memoir, Satrapi recounts her childhood in Iran during the Islamic Revolution when the fundamentalists took power. The family experiences violence and oppression, and the young Satrapi questions her own developing identity and ideals as the cultural, legal, and moral code of her country changes.

- **A Remembrance of Things Past,** Marcel Proust. In his monumental work, Proust attempted to capture a complete life. The novel addresses many themes related to consciousness and identity, including how we develop self-understanding and knowledge of other people; the role of memory and sensory perception in identity creation; phenomenological issues regarding the nature of reality; whether there is a single "self" that is consistent both in the present and across time; and how to articulate the complexity of capturing life in art.

Baron d'Holbach
Freedom is an illusion: All human actions are brought about by previous events in accordance with universal causal laws.

William James and Jean-Paul Sartre
Freedom is possible: At least some human actions are not necessarily determined by previous events in accordance with universal causal laws.

Determinism

Indeterminism

are you free?

FREEDOM AND DETERMINISM

Compatibilism

Although all human actions are brought about by previous events in accordance with universal causal laws, freedom is possible . . .

IF

W. T. Stace
. . . actions are independent of external coercion or restraint.

Moritz Schlick
. . . actions are independent of internal irrational compulsion.

◀ **Who controls your life?** The puppet, created for the Tblisi Marionette Theatre, is controlled by forces hidden from public view. In this chapter, you will explore whether this metaphor is applicable to your life and the choices you make.

4

chapter

PHILOSOPHERS AND THINKERS IN THIS CHAPTER	
Baron d'Holbach	■ 1723–1789
John Stuart Mill	■ 1806–1873
William James	■ 1842–1910
Moritz Schlick	■ 1882–1936
Walter Stace	■ 1886–1967
Jean-Paul Sartre	■ 1905–1980
Mary Daly	■ 1928–2010
Kate Millet	■ B. 1934
Daniel C. Dennett	■ B. 1942
Marilyn Frye	■ B. 1941
Jean Grimshaw	■

4.1 Are You the Master of Your Fate?

Are you free? Unquestionably, most of us *want* to believe that we are free. We connect to poet William Ernest Henley's notion that "I am the master of my fate; I am the captain of my soul"; we intend to create a bold, vibrant life through wise choices and principled commitments. Yet, at the same time, many of us believe that our freedom is restricted by forces outside our control—by the social structure or even our own unconscious minds. We may feel that we are free—and responsible—when things are going well, but that feeling changes when we experience failure; as the Chinese adage observes, "Success has a thousand fathers, but failure is an orphan."

Whether we are free is a philosophical (and psychological) question that requires thoughtful reflection and rigorous analysis. Are we able to make authentically free choices, or are our actions determined by factors beyond our control? Given exactly the same conditions or circumstances, could we have chosen otherwise than we did? Are we responsible for the choices we make and their outcomes, or should we be excused from responsibility? We will explore these central issues in this chapter. Of course, as with most philosophical explorations, we will soon see that the questions—and potential answers—are a great deal more complex than the simple conclusion "We're free" or "We're not free."

Every day we are confronted with the mystery of human action. One person commits an armed robbery, killing a guard in the process. A firefighter risks her life to save the life of an infant trapped in a burning building. A peaceful protest gets out of control and turns into a violent and destructive altercation. A respected member of the community is accused of abusing the children on the teams that he coached. A man leaps off a subway platform to save another man from an oncoming train. Two teenagers are accused of murdering their newborn infant and dumping the body in a garbage container. An eighty-four-year-old woman who spent her life cleaning the homes of others donates her life savings—$186,000—to a local college with which

Human Nature
People are born with certain basic instincts that influence how they behave.

Environmental Influences
People are shaped by their environment, conditioned by their experiences to be the kind of people they are.

Theories Explaining Human Behavior

Psychological Forces
People are governed by psychological forces, some of them unconscious, that cause them to think, feel, and act in certain ways.

Social Dynamics
People are social creatures who are influenced by the social forces around them.

Free Will
People make free choices that reflect and shape who they are, and they are responsible for the consequences of these choices.

she had no previous relationship. In each of these instances, and countless others, we struggle to understand "why" people acted the way they did. Our answers typically depend on our deepest beliefs about the nature of the human self. Some people believe that genuine freedom of choice is not always possible because our decisions and actions are determined by factors beyond our control. This view is known as **determinism**; and, at its most extreme form, "hard determinism." Hard determinists believe that every behavior can be traced to a cause, although they may disagree about what those causes are. Here are some popular explanations of human behavior that exemplify the determinist view:

Determinism The view that every event, including human actions, is brought about by previous events in accordance with universal causal laws that govern the world. Human freedom is an illusion.

12R-12210-00

- *Human nature:* "People are born with certain basic instincts that influence and determine how they behave." Based on this view, the actions described above, whether "good" or "evil," are no more than the natural expression of a *universal nature* that is genetically hardwired into every person. There is no possibility of free choice because our actions necessarily follow from our inborn nature, and we cannot be other than we are. Whether we do good or ill in life is really beyond our control, and we cannot alter our fundamental character.

- *The environment:* "People are shaped by their environment, conditioned by their experiences to be the kind of people they are." This explanation holds that behaviors are the direct products of the *life experiences* that people have. If the environment in which someone developed was deprived or abusive, then it follows that the person would act with little regard for the rights or lives of others. On the other hand, if a person was fortunate enough to grow up in a loving and nurturing environment, the good that person does is the result of this upbringing. In either case, people cannot be held responsible for how they behave because they didn't choose their environment; they were a *passive agent* molded by forces beyond their control. We should no more condemn the armed robber than we should reward the firefighter because each is merely a product of his or her environment.

- *Psychological forces:* "People are governed by psychological forces, many of them unconscious, that cause them to think, feel, and act in certain ways." Based on this point of view, the actions described above are the direct result of deep psychological impulses that have been formed by people's earliest relationships and experiences. Although these people may *think* they are choosing to do the things they are, in reality they are puppets manipulated by unseen psychological strings. So when the coach sexually abused the children on his teams, he was not actually *choosing* this reprehensible course of action, he was impelled by *psychological forces* over which he had no control. In this view, behavior results from psychological motivations, often repressed, that form the basic structure of personality. Feelings of freedom are illusory.

- *Social dynamics:* "People are social creatures who are greatly influenced by the people around them." The need to conform to the prevailing norms, to be accepted by peer groups, to please those who are close to them, to obey those in positions of authority—these and other social needs determine people's behavior and define who they are as individuals. For example, the violent actions of the initially peaceful demonstrators can be understood only by examining the dynamics of *social interaction.* Because the group as a whole is to blame, responsibility is removed from the individuals. In the same way, individuals who act illegally (or immorally) within an

Compatibilism The view that all events, including human actions, are caused. However, we can consider human actions *free* if they are the result of internal motivations, not the product of external influences or constraints.

Indeterminism The view that some events, including human actions, are not necessarily determined by previous events in accordance with universal causal laws.

Libertarianism The view that humans are able to make authentically free choices that are not determined by previous events in accordance with universal causal laws, that there is a meaningful sense that though we made one choice, we "could have done otherwise."

organization often seek to be exonerated on the grounds that they were merely acting as cogs in the machine, not independent agents. An extreme version of this occurred after World War II at the Nuremberg trials when many people accused of wartime atrocities explained that they were "only following orders."

An alternative version of determinism is called **compatibilism**, a view that has also been referred to as "soft determinism." Compatibilists agree with hard determinists that all events, including human actions, are caused. However, compatibilists assert that we can consider human actions "free" if they are the result of internal motivations, not the product of external influences or constraints. These thinkers agree with the determinists that all human behavior is caused by previous events; however, compatibilists contend that we can still distinguish between actions that are compelled by external constraints and actions that are not. Actions that are externally compelled—for example, as the result of threats—are *unfree*. In contrast, actions that are not compelled by external factors are *free*. Freedom means the opposite of compulsion: People are free if they are not prevented from acting on their unimpeded natural desires, even though these natural desires may be causally determined by factors in their personal history.

A third view of human freedom holds that we are fully able to make decisions and initiate actions independently of any influences on our thinking. This position holds that in precisely the same choice situations an individual "could have done otherwise" had he or she freely chosen to. As a result, people are absolutely responsible for what they do. This view is known as **indeterminism**. Some philosophers make a distinction between "indeterminism" and "**libertarianism**." For them, all libertarians are indeterminists but not vice versa. Indeterminism is the position that at least some of our actions are not determined, leaving open the possibility that these undetermined actions are random. The indeterminist need not admit the existence of free will, whereas this is precisely what the libertarian is committed to. Let's revisit the examples identified above and analyze them from the libertarian perspective:

Can freedom and responsibility be taught? Most people are taught to take responsibility for their actions at an early age. But some parents stress the importance of thinking independently, while others stress following authority. How might your background affect your beliefs about free will and responsibility?

- The person who committed the armed robbery and murdered the guard *freely chose* to steal money, and he is completely *responsible*. He was not compelled to act in this fashion: He could have chosen not to steal.

- The heroic firefighter *freely chose* to overcome her natural fear of death and risk her life to save someone else's, and she should be awarded full credit for her heroism.

- The subway "savior" *freely chose* to risk his life to save another's.

- The child abuser *freely chose* to surrender to his destructive sexual impulses, and he deserves to be condemned and fully punished.

- The infant-murdering teenagers *freely chose* to deal with their fear of having an unwanted child by killing it and trying to hide the body (despite having many other alternatives available), and they should be held fully responsible for their choice.

Views of Free Will	
Hard Determinism	1. All events and human actions are brought about by previous events in accordance with universal causal laws.
	2. Human freedom is an illusion.
Compatibilism	1. All events and human actions are brought about by previous events in accordance with universal causal laws.
	2. Human actions are free if they are the result of internal motivations, not the product of external influences or constraints.
Indeterminism and Libertarianism	1. At least some human actions are not determined by previous events in accordance with universal causal laws.
	2. *Indeterminist:* Human freedom is possible because some actions may be random.
	Libertarian: Human freedom is possible because people are able to make genuinely free choices by exercising their free will.

- The philanthropic senior citizen *freely chose* to donate her money to improve educational opportunities for underprivileged young people rather than spending the money on herself, and she deserves to be praised for her altruism.

In addition to these three standard positions, some thinkers are convinced that both determinists and indeterminists make valid points but represent extreme perspectives that need to be synthesized into an integrated whole. We will look at one possible synthesis at the end of the chapter.

Explore your beliefs and assumptions about human behavior and personal freedom by completing the adjacent Thinking Philosophically box. Your experience with this activity may reveal to you how complex the subject of personal freedom actually is. For example, you might find that some of your beliefs and assumptions are in apparent conflict with one another, that a conclusion you had previously felt confident about now seems less certain, and that you end up more confused about the concepts of "freedom" and "responsibility" than when you began the activity. If so, congratulations! These are healthy signs that you are thinking seriously about these issues and that you are getting below the level of superficial platitudes ("Of course I'm free—I do what I want!") where many people reside. To gain a genuinely sophisticated philosophical understanding

thinking philosophically

WHAT ARE YOUR ASSUMPTIONS ABOUT FREEDOM?

Think critically about your own assumptions regarding personal freedom by responding to the following questions:

- How would you explain the actions discussed on pages 172–174? Do you believe that people's decisions are determined by factors such as human instincts, their environment, their psychological makeup, or social dynamics? Do you think this is always the case?

- Do you believe that you can improve yourself by establishing goals and making intelligent choices to achieve those goals? If so, do you believe that you are personally responsible for both the positive and "less positive" aspects of yourself? Why or why not?

- Do you accept full responsibility for all of the moral choices you have made, even those you may regret having made? Why or why not?

of the subject of freedom, you need to first abandon the simplistic notions and clichés that are so prevalent in our culture and have the courage to openly and honestly explore these crucial yet challenging themes. As you enhance your understanding of freedom, your evolving insights may have a significant impact on your own life.

4.2 Determinism

The determinist view of human freedom is typically based on the scientific model of the physical universe. Most modern cultures assume that the universe is governed by causal laws that can be discovered and that we can use to predict what will happen in the future. When you set your alarm clock, adjust the thermostat, turn off the light switch, bring an umbrella, turn the key in the ignition of your car, make plans for the evening after the sun disappears—all of these actions and countless others are based on your general belief that everything that occurs in the physical world has a cause (or causes) and that by discovering these causal relationships between events, we can predict and influence what will happen in the future. Imagine your surprise if your auto mechanic informed you that there was no cause for your car's difficulties, nor would any cause ever be discovered, so you might as well junk it. Time for a new mechanic, you would likely conclude!

Similarly, when you take vitamins, eat a balanced diet, limit your alcohol intake, take prescribed antibiotics, and get enough sleep—all of these actions, and many others—you are acting on the belief that your physical body is also governed by causal relationships. Again, imagine your surprise if your physician informed you that although you may be feeling ill, there was nothing causing your sickness and so there was absolutely nothing that could be done to improve your health. It's likely that you would seek a second opinion, don't you think?

Those who take a determinist view of personal freedom use these generally accepted areas of causal determinism as a framework for understanding the mainsprings of human action. Their reasoning can be summarized thus:

- Events in the physical universe consistently display well-defined causal connections. There are scientific exceptions to this precise causal determinism at subatomic levels, but it's a scientific perspective generally accepted for the rest of the universe.
- Events in the biological realm also consistently display causal connections, though as we saw in the last chapter, the complex and intimate relationship between the mind and body makes this a much more complicated situation.
- Because humans are a part of the physical universe and the biological realm, it's reasonable to assume that all of our actions (and the choices that initiated the actions) are also causally determined, eliminating the possibility of free choice.

Just as your alarm clock lacks the possibility to choose freely whether it will sound the alarm, so you lack the power to choose freely, because everything that you think, feel, and do is caused by other factors beyond your control. This determinist view has enjoyed passionate support from a wide variety of individuals, including psychologists like B. F. Skinner and Sigmund Freud, and a number of prominent philosophers, including **John Stuart Mill**. In his "On Causation and Necessity," Mill summarized the determinist position:

> *Given the motives which are present to an individual's mind, and given likewise the character and disposition of the individual, the manner in which he will act*

John Stuart Mill
(1806–1873). British philosopher known for his writing on utilitarianism, the view that we should act to promote the greatest amount of happiness and create the least amount of suffering possible for the greatest number of people.

might be unerringly inferred; that if we knew the person thoroughly, and knew all the inducements which are acting upon him, we could foretell his conduct with as much certainty as we can predict any physical event. . . . No one who believed that he knew thoroughly the circumstances of any case, and the characters of the different persons concerned, would hesitate to foretell how all of them would act. Whatever degree of doubt he may in fact feel, arises from the uncertainty whether he really knows the circumstances, or the character of some one or other of the persons, with the degree of accuracy required; but by no means from thinking that if he did know these things, there could be any uncertainty what the conduct would be.

Loeb and Leopold in the courtroom: Are we victims of circumstances? Clarence Darrow convinced the clients to plead guilty to their crimes so that one person—the judge—would feel the full weight of responsibility for deciding whether to apply the death penalty. The judge chose life imprisonment over the death penalty, but he claimed that the determinist argument was not a factor in his decision; rather, it was "beyond the province of this court" to "predicate ultimate responsibility for human acts." Do you agree that the court cannot decide why criminals act as they do?

Determinism has worked its way into other aspects of our culture, such as the criminal justice system. For example, in the early part of the twentieth century, the dramatic case of Richard Loeb and Nathan Leopold transfixed the United States. These two young men, who were from privileged families and who had attended the best schools, abducted and murdered a fourteen-year-old boy just to experience the thrill of killing someone. The country was outraged at such a cold-blooded and senseless killing, and public opinion favored giving them the death penalty. Hired to defend them, and save their lives, was the famed attorney, Clarence Darrow. In his famous summation, he passionately employed the hard determinist argument to convince the judge that the defendants were victims of circumstances beyond their control, not autonomous agents making free choices:

We are all helpless. . . . This weary old world goes on, begetting, with birth and with living and with death; and all of it is blind from the beginning to the end. I do not know what it was that made these boys do this mad act, but I do know there is a reason for it. I know they did not beget themselves. I know that any one of an infinite number of causes reaching back to the beginning might be working out in these boys' minds, whom you are asked to hang in malice and hatred and injustice. . . .

Nature is strong and she is pitiless. She works in her own mysterious way, and we are her victims. We have not much to do with it ourselves. Nature takes this job in hand, and we play our parts. In the words of old Omar Khayyam, we are:

> *But helpless pieces in the game He plays*
> *Upon this checkerboard of nights and days:*
> *Hither and thither moves, and checks, and slays,*
> *And one by one back in the closet lays.*

What had this boy to do with it? He was not his own father, he was not his own mother; he was not his own grandparents. All of this was handed to him. He did not surround himself with governesses and wealth. He did not make himself. And yet he is to be compelled to pay.

Darrow's argument moved the courtroom, and many other defense lawyers have used similar approaches in the decades since.

However, most people don't live their lives based on the assumption that all of their thoughts and actions are determined and, as a result, unfree. Most people act as if they—and others—have some degree of personal freedom, believing that it makes sense:

- to choose to improve yourself.
- to hold people morally responsible and educate them to be more enlightened.
- to seek to achieve spiritual transformation and enlightenment.
- to work to create a better world.
- to raise children to be thoughtful individuals who accept responsibility.
- to hold wrongdoers responsible and to punish and/or rehabilitate them.

For the determinist, these commonly held ideals are based on an illusion of freedom. Yet even though determinism may rub against our deeply held beliefs, to truly understand the nature of human freedom we must approach the determinist argument with an open mind and subject it to philosophical analysis. Consider, then, one of the most compelling and entertaining defenses of determinism, presented by the French philosopher **Paul Henri Thiry, Baron d'Holbach**, in his book *The System of Nature*, which his critics called "The Atheist's Bible."

Paul Henri Thiry, Baron d'Holbach (1723–1789). This French philosopher and translator played a major role in the Enlightenment as a contributor to the *Encyclopedie*, a compendium of progressive ideas and knowledge. He published his own radical writings anonymously, and his *System of Nature* and *Common Sense* were publicly condemned and burned. *(Paul Henry Tiry ([1723–1789]) Baron d'Holbach, 1766 [wic on paper] by Carmontelle [Louis Carrogis] [1717–1806]*

Baron d'Holbach, from *The System of Nature*

Motives and the Determination of the Will

In whatever manner man is considered, he is connected to universal nature, and submitted to the necessary and immutable laws that she imposes on all the beings she contains, according to their peculiar essences or to the respective properties with which, without consulting them, she endows each particular species. Man's life is a line that nature commands him to describe upon the surface of the earth, without his ever being able to swerve from it, even for an instant. He is born without his own consent; his organization does in nowise depend upon himself; his ideas come to him involuntarily; his habits are in the power of those who cause him to contract them; he is unceasingly modified by causes, whether visible or concealed, over which he has no control, which necessarily regulate his mode of existence, give the hue to his way of thinking, and determine his manner of acting. He is good or bad, happy or miserable, wise or foolish, reasonable or irrational, without his will being for anything in these various states. Nevertheless, in spite of the shackles by which he is bound, it is pretended he is a free agent, or that independent of the causes by which he is moved, he determines his own will, and regulates his own condition.

However slender the foundation of this opinion, of which everything ought to point out to him the error, it is current at this day and passes for an incontestable truth with a great number of people, otherwise extremely enlightened; it is the basis of religion, which, supposing relations between man and the unknown being she has placed above nature, has been incapable of imagining how man could merit reward or deserve punishment from this being if he was not a free agent. Society has been believed interested in this system; because an idea has gone abroad, that if all the actions of man were to be contemplated as necessary, the right of punishing those who injure their associates would no longer exist. At length human vanity accommodated itself to a hypothesis which, unquestionably, appears to distinguish man from all other physical beings, by assigning to him the special privilege of total independence of all other causes, but of which a very little reflection would have shown him the impossibility. . . .

The keystone of d'Holbach's view is that we are inextricably "connected to universal nature" and so are subject to the "necessary and immutable laws that she imposes on all the beings she contains." In other words, when we consider the natural order, it is clear that humans are woven into the fabric of the universe with countless threads. We fit into the natural world along with all other living beings. And because we assume that all other dimensions of the universe, both physical and biological, are subject to causal laws that necessarily define their natures and relationships, it only makes sense to include ourselves in this natural causal system. Why should humans alone be considered exceptions to immutable laws that govern every other aspect of the universe? We shouldn't, according to d'Holbach, any more than we should believe that certain people are exempt from the law of gravity.

D'Holbach acknowledges that humans don't believe or act as if their thinking actions are causally determined, and he even cites the arguments for indeterminism that we have already explored. It's true, he observes, that cultural beliefs like religion, morality, and criminal justice are founded on the concepts of personal freedom—it's just that the foundation of these beliefs is wrong. Simply wanting something to be true doesn't make it true. By operating as if we are free agents, we are similar to actors playing a role, perpetuating an illusion that everyone wants to believe.

But what about our "will"? Isn't that independent of the causal laws of the universe? Absolutely not, according to d'Holbach!

> The will, as we have elsewhere said, is a modification of the brain, by which it is disposed to action, or prepared to give play to the organs. This will is necessarily determined by the qualities, good or bad, agreeable or painful, of the object or the motive that acts upon his senses, or of which the idea remains with him, and is resuscitated by his memory. In consequence, he acts necessarily, his action is the result of the impulse he receives either from the motive, from the object, or from the idea which has modified his brain, or disposed his will. When he does not act according to this impulse, it is because there comes some new cause, some new motive, some new idea, which modifies his brain in a different manner, gives him a new impulse, determines his will in another way, by which the action of the former impulse is suspended: thus, the sight of an agreeable object, or its idea, determines his will to set him in action to procure it; but if a new object or a new idea more powerfully attracts him, it gives a new direction to his will, annihilates the effect of the former, and prevents the action by which it was to be procured. This is the mode in which reflection, experience, reason, necessarily arrests or suspends the action of man's will: without this he would of necessity have followed the anterior impulse which carried him towards a then desirable object. In all this he always acts according to necessary laws from which he has no means of emancipating himself.

Baron d'Holbach,
from *The System of Nature*

> " [Man] always acts according to necessary laws. . . . "

Writing 250 years ago, d'Holbach clearly did not have access to the latest in brain/mind research, but his logic is still clear. Our "will," along with all of the other mental states of consciousness such as "motive," "reflection," and "reason," are produced by the chemistry of the brain, and they are necessary products of the brain's interaction with the environment. Certain sets of circumstances in the environment produce one sort of mental response; other sets of circumstances produce a different kind of mental response. In either case, there is not room for personal freedom: the particular mental states—will, motive, reflection, reason, and so on—are determined by necessary causal laws. d'Holbach goes on to provide an example to illustrate his reasoning.

Baron d'Holbach, from *The System of Nature*

If when tormented with violent thirst, he figures to himself in idea, or really perceives a fountain, whose limpid streams might cool his feverish want, is he sufficient master of himself to desire or not to desire the object competent to satisfy so lively a want? It will no doubt be conceded, that it is impossible he should not be desirous to satisfy it; but it will be said—if at this moment it is announced to him that the water he so ardently desires is poisoned, he will, notwithstanding his vehement thirst, abstain from drinking it: and it has, therefore, been falsely concluded that he is a free agent. The fact, however, is, that the motive in either case is exactly the same: his own conservation. The same necessity that determined him to drink before he knew the water was deleterious upon this new discovery equally determined him not to drink; the desire of conserving himself either annihilates or suspends the former impulse; the second motive becomes stronger than the preceding, that is, the fear of death, or the desire of preserving himself, necessarily prevails over the painful sensation caused by his eagerness to drink: but, it will be said, if the thirst is very parching, an inconsiderate man without regarding the danger will risk swallowing the water. Nothing is gained by this remark: in this case, the anterior impulse only regains the ascendancy; he is persuaded that life may possibly be longer preserved, or that he shall derive a greater good by drinking the poisoned water than by enduring the torment, which, to his mind, threatens instant dissolution; thus the first becomes the strongest and necessarily urges him on to action. Nevertheless, in either case, whether he partakes of the water, or whether he does not, the two actions will be equally necessary; they will be the effect of that motive which finds itself most puissant; which consequently acts in the most coercive manner upon his will.

D'Holbach's analysis of this "thirst" example is in response to indeterminists who want to argue that this kind of example proves the existence of free will. The indeterminist's reasoning is something like this: If you place a bowl of water before a thirsty animal like a dog, he will drink. His action is the result of inborn instinct, conditioned behavior, brain chemistry—not free will. *However*, if you present a cold drink to a thirsty human, and then tell her that the drink is poisoned, she will likely *choose freely* not to drink, overriding her instinct to quench her thirst.

Far from proving the existence of free will, d'Holbach believes that the example simply strengthens his case for determinism. The impulse to drink and the impulse not to drink upon discovering that the water is poisoned are both driven by the same need—self-preservation. And it is this underlying need that causes the individual to drink or not to drink. D'Holbach's model of human functioning is mechanical: Each action is the net result of the forces that are driving it. In the case of conflicting forces, it is the strongest ones that will win out. Most rational, well-adjusted people will be motivated to refrain from drinking the poisoned water because they don't want to die. This is not a free choice, simply the outcome of their psychological state, undergirded by their brain chemistry. But people who are emotionally disturbed, who are not thinking clearly, or who are self-destructive may very well drink the poisoned water. Again, their decision is not freely made but rather is determined by their psychological state. That's why d'Holbach is able to conclude that "the actions of fools are as necessary as the most prudent individuals."

In passages foreshadowing modern theories in psychology, anthropology, and philosophy, d'Holbach goes on to further develop his view that we are completely shaped by social forces beyond our control.

In short, the actions of man are never free; they are always the necessary consequence of his temperament, of the received ideas, and of the notions, either true or false, which he has formed to himself of happiness; of his opinions strengthened by example, by education, and by daily experience. So many crimes are witnessed on the earth only because every thing conspires to render man vicious and criminal; the religion he has adopted, his government, his education, the examples set before him, irresistibly drive him on to evil: under these circumstances, morality preaches virtue to him in vain. In those societies where vice is esteemed, where crime is crowned, where venality is constantly recompensed, where the most dreadful disorders are punished only in those who are too weak to enjoy the privilege of committing them with impunity, the practice of virtue is considered nothing more than a painful sacrifice of happiness. Such societies chastise, in the lower orders, those excesses which they respect in the higher ranks; and frequently have the injustice to condemn those in the penalty of death, whom public prejudices, maintained by constant example, have rendered criminal.

Man, then, is not a free agent in any one instant of his life; he is necessarily guided in each step by those advantages, whether real or fictitious, that he attaches to the objects by which his passions are roused: these passions themselves are necessary in a being who unceasingly tends towards his own happiness; their energy is necessary, since that depends on his temperament; his temperament is necessary, because it depends on the physical elements which enter into his composition; the modification of this temperament is necessary, as it is the infallible and inevitable consequence of the impulse he receives from the incessant action of moral and physical beings.

Baron d'Holbach,
from The System of Nature

> **Man, then, is not a free agent in any one instant of his life. . . .**

Humans, in other words, are simply malleable lumps of clay that are shaped and molded by their personal and cultural experiences. If any one of us had grown up in a different family or a different culture, we would be radically different because the shaping forces would be different—not because of any choices that we made. But what about situations in which we choose one of a number of options after careful thought and analysis—doesn't this "prove" that personal freedom is possible? Definitely not, d'Holbach argues. We are compelled by "interior motives" to make that choice.

Imagine that you are engaged in a conversation with d'Holbach, trying to convince him that you are free. "I could throw myself out of that window if I wanted to—it's my choice!" you say. "That proves I'm free!" "Not really," replies d'Holbach. "Your choice is completely determined. If you retain your rationality and sanity, then I can assure you that your forces of self-preservation will prevent you from throwing yourself out of the window. On the other hand, if you are irrational and emotionally disturbed, then these mental forces will compel you to defenestrate yourself. As a third possibility, you may be rational but so intent on proving me wrong that you are willing to sacrifice your life by hurling yourself out of the window. In any case, your action will be necessarily determined by whichever psychic forces are the strongest, not by a free choice on your part."

D'Holbach goes on to explore another common definition of free choice, namely, the absence of constraint. In other words, people often say an action is free if the action is not being compelled by outside forces, a philosophical position known as "compatibilism" that we will explore more fully in the next section. D'Holbach dismisses this distinction as irrelevant. It's difficult not to be amused by d'Holbach's use of Socrates' death as an example to prove his point, an analysis so contrary to Socrates' beliefs regarding the nature of free choice and personal responsibility that Socrates himself doubtless would have been fascinated by d'Holbach's audacity!

Socrates' decision to accept the sentence of death rather than cease his teachings or be banished to another country is considered by many (including Socrates, in all likelihood) to be the paradigm of a thoughtful, principled, and *free* choice. For d'Holbach to use this archetypal moment as evidence to support his belief in causal determinism is dramatically ironic.

Baron d'Holbach,
from *The System of Nature*

Absence of Restraint Is Not Absence of Necessity

The partisans of the system of free agency appear ever to have confounded constraint with necessity. Man believes he acts as a free agent, every time he does not see any thing that places obstacles to his actions; he does not perceive that the motive which causes him to will, is always necessary and independent of himself. A prisoner loaded with chains is compelled to remain in prison; but he is not a free agent in the desire to emancipate himself; his chains prevent him from acting, but they do not prevent him from willing; he would save himself if they would loose his fetters; but he would not save himself as a free agent; fear or the idea of punishment would be sufficient motives for his action.

Man may, therefore, cease to be restrained, without, for that reason, becoming a free agent. In whatever manner he acts, he will act necessarily, according to motives by which he shall be determined. He may be compared to a heavy body that finds itself arrested in its descent by any obstacle whatever. Take away this obstacle, it will gravitate or continue to fall; but who shall say this dense body is free to fall or not? Is not its descent the necessary effect of its own specific gravity? The virtuous Socrates submitted to the laws of his country, although they were unjust; and though the doors of his jail were left open to him, he would not save himself; but in this he did not act as a free agent. The invisible chains of opinion, the secret love of decorum, the inward respect for the laws, even when they were iniquitous, the fear of tarnishing his glory, kept him in his prison; they were motives sufficiently powerful with this enthusiast for virtue, to induce him to wait death with tranquility; it was not in his power to save himself, because he could find no potential motive to bring him to depart, even for an instant, from those principles to which his mind was accustomed.

D'Holbach's sophisticated analysis foreshadows important elements of the contemporary discussion regarding free choice. To begin with, d'Holbach distinguishes **"external" constraints** on our free choice from **"internal" constraints**. For the person behind bars and shackled in chains, freedom of choice is clearly circumscribed. He can't stroll down to Ben & Jerry's for an ice cream cone, take a leisurely walk in the park, or make an appointment for a pedicure. Philosophers who are compatibilists argue that these external constraints are limiting his natural freedom of choice and, when they are removed—for example, on being released from prison—he is then able to make these free choices that are consistent with his own natural desires. D'Holbach disagrees. Whether in prison or out, the man's actions are still causally determined in exactly the same way: It's just that the context has changed. Again he uses an analogy from physics: We may suspend an object in midfall by arresting its descent; but, as soon as we remove the support, the object will continue to fall. It's the same with humans: The man in prison is not free, and when he gets out of prison he's still not free because in both cases his actions are caused by inexorable and irresistible forces of nature.

D'Holbach uses Socrates' death to argue that internal constraints are just as powerful as external constraints, if not as obvious. Although Socrates had a number

External constraints External forces that limit human freedom, such as incarceration, threats, or coercion.

Internal constraints Limits on freedom that are within the individual such as compulsions, obsessions, or uncontrolled anxiety.

of opportunities to escape the external constraints of his death sentence, he didn't take advantage of them because internal constraints kept him from fleeing or pleading for his life. D'Holbach maintains that Socrates "did not act as a free agent" because "the invisible chains of opinion, the secret love of decorum, the inward respect for the laws, even when they were iniquitous, the fear of tarnishing his glory, kept him in his prison; they were motives sufficiently powerful with this enthusiast for virtue, to induce him to wait death with tranquility." Socrates' entire history led up to the end of his life, and his "choice" to drink the hemlock was determined by all of the elements of his personality, as d'Holbach contends: ". . . it was not in his power to save himself, because he could find no potential motive to bring him to depart, even for an instant, from those principles to which his mind was accustomed."

Most people in Western societies are convinced that they have at least some degree of freedom, some power to direct their destiny and make independent choices based on their needs and desires. How does d'Holbach explain this nearly universal belief in freedom? It doesn't seem adequate to simply assert that all of these people are suffering from a mass illusion of being free. D'Holbach's explanation is that people are not able to recognize the causal necessity of their actions because the human mind is so infinitely complex. This complexity makes a clear causal analysis of their behavior nearly impossible to achieve, and it contributes to the inaccurate belief that free choice is possible. D'Holbach explains:

Are free choices an illusion? D'Holbach concludes his essay with a striking metaphor: We are all swimming in the river of the universe, carried along by powerful currents of which we are often unaware. Sometimes we believe we're acting freely by struggling momentarily against the current, but in the end we are simply carried downstream, trying to keep our heads above water. Evaluate the effectiveness of this metaphor in explaining your own experience in life. What metaphor would you use to explain your own experience of moving through life?

The Complexity of Human Conduct and the Illusion of Free Agency

Baron d'Holbach, from *The System of Nature*

It is the great complication of motion in man, it is the variety of his action, it is the multiplicity of causes that move him, whether simultaneously or in continual succession, that persuades him he is a free agent. If all his motions were simple, if the causes that move him did not confound themselves with each other, if they were distinct, if his machine were less complicated, he would perceive that all his actions were necessary, because he would be enabled to recur instantly to the cause that made him act. A man who should be always obliged to go towards the west, would always go on that side; but he would feel that, in so going, he was not a free agent. If he had another sense, as his actions or his motion, augmented by a sixth, would be still more varied and much more complicated, he would believe himself still more a free agent than he does with his five senses . . .

Fatality is the eternal, the immutable, the necessary order, established in nature; or the indispensable connexion of causes that act, with the effects they operate. Conforming to this order, heavy bodies fall, light bodies rise; that which is analogous in matter reciprocally attracts; that which is heterogeneous mutually repels; man congregates himself in society, modifies each his fellow; becomes either virtuous or wicked either contributes to his mutual happiness, or reciprocates his misery; either loves his neighbour, or hates his companion necessarily, according to the manner in which the one acts upon the other. From whence it may be seen, that the same necessity which regulates the physical, also regulates the moral world, in which every thing is in consequence submitted to fatality. Man, in running over, frequently without his own knowledge, often in spite of himself, the route which nature has marked out for him, resembles a swimmer who is obliged to follow the current that carries him along. He believes himself a free agent, because he sometimes consents, sometimes does not consent, to glide with the stream, which, notwithstanding, always hurries him forward; he believes himself the master of his condition, because he is obliged to use his arms under the fear of sinking.

thinking philosophically

DO YOU CHOOSE FREELY?

- Consider a situation in which you felt you were at a crossroads, having to decide what path to take. D'Holbach argues that whatever choice you made, you *had* to make that choice because of the circumstances and motivations driving your action. Do you agree with this analysis? Why or why not? Do you believe that if you were able to be placed in an identical situation (with no recollection of the initial situation) that you would have the freedom to choose differently, or would your choice be the same? Why or why not?

- Imagine that you are engaged in a discussion with a determinist like d'Holbach over your freedom to choose. If that person says to you, "I know that you would never _____ because of the person you are," and you then go and _____, does that prove that you are capable of free choice? Why or why not?

- How do you think Socrates would respond to d'Holbach's suggestion that in accepting his death sentence, he was not making a free choice?

- D'Holbach contends that philosophers have made the mistake of believing that human *will* is "the original motive of his actions." Instead, d'Holbach believes that the *self* is passive, serving only as a vehicle for the interplay of psychic forces that determine one's thoughts, feelings, and actions. How does this analysis compare to your own experiences? When you initiate an action, such as rousing yourself from sleep, do you have the sense that your *self* is a passive spectator, a "theatre" (in Hume's terms) for psychic forces? Or are you convinced that your *self* is actively "willing" your actions?

< READING CRITICALLY >

Analyzing Baron d'Holbach on the Illusion of Freedom

- D'Holbach's core explanation of why people don't readily see and acknowledge that their actions are causally determined is because their minds are so complex. Do you find this explanation persuasive? Why or why not?

- Seen from another perspective, could the complexity of the human mind be seen as an argument supporting a belief in free choice? How? Would it be reasonable to argue that d'Holbach is trying to impose an overly simplistic model onto the rich complexity of human experience?

- D'Holbach's entire case for determinism is based on applying a causal model used in understanding the physical universe to the realm of human experience and behavior. How successful do you think this approach is?

- Some philosophers have argued that the concept of "cause" is appropriate for the physical universe but not for human behavior. Instead of "cause," they maintain that we should use the concept "reason," which does not have the same deterministic implications as "cause." Do you think that this criticism of determinism makes sense? Why or why not?

4.3 Compatibilism

There's no question that d'Holbach's unrelenting determinism might lead to some potentially disturbing conclusions, as he freely admits. If d'Holbach's frontal assault on free will is successful, doesn't that have the culminating effect of draining out of our lives many of the qualities that give it meaning, rendering us little better than complex automatons just going through the motions of living?

These are, in fact, disturbing possibilities even to those thinkers who are scientifically inclined in their approach to the human mind and will. And so, beginning with David Hume, some thinkers have modified the determinist position, arguing that free choice is possible even as they endorse the general deterministic assumption that "All events and human actions are brought about by previous events in accordance with universal causal laws." Because the goal of this approach is to find a common ground between "hard" determinism and indeterminism (or libertarianism), it has been given the name "compatibilism" by its supporters and the somewhat less complimentary "soft determinism" by its detractors. In either case, compatibilism is a worthy effort to understand the nature of personal freedom and one that deserves our careful consideration.

External Constraints May Limit Freedom: Stace

We'll begin by exploring some passages from the Anglo-American philosopher **W. T. Stace**'s book, *Religion and the Modern Mind*. Although Stace is a determinist in the tradition of d'Holbach, he nevertheless wants to establish the existence of free will and personal responsibility within this deterministic framework.

> ### W. T. Stace, from *Religion and the Modern Mind*
>
> I shall first discuss the problem of free will, for it is certain that if there is no free will there can be no morality. Morality is concerned with what men ought and ought not to do. But if a man has no freedom to choose what he will do, if whatever he does is done under compulsion, then it does not make sense to tell him that he ought not to have done what he did and that he ought to do something different. All moral precepts would in such case be meaningless. Also if he acts always under compulsion, how can he be held morally responsible for his actions? How can he, for example, be punished for what he could not help doing?
>
> It is to be observed that those learned professors of philosophy or psychology who deny the existence of free will do so only in their professional moments and in their studies and lecture rooms. For when it comes to doing anything practical, even of the most trivial kind, they invariably behave as if they and others were free. They inquire from you at dinner whether you will choose this dish or that dish. They will ask a child why he told a lie, and will punish him for not having chosen the way of truthfulness. All of which is inconsistent with a disbelief in free will. This should cause us to suspect that the problem is not a real one; and this, I believe, is the case. The dispute is merely verbal, and is due to nothing but a confusion about the meanings of words. It is what is now fashionably called a semantic problem.

W.T. Stace (1886–1967). This British philosopher wrote influential books on Hegel, mysticism, aesthetics, and philosophy of religion. His books include *Mysticism and Philosophy* and *The Meaning of Beauty*.

Stace's introduction reads as if it could have been written by a libertarian, not a determinist, a measure of his concern that extreme determinism is a philosophical dead end. To begin, Stace thinks it is clear that a commitment to *hard determinism* undermines the reality of the moral enterprise in human affairs because, if free will is indeed an illusion, then it makes no sense to encourage people to make enlightened moral choices nor to hold them morally responsible when they fail to. But Stace doesn't think hard determinists, even the most vocal like d'Holbach, actually believe the philosophical theory they have constructed. Why? Because, Stace contends, if we examine their personal lives, we find that these so-called disbelievers in free will actually—in their lived experience—think, behave, and live their lives as if the reality of making free choices was never in doubt. How does one explain this philosophical hypocrisy? Stace thinks the apparent conflict can be traced to a confusion in language use.

W. T. Stace, from *Religion and the Modern Mind*

Throughout the modern period, until quite recently, it was assumed, both by the philosophers who denied free will and by those who defended it, that *determinism is inconsistent with free will.* If a man's actions were wholly determined by chains of causes stretching back into the remote past, so that they could be predicted beforehand by a mind which knew all the causes, it was assumed that they could not in that case be free. This implies that a certain definition of actions done from free will was assumed, namely that there are actions *not* wholly determined by causes or predictable beforehand. Let us shorten this by saying that free will was defined as meaning indeterminism. This is the incorrect definition which has led to the denial of free will. As soon as we see what the true definition is we shall find that the question whether the world is deterministic, as Newtonian science implied, or in a measure indeterministic, as current physics teaches, is wholly irrelevant to the problem.

Of course, there is a sense in which one can define a word arbitrarily in any way one pleases. But a definition may nevertheless be called correct or incorrect. It is correct if it accords with a *common usage* of the word defined. It is incorrect if it does not. And if you give an incorrect definition, absurd and untrue results are likely to follow. For instance, there is nothing to prevent you from arbitrarily defining a man as a five-legged animal, but this is incorrect in the sense that it does not accord with the ordinary meaning of the word. Also it has the absurd result of leading to a denial of the existence of men. This shows that *common usage is the criterion for deciding whether a definition is correct or not.* And this is the principle which I shall apply to free will. I shall show that indeterminism is not what is meant by the phrase "free will" *as it is commonly used.* And I shall attempt to discover the correct definition by inquiring how the phrase is used in ordinary conversation.

Here are a few samples of how the phrase might be used in ordinary conversation. It will be noticed that they include cases in which the question whether a man acted with free will is asked in order to determine whether he was morally and legally responsible for his acts.

> **Jones:** I once went without food for a week.
> **Smith:** Did you do that of your own free will?
> **Jones:** No. I did it because I was lost in a desert and could find no food.

But suppose that the man who had fasted was Mahatma Gandhi. The conversation might then have gone:

> **Gandhi:** I once fasted for a week.
> **Smith:** Did you do that of your own free will?
> **Gandhi:** Yes. I did it because I wanted to compel the British Government to give India its independence.

Take another case. Suppose that I had stolen some bread, but that I was as truthful as George Washington. Then, if I were charged with the crime in court, some exchange of the following sort might take place:

> **Judge:** Did you steal the bread of your own free will?
> **Stace:** Yes. I stole it because I was hungry.

Or in different circumstances the conversation might run:

Judge: Did you steal of your own free will?

Stace: No. I stole because my employer threatened to beat me if I did not.

At a recent murder trial in Trenton some of the accused had signed confessions, but afterwards asserted that they had done so under police duress. The following exchange might have occurred:

Judge: Did you sign this confession of your own free will?

Prisoner: No. I signed it because the police beat me up.

Now suppose that a philosopher had been a member of the jury. We could imagine this conversation taking place in the jury room.

Foreman of the jury: The prisoner says he signed the confession because he was beaten, and not of his own free will.

Philosopher: This is quite irrelevant to the case. There is no such thing as free will.

Foreman: Do you mean to say that it makes no difference whether he signed because his conscience made him want to tell the truth or because he was beaten?

Philosopher: None at all. Whether he was caused to sign by a beating or by some desire of his own—the desire to tell the truth, for example—in either case his signing was causally determined, and therefore in neither case did he act of his own free will. Since there is no such thing as free will, the question whether he signed of his own free will ought not to be discussed by us.

The foreman and the rest of the jury would rightly conclude that the philosopher must be making some mistake. What sort of a mistake could it be? There is only one possible answer. The philosopher must be using the phrase "free will" in some peculiar way of his own which is not the way in which men usually use it when they wish to determine a question of moral responsibility. That is, he must be using an incorrect definition of it as implying action not determined by causes. Suppose a man left his office at noon, and were questioned about it. Then we might hear this:

Jones: Did you go out of your own free will?

Smith: Yes. I went out to get my lunch.

But we might hear:

Jones: Did you leave your office of your own free will?

Smith: No. I was forcibly removed by the police.

We have now collected a number of cases of actions which, in the ordinary usage of the English language, would be called cases in which people have acted of their own free will. We should also say in all these cases that they *chose* to act as they did. We should also say that they could have acted otherwise, if they had chosen. For instance, Mahatma Gandhi was not compelled to fast; he chose to do so. He could have eaten if he had wanted to. When Smith went out to get his lunch, he chose to do so. He could have stayed and done some more work, if he had wanted to. We have also collected a number of cases of the opposite kind. They are cases in which men were not able to exercise their free will. They had no choice. They were compelled to do as they did. The man in the desert did not fast of his own free will. He had no choice in the matter. He was compelled to fast because there was nothing for him to eat. And so with the other cases. It ought to be quite easy, by an inspection of these cases, to tell what we ordinarily mean when we say that a man did or did not exercise free will. We ought therefore to be able to extract from them the proper definition of the term. Let us put the cases in a table:

Free Acts	**Unfree Acts**
Gandhi fasting because he wanted to free India.	The man fasting in the desert because there was no food.
Stealing bread because one is hungry.	Stealing because one's employer threatened to beat one.
Signing a confession because one wanted to tell the truth.	Signing because the police beat one.
Leaving the office because one wanted one's lunch.	Leaving because forcibly removed.

It is obvious that to find the correct definition of free acts we must discover what characteristic is common to all the acts in the left-hand column, and is, at the same time, absent from all the acts in the right-hand column. This characteristic which all free acts have, and which no unfree acts have, will be the defining characteristic of free will.

Is being uncaused, or not being determined by causes, the characteristic of which we are in search? It cannot be, because although it is true that all the acts in the right-hand column have causes, such as the beating by the police or the absence of food in the desert, so also do the acts in the left-hand column. Mr. Gandhi's fasting was caused by his desire to free India, the man leading his office by his hunger, and so on. Moreover, there is no reason to doubt that these causes of the free acts were in turn caused by prior conditions, and that these were again the results of causes, and so on back indefinitely into the past. Any physiologist can tell us the causes of hunger. What caused Mr. Gandhi's tremendously powerful desire to free India is no doubt more difficult to discover. But it must have had causes. Some of them may have lain in peculiarities of his glands or brain, others in his past experiences, others in his heredity, others in his education. Defenders of free will have usually tended to deny such facts. But to do so is plainly a case of special pleading, which is unsupported by any scrap of evidence. The only reasonable view is that all human actions, both those which are freely done and those which are not, are either wholly determined by causes, or at least as much determined as other events in nature. It may be true, as the physicists tell us, that nature is not as deterministic as was once thought. But whatever degree of determinism prevails in the world, human actions appear to be as much determined as anything else. And if this is so, it cannot be the case that what distinguishes actions freely chosen from those which are not free is that the latter are determined by causes while the former are not. Therefore, being uncaused or being undetermined by causes, must be an incorrect definition of free will.

What, then, is the difference between acts which are freely done and those which are not? What is the characteristic which is present to all the acts in the left-hand column and absent from all those in the right-hand column? Is it not obvious that, although both sets of actions have causes, the causes of those in the left-hand column are *of a different kind* from the causes of those in the right-hand column? The free acts are all caused by desires, or motives, or by some sort of internal psychological states of the agent's mind. The unfree acts, on the other hand, are all caused by physical forces or physical conditions, outside the agent. Police arrest means physical force exerted from the outside; the absence of food in the desert is a physical condition of the outside world. We may therefore frame

Mahatma Gandhi (1869–1948). A political and spiritual leader, Gandhi helped India achieve independence through nonviolent civil protest and disobedience. What were the factors in his background that influenced his decisions? Were these choices free?

the following rough definitions. *Acts freely done are those whose immediate causes are psychological states in the agent. Acts not freely done are those whose immediate causes are states of affairs external to the agent.*

It is plain that if we define free will in this way, then free will certainly exists, and the philosopher's denial of its existence is seen to be what it is—nonsense. For it is obvious that all those actions of men which we should ordinarily attribute to the exercise of their free will, or of which we should say that they freely chose to do them, are in fact actions which have been caused by their own desires, wishes, thoughts, emotions, impulses, or other psychological states.

Here, then, is Stace's "compatible" solution to the challenge of retaining free choice and responsibility while retaining the conviction that "all human actions, both those which are freely done and those which are not, are either wholly determined by causes, or at least as much determined as other events in nature." For Stace, and other compatibilists, *free choices* are those that are not compelled by forces or circumstances external to the individual, while *unfree choices* are those that are compelled. In both cases the actions are causally determined: What distinguishes free choices from unfree choices is the nature of the causal factors. In the case of the individual lost in the desert, his failure to eat was the result of his circumstances, not his natural desires. But in the case of Gandhi, his failure to eat was a choice on his part, the result of his desire to make a political statement and influence the policies of the British government.

This approach is similar to the distinction that d'Holbach makes when analyzing the case of Socrates. When Socrates was found guilty at his trial and incarcerated awaiting his cup of hemlock, his choices were constrained by factors external to him—*external constraints*. But when his friends arranged for him to escape from his guarded room and flee the country, and he didn't, his choice not to escape was still constrained, not by external factors but by internal factors, as d'Holbach notes— "The invisible chains of opinion, the secret love of decorum, the inward respect for the laws, even when they were iniquitous, the fear of tarnishing his glory . . . all of these *internal constraints* served to keep Socrates in his prison cell in the same way that Gandhi's own *internal constraints* compelled him not to eat until the British government had changed its policy toward India. Seen in this way, both the "hard determinist" d'Holbach and the "compatibilist" Stace are in agreement regarding the fundamental psychological processes at work: Where they differ is how to *classify* these processes. For d'Holbach—and other hard determinists—whether the choices by Socrates and Gandhi were the causal results of external factors or internal factors, they were *unfree*. For Stace—and other compatibilists—when the choices of Socrates and Gandhi were the causal results of external factors, those choices were *unfree*. But when those choices were not compelled externally, and instead were the result of only internal factors, their choices were *free*. Thus, for the compatibilist, when we make choices that express our natural desires, those choices are free and we are responsible for those choices, even though the desires and impulses that cause those choices may not be in our conscious control.

Does this proposed compatibilist solution to the challenge of reconciling hard determinism and free choice actually work? How do hard determinists and libertarians respond to the compatibilist definition of free choices as those choices that are not compelled externally and instead fully reflect our natural desires? From the standpoint of the hard determinists, the compatibilist "solution" is unlikely to have much of an impact. As we noted, d'Holbach already acknowledges the distinction between external constraints and internal constraints, and he considers them both to be equally determined and equally unfree.

The libertarians have traditionally been even less sympathetic to the compatibilist efforts. It was the passionate libertarian William James who coined the term *soft determinism* in the following passage dripping with contempt:

> *To begin, then, I must suppose you are acquainted with all the usual arguments on the subject [of free will]. I cannot stop to take up the old proofs from causation, from statistics, from the certainty with which we can foretell one another's conduct, from the fixity of character, and all the rest. . . . Old-fashioned determinism was what we may call **hard** determinism. It did not shrink from such words as fatality, bondage of the will, necessitation, and the like. Nowadays, we have a **soft** determinism which abhors harsh words, and, repudiating fatality, necessity, and even predetermination, says that its real name is freedom; for freedom is only necessity understood, and bondage to the highest is identical with true freedom . . .*

Certainly the libertarian would raise the following points, which we will explore more fully in the pages ahead:

- Stace maintains that *"common usage is the criterion for deciding whether a definition is correct or not."* Does it really make sense to consider popular language use to be the ultimate arbiter of philosophical truth? Most philosophers would say that one of our major challenges is to clarify all of the confusions, conflicts, ambiguities, and opaqueness embedded in the common usage of language. In fact, that insight is one of the central truths contributed by Socrates and the Socratic Method, as we saw in Chapter 2. So while ordinary language and common usage may be an appropriate starting point for philosophical analysis, it is rarely thought of by philosophers as an appropriate endpoint.

- It's likely that libertarians would agree that "not being compelled by external factors" only captures a portion of what most people think of as making a "free choice." For the compatibilist, our free choices are simply the result of our strongest desires, whatever they may be. But when most people reflect on making a free choice, they typically think of a process that involves the thoughtful consideration of multiple possibilities and then the active willing of a choice based on their deliberations—a complex process not encompassed by "simply following the strongest desires." Of course, this differs from d'Holbach's conception that the entire process of making a choice is simply a complex illusion masking a causally determined process. But it does suggest that the compatibilist definition of free choice addresses only a limited dimension of what that concept means to most people.

Internal Constraints May Also Limit Freedom: Schlick

Moritz Schlick (1882–1936). A founder of the Vienna Circle, Schlick—who had a Ph.D. in physics—was interested in creating a theory of knowledge based on direct observation and logic.

It's not only hard determinists and libertarians who have problems with the traditional version of the compatibilist analysis of freedom as articulated by Stace: Even some other compatibilists consider it to be a somewhat oversimplified analysis in need of clarification. One such philosopher is **Moritz Schlick**, whose views are encapsulated in his essay, "When Is a Man Responsible?" Schlick agrees with mainstream compatibilists that freedom means the opposite of compulsion: People are "free" if they do not act under compulsion, and they are compelled or "unfree" when they are inhibited from without in the realization of their natural desires. Schlick agrees that the consciousness of freedom is the knowledge of having acted on one's own desires—"those desires that have their origin in the regularity of one's character in a given situation." The feeling of freedom says that if we are being constrained externally, then we "could have done otherwise" if that constraint was not present. However, Schlick contends, the feeling of freedom does *not* say that under exactly the same inner and outer condition we could have willed something else. As a result, Schlick's views in this regard accord with determinism, which holds that all human actions are brought about by previous events in accordance with universal causal laws. In Schlick's words:

When are choices free and when are they unfree?
In January 2007, Cameron Hollopeter fell onto the subway tracks in New York as he was having an epileptic seizure. A bystander, Wesley Autrey (shown above), jumped onto the tracks and rescued Hollopeter from the wheels of an oncoming train. This story illustrates how the same action—moving from a subway platform onto the tracks—can be unfree for one and free for another.

> *This feeling is **not** the consciousness of the absence of a cause, but of something altogether different, namely of freedom, which consists in the fact that I can act as I desire. Thus the feeling of responsibility assumes that I acted freely, that my desires impelled me . . . If decisions were causeless there would be no sense in trying to **influence** men; and we see at once that this is why we could not hold such a man responsible, but would always have only a shrug of the shoulders in answer to his behavior. In practice, we make an agent the more responsible the more motives we can find for his conduct.*

However, where Schlick's views diverge from Stace's and other compatibilists is in his recognition that there are times when *internal constraints* in the form of mental illness or even neuroses can act as a disturbing factor that hinders the normal functioning of our natural tendencies. In such cases, we hold the illness responsible, not the individual: for example, a clinically depressed individual who attempts suicide, or a schizophrenic who retreats into the confines of his own reality. Thus, Schlick believes, we need to amend the compatibilist definition of free choice to include not just the absence of *external constraints* but also the absence of serious and debilitating *internal constraints*. To say that an action is genuinely free is to say that it is the expression of a person's *unimpeded rational desires*. If an action is the result of deeply disturbed irrational desires, then, Schlick believes, it is not accurate to say that the action is free, and as a consequence we cannot hold the individual responsible for his or her choice.

The question is now, however, if by adding this "clarification" to the compatibilist account, whether Schlick opened a philosophical Pandora's box of trouble. For the truth is that we all suffer our own peculiar recipe of addictions, neuroses, compulsions, and obsessions that interfere with our making rational decisions. There is a real sense in which these *internal constraints* limit our freedom by preventing us from making the choices that are in our rational self-interest. And this insight seems to suggest that we can actually *increase* our freedom, not only by removing *external constraints* but by removing or diminishing *internal constraints* as well. Instead of freedom being an absolute, unchanging condition—either we're free or we're not free—this

Daniel C. Dennett
(b. 1942). The research of
this American philosopher
centers on the philosophy
of mind, particularly as it
relates to evolutionary biology and cognitive science.

line of thinking suggests that there may be *degrees of freedom*, and that it may be in our self-interest to increase to the optimal level the degree of freedom of which we are capable. These are complex and important themes that we're going to explore later in the chapter. For now, it's enough to notice how far away from the original compatibilist formulation Schlick's "clarification" has taken him.

Free Will Is a Human Creation: Dennett

Compatibilism is vibrantly alive today in the work of such individuals as **Daniel C. Dennett**, a philosopher with an evolutionary perspective on the human mind. Dennett is a materialist who believes that humans are at essence evolved organisms lacking a spiritual self or immortal soul, the mind nothing more than the workings of the brain, created through the natural selection by the "blind watchmaker" of evolution. As a result, Dennett is committed to determinism in the sense that "there is at any instant exactly one physically possible future." But Dennett also believes that "Human freedom is not an illusion; it is an objective phenomenon, distinct from all other biological conditions and found in only one species, us." Because human freedom is real, he believes that it can be studied and understood objectively from a scientific point of view. Thus, Dennett is seeking to achieve the same "compatibility" between determinism and freedom that other thinkers have but within the context of evolutionary theory and modern research into the relationship between the brain and the mind. Here's how Dennett describes the goals of his undertaking, which are described in his book, *Freedom Evolves*:

> . . . my task will be to bring this churning of perspectives to a halt and provide a unified, stable, empirically well-grounded coherent view of human free will, and you already know the conclusion I will reach: Free will is real, but it is not a preexisting feature of our existence, like the law of gravity. It is also not what tradition declares it to be: a God-like power to exempt oneself from the causal fabric of the physical world. It is an evolved creation of human activity and beliefs, and it is just as real as such other human creations as music and money. And even more valuable. From this evolutionary perspective, the traditional problem of free will can be broken into some rather unusual fragments, each of some value in illuminating the **serious** problems of free will . . .

Dennett's argument is complex, empirically grounded, and not easily summarized, but his work shows that free will is still a vital and vigorous issue in philosophy, and in other disciplines as well.

● **Watch** the **Interview**
*Robert Wright Inter-
views Daniel Dennett
on Free Will* on
mysearchlab.com

< READING CRITICALLY >

Evaluating Compatibilism

■ Even though W. T. Stace believes that all events are causally determined, he also believes that, if free will did not exist, "All moral precepts would in such case be meaningless." Do you agree with his conclusion? Stace then goes on to argue that as long as an action is not compelled by an outside force, the action is free, even though it is causally determined by previous events beyond the person's control. Does his definition of "free choice" as "uncompelled" agree with your own sense of free choice? Why or why not?

- D'Holbach would contend that when Socrates refused to escape from his prison and Gandhi refused to eat, both individuals were not making free choices because they were being compelled by internal impulses that were causing their actions. Stace and other compatibilists, on the other hand, believe that even though their actions may have been causally determined by their personal histories, the actions were nevertheless freely chosen because they were not being compelled by external forces. Which perspective do you believe is more likely to be accurate: the hard determinist's or the compatibilist's? Why? If instead of saying their actions were "caused" we say that Socrates and Gandhi had "reasons" for actions they took, does that change your perspective? Why?

- According to Moritz Schlick, actions that are the result of "internal constraints," as well as those that are compelled by "external constraints," are unfree because they do not express the "unimpeded rational desires" of the person acting. Do you agree with his analysis? If a person is emotionally disturbed, should we consider his actions to be free or unfree? Why or why not?

- Are there times in your life when you feel that you are in the grip of internal constraints—obsessions, compulsions, neuroses, depressions—that you cannot consciously control despite your best efforts to choose otherwise? If so, would you say that your actions in these situations are free or unfree? Why?

- Hard determinists like d'Holbach define determinism as meaning that "all human actions are caused by previous events," and that as a result free will is an illusion that does not exist. A compatibilist like Daniel Dennett defines determinism as meaning "there is at any instant exactly one physically possible future" and yet free will is still not an illusion, it is real. Is there a meaningful difference in these two somewhat different definitions of "determinism"? Might one's definition of determinism influence whether one believes free will is real or an illusion? Why or why not?

4.4 Indeterminism and Libertarianism

While determinists, both "hard" and "soft," view all human actions as necessarily caused by preceding events, indeterminists are convinced that at least some human actions are independent and that freedom of choice is a genuine possibility, at least in certain circumstances. For example, when you find yourself at a decision crossroads, the indeterminist believes that your choice is at least potentially independent of any external or internal events. *You* choose which path to take, and you are as a result responsible for that choice. If you found yourself in exactly the same situation, you might very well choose another path. In other words, whichever option you choose, there is the conviction that *you could have chosen otherwise.* As we noted on page 142, some philosophers make a distinction between "indeterminism" and "libertarianism." Indeterminists leave open the possibility that undetermined actions are simply random, while libertarians are convinced that people are able to make genuinely free choices by exercising their free wills. While keeping this important distinction in mind, the more common term "indeterminism" will be used in this chapter to refer to both kinds of freedom. We are going to explore indeterminism through the eyes of two influential philosophers, William James and Jean-Paul Sartre.

((•—[**Listen** to the **Interview** *Book Explores Intellectual Power of William James* on **mysearchlab** .com

We Live in a World of Possibilities: James

William James
(1842–1910). An American thinker whose work blends science, psychology, and philosophy. James was one of the founders of Pragmatism, a school of philosophy that connects questions of meaning and truth to practical applications and consequences. Among his writings is *The Principles of Psychology* (1890), a 1,200-page work that introduced the concept of "stream of thought."

William James was an American philosopher, psychologist, and medical doctor who explored a wide variety of issues, including the varieties of religious experience, pragmatism, and the possibility of personal freedom. In the following selections, taken from *The Will to Believe,* James mounts a strong offensive for believing in the reality of human freedom.

James begins his defense of free will at precisely the point where determinism is most vulnerable: how well it explains the reality of our experience. For James, the testimony of our direct, lived experience provides the most compelling grounds for free will, providing there are no sufficiently persuasive intellectual arguments to convince us otherwise. In other words, the fact that most humans live their lives based on the assumption that personal freedom and responsibility are valid concepts is a compelling reason for believing in the reality of these concepts. Our belief in free choice and personal responsibility infuses our beliefs in self-improvement, morality, religion, social improvement, crime and punishment, and countless other dimensions of our private and public lives. Consider the following:

- *Self improvement:* We try to improve ourselves and the quality of our lives, which depends on believing that we possess the freedom to make different choices from those we have previously made.

- *Morality:* As a society, we develop moral ideals, rewards, and punishments to help people live together in a harmonious and productive fashion. But if people's actions are caused by genes or uncontrolled impulses, then there is little point in trying to develop an ethical world.

- *Religion:* Most religions require that individuals have the ability to choose freely in determining their spiritual destiny. In the absence of freedom, religion becomes irrelevant.

- *Social improvement:* Many people want to create a better world, free from poverty, crime, discrimination, and other destructive forces, but to do so requires the ability to change the past and present. Without it, there is no point in trying to solve social problems.

The question is, are there in fact intellectual grounds for believing that the compelling testimony of our lived experience is mistaken? James thinks not.

William James, from *The Will to Believe*

The thesis I defend is, briefly stated, thus: *Our passional nature not only lawfully may, but must, decide an option between propositions, whenever it is a genuine option that cannot by its nature be decided on intellectual grounds; for to say, under such circumstances, "Do not decide, but leave the question open," is itself a passional decision,—just like deciding yes or no,—and is attended with the same risk of losing the truth.*

A common opinion prevails that the juice has ages ago been pressed out of the free-will controversy, and that no new champion can do more than warm up stale arguments which everyone has heard. This is a radical mistake. I know of no subject less worn out, or in which inventive genius has a better chance of breaking open new ground,—not, perhaps, of forcing a conclusion or of coercing assent, but of deepening our sense of what the issue between the two parties really is, of what the ideas of fate and free-will imply. . . . Our first act of freedom, if we are free, ought in all inward propriety to be to affirm that we are free. . . .

What a stirring rallying cry for indeterminists, who often seem on the defensive against the mechanistic onslaughts of deterministic arguments: "Our first act of freedom, if we are free, ought . . . to be to affirm that we are free. . . ." But James's affirmation is more than a rallying cry: He is making an epistemological statement about the free-will controversy. His philosophical point is that, if free will genuinely exists, then the exercise of it is the strongest evidence for its existence. He has no tolerance for those who are not prepared to commit themselves one way or the other regarding free will, for "not committing" is itself a free choice—just not a very authentic or courageous choice, in James's eyes. If you live your life as though free will exists, then you should come forward and affirm in a loud and clear voice, "I believe that I am able to make free choices." This primal affirmation is itself the ground for believing that your statement is true. The testimony of your direct, lived experience confirms its validity.

This resounding affirmation of free will is the cornerstone of James's overall position, and he next proceeds to lay the foundation of his general argument.

With this much understood at the outset, we can advance. But not without one more point understood as well. The arguments I am about to urge all proceed on two suppositions: first, when we make theories about the world and discuss them with one another, we do so in order to attain a conception of things which shall give us subjective satisfaction; and second, if there be two conceptions, and the one seems to us, on the whole, more rational than the other, we are entitled to suppose that the more rational one is the truer of the two. . . .

William James,
from *The Will to Believe*

James is setting out his basic epistemological criteria for determining truth and knowledge, and his view is remarkably similar to that of phenomenologists such as Edmund Husserl and Maurice Merleau-Ponty, whom we examined in Chapter 3. From this perspective, humans use their intellectual abilities to create concepts and create theories to help them understand and give meaning to their lived experience. When theories conflict with one another, how do we decide which theories are the "best"? In the final analysis, we should endorse those theories that provide the most rational, clearest, complete, and persuasive understanding of our lived experience.

By setting out his basic criteria of evaluation, James is making clear the direction his argument is going to take with respect to free will. Deterministic theories such as those advanced by Baron d'Holbach are, in the final analysis, inferior to indeterminist theories because they do an inferior job of helping us understand our lived experience. In fact, as we have seen, and as the determinists openly acknowledge, their theories consistently contradict and clash with our lived experience. Why should we give epistemological precedence to these determinist theories over testimony of our lived experience, which tends to support an indeterminist point of view? We *shouldn't*, James believes. And when people do commit themselves to theories that provide an inadequate account of our experience, they have completely lost sight of the essential purpose of concepts and theories—to help us clarify our experience, not distort it.

James continues to build his case by reviewing the traditional arguments for and against free will.

William James, from
The Will to Believe

> To begin, then, I must suppose you are acquainted with all the usual arguments on the subject. I cannot stop to take up the old proofs from causation, from statistics, from the certainty with which we can foretell one another's conduct, from the fixity of character, and all the rest. . . . Old-fashioned determinism was what we may call *hard* determinism. It did not shrink from such words as fatality, bondage of the will, necessitation, and the like. Nowadays, we have a *soft* determinism which abhors harsh words, and, repudiating fatality, necessity, and even predetermination, says that its real name is freedom; for freedom is only necessity understood, and bondage to the highest is identical with true freedom. . . .

As we have noted previously, *hard determinists* believe that all events, including human actions, are caused, precluding the possibility of free choice. *Soft determinists* agree with hard determinists that all events, including human actions, are caused. However, soft determinists assert that we can consider human actions "free" if they are the result of internal motivations, not the product of external influences or constraints.

With disdain, James dismisses this as a meaningless distinction because soft determinists still deny the possibility of free will independent of a causal chain of events. We act the way that we do because we are compelled by internal forces: There is no meaningful sense in which we could have freely chosen "to do otherwise." So for James, "hard" and "soft" determinism are simply variations of the same unacceptable point of view.

William James, from
The Will to Believe

> Determinism professes that those parts of the universe already laid down absolutely appoint and decree what the other parts shall be. The future has no ambiguous possibilities hidden in its womb: the part we call the present is compatible with only one totality. Any other future complement than the one fixed from eternity is impossible. The whole is in each and every part, and welds it with the rest into an absolute unity, an iron block, in which there can be no equivocation or shadow of turning.
>
> With earth's first clay they did the last man knead,
>
> And there of the last harvest sowed the seed.
>
> And the first morning of creation wrote
>
> What the last dawn of reckoning shall read.
>
> Indeterminism, on the contrary, says that the parts have a certain amount of loose play on one another, so that the laying down of one of them does not necessarily determine what the others shall be. It admits that possibilities may be in excess of actualities, and that things not yet revealed to our knowledge may really in themselves be ambiguous. Of two alternative futures which we conceive, both may now be really possible; and the one become impossible only at the very moment when the other excludes it by becoming real itself. Indeterminism thus denies the world to be one unbending unit of fact. It says there is a certain ultimate pluralism in it; and, so saying, it corroborates our ordinary unsophisticated view of things. To that view, actualities seem to float in a wider sea of possibilities from out of which they are chosen; and, somewhere, indeterminism says, such possibilities exist, and form a part of the truth.
>
> Determinism, on the contrary, says they exist *nowhere*, and that necessity on the one hand and impossibility on the other are the sole categories of the real. Possibilities that fail to get realized are, for determinism, pure illusions: they never were possibilities at all. There is nothing inchoate, it says, about this universe of ours, all that was or is or shall be actual in it having been from eternity virtually there. The cloud of alternatives

our minds escort this mass of actuality withal is a cloud of sheer deception, to which "impossibilities" is the only name that rightfully belongs.

The issue, it will be seen, is a perfectly sharp one, which no eulogistic terminology can smear over or wipe out. The truth *must* lie with one side or the other, and its lying with one side makes the other false.

The question related solely to the existence of possibilities, in the strict sense of the term, as things that may, but need not, be. Both sides admit that a volition, for instance, has occurred. The indeterminists say another volition might have occurred in its place: the determinists swear that nothing could possibly have occurred in its place. Now, can science be called in to tell us which of these two point-blank contradicters of each other is right? Science professes to draw no conclusions but such as are based on matters of fact, things that have actually happened; but how can any amount of assurance that something actually happened give us the least grain of information as to whether another thing might or might not have happened in its place? Only facts can be proved by other facts. With things that are possibilities and not facts, facts have no concern. If we have no other evidence than the evidence of existing facts, the possibility-question must remain a mystery never to be cleared up.

And the truth is that facts practically have hardly anything to do with making us either determinists or indeterminists. Sure enough, we make a flourish of quoting facts this way or that; and if we are determinists, we talk about the infallibility with which we can predict one another's conduct; while if we are indeterminists, we lay great stress on the fact that it is just because we cannot foretell one another's conduct, either in war or statecraft or in any of the great and small intrigues and business of men, that life is so intensely anxious and hazardous a game. But who does not see the wretched insufficiency of this so-called objective testimony on both sides? What fills up the gaps in our minds is something not objective, not external. What divides us into possibility men and anti-possibility men is different faiths or postulates,—postulates of rationality. To this man the world seems more rational with possibilities in it,—to that man more rational with possibilities excluded; and talk as we will about having to yield to evidence, what makes us monists or pluralists, determinists or indeterminists, is at bottom always some sentiment like this. . . .

In reviewing the traditional positions of determinism and indeterminism, James casts the debate in a fresh light that helps to clarify the underlying issues. There are two ways of viewing the universe:

- A universe of *actualities*, in which no other possibilities exist other than those that occur. If the events of the universe were a story, there is one way and one way only that this story could ever be told. This is the determinist view.

- A universe of *possibilities*, in which no matter what events have occurred in the past, there are still multiple possibilities in the future. If the events of the universe were a story, the past has been written, but we will not be able to write the future until it occurs because we need to see which of the multitude of possibilities become actualities. This is the indeterminist view.

How can we tell which of these two universes is the "real" universe? Facts won't help because facts can't tell us anything about possibilities: They can tell us only about other facts. Baron d'Holbach can cite facts about what has occurred previously in the universe, but he cannot marshal any facts to prove that what occurred was the *only* possible sequence of events. Nor can he use facts to predict which of the limitless number of possibilities will end up becoming actualities in the future.

On the other hand, there are no facts that the indeterminist can present to prove that what occurred *wasn't* the only possible sequence of events. Nor can the indeterminist cite facts to prove that the future has more than one set of possibilities that can occur.

But if facts can't decide the issue for us, then what can? James now returns to the original criteria for truth and knowledge that he introduced at the beginning. We choose the theory based on our lived experience: Which universe makes the most sense to us, seems the most rational, is consistent with our deepest convictions? Is it a universe *without* possibilities or a universe *with* possibilities? Determinists claim that it is the former; indeterminists claim it is the latter.

James begins to address this central question—"Which universe is more rational and makes the most sense?"—by exploring (with good humor) the practical implications of each theory.

William James, from *The Will to Believe*

Nevertheless, many persons talk as if the minutest dose of disconnectedness of one part with another, the smallest modicum of independence, the faintest tremor of ambiguity about the future, for example, would ruin everything, and turn this goodly universe into a sort of insane sand-heap or nulliverse, no universe at all. Since future human volitions are as a matter of fact the only ambiguous things we are tempted to believe in, let us stop for a moment to make ourselves sure whether their independent and accidental character need be fraught with such direful consequences to the universe as these.

What is meant by saying that my choice of which way to walk home after the lecture is ambiguous and matter of chance as far as the present moment is concerned? It means that both Divinity Avenue and Oxford Street are called; but that only one, and that one, *either* one, shall be chosen. Now I ask you seriously to suppose that this ambiguity of my choice is real; and then to make the impossible hypothesis that the choice is made twice over, and each time falls on a different street. In other words, imagine that I first walk through Divinity Avenue, and then imagine that the powers governing the universe annihilate ten minutes of time with all that it contained, and set me back at the door of this hall just as I was before the choice was made. Imagine then that, everything else being the same, I now make a different choice and traverse Oxford Street. You, as passive spectators, look on and see the two alternative universes,—one of them with me walking through Divinity Avenue in it, the other with the same me walking through Oxford Street. Now, if you are determinists you believe one of these universes to have been from eternity impossible: you believe it to have been impossible because of the intrinsic irrationality or accidentality somewhere involved in it. But looking outwardly at these universes, can you say which is the impossible and accidental one, and which the rational and necessary one? I doubt if the most ironclad determinist among you could have the slightest glimmer of light on this point. In other words, either universe *after the fact* and once there would, to our means of observation and understanding, appear just as rational as the other. There would be absolutely no criterion by which we might judge one necessary and the other matter of chance. Suppose now we relieve the gods of their hypothetical task and assume my choice, once made, to be made forever. I go through Divinity Avenue for good and all. If, as good determinists, you now begin to affirm, what all good determinists punctually do affirm, that in the nature of things I *couldn't* have gone through Oxford Street,—had I done so it would have been chance, irrationality, insanity, a horrid gap in nature,—I simply call your attention to this, that your affirmation is what the Germans call a *Machtspruch*, a mere conception fulminated as a dogma and based on no insight into details. Before my choice, either street seemed as natural to you as to me. Had I happened to take Oxford Street, Divinity Avenue would have figured in your philosophy as the gap in nature; and you would have so proclaimed it with the best deterministic conscience in the world. . . .

And this at last brings us within sight of our subject. We have seen what determinism means: we have seen that indeterminism is rightly described as meaning chance; and we have seen that chance, the very name of which we are urged to shrink from as from a metaphysical pestilence, means only the negative fact that no part of the world, however big, can claim to control absolutely the destinies of the whole. But although, in discussing the word "chance," I may at moments have seemed to be arguing for its real existence, I have not meant to do so yet. We have not yet ascertained whether this be a world of chance or not; at most, we have agreed that it seems so. And I now repeat what I said at the outset, that, from any strict theoretical point of view, the question is insoluble. To deepen our theoretic sense of the *difference* between a world with chances in it and a deterministic world is the most I can hope to do; and this I may now at last begin upon, after all our tedious, clearing of the way.

James's analysis of a concrete example is both ingenious and effective, bringing the core issues in the free-will debate into relief. After gently poking fun at the determinist's phobic reactions to the possibility of chance and ambiguity in the universe, he asks us to visualize two superimposed universes: one in which he chooses to take Divinity Avenue home and the other in which he opts for Oxford Street. He then asks the determinists: "How can you tell the difference between the selections? Is one more rational than the other? How can you determine which is necessary and which is impossible?" The answer is, James believes, they *can't* tell the difference. They can only tell the difference *after the fact*, once the event has taken place. But, of course, using a theory to explain something that has already occurred typically is not very informative. It is the ability to *predict* events in advance that provides more reliable support for a theory. Many theories confidently proclaim explanations of events after they have taken place, including

- psychological theories ("Unconscious impulses made you . . .").
- astrological theories ("The position of the planets shaped your personality . . .").
- sociological theories ("Social forces molded you into the person you are . . .").
- economic theories ("Economic forces account for your current income level . . .").

Are decisions in life free choices or predetermined by factors beyond our control? Assume that both roads in the picture take you to your destination in the same amount of time. According to James, the determinist would say that, at a particular moment, everything that happened previously would lead you to choose only one of the roads; the indeterminist would say that at the same moment, you might choose either of them. Which theory makes the most sense to you? Why?

But all of these theories are typically much less successful in accurately predicting what is going to occur in the future, which brings us back to the theories of determinists like d'Holbach. By advancing all-encompassing theoretical explanations for every event that occurs, they are making it impossible to ever assess the truth or falsity of their theories. And if a theory cannot establish clear criteria for evaluating its truth and falsity, then it amounts to little more than what James terms a *Machtspruch*—"a mere conception fulminated as a dogma and based on no insight into details." This conceptual dilemma poses a serious challenge to determinism, but James finds additional difficulties that pose an even more devastating threat.

William James, from
The Will to Believe

I wish first of all to show you just what the notion that this is a deterministic world implies. The implications I call your attention to are all bound up with the fact that it is a world in which we constantly have to make what I shall, with your permission, call judgments of regret. Hardly an hour passes in which we do not wish that something might be otherwise; and happy indeed are those of us whose hearts have never echoed the wish of Omar Khayyam—

That we might clasp, ere closed, the book of fate,

And make the writer on a fairer leaf

Inscribe our names, or quite obliterate,

Ah! Love, could you and I with fate conspire

To mend this sorry scheme of things entire,

Would we not shatter it to bits, and then

Remould it nearer to the heart's desire?

Now, it is undeniable that most of these regrets are foolish, and quite on a par in point of philosophic value with the criticisms on the universe of that friend of our infancy, the hero of the fable The Atheist and the Acorn,—

Fool! Had that bough a pumpkin bore,

Thy whimsies would have worked no more, etc.

Even from the point of view of our own ends, we should probably make a botch of remodeling the universe. How much more then from the point of view of ends we cannot see! Wise men therefore regret as little as they can. But still some regrets are pretty obstinate and hard to stifle,—regrets for acts of wanton cruelty or treachery, for example, whether performed by others or by ourselves. Hardly any one can remain *entirely* optimistic after reading the confession of the murderer at Brockton the other day: how, to get rid of the wife whose continued existence bored, he inveigled her into a desert spot, shot her four times, and then, as she lay on the ground and said to him, "you didn't do it on purpose, did you, dear?" replied, "No, I didn't do it on purpose," as he raised a rock and smashed her skull. Such an occurrence with the mild sentence and self-satisfaction of the prisoner, is a field for a crop of regrets, which one need not take up in detail. We feel that, although a perfect mechanical to fit to the rest of the universe, it is a bad moral fit, and that something else would really have been better in its place.

To answer the question of which universe is more rational and makes more sense—the determinist's or the indeterminist's—James wants us to fully appreciate the implications of a deterministic world, and he does this by analyzing our "judgments of regret." What are "judgments of regret"? Simply the desire that events might have occurred differently or might have had other, more desirable, outcomes. For example, think of mistakes you have made in the past: Do you wish you had made different choices? Do you imagine that you would select different courses of action, if you had the opportunity? If so, you are experiencing "judgments of regret."

Analogously, consider the human catastrophes that have occurred, both natural and human-made: earthquakes and famines that wreaked havoc on countless lives; diseases such as the bubonic plague, smallpox, and AIDS that have resulted in endless human misery; wars and mindless acts of terror that have left senseless death and destruction in their wake. If you had the power, would you have prevented these calamitous events from occurring? Do you wish they had not occurred and fervently hope that they will not occur in the future? If so, you are experiencing "judgments of regret."

It is the same with the murderer at Brockton that James describes. How could any sentient being, on hearing of the accused man's savage murder of his wife, not wish that events had been otherwise, that he had not murdered her? And who among us

Do our "judgments of regret" support the belief that free will is real? Hurricane Katrina caused a great deal of misery that many people wished could have been avoided.

wouldn't regret *any* such murder of an innocent person that has occurred and hope that such evil actions would not occur in the future? Such horrendous events violate our moral sense of the way the world *should* be and spur us to hope for a more enlightened future.

But for the determinist, none of these "judgments of regret" and the hopes and desires for the future that emanate from them have any validity or ultimately make any sense. From a determinist point of view, everything that happens in the universe *has* to occur exactly the way in which it does, and the same holds true for the future as well. To think otherwise, to regret an occurrence in the past or hope for an altered future, are ideas and emotions that are futile and illogical.

But for the deterministic philosophy the murder, the sentence, and the prisoner's optimism were all necessary from eternity; and nothing else for a moment had a ghost of a chance of being put into their place. To admit such a chance, the determinists tell us, would be to make a suicide of reason; so we must steel our hearts against the thought. And here our plot thickens, for we see the first of those difficult implications of determinism and monism which is my purpose to make you feel. If this Brockton murder was called for by the rest of the universe, if it had to come at its preappointed hour, and if nothing else would have been consistent with the sense of the whole, what are we to think of the universe? Are we stubbornly to stick to our judgment of regret, and say, though it *couldn't* be, yet it *would* have been a better universe with something different from this Brockton murder in it? That, of course, seems the natural and spontaneous thing for us to do; and yet it is nothing short of deliberately espousing a kind of pessimism. The judgment of regret calls the murder bad. Calling a thing bad means, if it means anything at all, that the thing ought not to be, that something else ought to be in its stead. Determinism, in denying that anything else can be in its stead,

William James, from *The Will to Believe*

virtually defines the universe as a place in which what ought to be is impossible,—in other words, as an organism whose constitution is afflicted with an incurable taint, an irremediable flaw. The pessimism of a Schopenhauer says no more than this,—that the murder is a symptom; and that it is a vicious symptom because it belongs to a vicious whole, which can express its nature no otherwise than by bringing forth just such a symptom as that at this particular spot. Regret for the murder must transform itself, if we are determinists and wise, into a larger regret. It is absurd to regret the murder alone. Other things being what they are, *it* could not be different. What we should regret is that whole frame of things of which the murder is one member. I see no escape whatever from this pessimistic conclusion, if, being determinists, our judgment of regret is to be allowed to stand at all.

For the determinist, the inescapable conclusion seems to be one of cosmic pessimism. Even though the universe *could* be better than it is if it were to be rid of natural catastrophes and human evil, the universe *never will* be better—or different in any way—than it is. All that happens occurs because it *must* happen in exactly the way in which it does. Recognizing that the universe is necessarily morally flawed and vicious, and that *nothing can ever be done to change it for the better*, necessarily leads a reflective person to a profound feeling of pessimism. We regret, but we recognize that our regrets will always be hopeless. Determinism, James concludes, fails miserably in explaining the beliefs and convictions of our lived experience, and it is also a perspective that is ultimately self-contradictory and not rational in any meaningful human sense. Which leaves us with indeterminism, in James's opinion, as the only plausible point of view of freedom.

William James, from
The Will to Believe

> **I cannot understand regret without the admission of real, genuine possibilities in the world.**

But this brings us right back, to the question of indeterminism. . . . For the only consistent way of representing a pluralism and a world whose parts may affect one another through their conduct being either good or bad is the indeterministic way. What interest, zest, or excitement can there be in achieving the right way, unless we are enabled to feel that the wrong way is also a possible and a natural way—nay, more, a menacing and an imminent way? And what sense can there be in condemning ourselves for taking the wrong way, unless we need have done nothing of the sort, unless the right way was open to us as well? I cannot understand the belief that an act is bad, without regret at its happening. I cannot understand regret without the admission of real, genuine possibilities in the world. Only *then* is it other than a mockery to feel, after we have failed to do our best, that an irreparable opportunity is gone from the universe the loss of which it must forever after mourn. The indeterminism I defend, the free-will theory of popular sense based on the judgment of regret, represents that world as vulnerable, and liable to be injured by certain of its parts if they act wrong. And it represents their acting wrong as a matter of possibility or accident, neither inevitable nor yet to be infallibly warded off. In all this, it is a theory devoid either of transparency or of stability. It gives us a pluralistic, restless universe, in which no single point of view can ever take in the whole scent; and to a mind possessed of the love of unity at any cost, it will, no doubt, remain forever unacceptable. . . . The great point is that the possibilities are really *here*. Whether it be we who solve them or he working through us, at those soul-trying moments when fate's scales seem to quiver, and good snatches the victory from evil or shrinks nevertheless from the fight, is of small account, so long as we admit that the issue is decided nowhere else than *here* and *now*. *That* is what gives the palpitating reality to our moral life and makes it tingle . . . with so strange and elaborate an excitement. This reality, this excitement, are what the determinists, hard and soft alike, suppress by their denial that *anything* is decided here and now, and their dogma that all things were foredoomed and settled long ago.

< READING CRITICALLY >

Analyzing James on Free Will

- Summarize James's argument that the determinists are unable to permit either judgments of regret or judgments of approval within their theoretical framework. Is this a compelling argument for indeterminism? Why or why not?

- James returns to his initial epistemological foundation when he states, "The great point is that the possibilities are really *here*. Whether it be we who solve them or he working through us, at those soul-trying moments when fate's scales seem to quiver, and good snatches the victory from evil or shrinks nevertheless from the fight, is of small account, so long as we admit that the issue is decided nowhere else than *here* and *now*." Explain the significance of James grounding his conclusions on the "*here* and *now*." Do you agree with his analysis? Why or why not?

- James believes that our "lived experience" confirms our belief in free will. But what is there in our lived experience to confirm free will? Is it that we do not notice any forces acting on us requiring one choice rather than another? Is that good evidence, or could we simply be blind to the inner springs behind our thinking? Is it that we "feel" free? But again, could that just be that we notice we are not externally constrained, we are able to do what we want, while being blind to the actual inner causes that lead us to have the wants we have? Or does critical reflection give us the means to differentiate genuinely autonomous choices from those choices that are constrained in some way?

- Determinists maintain that people believing in free will are deluded and in denial about their lack of freedom. James maintains the reverse: The vitality of our moral lives makes clear that it is determinists who are deluded and in denial about their genuine freedom: "This reality, this excitement, are what the determinists, hard and soft alike, suppress by their denial that *anything* is decided here and now, and their dogma that all things were foredoomed and settled long ago." Who do you think is ultimately deluded and in denial, determinists or indeterminists? Why?

We Create Ourselves Through Our Choices: Sartre

Jean-Paul Sartre was a French philosopher who also expressed his philosophical principles in plays such as *No Exit* and novels such as *Nausea*. Sartre is generally considered to be a chief exponent of modern **existentialism**, a philosophical movement that emphasizes the challenge and responsibility of all people to create a meaningful existence through the free choices they make. In seeking meaning, existentialists believe that we cannot look outward to a supernatural creator or an intelligible universe: We must look inward, to our own resources and possibilities, as we struggle to create meaning in a world that often seems chaotic and absurd. Sartre's core philosophical text is *Being and Nothingness*, but the following excerpts are taken from a much briefer work, *Existentialism Is a Humanism*, which presents a lucid summary of his central beliefs regarding the role of personal freedom in our lives.

In certain respects, Sartre begins his exploration of human freedom where William James leaves off. James makes a compelling case for why believing in the possibility of human freedom is a more rational view of the world than not believing in it. Using the same foundation as James—the testimony of lived experience—Sartre assumes that human freedom is a reality, and then goes on to develop an entire worldview based on this conviction. And while James is most concerned with establishing the

Jean-Paul Sartre (1905–1980). Sartre was a French philosopher and founder of Existentialism, a school of thought based on the idea that "existence precedes essence." His *Being and Nothingness* (1943) offers a full exploration of this view. Sartre also wrote literary criticism, plays, and novels and was awarded the Nobel Prize for Literature in 1954 (which he declined.)

((•●[**Listen** to the **Podcast**
*Mary Warnock on
Sartre's Existentialism*
on **mysearchlab.com**

possibility of freedom, Sartre's view of freedom is extreme: We are "condemned" to be *totally* free, a radical view of freedom that makes us completely responsible for who we are.

Sartre begins his essay by defining existentialism.

Jean-Paul Sartre, from *Existentialism Is a Humanism*

. . . There are two kinds of existentialists; first, those who are Christian, among whom I would include Jaspers and Gabriel Marcel, both Catholic; and on the other hand the atheistic existentialists, among whom I class Heidegger, and then the French Existentialists and myself. What they have in common is that they think that existence precedes essence, or, if you prefer, that subjectivity must be the starting point.

Just what does that mean? Let us consider some object that is manufactured, for example, a book or a paper-cutter [letter-opener]: here is an object which has been made by an artisan whose inspiration came from a concept. He referred to the concept of what a paper-cutter is and likewise to a known method of production, which is part of the concept, something which is, by and large, a routine. Thus, the paper-cutter is at once an object produced in a certain way and, on the other hand, one having a specific use; and one can not postulate a man who produces a paper-cutter but does not know what it is used for. Therefore, let us say that, for the paper-cutter, essence—that is, the ensemble of both the production routines and the properties which enable it to be both produced and defined—precedes existence. Thus, the presence of the paper-cutter or book in front of me is determined. Therefore, we have here a technical view of the world whereby it can be said that production precedes existence.

Though it's not initially obvious, Sartre is using this example of producing a paper-cutter as a way of illustrating a larger metaphysical framework within which he will situate people. In the production of a paper-cutter—or any physical object that is manufactured—there must first be an initial concept of the object and then a production formula for bringing it into existence. Thus, in general terms, we can say that the "essence" of the paper-cutter (the initial concept and the production formula) *precedes* its existence. Humans, according to Sartre, are very different from paper-cutter, but people often still use this same metaphysical framework as a model for understanding human development, even though this "essence precedes existence" model is appropriate only for inanimate objects.

Jean-Paul Sartre,
from *Existentialism Is
a Humanism*

When we conceive God as the Creator, He is generally thought of as a superior sort of artisan. Whatever doctrine we may be considering, whether one like that of Descartes or that of Leibnitz, we always grant that will more or less follows understanding or, at the very least, accompanies it, and that when God creates He knows exactly what He is creating. Thus, the concept of man in the mind of God is comparable to the concept of paper-cutter in the mind of the manufacturer, and, following certain techniques and a conception, God produces man, just as the artisan, following a definition and a technique, makes a paper-cutter. Thus, the individual man is the realization of a certain concept in the divine intelligence.

When people imagine human existence as being the product of God's creation, Sartre believes they are unwittingly—and mistakenly—using the letter-opener metaphysic to understand human creation. Prior to our physical conception and birth, we "exist" in the omniscient (all-knowing) mind of God, both as a concept and as a formula for production. Thus, just like the letter-opener, our "essence" precedes our "existence"; that is, our *soul* or *spirit* is a reality prior to our physical existence on earth. Our thoughts, ideas, choices, and actions are a direct reflection of our preexisting *soul* or *spirit*.

But according to Sartre, those who believe in a divine Creator are not the only ones guilty of misunderstanding the nature of human existence in such a profound way. There are also those who, while denying the existence of a divine Creator, nevertheless believe that we each possess an essential and universal human nature that precedes our actual historical existence. This essential nature forms the structure of our personalities, and our thoughts, ideas, choices, and action are a direct result of its influence. Thus, this is also a view in which, like the letter-opener, our "essence" precedes our "existence."

((•—[**Listen** to the **Interview** *Jean Paul Sartre* with *Melvyn Bragg* on **mysearchlab.com**

In the eighteenth century, the atheism of the *philosophes* discarded the idea of God, but not so much for the notion that essence precedes existence. To a certain extent, this idea is found everywhere; we find it in Diderot, in Voltaire, and even in Kant. Man has a human nature; this human nature, which is the concept of the human, is found in all men, which means that each man is a particular example of a universal concept, man. In Kant, the result of this universality is that the wildman, the natural man, as well as the bourgeois, are circumscribed by the same definition and have the same basic qualities. Thus, here too the essence of man precedes the historical existence that we find in nature.

Jean-Paul Sartre, from *Existentialism Is a Humanism*

All of these "essence precedes existence" views of human existence are, according to Sartre, irretrievably flawed and confused. In fact, their view of human existence is completely the opposite of what it should be. For Sartre, an accurate view of human experience is based on the principle "existence precedes essence," not the reverse!

Atheistic existentialism, which I represent, is more coherent. It states that if God does not exist, there is at least one being in whom existence precedes essence, a being who exists before he can be defined by any concept, and that this being is man, or, as Heidegger says, human reality. What is meant here by saying that existence precedes essence? It means that, first of all, man exists, turns up, appears on the scene, and, only afterward, defines himself. If man, as the existentialist conceives him, is indefinable, it is because at first he is nothing. Only afterward will he be something, and he himself will have made what he will be. Thus, there is no human nature, since there is no God to conceive it. Not only is man what he conceives himself to be, but he is also only what he wills himself to be after this thrust toward existence.

Man is nothing else but what he makes of himself. Such is the first principle of existentialism. It is also what is called subjectivity, the name we are labeled with when charges are brought against us. But what do we mean by this, if not that man has a greater dignity than a stone or table? For we mean that man first exists, that is, that man first of all is the being who hurls himself toward a future and who is conscious of imagining himself as being in the future. Man is at the start a plan which is aware of itself, rather than a patch of moss, a piece of garbage, or a cauliflower; nothing exists prior to this plan; there is nothing in heaven; man will be what he will have planned to be. Not what he will want to be. Because by the word "will" we generally mean a conscious decision, which is subsequent to what we have already made of ourselves. I may want to belong to a political party, write a book, get married; but all that is only a manifestation of an earlier, more spontaneous choice that is called "will." But if existence really does precede essence, man is responsible for what he is. Thus, existentialism's first move is to make every man aware of what he is and to make the full responsibility of his existence rest on him. And when we say that a man is responsible for himself, we do not only mean that he is responsible for his own individuality, but that he is responsible for all men.

Jean-Paul Sartre, from *Existentialism Is a Humanism*

" **Man is nothing else but what he makes of himself.** "

The essential problem with nonexistentialist views of human existence, according to Sartre, is that they focus on our historical existence in the past, not our orientation toward the future. But it is our focus on the future, the way our minds naturally leap ahead imaginatively, that distinguishes our essential natures. It is through imagining a future that we then weigh alternatives and select options to make this imagined future a reality. It is this ongoing projection toward the future that renders us uniquely human, and it is the ability to imagine a nearly limitless number of future paths, and to select from among them, that makes us uniquely free. Although our past experiences and developed personality have set the stage for our moment of choice, it is the beckoning future that defines our spirit.

For example, consider your current state of consciousness. Though you may reflect on your past, it is your future goals and dreams that define your essence. What will you be doing this evening, next week, next year, and beyond? And what actions will you have to take to reach these goals and achieve these dreams? And how can you ensure that the choices you make reflect your authentic self, your deepest values and highest aspirations?

This perspective on human existence is contrary to many common views that hold that our history defines our present and our future. For example, the view of God as supernatural creator often assumes that each individual's soul is crafted and defined prior to his or her existence on Earth, and so the individual's "essence" precedes his or her "existence." The same is true, to one degree or another, of the main theories of human behavior that we explored at the beginning of the chapter:

- *Human nature:* "People are born with certain basic instincts that influence and determine how they behave."
- *The environment:* "People are shaped by their environment, conditioned by their experiences to be the kind of people they are."
- *Psychological forces:* "People are governed by psychological forces, many of them unconscious, that cause them to think, feel, and act in certain ways."
- *Social dynamics:* "We are social creatures that are greatly influenced by the people around us."

Each of these theories is designed to explain who we are by reference to factors that predate the choices we are making. Why do we act the way we do, according to these theories? Why do you choose a certain group of friends, select a given career, engage in a romantic relationship, not to mention the countless choices you make on an a daily basis? Because of the influence of

- genetically programmed instincts that make up our human nature.
- experiential forces that have shaped and molded our personalities.
- deep-seated drives and emotions, of many of which we are unaware.
- social pressures from other people.

In all of these instances the underlying assumption is that "essence precedes existence"—that is, factors such as human nature, past experiences, psychological forces, or social dynamics determine who we are and the choices we make. In other words, all of these theories assume that your "essence" as a person, as defined by the factors identified above, comes *before* your actual "existence" in the moment that choices are made and actions are taken.

There are serious consequences to such an "essence precedes existence" framework, as we noted earlier. To begin with, all of these beliefs about the human self have the effect of removing—or diminishing—responsibility from the individual for her or his actions. If the choices you make, the actions you take, are the direct result of human nature, past experiences, psychological forces, or social dynamics, then you cannot be held responsible (or fully responsible) because these influences were beyond your control. Analogously, an "essence precedes existence" framework limits future possibilities for people. To the extent that our choices and actions are the result of preexistent influences that are beyond our control, we are limited in our power to think independently and choose freely the directions we want to take in life.

Do we have a greater responsibility to humankind in the choices we make? According to Sartre, we create "a certain image of man" with every action. Do you think this is true? In what sense might our actions allow for situations like those depicted in the film *Slumdog Millionaire*?

For Sartre, to explain your human essence and the choices you make (which define your existence) in terms of any "essence precedes existence" theory is to place yourself in the same category as unreflective life forms like moss and cauliflower. But such perspectives, no matter how well intentioned, miss entirely the essence of who you are. You are a thinking being, capable of reflective thought, propelled toward a future of your own creation, making free choices independent of any prior influences. *That's* who you are, a being whose existence from moment to moment precedes your essence, which you are in the process of creating and recreating with every choice you make. Whatever influences are a part of your history—inborn instincts, environmental conditioning, psychological forces, social influences—you have the capacity to separate yourself from them and to make genuinely independent and free choices. Rather than looking at your history in the rearview mirror, you should be looking ahead to the person you are in the process of creating.

The consequence of this radical view of freedom is a radical responsibility. If every choice you make is genuinely free, independent of any historical influence, then you are completely responsible for your choices and their consequences. There is no point in seeking escape from your responsibility by blaming your human nature, past experiences, psychological forces, or social dynamics. You chose freely; therefore your choice is your **responsibility**.

But isn't this a potentially dangerous theory? After all, if we give people unlimited license to choose whatever they want, as long as they accept responsibility for their choices, how can we condemn the actions of evil people like Hitler? When confronted regarding their moral evil, couldn't they respond: "I'm an existentialist: My choices are completely free, and I accept responsibility for them. So you have no grounds for condemning me."

This is a serious issue for Sartre, one that we will examine more closely in the chapters on moral philosophy. But for now we can look briefly at Sartre's approach to dealing with this potentially devastating critique, for he is clearly aware of its threat. Sartre himself was a person of strong moral principles, which led him to become a fighter for the French Resistance during World War II, following the invasion of France by Nazi Germany. For Sartre, choosing freely and accepting one's responsibility is not a solely individual project: It takes place in a social context and embodies an enlightened sense of moral responsibility to humanity as a whole.

Responsibility Humans are accountable for their actions, which they freely choose.

Jean-Paul Sartre,
from *Existentialism Is
a Humanism*

> When we say that man chooses his own self, we mean that every one of us does likewise; but we also mean by that that in making this choice he also chooses all men. In fact, in creating the man that we want to be, there is not a single one of our acts which does not at the same time create an image of man as we think he ought to be. To choose to be this or that is to affirm at the same time the value of what we choose, because we can never choose evil. We always choose the good, and nothing can be good for us without being good for all.
>
> . . . If we grant that we exist and fashion our image at one and the same time, the image is valid for everybody and for our whole age. Thus, our responsibility is much greater than we might have supposed, because it involves all mankind. . . . If I want to marry, to have children; even if this marriage depends solely on my own circumstances or passion or wish, I am involving all humanity in monogamy and not merely myself. Therefore, I am responsible for myself and for everyone else. I am creating a certain image of man of my own choosing. In choosing myself, I choose man.

Sartre is invoking a bold blend of Immanuel Kant and Plato in his effort to save his theory from amorality. Kant founded his ethical theory on what he termed his categorical imperative: "Act as if the maxim of your action were to become by your will a universal law of nature." In other words, Kant is suggesting that the standard we use in making moral decisions is to ask ourselves: "Would I be rationally able to endorse *everyone* making the same choice as I?" For example, if you're contemplating gossiping about someone you don't care for, you would have to support, as a rational requirement, that *everyone* gossip in all comparable situations. Or if you're thinking about purchasing a term paper online and submitting it as your own, you would have to endorse as a rational law that *everyone* is doing exactly the same thing.

Sartre seems to be trying to attach his theory of free choice to this same "universalizing" concept when he states:

Jean-Paul Sartre,
from *Existentialism Is
a Humanism*

> When we say that man chooses his own self, we mean that every one of us does likewise; but we also mean by that that in making this choice he also chooses all men. In fact, in creating the man that we want to be, there is not a single one of our acts which does not at the same time create an image of man as we think he ought to be.

When you make a choice, according to Sartre, you are not simply creating and defining yourself as a person—you are also creating and defining your image of the way all humans *should* be. So if you choose to gossip or cheat, you are by implication suggesting that all humans should be gossips and cheats.

Sartre also seems to be drawing on Plato's ethical perspective that no person does evil intentionally. Plato was convinced that when people act immorally it is due to ignorance because they are unenlightened and don't know better. When you educate people and show them a more enlightened path, they cannot help but take it. Sartre seems to be making the same point when he states, "To choose to be this or that is to affirm at the same time the value of what we choose, because we can never choose evil. We always choose the good, and nothing can be good for us without being good for all." The idea that no one does evil voluntarily is a provocative but also problematic view, for both Plato and Sartre, and we will analyze it further in later chapters.

For now, let's continue our exploration of Sartre's concept of radical freedom. For Sartre, an existentialist perspective illuminates the deeply felt emotions that are an inescapable part of the human condition. Sartre identifies three such fundamental emotions that define our experience when we discover that we are condemned to be free: *anguish, abandonment,* and *despair.*

First, what is meant by anguish? The existentialists say at once that man is anguish. What that means is this: the man who involves himself and who realizes that he is not only the person he chooses to be, but also a law-maker who is, at the same time, choosing all mankind as well as himself, cannot help escape the feeling of his total and deep responsibility. Of course, there are many people who are not anxious; but we claim that they are hiding their anxiety, that they are fleeing from it. Certainly, many people believe that when they do something, they themselves are the only ones involved, and when someone says to them, "What if everyone acted that way?" they shrug their shoulders and answer, "Everyone doesn't act that way." But really, one should always ask himself, "What would happen if everybody looked at things that way?" There is no escaping this disturbing thought except by a kind of double-dealing. A man who lies and makes excuses for himself by saying "not everybody does that," is someone with an uneasy conscience, because the act of lying implies that a universal value is conferred upon the lie.

Jean-Paul Sartre, from *Existentialism Is a Humanism*

Throughout our lives we are called on to make difficult decisions in complex circumstances. How can we be sure we're doing the right thing? In the final analysis, we can't be sure. We can't really depend on the advice of others; who is to say that they are right? And even the prevailing norms, moral codes, and holy books that we are familiar with typically provide guidance that is conflicting, ambiguous, or too general to be of practical use.

If we are truly honest with ourselves, we realize the distressing and inescapable fact that we alone have to decide what is the right thing to do and that there is no one to rely on for advice other than ourselves. The result of this searing insight? A profound, existential anguish. And not only do we shoulder the burden of responsibility for ourselves when we make what we hope are the "right" choices, we are also assuming the responsibility of creating an image for all humankind. And what makes this intimidating responsibility nearly unbearable is the certainty of our uncertainty—we will never be sure that we're doing the right thing.

But what about people who don't seem to be experiencing this overwhelming feeling of anguish, who seem to simply live their lives on the surface, making choices without any apparent sense of profound responsibility? How does Sartre account for these individuals? He believes that they're "in denial."

For every man, everything happens as if all mankind had its eyes fixed on him and were guiding itself by what he does. And every man ought to say to himself, "Am I really the kind of man who has the right to act in such a way that humanity might guide itself by my actions?" And if he does not say that to himself, he is masking his anguish.

Jean-Paul Sartre, from *Existentialism Is a Humanism*

Those who deny their experience of existential anguish are striving desperately to escape from their freedom. But their strivings are doomed to failure. We are "condemned to be free," and our freedom is a lifetime sentence. We can try to hide from our freedom, attempt to assign it to others, pretend that our actions are determined by forces beyond our control, claim that we were only following the directions of others— but whatever efforts we make to escape from our freedom, *we are still free,* and nothing will ever change this simple fact. Those people who live their lives seeking to deny and escape from their freedom are living lives that are false, diminished, *inauthentic.*

On the other hand, embracing your freedom and experiencing the anguish of your profound responsibility in life does not entail becoming paralyzed with fear, frozen into inaction. Quite the contrary, according to Sartre.

Jean-Paul Sartre,
from *Existentialism Is a Humanism*

> There is no question here of the kind of anguish which would lead to quietism, to inaction. It is a matter of a simple sort of anguish that anybody who has had responsibilities is familiar with. For example, when a military officer takes the responsibility for an attack and sends a certain number of men to death, he chooses to do so, and in the main he alone makes the choice. Doubtless, orders come from above, but they are too broad; he interprets them, and on this interpretation depend the lives of ten or fourteen or twenty men. In making a decision he can not help having a certain anguish. All leaders know this anguish. That doesn't keep them from acting; on the contrary, it is the very condition of their action. For it implies that they envisage a number of possibilities, and when they choose one, they realize that it has value only because it is chosen. We shall see this kind of anguish, which is the kind that existentialism describes, is explained, in addition, by a direct responsibility to the other men whom it involves. It is not a curtain separating us from action, but is part of the action itself.

This deep and abiding sense of responsibility should bring out the best in you, encouraging you to be thoughtful and serious about the choices you make. Your life is not trivial: It is your contribution to the human world, your record in history. The self you create, the life that you lead demands your total commitment. This is *your* life—no one else's—and you are responsible for crafting a life of which you can be proud and that will earn the admiration of others. This is Sartre's message. For those who decide to think in limited and myopic ways, to run from their freedom and responsibility, to make choices with only their own selfish needs in mind—these people are living inauthentic lives of diminished value.

Consistent with Sartre's atheistic existentialism is the second profound emotion that he believes is an unavoidable part of the human condition: *abandonment.* Sartre explains:

Jean-Paul Sartre,
from *Existentialism Is a Humanism*

> When we speak of abandonment, a term Heidegger was fond of, we mean only that God does not exist and that we have to face all the consequences of this. The existentialist is strongly opposed to a certain kind of secular ethics which would like to abolish God with the least possible expense. . . .
>
> The existentialist, on the contrary, thinks it very distressing that God does not exist, because all possibility of finding values in a heaven of ideas disappears along with Him; there can no longer be an *a priori* Good, since there is no infinite and perfect consciousness to think it. Nowhere is it written that the Good exists, that we must be honest, that we must not lie; because the fact is we are on a plane where there are only men. Dostoevsky said, "If God didn't exist, everything would be possible." That is the very starting point of existentialism. Indeed, everything is permissible if God does not exist, and as a result man feels abandoned, because neither within him nor without does he find anything to cling to. He can't start making excuses for himself.
>
> If existence really does precede essence, there is no explaining things away by reference to a fixed and given human nature. In other words, there is no determinism, man is free, man is freedom. On the other hand, if God does not exist, we find no values or commands to turn to which legitimize our conduct. So, in the bright realm of values, we have no excuse behind us, nor justification before us. We are alone, with no excuses.

When was the last time that you felt abandoned? It's a devastating experience, feeling not just alone, but having been *left alone.* Abandonment is the absence of a caring presence that we had become accustomed to, a caring presence that is suddenly torn away. For Sartre, this is another fundamental emotion of the human condition. Why? Because most of us have been raised to believe that there is an ultimate caring presence to guide, nurture, and take care of us. For many, this caring presence has been a supreme being—"God(s)"—in some form. For others, the caring presence has been a cultural identity that has provided a clear moral framework. For others, it has been a sharply defined natural philosophy that has included universal values independently of religion. All of these caring presences, according to Sartre, provide a false and illegitimate sense of security. When we honestly understand the human predicament, we realize that we are utterly alone, with no one to turn to for support other than ourselves.

A radical act of free will? On June 11, 1963, Thich Quang Duc set himself on fire to draw the world's attention to the persecution of Buddhists under the U.S.-backed South Vietnamese regime. What is your reaction to this action? How might Sartre have interpreted it?

Sartre claims that some people try to maintain the moral advantages of God without believing in God's existence. These efforts are doomed to fail. It is not possible to proclaim universal moral values inscribed in the structure of the universe because such a proclamation makes no sense without a supernatural being to authenticate these values. Similarly, we cannot ground values in a universal human nature because, according to Sartre, there is no human nature. Each person creates his or her self through the choices that they make on a daily basis. We must accept our abandonment, forge our own set of values through our free choices, and accept our responsibility.

The final existential emotion that helps define the human condition is *despair*. Sartre explains:

> As for despair, the term has a very simple meaning. It means that we shall confine ourselves to reckoning only with what depends upon our will, or on the ensemble of probabilities which make our action possible. When we want something, we always have to reckon with probabilities. I may be counting on the arrival of a friend. The friend is coming by rail or street-car; this supposes that the train will arrive on schedule, or that the street-car will not jump the track. I am left in the realm of possibility; but possibilities are to be reckoned with only to the point where my action comports with the ensemble of these possibilities, and no further. The moment the possibilities I am considering are not rigorously involved by my action, I ought to disengage myself from them, because no God, no scheme, can adapt the world and its possibilities to my will. When Descartes said, "Conquer yourself rather than the world," he meant essentially the same thing.

Jean-Paul Sartre, from *Existentialism Is a Humanism*

For Sartre, despair results from recognizing that there are many elements in life that are completely outside of our control. No matter how clear our vision, how determined our will, there will be factors that we cannot influence. We may train for a career and then not be able to find a suitable position. We may embark on marriage with great hope and then have the marriage unravel despite our best efforts. We may develop a detailed, long-term plan for ourselves and then endure an accident or illness that makes the plan untenable. Does this recognition and the accompanying feeling of despair mean that we should approach life pessimistically, cynical about our power to influence, fearful of what may befall us? Absolutely not!

Jean-Paul Sartre, from *Existentialism Is a Humanism*

> The doctrine I am presenting is the very opposite of quietism, since it declares, "There is no reality except in action." Moreover, it goes further, since it adds, "Man is nothing else than his plan; he exists only to the extent that he fulfills himself; he is therefore nothing else than the ensemble of his acts, nothing else than his life."

Despite the ever-present threat of the unknown, Sartre believes that this recognition of both our absolute freedom and the limitations of our control should spur us to positive action. Why? Because our actions are the only genuine part of ourselves that define our lives. We truly exist only to the extent that we have acted boldly, forcefully, courageously, creatively, and lovingly. Everything else is of little consequence; and, for those individuals who choose a life of trivial action, their lives and their selves are also trivialized. Sartre recognizes that his perspective is not going to be very popular.

Jean-Paul Sartre, from *Existentialism Is a Humanism*

> According to this, we can understand why our doctrine horrifies certain people. Because often the only way they can bear their wretchedness is to think, "Circumstances have been against me. What I've been and done doesn't show my true worth. To be sure, I've had no great love, no great friendship, but that's because I haven't met a man or woman who was worthy. The books I've written haven't been very good because I haven't had the proper leisure. I haven't had children to devote myself to because I didn't find a man with whom I could have spent my life. So there remains within me, unused and quite viable, a host of propensities, inclinations, possibilities, that one wouldn't guess from the mere series of things I've done."
>
> Now, for the existentialist there is really no love other than one which manifests itself in a person's being in love. There is no genius other than one which is expressed in works of art; the genius of Proust is the sum of Proust's works; the genius of Racine is his series of tragedies. Outside of that, there is nothing. Why say that Racine could have written another tragedy, when he didn't write it? A man is involved in life, leaves his impression on it, and outside of that there is nothing. To be sure, this may seem a harsh thought to someone whose life hasn't been a success. But, on the other hand, it prompts people to understand that reality alone is what counts, that dreams, expectation, and hope warrant no more than to define a man as a disappointed dream, as miscarried hopes, as vain expectations. In other words, to define him negatively and not positively. However, when we say "You are nothing else than your life," that does not imply that the artist will be judged solely on the basis of his works of art; a thousand other things will contribute toward summing him up. What we mean is that a man is nothing else than a series of undertakings, that he is the sum, the organization, the ensemble of the relationships which make up these undertakings.

> **[Existentialism] prompts people to understand that reality alone is what counts. . . .**

You are the sum of your actions and accomplishments, not your wishes, dreams, or intentions. It's a harsh message but one that Sartre believes is ultimately uplifting because it encourages people to strive mightily to achieve great things and live a full life. Such a philosophy removes the temptation to remain passively in a fantasy life of "if only." It is the embodiment of the metaphor of you being the artist of your life, encouraging you to make yourself a masterpiece.

Analyzing Sartre on Freedom, Choice, and Responsibility

- Reflect on Sartre's core belief that "existence precedes essence." Do you believe that your *self* (*soul*, *spirit* or *personality*) already existed before or at the moment of your birth? Or do you believe that you create your *essence* through the choices that you freely make? Explain the reasons for your response.

- A number of factors seem to influence a person's development, including environmental experiences and learning, genetic programming and inborn instincts, social pressures and cultural socialization, and free choices. Think about the blending of factors that has produced you as a person. Which factors have been most influential in your development? How would Sartre respond to the idea that factors other than free choice contributed to your development (if you believe that they have)?

- Have you ever experienced the emotions of *anguish*, *abandonment*, and *despair* in the profound, existential sense that Sartre believes is part of the human condition? Do you think experiencing these emotions is a useful barometer for determining your efforts to escape from your freedom?

- Later in life Sartre became a Marxist and modified his radical views on freedom, arguing that economic and political forces can limit freedom. Should this biographical fact influence our evaluation of these earlier views? Why or why not?

- Some people believe that Sartre's message, while disturbing, is ultimately inspiring and uplifting because of its emphasis on personal freedom and personal responsibility. What is your response to Sartre's basic ideas? Do you agree that we are "condemned" to be completely free?

4.5 A Feminist Analysis of Freedom

Feminist thought has explored the complexities of freedom in some depth, particularly with respect to the manner in which internal constraints limit the possibility of genuine freedom. In the following reading, the philosopher **Jean Grimshaw** analyzes the ways in which repressive social forces can erode an individual's psychological autonomy—that is, their ability to think independently. Grimshaw, along with many other feminists, believe that many of these repressive forces are patriarchical, originating from men in male-dominated societies.

Jean Grimshaw, from *Autonomy and Identity in Feminist Thinking*

Issues about women's autonomy have been central to feminist thinking and action. Women have so often been in situations of powerlessness and dependence that any system of belief or programme of action that could count as "feminist" must in some way see this as a central concern. But what is meant by "autonomy" and under what conditions is it possible? This has been an important and contentious question in philosophy. But questions about autonomy, and related questions about self and identity, have also been important to feminism, and within feminist thinking it is possible to find radically different ways of thinking about these things. . . .

Feminist thinking does not, of course, exist in a vacuum, and in thinking about women's autonomy, feminists have drawn on different (and conflicting) approaches to questions about the human self, some of which have a long history. I want to begin by going back to an argument that Aristotle put forward in the *Ethics*, since I think that the point at which his argument breaks down can illuminate the nature of the problem some feminist thinking has faced.

Aristotle's argument concerns the question of what it is that makes an action "voluntary," done of a person's own free will, and in order to answer this question, he distinguished between actions whose origin was "inside" a person, and those whose origin was "outside," which resulted from external influences or pressure or compulsion. He discussed at some length the problems that arise over trying to define ideas such as "compulsion," and in estimating the degree of severity of pressure that could make an action not voluntary. But in this sort of model of autonomy, what defines an action as autonomous is seen as its point of *origin*; it must have an "immaculate conception," as it were, from *within* the self.

Now ultimately I think that it is this definition of "autonomy" in terms of origin and the associated distinction between an "inner" self which can in some way spontaneously generate its "own" actions, and "external" influences which are not "part" of the self, that will need challenging. But I think it is possible to defend the Aristotelian version of autonomy up to a point, provided notions of "inside" and "outside" the self are defined in a certain way. If a person is prevented from doing what they would otherwise intend or desire to do, or if they are coerced into doing what they would *not* otherwise want to desire to do, they are not acting autonomously. Under this interpretation, actions which originate from "inside" the self are those which are seen as in accordance with conscious desires or intentions, and those which originate from "outside" the self are those which one would not do if one were not coerced. The pressure here is to consider the sorts of circumstances which do, in fact, coerce people in these sorts of ways. And, of course, a central concern of feminism has been to identify and fight against the kinds of coercion to which women have been subjected, including things like physical violence and economic dependence.

But it is at this point that an Aristotelian-type argument fails to be able to deal with the most difficult questions about autonomy. The Aristotelian view, as I have interpreted it, "works" only to the extent that it is assumed that there is no problem about what I shall call "the autonomy of desires." Autonomy is defined as acting in accordance with desire (or intention). But what of the desires themselves? Are there *desires* (or intentions) which are not "autonomous," which do not originate from "within" the self, which are not authentic, not really "one's own"?

Grimshaw is delineating here the distinction between *external constraints* and *internal constraints*, which we explored in previous sections. As we have seen, *soft determinists* agree with Aristotle: Voluntary choices are those made by an individual that are not the result of external pressures or compulsions. But Grimshaw is asking the same question that many have asked: Can't choices that are not *externally constrained* nevertheless be "involuntary" or "unfree" because they are *internally constrained*? Can we assume that an individual's desires are always autonomous, or is it possible that there are "*desires*" (or intentions) which are not "autonomous," which do not originate from "within" the self, which are not authentic, not really "one's own"? Grimshaw proceeds to explore the "psychic coercion" that she believes can and does occur, an *internal constraint* that compromises individual autonomy and limits personal freedom.

Jean Grimshaw,
from *Autonomy and Identity in Feminist Thinking*

Feminist writers have wanted, of course, to indict the various forms of brutality and coercion from which women have suffered. But this brutality and coercion has been seen not merely as a question of physical or "external" coercion or constraint; the force of subjection has also been seen as a psychic one, invading women's very selves. The language of "conditioning," "brainwashing," "indoctrination," and so forth, has been used to describe this force. The female self, under male domination, is riddled through and through with false or conditioned desires. But set against this conditioned, nonautonomous female self are various images of a female self that would be authentic, that would transcend or shatter this conditioning. I want now to look at some of these images of the female self in feminist discourse: my particular examples are from the work of **Mary Daly, Marilyn Frye** and **Kate Millett**.

Daly, Frye, and Millett all stress the way in which women have been subject to the *power* of men. Much of Daly's book, *Gyn/Ecology* (1979), is an account of the barbarities inflicted on women such as suttee, clitorectomy, footbinding and other forms of mutilation. Millett, in *Sexual Politics* (1977), sees patriarchal power as something so historically all-embracing that it has totally dominated women's lives. Frye, in *The Politics of Reality* (1983) uses the situation of a young girl sold into sexual slavery and then systematically brutalized and brainwashed into a life of service to her captors as an analogy for the situation of all women. And all three writers stress the way in which they see the female self as "invaded" by patriarchal conditioning. Millett writes:

> When in any group of persons, the ego is subjected to such invidious versions of itself through social beliefs, ideology and tradition, the effect is bound to be pernicious. This should make it no very special cause for surprise that women develop group characteristics common to those who suffer minority status and a marginal existence.

Women, she argues, are deprived of all but the most trivial sources of dignity or self-respect. In her discussion of Lawrence's depiction of Connie in *Lady Chatterly's Lover*, what she sees Connie as relinquishing is "self, ego, will, individuality" (243); all those things which, Millett argues, women had but recently achieved (and for which Lawrence had a profound distaste).

Mary Daly's picture of the way in which women's selves are invaded by patriarchal conditioning is even more striking. She describes women, for example, as "moronized," "robotized," "lobotomized," as "the puppets of Papa." At times she seems to see women as so "brainwashed" that they are scarcely human; thus she describes them as "fembots," even as "mutants." In Millett, Daly, and Frye, women are seen primarily as *victims*; the monolithic brutality and psychological pressures of male power have reduced women almost to the state of being "non-persons." And indeed, as Daly sees women as having become "mutants" or "fembots," so Millett sees them as not having been allowed to participate in fully "human" activities, as Frye sees them as simply "broken" and then "remade" in the way that suits her masters.

But behind this victimized female self, whose actions and desires are assumed to be not truly "her own," since they derive from processes of force, conditioning or psychological manipulation, there is seen to be an authentic female self, whose recovery or discovery it is one of the aims of feminism to achieve. The spatial metaphor implicit in the word "behind" is not accidental, since this model of self is premised on the possibility of making a distinction between an "inner" and an "outer" self. Ibsen's Peer Gynt compared his quest for identity to the process of peeling layers off an onion; but after shedding all the "false selves," he found that there was nothing inside, no "core." The sort of spatial metaphor implicit in Peer Gynt's account of himself is also apt in the accounts of self given by Daly, Millett, and Frye, except that there *is* assumed to be a

How can social images and roles like the "Happy Housewife" restrict people's freedom? Many feminists believe that the freedom of women has been constrained by the coercive forces of social conditioning and psychological manipulation.

"core." This is the clearest in the work of Daly. In *Gyn/Ecology*, discovering or recovering one's own self is seen as akin to a process of salvation or religious rebirth, and Daly writes of what she calls the unveiling or unwinding of the "shrouds" of patriarchy to reveal the authentic female Spirit-Self underneath. And this Self is seen as a unitary and harmonious one. Splits and barriers within the psyche, she argues, as well as those between Selves, are the result of patriarchal conditioning. In the unitary and harmonious female Spirit-Self there will be no such splits. . . .

The paradigm of coercion, writes Frye, is *not* the direct application of physical force. Rather, it is a situation in which choice and action *do* take place, and in which the victim acts under her own perception and judgment. Hence, what the exploiter needs is that

> The will and intelligence of the victim to be disengaged from the projects of resistance and escape but that they not be simply broken or destroyed. Ideally, the disintegration and misintegration of the victim should accomplish the detachment of the victim's will and intelligence from the victim's own interests and their attachment to the interests of the exploiter. This will effect a displacement or dissolution of self-respect and will undermine the victim's intolerance of coercion. With that, the situation transcends the initial paradigmatic form or structure of coercion; for if people don't mind doing what you want them to do, you can't really be *making* them do it.

And, she writes:

> The health and integrity of an organism is a matter of its being organized largely towards its own interests and welfare. She is healthy and "working right" when her substance is organized primarily on principles which align it to *her* interests and welfare. Co-operation is essential of course, but it will not do that I arrange everything so that *you* get enough exercise: for me to be healthy, *I* must get enough exercise. My being adequately exercised is logically independent of your being so.

Frye is writing here as if it were possible to distinguish the interests of one self sharply from those of another, and as if, were the effects of male domination to be undone, it would not be too much of a problem for the self to know what its interests were.

In various ways then, underlying much of the work of these three writers is a set of assumptions about the self. First, that it is, at least potentially, a unitary, rational thing, aware of its interests. Second, that "splits" within the psyche should be seen as resulting from the interference of patriarchal or male-dominated socialization or conditioning. Third, that the task of undoing this conditioning is one that can be achieved solely by a rational process of learning to understand and fight against the social and institutional effects of male domination. And implicit in these assumptions about the self, I think, is a conception of autonomy. Frye writes that "left to themselves" women would not want to serve men. Daly writes of unveiling or unwinding the "shrouds" of patriarchy. Millett writes of the individuality and ego that women can discover in themselves once they recognize the effects of their patriarchal socialization. And in all three, what is autonomous (or authentic) is what is seen as originating in some way from *within* the self; what is in some way *untainted* by the conditioning or manipulation to which a woman has previously been subjected.

Grimshaw's article, and the voices of Frye, Daly, and Millett that are woven into it, present a compelling and disturbing analysis of the ways in which women in most cultures have been subjugated, denied independent thought and action, and subjected to brutalizing forces that have had the cumulative effect of alienating them from their authentic female selves. The possibility of free choice represents perhaps the only viable vehicle to eliminate these negative constraints, both external and internal. But the meaningful exercise of free choice is contingent on becoming aware of the fact and nature of repressive forces and then making consistent, determined choices to liberate oneself from them. These are central themes that we will be exploring in the next sections of the chapter.

< READING CRITICALLY >

Analyzing Jean Grimshaw on Autonomy

- Why does Grimshaw consider Aristotle's definition of "autonomy" to be inadequate from a feminist perspective?

- Grimshaw poses the question: "Are there *desires* (or intentions) which are not 'autonomous,' which do not originate from 'within' the self, which are not authentic, not really 'one's own'?" How does this question relate to the following observation from Erich Fromm?

   A great number of our decisions are not really our own but are suggested to us from the outside; we have succeeded in persuading ourselves that it is we who have made the decision, whereas we have actually conformed with expectations of others, driven by the fear of isolation and by more direct threats to our life, freedom, and comfort.

- Grimshaw observes that "Ibsen's Peer Gynt compared his quest for identity to the process of peeling layers off an onion; but after shedding all of the 'false selves,' he found that there was nothing inside, no 'core.'" In contrast, the authors referred to by Grimshaw all believe that there is an "authentic female Spirit-Self" at the core of each woman and that women can discover their "core" by freeing themselves from social and psychological oppression. Do you agree with their conviction regarding the existence of an authentic core self? Do you think this same argument can be extended to include people in general, including men? Why or why not?

4.6 Making Connections: Creating a Synthesis

At the beginning of the chapter, we noted that the question of whether we are capable of making free choices was one that becomes progressively more complicated the deeper we delve into it. There are a number of influential thinkers, such as Baron d'Holbach, who believe that personal freedom is an illusion, that all of our actions are necessarily determined by factors outside of our control. Some of these thinkers believe that it is our genetic heritage that plays a dominant role in who we become and the actions we take. Others, such as behavioral psychologists John Watson and B. F. Skinner, believe that we are entirely the products of conditioning experiences that have molded us and determined our actions. Some thinkers, such as Sigmund Freud, view the locus of control in unconscious instincts and drives that influence us without our even being aware of it. And many believe that who we are is the result of the *interaction* of these various factors. The genetic blueprint with which you begin life— your gender, race, basic temperament, physical qualities—dynamically interacts with environmental factors to gradually shape your development in complex ways. All of these thinkers can be considered *determinists* because they all believe that every choice you make is the necessary consequence of antecedent factors in your experience—a genetic blueprint, conditioning experiences, unconscious drives. There is no room for freedom of choice in these deterministic systems, and any feelings of freedom that we experience are mere illusions, without substance or reality.

And we have also seen that there is an entirely different group of thinkers, such as William James and Jean-Paul Sartre, who are convinced that personal freedom is real and that we are capable of making free choices independent of any influencing factors beyond our control. These thinkers, *indeterminists* (or *libertarians*), believe that until cogent evidence to the contrary is presented, we are entitled to put our trust in our belief in freedom (and responsibility), which is so deeply embedded in our experience as practical beings. We live our lives as if people are free and responsible, at least to some extent. Our core beliefs in morality, religion, self-improvement, social improvement, personal responsibility, criminal and civil justice, child rearing, and many other areas are founded on the conviction that people can make free choices and that they are responsible for the free choices that they make.

We also saw that there is a third perspective on the possibility of human freedom— *compatibilists (soft determinists)*—who believe that freedom means the opposite of compulsion: People are free if they are not prevented from acting on their unimpeded natural desires, even though these natural desires may be causally determined by factors in their personal history in accordance with universal laws.

You may recall that William James dismisses compatibilists as thinly disguised "soft" determinists because they agree with the fundamental deterministic principles. For the compatibilist, when you choose a major, a person to date, or an item on the menu, you are making a choice that is necessarily determined by factors in your history— you could not choose otherwise. However, if you are not being threatened or coerced to make your choice, then as far as soft determinists are concerned, your choice is free. Many indeterminists agree with James: Soft determinism defines free choice in such a narrow, limited way that it is really just a variation of determinism.

Overcoming Limitations to Your Freedom

So what is the answer? Is personal freedom a reality or an illusion? Are you capable of making genuinely free choices, or are your choices influenced and determined by causal factors woven into your personal history? Perhaps the most enlightened view is one that recognizes that the question is not either/or: Rather than people being completely free or completely unfree, perhaps there are *degrees* of freedom and nonfreedom. And that by developing your self-awareness you can *increase your freedom*. Let's explore how we might conceptualize and articulate such a perspective.

Most people have the deep-seated conviction that they are capable of making free choices. But how can we be sure? We are certainly born with a *genetic heritage* that not only determines our gender, race, and physical characteristics but also influences our personality. For example, studies of identical twins (thus possessing identical genetic "fingerprints") who were separated at birth and reared in different environments have revealed

Is heredity destiny? Do you think we are able to transcend the effects of these influences to make free, independent choices? Why?

provocative (although complex) results. Years later, despite great differences in their experiences since birth, some twins have exhibited remarkable similarities: identical gestures and senses of humor; the same number (and even names) of children; similar careers and hobbies—all underscoring the influence of genetic factors. We also know that the *environment* also plays a significant role in shaping people's characters and personalities. Young children are indeed like sponges, absorbing all of the information and influences around them and incorporating these elements into their thinking and behavior. Our attitudes, values, beliefs, interests, ways of relating to others—these and many other qualities are influenced by family, friends, and culture. This is the process by which positive values such as empathy and commitment get transmitted from generation to generation, and it is also how negative beliefs such as racism, sexism (as described in the article by Grimshaw), and violence are perpetuated.

If your genetic heritage and environmental background are such powerful forces in molding who you are, how is it possible to think that you are capable of making free choices in any meaningful sense? The answer to this enigma is that despite the early influences on your personal development, your mind and your thinking continue to mature. You have not only ongoing experiences but also the ability to *reflect* on these experiences and *learn* from them. Instead of simply accepting the views of others, you gradually develop the ability to *examine* this thinking and to *decide* whether it makes sense to you and whether you should accept it. So although you might share many beliefs with your parents or the prevailing culture in which you were raised, you likely disagree with many other areas. Although your parents might believe that sexual activity should begin with marriage or that the most important thing about a career is job security, you might have gradually developed very different perspectives on these issues.

The same is true of your personality. Although your genetic background and early experiences might have *contributed* to shaping the framework of your personality, it is up to you to *decide* who your future self will be. For example, your personality may incorporate many positive qualities from your parents as well as some that you dislike—such as a quick temper. But you can decide not to let this temper dominate your personality or be expressed inappropriately. With sufficient determination, you can be successful in controlling and redirecting this temper, though you may have occasional lapses. In other words, you can take a personality tendency formed early in your development and reshape it according to your own personal goals. In the same way, if your early history created qualities of insecurity, shyness, pessimism, insensitivity, passivity, or other qualities that you are unhappy about, you should realize that these traits do not represent a life sentence! You have it within your power to *remold* yourself, creating yourself to be the kind of person that you wish and choose to be. *This is the essence of freedom.* Free choice means dealing with an existing situation, selecting from a finite number of options, and working to reshape the present into the future.

Of course change often doesn't occur immediately. It took a long time for your personality to evolve into its present state, and it's going to take a while for you to reconceptualize and redirect it. It's like changing the course of a large ship: You need to turn the rudder to change course, but the past momentum of the ship makes the turn a gradual process, not a radical change of direction. The same is true with the human personality; meaningful change is a complex process, but by choosing to set the rudder on a new course and maintaining its position, you can change.

The first step in increasing your freedom is to become *aware* of the existence of constraints. For example, if someone is manipulating you to think or feel a certain way, you can't begin to deal with the manipulation until you become aware that it exists. Similarly, you can't solve a personal problem such as insecurity or emotional immaturity without first acknowledging that it *is* a problem and then developing insight into the internal forces that are driving your behavior. Once you have achieved this deeper level of understanding, you are then in a position to *choose* a different path for yourself, using appropriate decision-making and problem-solving approaches.

Confronting External Constraints

Many times we make choices that are not free because the choices are compelled by others. For example, if you are threatened with bodily harm by a mugger or an abusive spouse, your choices are made in response to these threats and clearly not free. Similarly, if you are being subjected to unreasonable pressure on the job by someone who has the power to fire you, the choices that you make are obviously constrained by the circumstances. As we have noted, these kinds of limitations on your freedom are known as *external constraints*, because they are external influences that force you to choose under duress. Although hostage tapes, ransom payments, and blackmail threats are extreme examples of this sort of coercion, there are many incipient forms of it as well. The appeal to fear used by political leaders, the subtle manipulations of an acquaintance, the implied threat by a panhandler, the sexual harassment perpetrated by someone in authority—these and countless other instances are testimony to the prevalence of external constraints on your freedom.

If you are limited by external forces, the way to free yourself is to *neutralize* or *remove* them, so that you can make choices that reflect your genuine desires. For example, if your choices are constrained by an unreasonable boss, you have to either change that person's coercive behavior or remove yourself from the situation to achieve genuine freedom. If you believe that your choices are excessively limited by the geographical location in which you live, you might have to move in order to increase your possibilities.

Confronting Internal Constraints

"No man is free who is a slave to himself." This saying captures the insight that, although you may believe that you are making a free choice because you are not the victim of visible *external constraints*, your choice may indeed be *un*free. How is this possible? Because your choice can be the result of *internal constraints*, irrational impulses that enslave you. Even though you may on one level be choosing what you "want," the "want" itself does not express your deepest desires and values. Consider the following examples:

- You are addicted to cigarettes and have been unable to quit despite many attempts.
- You are consumed by jealousy and find yourself unable to break free of your obsession.
- You can't go to bed without checking all of the locks three times.
- Whenever you think about speaking in front of a group of people, you are paralyzed by anxiety and you perform miserably.
- You have frequent and lasting episodes of depression from which you are unable to rouse yourself and that sap your interest in doing anything.

This is just a small sampling of common behaviors that are clearly in some sense "unfree," despite the fact that there are no external threats that are compelling people to make their choices. Instead, in these instances and countless others like them, the compulsions come from *within* the person, inhibiting them from making choices that originate from their genuine desires and values. How can you tell if your choice originates from your genuine desires and values or whether it is the result of an internal constraint? There is no simple answer. You have to think critically about your situation to understand it fully, but here are some questions to guide your reflective inquiry:

- Do you feel that you are making a free, unconstrained choice and that you could easily "do otherwise" if you wanted to? Or do you feel that your choice is in some sense *beyond* your conscious control, that you are "in the grip of" a force that does not reflect your genuine self, a compulsion that has in some way "taken possession" of you?

- Does your choice add positive qualities to your life: richness of experience, success, happiness? Or does your choice have negative results that undermine many of the positive goals that you are striving for?

- If you are asked "why" you are making the choice, are you able to provide a persuasive, rational explanation? Or are you at a loss to explain why you are behaving this way, other than to say, "I can't help myself"?

Let's apply these criteria to the example of smoking cigarettes.

- When people are addicted to cigarettes, they usually feel that they are *not* making a fully free, unconstrained choice to smoke because it is very difficult for them to stop smoking. Instead, they generally feel that they are "enslaved" by the habit, despite their numerous and determined attempts to quit.

- Smoking cigarettes adds many negative elements to a person's life, including health risks to themselves and others near them, stained teeth, and bad breath. On the positive side, people cite reduced anxiety, suppressed appetite, and lessened social awkwardness. But smoking only deals with the symptoms of these problems, not the causes. On balance, the bottom line on smoking is clearly negative.

- Most people who want to stop are at a loss to explain why they smoke, other than to say, "I can't help myself."

Using these criteria, habitual smoking clearly seems to be an example of an internal constraint. Of course, although smoking might not be your concern, it is likely that there are other elements of your life that are. Although you might find it easy to advise, "Just say no!" to cigarettes, you might have great difficulty accepting this same simple advice when confronted with an urge for

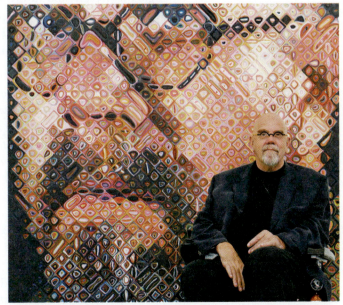

How can personal freedom transcend physical limitations? The painter Chuck Close exemplifies Viktor Frankl's belief that "No matter what the circumstances we find ourselves, we always retain the last of human freedoms—the ability to choose one's attitude in a given set of circumstances. [Note that he painted the portrait on page 100.]

WHAT ARE THE LIMITATIONS TO YOUR FREEDOM?

Making full use of your freedom involves first identifying the constraints that limit your freedom. Use this thinking activity to begin this self-reflective process, which will prepare you for increasing your freedom.

- Identify some of the important *external constraints* or limitations on your options that are imposed by people or circumstances outside of you. Are there people in your life who actively seek to limit your freedom? Are you locked into situations that present limited opportunities?

- Identify some of the important *internal constraints* in your life. Which behaviors feel out of your conscious control and have a negative effect on your life, undermining many of the positive goals that you are striving for? If you are asked "why" you are making the choice, are you able to provide a persuasive, rational explanation? Or are you at a loss to explain why you are behaving this way, other than to say, "I can't help myself"?

a chocolate éclair, a panicked feeling of insecurity, or a deep depression. Or to take another example: In analyzing your personality, you may feel that you too often lack confidence and are beset with feelings of insecurity. In reviewing your personal history, you may discover that these feelings stem in part from the fact that your parents were excessively critical and did not provide the kind of personal support that leads to a solid sense of security and self-worth. You might discover other factors in your history that contributed to these feelings as well: painful disappointments, such as a divorce or a career rejection. All of these experiences will have influenced who you are, and these historical events cannot now be changed. With this knowledge, you can move to the next level: *What are you going to do now?* How are you going to respond to the results of these events as embodied in your current thinking and behavior? This is where free choice enters in. Although you can't change what has previously happened, you can control *how you respond* to what happened. You can choose to let these historical influences continue to control your personality, like specters long dead reaching from the grave to influence and entangle the present and future. Or you can choose to move beyond these historical influences, to choose a different path for yourself that transcends their influence and liberates your future. As Viktor Frankl, a psychiatrist who survived the horrors of a Nazi concentration camp, explains in his book *Man's Search for Meaning*:

> *Man is not fully conditioned and determined but rather determines himself whether he gives in to conditions or stands up to them. In other words, man is ultimately self-determining. Man does not simply exist but always decides what his existence will be, what he will become in the next moment. No matter what the circumstances we find ourselves, we always retain the last of human freedoms—the ability to choose one's attitude in a given set of circumstances.*

writing about philosophy: Understanding Personal Freedom

The Assignment

As we have seen in this chapter, every person has certain beliefs regarding the possibility of free choice, though these beliefs have not necessarily been critically evaluated. This is an opportunity to express your own view of freedom and determinism in a form that is thoughtful and coherent. After reviewing, discussing, and reflecting on the various perspectives regarding personal freedom, compose a paper that reflects your own synthesis of these issues. Your point of view should be well reasoned and take into account all of the central arguments regarding whether people are free. One such student synthesis, entitled "Freedom and Science," can be found on MySearchLab.

MySearchLab Connections

Watch. Listen. Explore. Read. Mysearchlab is designed just for you. Each chapter features a customized study plan to help you learn and review key concepts and terms. Dynamic visual activities, videos, and readings found in the multimedia library will enhance your learning experience.

Here are a few questions and activities to help you understand this chapter:

1. **Watch** the **Interview** *Robert Wright Interviews Daniel Dennett* on *Free Will* on **mysearchlab.com** Why, according to Dennett, is the statement "determinism implies inevitability" false?

2. **Listen** to the **Interview** *Book Explores Intellectual Power of William James* on **mysearchlab.com** Describe James's beliefs regarding the classic mind/body problem.

3. **Listen** to the **Podcast** *Mary Warnock on Sartre's Existentialism* on **mysearchlab.com**   Explain Sartre's concept of "bad faith" as it relates to duty and obligation.

4. **Listen** to the **Interview** *Jean Paul Sartre with Melvyn Bragg* on **mysearchlab.com**   How did Sartre's experiences during WW II affect the development of his philosophical beliefs?

Are You the Master of Your Fate?

- Philosophical inquiry into the nature of human freedom attempts to define and explain how and why we make choices—are we truly free to choose a course of action, or is there some larger factor that determines what we do and why we do it?

- If we believe that human behavior is completely dependent on external forces (such as social dynamics or past psychological trauma), then we cannot ever truly be free to make independent choices. However, if we believe that we are capable of being the arbiters of our own actions, responsible for the choices we make (whatever their outcome), then personal freedom becomes a possibility for us.

- Your own beliefs about the nature of personal freedom have a substantial impact on your ability to change and grow as a person, to develop a consistent moral outlook, to relate to a specific spiritual tradition, and to participate in a just and fair society.   [pp. 140–144]

KEY TERMS
determinism
compatibilism
indeterminism
libertarianism

Determinism

- Determinists such as Baron d'Holbach argue that there cannot be true freedom, because none of the choices we make are truly "free": our actions are dependent on, or caused by, factors beyond our control.

- A determinist view of human freedom further holds that humans are inhibited in their ability to choose freely by both internal and external constraints. External constraints are those imposed by your environment and your circumstances; internal constraints involve limitations to our autonomy that we impose on ourselves.   [pp. 144–153]

KEY TERMS
external constraints
internal constraints

for further reading, viewing & research

Read the Primary Source on MySearchLab

- *The System of Nature*, Baron d'Holbach
- *Religion and the Modern Mind*, W. T. Stace
- *The Will to Believe*, William James
- *Existentialism Is a Humanism*, Jean-Paul Sartre
- *Autonomy and Identity in Feminist Thinking*, Jean Grimshaw

Films

- *Chinatown* (1974) Is a free and ethical existence possible? In Roman Polanski's neo-noir film, a private detective is hired by a woman to spy on her husband, and then finds himself at the center of a complex conspiracy in which he quickly becomes a pawn. As the detective attempts to uncover the truth, he encounters pervasive corruption, dishonesty, and evil.

- *Gattaca* (1997) Are we defined by our DNA? In the future envisioned by this science fiction film, genetic engineering and DNA determine people's social classes and life possibilities. One of the few naturally born humans, Vincent, faces prejudice and genetic discrimination due to his congenital heart disease. Vincent refuses to accept the lot he is dealt and attempts to defy society's laws in order to achieve the life he wants.

- *A Simple Plan* (1998) How do the choices that we make affect our freedom? When three men find millions of dollars in a crashed plane, they devise a plan to keep the money. Tension rises as concealing the secret becomes more complex and their choices lead to increasingly disastrous consequences.

- *Thelma and Louise* (1991) What are the constraints on freedom? Two women who feel trapped and unfulfilled decide to take their future into their own hands on a weekend getaway. The trip is one of self-discovery, possibility, and the strength of friendship. When they become outlaws due to unforeseen circumstances, the friends must decide what path to take.

- *Slumdog Millionaire* (2008) Is it possible to obtain freedom in spite of economic, social, and physical constraints? Jamal Malik, a teenager growing up in the slums of Mumbai, is one question away from winning India's equivalent

Compatibilism

- Compatibilists like W. T. Stace, Moritz Schlick, and Daniel Dennett assert that we can consider human actions "free" if they are the result of internal motivations, not the product of external influences or constraints.

- There are some compatibilists, like Moritz Schlick, who believe that we must also consider "internal constraints" as well as "external constraints" when determining whether an action is freely chosen. Freedom means "acting in accord with one's unimpeded rational desires." **[pp. 153–161]**

Indeterminism and Libertarianism

- Indeterminism holds that your choices, or at least some of your choices, are made (or can be made) freely. In other words, whichever option you choose, you might still have chosen otherwise. Some philosophers make a distinction between "indeterminism" and "libertarianism." The indeterminist need not admit the existence of free will, whereas this is precisely what the libertarian is committed to.

- William James argued that indeterminism was the more rational belief about human freedom, as most aspects of the way we live our

(continued)

lives assume that we all have some degree of freedom of choice. James bolstered his argument by pointing out that, in a deterministic universe, neither judgments of approval nor judgments of regret are possible; determinism leads to a radical pessimism that simply does not explain lived human experience.

- Jean-Paul Sartre argues that we are, in fact, radically free, "condemned to be free." In arguing against the view that "essence precedes existence"—that our choices, our selves, and our actions exist in some cosmic, predetermined realm before we were even born—Sartre posits instead that "existence precedes essence." We are oriented toward the future, continually weighing options and considering our choices; that faculty of consideration and choosing is what makes us truly free, in Sartre's view. As a result, however, we are each uniquely and completely responsible for the actions we choose to take. **[pp. 161–182]**

A Feminist Analysis of Freedom

- Feminist philosopher Jean Grimshaw argues that repressive social forces can erode an individual's psychological autonomy, creating false desires and pseudo-selves. She surveys the kinds of psychic coercion that has forced women to think of themselves as subordinate to men. **[pp. 182–186]**

---

of *"Who Wants to Be a Millionaire?"* when he is accused of cheating and interrogated. Jamal recounts his life story to his interrogators in an attempt to prove that he has, in fact, acquired the knowledge necessary to be successful in spite of a challenging background, limited education, and limited resources.

Literature

- ***Tess of the D'Urbervilles,*** Thomas Hardy. A young woman, Tess, attempts to live an ethical life in a world of societal double standards, religious uncertainty, and hypocrisy. Both Hardy and his protagonist walk the line between free choice and fatalism, and pose some of the most essential questions regarding the human condition, including the possibility of obtaining freedom in an unjust society and unjust universe.

- ***The Odyssey,*** Homer. Homer's epic recounts the journey of the Greek hero, Odysseus, following the Trojan War. The tale explores essential themes of ancient Greek culture, including notions of freedom, as Odysseus is continually challenged by the obstacles created by indifferent and amoral gods, who represent the unpredictable, and often cruel, nature of the universe.

- ***Reading Lolita in Tehran: A Memoir in Books,*** Azar Nafisi. After resigning from her job at a university in Tehran, literature professor Azar Nafisi began a book group for Iranian women to study works banned by the government. In this memoir, Nafisi recounts her experience with the group, which became an empowering forum for discussing political, social, and cultural issues through the lens of literature. Her story speaks to the possibility of maintaining one's freedom in spite of oppressive external constraints.

- ***No Exit,*** Jean-Paul Sartre. In this existentialist play, three characters find themselves trapped in a sort of hell. This torturous existence is not created by external pain or punishment, however, but rather by their interactions with each other. Sartre's work addresses issues of freedom and responsibility, the power of others to limit our freedom, and the absurdity of existence.

- ***Native Son,*** Richard Wright. Bigger Thomas, a black man living in a racist society in twentieth-century America, feels that he has no control over his existence and fears there is no hope of escaping poverty and oppression. Bigger attempts to free himself of the social and economic restraints on his freedom, but his life begins to unravel as a result of the devastating psychological effects of prejudice and oppression.

Metaphysics

What is *real*?

Epistemology

What is *true*?

how can we know the nature of reality?

PHILOSOPHICAL FOUNDATIONS

Plato

Reality is the eternal realm of the forms.

Truth is knowledge of the forms gained through rational intuition.

Aristotle

Reality is the natural world.

Truth is knowledge of the natural world gained through empirical investigation.

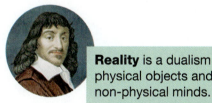

Descartes

Reality is a dualism of physical objects and non-physical minds.

Truth is knowledge gained through radical doubt and rational intuition.

◀ **Heaven or earth?** In this detail from Raphael's *School of Athens*, Plato points to the heavens and Aristotle motions toward the earth. While both philosophers believed that there was an ultimate reality, they disagreed about which way to discover it. This chapter will introduce you to their debate and others.

5

chapter

5.1 What Is the Nature of Reality?

Reality and *truth* are two of the most misunderstood and misused words in the English language. Think about the many ways that you use these terms, and that you hear them used, in our culture. Can you detect any core meanings for these terms? Or do you simply have a collection of diverse examples with some very general resemblance, such as

* *Reality* refers to things the way they really are.
* *Truth* refers to those statements that are one hundred percent accurate.

If you're having difficulty getting a clear grasp on these rich and complex concepts, don't despair: Philosophers have been discussing—and sometimes arguing—over the meaning of these terms for several thousand years without yet reaching a definitive agreement.

In philosophy, questions regarding the nature of reality fall under the category of **metaphysics**, which, as we saw in the first chapter, involves the study of the most general or ultimate characteristics of existence. Metaphysics explores issues beyond the physical world, such as the meaning of life, the existence of free will, the nature of mind, the fundamental principles of the universe, and the possibility of life beyond death. We can trace the origins of the term back to the Greek philosopher Aristotle, who wrote on a vast range of topics. One set of writings, the *Physics* (from the Greek word *physika*, "of nature"), deals with subjects pertaining to the natural world. Another set of writings, which he sometimes referred to as "first philosophy" or "wisdom," deals with subjects that are more abstract and theoretical than those dealt with in the *Physics*. In time, this set of writings became known as "the books after the books on nature" (in Greek, *ta meta ta physika biblia*), which eventually became shortened to *Metaphysics*. Metaphysics deals with a variety of important philosophical questions, which include those listed below. We have already explored a number of these questions in the preceding chapters, while others we will be taking up in this and subsequent chapters.

* What is the nature of reality?
* What is the place of humans in the universe?
* Does life have meaning?
* Do we have free wills that enable us to make independent choices?
* How are the mind and body related to each other?
* Is there life after death?
* Does God exist?
* What is the nature of the "self"?

Metaphysics Most generally, the philosophical investigation of the nature, constitution, and structure of reality.

The question that we will be focusing on in this and the next chapter is the first one: "What is the nature of reality?" When philosophers ask this question, they typically are trying to discover "the way the world really is." Although the world has a certain *appearance* to us, many philosophers (and scientists) believe that the *reality* of the world is something very different. This leads to such questions as:

- What is the ultimate "stuff" or "substance" of the universe?
- What aspects of the universe are eternal and unchanging?
- What aspects of the universe change and what principles govern this change?
- How did substances come into being?
- What is the relation of the material and the nonmaterial dimensions of the universe? (For example, what are the relations between our minds and our bodies, or God and ourselves?)

In philosophy, questions regarding the nature of Truth fall under the category of **epistemology**, which, as we saw in the first chapter, involves the study of knowledge. The term *epistemology* is derived from the Greek *episteme*, "knowledge," and *logos*, "explanation." It seeks to establish a framework that we can use to construct genuine and accurate understanding, and this entails identifying and developing criteria and methodologies for determining what we know and why we know it. Here are some of the questions epistemology attempts to answer:

- Can we ever really *know* anything?
- How do we know when we *don't* know something?
- What is the difference between *belief* and *knowledge*?
- Is truth possible?
- What are the roles of reason and experience in constructing knowledge and determining truth?
- Does truth evolve or is it unchanging?
- Can there be different "truths" for different people, or is "truth" the same for all?

What is reality? What is appearance? How do we tell the difference? A rainbow appears to have form and substance but in reality is a phenomenon of light.

Epistemology The study of the nature of knowledge and justification.

Metaphysics and epistemology are interdependent, and answering the questions in the one area frequently involves answering the questions in the other area. For example, determining the ultimate "substance" of the universe, whether it's eternal or subject to change, the relation of the material to the immaterial—none of these questions can be answered without addressing the questions of knowledge and truth that are a part of epistemology. So as we think our way through the next two chapters, we will be addressing both metaphysical and epistemological issues in an integrated context, exactly the way they naturally occur, rather than trying to impose an artificial separation.

Metaphysics and epistemology in Western culture begin with the ancient Greeks, in particular Socrates, Plato, and Aristotle. But as we noted in Chapter 2 (pages 55–56), it was the thinkers before them—collectively known as the "pre-Socratic Philosophers" who served as intellectual catalysts for Socrates, Plato, and Aristotle, and laid the foundation for much of their thinking. The pre-Socratic thinkers were preeminently concerned with identifying the ultimate "substance" of the universe, and they wrestled with the apparent contradictions between the eternal and the finite, the immutable and the changing, appearance and reality. They were distinctive because they introduced a new way of inquiring into the world and the place of human beings in it. Instead of appealing to gods, supernatural forces, myths or magic to explain the world and the events in it, they sought explanations that were *within* the natural world and used *reason* as the methodological tool to make sense of things. In the words of one of the most influential pre-Socratics, Heraclitus, "Those who are lovers of wisdom must be inquirers into many things," and it was in this spirit that these remarkable individuals proposed views of the natural world that encompassed the present day disciplines of physics, astronomy, geology, chemistry, meteorology, and embryology. It was because of their focus on the natural world that they are sometimes termed the "nature philosophers," and they were in this sense the first scientists in Western culture. But they also developed philosophical views in the areas of metaphysics, epistemology, and ethics, so we might term them the first scientist/philosophers. They themselves did not make a distinction between the questions they sought to answer and the answers they proposed. And although they proposed a diversity of world views, they were all in agreement that any explanation be within the natural world, without reference to gods, supernatural forces, myths or magic. They viewed the world as a *kosmos*, an ordered natural arrangement that that could be understood with the power of human reason: references to gods or mystical forces were not relevant and not welcome. As Aristotle noted, this remarkable collection of early thinkers were revolutionary "inquirers into nature" rather than traditional "poetical myth-makers," and it is because of this fundamental difference in perspective that they are credited with creating the foundation that made possible the work of subsequent scientists and philosophers. They sought to answer the same questions as religious and mythic beliefs did, it's just that they thought these questions should be answered within the natural world by using careful observation and

Thales
(c. 585 B.C.E.) Considered to be the first philosopher because he introduced a different mode of thinking that relied on reason and observation of nature. Argued that the primary substance of the universe was water.

Anaximenes
(c. sixth century B.C.E.) Held the belief that air is the one substance out of which the entire universe is formed.

Heraclitus
(c. 540–c. 480 B.C.E.) The most influential of pre-Socratic philosophers; maintained all things were in a constant state of flux and that the governing principle of the universe is what he called *logos*.

Democritus
(c. mid-fifth–fourth century B.C.E.) Advanced the doctrine of atomism, maintaining that all matter is composed of indivisible atoms in motion.

Pre-Socratic Philosophers

Parmenides
(510–450 B.C.E.) An accomplished mathematician and influential pre-Socratic thinker who posited a necessary, static, unchanging unity running throughout all of what is in flux. Reality must necessarily be eternal and unchanging: Therefore, the changing world of our experience must be in some sense illusory.

Pythagoras
(c. 570–c. 497 B.C.E.) Heavily influenced Plato; maintained that the human soul was immortal and transmigrated after death.

Anaxagoras
(500–428 B.C.E.) Maintained that the entire universe is composed of matter in motion, governed by the principle of mind (*nous*).

analytical reasoning: What is the true nature of reality? How did this ordered, intelligible world emerge out of chaos? How do we distinguish reality from appearance? How can we come to understand reality? How do we reconcile the underlying unity of the cosmos with the plurality and diversity of it? How do humans fit into the world? Is there meaning to existence? How ought we to live our lives?

The Milesians: Thales (c. 625–547 B.C.E.), Anaximander (610–546 B.C.E), Anaximenes (585–528 B.C.E.)

The earliest group of pre-Socratic thinkers came from Miletus, a city in Ionia, on the west coast of what is now Turkey. Since most of the writings of these and the other pre-Socratics did not survive, their views have been pieced together with fragments of their surviving "books" and "poems," as well as accounts for their views from other ancient philosophers like Plato and Aristotle who had access to their full texts. The first of these early philosophers, **Thales** proposed that the world was floating on water, and that everything was derived from and composed of water. Aristotle speculates that Thales's view that water was the *arche* or "fundamental principle" was based on water's essential role in the germination and growth of living things and its role in nutrition. In addition, water changes form through its own inherent nature, going from liquid, to solid, to mist, to gas in the various roles it plays in the world. Water, Thales believed, is the basic "stuff" of the universe and explains why things are the way they are. Although Aristotle considered Thales' specific view to be amateurish, he recognized its radical and revolutionary nature. For the first time, humans were seeking to understand the world in its own terms, as a complete and self-ordering system that could be explored and understood through our ability to reason. The traditional gods and supernatural forces existing outside of the natural world were not needed to achieve an accurate understanding of the world and humans' place in it.

Thales's student **Anaximander** agreed with Thales' basic nature philosophy approach that eliminated gods and supernatural forces from our understanding of the universe, but he took issue with his teacher's specific views on obvious grounds: how could water be considered the basic "stuff" of the universe when so many things are obviously *not* made of water? Instead, Anaximander proposed that the ultimate "stuff" of the universe is *apeiron*, which is generally translated as the "indefinite," the "unlimited," the "boundless." The philosopher **Simplicius**, a sixth- century C.E. commentator on Aristotle's *Physics*, observes about Anaximander:

> *Of those who say that (the first principle) is one and moving and indefinite, Anaximander, son of Praxiades, a Milesian who became successor and pupil to Thales, said that the indefinite* **(to apeiron)** *is both principle* **(arche)** *and element* **(stoicheion)** *of the things that are, and he was the first to introduce this name of the principle. He says that it is neither water nor any other of the so-called elements, but some other indefinite* **(apeiron)** *nature, from which come to be all the heavens and the worlds in them; and those things, from which there is coming-to-be for the things that are, are also those into which is their passing-away, in accordance with what much be. For they give penalty (dike) and recompense to one another for their injustice* **(adikia)** *in accordance with the order of time—speaking of them in rather poetical terms. It is clear that having seen the change of the four elements into each other, he did not think it fit to make some one of these underlying subject, but something else, apart from these.* (**Simplicius, Commentary on Aristotle's Physics 24,** *lines 13ff. 5 12A9 and B1*)

Aristotle gives further clarification of Anaximander's concept of the "indefinite" as being the beginning and fundamental element of all things:

> *Everything either is a beginning or has a beginning. But there is no beginning of the infinite; for if there were one, it would limit it. Moreover, since it is a beginning, it is unbegotten and indestructible. . . . Hence, as we say, there is no source of this, but this appears to be the source of all the rest, and "encompasses all things" and "steers all things," as those assert who do not recognize other causes besides the infinite. . . . And this, they say, is the divine; for it is "deathless" and "imperishable," as Anaximander puts it, and most of the physicists agree with him. (DK 12 A 15, **IEGP**, 24)*

In addition to positing this boundless, indefinite "stuff" and the fundamental constituent of the universe, Anaximander believed the universe to be an intrinsically ordered one, with the cycles of the seasons, the rotations of the heavens, and other sorts of cyclical change (such as coming into being and passing away) displaying a structured and intelligible organization that could be understood through rational investigation.

The third Milesian in this pre-Socratic group, **Anaximenes,** was the student of Anaximander. In the same way that Anaximander had critiqued his teacher Thales for proposing water as the fundamental stuff of the universe, Anaximenes takes issue with his teacher Anaximander for proposing the "indefinite" as the fundamental stuff as being too abstract and vague, so lacking in properties as to be nothing at all. Instead, Anaximenes proposes "air" as being the fundamental element of the universe in part because air can apparently take on various properties of color, temperature, humidity, motion, taste, and smell. In addition, air is the natural mechanism for change. It is the condensation and rarefaction of air that naturally determine the particular characters of the things produced from air, the original stuff.

Xenophanes of Colophon (570–475 B.C.E.) and Heraclitus of Ephesus (535–475 B.C.E.)

Xenophanes and **Heraclitus** continued on the path established by the Milesians, focusing on the nature of the physical world and offering their own cosmological accounts of it. But they advanced the foundations created by the Milesians by offering an expanded range of physical explanations, by focusing more attention on the role of the human subject in their worldviews, and, most significantly, by analyzing the nature of the thinking and reasoning process itself. In so doing, they addressed directly epistemological questions like: What can we know and how can we know it? What are the limits of human understanding? What knowledge is possible within these limits and how can we best achieve it? By investigating the process of human inquiry itself, they introduced an entirely new era in philosophical thinking.

"She whom they call Iris, this too is by nature (*pephuke*) cloud purple, and red, and greeny-yellow to behold." (21B32). In this one stunning statement, Xenophanes extinguishes the ties to traditional explanations of the world that invoked gods or mystical forces. Iris is a minor goddess in the Greek pantheon who had come to be identified with the rainbow, which many cultures interpreted as a sign from the gods. Not so, Xenophanes announces! Rainbows are natural phenomena within the natural order that we can understand and explain without reference to supernatural beings or forces. This rainbow explanation is one instance of Xenophanes's general view that all meteorological phenomena are clouds, colored, moving, incandescent. Clouds are fed by exhalations from the land and sea (mixtures of earth and water).

The motions of earth and water, and hence of clouds, account for all the things we find around us.

In the same way that Xenophanes wants to replace a god-dominated mystical account of the world with a naturalistic science, so also does he want to demystify the gods themselves. In contrast to the prevailing religious belief that gods create men (and women) in their own images, Xenophanes suggests the converse, namely that man creates gods in his own image, and he provides some concrete examples to support his anthropomorphic view.

> *"Mortals suppose that the gods are born, and have their own dress, voice, and body. (DK 21 B 14, EGP, 52)*

> *"The Ethiopians make their gods snub-nosed and black; the Thracians make theirs gray-eyed and red-haired." (DK 21 B 16, IEGP, 52)*

> *"And if oxen and horses and lions had hands, and could draw with their hands and do what man can do, horses would draw the gods in the shape of horses, and oxen in the shape of oxen, each giving the gods bodies similar to their own." (DK 21 B 15, IEGP, 52)*

While dismissing the diversity of culturally specific gods as human psychological projections (a view espoused by modern philosophers/thinkers like Ludvig Feuerbach, Karl Marx, and Sigmund Freud), Xenophanes advances the concept of one supreme god who does not in any recognizable way resemble human beings:

> *One god greatest among gods and men,*
> *Resembling mortals neither in body nor in thought.*
> *. . . whole he sees, whole he thinks, and whole he hears*
> *but completely without toil he agitates all things by the thought of his mind.*
> *. . . always he remains in the same (state), agitated not at all,*
> *nor is it fitting that he come and go to different places at different times. (B23, 24, 25, 26)*

In sharp contrast to other gods in Greece and other cultures, Xenophanes' supreme god is indifferent to the affairs of the human world. This god understands and controls the cosmos, infusing it with a divine intelligence that gives the cosmos its order and organization. Although this god does not reveal any knowledge of the cosmos to us, we can make use of our own intellectual abilities to discover knowledge of the cosmos, at least to some degree.

> *"Indeed not even from the beginning did the gods indicate all things to mortals, but, in time, inquiring, they discover better."*

There is a limit to what human understanding can achieve; however, this does not mean that we should surrender our quest for understanding or attempt to return to the god-dominated cosmologies of the past.

> *And of course the clear and certain truth no man has seen*
> *Nor will there be anyone who knows about the gods and what I say about all things;*
> *For even if, in the best case, he should chance to speak what is the case,*
> *All the same, he himself does not know; but opinion is found over all.*

"You cannot step into the same river, for other waters are continually flowing on." With this memorable observation, the enigmatic **Heraclitus** summed up his belief that the world is in a constant state of flux. "All is change" and "Change alone is unchanging," he declared, and if we examine the physical world in which we live, that certainly seems to be the case. Nothing in the world remains static: life forms are continually being born, aging, and dying; even the physical aspects of the universe are in a continual state of change. But if all is flux, then how can we ever hope to achieve permanent, universal knowledge? "It is in changing that all things find repose." Does this mean that, other than acknowledging that change is the defining attribute of the cosmos, we must abandon attempts to discover knowledge of reality? Not exactly.

Heraclitus also believes that the universe has an intrinsic structure and organizing principle that he identifies with the meaning-rich Greek word *logos*, and in fact the opening of his book refers to a "*logos* which holds forever." What exactly is *logos*, according to Heraclitus? It's an objective lawlike principle that governs the universe, and which it is possible (but difficult) for humans to come to understand. There is a single order that directs all events in the cosmos—"All things are one"—and this order is "divine" in the sense that it is immortal. It is because of this intrinsic order that steers and controls the universe that the universe is intelligible and rational rather than capricious and accidental. Which means that, in principle, humans can use their rational faculties to develop an understanding of our world.

But Nature doesn't make it easy! "Nature is accustomed to hide itself" (DK 22 B 123, *IEGP*, 96) and "Though the logos is as I have said, men always fail to comprehend it, both before they hear it and when they hear it for the first time. For though all things come into being in accordance with this logos, they seem like men without experience" (DK 22 B 1, *IEGP*, 94).

"Fire" is another metaphor that Heraclitus uses to communicate the intelligent, rational *logos* that is the inner eternal form of the ever-changing cosmos. "This world that is the same for all, no god made or any man, but it ever was and is and shall be ever-living fire that kindles in regular measures and goes out by regular measures." (DK 22 B 30, *IEGP*, 90) Although the fire is ever changing, like the physical world as a whole, there is nevertheless a structuring pattern and rhythm that insures the continuity and intelligibility of the world.

Heraclitus (c. 540–c. 480 B.C.E.) The most influential of pre-Socratic philosophers; maintained all things were in a constant state of flux and that the governing principle of the universe is what he called *logos*.

The dynamic quality of the fire also relates to Heraclitus's belief that the world is produced by the ongoing conflict of opposing forces, a unity of opposites that are continually at odds with one another. "It is right to know that war is common and justice strife, and that all things come to be through strife and are so ordained" (DK 22 B 80, *IEGP*, 93). "War is the father and king of all" (DK 22 B 53, *IEGP*, 93). In order to understand the cosmos on this deeper, more profound level governed by the *logos*, we must embrace this essential contradiction of the world. "The road up and down are one and the same" (DK 22 B 60, *IEGP*, 94); "The path of writing is both straight and crooked" (DK 22 B 59, *IEGP*, 93); "Sea water is very pure and very foul" (DK 22 B 61, *IEGP*, 93).

However, most people are not able to understand the *logos*-driven deeper unity and order of the cosmos to achieve genuine wisdom. "Wisdom is one thing: to understand the thought which steers all things through all things" (DK 22 B 41, *IEGP*, 88). Instead, they focus on the superficial level of experience most immediate to them, which is characterized by continual change and transience.

"Though they are in daily contact with the *logos* they are at variance with it, and what they meet appears alien to them" (DK 22 B 73, *IEGP*, 94).

"To those who are awake the world-order is one, common to all; but the sleeping turn aside each into a world of his own." (DK 22 B 89, *IEGP*, 95)

"We ought to follow what is common to all; but though the *logos* is common to all, the many live as though their thought were private to themselves." (DK 22 B 2, *IEGP*, 88)

How do we gain insight into the deeper *logos* level of the universe? Although we cannot see it, hear it, touch it, we can develop some understanding through flashes of unexpected insight. "Unless you expect the unexpected you will never find truth, for it cannot be found by search or trail." For Heraclitus, truth and knowledge are hidden and elusive and cannot be captured through systematic study. And with those flowing waters goes any possibility of achieving knowledge in any comprehensive and permanent sense.

Is there anything in life that is permanent, or is the world constantly changing? Heraclitus said, "You cannot step into the same river, for other waters are continually flowing on." Can you think of anything that *doesn't* change over time?

Parmenides of Elea (510 B.C.E.–)

Parmenides, an accomplished mathematician, had a different view from Heraclitus, positing a necessary, static, unchanging unity running throughout all of what is in flux. He assumed that reality must necessarily be eternal and unchanging: Therefore the changing world of our experience cannot be real—it is an illusion! What *is* real is "Being," which is a single coherent reality, "The One." *Being* is perfect, complete, permanent, and unchanging—it's what *is*. "It is the *being* of the visible cosmos, immobilized, and to a great extent purified, but still clearly recognizable." Parmenides reasons, "How could *being* perish? How could it come into being? If it came into being, it is not; and so too if it is about to be at some future time" (DK 28 B 8, *IEGP*, 113). But like Heraclitus, Parmenides does not believe that we can achieve extensive knowledge of "The One" in areas other than mathematics. What is the relation of "Being" to "change"? Parmenides seems to have believed that everything is somehow one, although just what is meant by one could be either holistic or a plurality somehow held together. This is Being, or what is. Read as a holistic unity, it is difficult to comprehend the relation of Being to beings or the particular things (like ourselves) that seem to partake of it. In what remains of his poem (as with Heraclitus, only fragments of Parmenides' writings have survived), Parmenides characterizes Being as imperishable, indivisible, and unchanging, but if the unity of Being is understood instead as the holding together of a plurality, then Being must include perishing, division, and change within itself. Being can then be pictured not simply as some form of perfect sphere but rather the unity that binds all things—the living and the dead, the changing and the static, the finite and the infinite—together. Just how this dialectical unity holds such remarkable opposites together is what Parmenides asks us to think about further.

Unlike Heraclitus, who believed it to be nearly impossible to attain authentic and comprehensive understanding of the underlying reality (*logos*), Parmenides believes that humans can achieve some knowledge in a meaningful sense by using our own reasoning abilities. In Parmenides' extended poem, he recounts how much of the poem had been revealed to him through a goddess intermediary. But instead of asking him to simply accept without question the religious principles announced from

Parmenides (c. 515 B.C.E.) Pre-Socratic philosopher. Maintained that only knowledge of "that which is" is possible and not of "that which is not," which led him to the belief that reality must be changeless and undifferentiated because, if it were not, then it would involve "that which is not."

on high, this goddess instructs him using the tools of reasoning suggested in the poem to test beliefs himself and arrive at his own thoughtful conclusions, to "judge by reasoning the much-contested argument that I have spoken."

> *Come now, and I will tell you, and you, hearing, preserve the story,*
> *The only routes of inquiry there are for thinking;*
> *The one that it is and that it cannot not be*
> *is the path of Persuasion (for it attends upon truth),*
> *The other, that it is not and that it is right that it not be*
> *This I point out to you is a path wholly inscrutable*
> *For you could not know what is not (for it is not to be accomplished)*
> *Nor could you point it out . . . For the same thing is for thinking and for being.*
> *(B2, B3)*

According to Parmenides, there are signs, hints, and tools of reason needed to gain and test knowledge claims that we should utilize in our investigation.

> *. . . a single account still*
> *remains of the route that it is; and on this route there are*
> *very many signs, that what-is is ungenerable and imperishable,*
> *a whole of a single kind, and unshaking and complete;*
> *nor was it or will it be, since it is now all together*
> *one, cohesive. (B8.1–6)*

But although there is a path to achieving knowledge, the journey is extremely difficult and most people are not able to travel it successfully. And for Parmenides, this includes philosophers like Heraclitus who he singles out in the following passage as believing "to be and not to be are the same."

> *Helplessness guides the wandering thought in their breasts; they are carried along*
> *deaf and blind alike, dazed, beasts without judgment, convinced that to be and not*
> *to be are the same and not the same, and that the road of all things is a backward—*
> *turning one. (DI 28 B 6, IEGP, 111)*

Pre-Socratic Atomism: Leucippus (Early Fifth Century B.C.E.) and Democritus (460–370 B.C.E.)

Although the pre-Socratic thinkers have been termed the "nature philosophers," this isn't completely accurate until we reach **Leucippus** and **Democritus**. Although the other thinkers had dramatically shifted the focus away from religious and magical explanations of the natural world and the lives of humans in it, many still assumed the existence of a deeper reality that was not evident on the immediate level of lived sense experience. For example, while focusing on the natural world, Anaximander identified the basic stuff of the universe to be the "unlimited," the "boundless," that "encompasses all things" and "steers all things." Similarly Xenophanes, while dismissing most gods and magical spirits as the psychological projections of the human mind, nevertheless ends up assuming the existence of one ultimate god who "sets all things in motion by the thought of his mind." And Heraclitus, while emphasizing the thorough-going flux and impermanence of ourselves and the world in which we live, still posits a divine *logos* that serves as a fundamental organizing principle of the universe that gives it rational intelligibility. Even Parmenides, who is committed to the permanent existence of Being, acknowledges that the changeable, transitory world in which we live is one of appearance: the "real" world is that of unchanging, eternal *Being*.

One consequence of these views is the distinction between "appearance" and "reality," an issue that is destined to become a permanent element in philosophical discourse up until the present time. If the natural world in which we live is only a world of "appearance," then what precisely is the "real" world, and how can we gain knowledge of it? This is a question that these early thinkers wrestle with, and as we have seen, they are not very optimistic about the human ability to grasp and understand the reality hidden deeper than mere sense experience. This deeper level of reality is hidden and illusive, requiring special abilities to achieve even limited awareness of it. For most people, they are not even aware that this deeper reality even exists.

Leucippus and Democritus also believe that there is a world of "appearance" and a world of "reality." The difference is that this world of reality is not divine, godlike, or even purposeful: it's entirely physical, just too small for us to see. For in a remarkable instance of seeing the future, and without the aid of electron microscopes or other scientific equipment, Leucippus and Democritus proposed an atomic theory to explain the nature of the universe. What is real is an infinite number of solid, permanent, uncuttable (*atomon*) physical units. All atoms are made of the same stuff—solid undifferentiated matter—differing from one another only in shape, position, and arrangement (later atomic theories include weight as an additional quality). The only thing that exists other than atoms is the "void" in which they exist and move. Everything is constructed of atoms and void: the shapes of the atoms and their arrangement with respect to each other give physical objects their apparent characteristics.

So, for example, the ancient Greek philosopher Theophrastus reported that according to the atomic theory, the flavors we taste vary according to the shapes of the atoms that compose various objects: "Democritus makes sweet that which is round and quite large, astringent that which large, rough, polygonal and not rounded (*de Caus. Plant.* 6.1.6 = 68A129). Analogously, atomists explained that iron is harder than lead because of the uneven arrangements of the atoms that make it up, and lighter than lead because it contains more void. Similarly, things composed of sharp and very fine atoms in comparable positions are hot and fiery; those composed of atoms with the opposite character come to be cold and watery.

Parmenides had argued a version of the principle of "Matter can neither be created nor destroyed." That is, it's not possible for Being to come from nothing (non-Being) and analogously, things that exist cannot disappear into non-Being, which led him to the perplexing conclusion that only Being—the One—exists and it cannot be separated, differentiated, or changed. As Aristotle explains, the atomic theory showed a way out of this conundrum: on the level of reality, atoms—and the void in which they exist and move—are permanent and indivisible. However, on the level of appearance—the physical world in which we live and experience through our senses—there is plurality, change, growth, decay, and mutability based on the types and arrangements of these immutable and indivisible atoms:

Watch the **Video**
Aristotle on
mysearchlab.com

> *Leucippus, however, thought he had arguments which, while consistent with sense perception, would not destroy coming into being or passing away or the multiplicity of existing things. These he conceded to be appearances, while to those who upheld the "one" he conceded that there can be no motion without a void, that the void is not-being, and that not-being is no part of being; for what is, in the strict sense, is completely full. But there is not one such being but infinitely many, and they are invisible owing to the smallness of their bulk. They move in the void (for void exists)*

and, by coming together and separating, effect coming into being and passing away.
*(DK 67 A 7, **IEGP**, 196)*

As noted above, Leucippus and Democritus were materialists who, unlike most of the other pre-Socratics, did not acknowledge the existence of gods, a cosmic mind, or an intelligent governing principle in the universe: all that exists is matter (atoms) in motion. But what of the human mind or soul? According to the atomists, these too had natural explanations: Democritus believed that the soul is composed of exceedingly fine and spherical atoms, permitting the soul to interpenetrate the whole of the body. He contends that "spherical atoms move because it is their nature never to be still, and that as they move they draw the whole body along with them, and set it in motion" (DK 68 A 104, *IEGP*, 222). It is in this sense that "soul-atoms" are similar to "fire-atoms," which are also small, spherical, and capable of penetrating solid bodies. In the final analysis, the soul—or mind—is ultimately material.

> *These two worlds—the "real" world of atoms and void, and the world of "appearance"—naturally have implications regarding the nature of truth and knowledge, as Democritus explains: "There are two forms of knowledge: one legitimate, one bastard. To the bastard sort belong all the following: sight, hearing, smell, taste, touch. The legitimate is quite distinct from this. When the bastard form cannot see more minutely, nor hear nor smell nor taste nor perceive through the touch, then another, finer form must be employed." (68B11)*

Thus, the world of truth and genuine knowledge is the atomic level of atoms and void: the world of "bastard knowledge" the level of sense experience, or as Democritus observes, "In truth we know nothing: for truth is in the depths" (68B 117). However, it is possible to be directed to this deeper level of knowledge: the evidence of the senses, when properly interpreted by reason, can be used as a guide to reality: "appearances are the sight of the unseen."

Legacy of the Pre-Socratic Philosophers

The pre-Socratics formed an indispensable "bridge" from an early cultural consciousness dominated by gods, mystical spirits and powers, magic and myth, to a cultural consciousness founded on reason and scientific investigation of the natural world. In so doing, they displayed an extraordinary diversity of interests, including all aspects of the natural world, the nature of human knowing and understanding, living the good life and other ethical issues, the nature and structure of the universe, and medicine. In so doing, they animated and led the transition from early consciousness to modern consciousness embodied in the fifth-century B.C.E. philosophy of Socrates, Plato, and Aristotle and ultimately the whole of Western scientific and philosophical thought.

---

thinking philosophically

WHAT IS YOUR CONCEPT OF REALITY?

- It may seem like an odd question, but how would you describe your idea of "ultimate reality"? Is it the physical reality of what you experience on a day-to-day basis? Or do you think of ultimate reality in terms of intellectual truths and insights? Or do you consider ultimate reality to be defined in terms of a spiritual metaphysic?

- Heraclitus was a passionate believer that "All is change"—that is, our world and our selves are continually changing, evolving, dying. Do you agree with his concept of reality? Why or why not? If so, does this continual flux mean that we can never know anything for certain?

- In contrast, Parmenides was convinced that there is an underlying principle of permanence that underlies all of the change and flux that we experience on a daily basis. Do you agree with Parmenides? If so, how would you describe the "underlying principle of permanence" that provides a metaphysical foundation for our world and in so doing holds everything together?

- Did you find thinking about these questions to be unfamiliar and challenging? If so, why do you feel this way?

5.2 Reality Is the Eternal Realm of the Forms: Plato

Plato was deeply versed in the thinking of these early philosophers through his teachers and mentors, who included Socrates, and profoundly aware of the questions regarding the eternal and the finite, the immutable and the changing. Plato's solution to this monumental conflict between reality-as-change and reality-as-eternal was both brilliant and problematic. Plato simply created the idea of "Two Worlds." One world, the world of *Becoming*, is the world we are familiar with, the physical world we inhabit. This world is continually changing, evolving, disappearing. This "Becoming" reality is taken in through our senses, and it is impossible to develop any genuine knowledge of it because we can merely describe its changing nature as it appears to us. This is the world of "appearance."

The other world, the world of "reality," is much different. This is the world of *Being*, a realm that is eternal, unchanging, and knowable through the faculty of reason. Plato doesn't suggest that the everyday world of Becoming is an illusion: It's just that this physical world of changing sensation is "less real" than the timeless world of Being. But what does the eternal world of Being contain, and what is its relation to the mutable world of Becoming? It is populated with *Forms*, the cornerstone of Plato's metaphysics and epistemology.

What precisely are **Forms**? The word *form* itself derives from the Greek word *eidos*, which is variously translated as idea, archetype, or essence. Plato considers Forms to be the ideal archetypes or essences of everything that exists. We can think of them as the perfect ideals of every meaningful object and idea. For example, there is an ideal Form for horses—the essence of what we mean when we use the term *horse*. This Form would include all of the essential qualities that constitute being a "horse," attributes that the tyrannical schoolmaster Thomas Gradgrind gets a terrified student, Bitzer, to enumerate in this passage from Charles Dickens's novel *Hard Times*:

> *"Bitzer," said Thomas Gradgrind. "Your definition of a horse."*
>
> *"Quadruped. Graminivorous. Forty teeth, namely twenty-four grinders, four eye-teeth, and twelve incisive. Sheds coat in the spring; in marshy countries sheds hoofs, too. Hoofs hard, but requiring to be shod with iron. Age known by marks in mouth." Thus (and much more) Bitzer.*
>
> *"Now girl number twenty," said Mr. Gradgrind, "you know what a horse is."*

Of course, Plato's ideal Form of "horse" would also include aesthetic qualities (physical beauty), functional qualities (strength, endurance, speed), and any other attributes that constitute the ideal, perfect idea of "horse."

For Plato, the Form of "horse" actually exists in the timeless and eternal world of Being. Although the Form for "horse"—and other Forms—do not exist in a material sense, they do exist independently of the minds of people. And, Plato believes, we can discover these Forms through disciplined study based on developing our ability to reason in

Plato (427–347 B.C.E.). An ancient Greek philosopher of extraordinary significance in the history of ideas. Plato not only preserved Socrates' teachings for future generations but also contributed original ideas on a wide range of issues such as morality, politics, metaphysics, and epistemology.

Form In Plato's metaphysics, the ideal essence of a thing.

What are examples of ideal forms? Judges at dog shows evaluate the contestants in terms of how well they conform to a breed standard. In what other areas are "examples" judged in terms of how closely they correspond to an ideal?

an enlightened fashion. That is to say, we can become familiar with the Form of "horse," and in so doing we have knowledge of the ideal pattern that we can use to understand and evaluate all of the actually existing horses in the world. For Plato, the relationship between the ideal Form of "horse," and the multitude of actual, existing horses, is complex and central to Plato's thought. He says that the actually existing horses *participate* in the ideal Form of horse. What exactly does "participate" mean? That's exactly the question that Plato's student Aristotle posed to Plato, and not receiving a satisfactory response, Aristotle vigorously criticized Plato's views:

> It is hard, too, to see how a weaver or a carpenter will benefit in regard to his own craft by knowing this (a form), or how the man who has viewed the Idea itself will be a better doctor or general thereby. For a doctor seems not even to study health in this way, but the health of man, or perhaps rather the health of a particular man; it is individuals that he is healing.

Plato uses other terms to elaborate this idea of "participation," including "to reflect," "to resemble," "to share in." But the precise nature of the Forms to the world of particulars is still ambiguous in Plato's writings.

One way to think about how the two worlds relate is conceptually: The ideal Form is the ultimate *concept* of the object or idea. Such a concept is defined by its boundaries, including, in the case of "horse," the qualities enumerated by young Bitzer. The actual horses in the world can then be seen as *examples* or *instances* of the concept. If someone tries to pass off a donkey or a zebra as a horse, we will be able to disqualify these pretenders, providing that we have developed knowledge of the Form/concept. "That's not a horse because it lacks the following necessary qualities . . ."

There are many different kinds of Platonic Forms: geometrical, mathematical, and logical relations (triangularity, equivalence, identity); human virtues (goodness, wisdom, courage); sensible properties (roundness, redness); and abstract concepts (justice, beauty, virtue, truth). In the sensible, day-to-day world of living, we see only imperfect examples of these perfect, eternal Forms, and the world of our senses can never yield authentic knowledge, only unsubstantial, changeable opinions.

It is in his doctrine of the Forms that we see the intersection of Plato's metaphysics and his epistemology. The existence of the Forms as transcendent, eternal archetypes enables Plato to distinguish genuine knowledge from mere, ill-informed opinion. We develop opinions through the simple experience of living and observing the world. But these opinions reflect the transitory nature of human life and so can never achieve the status of universal knowledge. Such knowledge comes only from knowledge of the eternal Forms, through our ability to use our reasoning abilities, as he describes:

> That which is apprehended by intelligence and reason is always in the same state, but that which is conceived by opinion with the help of sensation and without reason is always in a process of becoming and perishing and never really is.

Scientific knowledge, in every area of human experience, consists of apprehending the necessary and universal truths of that discipline. For example, gaining knowledge of various forms of government requires developing a grasp of the fundamental concepts of the discipline, as well as the principles and laws that characterize it. Thus,

◉ **Watch** the **Video**
Plato and Metaphysics
on **mysearchlab.com**

we must use our reasoning capacities to go beyond the world of appearance and opinion, to grasp the essence of the Forms that define that discipline:

> *The true lover of knowledge naturally strives for truth, and is not content with common opinion, but soars with undimmed and unwearied passion till he grasps the essential nature of things.*

Plato's metaphysical view enables him to achieve his epistemological goals, employing clear rational criteria to distinguish unsubstantiated and transient *opinion* from the eternal realm of *knowledge*. Even when our opinions happen to be accurate, this does not mean we have achieved knowledge:

> *Haven't you noticed that opinion without knowledge is blind—isn't anyone with a true but unthinking opinion like a blind man on the right road?*

Plato's metaphysical doctrine of the Forms provides him with a rational grounding for true knowledge, which enables him to escape from the snare of relativism and "unanchored" changeable opinions.

The Divided Line

Plato provides a visual analogy to illustrate the corresponding levels in his metaphysics and epistemology, which is reproduced in Figure 5.1. Levels C and D represent the world of Appearance, the Visible World in which we live our lives. Despite our best efforts, the highest form of knowing that we can achieve in this world of sense experience is Opinion. This is the world of Becoming, where everything is continually changing, evolving, disappearing, reappearing. The lowest level of Knowing and Being (Level D) is that of images produced by the human faculty of Imagination. This is the level of illusion, composed of unsubstantiated beliefs, transitory images, and fragmentary impressions that are received uncritically. For example, as we saw in *The Apology* in Chapter 2, Socrates acknowledged that there were many different images of who he was, conflicting perspectives of his character and reputation. He saw his challenge to be clarifying these unsubstantiated views of him but realized the difficulty of his task in a realm where people state their opinions without trying to provide compelling reasons and evidence. Plato was convinced that much of what people consider to be "knowledge" in the world is actually at this lowest level of opinion but that they deceive themselves into thinking that their unsupported impressions have genuine merit.

The next level in Plato's hierarchy of metaphysics and epistemology is Level C, that of Perception, which is effected by means of our five senses. Unlike the images produced by the imagination, perceptions have a grounding in the actual world in which we

Metaphysics		Epistemology			
Being	Higher Forms e.g. Wisdom	Level A	Understanding	Knowledge	INTELLIGIBLE WORLD
Being	Lower Forms e.g. Human form	Level B	Reasoning	Knowledge	INTELLIGIBLE WORLD
Becoming	Sensible Objects e.g. Socrates	Level C	Perception	Opinion	VISIBLE WORLD
Becoming	Images e.g. Socrates' reputation	Level D	Imagination	Opinion	VISIBLE WORLD

Figure 5.1 Plato's Divided Line

live. We see, hear, touch, taste, and smell things on an ongoing basis. Thus, Socrates was an actual, physical human being whom people in Athens could experience directly. But although the beliefs about the world based on our perceptions are more substantial than those produced by our imaginations, these perceptual beliefs still fall far short of knowledge. As we shall see, our perceptions are typically fragmentary and incomplete, and the conclusions that we reach based on them are typically subjective and biased. For example, although many people in Athens had seen, heard, and spoken to Socrates over a period of fifty years, people still had a diverse variety of perspectives on him. And, of course, the same principle applies in our lives. For example, interview a number of people who have witnessed the same event, and you'll likely hear a wide variety of different perceptions. Ask a number of people their opinion of the president, and you will no doubt receive many different points of view. Compare people's opinions with respect to a movie they saw or a college class they took, and you will no doubt find a range of different perceptions. When people's perceptions conflict, how can we tell which are "true" and rise to the level of Knowledge? That's the challenge of epistemology, and Plato believed that it was impossible to achieve at this level of metaphysics and epistemology.

According to Plato, the realm of human experience where knowledge begins to exist is Level B, the level of the "Lower" Forms. Lower Forms are those universals that we find exemplified in our physical world. For example, Socrates was a man who was an example of the universal form of "Human Being." And for us to understand the essence of Socrates, we need to use our reasoning ability to develop a clear idea of what it means to be a human being: What are the essential qualities that constitute this Form? Of course, Socrates isn't the only example of this form: All human beings illustrate or "participate" in the form of Human Being. And this Form qualifies as "Knowledge," according to Plato, because it represents a form of knowing that is universal and unchanging, unlike the transitory perceptions and images of Levels C and D.

The highest realm of Knowledge in Plato's metaphysics and epistemology is that of the "Higher" Forms, Level A. Universals such as Truth, Beauty, Good, and Justice are all examples of Higher Forms. Like the Lower Forms, the Higher Forms represent universals that are unchanging and eternal. The difference is that the Higher Forms refer to abstract ideals rather than actual physical objects in the world. Thus, although many people considered Socrates to illustrate the form of Wisdom by being a wise man, "wisdom" is not the essence of a physical object in the world that we can experience. It—like truth, beauty, justice, and good—exists on a much higher intellectual level, and understanding these ideals requires a lifetime of rational exploration and reflection. There are few people who can achieve this supreme understanding of these highest Forms. When you reach this exalted level of understanding, you "directly apprehend" these supreme, absolute Forms.

The Theory of Innate Ideas

Plato's belief that genuine knowledge can only be achieved through our reasoning abilities means that, in epistemological terms, he is a *rationalist*. In contrast, philosophers who, like Aristotle, believe that we can gain true knowledge through our sense experience are known as *empiricists* (though Aristotle was, like Plato, also seeking universal knowledge). As we will see in the pages ahead, this division between

rationalism and **empiricism** has endured since first introduced by Plato and Aristotle, and it has remained one of the core issues in epistemology.

One of the strongest arguments that rationalists advance to support their view that genuine knowledge is based on reason, not sense experience, is that humans seem to possess knowledge that could not possibly be derived solely from our experiences in the world. For example, the principles of mathematics and logic have for the most part been developed independently of experience. And although these principles can be *applied* to objects and events in the world, their truth is not dependent on these objects or events. In the dialogue *Meno*, Plato uses a dramatic example to illustrate this very point. Socrates is discussing his belief in the immortality of the soul with his friend Meno, along with his conviction that each soul begins life with essential knowledge. Such knowledge is *latent* in the sense that it requires experience to activate it, but it is in no way dependent on experience for its existence or truth. We need only to remember or "recollect" this knowledge for it to be brought to consciousness and used by us. Such knowledge is considered to be *innate* because it is present at birth. How can the existence of such knowledge be demonstrated? Socrates' solution is ingenious. He calls over an illiterate slave boy and presents him with the following problem: Socrates draws on the ground a square two feet by two feet (four feet square) and asks the boy to draw a second square that is exactly twice the size of the first square. The boy's first idea is to double the sides of the square to four feet by four feet, but he sees immediately that this solution is wrong. Through careful questioning, Socrates guides the boy through a systematic solution and geometric proof of the problem. Each step of the way, the boy seems to "know" the correct response, though he has never been taught any form of mathematics. Socrates then reflects on the entire process and its implications for innate knowledge:

Why do we view the universe the way we do? The world of the ancient Greeks comprised, primarily, islands and seas, thus leading them to infer that the whole world floated on water. In what ways might our current understanding of the universe also be inaccurate?

Rationalism The position that reason has precedence over other ways of acquiring knowledge or, more strongly, that it is the unique path to knowledge.

Empiricism The position that the senses (and sense experience) are primary in acquiring knowledge.

Plato, from *Meno*

Socrates: What do you think, Meno? Has he, in his answers, expressed any opinion that was not his own?

Meno: No, they were all his own.

Socrates: And yet, as we said, he did not know a short time ago?

Meno: That is true.

Socrates: So these opinions were in him, were they not?

Meno: Yes.

Socrates: So the man who does not know has within himself true opinions about the things that he does not know?

Meno: So it appears.

Socrates: These opinions have now just been stirred up like a dream, but if he were repeatedly asked these same questions in various ways, you know that in the end his knowledge about these things would be as accurate as anyone's.

Meno: It is likely.

Socrates: And he will know it without having been taught but only questioned, and find the knowledge within himself?

Meno: Yes.

Socrates: And is not finding knowledge within oneself recollection?

Meno: Certainly.

Socrates: Must he not either have at some time acquired the knowledge he now possesses, or else have always possessed it?

Meno: Yes.

Socrates: If he always had it, he would always have known. If he acquired it, he cannot have done so in his present life. Or has someone taught him geometry? For he will perform in the same way about all geometry, and all other knowledge. Has someone taught him everything? You should know, especially as he has been born and brought up in your house.

Meno: But I know that no one has taught him.

Socrates: Yet he has these opinions, or doesn't he?

Meno: That seems indisputable, Socrates.

Socrates: If he has not acquired them in his present life, is it not clear that he had them and had learned them at some other time?

Meno: It seems so.

Socrates: Then that was the time when he was not a human being?

Meno: Yes.

Socrates: If then, during the time he exists and is not a human being he will have true opinions which, when stirred by questioning, become knowledge, will not his soul have learned during all time? For it is clear that during all time he exists either as a man or not.

Meno: So it seems.

Socrates: Then if the truth about reality is always in our soul, the soul would be immortal so that you should always confidently try to seek out and recollect what you do not know at present—that is, what you do not recollect?

Meno: Somehow, Socrates, I think that what you say is right.

Socrates: I think so too, Meno.

Where does this knowledge come from? Plato's theory is that each soul existed in a perfect world before birth where such knowledge was learned, as he explains:

Plato, from *Meno*

For as all nature is akin, and the soul has (already) learned all things, there is no difficulty in learning all the rest, if a man is strenuous and does not faint; for all enquiry is but recollection.

Most philosophers—as well as psychologists, anthropologists, and linguists—who believe in some sort of innate knowledge *do not* accept these metaphysical beliefs of Plato. Instead, they tend to believe that such innate knowledge is simply part of the biological/cognitive "software" that humans come programmed with. But jettisoning Plato's metaphysical "perfect world" where immortal souls learn their innate knowledge leaves the core argument he is making in this passage untouched: How *do* we acquire knowledge that cannot be accounted for by sense experience if it is not innate and known through reason?

< **READING CRITICALLY** >

Analyzing Plato's Theory of Innate Ideas

- Do you find to be persuasive the example of the slave boy's "recollection" of geometric principles that he has not been explicitly taught? Why or why not? Can you think of an alternative explanation for the slave boy's "knowledge"?

- Reflect on your own intellectual development. Can you identify knowledge of which you became aware that you did not learn from experience? An example might be your belief in the scientific law of cause and effect. Although you may experience events connected to other events, there is nothing in experience that "teaches" you that this connection is a necessary one. Other examples might include your knowledge of logic, mathematics, language, or moral principles.

- Imagine that you disagreed with Plato's concept of innate knowledge learned in a previous perfect world before birth. Explain how you would go about trying to convince him that he was wrong.

- If you believe that there is innate knowledge independent of experience, and you reject Plato's idea of a perfect world where immortal souls exist before birth, then how would you explain the origin of these innate ideas—in other words, where did they come from?

The Path to Knowledge of Reality: The Cave Allegory

For Plato, ascending to the realm of the Forms to achieve genuine knowledge is a challenging, arduous process. Most people are submerged in the shadowy world of illusion and mere opinion, completely unaware of their own lack of enlightenment. It is possible for people to move from ignorance to rationally based knowledge and wisdom, but it requires willingness, dedication, and wise teachers as guides. Plato used a variety of metaphors and allegories to describe this intellectual journey of discovery. The most powerful and enduring of these is "The Allegory of the Cave," which has become a touchstone of Western thinking. The allegory communicates in rich and symbolic terms the journey through the various stages of knowledge, which echo the metaphysical and epistemological structure of the Divided Line analogy.

Plato, from *The Republic*

Socrates: Imagine men to be living in an underground cavelike dwelling place, which has a way up to the light along its whole width, but the entrance is a long way up. The men have been there from childhood, with their neck and legs in fetters, so that they remain in the same place and can only see ahead of them, as their bonds prevent them turning their heads. Light is provided by a fire burning some way behind them, and on a higher ground, there is a path across the cave and along this a low wall has been built, like the screen at a puppet show in front of the performers who show their puppets above it.

Glaucon: I see it.

Socrates: See then also men carrying along that wall, so that they overtop it, all kinds of artifacts, statues of men, reproductions of other animals in stone or wood fashioned in all sorts of ways, and, as is likely, some of the carriers are talking while others are silent.

How is the allegory of the cave a metaphor for achieving intellectual insight and wisdom? After reading the passage from *The Republic*, can you describe what is happening in this painting?

Glaucon: This is a strange picture, and strange prisoners.

Socrates: They are like us, I said. Do you think, in the first place, that such men could see anything of themselves and each other except the shadows which the fire casts upon the wall of the cave in front of them?

Glaucon: How could they, if they have to keep their heads still throughout life?

Socrates: And is not the same true of the objects carried along the wall?

Glaucon: Quite.

Socrates: If they could converse with one another, do you not think that they would consider these shadows to be the real things?

Glaucon: Necessarily.

Socrates: What if their prison had an echo which reached them from in front of them? Whenever one of the carriers passing behind the wall spoke, would they not think that it was the shadow passing in front of them which was talking? Do you agree?

Glaucon: By Zeus, I do.

Socrates: Altogether then, I said, such men would believe the truth to be nothing else than the shadows of the artifacts?

Glaucon: They must believe that.

Socrates: Consider then what deliverance from their bonds and the curing of their ignorance would be if something like this naturally happened to them. Whenever one of them was freed, had to stand up suddenly, turn his head, walk, and look up toward the light, doing all that would give him pain, the flash of the fire would make it impossible for him to see the objects of which he had earlier seen the shadows. What do you think he would say if he was told that what he saw was foolishness, that he was now somewhat closer to reality and turned to things that existed more fully, that he saw more correctly? If one then pointed to each of the objects passing by, asked him what each was, and forced him to answer, do you not think he would be at a loss and believe that the things which he saw earlier were truer than the things now pointed out to him.

Glaucon: Much truer.

Socrates: If one then compelled him to look at the fire itself, his eyes would hurt, he would turn round and flee toward those things which he could see, and think that they were in fact clearer than those now shown to him.

Glaucon: Quite so.

Socrates: And if one were to drag him thence by force up the rough and steep path, and did not let him go before he was dragged into the sunlight, would he not be in physical pain and angry as he was dragged along? When he came into the light, with the sunlight filling his eyes, he would not be able to see a single one of the things which are now said to be true.

Glaucon: Not at once, certainly.

Socrates: I think he would need time to get adjusted before he could see things in the world above; at first he would see shadows most easily, then reflections of men and other things in water, then the things themselves. After this he would see objects in the sky and the sky itself more easily at night, the light of the stars and the moon more easily than the sun and the light of the sun during the day.

Glaucon: Of course.

Socrates: Then, at last, he would be able to see the sun, not images of it in water or in some alien place, but the sun itself in its own place, and be able to contemplate it.

Glaucon: That must be so.

Socrates: After this he would reflect that it is the sun which provides the seasons and the years, which governs everything in the visible world, and is also in some way the cause of those other things which he used to see.

Glaucon: Clearly that would be the next stage.

Socrates: What then? As he reminds himself of his first dwelling place, of the wisdom there and of his fellow prisoners, would he not reckon himself happy for the change, and pity them?

Glaucon: Surely.

Socrates: And if the men below had praise and honours from each other, and prizes for the man who saw most clearly the shadows that passed before them, and who could best remember which usually came earlier and which later, and which came together and thus could most ably prophesy the future, do you think our man would desire those rewards and envy those who were honoured and held power among the prisoners, or would he feel, as Homer put it, that he certainly wished to be "serf to another man without possessions upon the earth" and go through any suffering, rather than share their opinions and live as they do?*

Glaucon: Quite so, I think he would rather suffer anything.

Socrates: Reflect on this too. If this man went down into the cave again and sat down in the same seat, would his eyes not be filled with darkness, coming suddenly out of the sunlight?

Glaucon: They certainly would.

Socrates: And if he had to contend again with those who had remained prisoners in recognizing those shadows while his sight was affected and his eyes had not settled down—and the time for this adjustment would not be short—would he not be ridiculed? Would it not be said that he had returned from his upward journey with his eyesight spoiled, and that it was not worthwhile even to attempt to travel upward? As for the man who tried to free them and lead them upward, if they could somehow lay their hands on him and kill him, they would do so.

---

*The Odyssey 11, 489–490, where Achilles says to Odysseus, on the latter's visit to the underworld, that he would rather be a servant to a poor man on Earth than king among the dead (trans. note).

Are reality shows "real"? Does the media tell the "truth"? How are the images we encounter on television and in the mass media similar to Plato's idea of a shadow puppet show? Why do some people who view television and read information sources uncritically tend to believe that what they are viewing is "real"? Recognizing that the perceptions we encounter in our daily lives are often incomplete, inaccurate, and distorted is essential to beginning our journey toward illumination.

Glaucon: They certainly would.

Socrates: This whole image, my dear Glaucon, must be related to what we said before. The realm of the visible should be compared to the prison dwelling, and the fire inside it to the power of the sun. If you interpret the upward journey and the contemplation of things above as the upward journey of the soul to the intelligible realm, you will grasp what I surmise since you were keen to hear it. Whether it is true or not only the god knows, but this is how I see it, namely that in the intelligible world the Form of the Good is the last to be seen, and with difficulty; when seen it must be reckoned to be for all the cause of all that is right and beautiful, to have produced in the visible world both the light and the fount of light, while in the intelligible world it is itself that which produces and controls truth and intelligence, and he who is to act intelligently in public or in private must see it.

Glaucon: I share your thought as far as I am able.

Socrates: Come then, share with me this thought also: do not be surprised that those who have reached this point are unwilling to occupy themselves with human affairs, and that their souls are always pressing upward to spend their time there, for this is natural if things are as our parable indicates.

Glaucon: That is very likely.

Socrates: Further, do you think it at all surprising that anyone coming to the evils of human life from the contemplation of the divine behaves awkwardly and appears very ridiculous while his eyes are still dazzled and before he is sufficiently adjusted to the darkness around him, if he is compelled to contend in court or some other place about the shadows of justice or the objects of which they are shadows, and to carry through the contest about these in the way these things are understood by those who have never seen Justice itself?

Glaucon: That is not surprising at all.

Socrates: Anyone with intelligence would remember that the eyes may be confused in two ways and from two causes, coming from light into darkness as well as from darkness into light. Realizing that the same applies to the soul, whenever he sees a soul disturbed and unable to see something, he will not laugh mindlessly but will consider whether it has come from a brighter life and is dimmed because unadjusted, or has come from greater ignorance into greater light and is filled with a brighter dazzlement. The former he would declare happy in its life and experience, the latter he would pity, and if he should wish to laugh at it, his laughter would be less ridiculous than if he laughed at the soul that has come from the light above.

Glaucon: What you say is very reasonable.

Socrates: We must then, if these things are true, think something like this about them, namely that education is not what some declare it to be; they say that knowledge is not present in the soul and that they put it in, like putting sight into blind eyes.

Glaucon: They sure say that.

> [T]he capacity to learn and the organ with which to do so are present in every person's soul.

Socrates: Our present argument shows that the capacity to learn and the organ with which to do so are present in every person's soul. It is as if it were not possible to turn the eye from darkness to light without turning the whole body; so one must turn one's whole soul from the world of becoming until it can endure to contemplate reality, and the brightest of realities, which we say is the Good.

Glaucon: Yes.

Socrates: Education then is the art of doing this very thing, this turning around, the knowledge of how the soul can most easily and most effectively be turned around; it is not the art of putting the capacity of sight into the soul; the soul possesses that already but it is not turned the right way or looking where it should. This is what education has to deal with.

5.3 Reality Is the Natural World: Aristotle

Aristotle was a devoted—and brilliant—student in Plato's Academy, and although he shared many philosophical convictions with his esteemed teacher, they also ended up having serious disagreements. Aristotle and Plato were both intent on determining the nature of reality, and they both agreed that genuine knowledge must be universal. But Aristotle was very disturbed at Plato's metaphysical dualism, his sharp division between

- the perfect world of Being constituted by the eternal Forms, and
- the imperfect world of Becoming, the sensible world of experience in which we live our lives, a world that is merely a pale reflection of the world of Being.

Aristotle was concerned that the net result of this division would be to devalue the world of experience as something "less real" and unworthy of

Aristotle (384–322 B.C.E.). This image, believed to be of Aristotle teaching an anatomy lesson, illustrates Aristotle's commitment to observation and his work in biology. One of the most important figures in the history of philosophy, Aristotle conceptualized the branches of philosophy and contributed to theories in logic, metaphysics, ethics, and political philosophy.

serious, systematic study. He feared that Plato's metaphysic would, in his words, push people toward

> *otherworldliness, to a chasm between the actual and the ideal . . . (which means)*
> *that discussion of what is can never amount to more than a "likely story," and*
> *knowledge of what **ought to be** has little or no relevance to pressing moral, politi-*
> *cal and social problems.*

This philosophical perspective was completely unacceptable to Aristotle, who was as much a scientist (he is often called "the father of science") as a philosopher: a great biologist, physicist, political theorist, and ethicist. Aristotle was focused on *this* world, committed to understanding it in all of its rich and complex splendor and using this knowledge to improve the quality of life both individually and socially. As a philosophical naturalist, he was convinced that reality consists of the natural world and that this natural world follows orderly principles and laws that we can use to understand it. For Aristotle, there *is* no separate, supernatural reality, such as Plato's world of Being and its eternal Forms. This sort of speculation is not only misguided, it is dangerous, because it deflects people from achieving genuine knowledge based on the actual facts of *this* world. Genuine knowledge, he argued, is derived through scientific exploration—careful observation, collection of data, systematic classification—not highly abstract and unprovable theories and speculation. Aristotle was convinced that Plato's epistemology was fatally flawed because Plato was never able to provide an intelligible account of the way the physical dimensions of this world "participate" in the eternal Forms. "Participation," Plato's keystone concept, was for Aristotle "a mere empty phrase and a poetic metaphor."

For Aristotle, this same naturalistic orientation extended to human beings themselves. As we saw, Plato's metaphysical belief in the world of Being and the eternal Forms is tied to

- his belief in an immortal soul separate from the physical body.
- an existence before birth in which the soul is exposed to universal truths, which need only be "recollected" in this life.
- the ability of the soul to ascend to the world of Being through rational inquiry and enlightenment.
- the continued existence of the soul after death.

Aristotle categorically rejects all of these intertwined metaphysical beliefs. From his perspective, there is indeed a human soul, but it cannot be separated from the body. We are entirely creatures of nature, just as all forms of life are. We are unique because of our ability to reason, but beyond that there is no other reality than this world, either before birth or after death. Metaphysics is not the study of nonphysical realms or entities—it is the study of the natural world, and the study of humans as an integral and inseparable part of the natural world.

Aristotle's Two Categories: Matter and Form

Like Plato, "forms" are an important part of Aristotle's metaphysic—with one significant difference. While Plato believed that Forms (with a capital *F*) embodied the highest order of reality in a timeless, transcendent realm knowable only through reason, Aristotle believed that forms (with a lowercase *f*) were embedded in physical objects, existing completely within the natural order. Every "thing" that exists has both a material element and a formal element; and, although we can separate these two in thought, they cannot be separated in reality. For example, "mortality" is a formal—or essential—aspect of living things. But although we can separate "mortality" and "living things" intellectually, they cannot be separated in reality. "Mortality"—or any formal element in nature—cannot exist independently, on its own. For Aristotle, this was Plato's fundamental mistake, believing that formal elements of things could be abstracted and then elevated to a transcendent status of ultimate reality. Or, as Aristotle expressed it, we must take care not to mistake "intellectual analysis" for "ontological status." And this is true for all of Plato's forms: Redness, Roundness, Justice, Beauty—although we can distinguish these concepts in our mind, they can't really *exist* on their own. They can only *exist* as a formal aspect of some material object: a *red* apple, a *round* ball, a *just* law, a *beautiful* sunset. Thus, in Aristotle's metaphysical system, there are two basic categories of things:

- Matter (in Greek, *hyle*), which refers to the common "stuff" that makes up the material universe
- Form, which refers to the essence of a thing, that which makes it what it is

Taken together, *matter* and *form* combine to create *formed matter* or *substance*—that is, all of the familiar things we see in the universe. For example, a piece of wood is composed of matter and certain formal elements that give the piece of wood shape, color, and texture. A craftsperson can take a number of pieces of wood and create a bed, reflecting the formal elements of design that he imposed on the wood. Similarly, a sculptor takes a block of marble (which itself embodies both matter and form), and then shapes it into a sculpture, reflecting the formal design she had in her mind.

Thus for Aristotle, matter and form require each other in order to exist. Matter provides the opportunity for formal elements to shape it into a purposeful design; or, in the case of living things, for a potential purposeful design to become actualized. A fertilized human egg has within it the *potential* to become an embryo; and, given the right conditions, this potential will become *actualized* into a *reality*. This general conceptual framework of Aristotle's has become known as **hylomorphism**, and it continues to have relevance in contemporary philosophy. The term "hylomorphism" is a compound derived from the Greek words *hyle* (matter) and *morphe* (form or shape). According to hylomorphism, individual organisms consist of both matter and form. One way of understanding this is in terms of *structure* and *structured*: form is a structure and matter is anything that admits of structuring and there can be no structure without something that is structured. According to hylomorphists, what we see when we look at the world is not simply the vast sea of matter and energy that the physicists describes. In fact, we see something more besides: the way the matter and energy are arranged, organized or structured.

Hylomorphism claims that structure, organization, or form is a basic ontological and explanatory principle. Some individuals, such as living things, consist of materials that are structured or organized in various ways. Human beings are not mere collections of physical particles; we are collections of physical particles (matter or body) with a certain organization or structure (form or soul). That structure is responsible for you and I being humans as opposed to dogs or rocks, and it is responsible for you and I possessing the particular capacities we have for development, metabolism, reproduction, perception, and cognition.

I am indebted to Emmanuel Nartey for this explication of Aristotle's concept of hylomorphism.

The structure or organization that distinguishes living things from nonliving ones is what Aristotle called "soul." As we saw at the beginning of this chapter, the pre-Socratic thinker Democritus grounded the living/nonliving distinction in differences at a more fundamental physical level. Living things, he said, had a greater number of *round atoms*. Platonists, on the other hand, grounded the difference in the presence of an additional nonmaterial "spooky" component in living things. Against both, Aristotle, who first developed hylomorphism as a conceptual framework, insisted that living things were composed of the same materials as nonliving ones, and that what distinguished the former from the latter was the way those materials were structured or organized. Understood in this way, hylomorphism enjoys a great deal of empirical support from current work in the biological, psychological, and social sciences.

Entelechy

Entelechy The creative drive or inner urge that impels all things to achieve their purpose in life.

For Aristotle, purpose through formal design is a basic principle of the universe. "Nature does nothing in vain" because every natural process has a goal. "Nature, like mind, always acts for a purpose, and this purpose is its end. That it should be so is according to nature." **Entelechy** is one of the core concepts on which Aristotle bases his entire philosophy. The word comes from the Greek for "having its end within itself," and Aristotle interpreted it to be a creative drive or inner urge that impels all things to achieve their purpose in life. "Such principles do not all make for the same goal, but each inner principle always makes for the same goal of its own (kind), if nothing interferes." That is, everything in the universe has its own unique purpose to fulfill: an acorn to be an oak tree, a fertilized egg to become a human being. Of course, achieving one's purpose is typically dependent on the right conditions being present: If an acorn isn't planted, or lacks sufficient water and light, its potential won't be actualized.

The same is true on a human level, as he observes in the first line from Book I of the *Metaphysics:* "All human beings by nature desire to know." Aristotle believed that each person has a potential to fulfill, in accordance with his or her own entelechy. In people, the formal element is the *soul*, which gives shape and purposeful direction to the body: ". . . for every part of a living body is an organ of the soul. Evidently then, all such parts are for the sake of the soul, which is their natural end." But the conditions for a person to fulfill her potential are much more complex and challenging than something like an acorn, and people's potentials are often not realized due to inhibiting experiences.

Aristotle believed that, as with every other aspect of nature, the soul is not immortal: It ceases to exist once the matter in which it is embedded (the body) stops functioning. And as we will see in Chapter 8, Aristotle believes that there is a "good life" for each of us to aspire to and achieve, a life of balance, fullness, and happiness.

Does everything in nature have a unique purpose (Entelechy)? An acorn is to be an oak tree, provided that the conditions are right for its potential to be realized. Aristotle believed that everything in the universe has its own unique purpose to fulfill.

The Four Causes

Aristotle integrated his central metaphysical ideas into a comprehensive framework that he termed *The Four Causes.* The Greek word for cause is *aitia*, which means "the reason for something happening." For Aristotle, this meant achieving a complete understanding of a thing. Although

Aristotle's concept of cause as "the reason for something happening" *includes* our modern concept of "one event bringing about another event," it also extends far beyond this notion. Aristotle's Four Causes include

- *Material Cause*—the "matter" of which a thing is made.
- *Formal Cause*—the embedded form that gives shape and purpose to the "matter."
- *Efficient Cause*—the "triggering" action that sets the thing in motion.
- *Final Cause*—the ultimate purpose for which a thing exists.

For Aristotle, a complete explanation for *why* something happens necessarily entails addressing all of these "causes," as he explains in his *Metaphysics*: "It is the business of the natural scientist to know about them all . . . (and to) give his answer to the question 'why?' in the manner of a natural scientist . . . (by referring to them all—to the matter, the form, the mover, and the purpose)."

Aristotle's four causes are different ways of answering or explaining *why-questions*, which seek to understand why things are how they are. Aristotle believes that we do not really come to know (or understand) a thing until we have known its causes or principles and we know a thing's causes or principles when we have grasped the "why" of it, as he explains in the following passage from the *Physics*:

> Now that we have established these distinctions, we must proceed to consider causes, their character and number. Knowledge is the object of our inquiry, and men do not think they know a thing till they have grasped the "why" of it (which is to grasp its primary cause). So clearly we too must do this as regards both coming to be and every kind of natural change, in order that, knowing their principles, we may try to refer to these principles each of our problems.

> Physics **II, 194ᵇ20**

Material Cause

As we have seen, Aristotle considers *matter* to be the basic "stuff" of the universe. However, *matter* requires *form* to shape it into something useful and purposeful. As he explains in the following passage, simply describing the material (wood or bronze) that something like a bed or statue is made of is *necessary* but in no way *sufficient* for providing a comprehensive explanation of the thing in question.

Aristotle, *from Metaphysics*

Some people regard the nature and substance of things that exist by nature as being in each case the proximate element inherent in the thing, this being itself unshaped; thus, (according to such a view) the nature of a bed, for instance, would be wood, and that of a statue, bronze. (Those who think this way offer) as evidence . . . the fact that if you were to bury a bed, and the moisture that got into it as it rotted gained enough force to throw up a shoot, it would be wood and not a bed that came into being. (According to this view, the bed's) arrangement according to the rules of an art . . . is an accidental attribute, whereas its substance is what remains permanently, and undergoes all these changes.

Formal Cause

As we discussed previously, *form* is the other major element in Aristotle's metaphysical system, representing the embedded shape or purpose of particular *matter*. In the bed and the sculpture, it is the design of the artisan that uses form to shape the material (wood and bronze) into something useful and purposeful. Before that happens, the material is only *potentially* a bed or sculpture. It is not until the artisan crafts the materials "according to the rules of an art" that the potential becomes an *actuality*. The same principle holds true for biological matter, such as flesh and bone, as well. Until nature shapes matter into the *formed matter* of flesh and bone, they exist only as potentials.

Aristotle, from
Metaphysics

> What is potentially flesh or bone does not yet have its own nature until it acquires the form that accords with the formula, by means of which we define flesh and bone; nor can it be said at this stage to exist by nature. So in another way, nature is the shape and form of things that have a principle of movement in themselves—the form being only theoretically separable from the object in question.

Efficient Cause

This is the concept that's closest to our modern idea of "cause"—the "triggering event" that sets things in motion or initiates change, transforming a *potential* into an *actuality*. Aristotle terms this immediate cause the "proximate mover." For example, the artisan is the "efficient cause" of the wood being crafted into a bed and the bronze being shaped into a sculpture.

Aristotle, from
Metaphysics

> Thus the answer to the question "why?" is to be given by referring to the matter, to the essence, and to the proximate mover. In cases of coming-to-be it is mostly in this last way that people examine the causes; they ask what comes to be after what, what was the immediate thing that acted or was acted upon, and so on in order.

The Four Causes. How does the process of forming an object through glassblowing illustrate Aristotle's concept of the Four Causes?

Final Cause

The Final Cause embodies the ultimate purpose of a thing's existence, its reason for being, its *telos* or final goal. For Aristotle, no description of an object is complete until we place it within the entire teleological framework of the universe. Every aspect of the cosmos is purposive, directed toward a goal, defined and driven by its entelechy. In humans, our soul or *psyche* is our entelechy, directing us toward our ultimate purpose in life. However, Aristotle's conception of "soul" or "ultimate purpose" is in no way supernatural: It simply describes our unique purpose within the natural order. As Aristotle observes: "If purpose is present in art, it must also be present in nature."

In summary, there are multiple types of causal relations in the world. But since our attempt to assign causes or grasp the "why" of a thing in question is inseparably connected with offering an explanation, the notion of a cause is inextricably tied to that of explanation. From Aristotle's perspective—and those philosophers who embrace his hylomorphic framework—these four causes are just different modes of explanation. So we can analyze and cite the cause or explain a thing, say Clara's activity of erecting a new building across the street by appealing to the material of which it is constructed (*material cause*); the structure, organization, or form of the building, and taken robustly its essence or nature (*formal cause*); the agent that brought it about *actually*, the builder, but *potentially* the owner of the building if the latter is not identical with the former (*efficient cause*); and finally the function or purpose for which the project was executed, for instance convening international conferences or providing shelter for the homeless (*final cause*).

Aristotle extends this concept of Final Cause to the universe as a whole, a cosmological concept that he variously characterizes as "first (Final) cause," "prime mover," and "pure thought, thinking thought." This is *not* a "God" as a Creator but rather an impersonal teleological principle that permeates the universe as a whole. Aristotle arrives at this conclusion through an intriguing—and famous—argument. If we examine each of the Four Causes, we can see that each one assumes the existence of something that came before. But to avoid what philosophers term an **infinite regress**, we need to posit a First Final Cause.

Infinite Regress A philosophical kind of argument purporting to show that a thesis is defective because it generates an infinite series when either no such series exists or, were it to exist, the thesis would lack the role (e.g., of justification) that it is supposed to play.

Aristotle, from *Metaphysics*

Moreover, it is obvious that there is some first principle, and that the causes of things are not infinitely many either in a direct sequence or in kind. For the material generation of one thing from another cannot go on in an infinite progression (e.g. flesh from earth, earth from air, air from fire, and so on without a stop); nor can the source of motion (e.g. man be moved by air, air by the sun, the sun by Strife, with no limit to the series). In the same way neither can the Final Cause (that is, purposes) recede to infinity—walking having health for its object, and health happiness, and happiness something else: one thing always being done for the sake of another. And it is just the same with the Formal Cause (that is, the essence). For in the case of all intermediate terms of a series which are contained between a first and last term, the prior term is necessarily the cause of those which follow it; because if we had to say which of the three is the cause, we should say "the first." At any rate it is not the last term, because what comes at the end is not the cause of anything. Neither, again, is the intermediate term, which is only the cause of one (and it makes no difference whether there is one intermediate term or several, nor whether they are infinite or limited in number). But of series which are infinite in this way, and in general of the infinite, all the parts are equally intermediate, down to the present moment. Thus if there is no first term, there is no cause at all.

5.4 Can Reality Be Known? Descartes

We were first introduced to this extraordinary philosopher in Chapter 3 along with his famous pronouncement, *Cogito, ergo sum* ("I think, therefore I am"). **René Descartes** was a mathematician by training, and he invented analytical geometry. He had a vibrant and wide-ranging intellect, and his influence on modern philosophy and Western thought in general has been profound. In fact, Descartes and Immanuel Kant are generally credited with establishing the intellectual framework for modern Western consciousness, which is still evident today in virtually every academic discipline.

It's a big leap between Socrates, Plato, Aristotle, and Descartes—over 2,000 years! And yet, in intellectual terms, Descartes is thought by many philosophers to represent the next significant advance in Western thinking. As we have seen, Plato constructed an ambitious vision of reality in which true knowledge is achieved by means of our rational faculties. It's a long and arduous journey that takes us through the shadowy and confusing world of sense experience to finally achieve a pure and complete understanding of the transcendent essences—the Forms—that make up true knowledge. This view, that reason is the primary source of all knowledge and that only our reasoning abilities can enable us to understand our experience and reach accurate conclusions, is known as *rationalism.*

Aristotle, on the other hand, was a naturalist who believed that we don't need to journey to the abstract realm of the Forms in order to achieve ultimate knowledge. Instead, it is by using our rational faculties to understand the natural world in a deep and profound way that we achieve true and lasting knowledge. Although Aristotle

René Descartes
(1596–1650). Descartes was a French philosopher considered the founder of modern philosophy. A mathematician and scientist as well, Descartes was a leader in the seventeenth-century scientific revolution. In his major work, *Meditations on First Philosophy* (1641), he rigorously analyzed the established knowledge of the time.

doesn't fit into a neat epistemological pigeonhole, his views were the precursor of *empiricism*, the view that sense experience can enable us to understand the world and achieve accurate conclusions.

Descartes was a rationalist, believing that true knowledge is produced by thinking which is reflective, logical, and analytical, independent of our sense experiences in the world, a view naturally reinforced by his training as a mathematician. And yet, despite the power and rigor of his thinking, Descartes was able to express his ideas in a very direct and personal way. The best examples of this are the *Meditations on First Philosophy* (1641), which are written in the form of a personal journal, even as he explores ideas that people are still discussing and debating today. He begins his Meditation I with the question that virtually every young person has posed to him- or herself at one time or another: Suppose every important thing I've been taught in my life to this point has been inaccurate and unreliable—what then? Descartes' response was dramatically unique. He decided to make every effort to dispose of everything he had been taught and start fresh, searching for a foundation point for knowledge that would be absolutely rock solid—clear, distinct, indubitable.

Listen to the **Podcast**
A.C. Grayling on Descartes' Cogito on **mysearchlab.com**

René Descartes, from *Meditations on First Philosophy*

Meditation I *Of the things which may be brought within the sphere of the doubtful*

1. It is now some years since I detected how many were the false beliefs that I had from my earliest youth admitted as true, and how doubtful was everything I had since constructed on this basis; and from that time I was convinced that I must once and for all seriously undertake to rid myself of all the opinions which I had formerly accepted, and commence to build anew from the foundation, if I wanted to establish any firm and permanent structure in the sciences. But as this enterprise appeared to be a very great one, I waited until I had attained an age so mature that I could not hope that at any later date I should be better fitted to execute my design. This reason caused me to delay so long that I should feel that I was doing wrong were I to occupy in deliberation the time that yet remains to me for action. To-day, then, since very opportunely for the plan I have in view I have delivered my mind from every care [and am happily agitated by no passions] and since I have procured for myself an assured leisure in a peaceable retirement, I shall at last seriously and freely address myself to the general upheaval of all my former opinions.

2. Now for this object it is not necessary that I should show that all of these are false—I shall perhaps never arrive at this end. But inasmuch as reason already persuades me that I ought no less carefully to withhold my assent from matters which are not entirely certain and indubitable than from those which appear to me manifestly to be false, if I am able to find in each one some reason to doubt, this will suffice to justify my rejecting the whole. And for that end it will not be requisite that I should examine each in particular, which would be an endless undertaking; for owing to the fact that the destruction of the foundations of necessity brings with it the downfall of the rest of the edifice, I shall only in the first place attack those principles upon which all my former opinions rested.

Descartes' attitude is so contemporary that he almost could have written the lyrics to the Paul Simon song, "Kodachrome," which begins, "When I think back on all the crap I learned in high school/it's a wonder I can think at all." Having had the growing suspicion that much of what he had been taught had been biased, incomplete, or downright wrong, Descartes resolves to try to wipe his epistemological "tablet" clean and begin anew. The "radical doubt" that he is employing is for the positive purpose of establishing a "firm and permanent structure in the sciences," *not* to end up mired in skepticism. In taking this approach, Descartes is modeling a very philosophical approach to knowledge first initiated by Socrates, which nonphilosophers often misunderstand. Rather than using doubt *destructively*, to simply disprove and undermine ways of thinking, doubt is used *constructively*, to identify, strengthen, and refine the best beliefs. It is this "trial by fire" that helps us develop beliefs that are tempered and firmly grounded. In the absence of genuine doubt, beliefs are left to exist uncritically and ill informed. It is also fascinating that Descartes recognized the need to wait until he had reached a level of intellectual maturity before calling into question the beliefs he had acquired growing up, as he wanted to ensure that his beliefs were not still in the process of evolution.

Is it really possible to suspend all of the beliefs we have been brought up with to start fresh in constructing our understanding of the world? No, of course not: Such a project would surely be impractical, and we would likely retain an abiding faith in many of the beliefs we had come to believe were true. Nevertheless, there is real merit in undertaking a "doubting project" like this, for it encourages us to begin questioning beliefs we may have been unwittingly taking for granted, and it also initiates what will hopefully become a lifelong process of critical reflection. And as Descartes is quick to point out, it is not necessary to question every individual belief, simply our core beliefs, such as:

- How is it possible to be certain of what I think I know?
- What is the reason for believing (or not believing) in a God?
- On what basis should I make ethical decisions?
- How do I know that there is a world that exists outside of my experience?

Having identified the general aim of his reflective analysis and established its basic ground rules, Descartes moves on to explore the reliability (and *un*reliability) of our sense experience.

René Descartes, from *Meditations on First Philosophy*

3. All that up to the present time I have accepted as most true and certain I have learned either from the senses or through the senses; but it is sometimes proved to me that these senses are deceptive, and it is wiser not to trust entirely to anything by which we have once been deceived.

4. But it may be that although the senses sometimes deceive us concerning things which are hardly perceptible, or very far away, there are yet many others to be met with as to which we cannot reasonably have any doubt, although we recognize them by their means. For example, there is the fact that I am here, seated by the fire, attired in a dressing gown, having this paper in my hands and other similar matters. And how could I deny that these hands and this body are mine, were it not perhaps that I compare myself to certain persons, devoid of sense, whose cerebella are so troubled and clouded by the violent vapours of black bile, that they constantly assure us that they think they are kings when they are really quite poor, or that they are clothed in purple when they are really without covering, or who imagine that they have an earthenware head or are nothing but pumpkins or are made of glass. But they are mad, and I should not be any the less insane were I to follow examples so extravagant.

5. At the same time I must remember that I am a man, and that consequently I am in the habit of sleeping, and in my dreams representing to myself the same

things or sometimes even less probable things, than do those who are insane in their waking moments. How often has it happened to me that in the night I dreamt that I found myself in this particular place, that I was dressed and seated near the fire, whilst in reality I was lying undressed in bed! At this moment it does indeed seem to me that it is with eyes awake that I am looking at this paper; that this head which I move is not asleep, that it is deliberately and of set purpose that I extend my hand and perceive it; what happens in sleep does not appear so clear nor so distinct as does all this. But in thinking over this I remind myself that on many occasions I have in sleep been deceived by similar illusions, and in dwelling carefully on this reflection I see so manifestly that there are no certain indications by which we may clearly distinguish wakefulness from sleep that I am lost in astonishment. And my astonishment is such that it is almost capable of persuading me that I now dream.

6. Now let us assume that we are asleep and that all these particulars, e.g. that we open our eyes, shake our head, extend our hands, and so on, are but false delusions; and let us reflect that possibly neither our hands nor our whole body are such as they appear to us to be. At the same time we must at least confess that the things which are represented to us in sleep are like painted representations which can only have been formed as the counterparts of something real and true, and that in this way those general things at least, i.e. eyes, a head, hands, and a whole body, are not imaginary things, but things really existent. For, as a matter of fact, painters, even when they study with the greatest skill to represent sirens and satyrs by forms the most strange and extraordinary, cannot give them natures which are entirely new, but merely make a certain medley of the members of different animals; or if their imagination is extravagant enough to invent something so novel that nothing similar has ever before been seen, and that then their work represents a thing purely fictitious and absolutely false, it is certain all the same that the colors of which this is composed are necessarily real. And for the same reason, although these general things, to wit, [a body], eyes, a head, hands, and such like, may be imaginary, we are bound at the same time to confess that there are at least some other objects yet more simple and more universal, which are real and true; and of these just in the same way as with certain real colors, all these images of things which dwell in our thoughts, whether true and real or false and fantastic, are formed.

7. To such a class of things pertains corporeal nature in general, and its extension, the figure of extended things, their quantity or magnitude and number, as also the place in which they are, the time which measures their duration, and so on.

Dreaming or awake? How would you respond to Descartes' question of "How can you be sure if you're dreaming or awake?" If we can't be sure, does this mean that we can never really know anything? *(Jacob Lawrence,* African American Bride Sleeping in Chair, Dreams No. 2, 1965. *Tempera on fiberboard, 35 3/4 × 24 in. Smithsonian American Art Museum, Washington, DC/Art Resource, NY/ © 2011 The Jacob and Gwendolyn Lawrence Foundation, Seattle/Artists Rights Society (ARS), New York.)*

What we experience through our senses is often incomplete, subjective, and inaccurate. Consider the many times during the day in which you think one thing is happening and it turns out to be something completely different. Or think about those many occasions in which you witnessed an event with others—an accident, a party, a walk downtown—and each person ended up with very different, and perhaps conflicting, perceptions of the experience. Or reflect on optical illusions (such as the "bent" straw in a glass) or the tricks performed by a magician. In all of these cases our sense experience reveals itself to be consistently unreliable and therefore completely unsuitable for Descartes' "firm and permanent" foundation for knowledge.

But Descartes then takes his radical doubt to the next level, with a provocative suggestion: Suppose what we consider to be our entire waking life is instead an illusion? What then? To support the plausibility of this possibility, Descartes first asks us to consider the plight of the mentally ill. Often they are convinced that their deranged perceptions of reality ("they have an earthenware head or are nothing but pumpkins or made of glass") are in fact true: How can we be sure that the same is not true for us? A disturbing notion, certainly. But Descartes recognizes that we need not go to this extreme to doubt the validity of our experience because we have another and very common altered state of consciousness that makes the same point just as well: dreaming. Think of the times your dream was so vivid and "real" that you woke up sweating and with a pounding heart. When you were fully absorbed in that dream, you were convinced that it was absolutely real—until you woke up. But, Descartes says, how can we be sure that when we believe we are awake we are not actually dreaming? How can we tell the difference? He contends that we can't:

René Descartes,
from *Meditations on First Philosophy*

. . . in dwelling carefully on this reflection I see so manifestly that there are no certain indications by which we may clearly distinguish wakefulness from sleep that I am lost in astonishment. And my astonishment is such that it is almost capable of persuading me that I now dream.

This is precisely the premise of the popular and influential film *The Matrix:* people believe that they are living real and authentic lives, when in fact they are suspended in tanks and having their brains stimulated to create a virtually real world. The Taoist philosopher and mystic Chuang-Tzu (fl. fourth century B.C.E.) makes this same point in the following passage:

> Once upon a time, I, Chuang-Tzu, dreamt I was a butterfly, fluttering hither and thither, to all intents and purposes a butterfly. I was conscious only of following my fancies as a butterfly, and was unconscious of my individuality as a man. Suddenly, I waked, and there I lay, myself again. Now I do not know whether I was then a man dreaming I was a butterfly, or whether I am now a butterfly dreaming I am a man.

But Descartes is not through with his doubting program: In fact, he is just getting ready to ratchet his radical doubt up to a level never before considered in philosophical writing until the moment that he conceived of it. He begins with a preliminary distinction between the relative certainty of the disciplines of arithmetic and geometry (which are independent of sense experience) in comparison with the natural sciences such as physics, astronomy, and medicine (which are dependent on sense experience). But Descartes soon erases the relevance of this distinction with his boldest move yet: the possibility that we are being systematically deceived by supernatural beings.

René Descartes,
from *Meditations on First Philosophy*

8. That is possibly why our reasoning is not unjust when we conclude from this that Physics, Astronomy, Medicine and all other sciences which have as their end the consideration of composite things, are very dubious and uncertain; but that Arithmetic, Geometry and other sciences of that kind which only treat of things that are very simple and very general, without taking great trouble to ascertain whether they are actually existent or not, contain some measure of certainty and an element of the indubitable. For whether I am awake or asleep, two and three together always form five, and the square can never have more than four

sides, and it does not seem possible that truths so clear and apparent can be suspected of any falsity [or uncertainty].

9. Nevertheless I have long had fixed in my mind the belief that an all-powerful God existed by whom I have been created such as I am. But how do I know that He has not brought it to pass that there is no earth, no heaven, no extended body, no magnitude, no place, and that nevertheless [I possess the perceptions of all these things and that] they seem to me to exist just exactly as I now see them? And, besides, as I sometimes imagine that others deceive themselves in the things which they think they know best, how do I know that I am not deceived every time that I add two and three, or count the sides of a square, or judge of things yet simpler, if anything simpler can be imagined? But possibly God has not desired that I should be thus deceived, for He is said to be supremely good. If, however, it is contrary to His goodness to have made me such that I constantly deceive myself, it would also appear to be contrary to His goodness to permit me to be sometimes deceived, and nevertheless I cannot doubt that He does permit this.

10. There may indeed be those who would prefer to deny the existence of a God so powerful, rather than believe that all other things are uncertain. But let us not oppose them for the present, and grant that all that is here said of a God is a fable; nevertheless in whatever way they suppose that I have arrived at the state of being that I have reached—whether they attribute it to fate or to accident, or make out that it is by a continual succession of antecedents, or by some other method—since to err and deceive oneself is a defect, it is clear that the greater will be the probability of my being so imperfect as to deceive myself ever, as is the Author to whom they assign my origin the less powerful. To these reasons I have certainly nothing to reply, but at the end I feel constrained to confess that there is nothing in all that I formerly believed to be true, of which I cannot in some measure doubt, and that not merely through want of thought or through levity, but for reasons which are very powerful and maturely considered; so that henceforth I ought not the less carefully to refrain from giving credence to these opinions than to that which is manifestly false, if I desire to arrive at any certainty [in the sciences].

11. But it is not sufficient to have made these remarks, we must also be careful to keep them in mind. For these ancient and commonly held opinions still revert frequently to my mind, long and familiar custom having given them the right to occupy my mind against my inclination and rendered them almost masters of my belief; nor will I ever lose the habit of deferring to them or of placing my confidence in them, so long as I consider them as they really are, i.e. opinions in some measure doubtful, as I have just shown, and at the same time highly probable, so that there is much more reason to believe in than to deny them. That is why I consider that I shall not be acting amiss, if, taking of set purpose a contrary belief, I allow myself to be deceived, and for a certain time pretend that all these opinions are entirely false and imaginary, until at last, having thus balanced my former prejudices with my

What would you choose: a harsh reality or a pleasant illusion? Descartes' "evil genius" bears an uncanny resemblance to the evil forces in *The Matrix*. In that film, the central character, Neo, is faced with a provocative choice: Does he want to continue existing in a "virtual" world, which is pleasant but unreal, a manipulated reality created by evil forces? Or does he wish to experience the real world, which is unpleasant and dangerous? If you were presented with these alternatives, which would you choose? Why?

latter [so that they cannot divert my opinions more to one side than to the other], my judgment will no longer be dominated by bad usage or turned away from the right knowledge of the truth. For I am assured that there can be neither peril nor error in this course, and that I cannot at present yield too much to distrust, since I am not considering the question of action, but only of knowledge.

12. I shall then suppose, not that God who is supremely good and the fountain of truth, but some evil genius not less powerful than deceitful, has employed his whole energies in deceiving me; I shall consider that the heavens, the earth, colors, figures, sound, and all other external things are naught but the illusions and dreams of which this genius has availed himself in order to lay traps for my credulity; I shall consider myself as having no hands, no eyes, no flesh, no blood, nor any senses, yet falsely believing myself to possess all these things; I shall remain obstinately attached to this idea, and if by this means it is not in my power to arrive at the knowledge of any truth, I may at least do what is in my power [i.e. suspend my judgment], and with firm purpose avoid giving credence to any false thing, or being imposed upon by this arch deceiver, however powerful and deceptive he may be. But this task is a laborious one, and insensibly a certain lassitude leads me into the course of my ordinary life. And just as a captive who in sleep enjoys an imaginary liberty, when he begins to suspect that his liberty is but a dream, fears to awaken, and conspires with these agreeable illusions that the deception may be prolonged, so insensibly of my own accord I fall back into my former opinions, and I dread awakening from this slumber, lest the laborious wakefulness which would follow the tranquility of this repose should have to be spent not in daylight, but in the excessive darkness of the difficulties which have just been discussed.

Thus enters Descartes' "evil genius," perhaps the most influential fictional creation in the history of philosophy. Although Descartes first proposes God as this arch deceiver, he concludes that such thoroughgoing duplicity would be inconsistent with God's essentially good nature. So the evil genius is born, a powerful device for extending radical doubt to all aspects of experience that we typically accept as incontrovertibly real:

René Descartes,
from *Meditations on First Philosophy*

I shall consider that the heavens, the earth, colors, figures, sound, and all other external things are naught but the illusions and dreams of which this genius has availed himself in order to lay traps for my credulity; I shall consider myself as having no hands, no eyes, no flesh, no blood, nor any senses, yet falsely believing myself to possess all these things . . .

The purpose of this extreme enterprise, Descartes reminds us, is to explicitly recognize and remind himself of the uncertainty of all beliefs based solely on sense experience and in so doing to "avoid giving credence to any false thing." Naturally, Descartes hopes to achieve "knowledge of truth," but, if that is not possible, he at least does not want to continue believing in the truth of things that in fact are corrupted by uncertainty, echoing Socrates' statement, "As for me, all I know is that I know nothing," and Confucius's observation, "He who knows he is a fool is not a great fool."

The closing passage, with its vivid image of an enslaved individual dreaming of freedom, is particularly compelling, as Descartes acknowledges the emotional difficulty of pressing on in his search for certainty. By placing his entire universe in doubt, he recognizes that he is risking the peace of mind that comes from assuming the stability and veracity of one's world. And although his intellect has urged him to destroy the illusion of security through unblinking questioning of all he believes in, on an emotional level he is reluctant to continue the quest, fearful of what he might find. And so, exhausted by his intellectual labors, he falls back into his previous state of consciousness, until he can marshal his courage and energy for another arduous and personally wrenching search for true knowledge. These are surely emotions with which all of us can identify: desirous of finding the truth, yet fearful of what we might discover. And that is precisely why committing ourselves to thinking philosophically in order to achieve an authentic understanding of reality requires uncommon courage.

Meditation II *Of the Nature of the Human Mind; and that it is more easily known than the Body*

1. The Meditation of yesterday filled my mind with so many doubts that it is no longer in my power to forget them. And yet I do not see in what manner I can resolve them; and, just as if I had all of a sudden fallen into very deep water, I am so disconcerted that I can neither make certain of setting my feet on the bottom, nor can I swim and so support myself on the surface. I shall nevertheless make an effort and follow anew the same path as that on which I yesterday entered, i.e. I shall proceed by setting aside all that in which the least doubt could be supposed to exist, just as if I had discovered that it was absolutely false; and I shall ever follow in this road until I have met with something which is certain, or at least, if I can do nothing else, until I have learned for certain that there is nothing in the world that is certain. Archimedes, in order that he might draw the terrestrial globe out of its place, and transport it elsewhere, demanded only that one point should be fixed and immovable; in the same way I shall have the right to conceive high hopes if I am happy enough to discover one thing only which is certain and indubitable.

Refreshed following his debilitating exertions recorded in Meditation I, Descartes is now ready to continue his reflective explorations with renewed energy. Yet a deep sense of unease accompanies his efforts, the result of turning his world upside down through his radical doubt. His metaphor of falling into deep water where one can neither swim nor touch the bottom is particularly apt, as he searches for a single certainty on which he can begin to rebuild the world he has deconstructed.

2. I suppose, then, that all the things that I see are false; I persuade myself that nothing has ever existed of all that my fallacious memory represents to me. I consider that I possess no senses; I imagine that body, figure, extension, movement and place are but the fictions of my mind. What, then, can be esteemed as true? Perhaps nothing at all, unless that there is nothing in the world that is certain.

3. But how can I know there is not something different from those things that I have just considered, of which one cannot have the slightest doubt? Is there not some God, or some other being by whatever name we call it, who puts these reflections into my mind? That is not necessary, for is it not possible that I am capable of producing them myself? I myself, am I not at least something? But I have already denied that I had senses and body. Yet I hesitate, for what follows from that? Am I so dependent on body and senses that I cannot exist without these? But I was persuaded that there was nothing in all the world, that there was no heaven, no earth, that there were no minds, nor any bodies: was I not then likewise persuaded that I did not exist? Not at all; of a surety I myself did exist since I persuaded myself of something [or merely because I thought of something]. But there is some deceiver or other, very powerful and very cunning,

René Descartes, from *Meditations on First Philosophy*

> **I shall have the right to conceive high hopes if I am happy enough to discover one thing only which is certain and indubitable.**

René Descartes, from *Meditations on First Philosophy*

who ever employs his ingenuity in deceiving me. Then without doubt I exist also if he deceives me, and let him deceive me as much as he will, he can never cause me to be nothing so long as I think that I am something. So that after having reflected well and carefully examined all things, we must come to the definite conclusion that this proposition: I am, I exist, is necessarily true each time that I pronounce it, or that I mentally conceive it.

Finally, a point of reference that Descartes believes exists beyond doubt: "I am, I exist, is necessarily true each time that I pronounce it, or that I mentally conceive it." Though everything in the world may be called into question, including the existence of his body and the external world, nevertheless the simple affirmation "I exist" *must* be true each time it is uttered or conceived as a primal statement of personal existence. Yet what precisely does it mean to affirm, "I exist"?

René Descartes, from *Meditations on First Philosophy*

4. But I do not yet know clearly enough what I am, I who am certain that I am; and hence I must be careful to see that I do not imprudently take some other object in place of myself, and thus that I do not go astray in respect of this knowledge that I hold to be the most certain and most evident of all that I have formerly learned. That is why I shall now consider anew what I believed myself to be before I embarked upon these last reflections; and of my former opinions I shall withdraw all that might even in a small degree be invalidated by the reasons which I have just brought forward, in order that there may be nothing at all left beyond what is absolutely certain and indubitable.

5. What then did I formerly believe myself to be? Undoubtedly I believed myself to be a man. But what is a man? Shall I say a reasonable animal? Certainly not; for then I should have to inquire what an animal is, and what is reasonable; and thus from a single question I should insensibly fall into an infinitude of others more difficult; and I should not wish to waste the little time and leisure remaining to me in trying to unravel subtleties like these. But I shall rather stop here to consider the thoughts which of themselves spring up in my mind, and which were not inspired by anything beyond my own nature alone when I applied myself to the consideration of my being. In the first place, then, I considered myself as having a face, hands, arms, and all that system of members composed on bones and flesh as seen in a corpse which I designated by the name of body. In addition to this I considered that I was nourished, that I walked, that I felt, and that I thought, and I referred all these actions to the soul: but I did not stop to consider what the soul was, or if I did stop, I imagined that it was something extremely rare and subtle like a wind, a flame, or an ether, which was spread throughout my grosser parts. As to body I had no manner of doubt about its nature, but thought I had a very clear knowledge of it; and if I had desired to explain it according to the notions that I had then formed of it, I should have described it thus: By the body I understand all that which can be defined by a certain figure: something which can be confined in a certain place, and which can fill a given space in such a way that every other body will be excluded from it; which can be perceived either by touch, or by sight, or by hearing, or by taste, or by smell: which can be moved in many ways not, in truth, by itself, but by something which is foreign to it, by which it is touched [and from which it receives impressions]: for to have the power of self-movement, as also of feeling or of thinking, I did not consider to appertain to the nature of body: on the contrary, I was rather astonished to find that faculties similar to them existed in some bodies.

6. But what am I, now that I suppose that there is a certain genius which is extremely powerful, and, if I may say so, malicious, who employs all his powers in deceiving me? Can I affirm that I possess the least of all those things which I have just

said pertain to the nature of body? I pause to consider, I revolve all these things in my mind, and I find none of which I can say that it pertains to me. It would be tedious to stop to enumerate them. Let us pass to the attributes of soul and see if there is any one which is in me? What of nutrition or walking [the first mentioned]? But if it is so that I have no body it is also true that I can neither walk nor take nourishment. Another attribute is sensation. But one cannot feel without body, and besides I have thought I perceived many things during sleep that I recognized in my waking moments as not having been experienced at all. What of thinking? I find here that thought is an attribute that belongs to me; it alone cannot be separated from me. I am, I exist, that is certain. But how often? Just when I think; for it might possibly be the case if I ceased entirely to think, that I should likewise cease altogether to exist. I do not now admit anything which is not necessarily true: to speak accurately I am not more than a thing which thinks, that is to say a mind or a soul, or an understanding, or a reason, which are terms whose significance was formerly unknown to me. I am, however, a real thing and really exist; but what thing? I have answered: a thing which thinks. . . . What is a thing which thinks? It is a thing which doubts, understands, [conceives], affirms, denies, wills, refuses, which also imagines and feels.

So here it is, the birth of the infamous Cartesian ego that is destined to bedevil philosophers and Western thinking as a whole from its gestation up until the present. Initially, it seems to be an innocent enough creation, and it does provide an apparent escape from the skepticism threatened by the "evil genius." For though the "evil genius" may force us to doubt the existence of our physical bodies, it cannot, by definition, cause us to doubt the existence of our thinking self, the "I think" that "doubts, understands, conceives, affirms, denies, wills, refuses which also imagines and feels." Of course, as we saw in Chapter 3, this concept of a pure, thinking self starts us down a slippery slope that leads inevitably to a full-blown dualism of mind and body, with all of its conceptual vexations.

But for the present, we're more concerned with whether Descartes has in fact discovered his philosopher's touchstone, that foundation of absolute certainty on which he can reconstruct his core beliefs about the world that were swept away by his radical doubt. He begins by addressing the existence of external objects, using a famous example to illustrate his reasoning.

11. Let us begin by considering the commonest matters, those which we believe to be the most distinctly comprehended, to wit, the bodies which we touch and see; not indeed bodies in general, for these general ideas are usually a little more confused, but let us consider one body in particular. Let us take, for example, this piece of wax: it has been taken quite freshly from the hive, and it has not yet lost the sweetness of the honey which it contains; it still retains somewhat of the odour of the flowers from which it has been culled; its colour, its figure, its size are apparent; it is hard, cold, easily handled, and if you strike it with the finger, it will emit a sound. Finally all the things which are requisite to cause us distinctly to recognise a body, are met with in it. But notice that while I speak and approach the fire what remained of the taste is exhaled, the smell evaporates, the colour alters, the figure is destroyed, the size increases, it becomes liquid, it heats, scarcely can one handle it, and when one strikes it, no sound is emitted. Does the same wax remain after this change? We must confess that it remains; none would judge otherwise. What then did I know so distinctly in this piece of wax? It could certainly be nothing of all that the senses brought to my notice,

René Descartes,
from *Meditations on First Philosophy*

since all these things which fall under taste, smell, sight, touch, and hearing, are found to be changed, and yet the same wax remains.

12. Perhaps it was what I now think, viz. That this wax was not that sweetness of honey, nor that agreeable scent of flowers, nor that particular whiteness, nor that figure, nor that sound, but simply a body which a little while before appeared to me as perceptible under these forms, and which is now perceptible under others. But what, precisely, is it that I imagine when I form such conceptions? Let us attentively consider this, and, abstracting from all that does not belong to the wax, let us see what remains. Certainly nothing remains excepting a certain extended thing which is flexible and movable. But what is the meaning of flexible and movable? Is it not that I imagine that this piece of wax being round is capable of becoming square and of passing from a square to a triangular figure? No, certainly it is not that, since I imagine it admits of an infinitude of similar changes, and I nevertheless do not know how to compass the infinitude by my imagination, and consequently this conception which I have of the wax is not brought about by the faculty of imagination. What now is this extension? Is it not also unknown? For it becomes greater when the wax is melted, greater when it is boiled, and greater still when the heat increases; and I should not conceive [clearly] according to truth what wax is, if I did not think that even this piece that we are considering is capable of receiving more variations in extension than I have ever imagined. We must then grant that I could not even understand through the imagination what this piece of wax is, and that it is my mind alone which perceives it. I say this piece of wax in particular, for as to wax in general it is yet clearer. But what is this piece of wax which cannot be understood excepting by the [understanding or] mind? It is certainly the same that I see, touch, imagine, and finally it is the same which I have always believed it to be from the beginning. But what must particularly be observed is that its perception is neither an act of vision, nor of touch, nor of imagination, and has never been such although it may have appeared formerly to be so, but only an intuition of the mind, which may be imperfect and confused as it was formerly, or clear and distinct as it is at present, according as my attention is more or less directed to the elements which are found in it, and of which it is composed.

Does the same candle exist after it is burned? Descartes notes how everything changes about a candle when it is burned, yet the same wax remains. How does this observation lead him to a theory about the mind and the external world?

Having established the existence of the thinking self, Descartes' next question is "What can the thinking self know that is beyond doubt?" The piece of wax serves his purposes well. From the standpoint of pure sense experience, the piece of wax poses a tangle of contradictions and confusions, as its physical properties change entirely as it is heated or cooled. However, our minds are nonetheless able to maintain a concept of the piece of wax, even as it goes through its various transformations, because its reactions to heat and cold are part of the concept of the wax itself. Therefore, Descartes is confident in saying that although pure sense experience is inadequate to understand the piece of wax, ". . . it is my mind alone which perceives it." How does the understanding mind perceive the piece of wax? Through an "intuition of the mind, which may be imperfect and confused as it was formerly, or clear and distinct as it is at present." And it is this "intuition of the mind" that forms the true foundation for all rationalist thinking and rationalist knowledge. In the case of the piece of wax—and the rest of the external world—our intuitions of the mind provide certain assurance that the external world exists, governed by the laws of mathematics and science. For Descartes, these intuitions of the mind are rationally based, not empirically based, for this is the only way that they could yield clear and certain knowledge.

Then, in Meditation III, Descartes reasons from his first premise—I exist as a thinking thing—to the conclusion that therefore God must exist because I could not exist without God. Descartes uses the "cosmological argument" for God, which argues that because the universe is orderly and apparently purposeful or teleological (from the Greek *telos*, meaning "purpose" or "end"), it is rational to assume that this order and purposefulness is the product of an intelligent Creator. He also uses the "ontological argument," which argues (essentially) that God must exist because we have a rational conception of a perfect Being, which necessarily entails God's existence.

Having established (in *his* mind, at least) the existence of God, Descartes next argues that we know by intuition that it is God's very nature to be perfectly good, which means that God would not deceive us. As a result, the world of physical objects and scientific laws must exist precisely the way our intuitions inform us they exist.

Meditation VI *Of the Existence of Material Things, and of the real distinction between the Soul and Body of Man*

René Descartes,
from *Meditations on First Philosophy*

Since He has given me a very strong inclination to believe that these ideas (of trees, houses, etc.) arise from corporeal objects, I do not see how he could be vindicated from the charge of deceit, if in truth they proceeded from any other source, or were produced by other causes than corporeal things? (For example, by the evil demon, or in dreams.)

Therefore,

We *cannot be deceived* (whether by the evil demon or whatever else).

. . . I cannot doubt but that there is in me a certain passive faculty of perception, that is, of receiving and recognizing the ideas of sensible things, but this would be useless to me if there were not either in me or in some other thing another active faculty capable of forming and producing these ideas. But this active faculty cannot exist in me [inasmuch as I am a thing that thinks] seeing that it does not presuppose thought, and also that those ideas are often produced in me without my contributing in any way to the same, and often even against my will; it is thus necessarily the case that the faculty resides in some substance different from me in which all the reality which is objectively in the ideas that are produced by this faculty is formally or eminently contained, as I remarked before. And this substance is either a body, that is, a corporeal nature in which there is contained formally [and really] all that which is objectively [and by representation] in those ideas, or it is God Himself, or some other creature more noble than body in which that same is contained eminently. But, since God is no deceiver, it is very manifest that He does not communicate to me these ideas immediately and by Himself, nor yet by the intervention of some creature in which their reality is not formally, but only eminently, contained. For since He has given me no faculty to recognise that this is the case, but, on the other hand, a very great inclination to believe [that they are sent to me or] that they are conveyed to me by corporeal objects, I do not see how He could be defended from the accusation of deceit if these ideas were produced by causes other than corporeal objects. Hence we must allow that corporeal things exist. However, they are perhaps not exactly what we perceive by the senses, since this comprehension by the senses is in many instances very obscure and confused; but we must at least admit that all things which I conceive in them clearly and distinctly, that is to say, all things which, speaking generally, are comprehended in the object of pure mathematics, are truly to be recognized as external objects.

Many philosophers have found these later arguments of Descartes to be less than convincing, for a variety of reasons. But as a rationalist, Descartes' key point is that we can achieve genuine knowledge through our rational intuition into the nature of beliefs. We can identify those beliefs that are true because they meet the standard of being "clear and distinct"; they are self-evident to our rational intuition, independent of experience. In fact, it is only through the faculty of reason that we can achieve true knowledge: Our sense experience on its own can never lead to authentic knowledge independent of our reasoning abilities. As we shall see, this view is the complete opposite of the epistemological views of the British empiricists, for whom knowledge is derived mainly from sense experience.

< READING CRITICALLY >

Analyzing Descartes' Radical Doubt

- Have you ever had the experience of wondering whether much of what you had been brought up to believe as true was in fact unreliable? If so, identify some of the main beliefs or values that you called into question. Was there a particular event that stimulated this process of doubt and examination? What was the outcome of your reflective questioning?

- Try to replicate Descartes' reflective process. Describe your current situation as you are reading this text, just as he does. Then try to trace his pattern of thinking: Can you imagine that what you think is real is actually a dream? How can you be sure? Haven't you had dreams that were at least as realistic as the current situation in which you now find yourself? Is there any clear criteria you can use to differentiate between when you are dreaming and when you are awake?

- Try to replicate Descartes' foundational starting point, "I think, therefore I am." Does your ability to think convince you, for once and for all, that you exist? What does it mean to you to say, "I exist"? Exactly how would you describe the "I" that exists?

5.5 Making Connections: Your Beliefs About the World

Plato, Aristotle, and Descartes constructed a framework for thinking about ourselves and the world that profoundly influenced the evolution of thought in Western culture. It is difficult to fully appreciate the extent to which our modern consciousness and the various disciplines devoted to constructing knowledge reflect the concepts and methodologies first introduced by these towering figures. Before we continue our exploration of other philosophers who have made significant contributions to metaphysics and epistemology, we are going to first take some time to reflect on the role that these areas play in our everyday lives, with particular attention to epistemology.

Though you may not fully realize it, you do have a theory of knowledge, your own epistemology. What does this mean? Simply that you—and everyone else—develop beliefs and construct knowledge based on certain principles. Of course, this doesn't mean that people necessarily construct the most enlightened beliefs possible—in fact, many times they don't! But that's the purpose of developing the abilities that will enable you to become a sophisticated critical thinker, as we explored in Chapter 1. It is these critical thinking abilities that will enable you to develop the most *informed* beliefs and construct the most *enlightened* knowledge of which you are capable. And because you have the advantage of taking an "Introduction to Philosophy" course, you will be able to integrate these critical thinking abilities into a coherent theory of knowledge—your own epistemology. Before we go any further, let us see these ideas in action in everyday life and then place them within a larger philosophical context.

It seems to be a natural human impulse to try to understand the world we live in, and beliefs are the conceptual tools humans use to accomplish this. For example, consider the following statements and answer "Yes," "No," or "Not sure" to each:

- A college education will improve your life.
- Alien life forms have visited our planet.
- Every person has a unique purpose in life.
- Developing your mind is as important as taking care of your body.
- You should treat other people the way you would like to be treated.

Your responses to these statements reflect certain beliefs you have, and these beliefs help you explain why the world is the way it is and how you ought to behave. The total collection of your beliefs represents your view of the world, your philosophy of life.

What exactly are "beliefs"? Beliefs represent an interpretation, evaluation, conclusion, or prediction about the world that we endorse as true. For example, the statement

- "I believe that, in the play *No Exit*, Jean-Paul Sartre is dramatizing the way other people can force us to acknowledge our personal 'bad faith' and thus create a personal hell on Earth"—represents an *interpretation* of that play.
- "I believe that a theory of human choice that allows for freedom of choice makes more sense than a theory that doesn't"—expresses an *evaluation* of rival philosophical theories.
- "I believe that one of the main reasons terrorism has become such a terrible threat is that primitive ways of thinking now have access to the most modern technology of destruction"—expresses a *conclusion* about the problem of world terrorism.
- "If drastic environmental measures are not undertaken to slow the global warming trend, then I believe that the polar ice caps will melt and Earth will be flooded"—represents a *prediction* about events that will occur in the future.

In addition to expressing an interpretation, evaluation, conclusion, or prediction about the world, beliefs also express an endorsement of the truth or accuracy of the beliefs by the speaker or author, based presumably on convincing reasons or evidence. The beliefs you develop in living your life help you explain why the world is the way it is, and they guide you in making decisions. But all beliefs are not equal. Some beliefs are certain ("Only women can give birth to babies") because they are supported by compelling reasons. Other beliefs are less certain ("I believe that aliens have visited Earth") because the support is not as solid. As you form and revise your beliefs, based on your experiences and your reflection on these experiences, it is important to make them as accurate as possible. The more accurate they are, the better you are able to understand what is taking place and to predict what will occur in the future.

The beliefs you form vary tremendously in accuracy. The idea of *knowing* is one of the ways humans have developed to distinguish beliefs supported by strong reasons or evidence from beliefs for which there is less support. Other beliefs are disproved by evidence to the contrary (such as the belief that men can give birth to babies). This distinction between "believing" and "knowing" can be illustrated by replacing

What degree of certainty? How would you go about justifying your belief that Earth is round? What degree of certainty would you give it?

the word *believe* with the word *know* in statements. For example, consider the following statements:

- "I *know* that, in the play *No Exit*, Jean-Paul Sartre is dramatizing the way other people can force us to acknowledge our personal 'bad faith' and thus create a personal hell on Earth."
- "I *know* that a theory of human choice that allows for freedom of choice makes more sense than a theory that doesn't."
- "I *know* that one of the main reasons terrorism has become such a terrible threat is that primitive ways of thinking now have access to the most modern technology of destruction."
- "If drastic environmental measures are not undertaken to slow the global warming trend, then I *know* that the polar ice caps will melt and Earth will be flooded."

When someone indicates that he or she thinks a belief is completely accurate by saying, "I *know*," your response is often, "*How do you know?*" If the person cannot give you a satisfactory answer to this question, you are likely to think to yourself that, "If this person can't explain how he knows it, then he doesn't *really* know it—he's just saying it." In other words, when you say that "you know" something, you mean at least two different things.

1. I think this belief is completely accurate.
2. I can explain to you the reasons or evidence that support this belief.

If either of these standards is not met, we would usually say that the person does not really "know." Or to state it another way, "You can *believe* what is not so, but you cannot *know* what is not so."

We work at evaluating the accuracy of our beliefs by examining the reasons or evidence that support them (known as the *justification* for the beliefs). Your beliefs can be thought of as forming a continuum based on their accuracy and justification. As you learn more about the world and yourself, you try to form beliefs that are increasingly accurate and justified. Looked at in this way, your beliefs form a range, as pictured:

Beliefs that you know are	**Beliefs that you are not sure are**	**Beliefs that you know are**
inaccurate	accurate	accurate
unjustified	justified	justified

Just as temperature is a scale that ranges from cold to hot with many degrees in between, so your beliefs can be thought of as forming a continuum based on their accuracy and justification. As you learn more about the world and yourself, you try to form beliefs that are increasingly more accurate and justified.

Of course, determining the accuracy and justification of your beliefs is a challenging business. How do we assess justification? We generally use a variety of criteria:

- To what extent is the belief supported by sound reasons and compelling evidence derived from reliable sources?
- How effectively does the belief explain what is taking place?

- To what extent is the belief consistent with other beliefs you have about the world?
- How effectively does your belief help you predict what will happen in the future?
- Is the belief falsifiable?

Let's apply these criteria to a sample belief to evaluate the degree of certainty we may ascribe to it:

I believe that someday I will die because death is the natural end of living.

- *To what extent is the belief supported by sound reasons and compelling evidence derived from reliable sources?* There is ample evidence that death is a natural and inevitable part of the life process. All living things eventually die, and this has been true for all people in all of history. Certainly there are those who hope that science will find ways to perpetuate eternal life, but at this point there is no compelling reason to believe that this is feasible.

- *How effectively does the belief explain what is taking place?* This belief does a very effective job of explaining why, every day, many people die, never to live again.

- *To what extent is the belief consistent with other beliefs you have about the world?* This belief is consistent with the complex web of beliefs that make up biological science, a discipline that details why (among other things) all living organisms eventually die.

- *How effectively does your belief help you predict what will happen in the future?* This is a belief that historically has had 100 percent predictive success. Every person who has lived before us has, at some point, died.

- *Is the belief falsifiable?* This criterion means that we can state conditions—tests—under which the beliefs could be disproved and the beliefs nevertheless *pass* those tests. Why is this important? Because it rules out beliefs that can never be proved or disproved. For example, if you believe that your destiny is related to the positions of the planets and stars (as astrologers do), it is not clear how we could conduct an experiment to determine if the belief is accurate. Because a belief that is not *falsifiable* can never be proved, such a belief is of questionable accuracy. Our sample belief is clearly falsifiable. Unfortunately, if our belief proves true, we won't be there to congratulate ourselves on the accuracy of our belief: We will have to let others perform that function.

Based on these criteria our sample belief that "I believe that someday I will die because this is the natural end of living" seems to be supported with such strong justification that we would likely be comfortable saying, "I *know* that someday I will die. . . ." To view a contrasting situation, use these same criteria to evaluate the following belief:

I believe that though our bodies may die, our spirits or souls continue to exist in some form.

What differences did you find from the first evaluation? Compare your responses to those of others in the class: Did you arrive at different conclusions regarding the relative certainty of the belief? Why or why not?

These criteria, and the two examples we used to illustrate them, constitute some of the epistemological standards we use in everyday life to evaluate our beliefs. We generally term "knowledge" those beliefs that we conclude best meet the criteria. And it is these "I know . . ." beliefs that we consider to be "true." A critical thinking perspective sees knowledge and truth as goals that we are striving to achieve, processes that we are all actively involved in as we construct our understanding of the world. Developing accurate knowledge about the world is often a challenging process of exploration and analysis in which our understanding grows and evolves over a period of time. As you continue your study of philosophy, including exploring the ideas of great philosophers as well as your own thoughtful reflections, you will discover that your ability to critically evaluate beliefs and construct well-founded knowledge is progressively enhanced. We began that process in this chapter and will continue it in the next when we examine the metaphysics and epistemologies of other noteworthy philosophers.

thinking philosophically

EVALUATING THE ACCURACY OF YOUR BELIEFS

State whether you think that each of the following beliefs is

- *completely accurate* (so that you would say, "I know this is the case"),
- *generally accurate* but not completely accurate (so that you would say, "This is often, but not always, the case"),
- *generally not accurate* but sometimes accurate (so that you would say, "This is usually not the case but is sometimes true"), and
- *definitely not accurate* (so that you would say, "I know that this is not the case").

After determining the degree of accuracy in this way, explain why you have selected your answer.

Beliefs to be evaluated

- I believe with Socrates that "the unexamined life is not worth living."
- I believe that the *self* is that unifying force that synthesizes our experiences into a personal identity.
- I believe in the existence of a supernatural Creator that I call "God."
- I believe that your astrological sign determines your basic personality traits.
- I believe that people are completely free and so completely responsible for their choices.
- Your example of a belief:

Example: I believe that if you treat other people with respect and consideration, that they will reciprocate and treat you the same way.

Degree of accuracy: Generally, but not completely, accurate.

Explanation: Although treating other people with respect and consideration may inspire many people to reciprocate with the same treatment, this is not likely to be true in all cases.

writing about philosophy: Analyzing Philosophical Themes in a Fictional Work

The Assignment

The core issues that metaphysics and epistemology are concerned with—Reality and Truth—are at the heart of life. In many ways our existence is framed and motivated by our ongoing efforts to answer the questions "What is real?" and "What is true?" Because these questions are of such central significance, they are explored not just in philosophy but in other aspects of culture as well, including films, plays, and books. This project will give you an opportunity to bring a philosophical lens to some aspect of culture that addresses the themes of reality and truth. Select a film, play, or novel that you believe focuses on metaphysical and epistemological themes and write an essay that analyzes the work philosophically. (See the list of stories and films on pages 278–279 for some ideas.) Be sure to make reference to specific philosophers to structure your analysis. The following essay by Sonja Tanner, entitled "Philosophy and the 'Desert of the Real,'" focuses on the film *The Matrix* and engages in just this sort of philosophical exploration, analyzing the film's themes in terms of the ideas of Plato, Descartes, Berkeley, and Kant. These last two philosophers are covered in the next chapter.

Student Essay

PHILOSOPHY AND THE "DESERT OF THE REAL"
by Sonja Tanner

Nearly two and a half millennia ago, Plato offered an image of the human condition in which our lives are likened to those of prisoners in a cave, bound by chains to remain where we are and to perceive the stimuli presented to us by hidden forces. One prisoner is described as somehow—mysteriously—being freed from bondage and undertaking the arduous journey out of the cave and toward the dazzling light of the sun. On doing so, this person is able to recognize his former state as one of illusion, as one does when waking up to recognize that what we thought to have transpired was only a dream. Waking up to face reality can be difficult, disorienting, and even, in the freed prisoner's case, a dangerous task.

Fast forward into contemporary times and into *The Matrix* where the choice between remaining a prisoner of sensory deception or becoming enlightened as to "true reality" is offered to Neo. Morpheus tells Neo that taking the blue pill will let him return to the matrix—a computer-generated simulation of reality—in which Neo had seemingly been leading a comfortable existence. Taking the red pill would enable Neo to expose the forces behind the illusions and so to encounter reality. This choice encapsulates several philosophical questions concerning reality and knowledge to which we will now turn. What kind of a choice is this? Can we be sure that taking the red pill would lead to reality, or might this be another simulation thereof? Is there an ethical dimension to this choice—that is, *should* you opt for one over the other? Which pill would you take?

Neo is offered two options, and to many people this means that whichever he chooses he has chosen freely; after all, he could have just as easily chosen the other. But is his choice really a reflection of free will? If we understand free will to refer to the capacity of someone to affect the future through his or her actions and choices, we can ask whether Neo's choice of the red pill amounts to his controlling the future. Is freedom a matter of having a choice? And is any choice necessarily a free one? Neo has already shown himself to be curious and trusting by following the white rabbit. Does his personality—something that it is extraordinarily difficult for any of us to change—not already influence him in the direction of the red pill?

A further wrinkle is added by two things we learn later. First, Neo has apparently chosen the red pill many, many times before. Second, Neo's actions and choices have been predicted by the Oracle (who, we learn in the second film, is herself part of the program). The more predictable someone's actions and choices are, the more it seems that those choices and actions are chosen for reasons beyond the agent's control. Above the kitchen door Neo enters to find the Oracle baking cookies is written the same imperative as is written above the door at the Delphic shrine which Oedipus visits: Know yourself. Does either Neo or Oedipus know who they are? Would such self-knowledge involve recognition of what may be their own arrogance at thinking themselves above the reaches of fate and determinism? Might being aware of how we are influenced or even determined by such forces lead to having control over them? Neo's encounter with the Oracle raises this question. For Sophocles' Oedipus Rex, about whom an oracle prophesizes that he will murder his father and sleep with his mother, it does not seem to matter what course of action is taken: The fated future is accomplished regardless of what choices are made. Indeed, it is precisely through their disbelief in fate and the belief that each can freely forge his own destiny that the futures of Oedipus and Neo are realized. It is only when the Oracle tells Neo not to worry about breaking the vase that he actually turns around and "accidentally" breaks it.

Regardless of whether the choice is a free one, we are compelled to ask whether the option is valid. How do we know that the red pill will really lead to reality and not simply to more deception? Whichever of the two Neo chooses, he must do so from a position of trusting that the choice he is being offered is a valid one. On a very base level, taking any kind of drug should raise questions as to what effect it will have on one's mental and physical condition. Can you believe in whatever is to follow the swallowing of the pill, or is this clouded by the fact that you need a capsule of some unknown chemical in order to have this "experience"? Another way of looking at this choice is whether the choice is a rupture in the matrix or yet another of its illusions.

For the sake of the argument, let's assume that the choice is a valid one. The question then becomes what is it a choice of. After taking the red pill, Neo is shown the true human condition. Like the prisoners in the cave, people in the matrix are enslaved and deceived. Morpheus shows Neo what he calls "the desert of the real," a world in which human bodies are forced to function as batteries—energy sources for the race of machines that keep humans placated by administering electrical signals to their brains. These signals are interpreted by human brains as actual sensory experiences of the outside world when in fact there is no such experience occurring. In other words, in "the desert of the real," the experience of eating a steak, which Cypher fondly recalls, does not involve actual consumption of a slab of beef. It is, rather, a combination of electrical impulses that simulate the taste, texture, smell, and resulting fullness of such a meal.

The question is one that has been asked before. Descartes asks us whether it is possible that some sort of evil genius is deceiving us to think that the sensory experiences we seem to have are real ones. What if, in other words, we are just brains in a bucket, deceived somehow into thinking that our inner mental states correspond to the outer world? Isn't it entirely possible that I am not truly sitting at my computer typing right now, but only, for example, dreaming that I am? How do I know that I ever wake up—couldn't that too be part of the dream? Unlike empiricism, which claims that sensory evidence is the most primary and reliable source of knowledge, Descartes and *The Matrix* express a skepticism as to sensory reliability. But then, if I can't trust my senses, what can I rely on?

It all depends, as Morpheus says to Neo, on what we mean by the word *real*. Morpheus suggests that to the enslaved human bodies, "the real" is nothing other than the electrical impulses interpreted by their brains. For these beings, Berkeley seems to be right: Reality is made up of nothing other than the ideas or sensory qualities

■ ■ ■   **Student Essay** (continued)

I perceive. A posteriori knowledge, or knowledge that depends on the senses, would then be our only and most reliable source of knowledge. It does not matter if these qualities don't correspond to the world outside my brain. Assuming Neo's experiences here are to be trusted as more than such electrical impulses—in other words, that his perceptions correspond to a world outside himself and are thus "real" in the ordinary sense of the word—then by what criterion can this distinction between reality and illusion be made? Are Rationalists right in suggesting a priori knowledge (knowledge that does not depend on any prior sensory or perceptual experience) not only exists but also is our most reliable source of knowledge?

Drawing on both Rationalism and Empiricism, Kant effects what he terms a "Copernican revolution" in understanding reality. Like the shift from thinking of Earth as occupying a central, stationary, and privileged position in the universe, around which the sun rotates to recognizing that Earth revolves around the sun, Kant suggests that we examine our role as being active in perception. Rather than thinking about how our representations conform to objects in the outer world, we should think of how it is that objects conform to our representations. In other words, reality does not consist simply of objects that our minds passively perceive. Our minds play an active role in how and what we perceive—we *construct* reality—and so inquiry into reality should begin with the mental faculties that allow us to register objects as such. Objects are understood here as phenomenal, or necessarily related to our experience of them, just as our experience of the sun makes it appear to be "rising" or "setting" in a rotation around Earth, when in fact it is just the other way around. Noumena, or objects as they are independent of human perception, are beyond the realm of human experience and thus also of human comprehension. At least to a degree, we actively shape phenomenal reality, and, to understand how our experience alters reality, we must explore our own minds: Knowing the world, then, requires knowing ourselves. "True reality"—reality understood as independent of our experience of it, or what Neo hopes to experience by swallowing the red pill—is thus not an option for anyone to experience.

The film doesn't so much answer the kinds of questions explored here as it raises them. While it may seem unlikely that any of us are having a collaborative and interactive hallucination, the questions themselves are worthwhile if we are to know ourselves and the world around us. Having once chosen the red pill, Cypher changes his mind and opts for the pleasant but illusory life—including the hallucinated experience of eating a steak—afforded those comfortably deceived about what reality truly is. Is Cypher wrong to do so? Is choosing the red pill morally better than choosing the blue? To answer such questions, we, too, face the choice of red or blue pills. Can we trust this choice to be a valid (and even a free) one, or should we be skeptical about ever acquiring true knowledge? The choice seems to be one of living a pleasant but thoroughly manipulated life in "the desert of the real" or of making the steep and rugged ascent out of the cave and into the light of truth. If there is such a thing as freedom, opting for the red pill—the route of philosophy and the questioning of reality, knowledge and ethics—is the only choice that can lead to it.

MySearchLab Connections

Watch. Listen. Explore. Read. Mysearchlab is designed just for you. Each chapter features a customized study plan to help you learn and review key concepts and terms. Dynamic visual activities, videos, and readings found in the multimedia library will enhance your learning experience.

Here are a few questions and activities to help you understand this chapter:

1. **Read** the **Profile** of *Heraclitus* on **mysearchlab.com** Explain Heraclitus's belief that "all is change."

2. **Watch** the **Video** *Aristotle* on **mysearchlab.com** For Aristotle, what is substance?

3. **Watch** the **Video** *Plato and Metaphysics* on **mysearchlab.com** Describe the two worlds that comprise Plato's metaphysics and how humans experience/gain knowledge about each world.

4. **Listen** to the **Podcast** *A.C. Grayling* on *Descartes' Cogito* on **mysearchlab.com** According to Descartes, how does one get from an internal private consciousness to an external world?

What Is the Nature of Reality?

- The philosophical study of metaphysics examines issues beyond the physical world such as the meaning of life, the existence of free will, and the fundamental principles of the universe. Metaphysicians attempt to explain the nature of reality itself. Aristotle laid the foundations for this branch of philosophy in his *Metaphysics*.

- Philosophical inquiry into the nature of truth is called *epistemology*. The study of *epistemology* attempts to describe and explain the nature of knowledge and truth, and whether it is possible to achieve genuine knowledge or perceive an ultimate truth.

[pp. 196–199]

KEY TERMS

metaphysics

epistemology

Reality Is the Eternal Realm of the Forms: Plato

- Plato attempted to resolve the conflict between an unchanging, ultimate truth and the everyday flux of our circumstantial lives by proposing two different "worlds": the world of "becoming," of our physical world; and the world of "being," a realm of eternal and unchanging truths that is knowable through the exercise of reason.

- This world of "being" is populated by ideal "forms," archetypes or essences of everything that exists. In our everyday world of the senses, we experience only imperfect examples of, or "participants" in, these "forms," but through careful study, reflection, and reasoning, we can begin

to apprehend the true and eternal nature of the forms. Plato's "Allegory of the Cave" is a vivid metaphor for this quest to understand the ultimate essences or truths of things.

- Plato's belief that genuine knowledge of the essential forms can be achieved through "innate" or inborn ideas and the faculty of reason makes him a *rationalist*. In contrast, philosophers who believe that true knowledge is best achieved through sense experience are *empiricists*. This conflict between rationalists and empiricists has both divided and enriched the study of epistemology since the time of Plato and Aristotle.

[pp. 199–209]

KEY TERMS

form

rationalism

empiricism

for further reading, viewing & research

Read the Primary Source on MySearchLab

- *Meno,* Plato
- *The Republic,* Plato
- *Metaphysics,* Aristotle
- *Meditations on First Philosophy,* Descartes

Films

- ***Babel*** **(2006)** What role does the media play in shaping our perceptions? How do false perceptions affect others? The stories of several families in different parts of the world are brought together by a single disaster. A young woman traveling with her husband in Morocco is the victim of a shooting. The media immediately portrays the event as a "terrorist attack." Meanwhile, the couple's children are stranded when taken by their nanny to

Mexico. As the police try to determine the origin of the gun used in the shooting, the story of a Japanese widower becomes a part of the intricate story web.

- ***Groundhog Day*** **(1993)** How can the same sequence of events be perceived differently? In this comedy, an egocentric weatherman hired to cover Groundhog Day is trapped, repeating the same day over and over again. As he tries to escape the cycle, he reconsiders himself and his life values.

- ***The Matrix*** **(1999)** Is a pleasant life based on a lie better than a difficult life based on the truth? In this futuristic film, a computer hacker, Neo, discovers that his reality might be a false existence created by artificial intelligence machines. He then must choose whether to remain in this fantasy world or attempt to liberate himself and humankind from this artificial existence.

- ***The Truman Show*** **(1998)** Is there any way to tell the difference between reality and virtual reality? Truman Burbank is an apparently normal man with a normal life who does not realize that his entire existence is the artificial creation of a production studio. When Truman begins to suspect that his life is not what it appears to be, he attempts to defy his scripted fate and take his existence into his own hands.

Reality Is the Natural World: Aristotle

- Aristotle broke with his teacher Plato's conception of a divided reality. As a philosophical naturalist, Aristotle was devoted to the idea that the nature of reality is best apprehended through close and careful attention to, and study of, sense experience, making him an empiricist.
- Whereas Plato believed, for example, in a changing and ultimately mortal human body that was inhabited by an unchanging and immortal soul, Aristotle argued that that the soul cannot be separated from the body; that we as humans are entirely creatures of nature.
- In Aristotle's metaphysical system, there are two categories of "things": matter (the physicality of a thing) and form (the essence of a thing). All things contain within themselves their potential, or *entelechy*. Aristotle's metaphysical framework consists of the Four Causes: Material Cause; Formal Cause; Efficient Cause; and Final Cause.

[pp. 209–215]

Can Reality Be Known? Descartes

- René Descartes established a constructively skeptical approach toward the nature of knowledge, vowing to begin with a "clean slate," or position of radical doubt, and from there to objectively evaluate everything he knew or believed to be true.
- Descartes' radical doubt led him to conceive of the possibility of an "evil genius," an entity that manipulates us into believing that our waking dream is "reality." Descartes only found his way out of this nightmarish possibility through his famous pronouncement, *Cogito, ergo sum* ("I think, therefore I am"), which he believed provided him with a foundation of absolute certainty on which he could construct a system of true beliefs through the power of reason.

[pp. 215–227]

- ***Twelve Monkeys*** (1995) Are memories true? How do we know? Set in a postapocalyptic world, this science fiction film addresses the subjective nature of memory and the effects of this on one's ability to understand reality and explores the nature of time and madness.
- ***Vanilla Sky*** (2001) What is the value of our dream existence? A successful publisher and playboy, David Aames survives a car crash orchestrated by a jilted lover but is left severely disfigured. After undergoing reconstructive surgery and gaining the support of a beautiful woman, David seems to be living his dream life. However, recurring hallucinations and strange occurrences cause him to question the reality and value of this dream existence.

Literature

- ***Labyrinths,*** Jorge Luis Borges. In this collection of stories and essays, Borges creates fantastical, bizarre, and brilliant worlds in which he explores the nature of reality, time, and existence; and questions the possibility of acquiring true knowledge. Borges addresses many philosophical movements and ideas, including epistemology, metaphysics, phenomenology, and relativism.

- ***One Hundred Years of Solitude,*** Gabriel García Márquez. Often labeled a magical realist work, this novel recounts 100 years in the life of an invented South American town as seen through the lens of a family. Márquez explores the subjectivity of reality as the story is narrated from multiple perspectives and redefines the idea of what is real as the magical and mythical enter the "truth" of the world of the story.
- ***The Crying of Lot 49,*** Thomas Pynchon. Nothing is what it appears to be in this postmodern mystery. When Oedipa is given the job of administering the estate of a deceased former lover, she uncovers a far-reaching conspiracy. Oedipa's investigation becomes a metaphor for the human experience as her inquiries and attempts at uncovering the truth are repeatedly undermined, calling into question the existence of any stable reality or meaning as well as the possibility of true communication.
- ***Oedipus the King,*** Sophocles. In this classic Greek tragedy, Oedipus unwittingly fulfills a tragic prophecy. As the horrific truth is revealed, Oedipus attempts to avoid and then come to terms with the reality of his actions.
- ***To the Lighthouse,*** Virginia Woolf. The life of a family is seen through shifting perspectives as Woolf explores the subjective nature of reality, the complexities of perception, and the possibility of capturing life in art.

Metaphysics

What is **real**?

Epistemology

What is **true**?

what is real? what is true?

FURTHER EXPLORATIONS

John Locke

Reality is the world which causes our sensations.

Truth is gaining knowledge of the world through mental ideas produced by empirical sensations.

George Berkeley

Reality is our perceptions and ideas. "To be is to be perceived."

Truth is gaining knowledge of our mental ideas.

David Hume

Reality is the world we experience.

Truth is knowledge of relations between ideas. Knowledge of the empirical world is limited.

Immanuel Kant

Reality is the world of experience that we actively construct.

We construct knowledge by applying the faculties of the mind to sense experience.

◄ **What is real and what is an illusion?** Surrealist paintings like this one can raise questions about how we make sense of our world. This chapter will explore a range of similarly mind-bending ideas in our search for "truth" and "reality."

6.1 Questioning Independent Reality

We began our exploration of metaphysics and epistemology in the previous chapter, examining the influential ideas of Plato, Aristotle, and Descartes. This chapter continues this exploration of metaphysics and epistemology, building on the foundation established in Chapter 5. Plato and Descartes are rationalists, believing that genuine, universal knowledge is discovered by using our reasoning abilities, independent of sense experience. In this chapter, we will initially be examining a number of empiricist philosophers, who believe that genuine knowledge can only be achieved through our sense experience. This was the crux of Aristotle's disagreement with Plato, because he (Aristotle) was convinced that while our reasoning process is indispensable in discerning the formal elements of knowledge and the teleological principles at work in the universe, sense experience is also crucial to constructing knowledge.

Despite their differences regarding the nature of reality and knowledge, Plato and Aristotle never doubted the existence of the external world. Plato believed that the sensible world of experience was an imperfect and transitory realm that could only yield opinion, never knowledge. We needed, he believed, to develop and employ our rational faculties to ascend to the perfect and eternal realm of the essences of things—the Forms—to achieve genuine knowledge. Aristotle, on the other hand, was just as convinced that knowledge could be achieved only by using our rational faculties to understand the universal truths embodied in the natural order, the sensible world in which we live. There was, he was convinced, no "higher" realm of truth and reality. Although they differed on the nature of knowledge and how to achieve it, both Plato and Aristotle assumed the *existence* of independent reality.

Descartes, on the other hand, did in fact pose the question, "How do I know the external world exists independently of my thinking about it?" For Descartes, questioning the existence of external reality was a necessary technique to discover his foundation of certainty on which he could build a system of knowledge that would be incontrovertibly true. It must have seemed like a good idea at the time, but Descartes' radical doubt opened up a gap between the knower (humans) and the known (the external world) that philosophers have spent centuries trying to bridge. According to Descartes, while we can be certain that we exist as thinking entities—*cogito ergo sum*—there is no way for us to be absolutely certain that external reality exists independently of our thinking about it.

The philosophers whom we turn to in this chapter—John Locke, Bishop George Berkeley, and David Hume (known collectively as the "British empiricists")—took the possibility that external reality might not exist and ran with it. Although these philosophers

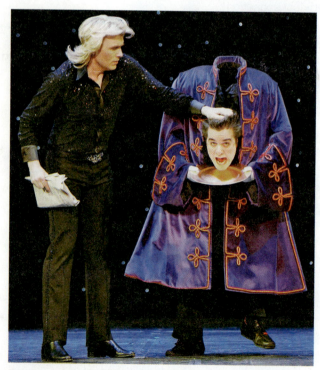

Reality? Illusion? How do we know? This magician's trick plays with the contradiction between the reality we take for granted (that a talking head belongs atop a body) and the appearance we obtain through our senses. Philosophy of knowledge asks us to explore the basis of knowledge about the world.

were empiricists who believed that all knowledge must come from experience, while Descartes was a rationalist who believed that truth can be discovered only by reason, they all agreed that there is no way to prove that external reality actually exists independently of our experience of it. It was left to Immanuel Kant to try and solve this conundrum, and he had to develop a radically different way of thinking about things to do so. We will explore Kant's solution in this chapter.

This may seem like a very odd question to you—"How can we prove the independent existence of the world in which we live?" But as **Bertrand Russell** explains in the following essay from his book, *Problems of Philosophy*, when you start thinking philosophically about these issues, the question of whether the external world exists and whether we can ever "know" it is not nearly so odd as first imagined.

Bertrand Russell, from *Appearance and Reality*

Is there any knowledge in the world which is so certain that no reasonable man could doubt it? This question, which at first sight might not seem difficult, is really one of the most difficult that can be asked. When we have realized the obstacles in the way of a straightforward and confident answer, we shall be well launched on the study of philosophy—for philosophy is merely the attempt to answer such ultimate questions, not carelessly and dogmatically, as we do in ordinary life and even in the sciences, but critically after exploring all that makes such questions puzzling, and after realizing all the vagueness and confusion that underlie our ordinary ideas.

In daily life, we assume as certain many things which, on a closer scrutiny, are found to be so full of apparent contradictions that only a great amount of thought enables us to know what it is that we really may believe. In the search for certainty, it is natural to begin with our present experiences, and in some sense, no doubt, knowledge is to be derived from them. But any statement as to what it is that our immediate experiences make us know is very likely to be wrong. It seems to me that I am now sitting in a chair, at a table of a certain shape, on which I see sheets of paper with writing or print. By turning my head I see out of the window buildings and clouds and the sun. I believe that the sun is about ninety-three million miles from the earth; that it is a hot globe many times bigger than the earth; that, owing to the earth's rotation, it rises every morning, and will continue to do so for an indefinite time in the future. I believe that, if any other normal person comes into my room, he will see the same chairs and tables and books and papers as I see, and that the table which I see is the same as the table which I feel pressing against my arm. All this seems to be so evident as to be hardly worth stating, except in answer to a man who doubts whether I know anything. Yet all this may be reasonably doubted, and all of it requires much careful discussion before we can be sure that we have stated it in a form that is wholly true.

To make our difficulties plain, let us concentrate attention on the table. To the eye it is oblong, brown and shiny, to the touch it is smooth and cool and hard; when I tap it, it gives out a wooden sound. Any one else who sees and feels and hears the table will agree with this description, so that it might seem as if no difficulty would arise; but as soon as we try to be more precise our troubles begin. Although I believe that the table is "really" of the same colour all over, the parts that reflect the light look much brighter than the other parts, and some parts look white because of reflected light. I know that, if I move, the parts that reflect the light will be different, so that the apparent distribution of colours on the table will change. It follows that if several people are looking at the table at the same moment, no two of them will see exactly the same distribution of colours, because no two can see it from exactly the same point of view, and any change in the point of view makes some change in the way the light is reflected.

Bertrand Russell, *The Problems of Philosophy* (Oxford: Oxford University Press, 1912). Copyright 1912. Reprinted by permission of Oxford University Press.

Bertrand Russell (1872–1970). British philosopher; one of the founders of modern logic. In *The Principles of Mathematics* (1903) and with Whitehead in the three-volume *Principia Mathematica* (1910–1913), Russell advanced the view that all of mathematics could be derived from logical premises. Also a political activist, he wrote many popular books on topics such as religion, ethics, and nuclear disarmament.

Listen to the **Audio-book** *Bertrand Russell Appearance and Reality* on **mysearchlab.com**

> **Here we have already the beginning of one of the distinctions that cause most trouble in philosophy—the distinction between 'appearance' and 'reality,' between what things seem to be and what they are.**

For most practical purposes these differences are unimportant, but to the painter they are all-important: the painter has to unlearn the habit of thinking that things seem to have the colour which common sense says they "really" have, and to learn the habit of seeing things as they appear. Here we have already the beginning of one of the distinctions that cause most trouble in philosophy—the distinction between "appearance" and "reality," between what things seem to be and what they are. The painter wants to know what things seem to be, the practical man and the philosopher want to know what they are; but the philosopher's wish to know this is stronger than the practical man's, and is more troubled by knowledge as to the difficulties of answering the question.

To return to the table. It is evident from what we have found, that there is no colour which preeminently appears to be *the* colour of the table, or even of any one particular part of the table—it appears to be of different colours from different points of view, and there is no reason for regarding some of these as more really its colour than others. And we know that even from a given point of view the colour will seem different by artificial light, or to a colour-blind man, or to a man wearing blue spectacles, while in the dark there will be no colour at all, though to touch and hearing the table will be unchanged. This colour is not something which is inherent in the table, but something depending upon the table and the spectator and the way the light falls on the table. When, in ordinary life, we speak of *the* colour of the table, we only mean the sort of colour which it will seem to have to a normal spectator from an ordinary point of view under usual conditions of light. But the other colours which appear under other conditions have just as good a right to be considered real; and therefore, to avoid favouritism, we are compelled to deny that, in itself, the table has any one particular colour.

The same thing applies to the texture. With the naked eye one can see the grain, but otherwise the table looks smooth and even. If we looked at it through a microscope, we should see roughnesses and hills and valleys, and all sorts of differences that are imperceptible to the naked eye. Which of these is the "real" table? We are naturally tempted to say that what we see through the microscope is more real, but that in turn would be changed by a still more powerful microscope. If, then, we cannot trust what we see with the naked eye, why should we trust what we see through a microscope? Thus, again, the confidence in our senses with which we began deserts us.

The *shape* of the table is no better. We are all in the habit of judging as to the "real" shapes of things, and we do this so unreflectingly that we come to think we actually see the real shapes. But, in fact, as we all have to learn if we try to draw, a given thing looks different in shape from every different point of view. If our table is "really" rectangular, it will look, from almost all points of view, as if it had two acute angles and two obtuse angles. If opposite sides are parallel, they will look as if they converged to a point away from the spectator; if they are of equal length, they will look as if the nearer side were longer. All these things are not commonly noticed in looking at a table, because experience has taught us to construct the "real" shape from the apparent shape, and the "real" shape is what interests us as practical men. But the "real" shape is not what we see; it is something inferred from what we see. And what we see is constantly changing in shape as we move about the room; so that here again the senses seem not to give us the truth about the table itself, but only about the appearance of the table.

Similar difficulties arise when we consider the sense of touch. It is true that the table always gives us a sensation of hardness, and we feel that it resists pressure. But the sensation we obtain depends upon how hard we press the table and also upon what part of the body we press with; thus the various sensations due to various pressures or various parts of the body cannot be supposed to reveal *directly* any definite property of the table, but at most to be signs of some property which perhaps *causes* all the sensations, but is not actually apparent in any of them. And the same applies still more obviously to the sounds which can be elicited by rapping the table.

Thus it becomes evident that the real table, if there is one, is not the same as what we immediately experience by sight or touch or hearing. The real table, if there is one, is not *immediately* known to us at all, but must be an inference from what is immediately known. Hence, two very difficult questions at once arise; namely, (1) Is there a real table at all? (2) If so, what sort of object can it be?

It will help us in considering these questions to have a few simple terms of which the meaning is definite and clear. Let us give the name of "sense-data" to the things that are immediately known in sensation: such things as colours, sounds, smells, hardnesses, roughnesses, and so on. We shall give the name "sensation" to the experience of being immediately aware of these things. Thus, whenever we see a colour, we have a sensation *of* the colour, but the colour itself is a sense-datum, not a sensation. The colour is that of which we are immediately aware, and the awareness itself is the sensation. It is plain that if we are to know anything about the table, it must be by means of the sense-data—brown colour, oblong shape, smoothness, etc.—which we associate with the table; but, for the reasons which have been given, we cannot say that the table is the sense-data, or even that the sense-data are directly properties of the table. Thus a problem arises as to the relation of the sense-data to the real table, supposing there is such a thing.

The real table, if it exists, we will call a "physical object." Thus we have to consider the relation of sense-data to physical objects. The collection of all physical objects is called "matter." Thus our two questions may be re-stated as follows: (1) Is there any such thing as matter? (2) If so, what is its nature?

The philosopher who first brought prominently forward the reasons for regarding the immediate objects of our senses as not existing independently of us was George Berkeley (1685–1753). His *Three Dialogues between Hylas and Philonous, in Opposition to Sceptics and Atheists*, undertake to prove that there is no such thing as matter at all, and that the world consists

What is the "real" shape of this table? In his painting *Breakfast*, Juan Gris presents multiple points of view on a single table, illustrating Russell's point that what we see changes in shape as we move about a room. Is there a "real" shape for this table? In what way is this fractured image "true"? *(Juan Gris [1887–1927] Breakfast 1914, cut-and-pasted paper, crayon and oil over canvas, 31 7/8 × 23 1/2 in. [80.9 × 59.7 cm.] The Museum of Modern Art/Licensed by Scala-Art Resource, NY. Acquired through the Lillie P. Bliss Bequest. Photograph © 1997 The Museum of Modern Art, New York.)*

of nothing but minds and their ideas. Hylas has hitherto believed in matter, but he is no match for Philonous, who mercilessly drives him into contradictions and paradoxes, and makes his own denial of matter seem, in the end, as if it were almost common sense. The arguments employed are of very different value: some are important and sound, others are confused or quibbling. But Berkeley retains the merit of having shown that the existence of matter is capable of being denied without absurdity, and that if there are any things that exist independently of us they cannot be the immediate objects of our sensations.

There are two different questions involved when we ask whether matter exists, and it is important to keep them clear. We commonly mean by "matter" something which is opposed to "mind," something which we think of as occupying space and as radically incapable of any sort of thought or consciousness. It is chiefly in this sense that Berkeley denies matter; that is to say, he does not deny that the sense-data which we commonly take

> **Berkeley retains the merit of having shown that the existence of matter is capable of being denied without absurdity, and that if there are any things that exist independently of us they cannot be the immediate objects of our sensations.**

as signs of the existence of the table are really signs of the existence of *something* independent of us, but he does deny that this something is non-mental, that it is neither mind nor ideas entertained by some mind. He admits that there must be something which continues to exist when we go out of the room or shut our eyes, and that what we call seeing the table does really give us reason for believing in something which persists even when we are not seeing it. But he thinks that this something cannot be radically different in nature from what we see, and cannot be independent of seeing altogether, though it must be independent of *our* seeing. He is thus led to regard the "real" table as an idea in the mind of God. Such an idea has the required permanence and independence of ourselves, without being—as matter would otherwise be—something quite unknowable, in the sense that we can only infer it, and can never be directly and immediately aware of it.

Other philosophers since Berkeley have also held that, although the table does not depend for its existence upon being seen by me, it does depend upon being seen (or otherwise apprehended in sensation) by *some* mind—not necessarily the mind of God, but more often the whole collective mind of the universe. This they hold, as Berkeley does, chiefly because they think there can be nothing real—or at any rate nothing known to be real except minds and their thoughts and feelings. We might state the argument by which they support their view in some such way as this: "Whatever can be thought of is an idea in the mind of the person thinking of it; therefore nothing can be thought of except ideas in minds; therefore anything else is inconceivable, and what is inconceivable cannot exist."

Such an argument, in my opinion, is fallacious; and of course those who advance it do not put it so shortly or so crudely. But whether valid or not, the argument has been very widely advanced in one form or another; and very many philosophers, perhaps a majority, have held that there is nothing real except minds and their ideas. Such philosophers are called "idealists." When they come to explaining matter, they either say, like Berkeley, that matter is really nothing but a collection of ideas, or they say, like Gottfried Leibniz (1646–1716), that what appears as matter is really a collection of more or less rudimentary minds.

But these philosophers, though they deny matter as opposed to mind, nevertheless, in another sense, admit matter. It will be remembered that we asked two questions; namely, (1) Is there a real table at all? (2) If so, what sort of object can it be? Now both Berkeley and Leibniz admit that there is a real table, but Berkeley says it is certain ideas in the mind of God, and Leibniz says it is a colony of souls. Thus both of them answer our first question in the affirmative, and only diverge from the views of ordinary mortals in their answer to our second question. In fact, almost all philosophers seem to be agreed that there is a real table. They almost all agree that, however much our sense-data—colour, shape, smoothness, etc.—may depend upon us, yet their occurrence is a sign of something existing independently of us, something differing, perhaps, completely from our sense-data whenever we are in a suitable relation to the real table. Now obviously this point in which the philosophers are agreed—the view that there is a real table, whatever its nature may be is vitally important, and it will be worth while to consider what reasons there are for accepting this view before we go on to the further question as to the nature of the real table. Our next chapter, therefore, will be concerned with the reasons for supposing that there is a real table at all.

Before we go farther it will be well to consider for a moment what it is that we have discovered so far. It has appeared that, if we take any common object of the sort that is supposed to be known by the senses, what the senses *immediately* tell us is not the truth about the object as it is apart from us, but only the truth about certain sense-data which, so far as we can see, depend upon the relations between us and the object. Thus what we directly see and feel is merely "appearance," which we believe to be a sign of some "reality" behind. But if the reality is not what appears, have we any means of knowing whether there is any reality at all? And if so, have we any means of finding out what it is like?

> **Philosophy, if it cannot answer so many questions as we could wish, has at least the power of asking questions which increase the interest of the world, and show the strangeness and wonder lying just below the surface even in the commonest things of daily life.**

Such questions are bewildering, and it is difficult to know that even the strangest hypotheses may not be true. Thus our familiar table, which has roused but the slightest thoughts in us hitherto, has become a problem full of surprising possibilities. The one thing we know about it is that it is not what it seems. Beyond this modest result, so far, we have the most complete liberty of conjecture. Leibniz tells us it is a community of souls: Berkeley tells us it is an idea in the mind of God; sober science, scarcely less wonderful, tells us it is a vast collection of electric charges in violent motion.

Among these surprising possibilities, doubt suggests that perhaps there is no table at all. Philosophy, if it cannot answer so many questions as we could wish, has at least the power of asking questions which increase the interest of the world, and show the strangeness and wonder lying just below the surface even in the commonest things of daily life.

< READING CRITICALLY >

How Do You Know What Is "Real"?

- After reading the Russell essay, look closely at a piece of furniture that is within your field of vision: Is the piece of furniture *real*? How do you *know* if it's real or not? Explain your reasoning for both responses.

- Russell analyzes the table near him in terms of its color, texture, and shape, and concludes:

  Thus it becomes evident that the real table, if there is one, is not the same as what we immediately experience by sight or touch or hearing. The real table, if there is one, is not *immediately* known to us at all, but must be an inference from what is immediately known.

  Do you agree with Russell's conclusion? Why or why not?

- Russell goes on to observe: "Hence, two very difficult questions at once arise; namely, (1) Is there a real table at all? (2) If so, what sort of object can it be?" Explain how you would respond to these two questions and explain the reasoning for your conclusions.

- Russell's essay emphasizes the significance of the philosophical distinction between *appearances* (what things seem to be) and *reality* (what they are). After "thinking philosophically" about these issues, do you see the world around you in a new light? Explain your response and the reasons for it.

6.2 All Knowledge Comes from Experience: Locke

*Let us suppose the mind to be, as we say, a blank tablet (**tabula rasa**) of white paper, void of all characters, without any ideas; how comes it to be furnished? Whence comes it by that vast store, which the busy and boundless fancy of man has painted on it with almost endless variety? Whence has it all the materials of reason and knowledge? To this I answer in one word, from **experience**: in that all our knowledge is founded, and from that it ultimately derives itself.*

John Locke

John Locke (1632–1704). This British philosopher and physician laid the groundwork for an empiricist approach to philosophical questions. Locke's revolutionary theory that the mind is a tabula rasa, a blank slate, on which experience writes is detailed in his *Essay Concerning Human Understanding* (1690).

This famous passage by **John Locke** captures his essential perspective on knowledge, an epistemological school of thought that came to be known as *empiricism*. For Locke and other empiricists, all human knowledge can ultimately be traced back to experiences we have had, transmitted through our five senses. This conviction sets

Innate knowledge The knowledge and ideas we were born with.

empiricists in direct opposition to the rationalists such as Plato and Descartes. Locke was passionately critical of the rationalist views that

- we enter the world with **innate knowledge** that we come to be aware of through experience.
- we can achieve true knowledge independent of sense experience by using our "rational intuition."

Locke was convinced that the rationalist view opened the door to all sorts of metaphysical speculations that were unsupportable and unprovable. He saw himself on a crusade to place philosophy in general, and epistemology in particular, on the firm footing of common sense. How can we have "innate" knowledge of which we are unaware? How can we define "rational intuition" in any precise and meaningful way? When we ask most people how they came to know something, they typically refer to experiences they have had: "I saw it . . . ," "I heard it . . . ," and so on. Common sense dictates that we focus on the direct data of experience to discover the source of all knowledge and thus avoid the speculative pitfalls of rationalism.

⊙ Watch the **Video**
Steven Pinker Chalks It Up to the Blank Slate on
mysearchlab.com

Locke's Critique of "Universality"

Locke expressed his views in the influential work, *An Essay Concerning Human Understanding* (1689), which had a dominant influence in philosophy and other fields in the eighteenth century. The idea for the book came to him following a long and energetic debate with friends over morality and religion when Locke announced, "If we can find out how far the understanding can extend its view; how far it has faculties to attain certainty; and in what cases it can only judge and guess, we may learn to content ourselves with what is attainable by us in this state."

The following passages represent a direct attack on the concept of innate ideas as expressed by Plato and other rationalists.

John Locke, from *An Essay Concerning Human Understanding*

Book I: Chapter II—No Innate Principles in the Mind

1. It is an established opinion amongst some men, that there are in the understanding certain innate principles; some primary notions . . . characters, as it were stamped upon the mind of man; which the soul receives in its very first being, and brings into the world with it. It would be sufficient to convince unprejudiced readers of the falseness of this supposition, if I should only show (as I hope I shall in the following parts of this Discourse) how men, barely by the use of their natural faculties, may attain to all the knowledge they have, without the help of any innate impressions; and may arrive at certainty, without any such original notions or principles. . . .

2. There is nothing more commonly taken for granted than that there are certain principles, both speculative and practical, (for they speak of both,) universally agreed upon by all mankind: which therefore, they argue, must needs be the constant impressions which the souls of men receive in their first beings, and which they bring into the world with them, as necessarily and really as they do any of their inherent faculties.

3. This argument, drawn from universal consent, has this misfortune in it, that if it were true in matter of fact, that there were certain truths wherein all mankind agreed, it would not prove them innate, if there can be any other way shown how men may come to that universal agreement, in the things they do consent in, which I presume may be done.

Locke announces straightaway that he intends to disprove the rationalist idea that there are "certain innate principles; some primary notions . . . characters, as it were stamped upon the mind of man; which the soul receives in its very first being, and brings into the world with it." He believes that the strongest rationalist argument for such innate knowledge is the idea that it is universally present in all humans. If everyone demonstrates an understanding of some law or principle—such as the logical principle "It is impossible for the same thing to be and not to be" (known since the time of Aristotle as the "Law of the Excluded Middle")—then Locke believes that the rationalist will argue that such a principle *must* be innate—otherwise, how did everyone come to acquire knowledge of it, even in the absence of formal education in logic or mathematics? Locke believes that it *is* possible to demonstrate how people could develop such universal knowledge based solely on experience. But he also believes that this rationalist argument of "universality" is even more seriously flawed because there are people who do *not* exhibit this supposedly universal knowledge.

John Locke, from
An Essay Concerning Human Understanding

4. But, which is worse, this argument of universal consent, which is made use of to prove innate principles, seems to me a demonstration that there are none such: because there are none to which all mankind give an universal assent. I shall begin with the speculative, and instance in those magnified principles of demonstration, "Whatsoever is, is," and "It is impossible for the same thing to be and not to be"; which, of all others, I think have the most allowed title to innate. These have so settled a reputation of maxims universally received, that it will no doubt be thought strange if any one should seem to question it. But yet I take liberty to say, that these propositions are so far from having an universal assent, that there are a great part of mankind to whom they are not so much as known.

5. For, first, it is evident, that all children and idiots have not the least apprehension or thought of them. And the want of that is enough to destroy that universal assent which must needs be the necessary concomitant of all innate truths: it seeming to me near a contradiction to say, that there are truths imprinted on the soul, which it perceives or understands not: imprinting, if it signify anything, being nothing else but the making certain truths to be perceived. For to imprint anything on the mind without the mind's perceiving it, seems to me hardly intelligible. If therefore children and idiots have souls, have minds, with those impressions upon them, they must unavoidably perceive them, and necessarily know and assent to these truths; which since they do not, it is evident that there are no such impressions. For if they are not notions naturally imprinted, how can they be innate? And if they are notions imprinted, how can they be unknown? . . .

At first glance (and perhaps, even at second glance), you might wonder at the wisdom of Locke's resting his major counterargument to innate ideas on the examples of "children and idiots." But he does. How might Plato and Descartes respond to such an attack? Well, surely they would want to point out that the argument for innate ideas is based on *normal* human development, not *abnormal* exceptions such as "idiots" (however Locke chooses to define them). Locke observes, "If therefore children and idiots have souls, have minds . . . ." Do idiots have minds like most people? Surely not. Do they have souls? That's something for Plato to puzzle out, but as we noted, a belief in innate ideas is in no way dependent on believing in an immortal soul.

Then what about children? They surely have souls and minds, as far as Plato and Descartes are concerned. But isn't it accurate to say that their minds are not yet fully developed? And when they are fully developed, won't they likely demonstrate the same understanding of the Law of Excluded Middle as everyone else (unless they turn out to be idiots)?

But Locke's more serious point is the following:

John Locke, from
*An Essay Concerning
Human Understanding*

> . . . To say a notion is imprinted on the mind, and yet at the same time to say, that the mind is ignorant of it, and never yet took notice of it, is to make this impression nothing. No proposition can be said to be in the mind which it never yet knew, which it was never yet conscious of.

Gottfried Wilhelm von Leibniz (1646–1716). As advisor and diplomat for several German barons, Leibniz traveled widely and was an influential intellectual in seventeenth-century Europe. He contributed to the fields of engineering, math, physics, linguistics, and history as well as philosophy. He maintained that the world, as created by God, is the best of all possible worlds.

What about this point? Is it possible to "know" something and yet not be aware you know it? In other words, does it make sense to say that innate knowledge can exist as *potential* knowledge, waiting to be activated? Have you ever had the experience of reaching an awareness of something and saying to yourself, "I knew that all the time—I just wasn't aware of it!" Clearly there are serious questions for Locke to face; but, rather than our posing them, let's turn this task over to a philosopher who was also one of Locke's contemporaries: **Gottfried Wilhelm von Leibniz**. It's a unique opportunity to see two historically influential philosophers square off and lock philosophical horns.

Leibniz's Case Against Locke

Leibniz was a rationalist with a very modern notion of innate ideas. Rather than viewing them as being "stamped" on the human mind (Locke's metaphor) in a static, fully formed fashion, Leibniz believes that the human mind at birth contains "inclinations, dispositions, tendencies, or natural potentials" to form these ideas. In a view that is stunningly consistent with modern theories in developmental psychology, cognitive psychology, and linguistics, Leibniz proposed an interactive concept of intellectual development in which, as people mature, their innate tendencies gradually evolve and become fully formed ideas through the mind's interaction with experience. In the following passage, written shortly after the publication of Locke's *Essay Concerning Human Understanding*, Leibniz does a masterful job of turning Locke's arguments against him.

Gottfried Wilhelm von Leibniz, from *New Essays Concerning Human Understanding*

> The questions at issue is whether the soul in itself is entirely empty, like the tablet upon which nothing has yet been written (*tabula rasa*), as is the view of Aristotle and the author of the *essay* (Locke), and whether all that is traced on it comes solely from the senses and from experience; or whether the soul contains originally the principles of various notions and doctrines which external objects merely awaken from time to time, as I believe, with Plato and even with the Schoolmen, and with all those who take in this sense the passage of St. Paul (Romans, 2:15) where he remarks that the law of God is written in the heart. . . .
>
> From this there arises another question, whether all truths depend on experience, that is to say, on induction and examples, or whether there are some that have some

other basis. For if some events can be foreseen before any trial has been made of them, it is clear that we must here contribute something of our own. The senses, although necessary for all our actual knowledge, are not sufficient to give us the whole of it, since the senses never give anything except examples, that is to say, particular or individual truths. All examples which confirm a general truth, however numerous they may be, are not enough to establish the universal necessity of this same truth; for it does not follow that what has happened will happen again in the same way.

Will the sun will rise tomorrow? Are you sure? "Cause and effect" vs. sense experience. Leibniz argued that we do not predict the rising of the sun based on observation but rather that we need the cognitive concept of "cause and effect." This principle of reason exists independently of sense experience.

Leibniz is making the same point to which we referred earlier: By itself, sense experience is incapable of validating any general principles or laws. Take, for example, the principle of "cause and effect." Even though we may see the sun rise each morning (except for cloudy days), sense experience provides no justification for concluding that there is a general law at work that permits us to predict with certainty that the sun will rise in the same way tomorrow and every day thereafter. To make such a prediction, we need the contribution of the cognitive concept "cause and effect," a concept that is nowhere to be found in our sense experience. In addition to the laws of science, other fields that are dependent on principles of reason that exist independently of sense experience include, according to Leibniz, pure mathematics, logic, ethics, and natural theology.

. . . It would seem that necessary truths, such as are found in pure mathematics, and especially in arithmetic and in geometry, must have principles the proof of which does not depend on examples, nor, consequently, on the testimony of the senses, although without the senses it would never have occurred to us to think of them. This ought to be well recognised; Euclid has so well understood it that he often demonstrates by reason what is obvious enough through experience and by sensible images. Logic also, together with metaphysics and ethics, one of which forms natural theology and the other natural jurisprudence, are full of such truths; and consequently their proof can only come from internal principles, which are called innate. It is true that we must not imagine that these eternal laws of the reason can be read in the soul as in an open book, as the edict of the praetor can be read in his *album* without difficulty or research; but it is enough that they can be discovered in us by dint of attention, for which opportunities are given by the senses. The success of experiments serves also as confirmation of the reason, very much as proofs serve in arithmetic for better avoiding error of reckoning when the reasoning is long. . . .

It seems that our able author claims that there is nothing potential in us and nothing even of which we are not at any time actually conscious; but he cannot mean this strictly, or his opinion would be too paradoxical; for acquired habits and the contents of our memory are not always consciously perceived and do not even always come to our aid at need, although we often easily bring them back to mind on some slight occasion which makes us remember them, just as we need only the beginning of a song to remember the song. Also he modifies his assertion in other places by saying that there is nothing in us of which we have not been at least formerly conscious. But besides the fact that no one can be sure by reason alone how far our past apperceptions, which we may have forgotten, may have gone, especially in view of the Platonic doctrine of reminiscence, which, mythical as it is, is not, in part at least, incompatible with bare reason; in addition to this, I say, why is it necessary that everything should be acquired by us through the

Gottfried Wilhelm von Leibniz, from *New Essays Concerning Human Understanding*

> perceptions of external things, and that nothing can be unearthed in ourselves? Is our soul, then, such a blank that, besides the images borrowed from without, it is nothing? . . . there are a thousand indications that lead us to think that there are at every moment numberless perceptions in us, but without apperception and without reflections; that is to say, changes in the soul itself of which we are not conscious, because the impressions are either too slight and too numerous, or too even, so that they have nothing sufficient to distinguish them one from the other; but, joined to others, they do not fail to produce their effect and to make themselves felt at least confusedly in the mass.

These are compelling points that Leibniz is making against Locke's concept of the tabula rasa. First, he points out that there are many things that we know—through habit or through our memory banks—that are not immediately before our perception. We can even act on this knowledge without being explicitly aware of it. For example, when an experienced motorist drives a car, she is performing extremely complex calculations and skilled movements while perhaps happily singing a favorite tune and thinking about what she'll be doing later that evening.

But the more penetrating question that Leibniz raises is why should we even try to account for all human knowledge based solely on sense experience, when so much argues against it? Ironically, it's the empirically rooted investigations in the twentieth century that have made such a strong case that the concept of a tabula rasa mind is pure fiction. Jean Piaget's work in developmental psychology; Noam Chomsky's work in linguistics; Claude Levi-Strauss's work in anthropology—plus the work of other thinkers—have developed exhaustive empirical evidence to suggest that humans come equipped with a whole array of innate conceptual structures that develop and become elaborated through their dynamic interaction with experience. These are points that we will consider more fully when exploring the epistemology of Immanuel Kant, who once again demonstrates his colossal status as a creative and prescient thinker in the history of philosophy. For now, we will move to an analysis of Locke's views on perception and its role in producing knowledge. Locke introduces some provocative ideas in these areas that end up having one significant unintended consequence—the disappearance of the external world.

Locke's Causal Theory of Perception

((•●— **Listen** to the **Audiobook** *Locke— An Essay Concerning Human Understanding by Nigel Warburton* on **mysearchlab.com**

Locke's epistemology is structured around a theory of perception that very much reflects the scientific worldview of Isaac Newton, a contemporary of his. Newton saw the universe in mechanistic terms, with discrete physical bodies relating to one another by means of particles and masses in motion ("force"). Thus for Locke, there are four independent elements in the knowing process, relating to one another in a mechanically causal fashion:

- The entity or object in the world
- Sensations (sense data, images, sensory impressions) emitted by the objects via "impulses" and transmitted to our five senses
- Ideas, which Locke characterizes as "the immediate object of perception, thought, or understanding"—in other words, the images and impressions produced in our minds by the impulses emitted by the objects
- The human subject, knower, or conscious mind who is able to perceive the ideas in his or her mind and "reflect" on them, thus constructing knowledge

Although such a theory may seem to have a certain commonsense logic, it contains within itself the conceptual seeds of its own destruction. But let's permit Locke to state his case before we attempt to dismantle it.

John Locke, from *An Essay Concerning Human Understanding*

Book II—Of Ideas: Chapter I—Of Ideas in General, and Their Original

1. *Idea is the object of thinking.* Every man being conscious to himself that he thinks; and that which his mind is applied about whilst thinking being the ideas that are there, it is past doubt that men have in their minds several ideas,—such as are those expressed by the words *whiteness*, *hardness*, *sweetness*, *thinking*, *motion*, *man*, *elephant*, *army*, *drunkenness*, and others: it is in the first place then to be inquired, How he comes by them?

I know it is a received doctrine, that men have native ideas, and original characters, stamped upon their minds in their very first being. This opinion I have at large examined already; and, I suppose what I have said in the foregoing Book will be much more easily admitted, when I have shown whence the understanding may get all the ideas it has; and by what ways and degrees they may come into the mind;—for which I shall appeal to every one's own observation and experience.

2. *All ideas come from sensation or reflection.* Let us then suppose the mind to be, as we say, white paper, void of all characters, without any ideas:—How comes it to be furnished? Whence comes it by that vast store which the busy and boundless fancy of man has painted on it with an almost endless variety? Whence has it all the materials of reason and knowledge? To this I answer, in one word, from EXPERIENCE. In that all our knowledge is founded; and from that it ultimately derives itself. Our observation employed either, about external sensible objects, or about the internal operations of our minds perceived and reflected on by ourselves, is that which supplies our understandings with all the materials of thinking. These two are the fountains of knowledge, from whence all the ideas we have, or can naturally have, do spring.

3. *The objects of sensation one source of ideas.* First, our Senses, conversant about particular sensible objects, do convey into the mind several distinct perceptions of things, according to those various ways wherein those objects do affect them. And thus we come by those ideas we have of yellow, white, heat, cold, soft, hard, bitter, sweet, and all those which we call sensible qualities; which when I say the senses convey into the mind, I mean, they from external objects convey into the mind what produces there those perceptions. This great source of most of the ideas we have, depending wholly upon our senses, and derived by them to the understanding, I call SENSATION.

4. *The operations of our minds, the other source of them.* Secondly, the other fountain from which experience furnisheth the understanding with ideas is,—the perception of the operations of our own mind within us, as it is employed about the ideas it has got;—which operations, when the soul comes to reflect on and consider, do furnish the understanding with another set of ideas, which could not be had from things without. And such are *perception*, *thinking*, *doubting*, *believing*, *reasoning*, *knowing*, *willing*, and all the different actings of our own minds;—which we being conscious of, and observing in ourselves, do from these receive into our understandings as distinct ideas as we do from bodies affecting our senses. This source of ideas every man has wholly in himself; and though it be not sense, as having nothing to do with external objects, yet it is very like it, and might properly enough be called internal sense. But as I call the other SENSATION, so I call this REFLECTION, the ideas it affords being such only as the mind gets by reflecting on its own operations within itself. . . .

5. *All our ideas are of the one or the other of these.* The understanding seems to me not to have the least glimmering of any ideas which it doth not receive from one of these two. External objects furnish the mind with the ideas of sensible qualities, which are all those different perceptions they produce in us; and the mind furnishes the understanding with ideas of its own operations.

Locke goes on to pose a provocative challenge for us in paragraph 5:

John Locke, from
*An Essay Concerning
Human Understanding*

Let any one examine his own thoughts, and thoroughly search into his understanding; and then let him tell me, whether all the original ideas he has there, are any other than of the objects of his senses, or of the operations of his mind, considered as objects of his reflection.

Let's try his suggestion. Examining your own thoughts, what do you find? Locke is confident that the only thing you find will be *images*, based directly on your senses, or what he terms your "reflection" on these images, with which he means cognitive operations such as *perception, thinking, doubting, believing, reasoning, knowing, willing.*

We can see right away that this challenge is problematic for Locke. For while you undoubtedly find in your consciousness direct sensory perceptions of your current situation—what you are currently seeing, hearing, touching, tasting, smelling—as well as memories of such experiences, you probably are also discovering all manner of ideas, concepts, and images that go far beyond anything you have directly experienced. Locke might respond that these additional contents of your mind are the results of the cognitive operations listed above: *But this is precisely the rationalist's point!* The rationalist contention is that there is no way we can account for the contents of our mind and the knowledge we have solely by looking at sense experience. We must necessarily introduce mental operations and concepts that *transform* sense experiences into an intelligible world. And because these mental operations and concepts are not to be found in sense experience, we must presume that they are somehow *innate* processes, present (at least potentially) at birth, *and* that these processes are essential for constructing knowledge in any meaningful way.

To further strengthen his case, Locke presents his analysis of the mental development of children. He asks us to imagine a child who has been raised in deprived circumstances, never viewing colors or tasting oysters. Such a child will have no idea of what these sights or tastes would be like.

Nature, nurture, or both? Is our evolving intelligence the result of innate structures or empirical experiences, through "nature" or "nurture"? The prevailing current view is that our evolving intelligence is the product of both innate elements and empirical experiences.

6. *Observable in children.* He that attentively considers the state of a child, at his first coming into the world, will have little reason to think him stored with plenty of ideas, that are to be the matter of his future knowledge. It is by degrees he comes to be furnished with them. And though the ideas of obvious and familiar qualities imprint themselves before the memory begins to keep a register of time or order, yet it is often so late before some unusual qualities come in the way, that there are few men that cannot recollect the beginning of their acquaintance with them.

And if it were worth while, no doubt a child might be so ordered as to have but a very few, even of the ordinary ideas, till he were grown up to a man. But all that are born into the world, being surrounded with bodies that perpetually and diversely affect them, variety of ideas, whether care be taken of it or not, are imprinted on the minds of children. Light and colours are busy at hand everywhere, when the eye is but open; sounds and some tangible qualities fail not to solicit their proper senses, and force an entrance to the mind;—but yet, I think, it will be granted easily, that if a child were kept in a place where he never saw any other but black and white till he were a man, he would have no more ideas of scarlet or green, than he that from his childhood never tasted an oyster, or a pine-apple, has of those particular relishes.

John Locke, from *An Essay Concerning Human Understanding*

Locke's point is that such data are not imprinted on the mind innately and require sense experience to familiarize an individual with them. But this only states the obvious. The rationalist would contend that it is obvious that the appropriate sense experiences are crucial for normal intellectual development but that these experiences are in no way sufficient for accounting for the mind's complex development. The only way to do this is to assume, using computer metaphors, innate "hard wiring" and "software" in the human mind that, working in partnership with sense experience, produce an intelligible world and the possibility of knowledge.

Locke then goes on to further analyze the qualities of independent objects and how these qualities relate to the perceiving subject. He distinguishes two types of physical qualities:

- **Primary qualities**, the "properties" of objects that reside in the objects, independent of our perceptions of the object. These include qualities that can be measured: size, shape, and weight.

- **Secondary qualities**, which do not reside within the objects themselves but instead are the power (or dispositions) of objects to produce sensations in our minds. These would include qualities such as color, smell, texture, and taste.

Primary qualities The "properties" of objects that reside in the objects (such as size, shape, weight), independent of our perceptions of the object.

Secondary qualities Properties that do not reside within the objects themselves but instead are the power of objects to produce sensations in our mind (such as color, smell, texture, and taste).

Book II: Chapter VIII—Primary and Secondary Qualities

8. *Our ideas and the qualities of bodies.* Whatsoever the mind perceives in itself, or is the immediate object of perception, thought, or understanding, that I call idea; and the power to produce any idea in our mind, I call quality of the subject wherein that power is. Thus a snowball having the power to produce in us the ideas of white, cold, and round,—the power to produce those ideas in us, as they are in the snowball, I call qualities; and as they are sensations or perceptions in our understandings, I call them ideas; which ideas, if I speak of sometimes as in the things themselves, I would be understood to mean those qualities in the objects which produce them in us.

9. *Primary qualities of bodies.* Qualities thus considered in bodies are, *First,* such as are utterly inseparable from the body, in what state soever it be; and such as in all the alterations and changes it suffers, all the force can be used upon it, it constantly keeps;

John Locke, from *An Essay Concerning Human Understanding*

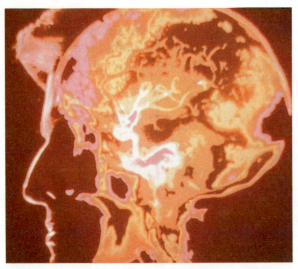

How do our minds create an intelligible world? Many philosophers and scientists believe that we must assume the existence of "hard wiring" and "innate software" in the mind which, working in partnership with sense experience, produces an intelligible world.

and such as sense constantly finds in every particle of matter which has bulk enough to be perceived; and the mind finds inseparable from every particle of matter, though less than to make itself singly be perceived by our senses: e.g. Take a grain of wheat, divide it into two parts; each part has still solidity, extension, figure, and mobility: divide it again, and it retains still the same qualities; and so divide it on, till the parts become insensible; they must retain still each of them all those qualities. For division (which is all that a mill, or pestle, or any other body, does upon another, in reducing it to insensible parts) can never take away either solidity, extension, figure, or mobility from any body, but only makes two or more distinct separate masses of matter, of that which was but one before; all which distinct masses, reckoned as so many distinct bodies, after division, make a certain number. These I call *original or primary qualities* of body, which I think we may observe to produce simple ideas in us, viz. Solidity, extension, figure, motion or rest, and number.

10. *Secondary qualities of bodies. Secondly*, such qualities which in truth are nothing in the objects themselves but power to produce various sensations in us by their primary qualities, i.e. by the bulk, figure, texture, and motion of their insensible parts, as colours, sounds, tastes, &c. These I call *secondary qualities*. To these might be added a *third* sort, which are allowed to be barely powers; though they are as much real qualities in the subject as those which I, to comply with the common way of speaking, call qualities, but for distinction, secondary qualities. For the power in fire to produce a new colour, or consistency, in *wax* or *clay*,—by its primary qualities, is as much a quality in fire, as the power it has to produce in *me* a new idea or sensation of warmth or burning, which I felt not before,—by the same primary qualities, viz. The bulk, texture, and motion of its insensible parts. . . .

15. *Ideas of primary qualities are resemblances; of secondary, not.* From whence I think it easy to draw this observation,—that the ideas of primary qualities of bodies are resemblances of them, and their patterns do really exist in the bodies themselves, but the ideas produced in us by these secondary qualities have no resemblance of them at all. There is nothing like our ideas, existing in the bodies themselves. They are, in the bodies we denominate from them, only a power to produce those sensations in us: and what is sweet, blue, or warm in idea, is but the certain bulk, figure, and motion of the insensible parts, in the bodies themselves, which we call so. . . .

17. *The ideas of the primary alone really exist.* The particular bulk, number, figure, and motion of the parts of fire or snow are really in them,—whether any one's senses perceive them or no: and therefore they may be called *real* qualities, because they really exist in those bodies. But light, heat, whiteness, or coldness, are no more really in them than sickness or pain is in manna. Take away the sensation of them; let not the eyes see light or colours, nor the ears hear sounds; let the palate

Primary vs. secondary qualities. Some empiricists, like Locke, distinguish between primary qualities (size, shape, weight) and secondary qualities (color, texture, smell) while other philosophers, like Berkeley, challenge this distinction.

not taste, nor the nose smell, and all colours, tastes, odours, and sounds, *as they are such particular ideas*, vanish and cease, and are reduced to their causes, i.e. bulk, figure, and motion of parts. . . .

This, in a nutshell, is Locke's theory of causal perception, the theoretical scaffolding that frames his empiricist theory. Given his dissatisfaction with rationalism as embodied in Plato and Descartes, combined with a Newtonian view of the universe, it must have seemed indeed like a plausible "commonsense" theory of knowledge. However, as we shall soon see in the writings of George Berkeley and David Hume, the logical consequences of Locke's theory are not at all what he intended, as his theory of causal perception leads inevitably to questioning whether the external world actually exists!

Locke was likely aware that establishing the existence of an external world might prove troublesome, and he does make an effort to reassure us of its existence in the following passages. Interestingly, he emulates Descartes in concluding that "intuition" provides knowledge of ourselves, and "reason" reveals the existence of God. But knowledge of the existence of everything else in the universe can only come through "sensation," as there is "no necessary connection of real existence" between the ideas produced in our minds and the objects that produced them.

Book IV: Chapter XI—Of Our Knowledge of the Existence of Other Things

John Locke, from
An Essay Concerning Human Understanding

1. *Knowledge of the existence of other finite beings is to be had only by actual sensation.* The knowledge of our own being we have by intuition. The existence of a God, reason clearly makes known to us, as has been shown.

The knowledge of the existence of *any other thing* we can have only by *sensation*: for there being no necessary connexion of real existence with any *idea* a man hath in his memory; nor of any other existence but that of God with the existence of any particular man: no particular man can know the existence of any other being, but only when, by actual operating upon him, it makes itself perceived by him. For, the having the idea of anything in our mind, no more proves the existence of that thing, than the picture of a man evidences his being in the world, or the visions of a dream make thereby a true history.

But if there is no necessary connection between physical objects and our mental impressions of these objects, then how can we be sure these objects actually exist? After all, our senses often provide partial or inaccurate information to us. Just consider all of those situations in which people experiencing the same event provide very diverse accounts of the experience. Or the times in which you were convinced you had experienced one thing and it turned out to be something very different. Locke appeals to the persuasiveness of common sense in asserting "the certainty of our senses, and the ideas we receive by them." But is this really convincing?

John Locke, from
An Essay Concerning Human Understanding

2. *Instance: whiteness of this paper.* It is therefore the *actual receiving* of ideas from without that gives us notice of the existence of other things, and makes us know, that something doth exist at that time without us, which causes that idea in us; though perhaps we neither know nor consider how it does it. For it takes not from the certainty of our senses, and the ideas we receive by them, that we know not the manner wherein they are produced: v.g. whilst I write this, I have, by the paper affecting my eyes, that idea produced in my mind, which, whatever object causes, I call white; by which I know that that quality or accident (i.e. whose appearance before my eyes always causes that idea) doth really exist, and hath a being without me. And of this, the greatest assurance I can possibly have, and to which my faculties can attain, is the testimony of my eyes, which are the proper and sole judges of this thing; whose testimony I have reason to rely

on as so certain, that I can no more doubt, whilst I write this, that I see white and black, and that something really exists that causes that sensation in me, than that I write or move my hand; which is a certainty as great as human nature is capable of, concerning the existence of anything, but a man's self alone, and of God.

Is there an external world? How do we know? Locke argues that the experience of pain caused by a burning candle proves the existence of an external world: Does it? This illustration depicts the bravery of the Roman soldier Gaius Mutius Scaevola, who plunged his hand into a flame in order to punish it for failing to kill the enemy's king.

Recognizing that "common sense" may not provide sufficient assurance regarding the external world, Locke brings God in for additional reinforcement: "As to myself, I think God has given me assurance enough of the existence of things without me." But is this really persuasive? Certainly not to those who have doubts in the existence of God!

Locke's next effort is to address Descartes' radical doubt regarding the external world. With barely concealed sarcasm directed toward the "dreamer" Descartes (a reference to Descartes' considering the possibility that our "reality" is actually a dream), Locke once again resorts to the persuasive powers of common sense: "And if our dreamer pleases to try whether the glowing heat of a glass furnace be barely a wandering imagination in a drowsy man's fancy, by putting his hand into it, he may perhaps be wakened into a certainty greater than he could wish, that it is something more than bare imagination." But has Locke missed the entire philosophical point of Descartes' radical doubt?

John Locke, from
An Essay Concerning Human Understanding

8. *This certainty is as great as our condition needs.* But yet, if after all this any one will be so sceptical as to distrust his senses, and to affirm that all we see and hear, feel and taste, think and do, during our whole being, is but the series and deluding appearances of a long dream, whereof there is no reality; and therefore will question the existence of all things, or our knowledge of anything. . . . For he that sees a candle burning, and hath experimented the force of its flame by putting his finger in it, will little doubt that this is something existing without him, which does him harm, and puts him to great pain; which is assurance enough, when no man requires greater certainty to govern his actions by than what is as certain as his actions themselves. And if our dreamer pleases to try whether the glowing heat of a glass furnace be barely a wandering imagination in a drowsy man's fancy, by putting his hand into it, he may perhaps be wakened into a certainty greater than he could wish, that it is something more than bare imagination. So that this evidence is as great as we can desire, being as certain to us as our pleasure or pain, i.e. happiness or misery; beyond which we have no concernment, either of knowing or being. . . .

Locke's final effort to put the question of the existence of an external world to rest consists in ridiculing anyone who even has the temerity to *ask* for proof—a very curious position for a philosopher to take! Such an approach is a clear indication of Locke's *lack* of compelling rationale for his position and the problems it engenders. The fact is that his theory of causal perception has created an excruciating dilemma for him.

If all knowledge comes from experience, and all we directly know are the mental impressions caused by the sense data emitted by external objects, then there is no way we can ever have direct knowledge of the external world. We are "locked" in a world of our own mental images, with no access to whatever is responsible for producing these images. Locke suggests in some places that our mental impressions are "copies" of external events—"resemblances," he calls them. But how can we ever be sure how accurate the copies are? We lack an external point of reference from which we can compare the objects and the copies. For example, suppose you have a hallucination: How could you tell whether your mental impression correlated to an external object under Locke's theory? The same principle holds true for *everything* you perceive: You have no way of determining to what extent your mental impressions reflect an external reality.

10. *Folly to expect demonstration in everything.* Whereby yet we may observe how foolish and vain a thing it is for a man of a narrow knowledge, who having reason given him to judge of the different evidence and probability of things, and to be swayed accordingly; how vain, I say, it is to expect demonstration and certainty in things not capable of it; and refuse assent to very rational propositions, and act contrary to very plain and clear truths, because they cannot be made out so evident, as to surmount even the least (I will not say reason, but) pretence of doubting. He that, in the ordinary affairs of life, would admit of nothing but direct plain demonstration, would be sure of nothing in this world, but of perishing quickly. The wholesomeness of his meat or drink would not give him reason to venture on it: and I would fain know what it is he could do upon such grounds as are capable of no doubt, no objection.

John Locke, from *An Essay Concerning Human Understanding*

Locke argues that the qualities we experience—both primary and secondary—must reside in *something*—therefore there must be external substances of which these qualities are a necessary part. But what are these "substances" that we can never directly experience actually like? Locke confesses: Such substances are "we know not what," "we have no clear or distinct idea," "nothing but the unknown support of those qualities." Locke's grand empiricist epistemology may have begun with a bang, but it surely ends with a whimper.

< READING CRITICALLY >

Analyzing Locke's Empirical View

- Locke believes that it is contradictory to believe that we might possess knowledge of which we are unaware. Do you agree with his position? Why or why not?
- Even though Locke believes that we can have direct knowledge only of the mental images and impressions in our mind, he does not believe this should cause us to doubt the existence of an external world that produces these images and impressions. Do you agree with his analysis? Why or why not?
- Locke provides at least four arguments for the existence of the external world of which we can have no direct knowledge. Identify these arguments and then evaluate which of his arguments you find most persuasive and the reasons why.
- Describe an instance in which you were convinced that you had perceived something that turned out to be very different from what you came to believe actually occurred. How does this sort of experience pose a problem for Locke?
- Describe, in your own words, your own epistemology. How do you think we gain knowledge?

6.3 Reality Depends on Perception: Berkeley

George Berkeley (1685–1753). Berkeley was an Irish philosopher and bishop known as one of the three great British empiricists. In *Treatise Concerning the Principles of Human Knowledge* (1710), Berkeley defends an idealist position that maintains there exists no matter, only sensible objects, whose existence is to be perceived.

George Berkeley was Ireland's most famous philosopher and was also a bishop in the Anglican Church (hence the title generally attached to his name). He was a remarkable individual, committed to education, particularly in America. He attempted to establish a college for Native Americans and the sons of English planters (it failed for lack of funding) and made important contributions to Harvard, Yale, and Columbia. In honor of his educational contributions, California even established a university in a city named after him—Berkeley.

Berkeley was well versed in the philosophy of John Locke (along with Descartes, Newton, and the other leading thinkers of the time), and Berkeley takes Locke's fundamental ideas to their logical—and astonishing—conclusion. He accepts Locke's basic empiricist perspective: All knowledge comes either through sense experience or by observing our own psychological states and operations (willing, doubting, loving, for example), and this knowledge is represented to us as "ideas." Berkeley follows Locke's definition of ideas as the images, feelings, or sense data that are directly present to our conscious minds, displayed as either vivid sensory or psychological experiences, or the less vivid form of memory and imagination.

But then Berkeley makes a radical departure from Locke's conclusions on two key points:

- Berkeley rejects Locke's distinction between primary qualities (inherent in physical objects) and secondary qualities (dependent on human minds).
- Berkeley rejects Locke's "commonsense" belief in external objects.

The startling result is Berkeley's denial of the existence of any independently existing external world. His reasoning is the logical extension of Locke's principles: Because all we know are the ideas we find presented to our conscious minds, then it follows that we can never know a material world that supposedly lies outside of our own personal experiences. Thus, the only things that exist are minds and ideas in the minds. "To be is to be perceived" (*esse est percipi*) is the cornerstone of Berkeley's epistemology, which has come to be known as **subjective idealism**. Objects do not exist independently of consciousness: The only things that exist are conscious minds and the ideas subjectively present to the conscious minds. An apple, for example, is simply an idea in our mind that combines the experiences of roundness, redness, hardness, and sweetness. The word *apple* simply names "recurring patterns" of sense experiences and nothing else. What most people interpret to be physical objects are actually groups of sense experiences, bundles of sense data that are present to our mind. To the age-old conundrum, "If a tree falls in the forest, does it make a sound?" Berkeley's response is not only doesn't it make a sound, but the tree and the forest don't actually exist independently of someone's perception of them. Berkeley outlines his views in the following passages taken from *A Treatise Concerning the Principles of Human Knowledge*.

Subjective idealism The belief that only ideas and conscious minds have actual existence.

((•⃝ **Listen** to the **Podcast** *John Campbell on Berkeley's Puzzle* on **mysearchlab.com**

>
>
> **George Berkeley,** from *A Treatise Concerning the Principles of Human Knowledge*
>
> 1. It is evident to any one who takes a survey of the objects of human knowledge, that they are either ideas actually imprinted on the senses; or else such as are perceived by attending to the passions and operations of the mind; or lastly, ideas formed by help

of memory and imagination—either compounding, dividing, or barely representing those originally perceived in the aforesaid ways. By sight I have the ideas of light and colours, with their several degrees and variations. By touch I perceive hard and soft, heat and cold, motion and resistance, and of all these more and less either as to quantity or degree. Smelling furnishes me with odours; the palate with tastes; and hearing conveys sounds to the mind in all their variety of tone and composition. And as several of these are observed to accompany each other, they come to be marked by one name, and so to be reputed as one thing. Thus, for example a certain colour, taste, smell, figure and consistence having been observed to go together, are accounted one distinct thing, signified by the name apple; other collections of ideas constitute a stone, a tree, a book, and the like sensible things—which as they are pleasing or disagreeable excite the passions of love, hatred, joy, grief, and so forth.

2. But, besides all that endless variety of ideas or objects of knowledge, there is likewise something which knows or perceives them, and exercises divers operations, as willing, imagining, remembering, about them. This perceiving, active being is what I call mind, spirit, soul, or myself. By which words I do not denote any one of my ideas, but a thing entirely distinct from them, wherein, they exist, or, which is the same thing, whereby they are perceived for the existence of an idea consists in being perceived.

3. That neither our thoughts, nor passions, nor ideas formed by the imagination, exist without the mind, is what everybody will allow. And it seems no less evident that the various sensations or ideas imprinted on the sense, however blended or combined together (that is, whatever objects they compose), cannot exist otherwise than in a mind perceiving them.—I think an intuitive knowledge may be obtained of this by any one that shall attend to what is meant by the term exists, when applied to sensible things. The table I write on I say exists, that is, I see and feel it; and if I were out of my study I should say it existed—meaning thereby that if I was in my study I might perceive it, or that some other spirit actually does perceive it. There was an odour, that is, it was smelt; there was a sound, that is, it was heard; a colour or figure, and it was perceived by sight or touch. This is all that I can understand by these and the like expressions. For as to what is said of the absolute existence of unthinking things without any relation to their being perceived, that seems perfectly unintelligible. Their *esse* is *percepi*, nor is it possible they should have any existence out of the minds or thinking things which perceive them.

What is the role of perception in knowing?
For Berkeley, an object such as an apple has no "existence outside of the minds or thinking things which perceive them." How does he defend this perplexing idea?

4. It is indeed an opinion strangely prevailing amongst men, that houses, mountains, rivers, and in a word all sensible objects, have an existence, natural or real, distinct from their being perceived by the understanding. But, with how great an assurance and acquiescence soever this principle may be entertained in the world, yet whoever shall find in his heart to call it in question may, if I mistake not, perceive it to involve a manifest contradiction. For, what are the fore-mentioned objects but the things we perceive by sense? And what do we perceive besides our own ideas or sensations? And is it not plainly repugnant that any one of these, or any combination of them, should exist unperceived?

One has to admire Berkeley's self-confidence in his ideas (or his sense of playfulness, perhaps), contending that a belief in an independently existing external world is "an opinion strangely prevailing amongst men," and that the misguided notion that anything should continue to exist unperceived by a mind is an idea that is "plainly repugnant." But the force of his argument clearly has to be reckoned with: Accepting Locke's empiricist causal theory of perception, isn't the unavoidable endpoint, *esse est percipi?*

Berkeley goes on to attack Locke's idea of "resemblances" directly, arguing in the following passages that it makes no sense to presume that there are things outside of the mind "like" our ideas—for "nothing is like an idea but another idea."

George Berkeley,
from *A Treatise Concerning the Principles of Human Knowledge*

6. Some truths there are so near and obvious to the mind that a man need only open his eyes to see them. Such I take this important one to be, viz., that all the choir of heaven and furniture of the earth, in a word all those bodies which compose the mighty frame of the world, have not any subsistence without a mind, that their being is to be perceived or known; that consequently so long as they are not actually perceived by me, or do not exist in my mind or that of any other created spirit, they must either have no existence at all, or else subsist in the mind of some Eternal Spirit—it being perfectly unintelligible, and involving all the absurdity of abstraction, to attribute to any single part of them an existence independent of a spirit. To be convinced of which, the reader need only reflect, and try to separate in his own thoughts the being of a sensible thing from its being perceived . . .

8. But, say you, though the ideas themselves do not exist without the mind, yet there may be things like them, whereof they are copies or resemblances, which things exist without the mind in an unthinking substance. I answer, an idea can be like nothing but an idea; a colour or figure can be like nothing but another colour or figure. If we look but ever so little into our thoughts, we shall find it impossible for us to conceive a likeness except only between our ideas. Again, I ask whether those supposed originals or external things, of which our ideas are the pictures or representations, be themselves perceivable or no? If they are, then they are ideas and we have gained our point; but if you say they are not, I appeal to any one whether it be sense to assert a colour is like something which is invisible; hard or soft, like something which is intangible; and so of the rest.

Berkeley next takes aim at Locke's distinction between "primary" and "secondary" qualities, making the persuasive point that the same arguments apply to both and that, in any case, our mind views them as inextricably tied together, posing the challenge: "But I desire any one to reflect and try whether he can, by any abstraction of thought, conceive the extension and motion of a body without all other sensible qualities."

George Berkeley,
from *A Treatise Concerning the Principles of Human Knowledge*

9. Some there are who make a distinction betwixt primary and secondary qualities. By the former they mean extension, figure, motion, rest, solidity or impenetrability, and number; by the latter they denote all other sensible qualities, as colours, sounds, tastes, and so forth. The ideas we have of these they acknowledge not to be the resemblances of anything existing without the mind, or unperceived, but they will have our ideas of the primary qualities to be patterns or images of things which exist without the mind, in an unthinking substance which they call Matter. By Matter, therefore, we are to understand an inert, senseless substance, in which extension, figure, and motion do actually subsist. But it is evident from what we have already shown, that extension, figure, and motion are only ideas existing in the mind, and that an idea can be like nothing but another idea, and that consequently neither they nor their archetypes can exist in an unperceiving substance. Hence, it is plain that the very notion of what is called Matter or corporeal substance, involves a contradiction in it. . . .

15. In short, let any one consider those arguments which are thought manifestly to prove that colours and taste exist only in the mind, and he shall find they may with

equal force be brought to prove the same thing of extension, figure, and motion. Though it must be confessed this method of arguing does not so much prove that there is no extension or colour in an outward object, as that we do not know by sense which is the true extension or colour of the object. But the arguments foregoing plainly shew it to be impossible that any colour or extension at all, or other sensible quality whatsoever, should exist in an unthinking subject without the mind, or in truth, that there should be any such thing as an outward object. . . .

But doesn't it make sense to assume some sort of independently existing "substance" that is responsible for our mental ideas? Predictably, Berkeley gives a vehement "no!" There are only two ways we can be aware of such substances:

- *Through our senses:* But, because our senses only produce mental ideas, they cannot, by definition, provide any indication of possible external "substances."
- *Through reason:* But even "the very patrons of Matter" (as Berkeley playfully terms Locke and others) admit the lack of necessary connection between mental ideas and external substances.

18. But, though it were possible that solid, figured, movable substances may exist without the mind, corresponding to the ideas we have of bodies, yet how is it possible for us to know this? Either we must know it by sense or by reason. As for our senses, by them we have the knowledge only of our sensations, ideas, or those things that are immediately perceived by sense, call them what you will: but they do not inform us that things exist without the mind, or unperceived, like to those which are perceived. This the materialists themselves acknowledge. It remains therefore that if we have any knowledge at all of external things, it must be by reason, inferring their existence from what is immediately perceived by sense. But what reason can induce us to believe the existence of bodies without the mind, from what we perceive, since the very patrons of Matter themselves do not pretend there is any necessary connexion betwixt them and our ideas?

George Berkeley, from *A Treatise Concerning the Principles of Human Knowledge*

Berkeley, once again, turns the commonly accepted way of viewing the world on its head, asserting that believing in an external world "must needs be a very precarious opinion; since it is to suppose, without any reason at all, that God has created innumerable beings that are entirely useless, and serve to no manner of purpose."

Finally, Berkeley acknowledges some of the inherent difficulties with his subjective idealist view of knowledge and reality. A common objection he encountered was the contention by people that his account of reality simply doesn't conform to common sense. We don't speak about eating or wearing "ideas"; we speak about eating food and wearing clothes—things, not ideas. Berkeley's response is direct: His priority is not to make people feel comfortable but to articulate a view of the world that he believes to be demonstrably true. His concepts, not the words used to describe his concepts, are significant. As long as people agree with his view of reality, it doesn't matter to him what language they use to describe his way of seeing things.

George Berkeley, from *A Treatise Concerning the Principles of Human Knowledge*

But after all, say you, it sounds very harsh to say we eat and drink ideas, and are clothed with ideas. I acknowledge it does so—the word idea not being used in common discourse to signify the several combinations of sensible qualities which are called things; and it is certain that any expression which varies from the familiar use of language will seem harsh and ridiculous. But this doth not concern the truth of the proposition, which in other words is no more than to say, we are fed and clothed with those things which we perceive immediately by our senses. The hardness or softness, the colour, taste, warmth, figure, or suchlike qualities, which combined together constitute the several sorts of victuals and apparel, have been shewn to exist only in the mind that perceives them; and this is all that is meant by calling them ideas; which word if it was as ordinarily used as thing, would sound no harsher nor more ridiculous than it. I am not for disputing about the propriety, but the truth of the expression. If therefore you agree with me that we eat and drink and are clad with the immediate objects of sense, which cannot exist unperceived or without the mind, I shall readily grant it is more proper or conformable to custom that they should be called things rather than ideas.

God taking the measure of the universe. Bishop Berkeley rests his epistemology on the belief that the world reflects the laws of nature as perceived by God, "author of nature." The poet and artist William Blake echoes this idea in his painting *Ancient of Days*. Do you find this to be a compelling argument?

Berkeley also deals with a second somewhat more serious objection to his views. Although the only things that supposedly exist according to his theory are minds and ideas, how do we account for the fact that we have no control over many of the most vivid ideas (of what appears to be the external world) that we experience? That is, they simply present themselves to our minds? And not only that: These ideas present themselves as a coherent whole, obeying what we observe to be certain regularities that we call the "laws of nature"? Berkeley finally concedes: The things of the world are nothing other than ideas in the mind of God, the "Author of nature," produced by "the will of another and more powerful spirit":

> There is a God, therefore he perceives all things: sensible things do really exist; and if they really exist, they are necessarily perceived by an infinite mind; therefor there is an infinite mind, or God.

Having consistently maintained his subjective idealism up until this point, Berkeley finally capitulates to conventional thought, bringing in God as a vehicle for insuring the existence of the external world. His last-minute failure of resolve was given a humorous statement by the English writer and priest Ronald Knox (1888–1957):

> There was a young man who said, "God
> Must think it exceedingly odd
> If he finds that this tree
> Continues to be
> When there's no one about in the Quad."

Reply

> Dear Sir:
>
> Your astonishment's odd:
> I am always about in the Quad.
> And that's why the tree
> Will continue to be,
> Since observed by
> >   Yours faithfully,
> >   GOD

Skepticism A school of thought that casts doubt on the possibility of achieving genuine knowledge.

< READING CRITICALLY >

Analyzing Berkeley's Subjective Idealism

- What is your reaction to Berkeley's claim that the only things that exist in the universe are minds and ideas that exist in the minds? If you are not comfortable with his eliminating an independently existing external world, how would you go about refuting his ideas?

- Unfortunately, Berkeley's major writings were published after Locke's death. If he had still been alive, how do you think Locke would have responded to Berkeley's criticism of his views?

- Samuel Johnson, a famous English writer who lived at the same time as Berkeley, responded to Berkeley's subjectivist idealism by kicking a stone and sending it flying into the air, while saying, "I refute him thus." Do you think this is a persuasive "argument" by Johnson? Why or why not?

6.4 Understanding Reality Demands Skepticism: Hume

The Scottish philosopher **David Hume** is widely considered to be one of the greatest philosophical skeptics of all time. (In epistemology, **skepticism** includes positions such as doubting all assumptions until proved or claiming that no knowledge is possible in any circumstances.) We first ran into his wrecking-ball logic in Chapter 3, where he cheerfully maintains that the "self" as a continuous identity through time simply does not exist. Instead, what we consider the "self" is really just a transient bundle of fragmentary sensations that parade across "the stage" of consciousness in a random stream.

Hume's skepticism naturally permeates his general views on epistemology as well. In fact, in the evolution of doubt and skepticism that began with Descartes and continued on through Locke and Berkeley, Hume can be seen as the final stage, announced with an emphatic exclamation point. As contrary as they are to established beliefs, Hume's views demand to be taken seriously, for they are argued with compelling reasoning and rigorous consistency. Writing 200 years later, the influential British philosopher Bertrand Russell observed about Hume's skepticism:

David Hume (1711–1776). This Scottish philosopher's skeptical examinations of religion, ethics, and history were to make him a controversial eighteenth-century figure. A prolific writer, his works include *Enquiry Concerning Human Understanding* (1748) and *Dialogue Concerning Natural Religion* (1779), held for publication until after his death.

To refute him has been, ever since he wrote, a favorite pastime among metaphysicians. For my part, I find none of their refutations convincing; nevertheless, I cannot but hope that something less skeptical than Hume's system may be discoverable.

Descartes championed radical doubt in epistemology, posing the possibility that we are caught in a dream and manipulated by an "evil genius." But Descartes was able to escape (in his own mind, anyway) from this skeptical nightmare by means of reason's *cogito, ergo sum* and the spiritual conviction that God would not permit a universe based on deception and illusion.

Locke took Descartes' radical doubt and applied it to an empiricist framework, concluding that all we can know are the ideas presented to the conscious mind. Hence, there is no evidence that an external world exists independently of the ideas we have of it, and substance is "something we know not what." Locke distinguished "primary qualities" (which reside in the external objects) from "secondary qualities," which reside only in our minds, a distinction that supports the existence of an external world. And to make sure that he avoided the unpalatable possibility of extreme skepticism, Locke also brought God into his epistemology to save the day—or the reality of the external world, anyway. According to Locke, God would not deceive us regarding the existence of an external world. And, he added for good measure, common sense tells us that such a world exists.

Berkeley, proposing an epistemology of subjective idealism, had no patience with two of Locke's three arguments for the existence of an external world. It is impossible to make a clear distinction between primary and secondary qualities, Berkeley contended: They are all ideas that exist only in our minds. And he soundly rejected Locke's commonsense argument for an external reality as being philosophically inconsistent with Locke's empiricist principles. No, Berkeley was convinced that only minds and ideas in minds exist: It is illogical and unsupportable to even consider the existence of an external world. Until . . . just before the external world is to be executed, an order of clemency is received: Not from the governor, but from God. The reality of the external world (and the laws of science, by the way) are preserved because they always exist in the mind of God.

When Hume storms onto the scene, he is outraged at what he considers to be the worst kind of philosophical hypocrisy. There is no empirical or rational evidence for God or traditional metaphysics, he thunders, and we have no good reason to believe in the laws of science that are used to organize, explain, and predict events in our world. Hume ends his monumental work, *An Enquiry Concerning Human Understanding*, with one of the most blistering attacks on God and metaphysics in the history of philosophy:

When we run over libraries, persuaded of these principles, what havoc must we make? If we take in our hand any volume; of divinity or school metaphysics, for instance; let us ask, Does it contain any abstract reasoning concerning quantity or number? No. Does it contain any experimental reasoning concerning matter of fact and existence? No. Commit it then to the flames: for it can contain nothing but sophistry and illusion.

The following passages from this same work detail his core arguments. In addition to attacking the possibility of knowing an external world, he also takes aim at two principles that are integral to understanding such a world:

- The *principle of universal causation*, which contends that every event has a cause or causes that can be discovered through observation or systematic investigation.
- The *principle of induction*, which contends that, using our understanding of causal relations, we can make justifiable inferences and predictions about future events.

Listen to the **Podcast**
Barry Stroud on Skepticism on
mysearchlab.com

So fasten your philosophical seat belts: Here comes David Hume.

David Hume, from *An Enquiry Concerning Human Understanding*

Section II—Of the Origin of Ideas

Every one will readily allow, that there is a considerable difference between the perceptions of the mind, when a man feels the pain of excessive heat, or the pleasure of moderate warmth, and when he afterwards recalls to his memory this sensation, or anticipates it by his imagination. These faculties may mimic or copy the perceptions of the senses; but they never can entirely reach the force and vivacity of the original sentiment. The utmost we say of them, even when they operate with greatest vigour, is, that they represent their object in so lively a manner, that we could almost say we feel or see it: But, except the mind be disordered by disease or madness, they never can arrive at such a pitch of vivacity, as to render these perceptions altogether undistinguishable. All the colours of poetry, however splendid, can never paint natural objects in such a manner as to make the description be taken for a real landskip. The most lively thought is still inferior to the dullest sensation.

We may observe a like distinction to run through all the other perceptions of the mind. A man in a fit of anger, is actuated in a very different manner from one who only thinks of that emotion. If you tell me, that any person is in love, I easily understand your meaning, and from a just conception of his situation; but never can mistake that conception for the real disorders and agitations of the passion. When we reflect on our past sentiments and affections, our thought is a faithful mirror, and copies its objects truly; but the colours which it employs are faint and dull, in comparison of those in which our original perceptions were clothed. It requires no nice discernment or metaphysical head to mark the distinction between them.

Here therefore we may divide all the perceptions of the mind into two classes or species, which are distinguished by their different degrees of force and vivacity. The less forcible and lively are commonly denominated Thoughts or Ideas. The other species want a name in our language, and in most others; I suppose, because it was not requisite for any, but philosophical purposes, to rank them under a general term or appellation. Let us, therefore, use a little freedom, and call them Impressions; employing that word in a sense somewhat different from the usual. By the term impression, then, I mean all our more lively perceptions, when we hear, or see, or feel, or love, or hate, or desire, or will. And impressions are distinguished from ideas, which are the less lively perceptions, of which we are conscious, when we reflect on any of those sensations or movements above mentioned.

As an empiricist, Hume wants to differentiate the various elements in our experience, and his empiricist criteria are "lively" and "vivid." "Impressions" refer to those phenomena directly experienced through the senses, or emotions that are directly felt, and they are the most lively and vivid. "Ideas," on the other hand, are the product of our memory or imagination, and they lack the liveliness and vividness of impressions. So, for example, the immediate perceptions of a sweltering hot day or a breathtaking sunset possesses a liveliness and vividness that the memory or imagination simply cannot duplicate. Similarly, no one is likely to confuse serenely contemplating the *idea* of love and directly experiencing "the real disorders and agitations of the passion." However, despite their difference in liveliness and vividness, both impressions and ideas are contents of the human mind and in no way suggest or validate the existence of an external world.

David Hume, from *An Enquiry Concerning Human Understanding*

Skeptical Doubts Concerning the Operations of the Understanding Part 1

All the objects of human reason or enquiry may naturally be divided into two kinds, to wit, *Relations of Ideas*, and *Matters of Fact*. Of the first kind are the sciences of Geometry, Algebra, and Arithmetic; and in short, every affirmation which is either intuitively or demonstratively certain. *That the square of the hypotenuse is equal to the square of the two sides*, is a proposition which expresses a relation between these figures. *That three times five is equal to the half of thirty*, expresses a relation between these numbers. Propositions of this kind are discoverable by the mere operation of thought, without dependence on what is anywhere existent in the universe. Though there never were a circle or triangle in nature, the truths demonstrated by Euclid would for ever retain their certainty and evidence.

Matters of fact, which are the second objects of human reason, are not ascertained in the same manner; nor is our evidence of their truth, however great, of a like nature with the foregoing. The contrary of every matter of fact is still possible; because it can never imply a contradiction, and is conceived by the mind with the same facility and distinctness, as if ever so conformable to reality. *That the sun will not rise to-morrow* is no less intelligible a proposition, and implies no more contradiction than the affirmation, *that it will rise*. We should in vain, therefore, attempt to demonstrate its falsehood. Were it demonstratively false, it would imply a contradiction, and could never be distinctly conceived by the mind.

Hume's division of human knowledge into "relations of ideas" and "matters of fact," along with his insistence that every justifiable belief meet the standards of one or the other, has sometimes been referred to in philosophy as "Hume's fork" (as in "fork in the road"). One fork, the "relations of ideas," includes the principles of mathematics and logic as well as simple tautologies ("A bachelor is an unmarried man"). These principles are discoverable by reason, without reference to experience, and they do not permit logical contradictions. For example, it doesn't make sense to simultaneously maintain that "A triangle has three sides" and "A triangle *does not* have three sides."

The second fork, "matters of fact," can be confirmed (or disconfirmed) by appeal to our experience. Unlike "relations of ideas," they necessarily involve sense experience, and their statements *do* permit logical contradictions, according to Hume. He believes it does make sense to maintain that "It will be cloudy tomorrow" and "It will *not* be cloudy tomorrow" in the sense that these two statements do not entail a *logical* contradiction.

But Hume is not about to leave things at this level of understanding. He wants to investigate the epistemological foundations of "matters of fact," an exploration that ultimately leads to his radical skepticism regarding empirical knowledge. But for now, he is committed to a completely open and honest inquiry, which he is convinced will "prove useful, by exciting curiosity, and destroying that implicit faith and security, which is the bane of all reasoning and free enquiry." He begins his analysis with what he considers to be a keystone of knowledge, the principle of "cause and effect."

All reasonings concerning matter of fact seem to be founded on the relation of *Cause and Effect*. By means of that relation alone we can go beyond the evidence of our memory and senses. If you were to ask a man, why he believes any matter of fact, which is absent; for instance, that his friend is in the country, or in France; he would give you a reason; and this reason would be some other fact; as a letter received from him, or the knowledge of his former resolutions and promises. A man finding a watch or any other machine in a desert island, would conclude that there had once been men in that island. All our reasonings concerning fact are of the same nature. And here it is constantly supposed that there is a connexion between the present fact and that which is inferred from it. Were there nothing to bind them together, the inference would be entirely precarious. The hearing of an articulate voice and rational discourse in the dark assures us of the presence of some person: Why? Because these are the effects of the human make and fabric, and closely connected with it. If we anatomize all the other reasonings of this nature, we shall find that they are founded on the relation of cause and effect, and that this relation is either near or remote, direct or collateral. Heat and light are collateral effects of fire, and the one effect may justly be inferred from the other.

If we would satisfy ourselves, therefore, concerning the nature of that evidence, which assures us of matters of fact, we must enquire how we arrive at the knowledge of cause and effect.

I shall venture to affirm, as a general proposition, which admits of no exception, that the knowledge of this relation is not, in any instance, attained by reasonings *a priori*; but arises entirely from experience, when we find that any particular objects are constantly conjoined with each other. Let an object be presented to a man of ever so strong natural reason and abilities; if that object be entirely new to him, he will not be able, by the most accurate examination of its sensible qualities, to discover any of its causes or effects. Adam, though his rational faculties be supposed, at the very first, entirely perfect, could not have inferred from the fluidity and transparency of water that it would suffocate him, or from the light and warmth of fire that it would consume him. No object ever discovers, by the qualities which appear to the senses, either the causes which produced it, or the effects which will arise from it; nor can our reason, unassisted by experience, ever draw any inference concerning real existence and matter of fact.

This proposition, *that causes and effects are discoverable, not by reason but by experience*, will readily be admitted with regard to such objects, as we remember to have once been altogether unknown to us; since we must be conscious of the utter inability, which we then lay under, of foretelling what would arise from them. Present two smooth pieces of marble to a man who has no tincture of natural philosophy; he will never discover that they will adhere together in such a manner as to require great force to separate them in a direct line, while they make so small a resistance to a lateral pressure. Such events, as bear little analogy to the common course of nature, are also readily confessed to be known only by experience; nor does any man imagine that the explosion of gunpowder, or the attraction of a loadstone, could ever be discovered

David Hume, from *An Enquiry Concerning Human Understanding*

Is breathing water dangerous? How do you know? Hume argues that we cannot know simply by observing water that it could suffocate us, nor can we infer that danger from using reason alone. Where does this observation lead him?

by arguments *a priori*. In like manner, when an effect is supposed to depend upon an intricate machinery or secret structure of parts, we make no difficulty in attributing all our knowledge of it to experience. Who will assert that he can give the ultimate reason, why milk or bread is proper nourishment for a man, not for a lion or a tiger?

But the same truth may not appear, at first sight, to have the same evidence with regard to events, which have become familiar to us from our first appearance in the world, which bear a close analogy to the whole course of nature, and which are supposed to depend on the simple qualities of objects, without any secret structure of parts. We are apt to imagine that we could discover these effects by the mere operation of our reason, without experience. We fancy, that were we brought on a sudden into this world, we could at first have inferred that one Billiard-ball would communicate motion to another upon impulse; and that we needed not to have waited for the event, in order to pronounce with certainty concerning it. Such is the influence of custom, that, where it is strongest, it not only covers our natural ignorance, but even conceals itself, and seems not to take place, merely because it is found in the highest degree.

But to convince us that all the laws of nature, and all the operations of bodies without exception, are known only by experience, the following reflections may, perhaps, suffice. Were any object presented to us, and were we required to pronounce concerning the effect, which will result from it, without consulting past observation; after what manner, I beseech you, must the mind proceed in this operation? It must invent or imagine some event, which it ascribes to the object as its effect; and it is plain that this invention must be entirely arbitrary. The mind can never possibly find the effect in the supposed cause, by the most accurate scrutiny and examination. For the effect is totally different from the cause, and consequently can never be discovered in it. Motion in the second Billiard-ball is a quite distinct event from motion in the first; nor is there anything in the one to suggest the smallest hint of the other. A stone or piece of metal raised into the air, and left without any support, immediately falls: but to consider the matter *a priori*, is there anything we discover in this situation which can beget the idea of a downward, rather than an upward, or any other motion, in the stone or metal?

And as the first imagination or invention of a particular effect, in all natural operations, is arbitrary, where we consult not experience; so must we also esteem the supposed tie or connexion between the cause and effect, which binds them together, and renders it impossible that any other effect could result from the operation of that cause. When I see, for instance, a Billiard-ball moving in a straight line towards another; even suppose motion in the second ball should by accident be suggested to me, as the result of their contact or impulse; may I not conceive, that a hundred different events might as well follow from that cause? May not both these balls remain at absolute rest? May not the first ball return in a straight line, or leap off from the second in any line or direction? All these suppositions are consistent and conceivable. Why then should we give the preference to one, which is no more consistent or conceivable than the rest? All our reasonings *a priori* will never be able to show us any foundation for this preference.

In a word, then, every effect is a distinct event from its cause. It could not, therefore, be discovered in the cause, and the first invention or conception of it, *a priori*, must be entirely arbitrary. And even after it is suggested, the conjunction of it with the cause must appear equally arbitrary, since there are always many other effects, which, to reason, must seem fully as consistent and natural. In vain, therefore, should we pretend to determine any single event, or infer any cause or effect, without the assistance of observation and experience.

> **The mind can never possibly find the effect in the supposed cause, by the most accurate scrutiny and examination. For the effect is totally different from the cause, and consequently can never be discovered in it.**

Hume explicitly acknowledges that our belief in the principle of cause and effect is woven into every aspect of our lives, and he provides unique and memorable examples to illustrate this:

- Receiving a letter confirms that your friend is in France.
- Finding a watch on a desert island suggests the previous presence of men.
- Hearing an articulate human voice in the dark convinces us that a person is there.
- Feeling the heat from a fire suggests that the fire is the cause of the heat.

Hume's first goal is to prove conclusively that our belief in cause and effect does not meet the criteria of his first "fork," "relations of ideas." There is no way that reason can inform us of these alleged causal connections between events. To see this, we need only imagine someone coming across a potential causal relation for the first time to understand that reason is useless in the face of such a situation. Again, Hume provides us with a sparkling example to illustrate his point. Imagine, he proposes, Adam coming across water for the first time: Despite his rational faculties, could he possibly be expected to infer from its "fluidity and transparency" that it would suffocate him? Or analogously, that the fire providing light and warmth would consume him? Absolutely not! Experience is required to make such inferences: ". . . nor can our reason, unassisted by experience, ever draw any inference concerning real existence and matter of fact."

Most people have difficulty appreciating this fact because of our familiarity with causally associated events in the world. We know that magnets attract iron, that gunpowder will explode when ignited, and that billiard balls will react in predictable ways when they strike one another. But what of completely new experiences: Suppose you were asked to "give the ultimate reason why milk or bread is proper nourishment for a man, not for a lion or tiger?" Lacking specialized knowledge, you would be at a complete loss to make this causal connection. As a result, we must conclude that the principle of cause and effect cannot be validated through the use of reason.

But Hume is not content to eliminate cause and effect from just one of his two forks of knowledge: He wants to eliminate it from the other fork, "matters of fact," as well, for which he is already laying the conceptual groundwork.

Is the principle of cause and effect unfounded?
Hume used the example of colliding billiard balls to argue that there is nothing in experience to support a belief in the principle of cause and effect because every causal event is independent of every other causal event. Do you agree with his reasoning? Why? (*English School*, The Billiard Room. *Oil on canvas. © Yale Center for British Art, Paul Mellon Collection, USA/ Bridgeman Art Library.*)

David Hume, from
*An Enquiry Concerning
Human Understanding*

> The mind can never possibly find the effect in the supposed cause, by the most accurate scrutiny and examination. For the effect is totally different from the cause, and consequently can never be discovered in it. Motion in the second Billiard-ball is a quite distinct event from motion in the first; nor is there anything in the one to suggest the smallest hint of the other. . . . In a word, then, every effect is a distinct event from its cause.

It is apparent where Hume is headed. Not only doesn't reason provide justification for explaining cause-and-effect connections, but experience isn't going to be able to either. When you independently examine a "cause" and an "effect," it is impossible to discover any properties that announce themselves as "causes" or "effects." It is only because these events happen to be conjoined in a particular way that we make the inference that they are causally related. But there is absolutely nothing in our direct observation of these objects and events to provide support for this inference. As a result, failing both "forks" in Hume's test for knowledge, it is not possible for us to say that we have knowledge of cause-and-effect relations in the world. It's a startling conclusion, with far-reaching reverberations. Welcome to Hume's radical skepticism!

Next on Hume's "hit list" is the "principle of induction," the type of reasoning in which we infer that "the water in ice cube trays always turns to ice when I place them in the freezer; so, when I place this new ice cube tray in the freezer, the water will also turn to ice." In other words, the "principle of induction" is the way we predict future events based on past experiences. And because these past experiences are generally based on the principle of cause and effect, it is apparent that Hume is going to discover the same epistemological flaws in the "principle of induction" as he found in that of cause and effect.

David Hume, from *An
Enquiry Concerning
Human Understanding*

Skeptical Doubts Concerning the Operations of the Understanding Part 2

. . . As to past *Experience*, it can be allowed to give *direct* and *certain* information of those precise objects only, and that precise period of time, which fell under its cognizance: but why this experience should be extended to future times, and to other objects, which for aught we know, may be only in appearance similar; this is the main question on which I would insist. The bread, which I formerly eat, nourished me; that is, a body of such sensible qualities was, at that time, endued with such secret powers: but does it follow, that other bread must also nourish me at another time, and that like sensible qualities must always be attended with like secret powers? The consequence seems nowise necessary. At least, it must be acknowledged that there is here a consequence drawn by the mind; that there is a certain step taken; a process of thought, and an inference, which wants to be explained. These two propositions are far from being the same. *I have found that such an object has always been attended with such an effect*, and *I foresee, that other objects, which are, in appearance, similar, will be attended with similar effects*. I shall allow, if you please, that the one proposition may justly be inferred from the other: I know, in fact, that it always is inferred. But if you insist that the

Why eat healthy? Questioning a basic assumption. Morgan Spurlock put this idea to the test in the documentary *Super Size Me,* when he subsists purely on fast food for thirty days.

inference is made by a chain of reasoning, I desire you to produce that reasoning. The connexion between these propositions is not intuitive. There is required a medium, which may enable the mind to draw such an inference, if indeed it be drawn by reasoning and argument. What that medium is, I must confess, passes my comprehension; and it is incumbent on those to produce it, who assert that it really exists, and is the origin of all our conclusions concerning matter of fact.

Hume states his case plainly. Our senses inform us that in the past, eating bread has been associated with our personal nourishment. We commonly believe that eating the bread *caused* our nourishment, but Hume believes we never actually witness the causal connection: We assume it to be there. But now it is apparent how Hume's same form of analysis applies to induction. Because we believe that eating bread has resulted in our healthy nourishment in the past, we believe that continuing to eat other things that resemble bread will nourish our body in the future. But again, Hume queries, where is the actual causal connection that warrants this belief? If we confine ourselves to analyzing our sense experience, such a connection is nowhere to be found. Hume details the "principle of induction":

- *I have found that such an object has always been attended with such an effect.*
- *I foresee, that other objects, which are, in appearance, similar, will be attended with similar effects.*

And then his query:

I shall allow, if you please, that the one proposition may justly be inferred from the other: I know, in fact, that it always is inferred. But if you insist that the inference is made by a chain of reasoning, I desire you to produce that reasoning. The connexion between these propositions is not intuitive.

David Hume, from *An Enquiry Concerning Human Understanding*

In other words, Hume freely acknowledges that we commonly make such inductive inferences: It is just that when called on to produce the actual connections that warrant such reasoning, we are unable to.

Critics of Hume's skepticism were no doubt quick to confront him with the apparent contradiction between his philosophical beliefs and the assumptions about the world reflected in the way he lived his life, along the lines of: "But Hume, isn't your skepticism refuted by the fact that you live your life as if the principles of cause and effect and induction were legitimate?" Hume's response? As a human being ("an agent") I am comfortable living my life assuming these principles to be warranted. *However*, as a philosopher, it is my responsibility to explore beneath the surface of unreflective existence, "to learn the foundation of this inference." And to this point, "no enquiry has yet been able to remove my difficulty, or give me satisfaction in a matter of such importance."

My practice, you say, refutes my doubts. But you mistake the purport of my question. As an agent, I am quite satisfied in the point; but as a philosopher, who has some share of curiosity, I will not say scepticism, I want to learn the foundation of this inference. No reading, no enquiry has yet been able to remove my difficulty, or give me satisfaction in a matter of such importance. Can I do better than propose the difficulty to the public, even though, perhaps, I have small hopes of obtaining a solution? We shall at least, by this means, be sensible of our ignorance, if we do not augment our knowledge.

David Hume, from *An Enquiry Concerning Human Understanding*

Hume goes on to elaborate this point in the following passage:

David Hume, from *An Enquiry Concerning Human Understanding*

Nature will always maintain her rights, and prevail in the end over any abstract reasoning whatsoever. Though we should conclude, for instance, as in the foregoing section, that, in all reasonings from experience, there is a step taken by the mind which is not supported by any argument or process of the understanding; there is no danger that these reasonings, on which almost all knowledge depends, will ever be affected by such a discovery. If the mind be not engaged by argument to make this step, it must be induced by some other principle of equal weight and authority; and that principle will preserve its influence as long as human nature remains the same. What that principle is may well be worth the pains of enquiry.

"Nature will always maintain her rights, and prevail in the end over any abstract reasoning whatsoever." That's an intriguing statement, particularly coming from one of the greatest skeptics of all time. It implicitly recognizes the limits of reason in the face of lived experience ("nature"). Yet though our reasoning ability may not solve all of nature's mysteries, that in no way absolves us of the intellectual responsibility to probe, analyze, and attempt to understand the foundations of knowledge and reality. That is why Hume finds philosophical appeals to "common sense" by thinkers like Locke to be so intellectually hypocritical. Going *beyond* common sense for more compelling explanations is precisely what philosophers are supposed to do! For Hume, the most rigorous and honest application of reason has led him to the conclusion that there is no sound reason to believe in the principles of cause and effect and induction. Instead, we must resign ourselves to the fact that these principles reflect custom and habit, not rational necessity. Nor, in fact, do we have a legitimate philosophical foundation for believing in the existence of an external world, the "self," or God. Does this mean that, lacking such rational evidence for the orderly and intelligible nature of the universe, that we should surrender ourselves to lives of quiet despondency? Just the opposite. In a famous passage that concludes his Treatise, Hume happily places his radical skepticism into the larger context of living one's life, acknowledging that after a delightful meal with friends, a few (or perhaps, more than a few) glasses of wine, and a congenial game of backgammon, his disturbing speculations "appear so cold, and strained, and ridiculous, that I cannot find in my heart to enter into them any farther."

David Hume, from *An Enquiry Concerning Human Understanding*

Most fortunately it happens, that since reason is incapable of dispelling these clouds, nature herself suffices to that purpose, and cures me of this philosophical melancholy and delirium, either by relaxing this bent of mind, or by some avocation, and lively impression of my senses, which obliterate all these chimeras. I dine, I play a game of backgammon, I converse, and am merry with my friends; and when after three or four hours' amusement, I would return to these speculations, they appear so cold, and strained, and ridiculous, that I cannot find in my heart to enter into them any farther.

Nevertheless, from a philosophical perspective, we are left with the profound question, "Can Hume's compelling case for skepticism be satisfactorily addressed?" Our next philosopher, Immanuel Kant, believes the answer is a resounding "yes!"

< READING CRITICALLY >

Analyzing Hume's Case for Skepticism

- Do you agree with Hume that appealing to the existence of God to support the belief that there is an external world (as Locke and Berkeley do) amounts to philosophical hypocrisy? Why or why not?

- Summarize Hume's arguments that it is impossible for us to ever have certain knowledge of the principle of cause and effect, whether we are rationalists or empiricists. Do you agree with his reasoning? Why or why not? Construct an argument to convince Hume that the principle of cause and effect is indeed valid, being sure to provide examples to support your point of view.

- Imagine that you truly believed that the principles of cause and effect and induction were in fact not "knowledge" at all but merely habitual associations. Would this conclusion influence any aspect of your life? Explain why or why not.

- Hume makes a sharp distinction between the skepticism of his philosophical reasoning and the contented optimism of the way he lives his life. What do you think of this "split" between rational/theoretical arguments and lived experience? Do you think that our choices in life should necessarily reflect our epistemological convictions? Describe an example to support your point of view.

- Hume believes that all metaphysical beliefs (that is, any belief not based on direct sense experience) should be "committed to the flames" because it cannot be empirically justified. This would include all beliefs regarding God, human freedom, universal moral laws, and so on. Do you agree with Hume? If not, explain how you would go about rebutting his arguments.

6.5 We Constitute Our World: Kant

We first encountered the brilliant German philosopher **Immanuel Kant** in Chapter 3, where we were introduced to his revolutionary views regarding epistemology and metaphysics. For Kant, the "self" is ultimately viewed as the synthesizing activity at the core of each one of us that integrates all of the disparate elements of experience into *our* experience, *our* world. He identifies this synthesizing "self" as the *"transcendental unity of apperception"*—not a very personal sounding term for an entity that we experience as intensely personal. But Kant is more concerned with constructing a metaphysical framework for the "self" that will account for the phenomena of experience, in particular what he describes as *"the unity of consciousness."*

In the same way that Hume's concept of the "self"—as a transitory stream of sensations moving randomly through the "theater" of our minds—is an integral part of his overall epistemology, so Kant's concept of the "self" is merely one dimension of an intricately and elaborately constructed philosophy that integrates both epistemology and metaphysics in a seamless integration. Kant's thinking is so revolutionary and profound in its implications that philosophies are typically classified as pre-Kantian

Immanuel Kant (1724–1804). A German philosopher considered by many to be the greatest thinker of the eighteenth century, Kant attempted to synthesize the two competing schools of the modern period, rationalism and empiricism, by showing the important role both experience and reason play in constructing our knowledge of the world. His works include the *Critique of Pure Reason* (1781; 1787) and *Prolegomena to Any Future Metaphysics* (1783).

and post-Kantian. Many of the modern movements in philosophy can trace their intellectual origins to Kant's thought, including existentialism, phenomenology, pragmatism, and linguistic philosophy.

At the time that Kant came onto the scene, the raging controversy in philosophy was between rationalism and empiricism, the twin movements that we have been exploring in these chapters through the philosophies of Plato and Descartes (rationalists) as well as Locke, Berkeley, and Hume (empiricists). Rationalists were convinced that genuine knowledge is best achieved through our rational capacities, whereas empiricists were equally certain that all knowledge is derived from sense experience. As we have seen, while the rationalists viewed the human mind as an active agent—reflecting, analyzing, deducing—the empiricists viewed the mind as a passive receiver of impressions and experiences.

Both approaches are vulnerable to serious conceptual problems and challenging questions when it comes to their ability to construct a coherent, compelling theory of knowledge. Once Descartes introduces the "evil genius" as a vehicle for his radical doubt of virtually everything, it's difficult for him to banish the "evil genius" from his epistemological kingdom of rational certainty. And the epistemological regression displayed in the thinking of Locke, Berkeley, and Hume culminates in the depressing conclusion that genuine knowledge of *anything* isn't possible: not of the external world, not scientific laws, not God, not even the "self." It is no wonder that Kant took the measure of this sad state of affairs and described it as "a scandal in philosophy."

But, unlike the other thinkers of his day, Kant also had the insight to fully appreciate the dire threat that Hume's virulent skepticism posed to epistemology and metaphysics in general, and to the "new physics" of science being championed by Isaac Newton and others. If Hume was right, and we are doomed to passively view the impressions and ideas presented to our minds, unable to connect them to each other, to an external world, or to anything else for that matter—then we might as well give up on discovering genuine and certain knowledge in any area of experience. It was the startling recognition of this threat that, in Kant's words, "first interrupted my dogmatic slumber, and gave my investigations in the field of speculative philosophy quite a new direction." Kant describes this intellectually galvanizing experience in the following passages from his *Prolegomena to Any Future Metaphysics* (1783).

Immanuel Kant, from *Prolegomena to Any Future Metaphysics*

However hasty and mistaken Hume's conclusion may appear, it was at least founded upon investigation, and this investigation deserved the concentrated attention of the brighter spirits of his day as well as determined efforts on their part to discover, if possible, a happier solution of the problem in the sense proposed by him, all of which would have speedily resulted in a complete reform of the science.

But Hume suffered the usual misfortune of metaphysicians, of not being understood. It is positively painful to see how utterly his opponents . . . missed the point of the problem; for while they were ever taking for granted that which he doubted, and demonstrating with zeal and often with impudence that which he never thought of doubting, they so misconstrued his valuable suggestion that everything remained in its old condition, as if nothing had happened.

* * *

Hume started from a single but important concept in Metaphysics, viz., that of Cause and Effect (including its derivatives force and action, etc.). He challenges reason, which pretends to have given birth to this idea from herself, to answer him by what right she thinks anything to be so constituted, that if that thing be posited, something else also must necessarily be posited; for this is the meaning of the concept of cause. He demonstrated irrefutably that it was perfectly impossible for reason to think a priori and by means of concepts a combination involving necessity. We cannot at all see why, in consequence of the existence of one thing, another must necessarily exist, or how the concept of such a combination can arise a priori. Hence he inferred, that reason was altogether deluded with reference to this concept, which she erroneously considered as one of her children, whereas in reality it was nothing but a bastard of imagination, impregnated by experience, which subsumed certain representations under the Law of Association, and mistook the subjective necessity of habit for an objective necessity arising from insight. Hence he inferred that reason had no power to think such combinations, even generally, because her concepts would then be purely fictitious, and all her pretended a priori cognitions nothing but common experiences marked with a false stamp. In plain language there is not, and cannot be, any such thing as metaphysics at all.

* * *

I openly confess, the suggestion of David Hume was the very thing, which many years ago first interrupted my dogmatic slumber, and gave my investigations in the field of speculative philosophy quite a new direction. I was far from following him in the conclusions at which he arrived by regarding, not the whole of his problem, but a part, which by itself can give us no information. If we start from a well-founded, but undeveloped, thought, which another has bequeathed to us, we may well hope by continued reflection to advance farther than the acute man, to whom we owe the first spark of light.

I therefore first tried whether Hume's objection could not be put into a general form, and soon found that the concept of the connection of cause and effect was by no means the only idea by which the understanding thinks the connection of things a priori, but rather that metaphysics consists altogether of such connections. I sought to ascertain their number, and when I had satisfactorily succeeded in this by starting from a single principle, I proceeded to the deduction of these concepts, which I was now certain were not deduced from experience, as Hume had apprehended, but sprang from the pure understanding. This deduction (which seemed impossible to my acute predecessor, which had never even occurred to any one else, though no one had hesitated to use the concepts without investigating the basis of their objective validity) was the most difficult task ever undertaken in the service of metaphysics; and the worst was that metaphysics, such as it then existed, could not assist me in the least, because this deduction alone can render metaphysics possible. But as soon as I had succeeded in solving Hume's problem not merely in a particular case, but with respect to the whole faculty of pure reason, I could proceed safely, though slowly, to determine the whole sphere of pure reason completely and from general principles, in its circumference as well as in its contents. This was required for metaphysics in order to construct its system according to a reliable method.

> " I openly confess, the suggestion of David Hume was the very thing, which many years ago first interrupted my dogmatic slumber, and gave my investigations in the field of speculative philosophy quite a new direction. "

Hume's Challenge to Philosophy

Hume's "Trojan Horse" into the bastion of rationalism is his devastating attack on the principle of cause and effect, which we examined in the previous section. Cause and effect is the bedrock principle of science. That's precisely what science attempts to achieve, articulating causal relationships between and among events in order to explain what has occurred in the past, what is happening in the present, and what will take place in the future. If we cannot rely on the power and authenticity of the cause-and-effect principle, then science is an endeavor doomed to epistemological

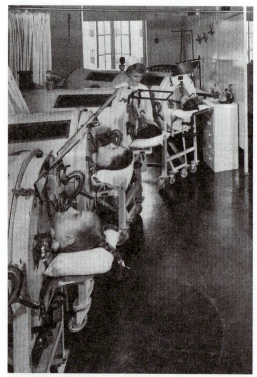

How does science discover? Polio treatment at the middle of the twentieth century, Baltimore Children's Hospital. The children in this photograph are each encased in an "iron lung," a machine that kept polio victims alive. Polio epidemics affected thousands in the first half of the twentieth century, until a vaccine was developed. Centuries earlier, Kant realized that if Hume's critique went unchallenged, it could have the effect of undermining scientific discovery and progress.

uncertainty. We will never be able to say that we "know" anything for sure about the physical world in which we live (nor, in fact, that there even *is* an external world).

The crux of Hume's critique of rationalism is as follows: When we examine events in the world that *seem* to be causally related, this assumption is in fact unwarranted if we rely solely on our reasoning abilities. Why? Because reason has no right to impose causal connections on events a priori—that is, independent of experience. Let's consider two examples that demonstrate this point:

- Imagine that you are introduced to a potential causal relationship regarding which you have no personal experience: for example, the behavior of electrons observed through an electron microscope; a potential chemical reaction involving the combining of a number of elements; or the potential effects on cancer cells of a new synthetic hormone. No matter how carefully you explore your a priori reasoning abilities independent of empirical experience, you will not be able to find a "rational intuition" that will inform you whether cause-and-effect relations exist.

- On the other hand, reflect on the times that you believed that your "rational intuition" was providing you with cause-and-effect knowledge that turned out to be bogus: for example, superstitious beliefs such as wearing your "lucky" shirt; experiencing an "intuition" regarding a dream you had and the lottery number; or acting on astrological advice. In these and countless other instances, people mistakenly believe that they "know" cause-and-effect relationships via their "rational intuitions," independent of confirming experiences.

To his great credit, Kant unflinchingly acknowledges the strength of these arguments with a vivid metaphor:

Immanuel Kant, from *Prolegomena to Any Future Metaphysics*

Hence he inferred, that reason was altogether deluded with reference to this concept (*cause and effect*), which she erroneously considered as one of her children, whereas in reality it was nothing but a bastard of imagination, impregnated by experience, which subsumed certain representations under the Law of Association, and mistook the subjective necessity of habit for an objective necessity arising from insight.

Describing the rationalist's attempt to have reason "give birth" to the principle of cause and effect as ". . . a bastard of the imagination, impregnated by experience" is strong language, to be sure! And yet Kant is convinced that to erect a legitimate framework for knowledge, he must begin by addressing directly and honestly Hume's incisive, relentless attack on the scope of reason, which he (Hume) considers to be the "slave of the passions." It is this open-eyed honesty that Kant found lacking in the other thinkers of the day, contemptible behavior that caused him to observe "was positively painful to see how utterly his opponents . . . missed the point of the problem."

Yet as concerned as Kant is to establish an irrefutable theory of knowledge that will serve as a legitimate grounding for modern science, he is just as intent on making sure this epistemological framework also incorporates other a priori knowledge. Kant considers such knowledge to be "metaphysical" in the sense that its ultimate justification and truth are based on reason, independent of sense experience, and it includes areas of experience such as

- Mathematics, arithmetic, logic
- Knowledge of the "self"
- The possibility of free will
- Moral principles
- The existence of God

Kant rightly realized that Hume's comprehensive discrediting of the validity and power of reason would prohibit discovering authentic knowledge in these metaphysical areas.

My object is to persuade all those who think Metaphysics worth studying, that it is absolutely necessary to pause a moment, and, neglecting all that has been done, to propose first the preliminary question, "Whether such a thing as metaphysics be at all possible? . . ."

I therefore first tried whether Hume's objection could not be put into a general form, and soon found that the concept of the connection of cause and effect was by no means the only idea by which the understanding thinks the connection of things a priori, but rather that metaphysics consists altogether of such connections.

Immanuel Kant, from *Prolegomena to Any Future Metaphysics*

For Kant, refuting Hume is not a trivial academic enterprise: It is an intellectual life-and-death struggle to make possible his most deeply held convictions about the universe and humanity's place in it. This is an intensely personal struggle for Kant, and underlying the extraordinary intellectual edifice that he ends up erecting is a profoundly human passion, revealed in his comment, "If man has the need of any science, then it is the one that can teach him what it means to be human."

Fortunately for Kant, he is not lacking in confidence. Kant viewed Hume's critique as a serious challenge, but more importantly he used it as an intellectual catalyst for his own thinking, a project that he believed to be supremely successful.

But as soon as I had succeeded in solving Hume's problem not merely in a particular case, but with respect to the whole faculty of pure reason, I could proceed safely, though slowly, to determine the whole sphere of pure reason completely and from general principles, in its circumference as well as in its contents. This was required for metaphysics in order to construct its system according to a reliable method.

Immanuel Kant, from *Prolegomena to Any Future Metaphysics*

To fully understand Kant's "solution," we need to fully appreciate Hume's critique, which was directed not only at rationalism but at empiricism as well. Recall that Hume established a two-pronged criterion for evaluating attempts to establish genuine knowledge ("Hume's fork"). The first category of knowledge was "relations

Transcendental idealism
Kant's epistemology that describes truths about the world that are both *necessary* and *universal*.

of ideas," which includes the principles of mathematics and logic as well as simple tautologies ("A bachelor is an unmarried man"). These principles are discoverable by reason, without reference to experience, and they do not permit logical contradictions. The force of Hume's argument against rationalism, noted above, was that claims to knowledge *other* than these, such as the principle of cause and effect, were not warranted.

The second category of knowledge, "matters of fact," can be confirmed (or refuted) by appeal to our experience. Unlike "relations of ideas," they necessarily involve sense experience, and their statements *do* permit logical contradictions, according to Hume. However, after careful analysis, Hume concluded that knowledge of such things as the principle of cause and effect are not warranted in this area either. When we investigate our sense experience, we discover that there is absolutely no evidence of causal relations between events. The best that we can say is that we link events by *association* or *habit*, but these connections are not necessary or lawlike, and we cannot legitimately draw inferences or make inductive predictions based on them. Thus, the project of making the universe scientifically intelligible is doomed.

Kant's Solution: Transcendental Idealism

For Kant to effectively commit Hume's critique "to the flames" (Hume's volatile image) and build a compelling theory of knowledge from the ashes, Kant needs to address both "forks" of Hume's attack on the possibility of knowledge. And this is precisely what Kant does through his theory of **transcendental idealism**—an epistemology that describes truths about the world that are both *necessary* and *universal*.

Is scientific knowledge necessary? Why? The advent of modern science challenged and replaced traditional religious and folklore explanations for the natural world with scientifically provable knowledge.

For all his intellectual power, Kant grounds his theory firmly in the world of lived experience. It is an incontrovertible fact that the world of objects exists, that objects are related in lawlike ways that science and common sense can discover (including cause and effect and induction), and that we can develop knowledge about the world that is compelling and verifiable. Yet rationalism and empiricism both run into dead ends, being forced to conclude that all these incontrovertible facts of experience are uncertain and ungrounded. For Kant, this conflict between the evidence of real-world experience and the epistemological skepticism of various theories could mean only one thing: The theories are profoundly flawed. So Kant turned the prevailing trend in epistemology upside down. Instead of questioning whether science could legitimately claim to discover knowledge, Kant initiates his inquiry with the following challenge: Science already has discovered knowledge that is necessary, universal, and certain: *How is this possible? What is the nature of the way the human mind works that makes the discovery of such knowledge a reality?*

Thus begins Kant's "Copernican revolution" in epistemology. As we noted in Chapter 3, the Polish astronomer Copernicus revolutionized the scientific study of the universe by declaring that the sun was the center of our solar system, around which planets in the system—including Earth—orbited. This was a reversal of accepted belief and directly contradicted the teachings of the Catholic Church, which steadfastly maintained that Earth was the center of our solar system, placed there by God as a symbol of the spiritual primacy of human life. In analogous fashion, Kant reversed the traditional approach of epistemology, changing the entire perspective. Rather than speculate on how the human mind can somehow connect to or match up with an (ultimately unknowable) external world, Kant decided to investigate precisely *how the human mind constructs a knowable world*. He explains:

> Hitherto it has been assumed that all our knowledge must conform to objects. But all attempts to extend our knowledge of objects by establishing something in regard to them by means of concepts have, on this assumption, ended in failure. We must, therefore, make trial whether we may not have more success if we suppose that objects must conform to our knowledge.

Immanuel Kant, from *Prolegomena to Any Future Metaphysics*

"... if we suppose that objects must conform to our knowledge." This is the core of Kant's revolution. He views the mind as an *active agent* in constructing the world and our knowledge about it. Empiricism, as expressed in the thinking of Locke, Berkeley, and Hume, had viewed the mind as a *passive agent*, a "blank slate" on which is recorded the sounds, images, and other sensations of experience. In *A Treatise of Human Nature*, Hume provides a graphic image to dramatize this view of the mind as passive agent:

> (The sensations in our senses) succeeded each other with an inconceivable rapidity and are in a perpetual flux and movement. . . . The mind is a kind of theater where several perceptions successively make their appearance, pass, re-pass, glide away, and mingle in an infinite variety of postures and situations.

Listen to the **Podcast** *Adrian Moore on Kant's Metaphysics* on **mysearchlab.com**

From Kant's perspective, this is precisely where the empiricists commit their fatal mistake, which culminates in epistemological skepticism and commonsense absurdity. A careful examination of how the mind operates makes clear that, as thinking beings, we don't simply "receive" and "record" impressions: Instead, we actively select, organize, order, structure, and interpret these sensations, shaping them into an intelligible world about which we can develop insight and knowledge. This is absolutely clear when we observe how science operates. Scientists don't simply record the data of experience: They actively pose questions, develop hypotheses, construct and implement experimental tests, create theories, and invent concepts to explain phenomena, continually revise their understanding in light of new information and countless other thinking operations. It is through the active use of the human mind *in interaction with the data of experience* that science discovers—and constructs—knowledge of the world.

We can see this active operation of the human mind in our daily lives as well. At almost every waking moment of your life, your senses are being bombarded by a tremendous number of stimuli: images to see, noises to hear, odors to smell, textures to feel, and flavors to taste. The experience of all these sensations happening at once creates what the nineteenth-century American philosopher William James called "a bloomin' buzzin' confusion." Yet for us, the world usually seems much more orderly and understandable. Why is this so?

In the first place, your sense equipment can receive sensations only within certain limited ranges. For example, there are many sounds and smells that animals can detect but you cannot, because their sense organs have broader ranges in these areas than yours do. A second reason you can handle this sensory bombardment is that from the stimulation available, you select only a small amount on which to focus your attention. To demonstrate this, try the following exercise. Concentrate on what you can see, ignoring your other senses for the moment. Focus on sensations that you were not previously aware of and then answer the first question. Concentrate on each of your other senses in turn, following the same procedure.

- What can you *see*? (For example, the shape of the letters on the page, the design of the clothing on your arm)
- What can you *hear*? (For example, the hum of the air circulator, the rustling of a page)
- What can you *feel*? (For example, the pressure of the clothes against your skin, the texture of the page on your fingers)
- What can you *smell*? (For example, the perfume or cologne someone is wearing, the odor of stale cigarette smoke)
- What can you *taste*? (For example, the aftereffects of a breath mint)

Compare your responses with those of the other students in the class. Do your classmates perceive sensations that differ from the ones you perceived? If so, how do you explain these differences?

By practicing this simple exercise, you can see that for every sensation on which you focus your attention there are countless other sensations that you are simply ignoring. If you were aware of everything that is happening at every moment, you would be completely overwhelmed. By selecting certain sensations, you are able to make sense of your world in a relatively orderly way. The activity of using your senses to experience and make sense of your world is known as "perceiving," and Kant believed this process is an *active* process of our minds, not passive. When we perceive we actively *select*, *organize*, and *interpret* what is experienced by our senses. Let's continue our exploration of this complex process that forms the foundation of our knowledge of the world.

It is tempting to think, as the empiricists did, that your senses simply record what is happening out in the world as if you were a human camera or voice recorder. You are not, however, a passive receiver of information, a "container" into which sense experience is poured. Instead, you are an active participant who is always trying to understand the sensations you are encountering. As you perceive your world, your experience is the result of combining the sensations you are having with the way you understand these sensations. For example, examine the collection of markings in Figure 6.1. What do you see? If all you see is a collection of black spots, try looking at the group sideways. After a while, you will probably perceive a familiar animal.

Figure 6.1

From this example you can see that when you perceive the world, you are doing more than simply recording what your senses experience. Besides experiencing sensations, you are also actively making sense of these sensations. That is why this collection of black spots suddenly became the figure of an animal—because you were able actively to organize these spots into a pattern you recognized. Or think about the times you were able to look up at the white, billowy clouds in the sky and see different figures and designs. The figures you were perceiving were not actually in the clouds but were the result of your giving a meaningful form to the shapes and colors you were experiencing.

The same is true for virtually everything you experience. Your perception of the world results from combining the information provided by your senses with the way you actively make sense of this information. And because making sense of information is what you are doing when you are thinking, you can see that perceiving your world involves using your mind in an active way. Of course, you are usually not aware that you are using your mind to interpret the sensations you are experiencing. You simply see the animal or the figures in the clouds as if they were really there.

When you actively perceive the sensations you are experiencing, you are usually engaged in three distinct activities:

- *Selecting* certain sensations to pay attention to
- *Organizing* these sensations into a design or pattern
- *Interpreting* what this design or pattern means to you

In Figure 6.1, you were able to perceive an animal because you selected certain of the markings to concentrate on, organized these markings into a pattern, and interpreted this pattern as representing a familiar animal.

Figure 6.2 *Archives of the History of American Psychology, The Center for the History of Psychology - The University of Akron*

Of course, when you perceive, these three operations of selecting, organizing, and interpreting are usually performed quickly, automatically, and often simultaneously. Also, you are normally unaware that you are performing these operations because they are so rapid and automatic. Kant understood that we needed to slow down this normally automatic process of perceiving so that we could understand how the process works.

Let's explore more examples that illustrate how you actively select, organize, and interpret your perceptions of the world. Carefully examine Figure 6.2. Do you see both the young woman and the old woman? If you do, try switching back and forth between the two images. As you switch back and forth, notice how for each image you are

- *selecting* certain lines, shapes, and shadings on which to focus your attention.
- *organizing* these lines, shapes, and shadings into different patterns.
- *interpreting* these patterns as representing things that you are able to recognize—a hat, a nose, a chin.

Another way for you to become aware of your active participation in perceiving your world is to consider how you see objects. Examine the illustration in Figure 6.3. Do you perceive different-sized people or the same-sized people at different distances? When you see someone who is far away, you usually do not perceive a tiny person. Instead, you perceive a normal-sized person who is far away from you. Your experience in the world has enabled you to discover that the farther

Figure 6.3

How do we construct a coherent reality? In his ingenious painting *Satire on False Perspective*, the eighteenth-century artist William Hogarth created a series of visual jokes by playing with the tricks used to create the illusion of space on a flat surface. How does this work reveal the active role our minds play in creating our intelligible world?

things are from you, the smaller they look. The moon in the night sky appears about the size of a quarter, yet you perceive it as being considerably larger. As you look down a long stretch of railroad tracks or gaze up at a tall building, the boundary lines seem to come together. Even though these images are what your eyes "see," however, you do not usually perceive the tracks meeting or the building coming to a point. Instead, your mind actively organizes and interprets a world composed of constant shapes and sizes, even though the images you actually see usually vary, depending on how far you are from them and the angle from which you are looking at them.

Examine carefully the engraving entitled *Satire on False Perspective*, completed by William Hogarth in 1754. In this engraving, the artist has changed many of the clues you use to perceive a world of constant shapes and sizes, thus creating some unusual effects. By analyzing how the artist has created these unusual perspectives, you gain insight into the way your mind actively takes fragmentary information and transforms it into the predictable, three-dimensional world that is so familiar to you.

So far, we have been exploring how your mind actively participates in the way you perceive the world. By combining the sensations you are receiving with the way your mind selects, organizes, and interprets these sensations, you perceive a world of things that is stable and familiar, a world that usually makes sense to you.

The process of perceiving takes place at a variety of different levels. At the most basic level, the concept of "perceiving" refers to the selection, organization, and interpretation of sensations: for example, being able to perceive the various objects in your experience, such as a basketball. However, you also perceive larger patterns of meaning at more complex levels, as in watching the action of a group of people engaged in a basketball game. Although these are very different contexts, both engage you in the process of actively selecting, organizing, and interpreting what is experienced by your senses—in other words, "perceiving."

To sum up, the cognitive processes of perceiving, developing beliefs, and constructing knowledge involve *both* the data of sense experience *and* what Kant terms the "faculties of the mind." It is through the active *interaction* of these two elements that we are able to "constitute" (Kant's term) an orderly and intelligible world. And it is through the active synthesis of our "self" that this world becomes *my* world, as Kant explains in his *Critique of Pure Reason*:

> *Sensations would be nothing to us, and would not concern us in the least, if they were not received into our (orderly) consciousness. Knowledge is impossible in any other way. . . . For perceptions could not be perceptions of anything for me unless they . . . could at least be connected together into (my) one consciousness. This principle stands firm* **a priori***, and may be called the "transcendental principle of unity" for all the multiplicity of our perceptions and sensations.*

We can now see how rationalism and empiricism created their own epistemological sinkholes because they didn't understand that constituting our world and constructing genuine knowledge involves the ongoing interaction of our thinking activities with sense experience. In science, and everyday life, our approach to making sense of the world is both rational and empirical, a fundamental insight that Kant captured with the memorable phrase, "Thoughts (*concepts*) without content (*sense data*) are empty; intuitions (*of sensations*) without conceptions, blind" (author's italics). Thus, a purely rationalist approach to knowledge is doomed to be "empty" because it fails to appreciate the need for sense experience to provide content for its thinking processes. Conversely, a purely empiricist approach to knowledge is doomed to be "blind" because it fails to understand the need for the structure, order, and interpretation provided by the rational categories of the mind. The only solution, Kant believes, is to recognize the essential role that each partner in the knowing process plays, which he describes in the opening passages of his extraordinary work, *Critique of Pure Reason.*

Immanuel Kant, from *Critique of Pure Reason*

Introduction: I. Of the Difference Between Pure and Empirical Knowledge

There can be no doubt that all our knowledge begins with experience. For how should our faculty of knowledge be awakened into action did not objects affecting our senses partly of themselves produce representations, partly arouse the activity of our understanding to compare these representations, and, by combining or separating them, work up the raw material of the sensible impressions into that knowledge of objects which is entitled experience? In the order of time, therefore, we have no knowledge antecedent to experience, and with experience all our knowledge begins.

But though all our knowledge begins with experience, it does not follow that it all arises out of experience. For it may well be that even our empirical knowledge is made up of what we receive through impressions and of what our own faculty of knowledge (sensible impressions serving merely as the occasion) supplies from itself. If our faculty of knowledge makes any such addition, it may be that we are not in a position to distinguish it from the raw material, until with long practice of attention we have become skilled in separating it. This, then, is a question which at least calls for closer examination, and does not allow of any off-hand answer:—whether there is any knowledge that is thus independent of experience and even of all impressions of the senses. Such knowledge is entitled *a priori*, and distinguished from the *empirical*, which has its sources *a posteriori*, that is, in experience.

Kant has an astonishing ability to incisively clarify and skillfully unravel what appears to be a hopeless conundrum. Descartes, Locke, Berkeley, Hume—all brilliant thinkers who had nevertheless managed to tie themselves up into philosophical knots, until Kant came along to disentangle them. And like most solutions to seemingly intransigent problems, once illuminated one is tempted to think: "It's so obvious: why didn't someone else think of that before?"

"There can be no doubt that all our knowledge begins with experience." Of course it does! Where else would knowledge originate? If we examine the cases of children who have been raised under experientially or educationally deprived circumstances, they don't "recollect," on their own, a profound understanding of truth and knowledge from the perfect preexistence, as Plato suggests. In fact, they can barely function, think, or communicate. Even the slave boy from whom Socrates elicits "knowledge" of geometric principles has lived a life filled with geometric objects and experiences

regarding them, along with the opportunity to discuss and reflect on these sensations and experiences. Knowledge of the world necessarily involves empirical experiences, and to suggest, as the rationalists maintain, that a wealth of a priori knowledge about the world is fully evolved in each person's head and completely independent of real-word sense experience seems extremely unlikely.

But the empiricists are no less confused and limited in how they understand the nature of constituting our world and constructing knowledge. *"But though all our knowledge begins with experience, it does not follow that it all arises out of experience."* No, of course it doesn't! Our minds are naturally active: That is what the thinking process is all about, performing complex mental (and linguistic) operations of the information provided through experience so that we can make sense of our world. And at the center of all these complex mental operations is the powerful impetus to *synthesize* everything that is taking place into a "picture" that makes sense to *me*, a picture that is being updated on an instantaneous basis based on new information and further mental processing. What an astonishingly powerful process! How could the empiricists—intelligent, thinking beings who were performing these complex mental operations at the very moment that they were writing that such processes don't exist—fail to see the obvious? Kant has a ready response.

Immanuel Kant,
from *Critique of Pure Reason*

> If our faculty of knowledge makes any such addition, it may be that we are not in a position to distinguish it from the raw material, until with long practice of attention we have become skilled in separating it. This, then, is a question which at least calls for closer examination, and does not allow of any off-hand answer:—whether there is any knowledge that is thus independent of experience and even of all impressions of the senses.

The reason the empiricists were unable to see the contributions of the human mind to constructing knowledge (and, conversely, the reason why rationalists were unable to fully credit the contributions of sensory experience) was that the world and our understanding of it is presented as an integrated package in which *sensory experience* and the *faculties of the mind* have already created their epistemological synthesis. As a result, we need to make an extraordinary effort to distinguish these two primary contributors to the knowing process "until with long practice of attention we have become skilled in separating it." That was our goal in performing some of the simple perceptual activities in the previous section, trying to slow the perceiving/believing/knowing process down to become aware of the various sensory and thinking components in these processes. Let's try a somewhat different approach that may prove to be even more effective.

Consider the (intentionally) ambiguous photograph in Figure 6.4. Describe what you think is going on and what you think will take place next. Now share your responses with other members of the class. Did they have different perceptions of what was taking place and what would happen next? Very likely. How do you account for these differences? Your response might be something like:

- People think differently (a rationalist analysis).
- People have had different experiences (an empiricist analysis).

For Kant, both responses are accurate; and, as we will see later in the chapter, modern developmental and cognitive psychology would agree. When you look at the

Figure 6.4

illustration you are gathering sensory information: the lines, the shading, the contours—data that your mind is actively organizing into images that are familiar to you.

But your mind is doing something else: It is *interpreting* the resulting images, giving them meaning. But, for the most part, you are *un*aware that these processes are taking place because they are instantaneous and present you with a finished product: an "interpreted image." What's more, if you are like most people, you assume that the interpretation that you are giving to this image is the "right one," that it somehow resides "in" the image, a necessary part of it. It is only when you compare your interpretation with those interpretations of others that you can begin to recognize the contribution of your active thinking process in projecting meaning onto the image. Where do those interpretations come from? Why do people experience the same events—in this case, looking at a simple image—and then register very different interpretations?

- Because people do, in fact, "think" differently. Although we may be using the same fundamental thinking processes, we can use these mental processes to interpret sensations in different ways.

- Because people have, in fact, had different experiences that they draw on in interpreting their experiences in the world. In this illustration, the unique experiences of the viewers contribute to *informing* their interpretations.

Comparing people's different perceptions of the same sensations is like dusting for fingerprints: The

Can you describe the suspect? In his cartoon *The Investigation*, John Jonik illustrates how the perceiving lenses of the people (and creature!) create conflicting views of the character at center.

fingerprints are there, but you can't "see" them until the right powder is brushed on. One useful image to help understand this knowing process is to realize each one of us views the world through our own unique perceiving/believing/knowing "lenses," which shape and influence every aspect of our experience. These lenses are permanently attached, and they reflect everything that has contributed to the person you are, including your past experiences and your uniquely individual use of your thinking abilities. No two pairs of lenses are exactly alike: They each embody a unique prescription that shapes and organizes each person's view of the world in distinctive ways. In a way, we can view the world we constitute as a dynamic coloring book. Because people have the same basic patterns and categories of thinking, they constitute their worlds in ways that are in basic agreement: I'm sitting in a class in philosophy with *x* other students discussing Immanuel Kant, and so on. These are the basic outlines of the coloring book, on which there is likely general agreement. (If a student jumped up and shouted, "Get me off this airplane!" we would probably wonder about his psychological stability.) But though we may agree on the basic outlines of life's events, we each "color" in these outlines in very individual ways, reflecting our perceiving lenses.

If we carefully examine the evidence of everyday experience, we see that the world we live in, both individually and collectively, is the product of an active mind interacting with empirical experience. What are the philosophical implications of this insight? That is precisely the question that Kant is attempting to answer, as he explains:

Immanuel Kant,
from *Critique of Pure Reason*

And thus I conclude the analytical solution of the main question which I had proposed: "How is metaphysics in general possible?" by ascending from the data of its actual use, as shown in its consequences, to the grounds of its possibility.

For Kant, metaphysics refers to necessary and universal knowledge that we can discover that is a priori—that is, obtained independently of experience. Of course, many empiricists accept the fact that tautologies ("A bald man has no hair") and the principles of formal logic and mathematics can claim a necessary and universal a priori truth. But Kant wants to claim another kind of a priori knowledge: a *synthetic a priori* knowledge. This is knowledge that is

- necessary and universally true.
- a priori—can be discovered independently of experience.
- *synthetic* in the sense that it provides us with genuine information regarding our experience of the world.

In other words, Kant is suggesting a phenomenological approach to epistemology and metaphysics. He's saying, in effect, "We know things about the world that are necessary and universal—such as the principles of cause and effect and induction—that do not depend on empirical experience. How is this possible?" It is possible because this *synthetic a priori* knowledge of the world reflects the way the human mind operates in constituting the orderly and intelligible world in which we live. The thinking process operates according to certain necessary and universal laws, categories that organize and structure the chaotic sensations of empirical experience. That is the heart of Kant's "Copernican revolution." Instead of trying to understand how to connect our minds to the external world, Kant is proposing that our minds actually *constitute* the world in accordance with certain fundamental *categories of understanding* that are an essential part of every human's thinking process. For example, one such "law" or "category" of the mind is *cause and effect*, which necessarily organizes the world in such a way that we are able to relate events according to this principle. When you (accidentally!) hit your thumb with a hammer, you have no doubt that the hammer blow is causing the excruciating pain in your thumb. Your understanding of this necessary connection is the product of the interaction of this cause-and-effect category of your mind with your experiences in the world. For example, at the age of five when I placed my hand on an iron that my mother had warned me was "hot" ("But it doesn't *look* hot," I reasoned), the pain alerted me that there was a connection between these events. And as I matured, my mind enabled me to understand the necessary and universal nature of that type of causal connection, as well as many others in the world.

Kant believes that there are twelve such basic categories of the mind, and that one of the goals of metaphysics is to become familiar with these categories so that we can understand how they shape, organize, and constitute our orderly and intelligible world. Other categories include induction, objects, space, and time. And the knowledge that we gain by analyzing these categories is *synthetic a priori* knowledge, because these "transcendental" categories are

- necessary and universally true.
- a priori—can be discovered independently of experience.
- *synthetic* in the sense that they provide us with genuine information regarding our experience of the world.

Does this mean that everyone lives in his or her own personal world? Kant believes that the answer to this is "no," because these twelve fundamental categories of the mind are universally present in every person of "normal" cognitive function. In contemporary terms, we might say that they are programmed into the human mind, an essential part of the brain "software" that we come equipped with. It doesn't matter where you were born, given the proper experiences, you will develop an understanding of the necessary, natural law principle of "cause and effect." This doesn't mean that people *apply* the principle correctly in all circumstances (as in the "lucky shirt") but that they have an accurate understanding of what the principle is and how it is supposed to be applied. This approach thus nullifies Hume's contention that we can never "know" that the principle of cause and effect is a true, lawlike relationship: We "know" that principle of cause and effect applies because that's exactly how our mind organizes our experience and constitutes our world. And because this principle is universal and necessary, a part of the mind's thinking equipment with which we are all born, we can be certain of its truth.

The same basic insights apply to Kant's other a priori categories of the mind, including "objects," "space," and "time." Kant reasons: We *know* that objects exist independently of our experience of them. How can we be so sure? Where does this certainty come from? Kant believes it comes from our mind, that the concept of an independently existing external object is an a priori "rule," "law," or "category" of thought that the mind imposes on the chaotic flux of experience to make the world an orderly and intelligible place.

Jean Piaget (1896–1980). Piaget used careful observations and interviews with infants and young children to trace the cognitive process by which humans constitute their world.

Empiricists such as Locke, Berkeley, and Hume wondered: How can we ever be sure that the external world exists, when all we encounter are sensations or impressions of this ultimately unknowable world? Kant's approach supersedes their concerns. Because our minds actively constitute the external world, there is no "gap" between mind and object, between our consciousness and the world of which we are conscious. We are dealing with a unified, integrated reality, in which our thinking and the external world it constitutes are necessary partners, inextricably connected one to the other. Because our minds actively *constitute* the world to include external objects that exist independently of our perception of them, we don't have to be concerned about whether these objects actually exist or how our minds connect to or "match up" with the external world. For example, recall Aristotle's image of the soul being the "form" of the body in the same way that a pattern-mold shapes wax in its image. Analogously, the human mind "shapes" the field of sensations into an intelligible and coherent whole. From a Kantian perspective, it makes no sense to question the existence of an external world because it is the human mind itself that gives shape and form to it, as a pattern-mold does to the wax: They are inseparable.

The research in developmental psychology in the twentieth century has provided an empirical foundation for Kant's philosophical analysis. The most influential thinker in this area is **Jean Piaget**, a Swiss psychologist who used painstakingly careful observations of infants and interviews with young children to trace the cognitive process by which humans constitute their world. In his work *The Child's Construction of Reality*, Piaget details the gradual process by which an infant's mind gradually develops the concepts of "object," "space," "time," "cause and effect," and other foundational ways of organizing experience. In Piaget's version of Kant's "categories," which he calls *schemata*, inherited cognitive structures evolve into more sophisticated and differentiated forms through interaction with experience. Thus an infant playing with an object becomes distressed if the object is covered up because she has not yet developed the concept of "object" as an independently existing entity. This will only happen later on. Similarly, such relations as cause and effect and induction are grounded in these basic *schemata*, but they need the interaction with empirical experience to gradually evolve into fully formed concepts. The same is true for the concepts of "space," "time," and the other conceptual building blocks of our world: Though they exist as *cognitive potentials* in our genetic equipment, they need the ongoing stimulation of experience to reach their fully evolved state. The ultimate result is the world that seems so familiar to us: objects contained in space, bounded by time, and governed by certain lawlike relationships. Yet this entire reality, which we assume to be completely independent of ourselves, is in fact, as Kant maintained, constituted by the active structuring of our minds. And because these mental forms—categories or *schemata*—are universally present in normally function-ing humans, we all share a common universe, constituted and defined by the same basic qualities and relations.

We see an analogous model in the development of human language. The lin-guist **Noam Chomsky's** theory, which has gained near universal acceptance among linguists, postulates that humans are born with the innate mental structures that provide for the *potential* of language development. These structures, which he refers to as "depth grammar," make possible the learning of any language. The particular language (or languages) that you learn to speak depends on your specific experi-ences: namely, the language to which you are exposed. Chomsky's theory is based on the reality that language is much too complex a phenomenon to be learned under a tabula rasa empiricist model. At the same time, language abilities will not develop on their own if an individual is not given ongoing experiences with spo-ken language, undermining the rationalist claim that knowledge exists fully formed at birth. (For those born hearing impaired, "sign language" is the equivalent of a spoken language.)

Finally, research in a variety of disciplines supports the view that although think-ing and language begin as distinct processes, they begin to intertwine very early in their evolution, and they quickly become so integrated that it is nearly impossible to disentangle them. Most thinking necessarily involves language and, conversely, most language involves thinking. So the fundamental cognitive categories with which we construct our world cannot be fully understood without simultaneously integrating the role of language into the mix.

Two Realities: Phenomenal and Noumenal

Although Kant's transcendental idealism, his Copernican revolution, solves the tradi-tional problems of knowledge posed by rationalism and empiricism, it creates other epistemological challenges. If our experience of the world—our "reality"—is the prod-uct of our categories of understanding actively ordering the sensations of experience, the question naturally leaps up: What can we know about the reality that is "outside" of our experience, independent of our perceptions? Kant's answer is that, from an empirical point of view, this reality is unknowable by us, and he calls it the *ding-an-sich*: "thing-in-itself." There is no way for us to "go beyond" the reality constituted by the categories of our mind as they transform sensations into an intelligible world. What-ever is "out there" by definition transcends our efforts to know and understand. Thus Kant ends up making a radical division between

- **phenomenal reality**—the world as we constitute it and experience it, and
- **noumenal reality**—the world beyond our perceptions, reality "in-itself."

Kant believes that we can achieve knowledge of the noumenal reality: It's just that we can't achieve it through our senses. The noumenal reality can be known only through the application of "pure reason," which in addition to confirming the existence of "objective reality" also gives us knowledge of the possibility of genuine personal free-dom and the existence of a universal moral law (the "categorical imperative"). This is essential for Kant because, as we will see in Chapter 9, he was fervently committed to constructing an ethical system, based on reason, that would have universal authority.

Noam Chomsky
(b. 1928). Philosopher of language, political activist. Chomsky maintains that humans possess a type of innate grammar and a "lan-guage faculty" that is involved in the acquiring and use of language.

((•—[**Listen** to the **Audiobook** *Kant—Critique of Pure Reason* by Nigel Warburton on **mysearchlab.com**

Phenomenal reality Kant's term for the world as we experience it.

Noumenal reality Kant's term for the world that exists beyond our perceptions.

And an integral part of such a system is the assumption that individuals are capable of making choices that are genuinely free. Otherwise, if we act only in ways that we are compelled to by forces beyond our control, an ethical system is irrelevant. Kant believed that we could never establish the possibility of genuine personal freedom or the existence of universal moral laws by remaining within phenomenal reality: The world that we constitute simply can't provide that sort of knowledge. It is necessary for us, using the power of pure reason, to go beyond the phenomenal world to the noumenal world.

In addition to the standard transcendental categories of understanding that we use to order sensations into an intelligible world, Kant also identifies three additional transcendental ideas that he believes we use to synthesize experience on a grand scale. These "super" transcendental ideas are "self," "cosmos," and "God," and they help us "bridge the gap" between the phenomenal and the noumenal realms. These "regulative ideas" are also essential for helping us constitute an epistemological framework that is comprehensive and inclusive.

Immanuel Kant,
from *Critique of Pure Reason*

Everything that has its basis in the nature of our powers must be appropriate to, and consistent with, their right employment—if we can only guard against a certain misunderstanding and so discover the proper direction of these powers. We are entitled, therefore to suppose that transcendental ideas . . . have an excellent, and indeed indispensably necessary, regulative employment, namely, that of directing the understanding towards a certain goal upon which the routes marked out by all its rules converge.

* * *

The first (regulative) idea is the "I" itself, viewed simply as thinking nature or soul. . .; in a word, the idea of a simple self-sustaining intelligence. (Reason operates) to represent all determinations as existing in a single subject, all powers, so far as possible, as derived from a single fundamental power, all change as belonging to the state of one and the same permanent being.

* * *

The second regulative idea of merely speculative reason is the concept of the world in general. . . .The absolute totality of the series of . . . conditions . . . is an idea which can never be completely realised in the empirical employment of reason, but which yet serves as a rule that prescribes how we ought to proceed in dealing with such series. . . . Cosmological ideas are nothing but simply regulative principles, and are very far from positing . . . an actual totality.

* * *

The third idea of pure reason, which contains a merely relative supposition of a being that is the sole and sufficient cause of all cosmological series, is the idea of *God*. We have not the slightest ground to assume in an absolute manner (the existence of) the object of this idea.

Kant is acknowledging that pure reason does not establish the actual *existence* of "cosmos" or "God," only that these are regulative ideas that are necessary to account for the world as we constitute it. These are universal a priori ideas that regulate and make possible the phenomenal world, but because they refer to possibilities that exist in the noumenal world they can never be empirically verified.

< **READING CRITICALLY** >

Analyzing Kant's Synthesizing Project

- Explain why Kant suggests that his approach embodies a "Copernican revolution" in epistemology. What are the central differences between his epistemology and that of the rationalists and the empiricists?

- What is the meaning of Kant's famous quote, "Thoughts (concepts) without content (sense data) are empty; intuitions (of sensations) without conceptions, blind"?

- Explain the significance of Kant's observation that "There can be no doubt that all our knowledge begins with experience. . . . But though all our knowledge begins with experience, it does not follow that it all arises out of experience."

- The empiricists concluded that we can never "know" that the principle of cause and effect is valid or that the external world exists independently of our perception of it. How does Kant's approach seek to overcome these troubling conclusions?

- Kant believes that the following transcendental ideas are necessary to explain our experience of the universe: Self, Cosmos, God. Considering each of these "regulative" ideas in turn, analyze whether or not you agree that the idea is required to explain the way we experience the world.

Applying Kant's Theory

For Kant, we constitute our world through the ongoing synthesis of the categories of our mind with the sensations of experience. We have seen in this section that this perceiving is a dynamic process in which we actively select, organize, and interpret sensations in a way that reflects our unique perceiving "lenses." To construct knowledge from the

What is your response to this photograph depicting the assassination of Malcolm X? Why? Even photographs, which seem unbiased and "real," are examples of constructed reality. The photographer actively selects a point of view on a scene, which the viewer then interprets. What does this photograph communicate about the assassination of Malcolm X?

information provided from experience, we must explore many different perspectives on the focus of our attention and take into account the "lenses" of the individuals or organizations that are providing the information—as well as being acutely aware of our own "lenses." This type of organized evaluation of contrasting sources and opinions—"perspective taking"—is an essential strategy of sophisticated thinking and one of the most powerful ways to construct well-supported beliefs and genuine knowledge. To experience this epistemological process in action, let's examine three different media accounts of the assassination of Malcolm X as he was speaking at a meeting in Harlem. As you read through the various accounts, pay particular attention to the different perceptions each one presents of this event. You will note that each account viewed the event through its own perceiving lenses, which shaped and influenced the information the writer selected, the way the writer organized it, his or her interpretations of the event and the people involved, and the language used to describe it. After you have finished reading the accounts, analyze some of the differences in these perceptions by answering the questions that follow the activity. As you do this, try to begin constructing your own "knowledge" of this event.

Three Accounts of the Assassination of Malcolm X

The *New York Times*

Malcolm X, the 39-year-old leader of a militant Black Nationalist movement, was shot to death yesterday afternoon at a rally of his followers in a ballroom in Washington Heights. The bearded Negro extremist had said only a few words of greeting when a fusillade rang out. The bullets knocked him over backwards. A 22-year-old Negro, Thomas Hagan, was charged with the killing. The police rescued him from the ballroom crowd after he had been shot and beaten. Pandemonium broke out among the 400 Negroes in the Audubon Ballroom at 160th Street and Broadway. As men, women and children ducked under tables and flattened themselves on the floor, more shots were fired. The police said seven bullets struck Malcolm. Three other Negroes were shot. Witnesses reported that as many as 30 shots had been fired. About two hours later the police said the shooting had apparently been a result of a feud between followers of Malcolm and members of the extremist group he broke with last year, the Black Muslims.

Life Magazine

His life oozing out through a half dozen or more gunshot wounds in his chest, Malcolm X, once the shrillest voice of black supremacy, lay dying on the stage of a Manhattan auditorium. Moments before, he had stepped up to the lectern and 400 of the faithful had settled down expectantly to hear the sort of speech for which he was famous—flaying the hated white man. Then a scuffle broke out in the hall and Malcolm's bodyguards bolted from his side to break it up—only to discover that they had been faked out. At least two men with pistols rose from the audience and pumped bullets into the speaker, while a third cut loose at close range with both barrels of a sawed-off shotgun. In the confusion the pistol man got away. The shotgunner lunged through the crowd and out the door, but not before the guards came to their wits and shot him in the leg. Outside he was swiftly overtaken by other supporters of Malcolm and very likely would have been stomped to death if the police hadn't saved him. Most shocking of all to the residents of Harlem was the fact that Malcolm had been killed not by "whitey" but by members of his own race.

The *New York Post*

They came early to the Audubon Ballroom, perhaps drawn by the expectation that Malcolm X would name the men who firebombed his home last Sunday, streaming from the bright afternoon sunlight into the darkness of the hall.

The crowd was larger than usual for Malcolm's recent meetings, the 400 filling three-quarters of the wooden folding seats, feet scuffling the worn floor as they waited impatiently, docilely obeying the orders of Malcolm's guards as they were directed to their seats.

I sat at the left in the 12th row and, as we waited, the man next to me spoke of Malcolm and his followers:

"Malcolm is our only hope," he said. "You can depend on him to tell it like it is and to give Whitey hell."

Then a man was on the stage, saying:

". . . I now give you Brother Malcolm. I hope you will listen, hear, and understand." There was a prolonged ovation as Malcolm walked to the rostrum past a piano and a set of drums waiting for an evening dance and stood in front of a mural of a landscape as dingy as the rest of the ballroom.

When after more than a minute the crowd quieted, Malcolm looked up and said, "A salaam aleikum (Peace be unto you)" and the audience replied "Wa aleikum salaam (And unto you, peace)."

Bespectacled and dapper in a dark suit, his sandy hair glinting in the light, Malcolm said: "Brothers and sisters. . ." He was interrupted by two men in the center of the ballroom, about four rows in front and to the right of me, who rose and, arguing with each other, moved forward. Then there was a scuffle in the back of the room and, as I turned my head to see what was happening, I heard Malcolm X say his last words: "Now, now brothers, break it up," he said softly. "Be cool, be calm."

Then all hell broke loose. There was a muffled sound of shots and Malcolm, blood on his face and chest, fell limply back over the chairs behind him. The two men who had approached him ran to the exit on my side of the room shooting wildly behind them as they ran.

I fell to the floor, got up, tried to find a way out of the bedlam.

Malcolm's wife, Betty, was near the stage, screaming in a frenzy. "They're killing my husband," she cried. "They're killing my husband."

Groping my way through the first frightened, then enraged crowd, I heard people screaming, "Don't let them kill him." "Kill those bastards." "Don't let him get away." "Get him."

At an exit I saw some of Malcolm's men beating with all their strength on two men. Police were trying to fight their way toward the two. The press of the crowd forced me back inside.

I saw a half-dozen of Malcolm's followers bend over his inert body on the stage, their clothes stained with their leader's blood. Then they put him on a litter while guards kept everyone off the platform. A woman bending over him said: "He's still alive. His heart's beating."

Four policemen took the stretcher and carried Malcolm through the crowd and some of the women came out of their shock long enough to moan and one said: "I don't think he's going to make it. I hope he doesn't die, but I don't think he's going to make it."

I spotted a phone booth in the rear of the hall, fumbled for a dime, and called a photographer. Then I sat there, the surprise wearing off a bit, and tried desperately to remember what had happened. One of my first thoughts was that this was the first day of National Brotherhood Week.

6.6 Emotions Shape Our Understanding: Jaggar

The views on epistemology that we have been considering in this chapter are for the most part clearly within the mainstream of traditional philosophical thought. Other perspectives on epistemology, particularly in contemporary thought, present very different points of view on efforts to construct knowledge and discover truth. Among the most vigorous of these newer epistemologies are those that fall under the general category of "feminist" perspectives.

The central point of feminist philosophers in this area is that traditional epistemologies have been selective and biased in their analyses, giving inadequate treatment to theoretical voices that fall outside the philosophical "mainstream," particularly the distinctive perspectives of women. If we are to accept in some form the Kantian view of knowledge, in which the mind is actively engaged in constituting the world and constructing knowledge, it is clear that this process is always susceptible to subjective interpretation. That is the significance of the metaphor of "perceiving lenses" that we introduced earlier in the chapter. We each view the world through lenses with unique prescriptions that shape and influence everything that we perceive, believe, and do. Every aspect of our personal history has contributed to creating our lenses, and we are generally unaware that we are wearing them. Instead, we (mistakenly) assume that the way we see (and constitute) the world is the way the world *is*. It is only when our lenses come into contact with contrasting lenses that we are challenged—and inspired—to critically examine them, evaluating their accuracy and objectivity.

The feminist argument is that the thinkers who have populated mainstream philosophical thought have shared certain basic assumptions—reflected in their epistemological lenses—which has resulted in an artificially narrow framework for knowledge. In the history of ideas, the voices of individuals who could have provided contrasting perspectives have been systematically repressed, ignored, or never given an opportunity to even speak. However, because the central discussion in the history of ideas is dynamic and ongoing, there is still opportunity for these voices to now be heard and included.

Alison M. Jaggar (b. 1942). Professor of Women's Studies and Philosophy at the University of Colorado, Boulder, Jaggar's areas of interest are contemporary social, moral, and political philosophy, usually from a feminist perspective.

This is the mandate that the philosopher **Alison M. Jaggar** is operating under in the following essay. Her central thesis is that Western tradition has, for the most part, omitted the entire realm of emotions in the mainstream discussion regarding the nature of knowledge. Instead, Western thinking has focused almost exclusively on the faculty of reason as the instrument for constructing knowledge and discovering truth. And when we consider that Western philosophy was initiated and propelled as a "love of wisdom," this systematic absence and denigration of emotions reveals a particularly jarring irony. Her goal in this paper is to display the central role of emotion in the construction of knowledge, a central premise that she believes every epistemology needs to take into consideration. Reflective analysis reveals that emotions—and their conceptual siblings such as values, motivations, and interests—influence every aspect of the knowing process, in science and everyday life. Emotions motivate and guide our cognitive explorations, influence the knowledge we construct, and are instrumental in evaluating both its certainty and relevance. As a result, emotion demands to be included as an integral partner with reason in the epistemological enterprise.

Alison M. Jaggar, from "Love and Knowledge: Emotion in Feminist Epistemology"

I. Introduction: Emotion in Western Epistemology

Within the Western philosophical tradition, emotions have usually been considered potentially or actually subversive of knowledge. From Plato until the present, with a few notable exceptions, reason rather than emotion has been regarded as the indispensable faculty for acquiring knowledge.

Typically, although again not invariably, the rational has been contrasted with the emotional, and this contrasted pair then often linked with other dichotomies. Not only has reason been contrasted with emotion, but it has also been associated with the mental, the cultural, the universal, the public and the male, whereas emotion has been associated with the irrational, the physical, the natural, the particular, the private and, of course, the female.

Although Western epistemology has tended to give pride of place to reason rather than emotion, it has not always excluded emotion completely from the realm of reason. In the *Phaedrus*, Plato portrayed emotions, such as anger or curiosity, as irrational urges (horses) that must always be controlled by reason (the charioteer). On this model, the emotions were not seen as needing to be totally suppressed, but rather as needing direction by reason: for example, in a genuinely threatening situation, it was thought not only irrational but foolhardy not to be afraid. The split between reason and emotion was not absolute, therefore, for the Greeks. Instead, the emotions were thought of as providing indispensable motive power that needed to be channeled appropriately. Without horses, after all, the skill of the charioteer would be worthless.

The contrast between reason and emotion was sharpened in the seventeenth century by redefining reason as a purely

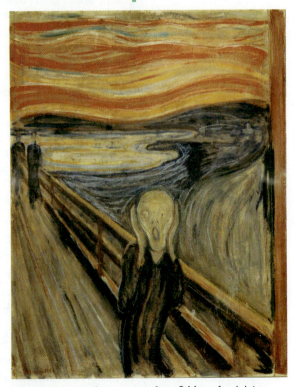

Where do emotions come from? Many feminists believe that modern science has contributed to inaccurately portraying emotions as irrational urges, like storms sweeping over a person, much like Edvard Munch's *The Scream*.

instrumental faculty. For both the Greeks and the medieval philosophers, reason had been linked with value in so far as reason provided access to the objective structure or order of reality, seen as simultaneously natural and morally justified. With the rise of modern science, however, the realms of nature and value were separated: nature was stripped of value and reconceptualized as an inanimate mechanism of no intrinsic worth. Values were relocated in human beings, rooted in their preferences and emotional responses. The separation of supposedly natural fact from human value meant that reason if it were to provide trustworthy insight into reality, had to be uncontaminated by or abstracted from value. Increasingly, therefore, though never universally, reason was reconceptualized as the ability to make valid inferences from premises established elsewhere, the ability to calculate means but not to determine ends. The validity of logical inferences was thought independent of human attitudes and preferences; this was now the sense in which reason was taken to be objective and universal.

The modern redefinition of rationality required a corresponding reconceptualization of emotion. This was achieved by portraying emotions as non-rational and often irrational urges that regularly swept the body, rather as a storm sweeps over the land. The common way of referring to the emotions as the "passions" emphasized that emotions happened to occur or were imposed upon an individual, something she suffered rather than something she did.

The epistemology associated with this new ontology rehabilitated sensory perception that, like emotion, typically had been suspected or even discounted by the Western tradition as a reliable source of knowledge. British empiricism, succeeded in the nineteenth century by positivism, took its epistemological task to be the formulation of rules of inference that would guarantee the derivation of certain knowledge from the "raw data" supposedly given directly to the senses. Empirical testability became accepted as the hallmark of natural science; this, in turn, was viewed as the paradigm of genuine knowledge. Often epistemology was equated with the philosophy of science, and the dominant methodology of positivism prescribed that truly scientific knowledge must be capable of intersubjective verification. Because values and emotions had been defined as variable and idiosyncratic, positivism stipulated that trustworthy knowledge could be established only by methods that neutralized the values and emotions of individual scientists.

Recent approaches to epistemology have challenged some fundamental assumptions of the positivist epistemological model. Contemporary theorists of knowledge have undermined once rigid distinctions between analytic and synthetic statements, between theories and observations and even between facts and values. However, few challenges have been raised thus far to the purported gap between emotion and knowledge. In this paper, I wish to begin bridging this gap through the suggestion that emotions may be helpful and even necessary rather than inimical to the construction of knowledge. . . .

Jaggar's central thesis is that the mainstream epistemology of Western thought has emphasized the role of reason in achieving knowledge and truth and deemphasized the role of emotions in this process. She notes that this division is not absolute, citing Plato's chariot metaphor in the *Phaedrus*. Although reason was clearly viewed as preeminent by the ancient Greeks, they also believed in the importance of cultivating the "higher" emotions. For example, as we noted in Chapter 1, the term *philosophy* is derived from Greek words meaning "love of wisdom," and the early philosophers clearly valued and embodied a passion for understanding. Nevertheless, it is true that in terms of philosophical *approach* and *methodology*, they place their faith in reason as the tool for discovering genuine knowledge, both universal (for example, Plato's "forms") and empirical (Aristotle's natural science).

Jaggar believes that the real split between reason and emotion was spawned by the rise of the "new science," pioneered by thinkers such as Isaac Newton and Galileo.

With the focus on making reliable scientific discoveries that could be validated and replicated by other scientists, the spiritual values that dominated the medieval consciousness were intentionally excised. Reason, in the form of experimental design and logical inferences, became the basic tool of science, whereas traditional spiritual values and personal emotions were perceived as threats to the hard-won objective methods of the new science. Jaggar believes that this ill-advised bifurcation of reason and emotion in the epistemology of science has continued to this day, a dualism that has seeped into modern consciousness in much the same way as the mind/body dualism of Descartes.

Alison M. Jaggar,
from "Love and Knowledge: Emotion in Feminist Epistemology"

II. What Are Emotions?

The philosophical question, "What are emotions?" requires both explicating the ways in which people ordinarily speak about emotion and evaluating the adequacy of those ways for expressing and illuminating experience and activity. Several problems confront someone trying to answer this deceptively simple question. One set of difficulties results from the variety, complexity, and even inconsistency of the ways in which emotions are viewed, both in daily life and in scientific contexts. It is in part this variety that makes emotions into a "question" at the same time that it precludes answering that question by simple appeal to ordinary usage. A second difficulty is the wide range of phenomena covered by the term "emotion": these extend from apparently instantaneous "knee-jerk" responses of fright to lifelong dedication to an individual or a cause; from highly civilized aesthetic responses to undifferentiated feelings of hunger and thirst; from background moods such as contentment or depression to intense and focused involvement in an immediate situation. It may well be impossible to construct a manageable account of emotion to cover such apparently diverse phenomena. . . .

III. Emotions as Intentional

Early positivist approaches to understanding emotions assumed that an adequate account required analytically separating emotion from other human faculties. Just as positivist accounts of sense perception attempted to distinguish the supposedly raw data of sensation from their cognitive interpretations, so positivist accounts of emotion tried to separate emotion conceptually from both reason and sense perception. As part of their sharpening of these distinctions, positivist construals of emotion tended to identify emotions with the physical feelings or involuntary bodily movements that typically accompany them, such as pangs or qualms, flushes or tremors; emotions were also assimilated to the subduing of physiological function or movement, as in the case of sadness, depression or boredom. The continuing influence of such supposedly scientific conceptions of emotion can be seen in the fact that "feeling" is often used colloquially as a synonym for emotion, even though the more central meaning of "feeling" is physiological sensation. On such accounts, emotions were not seen as being *about* anything: instead, they were contrasted with and seen as potential disruptions of other phenomena that *are* about some thing, phenomena such as rational judgments, thoughts, and observations. The positivist approach to understanding emotion has been called the Dumb View (Spelman, 1982). . . .

In recent years, contemporary philosophers have tended to reject the Dumb View of emotion and have substituted more intentional or cognitivist understandings. These newer conceptions emphasize that intentional judgments as well as physiological disturbances are integral elements in emotion. They define or identify emotions not by the quality or character of the physiological sensation that may be associated with them, but rather by their intentional aspect, the associated judgment. Thus, it is the content of my associated thought or judgment that determines whether my physical agitation and restlessness are defined as "anxiety about my daughter's lateness" rather than as "anticipation of tonight's performance.". . .

To discern the role of emotion in constructing knowledge, it is essential to develop an intelligent working definition of "emotion." As Jaggar makes apparent, "emotion" is a very complex concept that needs to be analyzed and articulated with care. One dimension of emotion is its "feeling" aspect: the physiological sensation that accompanies the experience of emotion, such as "pangs or qualms, flushes or tremors . . . sadness, depression or boredom." Yet although physiological "feelings" may accompany emotions, they are clearly not the same phenomenon. As Jaggar notes, feelings are "episodic" in the sense that they occur at a given moment in time, whereas emotions are "dispositional" in the sense that they extend over time: "For instance, we may assert truthfully that we are outraged by, proud of or saddened by certain events, even if at the moment we are neither agitated nor tearful." In addition, although people may be unaware of their emotional state—angry, ambivalent, depressed—they are (nearly) always aware of what they are feeling at any given moment in time.

If emotions include but also transcend episodic feelings, what else are they? One perspective—the *cognitivist* point of view—sees emotions as involving intentional judgments as well as physiological sensations. So, for example, you may be *feeling* anxious or agitated—but is the emotion involved related to concern about an upcoming exam or concern about an upcoming romantic date? In other words, an important component in emotions is the *intentional judgment* that is associated with the physiological feeling. We may conclude, for instance, that it is our (intentional) evaluation of an upcoming date that is responsible for the anxiety ("butterflies") we are feeling. Yet as important as "intentional judgments" are for understanding the nature of emotions, we still have not fully accounted for the complex nature of emotional experience.

Alison M. Jaggar, from "Love and Knowledge: Emotion in Feminist Epistemology"

IV. Emotions as Social Constructs

. . . Mature human emotions can be seen neither as instinctive nor as biologically determined. Instead, they are socially constructed on several levels.

The most obvious way in which emotions are socially constructed is that children are taught deliberately what their culture defines as appropriate responses to certain situations: to fear strangers, to enjoy spicy food or to like swimming in cold water. On

Are emotions social constructs? According to Alison M. Jaggar, emotions are in part social constructs, thus accounting for cultural differences in emotional responses to events like weddings.

a less conscious level, children also learn what their culture defines as the appropriate ways to express the emotions that it recognizes. Although there may be cross-cultural similarities in the expression of some apparently universal emotions, there are also wide divergences in what are recognized as expressions of grief, respect, contempt or anger. On an even deeper level, cultures construct divergent understandings of what emotions are. For instance, English metaphors and metonymies are said to reveal a "folk" theory of anger as a hot fluid contained in a private space within an individual and liable to dangerous public explosion (Lakoff and Kovecses, 1987). By contrast, the Ilongot, a people of the Philippines, apparently do not understand the self in terms of a public/private distinction and consequently do not experience anger as an explosive internal force: for them, rather, it is an interpersonal phenomenon for which the individual may, for instance, be paid (Rosaldo, 1984).

Further aspects of the social construction of emotion are revealed through reflection on emotion's intentional structure. If emotions necessarily involve judgments, then obviously they require concepts, which may be seen as socially constructed ways of organizing and making sense of the world. For this reason, emotions are simultaneously made possible and limited by the conceptual and linguistic resources of a society. This philosophical claim is borne out by empirical observation of the cultural variability of emotion. Although there is considerable overlap in the emotions identified by many cultures (Wierzbicka, 1986) at least some emotions are historically or culturally specific, including perhaps *ennui*, *Angst*, the Japanese *amai* (in which one clings to another, affiliative love), and the response of "being a wild pig," which occurs among the Gururumba, a horticultural people living in the New Guinea Highlands (Averell, 1980, p. 158). Even apparently universal emotions, such as anger or love, may vary cross-culturally. We have just seen that the Ilongot experience of anger is apparently quite different from the contemporary Western experience. Romantic love was invented in the Middle Ages in Europe and since that time has been modified considerably; for instance, it is no longer confined to the nobility. In some cultures, romantic love does not exist at all. . . .

In addition to immediate feelings and intentional judgments, emotions are also constituted by the social context in which they occur. For example, individuals in each culture are taught the appropriate emotional responses to people (strangers, authorities, religious figures, romantic interests) as well as situations (competitive sports, academic achievement, perceived insults). Each culture has its own unique "emotional vocabulary" that members of the culture learn at an early age, and this emotional vocabulary is an essential component in what emotions are all about. This vocabulary is expressed in the concepts and language of the culture, as well as in the actions and attitudes of the members. Jaggar's example of the emotion "romantic love" is pertinent here. Although there is general agreement regarding what this emotional concept means, each culture also tends to define the emotion—and its affiliated attitudes and behavior—in ways that are distinctive to that culture. The net result is that these social influences are integral elements in the construction of human emotions: hence the notion of "emotions as social constructs."

V. Emotions as Active Engagements

We often interpret our emotions as experiences that overwhelm us rather than as responses we consciously choose: that emotions are to some extent involuntary is part of the ordinary meaning of the term "emotion." Even in daily life, however, we recognize that emotions are not entirely involuntary and we try to gain control over them in various ways ranging from mechanistic behavior-modification techniques designed to

Alison M. Jaggar,
from "Love and Knowledge: Emotion in Feminist Epistemology"

sensitize or desensitize our feeling responses to various situations to cognitive techniques designed to help us to think differently about situations. For instance, we might try to change our response to an upsetting situation by thinking about it in a way that will either divert our attention from its more painful aspects or present it as necessary for some larger good. . . .

Emotions, then, are wrongly seen as necessarily passive or involuntary responses to the world. Rather, they are ways in which we engage actively and even construct the world. They have both "mental" and "physical" aspects, each of which conditions the other; in some respects they are chosen but in others they are involuntary; they presuppose language and a social order. Thus, they can be attributed only to what are sometimes called "whole persons," engaged in the on-going activity of social life.

Another component of emotions are the conscious decisions we make to engage in them—while pretending that they are natural forces over which we have little control. For example, have you ever had the experience of intentionally "working yourself up" into a state of righteous anger or indignation? And then acting as if it was the situation (a person's inconsiderate behavior, for example) that is responsible? Although the experience of the emotion may appear and feel genuine, it might never have come about if you hadn't made a conscious and active choice to engage the emotion.

VI. Emotion, Evaluation, and Observation

Emotions and values are closely related. . . . Indeed, many evaluative terms derive directly from words for emotions: "desirable," "admirable," "contemptible," "despicable," "respectable," and so on. Certainly it is true (*pace* J. S. Mill) that the evaluation of a situation as desirable or dangerous does not entail that it is universally desired or feared, but it does entail that desire or fear is viewed generally as an appropriate response to the situation. If someone is unafraid in a situation perceived generally as dangerous, her lack of fear requires further explanation; conversely, if someone is afraid without evident danger, then her fear demands explanation; and, if no danger can be identified, her fear is denounced as irrational or pathological. Thus, every emotion presupposes an evaluation of some aspect of the environment while, conversely, every evaluation or appraisal of the situation implies that those who share that evaluation will share, *ceteris paribus*, a predictable emotional response to the situation. . . .

Just as observation directs, shapes, and partially defines emotion, so too emotion directs, shapes, and even partially defines observation. Observation is not simply a passive process of absorbing impressions or recording stimuli; instead it is an activity of selection and interpretation. What is selected and how it is interpreted are influenced by emotional attitudes. On the level of individual observation, this influence has always been apparent to common sense, which notes that we remark very different features of the world when we are happy, depressed, fearful, or confident. . . .

Having articulated a multidimensional definition of "emotions," Jaggar is now ready to examine the implications of this enriched concept of emotions for epistemology. Most philosophers and probably all scientists believe that knowledge originates in sensory experience, through perception. Yet, as we have seen in this chapter, perceiving is an active process, not passive. We are continually selecting, organizing, and interpreting the sensations with which we are presented in our everyday experience, a process that is filtered through our uniquely constructed perceiving "lenses."

Analogously, there is an intimate and interactive relationship between perceiving and emotions. Imagine, for example, that you are waiting patiently in line for a bus when you feel a vigorous shove from behind: What is your emotion? Annoyance? When you turn around, you see that the "shover" is wearing dark glasses and is holding a cane used for the blind. Now what is your emotion? Sheepish embarrassment?

You help the individual onto the bus, guiding him to the last available seat, whereupon the "blind" person takes out a newspaper and begins reading. Now what is your emotional state? Anger? The point is that what we perceive in the world—and our judgments about these perceptions—influence our emotional reactions. And conversely, our emotions have a dramatic influence on what we perceive and how we interpret it. And because our knowledge of the world begins with perceptions, values and emotions are a natural and inseparable part of this knowing process. Jaggar next extends this fundamental insight to the project of constructing scientific knowledge.

VII. The Myth of Dispassionate Investigation

As we have already seen, Western epistemology has tended to view emotion with suspicion and even hostility. This derogatory Western attitude toward emotion, like the earlier Western contempt for sensory observation, fails to recognize that emotion, like sensory perception, is necessary to human survival. Emotions prompt us to act appropriately, to approach some people and situations and to avoid others, to caress or cuddle, fight or flee. Without emotion, human life would be unthinkable. Moreover, emotions have an intrinsic as well as an instrumental value. Although not all emotions are enjoyable or even justifiable, as we shall see, life without any emotion would be life without any meaning.

Within the context of Western culture, however, people have often been encouraged to control or even suppress their emotions. Consequently, it is not unusual for people to be unaware of their emotional state or to deny it to themselves and others. This lack of awareness, especially combined with a neopositivist understanding of emotion that construes it as just a feeling of which one is aware, lends plausibility to the myth of dispassionate investigation. But lack of awareness of emotions certainly does not mean that emotions are not present subconsciously or unconsciously, or that subterranean emotions do not exert a continuing influence on people's articulated values and observations, thoughts, and actions.

Within the positivist tradition, the influence of emotion is usually seen only as distorting or impeding observation or knowledge. Certainly it is true that contempt, disgust, shame, revulsion or fear may inhibit investigation of certain situations or phenomena. Furiously angry or extremely sad people often seem quite unaware of their surroundings or even of their own conditions; they may fail to hear or may systematically misinterpret what other people say. People in love are notoriously oblivious to many aspects of the situation around them.

In spite of these examples, however, positivist epistemology recognizes that the role of emotion in the construction of knowledge is not invariably deleterious and that emotions may make a valuable contribution to knowledge. But the positivist tradition will allow emotion to play only the role of suggesting hypotheses for investigation. Emotions are allowed this because the so-called logic of discovery sets no limits on the idiosyncratic methods that investigators may use for generating hypotheses.

When hypotheses are to be tested, however, positivist epistemology imposes the much stricter logic of justification. The core of this logic is replicability, a criterion believed capable of eliminating or cancelling out what are conceptualized as emotional as well as evaluative biases on the part of individual investigators. The conclusions of Western science thus are presumed "objective," precisely in the sense that they are uncontaminated by the supposedly "subjective" values and emotions that might bias individual investigators (Nagel, 1968, pp. 33–34).

But if, as has been argued, the positivist distinction between discovery and justification is not viable, then such a distinction is incapable of filtering out values in science. For example, although such a split, when built into the Western scientific method, is generally successful in neutralizing the idiosyncratic or unconventional values of individual investigators, it has been argued that it does not, indeed, cannot, eliminate generally

Alison M. Jaggar,
from "Love and Knowledge: Emotion in Feminist Epistemology"

> [E]motions have an intrinsic as well as an instrumental value. Although not all emotions are enjoyable or even justifiable, as we shall see, life without any emotion would be life without any meaning.

accepted social values. These values are implicit in the identification of the problems that are considered worthy of investigation, in the selection of the hypotheses that are considered worthy of testing and in the solutions to the problems that are considered worthy of acceptance. The science of past centuries provides ample evidence of the influence of prevailing social values, whether seventeenth-century atomistic physics (Merchant, 1980) or nineteenth-century competitive interpretations of natural selection (Young, 1985).

Of course, only hindsight allows us to identify clearly the values that shaped the science of the past and thus to reveal the formative influence on science of pervasive emotional attitudes, attitudes that typically went unremarked at the time because they were shared so generally. For instance, it is now glaringly evident that contempt for (and perhaps fear of) people of color is implicit in nineteenth-century anthropology's interpretations and even constructions of anthropological facts. Because we are closer to them, however, it is harder for us to see how certain emotions, such as sexual possessiveness or the need to dominate others, are currently accepted as guiding principles in twentieth century sociobiology or even defined as part of reason within political theory and economics (Quinby, 1986). . . .

Positivism views values and emotions as alien invaders that must be repelled by a stricter application of the scientific method. If the foregoing claims are correct, however, the scientific method and even its positivist construals themselves incorporate values and emotions. Moreover, such an incorporation seems a necessary feature of all knowledge and conceptions of knowledge. Therefore, rather than repressing emotion in epistemology it is necessary to rethink the relation between knowledge and emotion and construct conceptual models that demonstrate the mutually constitutive rather than oppositional relation between reason and emotion. Far from precluding the possibility of reliable knowledge, emotion as well as value must be shown as necessary to such knowledge. Despite its classical antecedents and as in the ideal of disinterested inquiry, the ideal of dispassionate inquiry is an impossible dream, but a dream none the less or perhaps a myth that has exerted enormous influence on Western epistemology. Like all myths, it is a form of ideology that fulfils certain social and political functions.

< READING CRITICALLY >

Analyzing Jaggar on the Role of Emotions

- Reflect on your study of philosophy to this point. Identify five emotions that you believe play a significant role in thinking philosophically and explain your rationale. Be sure to include specific examples to illustrate your points.

- Jaggar believes that both philosophy and modern science have artificially separated reason and emotion and have designated reason as the one true way of achieving knowledge and truth. Do you agree with her reasoning? Why or why not?

- Jaggar identifies the following components of what we mean by the term/concept *emotion*: a physiological sensation or feeling, intentional judgment, social construct, and active engagement/conscious choice. Select a complex emotion and analyze its structure by explaining how each of these factors contributes to its meaning.

- Jaggar believes that modern science needs to elevate emotions to a prominent role in every aspect of scientific exploration, though she doesn't provide many concrete examples to examine. Identify one emotion that you believe should be an essential and consistent element in scientific inquiry and explain (briefly) how this emotion might be better integrated into the process of constructing knowledge.

6.7 Making Connections: Developing Informed Beliefs

We have seen in these last two chapters that "knowledge" and "truth" are complex and elusive entities. Although there are compelling reasons to view knowledge and truth as goals toward which we challenge ourselves to strive, many people resist this insight. Either they take refuge in a belief in the absolute, unchanging nature of knowledge and truth, as presented by the appropriate authorities, or they conclude that there is no such thing as knowledge or truth and that trying to seek either is a futile enterprise. In this latter view of the world, known as *relativism,* all beliefs are considered to be "relative" to the person or context in which they arise. For the relativist, all opinions are equal in truth to all others; we are never in a position to say with confidence that one view is right and another view is wrong. Although a relativistic view is appropriate in some areas of experience—for example, in matters of taste such as fashion—in many other areas it is not. Knowledge in the form of well-supported beliefs is often difficult to achieve, but it does exist in some form. Some beliefs *are* better than others, not because an authority has proclaimed them so but because they can be analyzed and evaluated in terms of the criteria we described above.

Do you want another you? When Dolly the sheep proved that cloning was possible, another ethical dilemma was born. Developing informed beliefs in our complex and rapidly evolving world is a challenging enterprise, particularly with respect to volatile social issues such as cloning, racial profiling, or immigration. Philosophy provides the intellectual abilities to think critically about all of the issues we encounter.

Each day we are called on to solve difficult problems, analyze tangled issues, and sift through a tidal wave of information. We are expected to make intelligent decisions, negotiate our way through a jungle of relationships, and communicate our ideas clearly and persuasively. It's no wonder that we often feel overmatched, unable to marshal the thinking abilities needed to succeed in all of these demanding contexts. Here, for example, are a few of the issues that appear daily in the media and about which we, as thoughtful and concerned citizens, ought to develop informed opinions:

On Cloning Humans and Genetic Engineering, "Never" Turns Swiftly into "Why Not?": *There has been an enormous change in attitudes since Dolly the lamb became the first animal cloned from a cell taken from an adult. Contrary to early fears of a Brave New World, scientists have become sanguine about the notion of cloning human beings. The frenzy seems to have died down. Some infertility centers are already conducting experiments with human eggs that lay the groundwork for cloning. Ultimately, scientists expect cloning to be combined with genetic enhancement, adding genes to give desired traits. As another dimension of the cloning controversy, the genetic engineering of animals for food has recently become a major issue, raising both health concerns and also ethical questions regarding whether we have the "right" to tamper with nature in this way.*

Arab Americans Protest "Profiling" at Airports: *When Dr. Hassan Abbass, a Veterans Affairs Department surgeon, and his wife arrived at the airport to leave for vacation they were pulled aside and forced to submit to a careful search before boarding the plane. They became one of thousands of Americans of Middle Eastern heritage who have complained that a secretive and wide-scale "profiling" system sponsored by the government and aimed at preventing air terrorism has caused them to be unfairly selected for extra scrutiny at airports. "Profiling" of this type is being used more frequently in many areas of law enforcement, raising fundamental questions of how a free society balances security fears with civil liberties and the desire to avoid offensive stereotyping.*

Immigration: Is It Time to Shut the Door? *The United States is a nation of immigrants, with only the historically mistreated Native Americans possessing anything approaching a birthright to be in this country. Yet recently, and especially since 9/11, there are increasing cries to "shut the door" on immigration, strident voices coming from the descendents of previous immigrants. Compounding the complexity of the issues is the presence of millions of "illegal immigrants" who have already settled and established lives in the United States. In these cases, objections to granting these illegal immigrants resident status often come from immigrants who have "played by the rules" and pursued the legitimate path to legal residency. What approach should be taken to sorting out all of these issues in a just and humane way?*

Developing informed beliefs about these and other issues is an ongoing challenge to our thinking abilities. In thinking about these and any other issues, we should ask ourselves two important questions:

- *What is my belief about this issue?* Do you believe that human cloning should be pursued? What about whether "profiling" is a legitimate technique for improving public safety?

- *Is my belief informed by evidence and reasons?* For each of the beliefs that you have regarding these (and other) issues, can you answer the question "*Why* do you have that belief?" with intelligent and compelling reasons?

The fact is that, although beliefs are easy to come by, *informed* beliefs are much more difficult to find. To express a belief you merely have to say, "Well, I think . . ." or "I believe . . ." People are more than willing to make such pronouncements on virtually any subject. But to express an informed belief means that you have some idea of what you're talking about: You have explored the subject, examined different points of view, evaluated the supporting reasons and evidence, and synthesized your analysis into a cogent and compelling conclusion.

To develop a well-informed set of beliefs that you can use to knowledgeably guide you through life's treacherous currents, you need to combine the critical thinking abilities introduced in the first chapter with the philosophical themes that you have been exploring in subsequent chapters to arrive at informed, intelligent perspectives in every area of life. The tools of critical thinking are powerful, but they need to be integrated with the content of philosophy so that you will be able to

- develop a thoughtful and well-reasoned philosophy of life.
- engage in Socratic analysis and emulate his personal and intellectual virtues.
- develop insight into your "self."
- understand the nature of freedom.
- construct an enlightened ethical perspective.
- develop a thoughtful approach to religion.
- understand the nature of knowledge and truth and how to achieve them.
- develop a sophisticated and integrated view of reality.
- construct an informed perspective on political and social issues.

To initiate this process of evaluating your philosophical beliefs, complete the

---

thinking philosophically

WHAT ARE THE LIMITS OF YOUR KNOWLEDGE?

One of the core elements of thinking philosophically is reflecting thoughtfully on your intellectual development. Make a list of the philosophical themes that you have studied in your Introduction to Philosophy course (your professor may choose to have the class do this as a group). Then, for each of these topics, write a paragraph assessing the relative strength (or weakness) of your beliefs in that area.

Be sure that your responses are both honest and specific. They represent a rough evaluation of the progress you have made in learning to think philosophically about the most difficult areas of life. This is a journey that you will continue for the rest of your life, and ongoing critical reflection is the tool you can use to chart your growth and ensure that you are on the path you wish to take.

"Thinking Philosophically" activity above. How did you evaluate your philosophical understanding in these various areas? If you found that you have ample room for growth, you are not alone. We live in a complex, challenging world that is extremely demanding intellectually. The philosopher's way means recognizing that there are no easy answers and taking the responsibility for developing enlightened decisions.

writing about philosophy: Constructing Knowledge

The Assignment

Locate four different newspaper or magazine accounts of an important event—a court decision, a crime, and a political demonstration are possible topics. Analyze each of the accounts with the questions listed next and then construct your own version of what you believe took place in your own words.

- Does the account provide a convincing description of what took place?
- What reasons and evidence support the account?

- How reliable is the source? What are the author's perceiving lenses that might influence his or her account?
- Is the account consistent with other reliable descriptions of this event?

Finally, explain how each of the following philosophers would explain and analyze the process you used to create your account:

- René Descartes
- David Hume
- Immanuel Kant

MySearchLab Connections

Watch. Listen. Explore. Read. Mysearchlab is designed just for you. Each chapter features a customized study plan to help you learn and review key concepts and terms. Dynamic visual activities, videos, and readings found in the multimedia library will enhance your learning experience.

Here are a few questions and activities to help you understand this chapter:

1. Listen to the **Audiobook** *Bertrand Russell Appearance and Reality* on **mysearchlab.com** Explain Russell's theory regarding the relationship between appearance and reality.

2. Watch the **Video** *Steven Pinker Chalks It Up to the Blank Slate* on **mysearchlab.com** What are human universals and how do they undercut the validity of "The Blank Slate"?

3. Listen to the **Audiobook** *Locke—An Essay Concerning Human Understanding by Nigel Warburton* on **mysearchlab.com** Compare and contrast empiricism, innatism, and rationalism.

4. Listen to the **Podcast** *John Campbell on Berkeley's Puzzle* on **mysearchlab.com** Explain Berkeley's view that we are not physical things and all we have are our ideas.

5. Listen to the **Podcast** *Barry Stroud on Skepticism* on **mysearchlab.com** Is knowing that you are not dreaming a requirement to having reliable perceptual information about the world? Why or why not?

6. Listen to the **Podcast** *Adrian Moore on Kant's Metaphysics* on **mysearchlab.com** What is the primary difference between synthetic and analytic knowledge?

7. Listen to the **Audiobook** *Kant—Critique of Pure Reason by Nigel Warburton* on **mysearchlab.com** What is the difference between phenomena and noumena?

Questioning Independent Reality

- In his essay "Appearance and Reality," Bertrand Russell explores the question of whether there is any knowledge in the world that is so certain that no reasonable person could doubt it. He demonstrates the strangeness and wonder lying just below the surface of even the commonest things of daily life by analyzing the apparent paradoxes of perceiving something as simple as a table.

[**pp. 282–297**]

Reality Depends on Perception: Berkeley

- Bishop George Berkeley's philosophy of "subjective idealism" attempted to resolve the fundamental difficulty with Locke's epistemology by rejecting Locke's distinction between primary and secondary qualities, and Locke's "commonsense" belief in external objects. According to Berkeley, all things exist only as minds, or as ideas within minds (*esse est percipi*, "to be is to be perceived"). Ultimately, for Berkeley, all things exist as ideas in the mind of God.

[**pp. 300–305**]

All Knowledge Comes from Experience: Locke

- John Locke's approach to epistemology is founded on empiricism, or the belief that we only achieve knowledge through the experience of the senses. He believed that we are all born with an intellectual "blank slate," or *tabula rasa.*

- Locke's contemporary Gottfried Wilhelm von Leibniz, on the contrary, pointed out that there are many things that we do seem to know innately, but experience and education are required for these ideas to fully develop. Modern work in psychology, anthropology, and linguistics supports Leibniz's contentions.

- For Locke, there are four elements to the process of perceiving or knowing the experiential world: (1) the object in the world; (2) sensations the object emits through "impulses," and that we detect through our five senses; (3) ideas, images, and impressions produced in our minds by these "impulses"; and (4) the conscious mind that perceives, reflects, and arranges these impulses and ideas.

- According to Locke, these objects are themselves composed of two types of physical qualities, primary qualities and secondary qualities. Yet Locke was unable to resolve the nature of the external "substances" in which these emitted qualities must ultimately reside.

[**pp. 297–299**]

KEY TERMS
innate knowledge
primary qualities
secondary qualities

KEY TERM
subjective idealism

for further reading, viewing & research

Read the Primary Source on MySearchLab

- *An Essay Concerning Human Understanding,* John Locke
- *New Essays Concerning Human Understanding,* Gottfried Wilhelm von Leibniz
- *A Treatise Concerning the Principles of Human Knowledge,* George Berkeley
- *An Enquiry Concerning Human Understanding,* David Hume
- *Critique of Pure Reason,* Kant
- *Appearance and Reality,* Bertrand Russell

Films

- ***Apocalypse Now* (1979)** What factors affect one's understanding of what is real and true? Based on the themes in Joseph Conrad's *Heart of Darkness,* this Vietnam-era film follows a U.S. Special Forces captain on his mission to find and assassinate a Green Beret, Colonel Kurtz, who has set up his own community and is playing god in the

forest of Cambodia. As the captain travels further and further into the jungle, he begins to lose his grip on reality.

- ***JFK* (1991)** What is the truth? How do we know? Based in fact and theory, this film explores the causes of the assassination of President John F. Kennedy. The film follows the investigation of former New Orleans district attorney, Jim Garrison, into the events leading up to the assassination and the possible conspiracy in covering up the perpetrators.

- ***Rashomon* (1950)** Is there a single knowable reality? In twelfth-century Japan, a woman is raped and her husband is killed. In the trial that follows, four witnesses give four completely different accounts of what occurred.

- ***The Thin Blue Line* (1988)** How can our knowledge of the world be mistaken? Errol Morris's documentary about an innocent man found guilty of murder and sentenced to death by a corrupt system. The film illustrates the different realities presented over the course of the investigation and

Understanding Reality Requires Skepticism: Hume

- David Hume's epistemology is profoundly skeptical, applying Descartes' radical doubt to an empiricist framework. In Hume's view, scientific knowledge is based on the flawed belief that the principles of universal causation and induction are true, but there is no evidence to support this belief. However, Hume acknowledged that his radical skepticism, while his responsibility as a philosopher, did not doom him to a life of confusion and despair; "I dine, I play a game of backgammon, I converse, and am merry with my friends."

[pp. 305–315]

We Constitute Our World: Kant

- Immanuel Kant sought to resolve the disputes between empiricism and rationalism by refuting Hume's radical skepticism and its bleak conclusions. Kant proposed a theory of "transcendental idealism," which holds that there are truths about the world that are both necessary and universal. Kant's "Copernican revolution" in epistemology was his belief that the core question was not "How does the human mind come to know an essentially unknowable world?" but rather "How does the human mind construct a knowable world?" That is, whereas the empiricists Locke, Berkeley, and Hume conceived of the human mind as a passive *tabula rasa*, Kant argued that the mind is an active agent in the construction of knowledge. We come to an understanding of the world through an interaction between the data of sense experience and what Kant describes as "the faculties of the mind" to sort, organize, and make sense of that data.

- Kant's metaphysics describes twelve basic categories of the mind that help us to gain synthetic a priori knowledge, which (1) is necessary and universally true, (2) can be discovered independently of experience: *a priori*, and (3) provides us with genuine information regarding our experience of the world: *synthetic.*

- Kant makes a distinction between two kinds of reality: phenomenal reality (the world as we constitute it and experience it) and noumenal reality (the world beyond our perceptions, about which we can achieve knowledge through the application of "pure reason").

[pp. 315–336]

Emotions Shape Our Understanding: Jaggar

- Feminist epistemology argues that traditional epistemology has excluded marginal or "othered" voices, experiences, and views (especially those of women). For example, the feminist philosopher Alison M. Jaggar argues that the realm of *emotional* experience has been left out of epistemological analysis. Emotions, she argues, are as important as the senses and reason in shaping our perceptions and understandings of the world.

[pp. 336–344]

conviction, and includes interviews with those involved as well as reenactments of the crime based on the testimony given. Morris explores the dangerous way in which perception and belief can be manipulated and altered.

- ***The Third Man*** (1949) How do we know what to believe? American author Holly Martins arrives in Vienna to find that his friend and host, Harry Lime, has been killed in an auto accident. Investigation produces questions about the death, and casts a shadow on Harry's character, and soon Holly begins to question the reality that has been presented to him. The film is based on Graham Greene's novella.

- ***Vertigo*** (1958) How can appearances deceive? In Alfred Hitchcock's psychological thriller, a former police detective, Scottie Ferguson, is hired by an old college friend to trail his wife, who has been acting strangely and sometimes appears possessed. Scottie's understanding of reality begins to unravel as he entertains the notion that the possession may be true; the people involved are revealed to be other than they appear; his own severe fear of heights literally skews his perception; and he becomes aware that he may be a pawn in a larger plot.

Literature

- ***Waiting for Godot,*** Samuel Beckett. In this dramatic existentialist work, two men contemplate life's purpose while waiting for a visitor whom they hope will provide an answer but whom they suspect will never arrive. Beckett explores the futility and possibility of finding meaning in an absurd and godless world.

- ***Heart of Darkness,*** Joseph Conrad. Marlow, a young captain, travels into the Congo to find Kurtz, a brilliant man who runs the inner station of a Belgian ivory trading company. As Marlow travels deeper into the heart of the jungle, his awareness of the company's brutal dealings grows, and his understanding of reality shifts. By the time he reaches the now mad Kurtz, everything that Marlow knows has been called into question.

- ***The Turn of the Screw,*** Henry James. A governess suspects that her young charges are aware of and able to commune with ghosts. This psychologically complex novella lets the reader decide whether the governess's perceptions are a product of her paranoia or are to be taken as truth.

- ***The Death of Ivan Ilyich,*** Leo Tolstoy. As Ivan faces his own mortality, he begins to question the way in which he has lived and to recognize the artificiality that pervaded much of his existence. In this novel, Tolstoy addresses themes of perception, truth, and reality.

(Sistine Chapel, The Last Judgment *[1538–1541]. Fresco pre restoration* Buonarroti, Michelangelo (1475–1564)/The Art Gallery Collection/Alamy

Thinking philosophically about religious beliefs

What is religion?

is there a spiritual reality?

EXPLORING THE PHILOSOPHY OF RELIGION

A survey of world religions

Faith and reason

The problem of evil

Arguments for God

Søren Kierkegaard

John Hick

St. Thomas Aquinas

chapter 7

◀ **What can philosophy tell us about religion?** Michelangelo's depiction of the Last Judgment reflects the Renaissance view of life after death. In this chapter, you will think critically about various dimensions of the religious experience.

351

7.1 Thinking Philosophically About Religious Beliefs

You very possibly were brought up in a religious tradition that has influenced your life in a variety of ways. It likely helped demarcate the major life passages for members of your family, including birth, coming of age, marriage, and death. You may have gathered on a regular basis in a sacred place with others of your faith to pray, meditate, sing, chant, read from a holy book, or listen to a religious leader speak about important themes. The teachings of your religion very likely provided moral guidelines to follow as you navigated your life. And these same teachings may have provided answers to some of life's most enduring and disturbing mysteries: What is the meaning of my life? Is there some form of continued existence after death? What path should I take to achieve spiritual enlightenment? If you were not raised in an organized religion, you probably encountered religion in a less formal and structured way.

If you already have religious beliefs or if you do not see the value of religion, why study the philosophy of religion? What is the purpose of this field of philosophy? Perhaps it's best to begin with what such study is *not* about. Studying the philosophy of religion is *not* designed to

- transform you into an atheist or agnostic.
- convert you from being an atheist or agnostic to a belief in God or gods.
- undermine your religious beliefs or "convert" you to another religion.
- engage you in emotional arguments with classmates over which is the one "true" religion.

Instead, the philosophy of religion *is* designed to

- develop your ability to think philosophically regarding the religious and/or spiritual dimension of experience.
- critically evaluate the reasons, evidence, and arguments with respect to religion, both pro and con.
- expand, enrich, and deepen your understanding of other religions in the world.
- encourage you to reflect on the nature and foundation of your own religious beliefs.

Philosophy and religion have had a volatile and at times contentious relationship with one another. As we saw in Chapter 2 when we examined the pre-Socratic thinkers, religion was a precursor to philosophy as well as organized science. Early religions tended to be rooted in superstition, encouraging a worldview that initially inhibited the development of philosophy and science as independent disciplines based on reason, systematic inquiry, and empirical/logical validation. This was, in Western culture, the beginning of a long and uneasy relationship among philosophy, science, and religion, a competition over what each considered to be its legitimate domain of expertise. Over the centuries, the "highlight" reel of these mutual tensions would include

- the execution of Socrates for allegedly not believing in the conventional gods of the time (in addition to "corrupting" the youth of Athens).

- the threatened execution of Galileo for asserting the same "blasphemous" truth as Copernicus. Because he publicly recanted this belief, announcing that Earth (and, symbolically, humankind) formed the center of the universe, he was able to have his death sentence commuted to a twenty-year house arrest. (However, he was reported to have muttered on leaving the Inquisition Tribunal, "But still Earth circles the sun.")

- the uproar over the publication and subsequent dissemination of Charles Darwin's *On the Origin of Species*, which contended that all life forms on Earth have evolved from simpler origins through a process of "natural selection."

But seen through a modern lens, many people believe that there is *in principle* no necessary and compelling reason philosophy, science, and religion can't coexist (relatively) peacefully. It's only when one of the three disciplines intentionally encroaches on one or both of the other areas that problems may arise. For example:

- If philosophy decrees, as the logical positivists did, that religious statements have no "truth value" because they cannot be verified empirically

Do you practice a religion that has a holy book? This copy of the Holy Bible was handwritten and illustrated by monks in the fifteenth century. The attention lavished on each page reflects the reverence given to the Bible as the word of God in the Christian faith.

thinking philosophically

WHAT ARE YOUR RELIGIOUS BELIEFS?

As you respond to the following questions, express your ideas thoughtfully and articulately. If you have no religious beliefs at this time, you can respond to these questions with reference to a religion with which you are familiar or simply from your own perspective on religion, whatever that might be.

- What is your definition of religion? What do you think is the purpose of religion?

- How would you describe your religious beliefs? Does it include a belief in "God"? If so, describe your concept of God.

- What was the origin of your religious beliefs (or lack of religious beliefs)? If your beliefs are different from those you were raised with, explain what caused you to change your religious views.

- What religious activities do you engage in (for example, worship, prayer, meditation, communion, singing, chanting, liturgy)?

- Describe the role that religious leaders and "holy books" play in your religion.

- Describe some of the "symbols" and "myths" of your religion.

- How does your religion view other religions?

Science versus religion: What accounts for the conflict and tension that have existed between them? This depiction of a sixth-century view of the universe shows Earth as the center of the universe with the sun circling Earth. Scientists like Galileo (1564–1643), who asserted that Earth circled the sun, were considered to be heretics.

Albert Einstein (1879–1955). This German-born physicist advanced the theories of special and general relativity and is best known for his formula $E = mc^2$. In addition to his scientific papers, he wrote about the relationship between science, religion, and ethics.

- If science proclaims, as scientific materialists have, that only physical matter exists in the universe: Entities such as souls, spirits, or gods are simply concocted fantasies
- If religion announces, as many religions have, that the conclusions of philosophy and science should be automatically dismissed if they appear to conflict with religious truths

Unfortunately, it is too often the loudest, most strident, and least-informed voices that capture the headlines and people's attention. In contrast, a solid group of serious, reflective, and informed philosophers, scientists, and religious leaders believe that we should be using these three frameworks to achieve a more integrated, synthesized, and enlightened view of the entirety of human experience. Many philosophers have had strong religious convictions, including Immanuel Kant, René Descartes, William James, and Søren Kierkegaard. And many scientists have likewise believed in the compatibility of science and religion, including **Albert Einstein**, as he reveals in his essay "Religion and Science":

It is easy to see why the churches have always fought science and persecuted its devotees. On the other hand, I maintain that the cosmic religious feeling is the strongest and noblest motive for scientific research. Only those who realize the immense efforts and, above all, the devotion without which pioneer work in theoretical science cannot be achieved are able to grasp the strength of the emotion out of which alone such work, remote as it is from the immediate realities of life, can issue. What a deep conviction of the rationality of the universe and what a yearning to understand, were it but a feeble reflection of the mind revealed in this world, Kepler and Newton must have had to enable them to spend years of solitary labor in disentangling the principles of celestial mechanics! Those whose acquaintance with scientific research is derived chiefly from its practical results easily develop a completely false notion of the mentality of the men who, surrounded by a skeptical world, have shown the way to kindred spirits scattered wide through the world and the centuries. Only one who has devoted his life to similar ends can have a vivid realization of what has inspired these men and given them the strength to remain true to their purpose in spite of countless failures. It is cosmic religious feeling that gives a man such strength. A contemporary has said, not unjustly, that in this materialistic age of ours the serious scientific workers are the only profoundly religious people.

So, as you approach the philosophy of religion, make a special effort to do so with an open mind. A person's religious beliefs are an intensely personal affair. We need to honestly and openly seek to understand the religious experience in its deepest dimensions, endeavoring with intellectual empathy to appreciate the many ways of being religious with which we are unfamiliar. In this regard, it is helpful to remind ourselves that the reason we believe one religion rather than another (or believe in *no* religion) is often due to *an accident of birth.* In short, we need to think critically and philosophically at the highest possible levels to navigate our way through the emotional minefield of religion.

What exactly does it mean to think critically and philosophically about religions and the religious experience? It entails examining the epistemological foundations for religious beliefs, the cogency and coherence of their metaphysics, the intelligibility and appropriateness of their ethical systems. Thinking critically involves asking—and trying to answer—significant questions such as:

- What is the nature of the religious impulse?
- How do we respond to differing claims to religious truth? Must there be only one true religion?
- Are there compelling proofs or evidence for the existence of God (or gods)?
- If you believe in an all-powerful, all-good supernatural Being, how is it possible to account for the existence of evil in the world?
- Is reason relevant to religious faith?

If we consistently embody the values of critical scrutiny, objectivity, tolerance, and a willingness to grow in our understanding, then exploring the philosophy of religion can be one of the most rewarding endeavors in which we can engage. And if we as individuals can become more enlightened and less myopic regarding religion, then we can share this more informed perspective with others who have not had the same opportunity to think philosophically about these issues. And by so doing we can elevate their understanding in an effort to create a more peaceful, tolerant world.

7.2 What Is Religion?

There are few concepts more complex and emotionally charged than the concept of *religion*. In this section, we will begin with an essay by philosopher Frederick Streng that lays out the problems with common definitions of religion. We will then consider different explanations for the religious impulse and conclude with an essay that joins Eastern and Western thought in conceptualizing religion as the quest for understanding of the ultimate nature of reality.

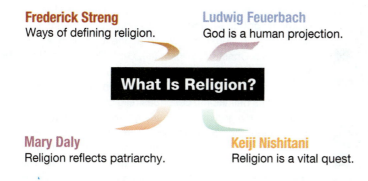

Frederick Streng
Ways of defining religion.

Ludwig Feuerbach
God is a human projection.

What Is Religion?

Mary Daly
Religion reflects patriarchy.

Keiji Nishitani
Religion is a vital quest.

Frederick Streng
(1933–1993). An American philosopher and professor at Southern Methodist University, Streng was a founding member of the Society of Asian and Comparative Philosophy and wrote and edited volumes on religious life across the world's religions.

Ways of Defining Religion

The twentieth-century philosopher **Frederick Streng** tackled the question of "What is religion?" in the following excerpt from his textbook *Ways of Being Religious*. Streng's work in comparative religions leads him to search for a definition that encompasses all of the world's religions, not just those in the Judeo-Christian tradition. In this selection, he challenges readers to subject their notion of what constitutes a religion to philosophical scrutiny.

Frederick Streng, from *Ways of Being Religious,* "What Is Religion?"

An African proverb, from the Ganda tribe in central Uganda, states, "He who never visits thinks his mother is the only cook." As with most proverbs, its meaning is larger than the explicit subjects referred to—in this case food and visiting. It suggests that a person is much the poorer for not having had exposure to and acquaintance with the ways of other people.

All of us have had some acquaintance with religious people, just as we have tasted our mother's food. But do we really understand very well what it means to be religious? The "Father of the Scientific Study of Religion," Max Mueller, once said: "He who knows one religion understands none." That is perhaps too extreme a statement as it stands, and yet it says about the study of religion what the African proverb says about the knowledge of life in general—that we sacrifice much if we confine ourselves to the familiar.

If a visit is to be fruitful, the "traveler" must do more than just move from place to place. He must respond to what he sees. But what is it that shapes the way we respond to new experiences? Our perception of things is often colored by our previous attitudes toward them. In this case, what do you, the reader, expect from an exposure to various expressions of religion? What sorts of things do you expect to see? How do you think you will respond to them? If you were asked to define, illustrate, or to characterize religious behavior, how would you do so? The answers to these questions, of course, reflect your preconceptions. To become conscious of your preconceptions, ask yourself the following four questions:

Does your definition *reduce* religion to what you happen to be acquainted with by accident of birth and socialization?
Perhaps that goes without saying. It may be true of anyone's "off-the-cuff" definition of religion. However, we ask this question to encourage you to consider whether your definition has sufficient *scope*. Is it broad enough to include the religious activities of human beings throughout the world? In surveying university students we have commonly gotten responses to the question, "What is religion?" as follows: "Being Christian, I would define it [religion] as personal relationship with Christ." "Religion [is]: God, Christ, and Holy Ghost and their meaning to each individual." Other students think of worship rather than belief. In this vein, one edition of Webster's dictionary, in the first of its definitions, describes religion as "the service and adoration of God or a god as expressed in forms of worship." If we were to accept any of the above definitions, many people in the world would be excluded—people who regard some of their most important activities as religious, but who do not focus upon a deity. That is to say, not all religions are **theistic**. It remains to be seen, of course, whether and to what extent this is true. But let us all be warned of taking our habits or our dictionary as the sole resource for defining religion. In some areas, the main lines of significant understanding are already well established. Therefore we have no serious quarrel with Webster's definition of food as "nutritive material taken into an organism for growth, work, or repair and for maintaining the vital processes." But in religion, interpretive concepts are more problematic. Therefore

Culture and religion: What are the connections? Many people participate in their parents' or culture's religion beginning in childhood, coloring their view of what constitutes religion. Streng suggests that we broaden our concept to include an understanding of other faiths.

we are suspicious of the adequacy of the dictionary's definition of religion.

Another common way to define religion is to regard it as "morality plus stories," or "morality plus emotion." These are ways of asserting that religion has to do mainly with ethics, or that its myths merely support the particular views of a people. There are, of course, persons for whom religion has been reduced to ethics, as when Thomas Paine stated (in *The Rights of Man*): "My country is the world, and my religion is to do good." But we should be cautious in assuming that this testimony would do for all religious people.

A final example of a definition that begins with personal experience is one that claims: "Religion is a feeling of security"; or, as one student put it: "Religion is an aid in coping with that part of life which man does not understand, or in some cases a philosophy of life enabling man to live more deeply." In locating the basis of religion in man's need for a sense of security, this approach suggests that the deepest study of religion is through psychology. It has been dramatically expressed by the psychiatrist and writer C. G. Jung when he wrote: "Religion is a relationship to the highest or strongest value . . . the value by which you are possessed unconsciously. That psychological fact which is the greatest power in your system is the god, since it is always the overwhelming psychic factor which is called 'god.'" Although this

What religious ceremonies have you participated in? As you examine this photo of a Hindu religious ceremony in the Ganges River, keep in mind Streng's point about "delaying to make an evaluation until you have understood why their expressions and processes have profound meaning for them—however strange those expressions may seem to you."

understanding of religion expresses a very important point, many theologians and religious philosophers point out that an interpretation that reduces all of religious experience to psychological, biological, or social factors omits the central reality exposed in that experience—the Sacred or Ultimate Reality. Thus, a student of religion should keep open the question of whether a familiar interpretation of religious life that fits into a conventional, social science perspective of man is adequate for interpreting the data.

Does your definition reflect a *bias* on your part—positive or negative—toward religion as a whole, or toward a particular religion?

There are many examples of biased definitions that could be cited. Some equate religion with superstition, thus reflecting a negative evaluation. One man defined religion as "the sum of the scruples which impede the free exercise of the human faculties." Another hostile view of religion is to see religion as a device of priests to keep the masses in subjection and themselves in comfort. Similarly, Karl Marx, while not actually attempting to define religion, called it "the opiate of the people," again reflecting a bias against (all) religion.

Still others, in defining religion, are stating their concept of *true* religion as opposed to what they regard as false or pagan faiths. Henry Fielding, in his novel *Tom Jones,* has the provincial parson Mr. Thwackum saying, "When I mention religion I mean the Christian religion; and not only the Christian religion, but the Protestant religion; and not only the Protestant religion; but the Church of England." Some Christians assume that their personal conviction comprises a definition of religion, so that religion is regarded as "the worship of God through His Son Jesus Christ," or "a personal relationship with Christ." A Muslim can point out that the essence of religion is to make peace with God through complete submission to God's will, a submission that he will insist is brought to fulfillment in Islam. (In Arabic the word "Islam" means "submission," "peace," "safety," and "salvation.")

Therefore the student interested in reflecting on religious experience that includes more than a single institutional or cultural expression should remember the distinction between descriptive (neutral) and evaluative definitions. A descriptive definition attempts to be as inclusive as possible about a class of items, such as religious forms. An evaluative definition, on the other hand, reflects one's own criteria for truth or falsity, for reality or illusion. In "visiting" religious people, we suggest that you delay making an evaluation until you have understood why their expressions and processes have profound meaning for them—however strange those expressions may seem to you. . . . Obviously the believer who advocates one religion to the exclusion of all others differs sharply from one who rejects all. Nevertheless, if either accepts his own convictions about what is best or worst in religion as a description of what religion in fact is everywhere and for everyone, he exhibits a common indifference to unfamiliar, and therefore potentially surprising, religious patterns. As a believer (or skeptic), you have a right to declare your own understanding of what is most important, most real, in religion. This declaration is, in fact, essential, for it guides you in your quest for whatever is most real in life. As a student, on the other hand, you have an obligation to carry your studies as far as necessary to include relevant data. In this role, your obligation is not only to your own perception of value but also to a common world of understanding in which men of many religious persuasions can converse with each other.

Does your definition *limit* religion to what it has been in the past, and nothing else, or does your definition make it possible to speak of emerging forms of religion?
In asking this question, we should observe two striking facts of the history of religion: there was a time when some present religions did not exist, and some of the religions which once emerged no longer exist (for example, the Egyptian and Babylonian religions). Human history, then, has witnessed the emergence and abandonment of several religions.

Even religious traditions that have maintained a sense of continuity over vast stretches of time (Hinduism, Buddhism, Judaism, Christianity, for example) have undergone important changes. Is it really as obvious as we tend to think that they are essentially the same now as they were at their origins? Do the terms naming these traditions even today point to a single entity, however complex? You are familiar with at least some instances of religious warfare *within* the Christian tradition. Roman Catholics have persecuted and killed Lutherans; Lutherans have persecuted and killed Calvinists; Calvinists, Anglicans; Anglicans, Quakers; and most have returned the act with interest. Are all of these groups expressions of "the one true church"? Are some more Christian than others? Is there only one form of Christianity? Are new movements violations of the tradition? Or is the one who speaks to his own time the one who is most faithful to the genius of his tradition? These questions can be asked of all religious traditions. All have experienced change and diversity. Furthermore, it seems likely that this will continue, and that new religious traditions will emerge. Therefore, the conventions of the past cannot be regarded as the limits of future religious forms.

In part because history has witnessed the emergence and internal changes of many religions, anthropologists and cultural historians commonly suggest that religion (and human culture in general) has attained only its adolescence. Likewise, philosophers and religious thinkers in both East and West point to the anxiety and tensions today that are expressed in political, social, economic, and intellectual upheaval. They raise a question of whether or not man's moral, psychic, and evaluative resources can catch up with his self-destructive potential seen in technologically advanced weapons and psychological-chemical techniques for social control. The most hopeful of these philosophers perceive the present turmoil as a lack of "maturity" in human consciousness, and express the hope that it is not too late (quite) to change the direction of man from self-destruction to self-fulfillment.

From this perspective most of mankind's experience is still in the future. The history of religious life to the present is only a beginning. But the basis of these projections is the recognition that man's survival requires him to recognize religious dynamics and processes for evaluations as major forces in human life. Should not a definition of religion aid us in looking at contemporary phenomena to see if any new ways of being religious are emerging? At least it should not inhibit persons with an interest in this matter, and we think an introduction to religion should encourage such reflection.

Does your definition have sufficient *precision?*

Are there any limits to the scope of religion, or are the limits so vague that they fail to mark out an object of study? In an attempt to be as broadminded as possible, many definitions are like a student's statement that religion is "the means man has of coping with his world." Or they are similar to the claim that religion is "believing in a way of life which involves understanding and caring for others," or "religion is love." Such definitions tell us a good deal, but without some qualification they might refer to many other expressions of human life than specifically religious ones. In order to find a focus and a set of limitations at the outer circumference of that focus, we need to designate what are those essential elements of religion that will expose the *religious* meaning of the evidence we look at.

When one has "visited" (seen) a wide range of religious life, from all parts of the world and throughout human history, it becomes apparent that religion is a way of life that involves many processes—all of which, in different ways, are directed toward a common end. The goal is to reach a state of being that is conceived to be the highest possible state or condition. Religion is the general term for the various ways by which people seek to become changed into that highest state. We understand *religion as a means toward ultimate transformation.* By this we are not claiming that every activity you think of as religious will in fact transform you ultimately. It might, but that is not our point. We mean that *any* reasonably specific means that *any* person adopts with the serious hope and intention of moving toward ultimate transformation should be termed "religious." We think it possible to speak of all religious activity (Eastern and Western, past, present, and emerging) without reducing religion to what is merely familiar to us and without putting a value judgment on one or more religions.

> **[M]ost of mankind's experience is still in the future. The history of religious life to the present is only a beginning.**

‹ READING CRITICALLY ›

Analyzing Streng on Definitions of Religion

- Describe your concept of *religion* as specifically as possible. Where did the concept originate for you? How did it evolve as you have matured? Explain the reasons or experiences that support your concept.

- Evaluate your concept of *religion* by answering the four questions posed by Streng:

  1. "Does your definition *reduce* religion to what you happen to be acquainted with by accident of birth and socialization?"

  2. "Does your definition reflect a *bias* on your part—positive or negative—toward religion as a whole, or toward a particular religion?"

  3. "Does your definition *limit* religion to what it has been in the past, and nothing else, or does your definition make it possible to speak of emerging forms of religion?"

  4. "Does your definition have sufficient *precision*?"

- Compare your definition of religion to the definitions of other students in your class. What are the similarities? What are the differences? How do you explain these similarities and differences?

- Streng defines religion as a "means toward ultimate transformation." What do you think this definition means? Explain how this definition relates to your definition.

Frederick Streng's essay suggests the variety of approaches that exist for thinking about religion, approaches that the philosopher John Hick has grouped into two camps. On one side is the idea that religion "is a projection upon the universe of our human hopes, fears, and ideals"; on the other side is the idea that religion is "a human response to a transcendent reality." The readings from Feuerbach and Nishitani that follow represent these two ideas.

God Is a Human Projection: Feuerbach

Ludwig Feuerbach (1804–1872). A German philosopher known for his radical critique of idealism and religion, Feuerbach's writing about religion led to his dismissal from his university job, and he spent much of his career as an independent scholar.

Many theistic religions assert that God created humans in God's image. The German philosopher **Ludwig Feuerbach** contended that the reverse is actually the case: That is, humans created God in their own image. Why? Because there is at the center of ourselves an "estrangement." We are divided into two selves: our actual selves—the way we are—and our idealized selves—the way would like to be. Our unconscious "solution" to this existential estrangement is to unconsciously project our idealized perfection (what we ought to be) as a divine being (God). At the same time, we project our own actual existence as one of sin and imperfection in comparison with this perfect being. In advancing this point of view, Feuerbach's goal was not to destroy traditional religion but to transform it into a secular humanism that he called "realized Christianity." When the "hidden truth" of theist religion was revealed through philosophical analysis, Feuerbach believed that this would liberate humans to turn their attention from worshipping a "God" that existed only as a projected image and redirect their love and devotion to all of humankind. Thus this new religion would be "secular" because it was not supernatural in nature and a "humanism" because it is devoted solely to the betterment of all fellow humans. The following selections are taken from Feuerbach's influential book, *The Essence of Christianity.*

Ludwig Feuerbach, from *The Essence of Christianity*

Religion is the dream of the human mind. But even in dreams we do not find ourselves in emptiness or in heaven, but on earth, in the realm of reality; we only see real things in the entrancing splendour of imagination and caprice, instead of in the simple daylight of reality and necessity. Hence I do nothing more to religion—and to speculative philosophy and theology also—than to open its eyes, or rather to turn its gaze from the internal towards the external, i.e., I change the object as it is in the imagination into the object as it is in reality . . . .

Following this initial statement of purpose, Feuerbach goes on to describe the process by which we "create" God: We identify the most revered values and emotions that humans are capable of, imagine these values in perfect form and then invest these values and emotions with a personal identity—God—a process known as **anthropomorphism**.

Anthropomorphism The assigning of human characteristics to nonhuman entities.

Ludwig Feuerbach, from *The Essence of Christianity*

You believe in love as a divine attribute because you yourself love; you believe that God is a wise, benevolent being because you know nothing better in yourself than benevolence and wisdom; and you believe that God exists, that therefore he is a subject—whatever exists is a subject whether it be defined as substance, person, essence, or otherwise—because you yourself exist, are yourself a subject. You know no higher human good than to love, than to be good and wise; and even so you know no higher happiness than to exist, to be a subject; for the consciousness of all reality, of all bliss, is for you bound up in the consciousness of being a subject of existing. God is an existence, a subject to you, for the same reason that he is to you a wise, a blessed, a personal being.

From this concept of perfection into which we have breathed supernatural life (the "subject"), we then proceed to elaborate our creation in more textured and personalized ways (the "divine predicates"). As part of this elaboration, we increasingly project ourselves as sinful and imperfect, needing blessings, mercy, and salvation from our divine creation to elevate ourselves and save us from the abyss.

. . . But here it is also essential to observe, and this phenomenon is an extremely remarkable one, characterizing the very core of religion, that in proportion as the divine subject is in reality human, the greater is the apparent difference between God and man; that is, the more, by reflection on religion, by theology, is the identity of the divine and human denied, and the human, considered as such, is depreciated. The reason of this is, that as what is positive in the conception of the divine being can only be human, the conception of man, as an object of consciousness, can only be negative. To enrich God, man must become poor; that God may be all, man must be nothing. But he desires to be nothing in himself, because what he takes from himself is not lost to him, since it is preserved in God. Man has his being in God; why then should he have it in himself? Where is the necessity of positing the same thing twice, of having it twice? What man withdraws from himself, what he renounces in himself, he only enjoys in an incomparably higher and fuller measure in God . . . .

Religion further denies goodness as a quality of human nature; man is wicked, corrupt, incapable of good; but, on the other hand, God is only good—the Good Being. Man's nature demands as an object goodness, personified as God; but is it not hereby declared that goodness is an essential tendency of man? If my heart is wicked, my understanding perverted, how can I perceive and feel the holy to be holy, the good to be good? . . . Either goodness does not exist at all for man, or, if it does exist, therein is revealed to the individual man the holiness and goodness of human nature.

Ludwig Feuerbach, from *The Essence of Christianity*

In this final section Feuerbach addresses the question of the source of religion: Why is it that humans naturally—and unconsciously—create a perfect being whom they can then worship and attempt to emulate? It's because we yearn to be free from ourselves, "from the limits and defects" of our individual, actual selves. It is through our imaginative creation of God that we transcend ourselves and soar to the realm of ultimate goodness and perfection.

Heavenly ideals. How might the idea of Heaven illustrate Feuerbach's thesis about the human longing for a realm of ultimate goodness and perfection?

Ludwig Feuerbach, from *The Essence of Christianity*

Man has his highest being, his God, in himself; not in himself as an individual, but in his essential nature, his species. No individual is an adequate representation of his species, but only the human individual is conscious of the distinction between the species and the individual; in the sense of this distinction lies the root of religion. The yearning of man after something above himself is nothing else than the longing after the perfect type of his nature, the yearning to be free from himself, i.e., from the limits and defects of his individuality. Individuality is the self-conditioning, the self-limitation of the species. Thus man has cognizance of nothing above himself, of nothing beyond the nature of humanity; but to the individual man this nature presents itself under the form of an individual man. Thus, for example, the child sees the nature of man *above itself* in the form of its parents, the pupil in the form of his tutor. But all feelings which man experiences toward a superior man, nay, in general, all moral feelings which man has towards man, are of a religious nature. Man feels nothing towards God which he does not also feel toward man. *Homo homini deus est.* Want teaches prayer; but in misfortune, in sorrow, man kneels to entreat help of man also. Feeling makes God a man, but for the same reason it makes man a God. How often in deep emotion, which alone speaks genuine truth, man exclaims to man: You are, you have been my redeemer, my saviour, my protecting spirit, by God! We feel awe, reverence, humility, devout admiration, in thinking of a truly great, noble man; we feel ourselves worthless, we sink into nothing, even in the presence of human greatness. The purely, truly human emotions are religious; but for that reason the religious emotions are purely human; the only difference is that the religious emotions are vague, indefinite; but even this is only the case when the object of them is indefinite. Where God is positively defined, is the object of positive religion, there God is also the object of positive, definite human feelings, the object of fear and love, and therefore he is a positively human being; for there is nothing more in God than what lies in feeling. If in the heart there is fear and terror, in God there is anger; if in the heart there is joy, hope, confidence, in God there is love . . . . Thus even in religion man bows before the nature of man under the form of a personal human being; religion itself expressly declares—and all anthropomorphisms declare this in opposition to Pantheism,—*quod supra nos nihil ad nos*: that is, a God who inspires us with no human emotions, who does not reflect our own emotions, in a word, who is not a man—such a God is nothing to us, has no interest for us, does not concern us.

Mary Daly (1928–2010). A feminist philosopher who wrote about the structure and myths of patriarchy and the historic oppression of women, Daly's books include *Gyn/ecology: The Metaethics of Radical Feminism* (1978) and *Amazon Grace: Recalling the Courage to Sin Big* (2006).

Patriarchy A form of social organization structured around the father; male-dominated.

> ### < READING CRITICALLY >
>
> #### Analyzing Feuerbach on Religion as Anthropomorphism
>
> - Why does Feuerbach believe that humans "created" God in their image rather than the reverse? How exactly does this process of "anthropomorphism" take place? Do you agree with his analysis? Why or why not?
> - According to Feuerbach, "To enrich God, man must become poor; that God may be all, man must be nothing." Why does he believe that humans have to become in their eyes imperfect and worthless sinners while God is elevated to the status of absolute perfection? Does his explanation make sense to you?
> - Feuerbach was not interested in destroying religion but in transforming it into a "realized Christianity" that he conceived of as a form of secular humanism. Explain as clearly as you can what he was trying to achieve. Do you think his approach an effective way to accomplish this goal? Why or why not?
> - The feminist philosopher **Mary Daly** argued not only that humans created God but also that the idea of God in Christianity reflects a **patriarchy**, a male-dominated society. In "Prolegomena to the Qualitative Leap Beyond Patriarchal Religion," she writes, "The myth of feminine evil, expressed in the story of the Fall, is reinforced by the myth of the salvation/redemption by a single human being of the male sex. The idea of a unique divining incarnation in a male, the God-man of the 'hypostatic union,' is inherently sexist and oppressive." Think critically about Daly's statement by providing reasons and examples to support both a "pro" and "con" view of it.

Religion Is a Vital Quest: Nishitani

Having examined the view that religion is a "projection upon the universe of our human hopes, fears, and ideals" in the writing of Feuerbach, it is now time for us to consider the alternate perspective on religion as a "human response to a transcendent reality." The Japanese philosopher **Keiji Nishitani** was strongly influenced by Buddhism but hoped to synthesize the philosophical and religious insights of both Western and Eastern traditions. For Nishitani, religion is a vital personal question that everyone must face when he or she encounters **nihility**—"that which renders meaningless the meaning of life." From his standpoint, each person is necessarily involved in the religious quest "to search for true reality in a *real* way."

Keiji Nishitani (1900–1990). A Japanese philosopher and professor at Kyoto University, Nishitani's work reflects Zen Buddhism, but he was also influenced by Western philosophers such as Kierkegaard.

Nihility Nothingness, nonexistence.

Keiji Nishitani, from *Religion and Nothingness*

"What is religion?" we ask ourselves, or, looking at it the other way around, "What is the purpose of religion for us? Why do we need it?" Though the question about the need for religion may be a familiar one, it already contains a problem. In one sense, for the person who poses the question, religion does not seem to be something he needs. The fact that he asks the question at all amounts to an admission that religion has not yet become a necessity for him. In another sense, however, it is surely in the nature of religion to be necessary for just such a person. Wherever questioning individuals like this are to be found, the need for religion is there as well. In short, the relationship we have to religion is a contradictory one: those for whom religion is *not* a necessity are, for that reason, the very ones for whom religion *is* a necessity. There is no other thing of which the same can be said.

When asked, "Why do we need learning and the arts?" we might try to explain in reply that such things are necessary for the advancement of mankind, for human happiness, for the cultivation of the individual, and so forth. Yet even if we can say why we need such things, this does not imply that we cannot get along without them. Somehow life would still go on. Learning and the arts may be indispensable to living well, but they are not indispensable to living. In that sense, they can be considered a kind of luxury.

Food, on the other hand, is essential to life. Nobody would turn to somebody else and ask him why he eats. Well, maybe an angel or some other celestial being who has no need to eat might ask such questions but men do not. Religion, to judge from current conditions in which many people are in fact getting along without it, is clearly not the kind of necessity that food is. Yet this does not mean that it is merely something we need to live *well.* Religion has to do with life itself. Whether the life we are living will end up in extinction or in the attainment of eternal life is a matter of the utmost importance for life itself. In no sense is religion to be called a luxury. Indeed, this is why religion is an indispensable necessity for those very people who fail to see the need for it. Herein lies the distinctive feature of religion that sets it apart from the mere life of "nature" and from culture. Therefore, to say that we need religion for example, for the sake of social order, or human welfare, or public morals is a mistake, or at least a confusion of priorities. Religion must not be considered from the viewpoint of its *utility,* any more than life should. A religion concerned primarily with its own utility bears witness to its own degeneration. One can ask about the utility of things like eating for the natural life, or of things like learning and the arts for culture. In fact, in such matters the question of utility should be of constant concern. Our ordinary mode of being is restricted to these levels of natural or cultural life. But it is in breaking through that ordinary mode of being and overturning it from the ground up, in pressing us back to the elemental source of life where life itself is seen as useless, that religion becomes something we need—a *must* for human life.

Two points should be noted from what has just been said. First, religion is at all times the individual affair of each individual. This sets it apart from things like culture, which, while related to the individual, do not need to concern each individual. Accordingly, we cannot understand what religion is from the outside. The religious quest alone is the key to understanding it; there is no other way. This is the most important point to be made regarding the essence of religion.

Second, from the standpoint of the essence of religion, it is a mistake to ask "What is the purpose of religion for us?" and one that clearly betrays an attitude of trying to understand religion apart from the religious quest. It is a question that must be broken through by another question coming from within the person who asks it. There is no other road that can lead to an understanding of what religion is and what purpose it serves. The counterquestion that achieves this breakthrough is one that asks, "For what purpose do I myself exist?" . . .

We become aware of religion as a need, as a must for life, only at the level of life at which everything else loses its necessity and its utility. Why do we exist at all? Is not our very existence and human life ultimately meaningless? Or, if there is a meaning or significance to it all, where do we find it? When we come to doubt the meaning of our existence in this way, when we have become a question to ourselves, the religious quest awakens within us. These questions and the quest they give rise to show up when the mode of looking at and thinking about everything in terms of how it relates to *us* is broken through, where the mode of living that puts us at the center of everything is overturned. This is why the question of religion in the form, "Why do we need religion?" obscures the way to its own answer from the very start. It blocks our becoming a question to ourselves.

The point at which the ordinarily necessary things of life, including learning and the arts, all lose their necessity and utility is found at those times when death, nihility, or sin—or any of those situations that entail a fundamental negation of our life, existence, and ideals, that undermine the roothold of our existence and bring the meaning of life into question—become pressing personal problems for us. This can occur through an illness that brings one face-to-face with death, or through some turn of events that robs one of what had made life worth living.

Take, for example, someone for whom life has become meaningless as a result of the loss of a loved one, or of the failure of an undertaking on which he had staked his all. All those things that had once been of use to him become good for nothing. This same process takes place when one comes face to face with death and the existence of the self—one's "self-existence"—stands out clearly in relief against the backdrop of nihility. Questions crowd in upon one: Why have I been alive? Where did I come from and where am I going? A void appears here that nothing in the world can fill; a gaping abyss opens up at the very ground on which one stands. In the face of this abyss, not one of all the things that had made up the stuff of life until then is of any use . . . .

Nihility refers to that which renders meaningless the meaning of life. When we become a question to ourselves and when the problem of why we exist arises, this means that nihility has emerged from the ground of our existence and that our very existence has turned into a question mark. The appearance of this nihility signals nothing less than that one's awareness of self-existence has penetrated to an extraordinary depth.

Normally we proceed through life, on and on, with our eye fixed on something or other, always caught up with something within or without ourselves. It is these engagements that prevent the deepening of awareness. They block off the way to an opening up of that horizon on which nihility appears and self-being becomes a question. This is even the case with learning and the arts and the whole range of other cultural engagements. But when this horizon does open up at the bottom of those engagements that keep life moving continually on and on, something seems to halt and linger before us. This something is the meaninglessness that lies in wait at the bottom of those very engagements

> **When we come to doubt the meaning of our existence in this way, when we have become a question to ourselves, the religious quest awakens within us.**

that bring meaning to life. This is the point at which that sense of nihility, that sense that "everything is the same" we find in Nietzsche and Dostoevsky, brings the restless, forward-advancing pace of life to a halt and makes it take a step back. In the Zen phrase, it "turns the light to what is directly underfoot."

In the forward progress of everyday life, the ground beneath our feet always falls behind as we move steadily ahead; we overlook it. Taking a step back to shed light on what is underfoot of the self—"stepping back to come to the self," as another ancient Zen phrase has it—marks a conversion in life itself. This fundamental conversion in life is occasioned by the opening up of the horizon of nihility at the ground of life. It is nothing less than a conversion from the self-centered (or man-centered) mode of being, which always asks what *use* things have for us (or for man), to an attitude that asks for what *purpose* we ourselves (or man) exist. Only when we stand at this turning point does the question "What is religion?" really become our own.

For Nishitani, religion is a dimension of human experience with which we are all necessarily involved because it has to do with the most fundamental questions that we encounter: Why do I exist? Does my life have meaning? Even when we seek to avoid engaging these questions, either submerged in the day-to-day details of living or actively trying to hide from these considerations, escape is not possible. "Religion has to do with life itself. Whether the life we are living will end up in extinction or in the attainment of eternal life is a matter of the utmost importance for life itself." But the religion Nishitani has in mind is not traditional, organized religion but rather the "religious quest" that is both intensely personal and ultimately profound. The challenge for each of us is to knowingly embrace this religious quest, seeking to disclose the meaning of our lives by halting the onward unreflective rush of life and instead "stepping back to come to the self." This personal exploration is not only cognitive in nature, but involves the whole self—mind and body—as Nishitani explains.

II

Being the multi-faceted reality that it is, religion can be approached from any number of different angles. It is commonly defined as the relationship of man to an absolute, like god. But as that definition may already be too narrow, there are those who prefer, for example, to speak in terms of the idea of the Holy. If this relationship is taken more concretely, however, still other possible angles of approach suggest themselves. For instance, the relationship of man to God may be spoken of as the abandonment of self-will in order to live according to the will of God; as the vision or knowledge of God; or, as the unveiling of God to the self, or in the self. Again, it may be thought of as the immediate perception of the absolute dependency of self-existence on divine existence, or as man's becoming one with God. One might as well pursue the view that it is only in religion that man becomes truly himself, that the self encounters it "original countenance." Furthermore, it is possible to regard the essence of religion, as Schleiermacher does in his *Reden uber die Religion*, as the intuition of the infinite in the finite, as "feeling the Universe." On a variety of counts, of course, each of these views is open to criticism. Rather than enter any further into their discussion here, I should like instead to approach religion from a somewhat different angle, as the self-awareness of reality, or, more correctly, the *real* self-awareness of reality.

Keiji Nishitani,
from *Religion and Nothingness*

What is the religious quest? Nishitani characterizes the religious quest as "man's search for true reality in a *real* way . . . not theoretically and not in the form of concepts." Do you think this kind of knowledge is possible?

By the "self-awareness of reality" I mean both our becoming aware of reality and, at the same time, the reality realizing itself in our awareness. The English word "realize," with its twofold meaning of "actualize" and "understand," is particularly well suited to what I have in mind here, although I am told that its sense of "understand" does not necessarily connote the sense of reality coming to actualization in us. Be that as it may, I am using the word to indicate that our ability to perceive reality means that reality realizes (actualizes) itself in us; that this in turn is the only way that we can realize (appropriate through understanding) the fact that reality is so realizing itself in us; and that in so doing the self-realization of reality itself takes place.

It follows that realization in its sense of "appropriation" differs from philosophical cognition. What I am speaking of is not theoretical knowledge but a real appropriation (the *proprium* taken here to embrace the whole man, mind and body). This real appropriation provides our very mode of being with its essential determination. The real perception of reality is our real mode of being itself and constitutes the realness that is the true reality of our existence. This perception of reality can constitute the realness of our existence because it comes into being in unison with the self-realization of reality itself. In this sense, the realness of our existence, as the appropriation of reality, belongs to reality itself as the self-realization of reality itself. In other words, the self-realization of reality can only take place by causing our existence to become truly real.

The question will no doubt arise as to what this "reality" signifies. If the question is posed merely in the form of the usual request for knowledge, in expectation of a simple, conceptual response, then it is inappropriate to the reality I am speaking of here. In order for it to become a *real* question, one that is asked with the whole self, body and mind, it must be returned to reality itself. The question that *asks about* reality must itself become something that *belongs to* reality. In that vein, I should like to try to interpret the religious quest as man's search for true reality in a *real* way (that is, not theoretically and not in the form of concepts, as we do in ordinary knowledge and philosophical knowledge), and from that same angle to attempt an answer to the question of the essence of religion by tracing the process of the real pursuit of true reality.

< READING CRITICALLY >

Analyzing Nishitani on the Religious Quest

- Have you ever experienced the "nihility" that Nishitani describes, the possibility that life—and our personal existence—is utterly meaningless? If so, what was your response to this profoundly disturbing possibility? Did it stimulate you to consider your reason for living, the meaning of your life?

- Nishitani seems to suggest that trying to answer questions dealing with the purpose of human existence and the meaning of our personal lives necessarily involves a religious quest. Do you agree with this perspective? Or do you believe that these questions might be answered without religion?

7.3 A Brief Survey of World Religions

Earlier in this chapter, Frederick Streng quoted the Ganda tribe's saying that "he who never visits thinks his mother is the only cook." Most of us do recognize that there are different religions in the world, but we may not have a sense of the different conceptions of spiritual reality that each presents. In this section, we will briefly overview the main ideas of the world's major religions.

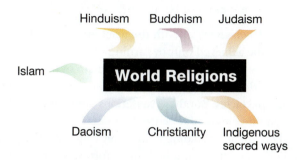

When we examine the history of the major religions of the world, we see that they have grown and been elaborated in an organic, evolutionary fashion, spreading from place to place and often changing in form and substance to accommodate their new cultural contexts. Additionally, in true evolutionary fashion, diversity has arisen within each of the various religious branches, so there is no one Christian or Buddhist system but rather important variations within each of the major religions. Thus, in the face of such complexity, any effort to summarize world religions in a few pages will be flawed. A detailed description of the world religions can be found in texts that specialize in world religions such as Mary Pat Fisher's *Living Religions*. As a further caution, learning *about* a religion is a very different sort of "knowing" than *living* a religion, so that even an exhaustive survey of world religions has unavoidable limitations. Nevertheless, despite these caveats, it is still helpful to have a basic understanding of the variety of religious conceptions of the world to think philosophically about questions of ultimate meaning, particularly since most of us were brought up in one religious tradition and know little of others.

Hinduism

Hinduism is the term used to designate the complex mosaic of religious beliefs and practices of the vast majority of the people of India. As one of the oldest living religions in the world, Hinduism is unique in that it had no single founder but evolved over a period of four thousand years, its history interwoven with religious and cultural movements. Other religions that originated on the Indian subcontinent include Buddhism, Jainism, and Sikhism.

The word *Hindu* is derived from the Sanskrit word *sindu*, which means "river," Hindu referring to the Indus River. An alternative label preferred today is **Sanatana Dharma**. *Sanatana* means "eternal religion," reflecting the belief that these religious ways have always existed, and *Dharma* embodies a holistic approach to both personal spiritual fulfillment and social harmony. Although there are literally millions of deities in Sanatana Dharma, it is common for followers to believe that they are all manifestations of a single God assuming different forms.

Sanatana Dharma The "eternal religion" of Hinduism.

Vedas Ancient scriptures revered by Hindus.

Upanishads The philosophical part of the *Vedas* in Hinduism, intended only for serious seekers.

Rishi A Hindu sage.

Brahman The impersonal Ultimate Principle in Hinduism.

Reincarnation The belief that the soul leaves the dead body and enters the new one, being born over and over in countless bodies.

Karma In Hinduism and Buddhism, our actions and their effects on this life and the lives to come.

Samsara The continual round of birth, death, and rebirth in Hinduism and Buddhism.

Moksha In Hinduism, liberation of the soul from illusion and suffering.

Nirvana The ultimate egoless state of bliss in Buddhism; the extinction of the self.

Central to Hindu teachings are the *Vedas*, a collection of ancient hymns in four parts. The *Upanishads* are commentaries on the *Vedas* and include the teaching of highly realized spiritual masters, the **rishis**, who explain the path to spiritual transformation. The *Upanishads* are thought to have developed between 600 and 400 B.C.E., about the same time that Gautama Buddha (c. 563–483 B.C.E.), the founder of Buddhism, lived on the Indian subcontinent. It is not surprising that these two world religions share certain common themes, though there are significant differences as well. We will consider five themes in Hinduism:

- *Contemplation of the luminous self.* As with the teachings of the Buddha, spiritual enlightenment can be achieved only by turning one's attention inward to discover a transcendent reality from within. The rishis explain in the *Upanishads* that the bodily senses are made for looking outward and are easily enticed by sensory pleasures and worldly spectacles. But these sensations are fleeting and impermanent, passing away when one dies, and obscure the search for the infinite, everlasting reality. This unseen but all-pervading reality they called **Brahman**, the Unknowable. From Brahman originate the multiplicity of all forms, including humans, and thus Brahman can be discovered in the soul (*atman*) within ourselves.

- *Reincarnation.* Central to all forms of Sanatana Dharma is the doctrine of **reincarnation**, the belief that the soul leaves the dead body and enters a new one, being born over and over in countless bodies. Whether the body is that of an animal or other life form, the self remains constant. But rebirth as a human being is a precious and rare opportunity for the soul to advance toward its ultimate goal of liberation from rebirth and merging with the Brahman.

- *Karma.* Progress toward a merging with Brahman is the result of **karma**, which refers to one's actions as well as the consequences of one's actions. Every action we take, even every thought we have—whether good or evil—shapes our present and also our future. The ultimate goal of creating ourselves through good choices is to escape from the *karmic* wheel of birth, death, and rebirth, which is called **samsara**. To escape from samsara is to achieve **moksha**, or liberation from the limitations of space, time, and matter through realization of the immortal absolute. Many lifetimes of upward-striving incarnations are required to reach this transcendence of earthly miseries. This desire for liberation from earthly existence is also one of the underpinnings of Buddhism, analogous to the Buddhist concept of **Nirvana** or *satori*, enlightenment through the realization of ultimate truth.

Why is prayer a common practice in religions? As depicted in this prayer room and shrine in India, Hindu homes typically contain a shrine to one or more of the thousands of Hindu deities. *(Barnabas Kindersley © DK)*

- *Yogic practices.* Spiritual seekers are generally encouraged to engage in disciplines that clear the mind and support a state of serene, detached awareness. This desired state of balance, purity, and peacefulness of mind is described as *sattvic*, in contrast with active, restless states or lethargic dull states. The practices for increasing *sattvic* qualities are known collectively as **yoga**, from the Sanskrit word for "union" (in this case the union of body, mind, and spirit). The physical and psychic practices of yoga are extremely ancient, dating back as long ago as the Neolithic Age. By 200 B.C.E., a yogi named Patanjali (or perhaps a series of people taking the same name) had described a coherent system for attaining the highest consciousness. Patanjali distinguishes eight "limbs" of the yogic path to making the mind absolutely clear and increasing the body's supply of life energy (*prana*): moral codes and observances (the *yamas* and *niyamas*), physical conditioning through yoga postures (*asana*), mindful breathing (*pranayama*), turning inward (*pratyahara*), concentration (*dharana*), meditation (*dhyana*), and the state of peaceful spiritual absorption (*samadhi*).

- *Fire sacrifices.* Ritual animal sacrifice around a fire was an essential part of ancient Sanatana Dharma practice, which has survived in various forms to the modern day. The practice of fire sacrifice is based on the idea that generous offerings to a deity will be rewarded by some specific results. Over time elaborate fire sacrifice rituals were created, controlled by **Brahmins** (priests) involving **mantras** (sacred chants) and sacred actions. The cumulative purpose of these practices was to invoke the breath behind all of existence, the absolute, the supreme reality.

Buddhism

Buddhism is a **nontheist** religion that does not believe in a supernatural God or Creator. Instead, the "ultimate transformation" to which Buddhists aspire is to escape the world of suffering through our own efforts until we finally achieve **Nirvana** (the ultimate egoless state of bliss).

The originator of Buddhism, Siddhartha Gautama, was born about 563 B.C.E., in the foothills of the Himalayas in India. After renouncing his princely life, he embarked on a spiritual quest that would transform him into a "**Buddha**," an enlightened being. This spiritual epiphany led to his developing the core beliefs on which Buddhism is founded: the Four Noble Truths about suffering; the Eightfold Path for liberation from suffering; the Wheel of Birth and Death; and Nirvana. He began a wandering ministry that was to last forty-five years, gathering disciples—the **sangha**—and teaching the truths of reality—the **dharma**—which revealed the path for each person's state of spiritual evolution.

The foundation for Buddha's religious philosophy is contained in the Four Noble Truths of Suffering, from which all other dimensions of his thinking flow.

1. *Life inevitably involves suffering, is imperfect and unsatisfactory.* Suffering and frustration—**dukkha**—is an unavoidable part of living: physical pain, sickness, grief, unfulfilled desires, and ultimately death. Happiness is fleeting, with unhappiness its constant shadow. Even the "self" is an impermanent illusion. In a view that foreshadows that of David Hume, what we view as our continual "I" is really a perpetually transient bundle of fleeting sensations, impressions, ideas, and feelings. The metaphor often used for the Buddhist concept of the self is that of a flame being passed from candle to candle in continual movement.

Yoga A systematic approach to spiritual realization, one of the major Hindu philosophical systems.

Brahmins Priests or members of the priestly caste in Hinduism.

Mantra A sound or phrase chanted to evoke the sound vibration of one aspect of creation or to praise a deity.

Nontheist A religion without the concept of a supernatural God or Creator.

Buddha Title meaning "Enlightened One."

Sangha The spiritual community of followers of the Buddha.

Dharma In Buddhism, the doctrine or law, as revealed by the Buddha; also the correct conduct for each person according to his or her level of awareness. In Hinduism, moral order, righteousness, religion.

Dukkha According to the Buddha, a central fact of human life, variously translated as discomfort, suffering, frustration, or lack of harmony with the environment.

Do we have immortal souls? This Buddhist wheel is symbolic of the Buddha's teachings on rebirth. The flames represent the idea of the self as a flame that is passed from candle to candle in continual movement.

2. *Suffering originates in our desires.* Desires are wishes for things to be different than they are. We wish for good health, riches and fame, eternal life, perpetual happiness, permanence and security, and many other things as well. But none of these wishes can be achieved in a permanent fashion because life and the universe are essentially impermanent. And because our wishes are continually thwarted and events in the world are beyond our control, frustration and suffering are unavoidable.

3. *Suffering will cease if all desires cease.* The only certain and final way to escape from suffering—*dukkha*—is by removing desire. This can be achieved only by realizing and accepting the fact that there is no unique, separate, permanent, immortal "self." Once we understand that our "self" is simply an impermanent flow of energy tied to the larger energies of the cosmos, we are freed to realize that desires and suffering are irrelevant. In practical terms, accepting the non-existence of a permanent self encourages us to live happily and fully in the moment, liberated from self-centeredness and full of compassion for others.

4. *There is a way to realize this state: the Noble Eightfold Path.* Extinguishing desire and suffering is a process that can be achieved by following the guidelines embodied in the Noble Eightfold Path, devoted to pursuing morality, focus, and wisdom. The Noble Eightfold Path is a systematic philosophy of life that enables people gradually to free themselves from desire and suffering and achieve the ultimate peace of Nirvana. This process typically extends over multiple lifetimes, as we are caught in the perpetual cycle of death and rebirth. Once again, the "self" is not a permanent, immortal entity but is akin to a flame being passed from moment to moment, lifetime to lifetime. The Noble Eightfold Path includes *right understanding, right thought and motives, right mindfulness,* and *right mediation.*

Daoism (Taoism)

At the time that India was giving birth to Hinduism and Buddhism, East Asia saw the creation of Daoism and Confucianism (in China) and Shinto (in Japan). Daoism, on the other hand, is a way of life inspired from the rhythms of natural phenomena. Daoism promotes a constant interaction with our environment and the importance of being aware of it.

Dao is believed to be the first cause of the universe. It is the "unnamable" and "eternally real" force that flows through life, and each believer's goal is to become one with the Dao. Although Dao can be translated as "path" or "the way," it is basically indefinable. Reality cannot be named or known through language, logic, or concepts—it must be experienced. Dao refers to a power that envelops and flows through all things, living and nonliving. The Dao regulates natural processes and balances the universe.

The founder of Daoism is believed by many to be **Laozi** (Lao Tsu). According to tradition, Laozi was a curator of the royal library of the Zhou dynasty who was searching for a way that would avoid the constant feudal warfare and other conflicts that were disrupting society during his lifetime. The result was his composing a book of five thousand characters known as the *Daode Jing* (*Tao-te Ching*). The book's central philosophy is a practical concern with improving harmony in life, attuning oneself to the natural energies of the cosmos by being receptive and quiet.

Laozi (604–531 B.C.E.) Founder of Daoism. This name means the "Old Master"; he is believed to be the author of the *Daode Jing*, translated as the "Classic of the Way and Virtue," which lays down the fundamental beliefs of Daoism.

Daoists do not pray to a Supreme Being; instead, they seek answers to life's problems through inner meditation and observation. For the Daoist, time is cyclical, not linear as in Western thinking. The entire cosmos is a manifestation of an impersonal self-generating energy called *qi* (*ch'i*). This force has two aspects whose interplay causes the ever-changing phenomena of the universe. *Yin* is the dark, receptive, "female" aspect; *Yang* is the bright, assertive, "male" aspect. The Yin is considered to be the breath that formed Earth, whereas the Yang is the breath that formed the heavens. These two forces symbolize the pairs of opposites that are seen throughout the universe, such as good and evil, light and dark, male and female. Wisdom lies in recognizing the ever-shifting, but regular and balanced, patterns of movement of Yin and Yang and moving along with them. The Dao is this creative rhythm of the universe.

Yin–Yang symbol. This image symbolizes the interplay of opposites that are seen throughout the universe.

Daoists follow the art of *wu-wei*, which is to let nature take its course, rather than trying to impede it. To take a metaphor from the natural world, one should allow a river to flow toward the sea unimpeded, instead of erecting a dam that would interfere with its natural flow. Analogously, we should be like flowing water ourselves, bypassing and gently wearing away obstacles rather than aggressively attacking them, effortlessly moving through life without struggling, leaving all accomplishment behind without trying to hold on to them. In fact, Laozi taught that all straining, all striving are not only vain but also counterproductive. We need to discern and follow the natural forces, as a butcher whose knife always stays sharp because he lets his hand be guided by the makeup of the carcass, finding the spaces between the bones where a slight movement of the blade will glide through without resistance. Even when difficulties arise, the Daoist does not panic and take unnecessary action. This is a philosophy that Daoists believe should be practiced on a social and political level as well.

Judaism

Judaism traces its roots to about 3,800 years ago, when, according to the holy scriptures known collectively as the TaNaKh, God entered into a covenant with Abraham. According to the covenant, Abraham and his descendants would give God (Yahweh) their exclusive devotion and obedience, and God would choose them to enjoy special consideration and protection (thus the idea that Jews are God's "chosen people"). Jewish scripture also states that God promised Canaan (now Israel) to the Jews as their homeland.

Jewish religious beliefs have evolved over time and even today embody a wide diversity ranging from highly orthodox to liberal, from legalistic to mystical. Nevertheless, there are certain core

Have you experienced or witnessed a religious "coming of age" ceremony? The Bar Mitzvah ceremony (or Bat Mitzvah for a young woman) marks the attainment of the status of Bar (or Bat) Mitzvah, in which one is recognized as a full member of the synagogue congregation.

Monotheism A belief in one God.

beliefs that are common threads through all of this diversity. First and foremost is **monotheism**, a belief in one Creator God, all-powerful, all-loving, and ever-present. In stories from scripture, this God demands obedience, metes out rewards and punishments, and issues a moral code (the Ten Commandments).

Religious holidays and rituals are based on key events in Jewish history as recorded in Jewish scriptures. These events serve as moral paradigms, symbolically rich stories that have continued relevance to contemporary lives. Divinely inspired laws that cover every aspect of Jewish social, communal, and religious life are another core element of Jewish religious faith. These laws have been codified in the *Torah*, a word which has a variety of meanings. One meaning refers to the first five books of the TaNaKh, believed to be the word of God as told to Moses. These teachings have evolved over time through the ongoing study and writings of Jewish scholars.

Christianity

Christianity emerged and split off from Judaism some 1,800 years after Abraham. At its core is the belief that Jesus is the son of God and savior whose sacrificial death and resurrection make it possible for souls to have eternal life in heaven. Christian scriptures consist of the Hebrew TaNaKh, which Christians refer to as the Old Testament, and the writings of Jesus's followers, known as the New Testament. Christianity is the largest of the world's religions, with approximately 2.1 billion adherents.

The New Testament contains the teachings of **Jesus**, a Jew who lived in Palestine under Roman rule at the beginning of the first millennium C.E. Jesus describes God as a loving Father who will take care of those who love Him and want to follow the path of righteousness. Jesus's message was to reveal this path, through words and actions, so that all could achieve spiritual perfection and salvation in preparation for life after death. He makes clear that each person's relationship with God is intensely personal, nurtured through worship, reflection, and personal prayer.

During the three years of his ministry, Jesus traveled around Palestine preaching, often with vivid parables, and, according to the biblical account, performing miracles. Among the miracles ascribed to Jesus are healing the sick and disabled, casting devils out of the possessed, restoring the dead to life, walking on water, cleansing lepers, and feeding 5,000 people with just a few loaves and fish. The miracles were widely interpreted as confirming his special spiritual status and possible divinity.

Jesus preached a radical ethic, focusing his attention on the most disinherited people of the day, including the poor, the outcasts, the prostitutes, and even the most despised people of the day, the Roman tax collectors. What's more, Jesus preached that, in the next life, the favored individuals would include the poor in spirit, the meek, the mourners,

Jesus Christ. Christianity is based on the teachings of Jesus of Nazareth, believed by Christians to be the son of God.

the seekers of righteousness, the pure in heart, the merciful, the peacemakers, and those who are persecuted for the sake of righteousness and for spreading the gospel. In addition to complete devotion to God, the core of Jesus' message was a love and devotion to others. In fact, Jesus preached that in extending ourselves to the less fortunate in society, we are symbolically worshiping God.

Although the Jews were expecting the Messiah to provide immediate relief from their current oppressed state under Roman rule, Jesus instead promised a spiritual kingdom that would be fully realized only in the future. By devoting themselves to God and following the path of righteousness, people could become spiritually transformed in this life and prepare themselves for eternal life at the end of time. The establishment of God's Kingdom will come at the apocalyptic end of the world, when Jesus returns triumphantly to fight the final battle of Armageddon and pass eternal judgment on the souls of all who have lived.

Islam

The world's second largest religion, Islam, views itself as the ultimate expression of the monotheistic tradition that began when God spoke to Abraham. Muslims believe that **Muhammad**, who lived in the Arabian Peninsula from 570 to 632 C.E., is the last and final prophet to receive the word of Allah *(Allah* is the Arabic word for God). Jesus is also viewed as a prophet, but Muslims believe that his message was corrupted by

Muhammad (570–632) Founder of Islam. Believed by Muslims to be the last of the great prophets from Abraham to Jesus and to have received the uninterpreted divine word of God.

Qur'an The holy book of Islam.

followers who insisted on his divinity. According to Islam, God revealed his messages to Muhammad through the angel Gabriel over the course of twenty-three years. These revelations constitute the text of the **Qur'an**, the unchanged, untranslated word of God.

The Qur'an is considered to be deeply symbolic, with multiple layers of meaning. The message of the Qur'an is spiritually inspiring but also contains vivid warnings. Those who choose to follow Allah are ensured an afterlife of splendid pleasures in Paradise. However, those who do not embrace and submit themselves to Allah will be called to account at the Last Judgment and will suffer the terrifying torments of hell.

The Qur'an reveals the central patterns of worship known as the Five Pillars of Islam. The Five Pillars is also known as the *outer practice* of Islam. It is set forth in the *Shari'ah,* the "straight path" of the divine law. Its main purpose is to bring remembrance of God into every aspect of daily life and practical ethics into the fabric of society. The Five Pillars spell out the way of Muslim life and its purposes:

- The First Pillar is *shahadah,* the profession of faith. "There is no God but Allah, and

Page from the Qur'an. Muslims believe that the Qur'an is the final word of God, delivered to Muhammad through the angel Gabriel.

Salat The principle of praying five times a day in a prescribed manner.

Zakat Spiritual tithing in Islam.

Sawm Fasting as a means of spiritual devotion.

Hajj The holy pilgrimage to Mecca, for Muslims.

Muhammad is his Prophet." This is the foundation stone of Islam, incorporating both a monotheistic belief in God and the recognition that while Muhammad is not divine, he is the last and greatest prophet of God. Although Islam believes that there might be many *names* for God, it is a religion built on the firm conviction that there is only *one* God, and it is our responsibility to *submit totally* to God's will in every dimension of our lives.

- The Second Pillar of Islam is **salat**, the performance of a continual round of prayers, a response to the natural yearning of the human heart to pour forth its love and gratitude toward its Creator. Regular prayer also keeps a Muslim's life in proper perspective, a reminder to submit to God's will as rightfully sovereign over his or her life. A Muslim should pray five times daily—on rising, at noon, in midafternoon, after sunset, and before retiring.

- The Third Pillar is **zakat**, the yearly setting aside of a portion of one's wealth for the benefit of others. There are always those who possess more material things than others, and Islam tries to bring a balance to this situation by asking those who have much to help lift the burden of those who have less. In addition to the zakat, Muslims are encouraged to give alms to charities.

- The Fourth Pillar is **sawm**, the observance of *Ramadan,* the holy month in the Arabian calendar. This was the period in which Muhammad received his initial commission as a prophet and ten years later made his historic flight from Mecca to Medina. To commemorate these two occasions, those who are physically able to fast during the entire month. From dawn to sunset, Muslims do not eat, drink, have sexual intercourse, or smoke. Fasting underscores humankind's dependence on God and, by experiencing what it is like to feel hunger and suffering, helps make us more compassionate.

- The Fifth Pillar is **hajj**, the pilgrimage to Mecca where one performs a set of rites. Once in a lifetime a Muslim is expected, if physical and economic conditions permit, to make this journey to Mecca, where God's ultimate revelation was first disclosed. Here again, similar to fasting during Ramadan, the purpose is to heighten the pilgrim's devotion to God and to His revealed will.

Like the other major world religions, Islam contains different branches, including Sunnis, Shiites, and Sufis, but all accept the five pillars.

Indigenous Sacred Ways

Indigenous religions Religions that have remained tied to the original people and location from which they developed. For the most part, indigenous religions practice sacred ways and a spiritual way of life that has remained virtually unchanged for centuries.

In contrast to the major religions of the world that have spread across geographical boundaries from their original points of origin, **indigenous religions** have for the most part remained tied to the original people and location from which they developed. Making up approximately 4 percent of the world population, these indigenous religions include Australian aborigines, Native Americans (Navajo, Hopi, Zuni, Lakota, Cheyenne, Iroquois), Inuit, Saami, African (Dagara, Dahomey, Ibo, Efe, Kung, Yoruba, Kikuyu), and others located in isolated pockets around the world. These religions are practiced by the original inhabitants of lands now controlled by larger political systems and dominated by one or more of the major world religions. Rather than relying on written texts or holy books, indigenous religions pass their core beliefs and secret practices down by an oral tradition entrusted to spiritual leaders.

What are the purposes of religious rituals? The men of the Kikuyu tribe in Kenya perform a ritual dance. Elaborate masks, costumes, and body paint are elements of these sacred performances, which bind the community of this indigenous sacred way.

Indigenous religions are fully integrated into the lives of those practicing them, rather than being discrete and separate activities. This includes a profound respect for their natural environment, which they tend to view as dynamic and alive. For indigenous people, religion, life, and the environment are all part of one integrated reality. They seek to maintain balance and harmony between all dimensions of their lives by developing *right relationships* with everything that exists: the unseen world of spirits, the land and weather, the people and creatures, and the power within.

We can generalize about four aspects of indigenous sacred ways:

- *Relationships with spirit.* For indigenous religions, the spirit world is central, the source of awesome power that influences every aspect of life. Many indigenous religions worship a Supreme Spirit whom they view as the Sacred Creator of the cosmos. Other religious views include a complex spirit world that includes unseen powers at work in the natural world or located in sacred places. The Supreme Spirit or Great Power is thought to be mysterious but all-powerful, penetrating into every element of the world. Maintaining harmonious relationships with the spirits of ancestors is another significant theme. Indigenous people tend to view themselves not as individuals but as integral members of a spiritual community of those both living and dead. Ancestors continue to serve as important guides, helpers, and influences, and they are revered and worshiped.

Shaman A "medicine person," a man or woman, who has undergone spiritual ordeals and can communicate with the spirit world to help the people in indigenous traditions.

- *Kinship with all creation.* For participants in indigenous religions, everything in the world is alive. The physical world is considered to be fully animate and spiritually interconnected with all life-forms in the universe. This spiritual view of "Mother Earth" encourages an ecological philosophy of the environment, in which human life is intended to interlock and mesh with the natural world, thus preserving the harmony and balance between people and their home, the natural world. Respect is due to all living creatures, and when trees are felled or animals are killed for food, one must explain one's intentions and ask for forgiveness.

- *Spiritual specialists.* In most indigenous religions, the average person has limited contact with the spirit world. Instead, this task is typically entrusted to spiritual specialists: priests, priestesses, and **shamans**. The spirit world is considered to be dangerous in the same way that a lightning bolt is both awesome and lethal. Only those who have undergone extensive training and preparation are thought to be able to act as intermediaries between this world and the unseen world. These spiritual specialists see themselves as human vessels for conducting spiritual communication and power. Preparing themselves for this role involves rituals of self-purification and self-emptying, applying the sacred knowledge that has been handed down for generations, from previous spiritual specialists.

- *Group observances.* A final dimension of indigenous religions are the group rituals that bind the community together in a shared participation in their spiritual life. These collective rituals include dances, ritual dramas, ritual purifications, pilgrimages to sacred sites, and, though undertaken individually, vision quests. The rituals typically occur at prescribed times or at defining moments in the life cycle: birth, naming, puberty, marriage, and death. The rituals constitute essential threads in the social fabric: They affirm the social bonds with each other, they honor the sacred, and they represent the group's harmony with the universe.

---

thinking philosophically

EXPANDING YOUR RELIGIOUS UNDERSTANDING

- Reflect on the religions that we reviewed in this chapter (Buddhism, Hinduism, Taoism, Judaism, Christianity, Islam, indigenous) as well as other religions with which you are familiar. Identify several common themes that you find to be particularly significant.

- Explain as best you can the reasons these themes resonate with you and describe how these themes might relate to your life. Provide specific examples.

7.4 Can We Prove the Existence of God?

How does one justify one's faith to nonbelievers, either atheists or those who practice other religions? And how does one strengthen one's own understanding of religious truths? Philosophers and theologians in the Christian tradition have argued for the truth of their belief in God using a variety of logical proofs, which we will explore here. The idea of finding proofs for the existence of God was of particular concern for medieval philosophers, who merged the Greek idea that the universe was governed by orderly principles and knowable through rational inquiry with the Judeo-Christian idea that universe was created and governed by an all-powerful, all-knowing God. We will look at some of these proofs here, as well as the objections to them raised by other philosophers. Keep in mind, however, that not all believers feel that reason is the path to spiritual understanding, and we will consider faith as an alternative path in the last section of the chapter.

Ontological argument   Argument from design   Cosmological argument

Arguments for the Existence of God

Argument from morality   Argument from gradations of perfection

Saint Anselm (1033–1109). Christian theologian who is known for his proofs for the existence of God. Anselm held the office of Archbishop of Canterbury in the last years of his life and openly opposed the Crusades to recapture Jerusalem from Muslim rule.

The Ontological Argument

First advanced by the medieval thinker **Saint Anselm**, the *ontological argument* for God's existence has generated debate that has spanned centuries. Saint Anselm rests his argument on the assumption that in general existence is "contingent," not "necessary." In other words, the things that currently exist in the universe don't necessarily "have to" exist: We can conceive of them as not existing. However, this analysis does not apply to the existence of the "ultimate reality"—God. Ultimate reality is the greatest possible reality that we can think of. Nothing greater than it can be conceived; that is why we characterize it as "ultimate." Because God is an ultimate reality "than which nothing greater can be conceived," God's existence must be necessary, not contingent. Therefore God must exist—not just inside our mind but outside of our mind as well—otherwise God would not be the greatest being that we can conceive.

If you find this to be a mind-twisting argument Saint Anselm is presenting, you are not alone. Included below is the critique of Saint Anselm's argument by a Christian monk named Gaunilo, a contemporary of Anselm, who offers a counterexample of a "perfect island" in order to illuminate the flaws in Saint Anselm's "proof." Included also is Saint Anselm's response to Gaunilo.

 Watch the **Video**
The Science of Being: Ontology on **mysearchlab.com**

Saint Anselm and Gaunilo, from *The Ontological Argument* ▮ ▮ ◢ ◆

Saint Anselm

Truly there is a God, although the fool has said in his heart, There is no God.

And so, Lord, do you, who does give understanding to faith, give me, so far as you know it to be profitable, to understand that you are as we believe; and that you are that which we believe. And, indeed, we believe that you are a being than which nothing greater can be conceived. Or is there no such nature, since the fool has said in his heart, there is no God? (Psalms xiii, 1). But, at any rate, this very fool, when he hears of this being of which I speak—a being than which nothing greater can be conceived—understands what he hears, and what he understands is in his understanding; although he does not understand it to exist.

For, it is one thing for an object to be in the understanding, and another to understand that the object exists. When a painter first conceives of what he will afterwards perform, he has it in his understanding, but he does not yet understand it to be, because he has not yet performed it. But after he has made the painting, he both has it in his understanding, and he understands that it exists, because he has made it.

Hence, even the fool is convinced that something exists in the understanding, at least, than which nothing greater can be conceived. For, when he hears of this, he understands it. And whatever is understood, exists in the understanding. And assuredly that, than which nothing greater can be conceived, cannot exist in the understanding alone. For, suppose it exists in the understanding alone: then it can be conceived to exist in reality; which is greater.

Therefore, if that, than which nothing greater can be conceived, exists in the understanding alone, the very being, than which nothing greater can be conceived, is one, than which a greater can be conceived. But obviously this is impossible. Hence, there is no doubt that there exists a being, than which nothing greater can be conceived, and it exists both in the understanding and in reality.

God cannot be conceived not to exist. — God is that, than which nothing greater can be conceived. — That which can be conceived not to exist is not God.

And it assuredly exists so truly, that it cannot be conceived not to exist. For, it is possible to conceive of a being which cannot be conceived not to exist; and this is greater than one which can be conceived not to exist. Hence, if that, than which nothing greater can be conceived, can be conceived not to exist, it is not that, than which nothing greater can be conceived. But this is an irreconcilable contradiction. There is, then, so truly a being than which nothing greater can be conceived to exist, that it cannot even be conceived not to exist; and this being you are, O Lord, our God.

So truly, therefore, you do exist, O Lord, my God, that you can not be conceived not to exist; and rightly. For, if a mind could conceive of a being better than you, the creature would rise above the Creator; and this is most absurd. And, indeed, whatever else there is, except you alone, can be conceived not to exist. To you alone, therefore, it belongs to exist more truly than all other beings, and hence in a higher degree than all others. For, whatever else exists does not exist so truly, and hence in a less degree it belongs to it to exist. Why, then, has the fool said in his heart, there is no God (Psalms xiii, 1), since it is so evident, to a rational mind, that you do exist in the highest degree of all? Why, except that he is dull and a fool?

How the fool has said in his heart what cannot be conceived. — A thing may be conceived in two ways: (1) when the word signifying it is conceived; (2) when the thing itself is understood. As far as the word goes, God can be conceived not to exist, in reality he cannot.

But how has the fool said in his heart what he could not conceive; or how is it that he could not conceive what he said in his heart? Since it is the same to say in the heart, and to conceive.

But, if really, nay, since really, he both conceived, because he said in his heart; and did not say in his heart, because he could not conceive; there is more than one way in which a thing is said in the heart or conceived. For, in one sense, an object is conceived, when the word signifying it is conceived; and in another, when the very entity, which the object is, is understood.

In the former sense, then, God can be conceived not to exist; but in the latter, not at all. For no one who understands what fire and water are can conceive fire to be water, in accordance with the nature of the facts themselves, although this is possible according to the words. So, then, no one who understands what God is can conceive that God does not exist; although he says these words in his heart, either without any

> **Therefore, he who understands that God so exists, cannot conceive that he does not exist.**

or with some foreign, signification. For, God is that than which a greater cannot be conceived. And he who thoroughly understands this, assuredly understands that this being so truly exists, that not even in concept can it be non-existent. Therefore, he who understands that God so exists, cannot conceive that he does not exist.

I thank you, gracious Lord, I thank you; because what I formerly believed by your bounty, I now so understand by your illumination, that if I were unwilling to believe that you do exist, I should not be able not to understand this to be true.

Gaunilo's Criticism

For example: it is said that somewhere in the ocean is an island, which, because of the difficulty, or rather the impossibility, of discovering what does not exist, is called the lost island. And they say that this island has an inestimable

The island metaphor. Gaunilo substitutes a "perfect island" for "God" to illustrate what he considers to be the flaws in Anselm's argument. Do you think Anselm's rejoinder is persuasive?

wealth of all manner of riches and delicacies in greater abundance than is told of the Islands of the Blest; and that having no owner or inhabitant, it is more excellent than all other countries, which are inhabited by mankind, in the abundance with which it is stored.

Now if someone should tell me that there is such an island, I should easily understand his words, in which there is no difficulty. But suppose that he went on to say, as if by a logical inference: "You can no longer doubt that this island which is more excellent than all lands exists somewhere, since you have no doubt that it is in your understanding. And since it is more excellent not to be in the understanding alone, but to exist both in the understanding and in reality, for this reason it must exist. For if it does not exist, any land which really exists will be more excellent than it; and so the island already understood by you to be more excellent will not be more excellent."

If a man should try to prove to me by such reasoning that this island truly exists, and that its existence should no longer be doubted, either I should believe that he was jesting, or I know not which I ought to regard as the greater fool: myself, supposing that I should allow this proof; or him, if he should suppose that he had established with any certainty the existence of this island. For he ought to show first that the hypothetical excellence of this island exists as a real and indubitable fact, and in no wise as any unreal object, or one whose existence is uncertain, in my understanding.

Saint Anselm's Rejoinder

A criticism of Gaunilo's example, in which he tries to show that in this way the real existence of a lost island might be inferred from the fact of its being conceived.

But, you say, it is as if one should suppose an island in the ocean, which surpasses all lands in its fertility, and which, because of the difficulty, or rather the impossibility, of discovering what does not exist, is called a lost island; and should say that there can be no doubt that this island truly exists in reality, for this reason, that one who hears it described easily understands what he hears.

Now I promise confidently that if any man shall devise anything existing either in reality or in concept alone (except that than which a greater cannot be conceived) to which he can adapt the sequence of my reasoning, I will discover that thing, and will give him his lost island, not to be lost again.

But it now appears that this being than which a greater is inconceivable cannot be conceived not to be, because it exists on so assured a ground of truth; for otherwise it would not exist at all.

Hence, if any one says that he conceives this being not to exist, I say that at the time when he conceives of this either he conceives of a being than which a greater is inconceivable, or he does not conceive at all. If he does not conceive, he does not conceive of the non-existence of that of which he does not conceive. But if he does conceive, he certainly conceives of a being which cannot be even conceived not to exist. For if it could be conceived not to exist, it could be conceived to have a beginning and an end. But this is impossible.

He, then, who conceives of this being conceives of a being which cannot be even conceived not to exist; but he who conceives of this being does not conceive that it does not exist; else he conceives what is inconceivable. The non-existence, then, of that than which a greater cannot be conceived is inconceivable.

< READING CRITICALLY >

Analyzing the Ontological Argument

- Describe in your own words Anselm's *ontological argument* for the existence of God. If you did not believe in God, or if your belief in God was shaky, would this argument help convince you that there is indeed a supreme being whom we have traditionally called God? Why or why not?

- Describe in your own words Gaunilo's critique of Anselm's *ontological argument* for the existence of God. Do you find Gaunilo's reasoning persuasive? Why or why not?

The Cosmological Argument

Cosmological arguments for the existence of God take as their starting point the orderly, coherent, intelligible nature of the cosmos. In his towering work, *Summa Theologica*, the medieval philosopher **Saint Thomas Aquinas** presents a number of different formulations of the Cosmological Argument which argues that if we examine the world in which we live—the cosmos—we will find compelling "proofs" for believing in God's existence. It should be noted that Aquinas's five arguments for God are taken almost directly from Aristotle's arguments for a Prime Mover. Aquinas wanted to show that faith and reason were consistent with one another—that rational arguments could be used to demonstrate, or explain, what he, as a Christian, accepted on faith.

Saint Thomas Aquinas (1225–1274). Aquinas was a Christian theologian who sought to synthesize philosophy and religion and offered detailed and systematic works on the natures of God, humanity, and the universe.

Aquinas's first three arguments are variations of a general argument known as the *argument from contingency* (he subsequently provides two additional proofs for God's existence, bringing the total to five proofs). In the broadest sense, *contingency* means "dependency."

The logic of the *argument from contingency* goes something like this: When we examine the universe, we see that everything that exists and occurs is dependent on something else. However, for the universe to exist as it does, there must be some ultimate reality that is necessary, not contingent. This ultimate reality is God. Aquinas provides, in the following passage from *Summa Theologica*, three different formulations of this argument, involving the concepts of motion, causality, and contingency.

Saint Thomas Aquinas, from *Summa Theologica*

The existence of God can be shown in five ways.

The first and more manifest way is the argument from motion. It is certain, and evident to our senses, that in the world some things are in motion. Now whatever is in motion is put in motion by another, for nothing can be in motion except it is in potentiality to that towards which it is in motion; whereas a thing moves inasmuch as it is in actuality. For motion is nothing else than the reduction of something from potentiality to actuality. But nothing can be reduced from potentiality to actuality, except by something in a state of actuality. Thus that which is actually hot, as fire, makes wood, which is potentially hot, to be actually hot, and thereby moves and changes it. Now it is not possible that the same thing should be at once in actuality and potentiality in the same respect, but only in different respects. For what is actually hot cannot simultaneously be potentially hot; but it is simultaneously potentially cold. It is therefore impossible that in the same respect and in the same way a thing should be both mover and moved, i.e. that it should move itself. Therefore, whatever is in motion must be put in motion by another. If that by which it is put in motion be itself put in motion, then this also must needs be put in motion by another, and that by another again. But this cannot go on to infinity, because then there would be no first mover, and, consequently, no other mover; seeing that subsequent movers move only inasmuch as they are put in motion by the first mover; as the staff moves only because it is put in motion by the hand. Therefore it is necessary to arrive at a first mover, put in motion by no other; and this everyone understands to be God.

The logic of this argument is straightforward: When we examine the universe, we observe that, as Heraclitus noted, "All is change," as everything is continually moving, evolving, changing. Each state of change is the result of a prior state, which is the result of a prior state, and so on. It is rational for us to assume (the proof argues) that at some point, there is an ultimate, unchanging source of all change; and that source is God.

The second argument mirrors the first, substituting the concept of "causation" for "motion."

> **Saint Thomas Aquinas,** from *Summa Theologica*
>
> The second way is from the nature of the efficient cause. In the world of sense we find there is an order of efficient causes. There is no case known (neither is it, indeed, possible) in which a thing is found to be the efficient cause of itself; for so it would be prior to itself, which is impossible. Now in efficient causes it is not possible to go on to infinity, because in all efficient causes following in order, the first is the cause of the intermediate cause, and the intermediate is the cause of the ultimate cause, whether the intermediate cause be several, or only one. Now to take away the cause is to take away the effect. Therefore, if there be no first cause among efficient causes, there will be no ultimate, nor any intermediate cause. But if in efficient causes it is possible to go on to infinity, there will be no first efficient cause, neither will there be an ultimate effect, nor any intermediate efficient causes; all of which is plainly false. Therefore it is necessary to admit a first efficient cause, to which everyone gives the name of God.

Both of these arguments rest on Aquinas's assumption that there must be an unchanging source of change or a "first cause" of all causal events because the alternative would be an "infinite regress," which is metaphysically and epistemologically unacceptable. Our understanding *demands* that there be a beginning point, whether it's an unchanging source of change or a "first cause" of all causal events. But is this

***The Creation of Adam* by Michelangelo.** Do you agree with Aquinas that there must be a source of all change and a first cause of all causal events and that the beginning point is God?

necessarily so? Why can't we simply accept that the universe is eternal, that things have been moving, and that causal events have been occurring forever? And even if we *do* accept the necessity of an unchanging source of change or a "first cause" of the universe's existence, why must we assume that such a beginning point is "God"? Perhaps it was simply some impersonal principle or phenomenon at the origin of things, something beyond our limited ability to comprehend—other than "God."

Another objection that has been raised against the *first cause argument* is that its conclusion ("Therefore God must be the First Cause") is contradicted by its premise ("Every event must be caused"). As Bertrand Russell expresses it in *Why I Am Not a Christian*: "If everything must have a cause, then God must have a cause. If there can be anything without a cause, it may just as well be the world as God, so there cannot be any validity in that argument."

The third argument of Aquinas is slightly more complex. Everything in the universe appears to be contingent, a possibility. But if something is *possible*, it means that it is not *necessary* that it exist. It might just as easily have *not* existed, and in fact, at one point it didn't exist. But if everything in the universe is only possible, and not necessary, then at some point everything in the universe would not have existed because that is what it means to be "possible"—not existing at some point. But because the universe *does* exist, it's rational to assume (according to the proof) that there is a Being that is a necessary (not merely contingent) Being that does not depend on anything else for its existence. That Being is God. However, this argument is going to be vulnerable to the same objections we noted have been raised against the first two arguments.

Saint Thomas Aquinas, from *Summa Theologica*

The third way is taken from possibility and necessity, and runs thus. We find in nature things that are possible to be and not to be, since they are found to be generated, and to corrupt, and consequently, they are possible to be and not to be. But it is impossible for these always to exist, for that which is possible not to be at some time is not. Therefore, if everything is possible not to be, then at one time there could have been nothing in existence. Now if this were true, even now there would be nothing in existence, because that which does not exist only begins to exist by something already existing. Therefore, if at one time nothing was in existence, it would have been impossible for anything to have begun to exist; and thus even now nothing would be in existence—which is absurd. Therefore, not all beings are merely possible, but there must exist something the existence of which is necessary. But every necessary thing either has its necessity caused by another, or not. Now it is impossible to go on to infinity in necessary things which have their necessity caused by another, as has been already proved in regard to efficient causes. Therefore we cannot but postulate the existence of some being having of itself its own necessity, and not receiving it from another, but rather causing in others their necessity. This all men speak of as God.

< READING CRITICALLY >

Analyzing the Cosmological Argument

Aquinas's arguments rest on the assumption that our understanding of the universe *demands* that there be a beginning point, whether it's an unchanging source of change or a "first cause" of all causal events, and that the alternative, an "infinite regress," would be metaphysically and epistemologically unacceptable to us. Do you agree with this assumption, or are you equally comfortable with the idea that there is no "first cause" or ultimate beginning source for the existence of the universe? Explain the reasons for your answer.

The Argument from Gradations of Perfection

Aquinas's fourth way to prove God's existence is his argument from the different degrees of perfection found in finite things. Humans commonly judge some things to be more perfect than other things. But judgment concerning the degree of perfection in things only makes sense if there exists a most perfect Being. To say that something is more perfect than something else is to say that it closer approximates the perfect. One cannot determine that something falls short of a perfect standard unless that perfect standard is known. Therefore, the perfect must exist. Whatever contains the most perfection must be the source of all the perfection that exists in other beings. Therefore, concludes Aquinas, there must exist a most perfect Being who is the cause of all the perfections that exist in beings containing lesser degrees of perfection.

The Argument from Design

In *Summa Theologica*, Aquinas also introduces a fifth proof known as the *argument from design*. This argument begins with the observation that the universe is orderly and apparently purposeful or *teleological* (from the Greek *telos*, meaning purpose or end). It is rational to assume (according to this proof) that this order and purposefulness did not simply happen by accident but is the product of an intelligent Creator: namely, God.

((•—[**Listen** to the **Podcast**
Anthony Kenny on Aquinas's Ethics on
mysearchlab.com

The fifth way is taken from the governance of the world. We see that things which lack intelligence, such as natural bodies, act for an end, and this is evident from their acting always, or nearly always, in the same way, so as to obtain the best result. Hence it is plain that not fortuitously, but designedly, do they achieve their end. Now whatever lacks intelligence cannot move towards an end, unless it be directed by some being endowed with knowledge and intelligence; as the arrow is shot to its mark by the archer. Therefore some intelligent being exists by whom all natural things are directed to their end; and this being we call God.

Saint Thomas Aquinas, from *Summa Theologica*

The design argument was further developed and refined almost six hundred years later by the theologian **William Paley**, who begins his analysis with a vivid image.

William Paley (1743–1805). Paley was a British theologian who developed the argument from design that asserts that the high level of order in the world is proof of an intelligent designer, God.

William Paley, from *Natural Theology*

In crossing a heath, suppose I pitched my foot against a *stone*, and were asked how the stone came to be there; I might possibly answer, that, for any thing I knew to the contrary, it had lain there for ever: nor would it perhaps be very easy to show the absurdity of this answer. But suppose I had found a *watch* upon the ground, and it should be inquired how the watch happened to be in that place; I should hardly think of the answer which I had before given, that, for any thing I knew, the watch might have always been there. Yet why should not this answer serve for the watch as well as for the stone? Why is it not as admissible in the second case, as in the first? For this reason, and for no other, viz. that, when we come to inspect the watch, we perceive (what we could not discover in the stone) that its several parts are framed and put together for a purpose, *e.g.* that they are so formed and adjusted as to produce motion, and that motion so regulated as to point out the hour of the day; that, if the different parts had been differently shaped from what they are, of a different size from what they are, or placed after any other manner, or in any other order, than that in which they are placed, either no motion at all would have been carried on in the machine, or none which would have answered the use that is now served by it. To reckon up a few of the plainest of these parts, and of their offices, all tending to one result:—We see a cylindrical box containing a coiled elastic spring, which, by its endeavour to relax itself, turns round the box. We next observe a flexible chain (artificially wrought for the sake of flexure), communicating the action of the spring from the box to the fusee. We then find a series of wheels, the teeth of which catch in, and apply to, each other, conducting the motion from the fusee to the balance, and from the balance to the pointer; and at the same time, by the size and shape of those wheels, so regulating that motion, as to terminate in causing an index, by an equable and measured progression, to pass over a given space in a given time. We take notice that the wheels are made of brass in order to keep them from rust; the springs of steel, no other metal being so elastic; that over the face of the watch there is placed a glass, a material employed in no other part of the work, but in the room of which, if there had been any other than a transparent substance, the hour could not be seen without opening the case. This mechanism being observed (it requires indeed an examination of the instrument, and perhaps some previous knowledge of the subject, to perceive and understand it; but being once, as we have said, observed and understood), the inference, we think, is inevitable, that the watch must have had a maker: that there must have existed, at some time, and at some place or other, an artificer or artificers who formed it for the purpose which we find it actually to answer; who comprehended its construction, and designed its use.

The argument from design. Paley uses the analogy of a watch to argue that the universe must have a creator. Do you think this is a good analogy?

< READING CRITICALLY >

Analyzing the Argument from Design

The *argument from design*, like the various formulations of the *cosmological* argument," asks us to consider two different views of the universe and choose the one that makes the most sense to us. In this case, the choice is between believing either that the order and organization of the universe are due to the design of a purposeful divine Creator or that the order and organization are simply due to chance or impersonal principles that govern the universe. Does one view make more sense to you than the other? How would you respond to Bertrand Russell's suggestion that if you were an all-knowing and all-powerful divine Creator, you could have done a better job in designing the universe?

Although some thinkers have found the design argument to be persuasive, others have raised objections. To begin with, can't we accept the fact that there is a certain *order* in the universe without concluding that this order is the result of *intelligent design*? Perhaps the order that we see simply evolved randomly, or perhaps the universe is governed by certain impersonal principles (such as the ancient Greek concept of *Logos*) that are expressed in the orderliness of the universe that we perceive. Neither possibility entails that we accept the existence of "God" as a supernatural creator or designer. Some thinkers have argued that the universe is actually *poorly* designed, with many elements that don't work as well as they could have if an intelligent designer had created them. Or, as Bertrand Russell expresses it in *Why I Am Not a Christian,*

> *When you come to look into this argument from design, it is a most astonishing thing that people can believe that this world, with all the things that are in it, with all its defects, should be the best that omnipotence and omniscience have been able to produce in millions of years. I really cannot believe it. Do you think that, if you were granted omnipotence and omniscience and millions of years in which to perfect your world, you could produce nothing better than the Ku Klux Klan or the Fascists?*

The Argument from Morality

Another type of argument that has been made for the existence of God is the *argument from morality*. Its beginning point is the deeply ingrained sense of morality that humans possess, and its conclusion is that this moral sense must be derived from a supremely moral mind—namely, God. This argument can be focused in a number of different ways. Natural law ethicists see a broad agreement among the major ethical systems of the world, embodied in writings as diverse as the *Daode Jing* of Laozi, the Ten Commandments, the Hindu Code of Manu, the Analects of Confucius, the Dharma of Buddha, and the Qur'an of Islam. Others point to the "conscience," the powerful, deeply ingrained conviction that we have the capacity to choose what is "right" and "good" over what is "wrong" and "bad." Both schools of thought point to God as the source of these teachings or feelings.

A final focus of the moral argument for God's existence was proposed by **Immanuel Kant** and is somewhat more intricate. For Kant, morality is grounded mainly in our ability to reason, hence his supreme moral principle, the categorical imperative, which we will explore in Chapter 9: *Act only on the principle that you can at the same time will it to be a universal law of nature.* But Kant also believes that our ability to reason gives us the ability to clearly recognize the "highest good," the summum bonum, a concept that integrates the balanced harmony of moral goodness and personal happiness. We have the absolute conviction that people who live virtuous, morally upright lives should be rewarded by happiness, whereas those who lead evil, immoral lives should endure misery and suffering. However, we also observe that at least in this current life on Earth, such a harmonious balance often does not exist: Virtuous people can endure great misery and unhappiness, whereas immoral people can be successful and even seem to be relatively happy. For Kant, our ability to reason demands that this seemingly unfair state of affairs be corrected, and this can only occur in an afterlife in which virtue will be rewarded and evil punished. Such a future life of rational justice can only be created by a supreme being: God. Kant explains this view in more

Immanuel Kant
(1724–1804). German philosopher, widely regarded as one of the greatest philosophers of the modern period. Kant attempted to synthesize two competing schools, rationalism and empiricism, by showing the important roles that both experience and reason play in constructing our knowledge of the world.

***The Good Samaritan,* by Delacroix.** In this Christian parable, a Samaritan acts with great kindness toward an injured stranger. Do you think that the moral impulse to help those in need comes from God? *(Eugene Delacroix,* The Good Samaritan *(Luke, X:34). 1852. Oil on canvas, 13 1/4 × 16 1/2 in. Victoria & Albert Museum, London. Art Resource, NY.)*

detail in the following selection from his *Critique of Practical Reason* entitled "God as a Postulate of Practical Reason."

Immanuel Kant, from *Critique of Practical Reason,* "God as a Postulate of Practical Reason"

The moral law led, in the foregoing analysis, to a practical problem which is assigned solely by pure reason and without any concurrence of sensuous incentives. It is the problem of the completeness of the first and principal part of the highest good, viz. Morality; since this problem can be solved only in eternity, it led to the postulate of immortality. The same law must also lead us to affirm the possibility of the second element of the highest good, i.e., happiness proportional to that morality; it must do just as disinterestedly as heretofore, by a cause adequate to this effect, i.e., it must postulate the existence of God as necessarily belonging to the possibility of the highest good (the object of our will which is necessarily connected with the moral legislation of pure reason). We proceed to exhibit this connection in a convincing manner.

Kant has complete confidence in the capacity of our rational abilities to describe the structure of reality. Because we are able to contemplate the "highest good" for humans in a clear and compelling way, we must assume the existence of those things that make such a "highest good" possible. In the section preceding this passage, Kant has argued that this means assuming that we have immortal souls: Otherwise, the concept of achieving the "highest good" would make no sense for humans. In this section, he is arguing that the "highest good" entails the idea of people being happy in direct proportion to their moral goodness: We believe such a formula to be a rational necessity. And because a direct correlation between happiness and moral goodness does not occur in this life, reason demands that we assume (or *postulate*) that this correlation will occur in the next life. And this means postulating the existence of God.

Immanuel Kant, from *Critique of Practical Reason,* "God as a Postulate of Practical Reason"

Happiness is the condition of a rational being in the world, in whose whole existence everything goes according to wish and will. It thus rests on the harmony of nature with his entire end and with the essential determining ground of his will. But the moral law commands as a law of freedom through motives wholly independent of nature and of its harmony with our faculty of desire (as incentives). Still, the acting rational being in the world is not at the same time the cause of the world and of nature itself. Hence there is not the slightest ground in the moral law for a necessary connection between the morality and proportionate happiness of a being which belongs to the world as one of its parts and as thus dependent on it. Not being nature's cause, his will cannot by its own strength bring nature, as it touches on his happiness, into complete harmony with this practical principle. Nevertheless, in the practical task of pure reason, i.e., in the necessary endeavor after the highest good, such a connection is postulated as necessary: we *should* seek to further the highest good (which therefore must be at least possible). Therefore also the existence is postulated of a cause of the whole of nature, itself distinct from nature, which contains the ground of the exact coincidence of happiness with morality. This supreme cause, however, must contain the ground of the agreement of nature not merely with actions moral in their form but also with their morality as the motives to such actions, i.e., with their supposition of a supreme cause of nature which has a causality corresponding to the moral intention. Now a being which is capable of actions by the idea of laws is an intelligence (a rational being), and the causality of such a being according to this idea of laws is his will. Therefore, the supreme cause of nature, in so far as it must be presupposed for the highest good, is a being which is the cause (and consequently the author) of nature through understanding and will, i.e., God. As a consequence, the postulate of the possibility of a highest derived good (the best world) is at the same time the postulate of the reality of a highest original good, namely, the existence of God. Now it was our duty to promote the highest good; and it is not merely our privilege but a necessity connected with duty as a requisite to presuppose the possibility of this highest good. This presupposition is made only under the condition of the existence of God, and this condition inseparably connects this supposition with duty. Therefore, it is morally necessary to assume the existence of God.

< READING CRITICALLY >

Analyzing the Argument from Morality

- Consider your "conscience" or your ingrained sense of morality. Do you believe that the existence of this deeply felt moral sense supports belief in the existence of a supremely moral mind—God? Why or why not?
- In line with Kant's reasoning, do you believe in "cosmic justice," the belief that good people must be rewarded with personal happiness, whether in this world or the next? Why or why not?

How could a loving Creator permit this?
Philosophers and theologians have grappled with questions regarding the existence of God and God's nature in the face of events of massive pain and suffering.

7.5 The Problem of Evil

Three centuries before the birth of Christ, the Greek philosopher Epicurus posed the following challenge regarding God and the existence of evil in the universe:

> *God either cannot or will not prevent evil. If God cannot prevent evil, then God is limited in power. If God will not prevent evil, then God is limited in benevolence. But if God is not limited in either power or benevolence, why is there evil in the world?*

The existence of evil in the world poses a serious threat to religion in general and to the concept of an all-loving, all-powerful God in particular. When human catastrophes happen, it is common for people to wonder, "How could God let this happen?" There are two general categories of evil in the world. The first is *natural evil,* the human calamities that are the result of natural disasters: earthquakes, hurricanes, tornadoes, disease, crop-destroying droughts and pestilence, starvation, and other aspects of the natural order that end up destroying lives and crushing human hopes. The second category is *moral evil,* the pain, suffering, and death inflicted by humans on humans through evil actions: murder, rape, physical abuse, theft, psychological torture, child abuse, warfare, genocide, discrimination, persecution, and other examples of human malevolence. Although these two types of evil are distinct, they are also related in complex ways. For example, starvation and poverty are often the result of human policies as well as natural disasters, and the failure of wealthy cultures to share their resources increases the death and disease in less affluent cultures.

Questions regarding the existence of God and God's nature apply to both kinds of evil. Regarding natural evil, it seems reasonable to ask: Why does God permit natural disasters to occur, with the loss of life and property of innocent people? If God is all-powerful (omnipotent), God should be able to exert some minimal planning and control to prevent hurricanes, earthquakes, disease, and other natural catastrophes from harming innocent people. And if God is all-benevolent, wouldn't God want to prevent such senseless disasters from occurring?

With respect to moral evil, it seems reasonable to ask: Why did God create humans with such primal, destructive impulses that result in such evil actions? Couldn't God have created everyone with a sufficiently moral nature to prevent such evil? Couldn't humans have been created with the ability to make free choices while still retaining a basic decency and empathy? And why does God permit the creation of such human monsters as Stalin and Hitler or serial killers and child abusers? Again, if God is omnipotent, preventing human evil on this scale should not be all that difficult; and if God is all-loving, God should certainly want to prevent this kind of unnecessary human suffering. The obvious responses to this dilemma include

- God does not exist, at least as a personal Creator involved in human affairs.
- God is not all-powerful and so is unable to influence events in the world.
- God is not all-loving and so is not interested in preventing evil in the world.

For people with a fervent belief in religions based on a supreme, omnipotent, all-loving Creator—such as Judaism, Christianity, and Islam—none of these alternatives are attractive. As a result, many thinkers have tried to construct alternative metaphysical/theological frameworks that will reconcile the existence of a Creator God with the existence of evil in the universe. The name of this field of inquiry is **theodicy**, which comes from the Greek words *theos* (God) and *dike* (righteous), which together mean the justification of God's goodness in the face of the fact of evil. However, there are other thinkers who believe that these efforts to rescue the existence of God from the threat posed by evil in the universe are destined to fail. This is precisely the position advocated for by the philosopher J. L. Mackie in the following essay.

Theodicy A defense of the justice or goodness of God in the face of doubts or objections arising from the phenomena of evil in the world.

J. L. Mackie, from *Evil Shows That There Is No God*

The traditional arguments for the existence of God have been fairly thoroughly criticized by philosophers. But the theologian can, if he wishes, accept this criticism. He can admit that no rational proof of God's existence is possible. And he can still retain all that is essential to his position, by holding that God's existence is known in some other, non-rational way. I think, however, that a more telling criticism can be made by way of the traditional problem of evil. Here it can be shown not that religious beliefs lack rational support, but that they are positively irrational, that the several parts of the essential theological doctrine are inconsistent with one another, so that the theologian can maintain his position as a whole only by a much more extreme rejection of reason than in the former case. He must now be prepared to believe, not merely what cannot be proved, but what can be *disproved* from other beliefs that he also holds.

The problem of evil, in the sense in which I shall be using the phrase, is a problem only for someone who believes that there is a God who is both omnipotent and wholly good. And it is a logical problem, the problem of clarifying and reconciling a number of beliefs: it is not a scientific problem that might be solved by further observations, or a practical problem that might be solved by a decision or an action. These points are obvious; I mention them only because they are sometimes ignored by theologians, who sometimes parry a statement of the problem with such remarks as "Well, can you solve the problem yourself?" or "This is a mystery which may be revealed to us later" or "Evil is something to be faced and overcome, not to be merely discussed."

In its simplest form the problem is this: God is omnipotent; God is wholly good; and yet evil exists. There seems to be some contradiction between these three propositions, so that if any two of them were true the third would be false. But at the same time all three are essential parts of most theological positions: the theologian, it seems, at once *must* adhere and *cannot consistently* adhere to all three. (The problem does not arise only for theists, but I shall discuss it in the form in which it presents itself for ordinary theism.)

However, the contradiction does not arise immediately; to show it we need some additional premises, or perhaps come quasi-logical rules connecting the terms "good," "evil," and "omnipotent." These additional principles are that good is opposed to evil, in such a way that a good thing always eliminates evil as far as it can. And that there are no limits to what an omnipotent thing can do. From these it follows that a good omnipotent thing eliminates evil completely, and then the propositions that a good omnipotent thing exists, and that evil exists, are incompatible.

A. Adequate solutions

Now once the problem is fully stated it is clear that it can be solved, in the sense that the problem will not arise if one gives up at least one of the propositions that constitute it.

If you are prepared to say that God is not wholly good, or not quite omnipotent, or that evil does not exist, or that good is not opposed to the kind of evil that exists, or that there are limits to what an omnipotent thing can do, then the problem of evil will not arise for you.

There are, then, quite a number of adequate solutions of the problem of evil, and some of these have been adopted, or almost adopted, by various thinkers. For example, a few have been prepared to deny God's omnipotence, and rather more have been prepared to keep the term "omnipotence" but severely to restrict its meaning, recording quite a number of things that an omnipotent being cannot do. Some have said that evil is an illusion, perhaps because they held that the whole world of temporal, changing things is an illusion, and that what we call evil belongs only to this world, or perhaps because they held that although temporal things *are* much as we see them, those that we call evil are not really evil. Some have said that what we call evil is merely the privation of good, that evil in a positive sense, evil that would really be opposed to good, does not exist. Many have agreed with (Alexander) Pope that disorder is harmony not understood, and that partial evil is universal good. Whether any of these views is *true* is, of course, another question. But each of them gives an adequate solution of the problem of evil in the sense that if you accept it this problem does not arise for you, though you may, of course, have *other* problems to face.

But often enough these adequate solutions are only *almost* adopted. The thinkers who restrict God's power, but keep the term "omnipotence," may reasonably be suspected of thinking, in other contexts, that his power is really unlimited. Those who say that evil is an illusion may also be thinking, inconsistently, that this illusion is itself an evil. Those who say that evil "evil" is merely privation of good may also be thinking, inconsistently, that privation of good is an evil . . . .

In addition, therefore, to adequate solutions, we must recognize unsatisfactory inconsistent solutions, in which there is only a half-hearted or temporary rejection of one of the propositions which together constitute the problem. In these, one of the constituent propositions is explicitly rejected, but it is covertly re-asserted or assumed elsewhere in the system.

G. Fallacious solutions

Besides these half-hearted solutions, which explicitly reject but implicitly assert one of the constituent propositions, there are definitely fallacious solutions which explicitly maintain all the constituent propositions, but implicitly reject at lease one of them in the course of the argument that explains away the problem of evil. . . . I propose to examine some of these so-called solutions, and to exhibit their fallacies in detail.

1. **"Good cannot exist without evil" or "Evil is necessary as a counterpart to good."** It is sometimes suggested that evil is necessary as a counterpart to good, that if there were no evil there could be no good either, and that this solves the problem of evil. It is true that it points to an answer to the question "Why should there be evil?" But it does so only by qualifying some of the propositions that constitute the problem.

   First, it sets a limit to what God can do, saying that God *cannot* create good without simultaneously creating evil, and this means either that God is not omnipotent or that there are *some* limits to what an omnipotent thing can do. It may be replied that these limits are always presupposed, that omnipotence has never meant the power to do what is logically impossible, and on the present view the existence of good without evil would be a logical impossibility. This interpretation of omnipotence may, indeed, be accepted as a modification of our original account which does not reject anything that is essential to theism, and I shall in general assume it in the subsequent discussion. It is, perhaps the most common theistic view, but I think that some theists at least have maintained that God can do what is logically impossible. Many theists, at any rate, have held that logic itself is created or laid down by God, that logic is the way in which God arbitrarily chooses to think. (This is, of course, parallel to the ethical view that morally right actions are those which God arbitrarily chooses to command, and the two views encounter similar difficulties.) And *this* account of logic is clearly inconsistent with the view that God is bound by logical necessities—unless it is possible for an omnipotent being to bind himself, an issue which we shall consider later, when we come to the Paradox of Omnipotence. This solution of the problem of evil cannot, therefore, be consistently adopted along with the view that logic is itself created by God.

2. **"Evil is necessary as a means to good."** It is sometimes suggested that evil is necessary for good not as a counterpart but as a means. In its simple form this has little plausibility as a solution of the problem of evil, since it obviously implies a severe restriction of God's power. It would be a *causal* law that you cannot have a certain end without a certain means, so that if God has to introduce evil as a means to good, he must be subject to at least some causal laws. This certainly conflicts with what a theist normally means by omnipotence. This view of God as limited by causal laws also conflicts with the view that causal laws are themselves made by God, which is more widely held than the corresponding view about the laws of logic. This conflict would, indeed, be resolved if it were possible for an omnipotent being to bind himself, and this possibility has still to be considered. Unless a favourable answer can be given to this question, the suggestion that evil is necessary as a means to good solves the problem of evil only by denying one of its constituent propositions, either that God is omnipotent or that "omnipotent" means what it says.

3. **"The universe is better with some evil in it than it could be if there were no evil."** Much more important is a solution which at first seems to be a mere variant of the previous one, that evil may contribute to the goodness of a whole in which it is found, so that the universe as a whole is better as it is, with some evil in it, than it would be if there were no evil. This solution may be developed in either of two ways. It may be supported by an aesthetic analogy, by the fact that contrasts heighten beauty, that in a musical work, for example, there may occur discords which somehow add to the beauty of the work as a whole. Alternatively, it may be worked out in connection with the notion of progress, that the best possible organization of the universe will not be static, but progressive, that the gradual overcoming of evil by good is really a finer thing than would be the eternal unchallenged supremacy of good.

In either case, this solution usually starts from the assumption that the evil whose existence gives rise to the problem of evil is primarily what is called physical evil, that is to say, pain. In (David) Hume's rather halfhearted presentation of the problem of evil, the evils that he stresses are pain and disease, and those who reply to him argue that the existence of pain and disease makes possible the existence of sympathy, benevolence, heroism, and the gradually successful struggle of doctors and reformers to overcome these evils. In fact, theists often seize the opportunity to accuse those who stress the problem of evil of taking a low, materialistic view of good and evil, equating these with pleasure and pain, and of ignoring the more spiritual gods which can arise in the struggle against evils.

But let us see exactly what is being done here. Let us call pain and misery "first order evil" or "evil (1)." What contrasts with this, namely, pleasure and happiness will be called "first order good" or "good (1)." Distinct from this is "second order good" or "good (2)" which somehow emerges in a complex situation in which evil (1) is a necessary component—logically, not merely causally, necessary. (Exactly how it emerges does not matter: in the crudest version of this solution good (2) is simply the heightening of happiness by the contrast with misery; in other versions it includes sympathy with suffering, heroism in facing danger, and the gradual decrease of first order evil and increase of first order good.) It is also being assumed that second order good is more important than first order good or evil, in particular that it more than outweighs the first order evil it involves.

Now this is a particularly subtle attempt to solve the problem of evil. It defends God's goodness and omnipotence on the ground that (on a sufficiently long view) this is the best of all logically possible worlds, because it includes the important second order goods, and yet it admits that real evils, namely first order evils, exist. But does it still hold that good and evil are opposed? Not, clearly, in the sense that we set out originally: good does not tend to eliminate evil in general. Instead, we have a modified, a more complex pattern. First order good (e.g., happiness) *contrasts with* first order evil (e.g., misery): these two are opposed in a fairly mechanical way; some second order goods (e.g., benevolence) try to maximize first order good and minimize first order evil; but God's goodness is not this, it is rather the will to maximize *second* order good. We might, therefore, call God's goodness an example of a third order goodness, or good (3). While this account is different from our original one, it might well be held to be an improvement on it, to give a more accurate description of the way in which good is opposed to evil, and to be consistent with the essential theist position.

There might, however, be several objections to this solution.

First, some might argue that such qualities as benevolence—and *a fortiori* the third order goodness which promotes benevolence—have a merely derivative value, that they are not higher sorts of good, but merely means to good (1), that is, to happiness, so that it would be absurd for God to keep misery in existence in order to make possible the virtues of benevolence, heroism, etc. The theist who adopts the present solution must, of course, deny this, but he can do so with some plausibility, so I should not press this objection.

Secondly, it follows from this solution that God is not in our sense benevolent or sympathetic: he is not concerned to minimize evil (1), but only to promote good (2), and this might be a disturbing conclusion for some theists.

But, thirdly, the fatal objection is this. Our analysis shows clearly the possibility of the existence of a *second* order evil, an evil (2) contrasting with good (2) as evil (1) contrasts with good (1). This would include malevolence, cruelty, callousness, cowardice, and states in which good (1) is decreasing and evil (1) increasing. And just as good (2) is held to be the important kind of good, the kind that God is concerned to promote, so evil (2) will, by analogy, be the important kind of evil, the kind which God, if he were wholly good and omnipotent, would eliminate. And yet evil (2) plainly exists, and indeed most theists (in other contexts) stress its existence more than that of evil (1). We should, therefore, state the problem of evil in terms of second order evil, and against this form of the problem the present solution is useless.

"Evil is due to human free will." Perhaps the most important proposed solution of the problem of evil is that evil is not to be ascribed to God at all, but to the independent actions of human beings, supposed to have been endowed by God with freedom of the will. This solution may be combined with the preceding one: first order evil (e.g., pain) may be justified as a logically necessary component in second order good (e.g., sympathy) while second order evil (e.g., cruelty) is not *justified*, but is so ascribed to human beings that God cannot be held responsible for it. This combination evades my third criticism of the preceding solution.

The free will solution also involves the preceding solution at a higher level. To explain why a wholly good God gave men free will although it would lead to some important evils, it must be argued that it is better on the whole that men should act feely, and sometimes err, than that they should be innocent automata, acting rightly in a wholly determined way. Freedom, that is to say, is now treated as a third order good, and as being more valuable than second order goods (such as sympathy and heroism) would be if they were deterministically produced, and it is being assumed that second order evils, such as cruelty, are logically necessary accompaniments of freedom, just as pain is a logically necessary pre-condition of sympathy.

I think that this solution is unsatisfactory primarily because of the incoherence of the notion of freedom of the will: but I cannot discuss this topic adequately here, although some of my criticisms will touch upon it.

First I should query the assumption that second order evils are logically necessary accompaniments of freedom. I should ask this: if God has made men such that in their free choices they sometimes prefer what is good and sometimes what is evil, why could he not have made men such that they always freely choose the good? If there is no logical impossibility in a man's freely choosing the good on one, or on several occasions, there cannot be a logical impossibility in his freely choosing the good on every occasion. God was not, then, faced with a choice between making innocent automata and making beings who, in acting feely, would sometimes go wrong: there was open to him the obviously better possibility of making beings who would act freely but always go right. Clearly, his failure to avail himself of this possibility is inconsistent with his being both omnipotent and wholly good.

If it is replied that this objection is absurd, that the making of some wrong choices is logically necessary for freedom, it would seem that "freedom" must here mean complete randomness or indeterminacy, including randomness with regard to the alternatives good and evil, in other words that men's choices and consequent actions can be "free" only if they are not determined by their characters. Only on this assumption can God escape the responsibility for men's actions; for if he made them as they are, but did not determine their wrong choices, this can only be because the wrong choices are not determined by men as they are. But then if freedom is randomness, how can it be a characteristic of *will*? And, still more, how can it be the most important good? What value or merit would there be in free choices if these were random actions which were not determined by the nature of the agent?

I conclude that to make this solution plausible two different senses of "freedom" must be confused, one sense which will justify the view that freedom is a third order good, more valuable than other goods would be without it, and another sense, sheer randomness, to prevent us from ascribing to God a decision to make men such that they sometimes go wrong when he might have made them such that they would always freely go right.

This criticism is sufficient to dispose of this solution. But besides this there is a fundamental difficulty in the notion of an omnipotent God creating men with free will, for if men's wills are really free this must mean that even God cannot control them, that is, that God is no longer omnipotent. It may be objected that God's gift of freedom to men does not mean that he *cannot* control their wills, but that he always *refrains* from controlling their wills. But why, we may ask, should God refrain from controlling evil wills? Why should he not leave me free to will rightly but intervene when he sees them beginning to will wrongly? If God could do this, but does not, and if he is wholly good, the only explanation could be that even a wrong free act of will is not really evil, that its freedom is a value which outweighs its wrongness, so that there would be a loss of value if God took away the wrongness and the freedom together. But this is utterly opposed to what theists say about sin in other contexts. The present solution of the problem of evil, then, can be maintained only insofar that God has made men so free that he *cannot* control their wills.

This leads us to what I call the Paradox of Omnipotence: can an omnipotent being make things which he cannot subsequently control? Or, what is practically equivalent to this, can an omnipotent being make rules which then bind himself? (These are practically equivalent because any such rules could be regarded as setting certain things beyond his control and *vice versa*) The second of these formulations is relevant to the suggestions that we have already met, that an omnipotent God creates the rules of logic or causal laws, and is then bound by them.

It is clear that this is a paradox: the questions cannot be answered satisfactorily either in the affirmative or in the negative. If we answer "Yes," it follows that if God actually makes things which he cannot control, or makes rules which bind himself, he is not omnipotent once he has made them: there are *then* things which he cannot do. But if we answer "No," we are immediately asserting that there are things which he cannot do, that is to say that he is already not omnipotent.

Conclusion

Of the proposed solutions of the problem of evil which we have examined, none has stood up to criticism. There may be other solutions which require examination, but this study strongly suggests that there is no valid solution of the problem which does not modify at least one of the constituent propositions in a way which would seriously affect the essential core of the theistic position.

Quite apart from the problem of evil, the paradox of omnipotence has shown that God's omnipotence must in any case be restricted in one way or another, that unqualified omnipotence cannot be ascribed to any being that continues through time. And if God and his actions are not in time, can omnipotence, or power of any sort, be meaningfully ascribed to him?

< READING CRITICALLY >

Analyzing Mackie on "Evil Shows That There Is No God"

Why does Mackie believe that the existence of evil in the world shows that there is no God? Do you agree that his reasoning is sound? If not, why do you disagree with his argument and conclusion?

1. Summarize the four ways Mackie identifies that believers in God try to account for the existence of evil in the world while still maintaining a belief in God.
2. Describe in each case why Mackie believes that the each of these four efforts fails in saving God's existence.
3. Explain what the Paradox of Omnipotence is. Does this pose a serious threat to a belief in God? Why or why not?

In the following essay, *John Hick* reviews some of the traditional theodicy theories and also presents his own approach to this complex and disturbing issue.

John Hick, from *Philosophy of Religion,* "God Can Allow Some Evil"

To many, the most powerful positive objection to belief in God is the fact of evil. Probably for most agnostics it is the appalling depth and extent of human suffering, more than anything else, that makes the idea of a loving Creator seem so implausible and disposes them toward one or another of the various naturalistic theories of religion.

As a challenge to theism, the problem of evil has traditionally been posed in the form of a dilemma; if God is perfectly loving, he must wish to abolish evil; and if he is all-powerful, he must be able to abolish evil. But evil exists; therefore God cannot be both omnipotent and perfectly loving . . . .

Theodicy, as many modern Christian thinkers see it, is a modest enterprise, negative rather than positive in its conclusions. It does not claim to explain, nor to explain away, every instance of evil in human experience, but only to point to certain considerations which prevent the fact of evil (largely incomprehensible though it remains) from constituting a final and insuperable bar to rational belief in God.

In indicating these considerations it will be useful to follow the traditional division of the subject. There is the problem of *moral evil* or wickedness; why does an all-good and all-powerful God permit this? And there is the problem of the *nonmoral evil* of suffering or pain, both physical and mental: why has an all-good and all-powerful God created a world in which this occurs?

Christian thought has always considered moral evil in its relation to human freedom and responsibility. To be a person is to be a finite center of freedom, and (relatively) free and self-directing agent responsible for one's own decisions. This involves being free to act wrongly as well as to act rightly. The idea of a person who can be infallibly guaranteed always to act rightly is self-contradictory. There can be no guarantee in advance that a genuinely free moral agent will never choose amiss. Consequently, the possibility of wrongdoing or sin is logically inseparable from the creation of finite persons, and to say that God should not have created beings who might sin amounts to saying that he should not have created people.

This thesis has been challenged in some recent philosophical discussions of the problem of evil, in which it is claimed that no contradiction is involved in saying that God might have made people who would be genuinely free and who could yet be guaranteed always to act rightly. A quotation from one of these discussions follows:

> *If there is no logical impossibility in a man's freely choosing the good on one, or on several occasions, there cannot be a logical impossibility in his freely choosing the good on every occasion. God was not, then, faced with a choice between making innocent automata and making beings, who, in acting freely, would sometimes go wrong: there was open to him the obviously better possibility of making beings who would act freely but always go right. Clearly, his failure to avail himself of this possibility is inconsistent with his being both omnipotent and wholly good. (Note: This quotation is taken from the preceding essay by J. L. Mackie.)*

A reply to this argument is suggested in another recent contribution to the discussion. If by a free action we mean an action which is not externally compelled but which flows from the nature of the agent as he reacts to the circumstances in which he finds himself, there is, indeed, no contradiction between our being free and our actions being "caused" (by our own nature), and therefore, being in principle

John Hick (B. 1922). A British philosopher and Christian theologian whose work has made a major contribution to contemporary philosophy of religion, Hick's books include *Evil and the God of Love* (4th ed., 2007) and *An Interpretation of Religion* (2nd ed., 2004).

September 11, 2001. Nearly 3,000 people died on the morning of September 11, 2001, as a direct result of the actions of nineteen individuals. How would Hick explain this event in terms of the existence of God?

John Hick, from *Philosophy of Religion,* "God Can Allow Some Evil"

predictable. There is a contradiction, however, in saying that God is the cause of our acting as we do but that we are free beings in relation to God. There is, in other words, a contradiction in saying that God has made us so that we shall of necessity act in a certain way, and that we are genuinely independent persons in relation to him. If all our thoughts and actions are divinely predestined, however free and morally responsible we may seem to be ourselves, we cannot be free and morally responsible in the sight of God, but must instead be his helpless puppets. Such "freedom" is like that of a patient acting out a series of posthypnotic suggestions: he appears, even to himself, to be free, but his volitions have actually been predetermined by another will, that of the hypnotist, in relation to whom the patient is not a free agent.

Hick's analysis in this passage relates directly to the discussion of freedom in Chapter 4. If God formed our characters in the process of creating us to ensure that we always chose the morally right alternative, we could not be considered as genuinely free. Even though we might not be limited by external constraints, our actions would have already been limited by God through internal constraints. Genuine freedom, we concluded in Chapter 4, means making choices that are truly autonomous, independent of both external and internal constraints.

A different objector might raise the question of whether or not we deny God's omnipotence if we admit that he is unable to create persons who are free from the risks inherent in personal freedom. The answer that has always been given is that to create such beings is logically impossible. It is no limitation upon God's power that he cannot accomplish the logically impossible, since there is nothing here to accomplish, but only a meaningless conjunction of words—in this case "person who is not a person." God is able to create beings of any and every conceivable kind; but creatures who lack moral freedom, however superior they might be to human beings in other respects, would not be what we mean by persons. They would constitute a different form of life which God might have brought into existence instead of persons. When we ask why God did not create such beings in place of persons, the traditional answer is that only persons could, in any meaningful sense, become "children of God," capable of entering into a personal relationship with their Creator by a free and uncompelled response to his love.

We may now turn more directly to the problem of suffering. Even though the major bulk of actual human pain is traceable to man's misused freedom as a sole or part cause, there remain other sources of pain which are entirely independent of the human will, for example, earthquake, hurricane, storm, flood, drought, and blight. In practice, it is often impossible to trace a boundary between the suffering which results from human wickedness and folly and that which falls upon mankind from without. Both kinds of suffering are inextricably mingled together in human experience. For our present purpose, however, it is important to note that the latter category does exist and that

Listen to the **Podcast** *Marilyn McCord Adams on Evil* on **mysearchlab.com**

it seems to be built into the very structure of our world. In response to it, theodicy, if it is wisely conducted, follows a negative path. It is not possible to show positively that each item of human pain serves the divine purpose of good; but, on the other hand, it does seem possible to show that the divine purpose as it is understood in Judaism and Christianity could not be forwarded in a world which was designed as a permanent hedonistic paradise.

An essential premise of this argument concerns the nature of the divine purpose in creating the world. The skeptic's assumption is that man is to be viewed as a completed creation and that God's purpose in making the world was to provide a suitable dwelling place for this fully formed creature. Since God is good and loving, the environment which he has created for human life to inhabit is naturally as pleasant and comfortable as possible. The problem is essentially similar to that of a man who builds a cage for some pet animal. Since our world, in fact, contains sources of hardship, inconvenience, and danger of innumerable kinds, the conclusion follows that this world cannot have been created by a perfectly benevolent and all-powerful deity.

Christianity, however, has never supposed that God's purpose in the creation of the world was to construct a paradise whose inhabitants would experience a maximum of pleasure and a minimum of pain. The world is seen, instead, as a place of "soul-making" in which free beings grappling with the tasks and challenges of their existence in a common environment, may become "children of God" and "heirs of eternal life." A way of thinking theologically of God's continuing creative purpose for man was suggested by some of the early Hellenistic Fathers of the Christian Church, especially Irenaeus. Following hints from St. Paul, Irenaeus taught that a man has been made as a person in the image of God but has not yet been brought as a free and responsible agent into the finite likeness of God, which is revealed in Christ. Our world, with all its rough edges, is the sphere in which this second and harder stage of the creative process is taking place.

This conception of the world (whether or not set in Irenaeus's theological framework) can be supported by the method of negative theodicy. Suppose, contrary to fact, that this world were a paradise from which all possibility of pain and suffering were excluded. The consequences would be very far-reaching. For example, no one could ever injure anyone else: the murderer's knife would turn to paper or his bullets to thin air; the bank safe, robbed of a million of dollars, would miraculously become filled with another million dollars (without this device, on however large a scale, proving inflationary); fraud, deceit, conspiracy, and treason would somehow always leave the fabric of society undamaged. Again, no one would ever be injured by accident: the mountain-climber, steeplejack, or playing child falling from a height would float unharmed to the ground; the reckless driver would never meet with disaster. There would be no need to work, since no harm could result from avoiding work; there would be no call to be concerned for others in time of need or danger, for in such a world there could be no real needs or dangers.

To make possible this continual series of individual adjustments, nature would have to work by "special providences" instead of running according to general laws which men must learn to respect on penalty of pain or death. The laws of nature would have to be extremely flexible: sometimes gravity would operate, sometimes not; sometimes an object would be hard and solid, sometimes soft. There could be no sciences, for there would be no enduring world structure to investigate. In eliminating the problems and hardship of an objective environment, with its own laws, life would become like a dream in which, delightfully but aimlessly, we would float and drift at ease.

One can at least begin to imagine such a world. It is evident that our present ethical concepts would have no meaning in it. If, for example, the notion of harming someone is an essential element in the concept of a wrong action, in our hedonistic paradise there could be no wrong actions—nor any right actions in distinction from wrong. Courage and fortitude would have no point in an environment in which there is, by definition, no danger or difficulty. Generosity, kindness, the *agape* aspect of love, prudence, unselfishness, and all other ethical notions which presuppose life in a

> **God is able to create beings of any and every conceivable kind; but creatures who lack moral freedom, however superior they might be to human beings in other respects, would not be what we mean by persons.**

stable environment, could not even be formed. Consequently, such a world, however well it might promote pleasure, would be very ill adapted for the development of the moral qualities of human personality. In relation to this purpose it would be the worst of all possible worlds.

It would seem, then, that an environment intended to make possible the growth in free beings of the finest characteristics of personal life, must have a good deal in common with our present world. It must operate according to general and dependable laws; and it must involve real dangers, difficulties, problems, obstacles, and possibilities of pain, failure, sorrow, frustration, and defeat. If it did not contain the particular trials and perils which—subtracting man's own very considerable contribution—our world contains, it would have to contain others instead.

To realize this is not, by any means, to be in possession of a detailed theodicy. It is to understand that this world, with all its "heartaches and the thousand natural shocks that flesh is heir to," an environment so manifestly not designed for the maximization of human pleasure and the minimization of human pain, may be rather well adapted to the quite different purpose of "soul-making."

At this point, theodicy points forward in two ways to the subject of life after death.

First, although there are many striking instances of good being triumphantly brought out of evil through a man's or a woman's reaction to it, there are many other cases in which the opposite has happened. Sometimes obstacles breed strength of character, dangers evoke courage and unselfishness, and calamities produce patience and moral steadfastness. But sometimes they lead, instead, to resentment, fear, grasping selfishness, and disintegration of character. Therefore, it would seem that any divine purpose of soul-making which is at work in earthly history must continue beyond this life if it is ever to achieve more than a very partial and fragmentary success.

Second, if we ask whether the business of soul-making is worth all the toil and sorrow of human life, the Christian answer must be in terms of a future good which is great enough to justify all that has happened on the way to it.

< READING CRITICALLY >

Analyzing Hick on the Problem of Evil

- Hick maintains that if God interfered with the creation or development of people that we would be like "helpless puppets" or patients "acting out a series of post-hypnotic suggestions" because it would undermine free choice. Do you agree with this reasoning? Couldn't God simply prevent the creation of truly evil individuals without affecting the freedom of the vast majority of people?

- Hick also maintains that if God prevented natural disasters from occurring it would mean negating all of the laws of science. Do you agree with this reasoning? For example, couldn't God have created a scientifically orderly world in which natural disasters did not cause such human catastrophes?

- According to Hick, the sorrows, tragedies, and disappointments of this world are necessary ingredients in "soul-making." Do you agree with this way of thinking? How have the tragedies in your life influenced you? Might some disasters be positive influences, whereas others are simply destructive?

- Because there is not enough time on this Earth for our souls to become sufficiently enlightened, Hick believes that this suggests there must be an afterlife in which this process is continued. Does this reasoning make sense to you? Why or why not?

- Does the problem of evil in the world influence your thinking about religion? Why or why not? If you have a belief in God, how do you reconcile the existence of evil with your concept of God?

Edward H. Madden and Peter H. Hare,
A Critique of Hick's Theodicy

The intellectual honesty of John Hick is impressive. Unlike the majority of Christian apologists he does not try to find safety in the number of solutions but instead searchingly criticizes and disowns many of the favorite solutions. He concludes, nevertheless, the apologetics reduced to fighting trim is all the more effective. He believes that a sophisticated combination of the character-building and free-will solutions will serve. They show evil to serve God's purpose of "soul-making."

According to Hick, man, created as a personal being in the image of God, is only the raw material for a further and more difficult stage of God's creative work. This is the leading of men as relatively free and autonomous persons through their own dealings with life in the world in which he has placed them, towards that quality of personal existence that is the finite likeness of God.

The basic trouble, he says, with antitheistic writers is that "they assume that the purpose of a loving God must be to create a hedonistic paradise." He concedes that evil is not serving any, even remote, hedonistic end, but insists that it is serving the end of the development of moral personalities in loving relation to God. It is logically impossible to do this either by forcing them to love him or by forcing them always to act rightly. A creature forced to love would not be genuinely loving and a creature forced to do the right would not be a moral personality. Only through freedom, suffering, and initial remoteness from God ("epistemic distance") can the sort of person God is looking for come about.

Before we discuss in detail the difficulties involved in Hick's position we will briefly describe three informal fallacies Hick adroitly uses in his solution. They are all fallacies which have been used in one form or another throughout the history of Christian apologetics. However, it will be convenient in discussing Hick's skillful and elaborate use of them to describe and label clearly these arguments: "All or nothing," "It could be worse," and "slippery slope."

All or nothing. This is the claim that something is desirable because its complete loss would be far worse than the evil its presence now causes. The erroneous assumption is that we must have this thing either in its present form and amount or not at all. But it is often the case that only some amount of the thing in some form is necessary to the achievement of a desirable end.

It could be worse. This is the claim that something is not really bad because it will be followed by all manner of desirable things. The erroneous assumption here is that showing that having these later desirable things is a great boon also shows that the original evil is a necessary and not gratuitous one. Actually it only shows that the situation would be still worse if the desirable things did not follow. To show that it could be worse does not show that it could not be better.

Slippery slope. This is the claim that if God once started eliminating evils of this world he would have no place to stop short of a "perfect" world in which only robots and not men were possible. The erroneous assumption is that God would have no criterion to indicate where on the slippery slope to stop and no ability to implement it effectively. The same argument is used in human affairs and the answer is equally clear. "Once we venture, as we sometimes must, on a dangerous course which may lead to our salvation in a particular situation but which may also be the beginning of our path to perdition, the only answer we can give to the question 'Where will you stop?' is 'Wherever our intelligence tells us to stop!'"

Hick's use of the free-will solution is an example of the "all or nothing" fallacy. He concedes that there is an appalling amount of moral evil in the world but insists that it would be logically impossible for God to achieve his purpose of soul-making by creating puppets who always acted rightly.

Hick says that the difficulty with criticisms of the free-will solution has been that they suppose God would have done better to create man as a "pet animal" in a cage, "as pleasant and healthful" as possible. Undeniably critics of the free-will solution have often made this mistake, but it is a mistake easily avoided. We are prepared to grant that a better world would not have been created by making men as pet animals. However, the damaging question is whether God had only two alternatives: to create men with the unfortunate moral inclinations they have at present or to create men as pet animals. There are clearly other alternatives. There are, after all, many different ways for a parent to guide his child's moral growth while respecting his freedom.

Perhaps an analogy will be helpful. God, as Hick views him, might be described as headmaster to a vast progressive school where the absolute freedom of the students is sacred. He does not want to force any children to read textbooks because, he feels, that will only produce students who are more motivated by fear of punishment than by love of knowledge for its own sake. Every student must be left to educate himself as much as possible. However, it is quite unconvincing to argue that because rigid regulation has horrible consequences, almost no regulation is ideal—there are dangers in either extreme. And it is just as much of a mistake to argue that because the possibility of God's creation of men as pet animals is ghastly to contemplate, God's creation of men with the sort of freedom they have now is the best possible choice.

Sometimes Hick feels the weakness of the "all or nothing" argument and accordingly shifts to the "it could be worse" strategy. "Christian theodicy must point forward to that final blessedness, and claim that this infinite future good will render worthwhile all the pain and travail and wickedness that has occurred on the way to it." To be sure, we should be grateful to God for not tormenting us for an eternity, but the question remains of why he is torturing us at all. However, this strategy is beside the point. Hick must still show us how all the suffering in this world is the most efficient way of achieving God's goal. Merely to assure the student who is threatening riot that in his old age he will some-how come to regard the indignities of his student days as rather unimportant is not to explain why those indignities must be visited upon him at all.

Hick, however, candidly admits to a feeling that neither of the two strategies discussed above is completely effective in the last analysis and realizes that he must face "excessive or dysteleologcal suffering." Consequently he moves on to the "slippery slope" argument. Unless God eliminated all evils whatsoever there would always be relatively outstanding ones of which it would be said that He should have secretly prevented them. If, for example, divine providence had eliminated Hitler in his infancy, we might now point instead to Mussolini. . . . There would be nowhere to stop, short of divinely arranged paradise in which human freedom would be narrowly circumscribed. He claims, in other words, that there would be no way of eliminating some evils without removing all of them with the effect of returning us to the "all or nothing" situation.

This argument fails because the erroneous assumption is made that in the process of removing evils God would not be able precisely to calculate the effect of each removal and stop at exactly the point at which soul making was most efficiently achieved. Presumably at that point men would still suffer and complain about their suffering, but it would be possible to offer them an explanation of the necessity of this amount of suffering as a means to the end of soul making.

< READING CRITICALLY >

Analyzing Madden and Hare's Critique of John Hick's Theodicy

1. It's always particularly valuable when philosophers directly critique one another's ideas. We saw John Hick critically evaluate J. L. Mackie's views on the problem of evil, and in this article Edward Madden and Peter Hare critically evaluate Hick's ideas. What are the three fallacies that the authors believe Hick is guilty of? How does Hick use this fallacious reasoning to argue for his views?

   In what way do the authors believe that Hick's view of God is analogous to that of a headmaster of a school? How does this comparison highlight the weakness of Hick's argument, according to the authors?

7.6 Faith and Religious Experience

For people who are not believers in a particular religion, all the proofs and evidence religions offer for their religious truths are likely to fall far short of absolute certainty. For example, the "proofs" for the existence of God that we previously considered might be viewed as suggestive by many people, but they are hardly air-tight arguments. Similarly, appeal to divinely inspired holy books may carry a certain weight, but there are a number of holy books—which one are we to consider to be the one "true" holy book? And why? The same reasoning applies to historical religious figures: There are many such figures throughout history—on what grounds can we determine the one individual to whom we should commit ourselves? And naturally, the same is true for appeals to miracles, mighty acts of God, prophecies, and the like—how can we be sure these events actually happened as described?

And yet, despite the lack of absolutely certain proof, many people still choose to commit themselves to religious beliefs, often with great fervor and determination. Why? In a word, "faith." For many religious believers, traditional proofs and evidence may play a role in their religious beliefs, but in the final analysis it is the power of faith that forms the core of their commitment, echoing the writer in the New Testament, "We walk by faith and not by sight." What is faith exactly? Faith has to do with the acceptance of a belief as true in situations in which one does not have direct empirical knowledge and where, perhaps, no empirical knowledge is even possible. As some philosophers would say, faith is a choice—an act of will—not in itself a type of knowledge in the traditional sense, although certainly the believer will be likely to talk about the "knowledge" derived from faith. In other words, faith is often thought to lead to a form of knowing that is fundamentally different from objective, rational analysis, one that transcends traditional categories of thought and language. For many religions, faith is based on experiencing a relationship with a supernatural force or Creator. It is analogous in some ways to having an authentically loving relationship with another person. It would be pointless to try and subject the relationship to an exhaustive, rational analysis or to attempt to "prove" the reality of the relationship with objective measures or logical arguments. Instead, we have "faith" in the other person and our relationship to them; we "know" truths about the relationship that cannot be fully articulated in language.

Watch the **Video** *Faith and Philosophy* on **mysearchlab.com**

Blaise Pascal
Faith is a high-stakes wager.

Soren Kierkegaard
Faith is an informed "leap."

Attitudes Toward Faith

W. K. Clifford
Faith is misconceived because beliefs must be based on compelling evidence.

William James
Faith is a legitimate way of knowing.

At the same time, faith necessarily involves risk. It is the very absence of conclusive, demonstrable proof that makes room for faith, for if we were objectively certain in our beliefs, faith would be unnecessary. Faith necessarily entails the possibility of our

Blaise Pascal (1623–1662) This renowned French physicist and mathematician became a passionate defender of Christianity. In this regard he is best known for "Pascal's Wager," the proposal that in deciding on our religious beliefs, we balance the infinite possibility of gaining eternal life and happiness against the finite possibility of securing some limited earthly pleasures.

being wrong, whether it is regarding religion or regarding love. Yet in spite of the risk, there is nevertheless a primal urge in many people to *believe*, to *have faith* in the reality of something larger than themselves.

Religious Faith as a Wager: Pascal

The issue of risk is the central theme of the following reading by **Blaise Pascal** (1623–1662), a renowned mathematician and physicist who had a life-changing religious experience at the age of thirty-one. On the question of whether God exists, Pascal the mathematician presents us with two possible bets or "wagers" and then weighs the costs and benefits of each:

> *A. We can wager that God exists and live our lives based on this belief. If we win our bet because God does in fact exist, then we will receive eternal life and happiness. The only "cost" to us are giving up certain finite "poisonous pleasures, glory and luxury," and striving to live our lives as people who are "faithful, honest, humble, grateful, generous, and sincere."*

> *B. On the other hand, we can wager that God does not exist and live our lives based on this belief. If we win our bet in this case, we will "win" the opportunity to pursue our own pleasures and glory, constraints and without punishment in an afterlife. However, if we lose the bet—that is, if God does in fact exist and we have chosen not to believe in God's existence—then we may have forfeited the opportunity for eternal life and happiness.*

In making our choice, Pascal believes that "Reason can decide nothing here. There is an infinite chaos which separates us." However, choosing to believe in God's existence is not irrational, even though we may not understand God's nature. When confronted with a choice between eternal life and happiness versus some finite pleasure and glory, only fools would not choose to believe in God and live their lives based on this assumption. What will you wager?

Blaise Pascal, from *Thoughts on Religion,* "A Wager"

Infinite—nothing.—Our soul is cast into a body, where it finds number, dimension. Thereupon it reasons, and calls this nature necessity, and can believe nothing else.

—Unity joined to infinity adds nothing to it, no more than one foot to an infinite measure. The finite is annihilated in the presence of the infinite, and becomes a pure nothing. So our spirit before God, so our justice before divine justice. There is not so great a disproportion between our justice and that of God as between unity and infinity.

—The justice of God must be vast like His compassion. Now justice to the outcast is less vast and ought less to offend our feelings than mercy towards the elect.

—We know that there is an infinite, and are ignorant of its nature. As we know it to be false that numbers are finite, it is therefore true that there is an infinity in number. But we do not know what it is. It is false that it is even, it is false that it is odd; for the addition of a unit can make no change in its nature. Yet it is a number, and every number is odd or even (this is certainly true of every finite number). So we may well know that there is a God without knowing what He is. Is there not one substantial truth, seeing there are so many things which are not the truth itself?—We know then the existence and nature of the finite, because we also are finite and have extension. We know the existence of the infinite and are ignorant of its nature, because it has extension like us, but not limits like us. But we know neither the existence nor the nature of God, because He has neither extension nor limits.

—But by faith we know His existence; in glory we shall know His nature. Now, I have already shown that we may well know the existence of a thing, without knowing its nature.

—Let us now speak according to natural lights.

—If there is a God, He is infinitely incomprehensible, since, having neither parts nor limits, He has no affinity to us. We are then incapable of knowing either what He is or if He is. This being so, who will dare to undertake the decision of the question? Not we, who have no affinity to Him.

—Who then will blame Christians for not being able to give a reason for their belief, since they profess a religion for which they cannot give a reason? They declare, in expounding it to the world, that it is a foolishness, stultitiam; [I Cor. 1. 21.] and then you complain that they do not prove it! If they proved it, they would not keep their word; it is in lacking proofs that they are not lacking in sense. "Yes, but although this excuses those who offer it as such and takes away from them the blame of putting it forward without reason, it does not excuse those who receive it." Let us then examine this point, and say, "God is, or He is not." But to which side shall we incline? Reason can decide nothing here. There is an infinite chaos which separated us. A game is being played at the extremity of this infinite distance where heads or tails will turn up. What will you wager? According to reason, you can do neither the one thing nor the other; according to reason, you can defend neither of the propositions.

—Do not, then, reprove for error those who have made a choice; for you know nothing about it. "No, but I blame them for having made, not this choice, but a choice; for again both he who chooses heads and he who chooses tails are equally at fault, they are both in the wrong. The true course is not to wager at all."

—Yes; but you must wager. It is not optional. You are embarked. Which will you choose then? Let us see. Since you must choose, let us see which interests you least. You have two things to lose, the true and the good; and two things to stake, your reason and your will, your knowledge and your happiness; and your nature has two things to shun, error and misery. Your reason is no more shocked in choosing one rather than the other, since you must of necessity choose. This is one point settled. But your happiness? Let us weigh the gain and the loss in wagering that God is. Let us estimate these two chances. If you gain, you gain all; if you lose, you lose nothing. Wager, then, without hesitation that He is. "That is very fine. Yes, I must wager; but I may perhaps wager too much." Let us see. Since there is an equal risk of gain and of loss, if you had only to gain two lives, instead of one, you might still wager. But if there were three lives to gain, you would have to play (since you are under the necessity of playing), and you would be imprudent, when you are forced to play, not to chance your life to gain three at a game where there is an equal risk of loss and gain. But there is an eternity of life and happiness. And this being so, if there were an infinity of chances, of which one only would be for you, you would still be right in wagering one to win two, and you would act stupidly, being obliged to play, by refusing to stake one life against three at a game in which out of an infinity of chances there is one for you, if there were an infinity of an infinitely happy life to gain. But there is here an infinity of an infinitely happy life to gain, a chance of gain against a finite number of chances of loss, and what you stake is finite. It is all divided; wherever the infinite is and there is not an infinity of chances of loss against that of gain, there is no time to hesitate, you must give all. And thus, when one is forced to play, he must renounce reason to preserve his life, rather than risk it for infinite gain, as likely to happen as the loss of nothingness.

—For it is no use to say it is uncertain if we will gain, and it is certain that we risk, and that the infinite distance between the certainty of what is staked and the uncertainty of what will be gained, equals the finite good which is certainty staked against the uncertain infinite. It is not so, as every player stakes a certainty to gain an uncertainty, and yet he stakes a finite certainty to gain a finite uncertainty, without transgressing against reason. There is not an infinite distance between the certainty staked and the uncertainty of the gain; that is untrue. In truth, there is an infinity between the certainty of gain and the certainty of loss. But the uncertainty of the gain is proportioned to the certainty of the stake according to the proportion of the chances of gain and loss. Hence it comes that, if there are as many risks on one side as on the other, the course is to play even; and then the certainty of the stake is equal to the uncertainty of the gain, so far is it from fact that there is an infinite distance between them. And so our proposition is of infinite force, when there is the finite to stake in a game where there are equal risks of gain and of loss, and the infinite to gain. This is demonstrable; and if men are capable of any truths, this is one.

—"I confess it, I admit it. But, still, is there no means of seeing the faces of the cards?" Yes, Scripture and the rest, etc. "Yes, but I have my hands tied and my mouth closed; I am forced to wager, and am not free. I am not released, and am so made that I cannot believe. What, then, would you have me do?"

—True. But at least learn your inability to believe, since reason brings you to this, and yet you cannot believe. Endeavour, then, to convince yourself, not by increase of proofs of God, but by the abatement of your passions. You would like to attain faith and do not know the way; you would like to cure yourself of unbelief and ask the remedy for it. Learn of those who have been bound like you, and who now stake all their possessions. These are people who know the way which you would follow, and who are cured of an ill of which you would be cured. Follow the way by which they began; by acting as if they believed, taking the holy water, having masses said, etc. Even this will naturally make you believe, and deaden your acuteness. "But this is what I am afraid of." And why? What have you to lose?

—But to show you that this leads you there, it is this which will lessen the passions, which are your stumbling-blocks.

The end of this discourse.—Now, what harm will befall you in taking this side? You will be faithful, humble, grateful, generous, a sincere friend, truthful. Certainly you will not have those poisonous pleasures, glory and luxury; but will you not have others? I will tell you that you will thereby gain in this life, and that, at each step you take on this road, you will see so great certainty of gain, so much nothingness in what you risk, that you will at last recognise that you have wagered for something certain and infinite, for which you have given nothing.

—"Ah! This discourse transports me, charms me," etc.

—If this discourse pleases you and seems impressive, know that it is made by a man who has knelt, both before and after it, in prayer to that Being, infinite and without parts, before whom he lays all he has, for you also to lay before Him all you have for your own good and for His glory, that so strength may be given to lowliness.

< READING CRITICALLY >

Analyzing "Pascal's Wager"

- Is God's existence something that we can choose to believe or not believe in without compelling evidence? If you believe in God, how did you arrive at your own personal belief regarding God's existence? Did the kind of cost–benefit analysis that Pascal recommends enter into your deliberations?

- Pascal suggests that we can "cure ourself of unbelief" by acting like believers, "taking the holy water, having masses said, etc." Do you think that Pascal is right, that acting as though you believe in God will ultimately foster authentic belief in God? Can you think of an example in your own life in which acting as though you believed helped you create a genuine belief (for example, in feeling confident about performing some activity, being concerned about the welfare of others, or nurturing feelings in a personal relationship)?

- Do you think that it is morally appropriate to try to believe in God not because of compelling evidence but simply because you believe it to be in your self-interest? If we do engage in this sort of activity, is there a danger of deceiving ourselves and being inauthentic?

the belief fro
other. No ma
a belief on or
really in doul
unfits a man

Nor is it t
who holds it,
the action to
immediately
a part of that
moment of a
it can be isol
No real beli∈
it prepares u
weakens oth
may some d

And no o
Our lives are
created by s
and modes
an heirloom
sacred trust
with some c
belief of ev
responsibili

In the tw
believe on in
investigatio
the belief he
belief held
believer, is c
no choice b
faculty whic
compacted
used on tru
which have
men togeth
given to un
the believe
a bright mi
deception
would des∈
very fanatic
catch a sta

It is no
bounden c
infrequent
race. Ever
shall knit s
station, ca

It is tru€
very bitter
strong. To
We feel mu
matter wh

Religious Beliefs Require Sufficient Evidence: Clifford

In striking contrast to Pascal's pragmatic justification for his belief in God—we should believe in God because it's in our self interest to do so—**William K. Clifford (1845–1879)**, a British philosopher and mathematician, argues that the only legitimate justification for beliefs is that which is based on solid evidence. His commitment to the epistemological theory known as "evidentialism" is extreme, as he proclaims: "To sum up: it is wrong always, everywhere and for anyone, to believe anything upon insufficient evidence." Such a view certainly makes sense with many of the issues and decisions we confront in life. In fact, using the "fierce light of free and fearless questioning" to develop the most accurate and enlightened beliefs possible embodies the philosopher's way. But suppose we attempt to apply this standard to an issue like the existence of God: that is, to demand incontrovertible proof for God's existence before committing ourselves to actually believing in God? Is there such incontrovertible proof? If not, then we would be forced to conclude that it's impossible to actually know if God exists and that the only logical position for us is that of the agnostic. And, in fact, Clifford's article was very influential during the Victorian period because it was seen as a compelling argument for an agnostic view of the existence of God. For Clifford, it doesn't matter what we have convinced ourselves to believe—if our belief is not supported by "sufficient evidence," then it is "sinful, because it is stolen in defiance of our duty to mankind." Clifford introduces his version of "evidentialism" with two arresting metaphors.

William K. Clifford (1845–1879). This British philosopher and mathematician was a proponent of "evidentialism," the epistemological view that all beliefs must be supported with "sufficient evidence" to be accepted as legitimate; beliefs that are endorsed without adequate justification are both unethical and a potential threat to humanity.

W. K. Clifford, from "The Ethics of Belief"

A shipowner was about to send to sea an emigrant-ship. He knew that she was old, and not over-well built at the first; that she had seen many seas and climes, and often had needed repairs. Doubts had been suggested to him that possibly she was not seaworthy. These doubts preyed upon his mind and made him unhappy; he thought that perhaps he ought to have her thoroughly overhauled and refitted, even though this should put him to great expense. Before the ship sailed, however, he succeeded in overcoming these melancholy reflections. He said to himself that she had gone safely through so many voyages and weathered so many storms that it was idle to suppose she would not come safely home from this trip also. He would put his trust in Providence, which could hardly fail to protect all these unhappy families that were leaving their fatherland to seek for better times elsewhere. He would dismiss from his mind all ungenerous suspicions about the honesty of builders and contractors. In such ways he acquired a sincere and comfortable conviction that his vessel was thoroughly safe and seaworthy; he watched her departure with a light heart, and benevolent wishes for the success of the exiles in their strange new home that was to be; and he got his insurance-money when she went down in mid-ocean and told no tales.

What shall we say of him? Surely this, that he was verily guilty of the death of those men. It is admitted that he did sincerely believe in the soundness of his ship; but the sincerity of his conviction can in no wise help him, because he had no right to believe on such evidence as was before him. He had acquired his belief not by honestly earning it in patient investigation, but by stifling his doubts. And although in the end he may have felt so sure about it that he could not think otherwise, yet inasmuch as he had knowingly and willingly worked himself into that frame of mind, he must be held responsible for it.

Let us alter the case a little, and suppose that the ship was not unsound after all; that she made her voyage safely, and many others after it. Will that diminish the guilt of her owner? Not one jot. When an action is once done, it is right or wrong for ever; no accidental

Is it ever :
believe wi
In the movi
Aloysius (p
Streep) is c
the parish |
a student,
evidence. E
is correct,
Clifford tha
belief woul

system, a ship, a college, an athletic team, all exist on this condition, without which not only is nothing achieved, but nothing is even attempted. A whole train of passengers (individually brave enough) will be looted by a few highwaymen, simply because the latter can count on one another, while each passenger fears that if he makes a movement of resistance, he will be shot before any one else backs him up. If we believed that the whole car-full would rise at once with us, we should each severally rise, and train-robbing would never even be attempted. There are, then, cases where a fact cannot come at all unless a preliminary faith exists in its coming. And where faith in a fact can help create the fact, that would be an insane logic which should say that faith running ahead of scientific evidence is the "lowest kind of immorality" into which a thinking being can fall. Yet such is the logic by which our scientific absolutists pretend to regulate our lives!

X.

In truths dependent on our personal action, then, faith based on desire is certainly a lawful and possibly an indispensable thing.

But now, it will be said, these are all childish human cases, and have nothing to do with great cosmical matters, like the question of religious faith. Let us then pass on to that. Religions differ so much in their accidents that in discussing the religious question we must make it very generic and broad. What then do we now mean by the religious hypothesis? Science says things are; morality says some things are better than other things; and religion says essentially two things.

First, she says that the best things are the more eternal things, the overlapping things, the things in the universe that throw the last stone, so to speak, and say the final word. "Perfection is eternal,"—this phrase of Charles Secrétan seems a good way of putting this first affirmation of religion, an affirmation which obviously cannot yet be verified scientifically at all.

The second affirmation of religion is that we are better off even now if we believe her first affirmation to be true.

Now, let us consider what the logical elements of this situation are in case the religious hypothesis in both its branches be really true. (Of course, we must admit that possibility at the outset. If we are to discuss the question at all, it must involve a living option. If for any of you religion be a hypothesis that cannot, by any living possibility be true, then you need go no farther. I speak to the "saving remnant" alone.) So proceeding, we see, first, that religion offers itself as a momentous option. We are supposed to gain, even now, by our belief, and to lose by our non-belief, a certain vital good. Secondly, religion is a forced option, so far as that good goes. We cannot escape the issue by remaining sceptical and waiting for more light, because, although we do avoid error in that way if religion be untrue, we lose the good, if it be true, just as certainly as if we positively chose to disbelieve. It is as if a man should hesitate indefinitely to ask a certain woman to marry him because he was not perfectly sure that she would prove an angel after he brought her home. Would he not cut himself off from that particular angel-possibility as decisively as if he went and married some one else? Scepticism, then, is not avoidance of option; it is option of a certain particular kind of risk. Better risk loss of truth than chance of error,—that is your faith-vetoer's exact position. He is actively playing his stake as much as the believer is; he is backing the field against the religious hypothesis, just as the believer is backing the religious hypothesis against the field. To preach scepticism to us as a duty until "sufficient evidence" for religion be found, is tantamount therefore to telling us, when in presence of the religious hypothesis, that to yield to our fear of its being error is wiser and better than to yield to our hope that it may be true. It is not intellect against all passions, then; it is only intellect with one passion laying down its law. And by what, forsooth, is the supreme wisdom of this passion warranted? Dupery for dupery, what proof is there that dupery through hope is so much worse than dupery through fear? I, for one, can see no proof; and I simply refuse obedience to the scientist's command to imitate his kind of option, in a case where my own stake is important enough to give me the right to choose my own form of risk. If religion be true and the evidence for it be still insufficient, I do not wish, by putting your extinguisher upon my nature (which feels to me as if it had after all some business in this matter), to forfeit my sole chance in life of getting upon the winning side,—that chance depending, of course, on my willingness to run the risk of acting as if my passional need of taking the world religiously might be prophetic and right.

All this is on the supposition that it really may be prophetic and right, and that, even to us who are discussing the matter, religion is a live hypothesis which may be true. Now, to most of us religion comes in a still further way that makes a veto on our active faith even more illogical. The more perfect and more eternal aspect of the universe is represented in our religions as having personal form. The universe is no longer a mere It to us, but a Thou, if we are religious; and any relation that may be possible from person to person might be possible here. For instance, although in one sense we are passive portions of the universe, in another we show a curious autonomy, as if we were small active centres on our own account. We feel, too, as if the appeal of religion to us were made to our own active good-will, as if evidence might be forever withheld from us unless we met the hypothesis half-way. To take a trivial illustration: just as a man who in a company of gentlemen made no advances, asked a warrant for every concession, and believed no one's word without proof, would cut himself off by such churlishness from all the social rewards that a more trusting spirit would earn,—so here, one who should shut himself up in snarling logicality and try to make the gods extort his recognition willy-nilly, or not get it at all, might cut himself off forever from his only opportunity of making the gods' acquaintance. This feeling, forced on us we know not whence, that by obstinately believing that there are gods (although not to do so would be so easy both for our logic and our life) we are doing the universe the deepest service we can, seems part of the living essence of the religious hypothesis. If the hypothesis were true in all its parts, including this one, then pure intellectualism, with its veto on our making willing advances, would be an absurdity; and some participation of our sympathetic nature would be logically required. I, therefore, for one, cannot see my way to accepting the agnostic rules for truth-seeking, or wilfully agree to keep my willing nature out of the game. I cannot do so for this plain reason, *that a rule of thinking which would absolutely prevent me from acknowledging certain kinds of truth if those kinds of truth were really there, would be an irrational rule.* That for me is the long and short of the formal logic of the situation, no matter what the kinds of truth might materially be.

I confess I do not see how this logic can be escaped. But sad experience makes me fear that some of you may still shrink from radically saying with me, in abstracto, that we have the right to believe at our own risk any hypothesis that is live enough to tempt our will. I suspect, however, that if this is so, it is because you have got away from the abstract logical point of view altogether, and are thinking (perhaps without realizing it) of some particular religious hypothesis which for you is dead. The freedom to 'believe what we will' you apply to the case of some patent superstition; and the faith you think of is the faith defined by the schoolboy when he said, "Faith is when you believe something that you know ain't true." I can only repeat that this is misapprehension. In concreto, the freedom to believe can only cover living options which the intellect of the individual cannot by itself resolve; and living options never seem absurdities to him who has them to consider. When I look at the religious question as it really puts itself to concrete men, and when I think of all the possibilities which both practically and theoretically it involves, then this command that we shall put a stopper on our heart, instincts, and courage, and wait—acting of course meanwhile more or less as if religion were not true—till doomsday, or till such time as our intellect and senses working together may have raked in evidence enough,—this command, I say, seems to me the queerest idol ever manufactured in the philosophic cave. Were we scholastic absolutists, there might be more excuse. If we had an infallible intellect with its objective certitudes, we might feel ourselves disloyal to such a perfect organ of knowledge in not trusting to it exclusively, in not waiting for its releasing word. But if we are empiricists, if we believe that no bell in us tolls to let us know for certain when truth is in our grasp, then it seems a piece of idle fantasticality to preach so solemnly our duty of waiting for the bell. Indeed we may wait if we will,—I hope you do not think that I am denying that,—but if we do so, we do so at our peril as much as if we believed. In either case we act, taking our life in our hands. No one of us ought to issue vetoes to the other, nor should we bandy words of abuse. We ought, on the contrary, delicately and profoundly to respect one another's mental freedom: then only shall we bring about the intellectual republic; then only shall we have that spirit of inner tolerance without which all our outer tolerance is soulless, and which is empiricism's glory; then only shall we live and let live, in speculative as well as in practical things.

I began by a reference to Fitz James Stephen; let me end by a quotation from him. "What do you think of yourself? What do you think of the world? . . . These are questions with which all must deal as it seems good to them. They are riddles of the Sphinx, and in some way or other we must deal with them. . . . In all important transactions of life we have to take a leap in the dark. . . . If we decide to leave the riddles unanswered, that is a choice; if we waver in our answer, that, too, is a choice: but whatever choice we make, we make it at our peril. If a man chooses to turn his back altogether on God and the future, no one can prevent him; no one can show beyond reasonable doubt that he is mistaken. If a man thinks otherwise and acts as he thinks, I do not see that any one can prove that he is mistaken. Each must act as he thinks best; and if he is wrong, so much the worse for him. We stand on a mountain pass in the midst of whirling snow and blinding mist, through which we get glimpses now and then of paths which may be deceptive. If we stand still we shall be frozen to death. If we take the wrong road we shall be dashed to pieces. We do not certainly know whether there is any right one. What must we do? "Be strong and of a good courage." Act for the best, hope for the best, and take what comes. . . . If death ends all, we cannot meet death better."

< READING CRITICALLY >

Analyzing James on the Will to Believe

- William James says that Pascal's wager "tries to force us into Christianity by reasoning as if our concern with truth resembled our concern with the states in a game of chance." What is James's opinion of this approach to religious beliefs?

- James confronts W. K. Clifford's pronouncement that "It is wrong always, everywhere, and for every one, to believe anything upon insufficient evidence." While James thinks that this skeptical approach is appropriate when evaluating scientific claims, he thinks it is more problematic when applied to religious beliefs. Why does James think Clifford's perspective ought not to be applied to religious beliefs?

- In evaluating the role of faith in forming beliefs, James observes, "Science says things are; morality says some things are better than other things; and religion says . . . that the best things are the more eternal things" and "that we are better off even now if we believe her first affirmation to be true." How you believe that we should approach this "religious hypothesis"?

- Near the end of his essay James states: "I therefore, for one, cannot see my way to accepting the agnostic rules for truth-seeking, or wilfully agree to keep my willing nature out of the game. I cannot do so for this plain reason, that *a rule of thinking which would absolutely prevent me from acknowledging certain kinds of truth if those kinds of truth were really there, would be an irrational rule.*" What other "kinds of truth" is James referring to? Do you agree that denying these other kinds of truth in exploring our religious beliefs would be "the queerest idol ever manufactured in the philosophic cave"? Why or why not?

Subjective Knowing: The Leap of Faith

Perhaps the most passionate voice for religious faith is **Søren Kierkegaard**, the Danish philosopher who is widely considered to be the father of modern existentialism. In the following excerpts from his essay "The Leap of Faith and the Limits of Reason," he argues that to fully understand human existence, we must recognize the limits of reason and be prepared to make a "leap of faith" toward belief and commitment when such a leap is required.

Søren Kierkegaard, from "The Leap of Faith and the Limits of Reason"

But what is this unknown something with which the Reason collides when inspired by its paradoxical passion, with the result of unsettling even man's knowledge of himself? It is the Unknown. It is not a human being, insofar as we know what man is; nor is it any other known thing. So let us call this unknown something: *God*. It is nothing more than a name we assign to it. The idea of demonstrating that this unknown something (God) exists could scarcely suggest itself to the Reason. For if God does not exist it would of course be impossible to prove it; and if he does exist it would be folly to attempt it. For at the very outset, in beginning my proof, I will have presupposed it, not as doubtful but as certain (a presupposition is never doubtful, for the very reason that it is a presupposition), since otherwise I would not begin, readily understanding that the whole would be impossible if he did not exist. But if when I speak of proving God's existence I mean that I propose to prove that the Unknown, which exists, is God, then I express myself unfortunately. For in that case I do not prove anything, least of all an existence, but merely develop the content of a conception. Generally speaking, it is a difficult matter to prove that anything exists; and what is still worse for the intrepid souls who undertake the venture, the difficulty is such that fame scarcely awaits those who concern themselves with it. The entire demonstration always turns into something very different from what it assumes to be, and becomes an additional development of the consequences that flow from (our) having assumed existence, whether I move in the sphere of palpable sensible fact or in the realm of thought. I do not, for example, prove that a stone exists, but that some existing thing is a stone. The procedure in a court of justice does not prove that a criminal exists, but that the accused, whose existence is given, is a criminal . . .

Søren Kierkegaard
(1813–1855). A Danish philosopher who challenged much of Christian philosophy while remaining deeply religious, Kierkegaard maintained that true belief in God required a leap of faith for which there is no rational justification.

For Kierkegaard, trying to prove that God "exists" is a pointless endeavor, as he observes: "For if God does not exist it would of course be impossible to prove it; and if he does exist it would be folly to attempt it." Why folly? Because "proof" involves reasoning, and our reasoning powers are limited when it comes to the metaphysical. The best that we can do is acknowledge these limits and recognize that beyond the powers of reason lies the Unknown. In addition, it is virtually impossible to "prove" that anything exists, especially God. Our only realistic goal is to "develop the content of a conception" of God. But how can we do this if our reasoning abilities are by definition not capable of describing the Unknown (God)? Kierkegaard believes that we must take an entirely different approach.

. . . between God and his works there exists an absolute relationship; God is not a name but a concept. Is this perhaps the reason that his (essence involves existence)? The works of God are such that only God can perform them. Just so, but where then are the works of God? The works from which I would deduce his existence are not immediately given. The wisdom of God in nature, his goodness, his wisdom in the governance of the world—are all these manifest, perhaps, upon the very face of things? Are we not here confronted with the most terrible temptations to doubt, and is it not impossible finally to

Søren Kierkegaard,
from "The Leap of Faith and the Limits of Reason"

Bernini, *Ecstasy of Saint Theresa.* One of the most famous mystics in the Christian tradition is Saint Theresa of Avila, depicted here in a mystical state of union with God. How does this image relate to the kind of religious experience that Søren Kierkegaard proposes that we strive to achieve?

((•— **Listen** to the **Podcast**
Clare Carlisle on Kierkegaard's Fear and Trembling on
mysearchlab.com

dispose of all these doubts? But from such an order of things I will surely not attempt to prove God's existence; and even if I began I would never finish, and would in addition have to live constantly in suspense, lest something so terrible should suddenly happen that my bit of proof would be demolished. From what works then do I propose to derive the proof? From the works as apprehended through an ideal interpretation, i.e., such as they do not immediately reveal themselves. But in that case it is not from the works that I prove God's existence. . . .

And how does God's existence emerge from the proof? Does it follow straightway, without any breach of continuity? Or have we not here an analogy to the behaviour of these toys, the little Cartesian dolls? As soon as I let go of the doll it stands on its head. As soon as I let it go—I must therefore let it go. So also with the proof for God's existence. As long as I keep my hold on the proof, i.e., continue to demonstrate, the existence does not come out, if for no reason than that I am engaged in proving it: but when I let the proof go, the existence is there. But this act of letting go is surely also something; it is indeed a contribution of mine. Must not this also be taken into the account, this little moment, brief as it may be—it need not be long, for it is a *leap*. However brief this moment, if only an instantaneous now, this "now" must be included in the reckoning.

For Kierkegaard, any attempt to prove God's existence by reasoning from the observed features of the universe are destined to fail as well. Why? Because we can never be certain that an unexpectedly terrible event might not occur that would demolish our carefully constructed arguments from design, contingency, or morality. So it is not God's actions that we use as a basis for inferring God's existence; instead, it is an "ideal interpretation" of God that we use, an imaginative construction of God's nature. But such an ideal construction already *presupposes* God's existence, so we are not really proving anything.

Then how do we achieve a confidence in God's existence? Kierkegaard says we must *let go* of our efforts to "prove" God's existence with logical, rational means and instead simply let the reality of his existence become manifest. But this act of letting go is difficult: We naturally strive for objective certainty, demonstrable proof that will satisfy the demands of reason. To let go of this compulsion requires an act of will, a *leap* of faith in God's reality. And when we truly let go of our rational efforts, our faith is rewarded by our experiencing the reality of God's existence in nonrational or suprarational ways. We can again see the analogy with nurturing a loving relationship: We need to "let go" of our need to analyze every dimension of the relationship for the authentic emotions to be released and suffuse our shared experiences.

Kierkegaard provides a fuller explication of his view in another book, *Concluding Unscientific Postscript*, in which he articulates the stark contrast between "objective knowing" (logical, rational) and "subjective knowing" (personal, passionate, experiential). For Kierkegaard, we can only achieve genuine understanding of God through subjective knowing.

Søren Kierkegaard, from *Concluding Unscientific Postscript* ▮ ▯ ◢ ◆

When the question of truth is raised in an objective manner, reflection is directed objectively to the truth, as an object to which the knower is related. Reflection is not focused upon the relationship, however, but upon the question of whether it is the truth to which the knower is related. If only the object to which he is related is the truth, the subject is accounted to be in the truth. When the question of the truth is raised subjectively, reflection is directed subjectively to the nature of the individual's relationship; if only the mode of this relationship is in the truth, the individual is in the truth even if he should happen to be thus related to what is not true.

Let us take as an example the knowledge of God. Objectively, reflection is directed to the problem of whether this object is the true God; subjectively, reflection is directed to the question whether the individual is related to a something *in such a manner* that his relationship is in truth a God-relationship. On which side is the truth now to be found? Ah, may we not here resort to a mediation, and say: It is on neither side, but in the mediation of both? Excellently well said, provided we might have it explained how an existing individual manages to be in a state of mediation. For to be in a state of mediation is to be finished, while to exist is to become. Nor can an existing individual be in two places at the same time—he cannot be an identity of subject and object. When he is nearest to being in two places at the same time he is in passion; but passion is also the highest expression of subjectivity.

For Kierkegaard, "objective knowing" can never achieve a genuine understanding of God because it treats God as an object to be proved and understood—an impossible task, given the limits of our reasoning capacities. "Subjective knowing," on the other hand, is the consequence of establishing a *relationship* with God by means of our leap of faith, a connection founded on *passion*, not dispassionate rational understanding. The objective knowing of reason can provide the illusion of understanding God, but this way of knowing will always be an approximation, an idealized and distorted intellectual construction. Only by surrendering ourselves to subjective knowing, through the leap of faith, can we achieve true knowledge of God through a personal relationship.

< READING CRITICALLY >

Analyzing Kierkegaard on Faith and Reason

- Do you agree with Kierkegaard's view that our powers of reason are limited when it comes to understanding or encountering a supernatural being (God)? Why or why not?

- Kierkegaard believes that we must let go of our rational efforts to prove God's existence in order to *experience* God's existence. Does this analysis make sense to you? Why or why not?

- For Kierkegaard, the traditional arguments for God's existence are disturbing, not reassuring. Why do you think he believes this to be the case? Do you agree with his perspective? Why or why not?

- Paradoxically, it is this "objective uncertainty" produced by reason's attempt to prove God's existence that makes it possible to experience the reality of God through the passion of faith. Explain in your own words Kierkegaard's reasoning in the following passage, which concludes with a stunning metaphor:

  Without risk there is no faith. Faith is precisely the contradiction between the infinite passion of the individual's inwardness and the objective uncertainty. If I am capable of grasping God objectively, I do not believe, but precisely because I cannot do this I must believe. If I wish to preserve myself in faith I must constantly be intent upon holding fast the objective uncertainty, so as to remain out upon the deep, over seventy thousand fathoms of water, still preserving my faith.

7.7 Making Connections: Reflections on the Philosophy of Religion

At the beginning of this chapter you were asked to respond to a number of questions, including:

- What is your definition of religion?
- What do you think is the purpose of religion?
- What are your religious beliefs?
- How do you view other religions?
- What is the relationship of religion to your daily life?

In reflecting on the various issues that you have explored in this chapter—through readings, writing assignments, class discussions, and personal reflection—how would you respond to these questions now? These questions do not assume that you believe that any religious beliefs are ultimately true. Religion is an integral dimension of virtually every culture, but you may believe that religion can claim no metaphysical reality, only cultural reality.

As we saw at the beginning of the chapter, philosopher Frederick Streng defines religion as "a means toward ultimate transformation." What precisely does he mean by that? He explains in the following passage:

> *The term "ultimate" points to what a religious person holds to be "real," to what has such significance that people define their lives on its terms. Whatever is "ultimate" is that without which life would be meaningless and dead because of such common human experiences as physical death, unfulfilled hopes, and the discomfort derived from a sense of not belonging. In this context, the "ultimate" is a power or force in man's life that is recognized by the religious person to undergird, to condition, to encompass life. This appears in the form of words, actions, social relations, and states of consciousness: and its distinguishing mark is that it is so real that one recognizes its power to have been effective before as well as after one has become conscious of it. This is recognized as the reality that (who) establishes a whole and integrated person who then exists in a mutually beneficial relation with other people and with nature.*

Religion, in sum, provides a framework for human life, helping us address the most profound and challenging questions that we encounter as existing beings:

- What is the meaning and purpose of my life?
- What is my destiny, both as an individual and as a member of a community of individuals?
- How ought I to conduct my life? What values should I live by?
- What happens to me when I die? What is the relation of death to life?

These questions, and others like them, are situated at the core of our consciousness, whether or not we are explicitly aware of them at any given moment. It is these questions that our souls yearn to comprehend, and it is to these questions that religion attempts to provide answers. Of course, as thinking individuals, we are not supposed to be satisfied with just *any* answers to make us feel better—we want the *right* answers. And that's why it is so essential that we think philosophically about the religious experience, bringing our critical judgment to bear in trying to understand things that may very well lie beyond the scope of reason. Nevertheless, we want to develop the most informed and intelligent understanding of the religious experience that we can. And to do this we need to make full use of *all* the capabilities of our minds. How do we achieve this authentic understanding of the ultimate? Streng explains:

Noetic Pertaining to the intellect or mind.

> *The term "transformation" implies that human life necessarily presents all of us a comprehensive task. This task may be variously conceived; one may speak of it as the quest for salvation, enlightenment, perfection, fulfillment, or joy, but the distinctively religious claim is that it cannot be escaped. In using the phrase "toward . . . transformation," then, we refer not only to "conversion experiences" especially prominent in prophetic (Western) religious traditions but also to significant changes that may happen either suddenly or slowly, individually or communally, in people's lives. Put more vividly, the claim is that one is threatened by illusion, but that he can move toward truth: by death, but that he can move toward life; by chaos, but that he can move toward meaning; by self-destruction, but that he can move toward an abundant life. These are, no doubt, concerns of the non-religious man as well. But the non-religious man fails (or refuses) to acknowledge the fundamental and comprehensive character of these tasks. He thinks of his humanity simply as given; the religious man insists that authentic humanity, although conditioned, must nevertheless be attained, released, or granted.*

As you reflect on your own religious evolution, consider the impact on your thinking—and your life—of the religions and philosophical issues that you explored in this course.

MySearchLab Connections

Watch. Listen. Explore. Read. Mysearchlab is designed just for you. Each chapter features a customized study plan to help you learn and review key concepts and terms. Dynamic visual activities, videos, and readings found in the multimedia library will enhance your learning experience.

Here are a few questions and activities to help you understand this chapter:

1. **Watch** the **Video** *The Science of Being: Ontology* on **mysearchlab.com**   What is ontological commitment?

2. **Listen** to the **Podcast** *Anthony Kenny on Aquinas's Ethics* on **mysearchlab.com**   According to Aquinas, how does one achieve happiness on earth?

3. **Listen** to the **Podcast** *Marilyn McCord Adams on Evil* on **mysearchlab.com**   Explain McCord's thesis that there has been very little human progress toward reducing the amount of evil in the world.

4. **Watch** the **Video** *Faith and Philosophy* on **mysearchlab.com**   Define and explain the three major areas in philosophy of religion—religious epistemology, metaphysics of religion, and theodicy.

5. **Listen** to the **Podcast** *Clare Carlisle on Kierkegaard's Fear and Trembling* on **mysearchlab.com**   Why did Kierkegaard's *Fear and Trembling* appeal to existential philosophers like Jean Paul Sartre?

Which of your moral values are clearly articulated and well-grounded? Which are ill-defined and tenuously rooted? Do your values form a coherent whole, consistent with one another, or do you detect fragmentation and inconsistency? Obviously, constructing a well-reasoned and clearly defined moral code is a challenging journey. But if we explore the ideas of great moral philosophers, and think philosophically about the central moral questions, we can make significant progress toward this goal.

Your responses to the questions in the "Thinking Philosophically" activity reveal your current values. Where did these values come from? Parents, teachers, religious leaders, and other authority figures have sought to inculcate values in your thinking, but friends, acquaintances, and colleagues do as well. And in many cases they have undoubtedly been successful. Although much of your values education was likely the result of thoughtful teaching and serious discussions, in many other instances people may have bullied, bribed, threatened, and manipulated you into accepting their way of thinking. It's no wonder that our value systems typically evolve into a confusing patchwork of conflicting beliefs.

In examining your values you probably also discovered that although you had a great deal of confidence in some of them ("I feel very strongly that animals should never be experimented on in ways that cause them pain because they are sentient creatures just like ourselves"), you felt less secure about other values ("I feel it's usually wrong to manipulate people, although I often try to influence their attitudes and behavior—I'm not sure of the difference"). These differences in confidence are likely related to how carefully you have *examined* and *analyzed* your values. For example, you may have been brought up in a family or religion with firmly fixed values that you have adopted but never really scrutinized or evaluated, wearing these values like a borrowed overcoat. When questioned, you might be at a loss to explain exactly *why* you believe what you do, other than "This is what I was taught." In contrast, you may have other values that you consciously developed, the product of thoughtful reflection and the crucible of experience. For example, doing volunteer work with a disadvantaged group of people may have led to the conviction that "I believe we have a profound obligation to contribute to the welfare of people less fortunate than ourselves."

In short, most people's values are not "systems" at all: They are typically a collection of *general principles* ("Do unto others . . . "), *practical conclusions* ("Stealing is wrong because you might get caught"), and *emotional pronouncements* ("Euthanasia is wrong because it seems heartless"). This hodgepodge of values may reflect the serendipitous way they were acquired over the course of your life, and these values likely comprise your current "moral compass" that you use to guide your decisions in moral situations, even though you may not be consciously aware of it. Your challenge is to create a more refined and accurate compass, an enlightened system of values that you can use to confidently guide your moral decisions. This is not to say that we should be seeking certitude in our ethical beliefs: The confusing and often contradictory labyrinth of ethical challenges in life makes complete accuracy an unrealistic ideal. Instead, we should seek the clearest and most justified moral beliefs that we can identify in our ethical quest, recognizing that even our best efforts may fall short of unambiguous certainty.

The next "Thinking Philosophically" activity presents several complex moral decision scenarios. As you think your way through these moral dilemmas, you will probably find yourself appealing to basic moral principles that you typically use to guide your actions. The "Thinking Philosophically" questions on the facing page are based on the following scenarios:

- *The Lifeboat:* In 1842, a ship struck an iceberg and sank. There were 30 survivors, crowded into a lifeboat designed to hold just 8. With the weather stormy and getting worse, it was obvious that many of the passengers would have to be thrown overboard or the boat would sink and everyone would drown. Imagine that you were the captain of the boat. Would you have people thrown over the side? If so, on what basis would you decide who would go? Age? Health? Strength? Gender? Size? Survival skills? Friendships? Family?

- *The Whistleblower:* Imagine that you are employed by a large corporation that manufactures baby formula. You suspect that a flaw in the manufacturing process results in contamination of the formula in a small number of cases, and that this contamination can result in serious illness and even death. You have been told by your supervisor that "Everything is under control," and you have been warned that if you "blow the whistle" by going public, you will be putting the entire company in jeopardy from multimillion-dollar lawsuits. You will naturally be fired and blackballed in the industry, and as the sole provider in your household, your family is depending on you. What do you do? Why?

- *The Patient:* As a clinical psychologist, you are committed to protecting the privacy of your patients. One afternoon, a patient tells you that her husband, a person who has been abusing her physically and mentally for years, has threatened to kill her, and she believes him. You try to convince her to leave him and seek professional help, but she tells you that she has decided to kill him. She is certain that he will find her wherever she goes and feels that she will only be safe when he is dead. What do you do?

- *The Friend:* As the director of your department, you are in charge of filling an important vacancy. Many people have applied, including your best friend, who has been out of work for over a year and needs a job desperately. Although your friend would likely perform satisfactorily, there are several more experienced and talented candidates who would undoubtedly perform better. You have always prided yourself in hiring the best people, and you have earned a reputation as someone with high standards who will not compromise your striving for excellence. Whom do you hire?

What makes each of these scenarios *dilemmas* is that both of the moral principles that you are

Whom would you save? Any situation where we must decide whom to help and whom to let suffer presents us with the lifeboat dilemma.

appealing to seem ethically sound and appropriate: The problem is that they *contradict* each other. "The Lifeboat" involves a conflict between the moral beliefs:

- It is wrong to take any innocent life.
- It is right to save *some* lives rather than threaten *all* the lives on board.

"The Whistleblower" involves a conflict between the moral beliefs:

- It is wrong to knowingly jeopardize the health of children.
- It is right to protect the welfare of your family and career.

"The Patient" involves a conflict between the moral beliefs:

- It is wrong to violate the confidentiality of a professional relationship.
- It is right to prevent someone from committing murder.

"The Friend" involves a conflict between the moral beliefs:

- It is wrong to hire someone who is not the best-qualified candidate for the job.
- It is right to try to help and support your friends.

What should you do when this happens? How do you decide which principle is *more* "right"? There is no simple answer to this question, any more than there is to the question, "What do you do when experts disagree?" In both cases, you need to *think critically* to arrive at intelligent and informed conclusions.

Naturally the moral dilemmas described in this activity are specifically designed to provoke intense *angst* and vigorous debate, but the situations nevertheless contain elements found in our everyday moral deliberations. For example, though you are unlikely to find yourself in a similar "Lifeboat" situation, you might be faced with the decision of which employees to fire in order to keep your company afloat. And though the "Whistleblower" example may seem extreme, the fact is that employees working for companies that manufacture baby formula, ephedra-based diet supplements, and tobacco products have often found themselves in precisely this moral dilemma. You yourself have likely been in a job situation where telling the truth or objecting to an unethical practice would jeopardize your position or opportunity for advancement. Many therapists, clergy, lawyers, and doctors wrestle daily with issues of confidentiality, analogous to that described in "The Patient," and we all have to deal with the question of under what circumstances is it morally appropriate to break our promises to avoid a greater evil or achieve a greater good. It requires little imagination to identify the issues of "The Friend." There are countless instances in which we are forced to balance our feelings of personal obligation with our objective or professional analysis.

In addition to these kinds of ethical situations, you will also undoubtedly confront other types of moral dilemmas that are at least as problematic. It is probable that at some point in your life you will have to make a "right to die" decision regarding a loved one nearing the end of his or her life. You might also find yourself in a situation in which you are torn between ending a difficult marriage or remaining as a full-time parent of young children. Or you might be tempted to take advantage of an investment opportunity that, although not completely illegal, is clearly unethical. Dealing with complicated, ambiguous moral challenges is an inescapable part of the human condition. Because these situations can't be avoided, you need to develop the insight and conceptual tools to deal with them effectively.

Making sense out of the confusing and emotionally charged territory of moral experience is the express purpose of moral philosophy. Moral philosophy—ethics—attempts to create coherent theoretical frameworks that we can apply to the moral decisions that we encounter in our daily lives. The ultimate goal of moral philosophy is for us to use these moral theories to accurately calibrate our moral compasses, sharpen our moral intuitions, and refine our moral consciences. In this way, when we are faced with moral decisions and ethical issues, we will be able to choose confidently, with decisions that are wise, enlightened, and justified. We should be able to provide a clear rationale for our decision and cite compelling reasons why our point of view is ethically appropriate. To reach this point of moral confidence, we need to familiarize ourselves with the core theories of moral reasoning that constitute moral philosophy.

This chapter and the next will introduce you to a number of ethical theories that have been formulated and critiqued by philosophers and other thinkers. In this chapter, we will explore the most commonly held beliefs that are used in moral decision making. These are beliefs that we may apply without being conscious of them or examining them critically. At the core of these beliefs are two opposing ideas about the basis of morality and the existence of moral truths. On one side is the idea that judgments about right and wrong depend on the individual or culture; on the other is the conviction that there exists a moral code that can apply to all people, whether given to us by God or formulated by philosophers. Do all beliefs have equal value, or are some beliefs better than others? We will begin with the idea that there are no universal moral truths.

8.2 Ethical Relativism

As you reflect on some of your deeply held ethical beliefs, consider whether you think they should apply to everyone. For example, if you believe that it is morally wrong to beat children, trap animals for fur coats, or ignore those less fortunate than ourselves, do you think that others should share those values? This question is at the core of a debate over whether or not there can be universal ethical values. In this section, we will consider the arguments for and against **ethical relativism**, the theory that ethical values depend on the individual or the culture.

Ethical Subjectivism: Each Person Determines What Is Morally Right

Does this conversation sound familiar?

Emily: Sometimes it's all right to have a flexible view of morality. For example, I bought a research paper for my history course from an online service and I even got an A– on it. I was totally swamped with work—I don't usually do things like that. And anyway, the professor shouldn't assign topics that you can buy papers for.

Jorge: Well, I don't think buying research papers and submitting them as your own is the right thing to do. We're in college to learn, and buying papers defeats the whole purpose of education.

Emily: Yeah, well, that is fine in theory. But what about when you're overwhelmed with work, and your teacher is ready to squash you like a bug if you turn your paper in late? What then?

> **"**What I feel is right is right. What I feel is wrong is wrong.
> **JEAN-JACQUES ROUSSEAU"**

Ethical relativism The view that all moral values are relative to the individual or specific culture.

Jorge: Well, you shouldn't have put yourself in this situation. And trying to get by with cheating is just plain wrong.

Emily: You're being naïve and overly rigid. I know we agree about the important issues: This is just a little disagreement on the fringes, in the "gray" area. In a way, we're both right, it just depends on what your point of view is. You have to go with your inner feeling, what feels right, and this feels okay to me.

Jorge: I guess you're right. Sometimes you do have to be flexible in your morality: What's right for one person may be wrong for someone else—that's just the way it is. As long as you're being true to yourself, then you're morally right. It all depends on your personal feelings. People can have different feelings, but they can't tell you that you're wrong. They simply have different feelings from yours.

The view of morality portrayed in this dialogue is both popular and problematic. It's typically referred to as **ethical subjectivism**, because the ultimate moral authority is considered to be the individual, the "subject." It is a popular view because it embodies some superficially attractive qualities. Many people enjoy the idea that they alone determine what's right and what's wrong in their lives, independent of the views and pressures of others. They also like romantic notions of "being true to myself," or "I have to go with what I truly believe." In addition, awarding each person the moral authority to determine right and wrong, good and evil, seems on the surface to be a tolerant and open-minded approach to the views of others: "I have my moral beliefs; you have your moral beliefs— who is to say which beliefs are better?" To many people, advocating ethical subjectivism seems to be equivalent to a "live and let live" moral policy. So what's the problem?

Actually, an ethical subjectivist view of morality has some serious philosophical difficulties. For example, consider the following exchange:

Emily: Somebody stole my laptop! I left it on the table here for a minute to get some coffee and now it's gone. Did you see someone take it?

Jorge: Actually, *I* took it. My laptop died yesterday and I needed a new one, so I took yours.

Emily: Are you crazy? Give it back! What were you thinking? How can you be so unethical?

Jorge: Actually, I'm being very ethical. I'm an ethical subjectivist, and I'm simply acting in accordance with my own moral convictions. Remember what you said? In making moral decisions, "You have to go with your inner feeling, what feels right." Well, taking your laptop feels right to me. You have a lot more money than I do, and you can simply buy another laptop. As far as my moral beliefs are concerned, the right thing to do is whatever advances my own interests. And taking your laptop is definitely advancing my own interests.

Emily: Well, in that case, be prepared for a visit from Campus Security, because getting my laptop back is in *my* best interests, even if it means getting you in serious trouble. But before I do that, maybe we should rethink the ethical subjectivism we thought was such a good idea!

Rethink indeed! The fatal flaw of ethical subjectivism is that it does not entail tolerance for the views or interests of others. It simply invests each individual with the moral authority to determine what is morally right and wrong, even if this means violating the rights or interests of others. Stealing a laptop is one example. But so are lying, cheating, mugging, raping, murdering, abusing children, being racist, being sexist, and virtually any other actions that are commonly considered to be "immoral"

Ethical subjectivism The view that the ultimate moral authority is the individual or the "subject."

or "unethical." We can see now that ethical subjectivism does not really mean advocating a "live and let live" point of view, because it does not guarantee a tolerant acceptance of the rights and interests of others. Such tolerance of others would be an ethical value that transcends any individual's point of view. **Mohandas Gandhi**, the man responsible for India's independence and an individual considered by many to be morally enlightened, makes this point clear in the following passage:

> *The golden rule of conduct, therefore, is mutual tolerance, seeing that we will never all think alike and we shall see Truth in fragments and from different angles of vision. Conscience is not the same thing for all. Whilst there, it is a good guide for individual conduct, imposition of that conduct upon all will be an insufferable interference with everybody's freedom of conscience.*

So although ethical subjectivism is attractive on the surface, it becomes rather unattractive just below the surface. In fact, it is a recipe for moral anarchy, a world in which everyone does whatever they want, even if this means threatening or harming others. Why is ethical subjectivism so popular? Because people who espouse it haven't really thought critically about the implications of their views. When they say things like, "With moral choices, you have to go with your inner feeling, what feels right," or "Everyone is entitled to have their own beliefs," or "You have to be true to yourself," they are generally *assuming* a universal principle of tolerance. But once you commit yourself to a universal principle of tolerance—something like the belief that we're entitled to our beliefs *as long as they don't infringe on the rights or interests of others*—we are no longer ethical subjectivists. The ultimate moral authority for beliefs does not reside in the individual. Instead, *all individuals* are answerable to a higher value, namely, the principle of tolerance. And if they violate that principle, then they are morally wrong. And *that* moral belief poses a mortal threat to ethical subjectivism.

What are the roots of ethical subjectivism, and why does it seem to be particularly popular on college campuses and in our culture as a whole? Part of the answer lies in the confusion between **descriptive ethics** (what *is* the case) and **normative ethics** (what *ought to be* the case). Individuals have a diverse array of moral beliefs, which vary from person to person and culture to culture. To say this is to simply *describe* what is the case. But this is very different from saying that this is the way things *ought* to be. Yet this is exactly what ethical subjectivism stands for, the idea that each individual *should* have their own moral beliefs and that these beliefs are by definition *morally right*. According to this view, simply having a sincere moral belief gives that belief a moral authority by definition. But this move from a statement about what *is* the case ("People *have* many different moral beliefs") to a conclusion about what *ought* to be the case ("People *should* have different moral beliefs and they *should* act on these beliefs because they are right for them") is illogical and is known in philosophy as committing "the naturalistic fallacy." The philosopher **John Searle** explains:

> *It is often said that one cannot derive an "ought" from an "is.". . . Put in more contemporary terminology, no set of descriptive statements can entail an **evaluative** statement without the addition of at least an evaluative premise. To believe otherwise is to commit the naturalistic fallacy.*

Another reason people are drawn to ethical subjectivism—or at least, what they *think* is ethical subjectivism—has to do with a misunderstanding about the nature and logic of moral beliefs. There is a temptation to think that because people have different

Mohandas Gandhi (1869–1948). As leader of India's struggles for independence from Britain, Gandhi's method of nonviolent resistance served as a model for twentieth-century civil rights leaders, including Martin Luther King Jr.

◉—⎤Watch the **Video** *Normative Ethics* on **mysearchlab.com**

Descriptive ethics An ethical approach that simply represents ethical beliefs without evaluating their accuracy or appropriateness.

Normative ethics An ethical approach that attempts to prescribe what ethical behaviors should be accepted or become cultural norms.

John Searle (B. 1932) Philosopher of mind. Has written influential articles on the philosophy of mind in which he rejects the notion that the mind can be understood as a computer program.

moral beliefs that these beliefs all have equal value, like matters of taste. The popular statement "Everyone is entitled to their own belief" suggests that no individual person has the right to say to another, "Your belief is wrong—you should believe *this* instead." In fact, it's often considered "bad manners" to question the beliefs of others, and to suggest that their beliefs are confused, unfounded, illogical, or outright wrong. This approach *seems* to be tolerant and democratic, and it often works well for matters of taste. However, as we noted earlier, it's an approach that doesn't work well for moral beliefs. For example, people's tastes in fashion, hairstyle, music, food, slang, and so on vary greatly. And by and large, most people acknowledge—in theory at least—that people are entitled to their individual preferences and that, as the old maxim states, "There is no accounting for taste." In other words, it doesn't make sense for you to say to someone else, "You are *wrong* to wear your hair in a mullet, sport a tattoo, and eat chunky peanut butter directly from the jar." You might reasonably say, "That's not my style," or "I prefer a different look," but not that a person with different tastes is *wrong*. As evidence, look at a photograph of yourself from four or five years ago: You probably thought at the time that you looked quite stylish—how does it look now? A little embarrassing?

But moral beliefs are very, very different. If someone says "I agree with Hitler— there is only one super-race and all others are inferior," it *does* make sense to disagree and say, "I think your belief is unethical and wrong. On what rationale do you base it?" Similarly, if someone says, "I think that the sexual abuse of children is all right," they are not simply stating a personal belief: They are enunciating a general moral value that they believe applies to *everyone*. That's the unique logic of moral beliefs: When I say that something is "right" or "wrong," I am by definition suggesting that it is right or wrong not just for me but for everyone.

In this way we can see that many people naïvely fall into ethical subjectivism because they fail to make a distinction between beliefs about taste and moral beliefs. Matters of taste reflect our personal preferences in fashion, music, ice-cream flavors, and so on. You're entitled to have whatever opinion you want about matters of taste without justifying your belief or providing an explanation. But if you are advocating a moral belief, it is your responsibility to explain why you think such a belief should be adopted by others: What are the reasons, evidence, or rationale for such a belief? Moral beliefs implicate and influence our relationships with others in a way that matters of taste never will. Since moral beliefs affect the treatment and well-being of others, they are held to a much higher standard of evaluation and justification than other types of beliefs.

This confused notion that "everyone is entitled to their opinion, and everyone's opinion is equally valuable, no matter how uninformed, illogical, or ignorant," has been encouraged by influences in our culture. Developing informed beliefs about all important issues—moral and otherwise—is an ongoing challenge to our thinking abilities. In thinking about these and any other issues, we should ask ourselves two important questions:

- *What is my opinion about this issue?* Do you believe that human cloning should be pursued? What about whether "profiling" is a legitimate technique for improving public safety?

- *Is my opinion informed by evidence and reasons?* For each of the opinions that you have regarding these (and other) issues, can you answer the question, "*Why* do you have that opinion?" with intelligent and compelling reasons?

The truth is that while opinions are easy to come by, *informed* opinions are much more difficult to find. To express an opinion you merely have to say, "Well, I think . . . " or "I believe. . . " People are more than willing to make such pronouncements on virtually any subject. But to express an *informed* opinion means that you have some idea of what you're talking about: You have *explored* the subject, *examined* different points of view, *evaluated* the supporting reasons and evidence, and *synthesized* your analysis into a cogent and compelling conclusion. You can provide a clear, articulate explanation to the question, *"Why do you believe that human cloning should be prohibited?"*

But isn't everyone "entitled to his or her opinion"? Yes and no. Living in a democracy with broad free-speech protections, people are allowed to think and express virtually *any* opinion, no matter how illogical, uninformed, or foolish. But this does not mean that they are entitled to have their uninformed opinions taken seriously, or that their opinions should be given the same consideration as *informed* opinions! We show respect for other people—and ourselves—by challenging them to think critically about their beliefs.

Ethical subjectivism can result in more damage to the social fabric of our lives than simply legitimating ignorant and ill-informed opinions. It can also encourage a sense of moral apathy. A famous instance of moral apathy occurred in Detroit in 1995 on the Belle Isle Bridge. Deletha Word, a 33-year-old woman, was involved in a minor traffic accident. The enraged 19-year-old male driver of the other car began to beat her mercilessly as a crowd of people gradually assembled to watch. Finally, in desperation to escape her attacker, Deletha Word jumped off the bridge and drowned. One man who jumped off after her in an unsuccessful attempt to save her observed that the crowd was "standing around like people taking an interest in sports." Once again, from the standpoint of ethical subjectivism, these morally indifferent people were doing what they "felt" was right by not "getting involved."

The point is that our moral beliefs, whether openly acknowledged or implicit, have real-world consequences. These beliefs are not simply academic exercises to be discussed in the hermetically

---

What are the consequences of "not getting involved"? Deletha Word's family and friends gathered to mourn a loss that might have been prevented had onlookers intervened. Do you think that a belief in ethical subjectivism results in a lack of caring for others?

sealed environments of college classrooms. A moral philosophy like ethical subjectivism can in fact contribute to the unraveling of our social fabric and undermining of our sense of community. Rather than viewing ourselves as tied to one another through a sense of social relationships and mutual responsibilities, people can come to see themselves as on their own, obligated to pursue only their own personal interests. They "don't want to get involved," do not consider themselves to be "their brother's (or sister's) keeper." Were this to become a prevalent moral philosophy, the quality of life for all would be greatly diminished.

But is ethical subjectivism in fact the prevalent norm in most cultures? The answer is a clear "no," a fact that casts doubt on its credibility as a moral theory. In all cultures, just because an individual "feels" like raping, robbing, assaulting, or murdering does not mean that the other members of the society believe that the actions are morally justified. Quite the contrary. Such individuals are morally condemned and generally punished for violating the accepted moral norms. When they consider the full implications of the theory, most people do not consider ethical subjectivism to be an appropriate or enlightened moral philosophy of life.

Cultural Relativism: Each Culture Determines What Is Morally Right

> For if anyone, no matter who, were given the opportunity of choosing from amongst all the nations of the world the set of beliefs which he thought best, he would inevitably, after careful consideration of their relative merits, choose that of his own country. Everyone without exception believes his own native customs . . . to be the best.
> **HERODOTUS**

Human sacrifice, slavery, cannibalism, torture, genocide, child abuse—these, and every other possible atrocity that humans are capable of, have been considered morally "right" in various times and various cultures. In less extreme categories we also find a nearly infinite variety of values and practices related to marriage (the number and age of brides), sexuality, treatment of children and the elderly, and every other dimension of human experience. This extraordinary diversity of ethical perspectives has led some people to conclude that moral values are nothing more than the mutual agreement of various groups of people and so are relative to each culture's unique context. In other words, if cannibalism or slavery or polygamy is a common practice in a certain culture, then this practice is *morally right* for that culture. No one outside that culture has the right to criticize or evaluate this practice as being "morally wrong." Any culture's moral values are right simply because they are that culture's values.

Cultural relativism is thus ethical subjectivism on a societal level. Ethical subjectivism contends that each individual determines what is morally right and wrong. Cultural relativism makes a similar argument with the exception that it is the entire culture—not each individual—that determines what is morally right and wrong. Both ethical theories are driven by the diversity of moral viewpoints that we find in the human species. Because we each have our unique set of moral values, ethical subjectivism argues that it doesn't make sense to search for universal moral standards that transcend individuals. Analogously, cultural relativism contends that because every culture has its own unique set of moral values, it doesn't make sense to try to identify universal moral standards that transcend all cultures.

One of the most passionate and articulate exponents of cultural relativism was **Ruth Benedict**, an American anthropologist whose book *Patterns of Cultures* (1935) was enormously influential. For Benedict, the term *morality* should be defined as "socially approved customs"—nothing more, nothing less. There are no universal values that we can use to evaluate the moral values of any culture; there are only the moral values that each culture creates.

Cultural relativism The view that cultural norms determine what is ethically right and wrong.

To a certain extent, Benedict (and other social scientists such as Emile Durkheim, Franz Boas, and William Graham Sumner) were reacting to what they perceived to be the cultural imperialism of the West—the assumption by some that the moral values of Western Europe and America were morally superior to the moral values of more "primitive" cultures. From this perspective, it was the moral "obligation" of Western culture to "educate" the rest of the world regarding these more "enlightened" values.

Many of these thinkers used as a framework the ideas of Charles Darwin, whose books *The Origin of the Species* (1859) and *The Descent of Man* (1871) introduced the theory of evolution to explain the biological development of life on earth. Appropriating the general concepts of evolutionary theory without its scientific detail, these "Social Darwinists" proposed that moral values also had evolved over time in the same way that forms of life had. The moral values of "primitive" cultures represented early stages of moral development, while modern Western culture represented the pinnacle of moral evolution.

For Benedict, the values of any one culture are neither superior nor inferior to those of another—they are all on the same moral plane. Each culture is thought of as a self-contained cultural entity, a social organism in which its values, practices, and belief systems have developed as an integrated whole. It is not possible, nor appropriate, for any culture to judge the moral enlightenment of other cultures. We must accept them as they are and try to understand how they evolved in their unique fashion.

Which perspective is right? Are there universal moral standards that can be applied to every culture? Or should we adopt the perspective of cultural relativism and acknowledge that all moral values are equal, no matter how offensive and unacceptable we may personally find them? To answer these crucial ethical questions, we need to let proponents of these views make their strongest possible case, and then engage in critical thinking and philosophical reflection. The following passages are taken from Ruth Benedict's essay, "Anthropology and the Abnormal." Benedict begins by articulating her central thesis and explaining her rationale.

Ruth Benedict
(1887–1948). This American anthropologist was one of the first women to become prominent in the social sciences. In *Patterns of Culture* (1945), Benedict advocated cultural relativism and attempted to apply individual psychological concepts to whole groups.

Ruth Benedict, from *Anthropology and the Abnormal*

Modern social anthropology has become more and more a study of the varieties and common elements of cultural environment and the consequences of these in human behavior. For such a study of diverse social orders primitive peoples fortunately provide a laboratory not yet entirely vitiated by the spread of a standardized world-wide civilization. Dyaks and Hopis, Figians and Yakuts are significant for psychological and sociological study because only among these simpler peoples has there been sufficient isolation to give opportunity for the development of localized social forms. In the higher cultures the standardization of custom and belief over a couple of continents has given a false sense of the inevitability of the particular forms that have gained currency, and we need to turn to a wider survey in order to check the conclusions we hastily based upon this near-universality of familiar customs. Most of the simpler cultures did not gain the wide currency of the one which, out of our experience, we identify with human nature, but this was for various historical reasons, and certainly not for any that gives us as its carriers a monopoly of social good or of social sanity. Modern civilization, from this point of view, becomes not a necessary pinnacle of human achievement but one entry in a long series of possible adjustments.

Benedict's central thesis is encapsulated in the last two sentences: Modern civilization does not embody an evolutionary "pinnacle of human achievement" but is rather "one entry in a long series of possible adjustments." From her perspective,

Is capital punishment immoral? In 2003, four countries were responsible for 84 percent of deaths by capital punishment: China, Iran, the United States, and Vietnam. The European Parliament has declared the death penalty to be "an inhuman, medieval form of punishment and unworthy of modern societies." Do you agree or disagree with the European assessment?

every culture uses its own unique cultural "recipe" to create its social structure and maintain its community. Moral beliefs are an essential ingredient in the recipe, as are customs, rituals, political structures, religious views, and other core beliefs. But it is not possible to say that one recipe is "better" than another—they simply represent different ways people use to organize themselves into social groups.

Ruth Benedict, from *Anthropology and the Abnormal*

The most spectacular illustrations of the extent to which normality may be culturally defined are those cultures where an abnormality of our culture is the cornerstone of their social structure. It is not possible to do justice to these possibilities in a short discussion. A recent study of an island northwest in Melanesia by Fortune describes a society built upon traits which we regard as beyond the border of paranoia. In this tribe the exogamic groups look upon each other as prime manipulators of black magic, so that one marries always into an enemy group which remains for life one's deadly and unappeasable foes. They look upon a good garden crop as a confession of theft, for everyone is engaged in making magic to induce into this garden the productiveness of his neighbors'; therefore no secrecy in the island is so rigidly insisted upon as the secrecy of a man's harvesting of his yams. Their polite phrase at the acceptance of a gift is, "And if you now poison me, how shall I repay you this present?" Their preoccupation with poisoning is constant; no woman ever leaves her cooking pot for a moment untended. Even the great affinal economic exchanges that are characteristic of this Melanesian culture area are quite altered in Dobu since they are incompatible with this fear and distrust that pervades the culture. They go farther and people the whole world outside their own quarters with such malignant spirits that all-night feasts and ceremonials simply do not occur here. They have even rigorous religiously enforced customs that forbid the sharing of seed even in one family group. Anyone else's food is deadly poison to you, so that communality of stores is out of the question. For some months before harvest the whole society is on the verge of starvation, but if one falls to the temptation and eats up one's seed yams, one is an outcast and a beachcomber for life. There is no coming back. It involves, as a matter of course, divorce and the breaking of all social ties.

Now in this society where no one may work with another and no one may share with another, Fortune describes the individual who was regarded by all his fellows as crazy. He was not one of those who periodically ran amok and, beside himself and frothing at the mouth, fell with a knife upon anyone he could reach. Such behavior they did not regard as putting anyone outside the pale. They did not even put the individuals who were known to be liable to these attacks under any kind of control. They merely fled when they saw the attack coming on and kept out of the way. "He would be all right tomorrow." But there was one man of sunny, kindly disposition who liked work and liked to be helpful. The compulsion was too strong for him to repress it in favor of the opposite tendencies of his culture. Men and women never spoke of him without laughing; he was silly and simple and definitely crazy. Nevertheless, to the ethnologist used to a culture that has, in Christianity, made his type the model of all virtue, he seemed a pleasant fellow.

What a fascinating example! Living in this Melanesian culture would, for most people, be like living in a world turned upside down. In sharp contrast to the values of kindness, social cooperation, harmonious collaboration, friendships, and family ties that are prized in many cultures, the Melanesians view all of these as dangerously abnormal. Their culture is paranoia personified, as all individuals assume that everyone else is out to do them harm. In this world of seemingly inverted values, the aberrant "crazy" person is the one who has a compulsion to be friendly, trusting, and helpful. Once again, Benedict's point is that moral values that we may assume to be a universal part of our divine or human natures are actually merely the consequence of the social adaptation of particular cultures. But in other cultures, like the Melanesians, these adaptations can take a very different—and equally legitimate—form.

A useful way to understand Benedict's point is to consider the case of language. People are born with a basic linguistic capacity, a genetically transferred ability that is hardwired into our DNA. This linguistic ability allows us to invest sounds with meaning and organize words together into syntactic combinations, giving us the ability to think and communicate. However, the *precise* language one learns is determined by the culture within which one is born. Each language has selected a distinct set of sounds to carry meaning and evolved its own set of grammatical rules to link individual words and ideas together into more complex combinations. Although these various languages seem very different on the surface, most linguists believe that they all reflect an underlying "depth grammar" and meaning-giving abilities.

Anthropologists like Benedict believe that the same is true of cultural customs, belief structures, and moral values. Faced with the need to develop ways to live together and survive as an integrated community, each culture has developed its own specific cultural adaptations. Seen in this way, it makes

thinking philosophically

CULTURAL RELATIVISM AND YOUR MORAL PERSPECTIVE

Several years ago a family that had immigrated to Minnesota was caught in a clash of cultural values. Consistent with cultural practices in his home country, the father of two daughters, aged thirteen and fourteen, arranged marriages for them with two men in their thirties. The twin marriage ceremonies were an event of great celebration, with many friends and relatives attending. The day after the ceremony, the two young "brides" went to local law enforcement authorities, complaining about their situation. Their parents were arrested and charged with child endangerment and the two "grooms" were charged with statutory rape. All four adults stated that it never occurred to them that they were doing anything wrong. Nevertheless, they were convicted. How would Ruth Benedict analyze this event? How would you analyze this event?

applies to all individuals and cultures. It doesn't matter if some individuals—or many individuals—believe that slavery is ethically acceptable: For the ethical absolutist, these individuals *must* be wrong because prohibiting slavery is a universal value. Analogously, it doesn't matter if human slavery is an integral component of a culture's social and economic fabric: Slavery is morally wrong, and this moral evaluation is independent of whatever customs and moral practices a particular culture holds. Finally, for the ethical absolutist, the period of time being evaluated does not matter—human slavery is morally wrong today and it was also morally wrong 200 years ago in the United States.

Which view is right? Are moral values

W. T. Stace (1886–1967). English-born philosopher who sought to reconcile naturalism with religious experience. His utilitarian theories, though empiricist in nature, acknowledged the necessity of incorporating mystical and spiritual interpretations.

relative to an individual or specific culture? Or are they universal, applying to all humans in all cultures and all time periods? In the Reading Critically box on Benedict, we suggested some difficulties that a moral relativist faces. In the following reading, the philosopher **W. T. Stace** examines some of these difficulties at some length, while also considering the arguments for ethical absolutism. Stace begins by providing a very clear and succinct analysis of the ethical absolutist perspective.

W. T. Stace, from *The Concept of Morals*

Ethical Absolutism

According to the absolutists there is but one eternally true and valid moral code. This moral code applies with rigid impartiality to all men. What is a duty for me must likewise be a duty for you. There is but one law, one standard, one morality, for all men. And this standard, this law, is absolute and unvarying.

Moreover, as the one moral law extends its dominion over all the corners of the earth, so too it is not limited in its application by any considerations of time or period. That which is right now was right in the centuries of Greece and Rome, nay, in the very ages of the cave man. That which is evil now was evil then. If slavery is morally wicked today, it was morally wicked among the ancient Athenians, notwithstanding that their greatest men accepted it as a necessary condition of human society. Their opinion did not make slavery a moral good for them. It only showed that they were, in spite of their otherwise noble conceptions, ignorant of what is truly right and good in this matter.

Stace then goes on to address the central thesis of Ruth Benedict and other cultural relativists—namely, the diversity of moral values and customs from culture to culture.

W. T. Stace, from *The Concept of Morals*

The ethical absolutist recognizes as a fact that moral customs and moral ideas differ from country to country and from age to age. This indeed seems manifest and not to be disputed. We think slavery morally wrong, the Greeks thought it morally unobjectionable. The inhabitants of New Guinea certainly have very different moral ideas from ours. But the fact that the Greeks or the inhabitants of New Guinea think something right does not make it right, even for them. Nor does the fact that we think the same things wrong make them wrong. They are *in themselves* either right or wrong. What we have to do is to discover which they are. What anyone thinks makes no difference. It is here just as it is in matters of physical science. We believe the earth to be a globe. Our ancestors may have thought it flat. This does not show that it *was* flat, and it is *now* a globe. What it shows is that men having in other ages been ignorant about the shape of the earth have now learned the truth. So if the Greeks thought slavery morally legitimate, this does not indicate that it was for them and in that age morally legitimate, but rather that they were ignorant of the truth of the matter.

This is a crucial point that Stace is making: The ethical absolutist believes that at least some moral values are independent of human belief and practice, just as the physical facts of the universe are independent. But what are the grounds for the independent status of moral values? We discover the truth of the physical universe through scientific investigation. How can we discover the truth about moral values? That is precisely the problem that most ethical theories are designed to solve, theories that we will be considering in these two chapters. Stace continues his analysis.

The ethical absolutist is not indeed committed to the opinion that his own, or our own, moral code is the true one. Theoretically at least he might hold that slavery is ethically justifiable, that the Greeks knew better than we do about this, that ignorance of the true morality lies with us and not with them. All that he is actually committed to is the opinion that, whatever the true moral code may be, it is always the same for all men in all ages. His view is not at all inconsistent with the belief that humanity has still much to learn in moral matters. If anyone were to assert that in five hundred years the moral conceptions of the present day will appear as barbarous to the people of that age as the moral conceptions of the middle ages appear to us now, he need not deny it. If anyone were to assert that the ethics of Christianity are by no means final, and will be superseded in future ages by vastly nobler moral ideals, he need not deny this either. For it is of the essence of his creed to believe that morality is in some sense objective, non man-made, not produced by human opinion; that its principles are real truths about which men have to learn—just as they have to learn about the shape of the world—about which they may have been ignorant in the past, and about which therefore they may well be ignorant now.

W. T. Stace, from *The Concept of Morals*

> [W]hatever the true moral code may be, it is always the same for all men in all ages.

Stace then proceeds to provide a similarly lucid account of ethical relativism, beginning with his belief that the motivation that powers these movements is a reaction *against* ethical absolutism. In fact, as we saw, it was Ruth Benedict and her colleagues' opposition to what they saw to be Western cultural imperialism—the view that Western values were superior to all others and should be universally adopted by all cultures—that helped shape her cultural relativist perspective.

Any ethical position which denies that there is a single moral standard which is equally applicable to all men at all times may fairly be called a species of ethical relativity. There is not, the relativist asserts, merely one moral law, one code, one standard. There are many moral laws, codes, standards. What morality ordains in one place or age may be quite different from what morality ordains in another place or age. The moral code of the Chinese is quite different from that of Europeans, that of Africans quite different from both. Any morality, therefore, is relative to the age, the place, and the circumstances in which it is found. It is in no sense absolute.

W. T. Stace, from *The Concept of Morals*

Stace goes on to emphasize a crucial dimension of ethical relativism, namely, that it is not simply providing a *descriptive account* of the diverse moral values of various cultures—it is also providing a *normative endorsement* of these values. Ethical relativism, in other words, is stating that each culture's moral values, whatever they may be, *are* morally right.

W. T. Stace, from *The Concept of Morals*

> This does not mean merely—as one might at first sight be inclined to suppose—that the very same kind of action which is *thought* right in one country and period may be *thought* wrong in another. This would be a mere platitude, the truth of which everyone would have to admit. Even the absolutist would admit this—would even wish to emphasize it—since he is well aware that different peoples have different sets of moral ideas, and his whole point is that some of these sets of ideas are false. What the relativist means to assert is, not this platitude, but that the very same kind of action which *is* right in one country and period may *be* wrong in another. And this, far from being a platitude, is a very startling assertion. . . . Moral right *means* what people think morally right. It has no other meaning.

At this point you might be finding that your views regarding moral values are becoming more confused rather than more clear. This is a perfectly natural process. Why? Because when people form views uncritically—as many do when it comes to moral values—their conclusions may not reflect their best thoughtful, insightful analysis. For example, you might believe that all values are relative to specific individuals or cultures, a misguided "live and let live" perspective, without fully appreciating the disturbing and unintended consequences of such a view. Or you might believe that you have a universal code in hand, derived from religion or respected authority such as the Ten Commandments, the Book of Mormon, or the Qur'an. But such moral codes pose problems of their own; what do we do when universal moral codes conflict? What is the justification for asserting that *our* moral code is the one, true universal set of values to which everyone ought to adhere? In short, once you begin the process of philosophical examination of the core issues of virtually any area of life experience, the initial effect is likely to be one of confusion, as you begin to appreciate the complexity of the situation. This questioning doubt and confusion is the engine that drives philosophical inquiry, and it stands in distinct contrast to the unreflectively simplistic views of nonphilosophical understanding. But be assured that as you continue your critical analysis of moral values—and other areas of philosophical investigation—that you are in the process of developing an informed understanding and building a solid foundation for your views, which you will be able to explain and justify through compelling analysis.

How do we decide which moral theory is correct: ethical relativism or ethical absolutism? We need to think critically, exploring and evaluating the rationale for each view, and come to an intelligent conclusion. To this end, Stace proceeds to critically evaluate the arguments supporting each of these ethical points of view.

W. T. Stace, from *The Concept of Morals*

> **Arguments in Favor of Ethical Relativity**
>
> . . . the first (argument) is that which relies upon the actual varieties of moral "standards" found in the world. It was easy enough to believe in a single absolute morality in older times when there was no anthropology, when all humanity was divided clearly into two groups, Christian peoples and the "heathen." . . . Greater knowledge has brought greater tolerance. We can no longer exalt our own morality as alone true, while dismissing all other moralities as false or inferior. The investigations of anthropologists have shown that there exist side by side in the world a bewildering variety of moral codes. On this topic endless volumes have been written, masses of evidence piled up. Anthropologists have ransacked the Melanesian islands, the jungles of New Guinea, the steppes of Siberia,

the deserts of Australia, the forests of central Africa, and have brought back with them countless examples of weird, extravagant, and fantastic "moral" customs with which to confound us. We learn that all kinds of horrible practices are, in this, that, or the other place, regarded as essential to virtue. We find that there is nothing, or next to nothing, which has always and everywhere been regarded as morally good by all men. Where then is our universal morality? Can we, in the face of all this evidence, deny that it is nothing but an empty dream?

This argument, taken by itself, is a very weak one. It relies upon a single set of facts—the variable moral customs of the world. But this variability of moral ideas is admitted by both parties to the dispute, and is capable of ready explanation upon the hypothesis of either party. The relativist says that the facts are to be explained by the nonexistence of any absolute moral standard. The absolutist says that they are to be explained by human ignorance of what the absolute moral standard is. And he can truly point out that men have differed widely in their opinions about all manners of topics including the subject-matters of the physical sciences—just as much as they differ about morals. And if the various different opinions which men have held about the shape of the earth do not prove that it has no one real shape, neither do the various opinions which they have held about morality prove that there is no one true morality.

Thus the facts can be explained equally plausibly on either hypothesis. There is nothing in the facts themselves which compels us to prefer the relativistic hypothesis to that of the absolutist. And therefore the argument fails to prove the relativist conclusion. If that conclusion is to be established, it must be by means of other considerations.

In the conflict between ethical relativism and ethical absolutism, this is a very important point that Stace is making. We saw that Ruth Benedict rested her entire argument for ethical relativism on the broad diversity of moral values across cultures, using this basic argument form:

- Ethical values vary from culture to culture and time period to time period in a bewildering and conflicting array of moral codes.

- Therefore, there are no universal values that exist independently—all moral values are relative to a specific culture and are "right" for that culture.

But ethical absolutism doesn't dispute the descriptive facts of cultural variation in moral values: It's in the *interpretation* of this data where the conflict lies. For the ethical relativist, this cultural diversity suggests the normative conclusion that there are no absolute moral values that can be applied to all cultures. But as we noted on page 437, this "leap of logic" commits the naturalistic fallacy: Simply describing a situation provides no evidence for concluding that this is the way things *should* be. And this is the ethical absolutist's point: Yes, there is a diversity of moral values across cultures; but this simply means that some cultures are not as morally enlightened as others because they have not accepted certain universal moral values that apply to all individuals, in all cultures, in all time periods.

Stace then goes on to consider a second argument for ethical relativity, which is in the form of a critique of ethical absolutism. The form of the argument is something like this:

- Ethical absolutists have never been able to establish a solid foundation or justification on which a universal set of values can be built.

- Therefore, there is no such foundation or justification for universal values, so we must conclude that all moral values are relative.

W. T. Stace, from *The Concept of Morals*

> (Another) argument in favor of ethical relativity . . . consists in alleging that no one has ever been able to discover upon what foundation an absolute morality could rest, or from what source a universally binding moral code could derive its authority.
>
> If, for example, it is an absolute and unalterable moral rule that all men ought to be unselfish, from whence does this *command* issue? For a command it certainly is, phrase it how you please. There is no difference in meaning between the sentence "You ought to be unselfish" and the sentence "Be unselfish." Now a command implies a commander. An obligation implies some authority which obliges. Who is this commander, what is this authority? Thus the vastly difficult question is raised of *the basis of moral obligation*. Now the argument of the relativist would be that it is impossible to find any basis for a universally binding moral law; but that it is quite easy to discover a basis for morality if moral codes are admitted to be variable, ephemeral, and relative to time, place, and circumstance.

Naturally, simply because a universally accepted set of moral values has not yet been developed does not mean that it *won't* be developed at some point in the future. And it also doesn't mean that such a moral code hasn't already been developed but has not yet been universally accepted. Nevertheless, the challenge to provide a compelling rationale is central for ethical absolutism. Traditional attempts to provide such a foundation have often been religious in nature, embedding the moral code within the metaphysic of a specific religion. In these cases, the universal authority for the moral values is typically divine or supernatural in nature: for example, "Killing is wrong because God prohibits it." But the fact that there are so many different religions with divergent codes of ethics tends to put this approach back in the ethical relativism quandary, namely, "Who is to say that *this* religion, along with its moral code, is the one true approach that should be universally accepted?" We will consider the key issues regarding the philosophy of religion in Chapter 7, but for now we are interested in approaches to ethical absolutism that are not dependent on accepting specific religious beliefs (that is, a *secular* approach to moral values).

((•⎯ **Listen** to the **Podcast**
Walter Sinnott-Armstrong on Morality Without God on
mysearchlab.com

To sum up, these are the two arguments in favor of ethical relativism:

- *The fact that moral values vary widely from culture to culture, age to age. But,* inferring from this descriptive statement of fact that this moral relativism represents the way morality *ought* to be viewed commits the naturalistic fallacy.

- The fact that no system of moral values has yet been universally accepted. *But,* although this is the central challenge confronting ethical absolutism, the fact that such a moral system has not yet been universally accepted doesn't mean that it shouldn't be or that it won't be at some point in the future.

Having considered arguments supporting ethical relativism, it's time to explore arguments critical of this view. Stace articulates several serious concerns with the ethical relativist position. The first argument is analogous to a point of view articulated by **William James** in his analysis of whether there is the possibility that we can make free choices. Those thinkers committed to determinism contend that all human actions are caused by influences beyond any person's control. Indeterminists counter that even though our actions may be subject to the effects of influences, we nevertheless retain the ability to make free choices independent of these influences, choices for which we are personally responsible. Which view is right? Are we free or not free? James frames his answer by stating what he

William James
(1842–1910) With C. S. Pierce, founded the philosophy of Pragmatism. Also contributed much to the psychology of religion in *The Varieties of Religious Experience* (1903).

considers to be the criteria we should use to evaluate theories and determine what is true.

> *The arguments I am about to urge all proceed on two suppositions: first, when we make theories about the world and discuss them with one another, we do so in order to attain a conception of things which shall give us subjective satisfaction; and second, if there be two conceptions, and the one seems to us, on the whole, more rational than the other, we are entitled to suppose that the more rational one is the truer of the two. . . .*

James's point is that humans use their intellectual abilities to create concepts and develop theories to help them understand and give meaning to their lived experience. When theories conflict with one another, how do we decide which theories are the "best"? In the final analysis, we should endorse those theories that provide the most rational, complete, and persuasive understanding of our lived experience. Stace employs analogous epistemological criteria to the questions of "Are moral values relative or absolute? Which theory is correct?"

Ethical relativity, in asserting that the moral standards of particular social groups are the only standards which exist, renders meaningless all propositions which attempt to compare these standards with one another in respect of their moral worth. And this is a very serious matter indeed. We are accustomed to think that the moral ideas of one nation or social group may be "higher" or "lower" than those of another. . . . We habitually compare one civilization with another and judge the sets of ethical ideas to be found in them to be some better, some worse. The fact that such judgments are very difficult to make with any justice, and that they are frequently made on very superficial and prejudiced grounds, has no bearing on the question now at issue. The question is whether such judgments have any *meaning*. We habitually assume that they have.

W. T. Stace, from *The Concept of Morals*

Is genocide morally evil?
According to Stace, our belief in absolute moral standards allows us to make moral judgments about genocide. Most of us would have no difficulty in judging Hitler's actions as morally wrong. What about the actions of those who followed his orders? Or those who supported Hitler but did not literally participate in killing Jews and other prisoners?

In the same way that James argues that humans live their lives based on the assumption that they are capable of making free choices, so Stace is arguing that we live our lives based on the assumption that *there are* absolute moral standards that are independent of individual or group preferences. It is because of our belief in absolute moral standards that we believe we are justified in making moral judgments, such as:

- The genocidal actions of Adolf Hitler and Slobodan Milosevic were morally reprehensible.
- Terrorist activities in which innocent lives are taken are morally indefensible.
- Cultures that systematically abuse children are morally inferior.

If ethical relativism is true, then we would not be able to make these judgments of moral evaluation. But *we do* make these sorts of moral evaluations all of the time, and we believe that we are justified in doing so. Let's apply the epistemological criteria suggested by William James and W. T. Stace in evaluating which view of moral values makes most sense: ethical relativism or ethical absolutism.

Criterion 1   Which theory provides the most *subjective satisfaction*?

Criterion 2   Which theory provides the *more rational* explanation?

James and Stace want to argue, with good reason, that because we believe that we are justified in making moral evaluations and comparisons of other cultures, a belief in ethical absolutism is going to provide us with more *subjective satisfaction*, and will provide a more *rational* explanation of the world. Otherwise, if we commit ourselves to ethical relativism, then we must conclude that our judgments of moral evaluation and comparison are illegitimate. And this *does not* provide us with as much subjective satisfaction or as rational an explanation of the world as that provided by ethical absolutism.

The same principle applies in evaluating moral values in different time periods and the possibility of moral progress. The fact is that most people believe that the barbaric treatment of mentally ill people in past centuries (to "drive the demons out of them") was morally inferior to the treatment of them today. And that practices such as slavery, human sacrifice, cannibalism, the burning of witches and widows, and the subjugation of women are morally inferior to current, more enlightened practices. Yet, if ethical relativism is accurate, then such moral comparisons are not valid and the concept of moral progress is an illusion—conclusions that are simply not consistent with our assumptions and beliefs about the world. In James's terms, these relativist conclusions provide less subjective satisfaction and present a less rational explanation than an absolutist perspective.

But a further difficulty with ethical relativism is just as serious as its inconsistency with our general epistemological framework. Ethical relativism contends that moral values are determined by "the group." But who precisely is "the group"? Ethical relativists assume that in most cultures, the majority of people agree about basic moral values. Although this may be true in smaller, simpler cultures, this seems untrue with large, complex, modern cultures. How would the ethical relativist determine the prevailing view on moral values in a culture that is deeply divided? What is the rationale for delimiting smaller groups within larger groups? Stace addresses these concerns in the following passage:

W. T. Stace, from *The Concept of Morals*

But even if we assume that the difficulty about defining moral groups has been surmounted, a further difficulty presents itself. Suppose that we have not definitely decided what are the exact boundaries of the social group within which a moral standard is to be operative. And we will assume—as is invariably done by relativists themselves—that this group is to be some actually existing social community such as a tribe or nation. How are we to know, even then, what actually *is* the moral standard within that group? How is anyone to know? How is even a member of the group to know? For there are certain to be within the group—at least this will be true among advanced peoples—wide differences of opinion as to what is right, what wrong. Whose opinion, then, is to be taken as representing *the* moral standard of the group? Either we must take the opinion of the majority within the group, or the opinion of some minority. If we rely upon the ideas of the majority, the results will be disastrous. Wherever there is found among a people a small band of select spirits, or perhaps one man, working for the establishment of higher and nobler ideals than those commonly accepted by the group, we shall be compelled to hold that, for that people at that time, the majority are right, and that the reformers are wrong and are preaching what is immoral. We shall have to maintain, for example, that Jesus was preaching immoral doctrines. . . . Moral goodness will have to be equated always with the mediocre and sometimes with the definitely base and ignoble. If on the other hand we say that the moral standard of the group is to be identified with the moral opinions of some minority, then what minority is this to be? We cannot answer that it is to be the minority composed of the best and most enlightened individuals of the group. This would involve us in a palpably vicious circle. For by what standard are these individuals to be judged the best and the most enlightened? There is no principle by which we could select the right minority. And therefore we should have to consider every minority as good as every other. And this means that we should have no logical right whatever to resist the claim of the gangsters of Chicago—if such a claim were made—that their practices represent the highest standards of American morality. It means in the end that every individual is to be bound by no standard save his own.

Stace's final concern regarding ethical relativism is less philosophical and more practical, posing the question, "What would be the effect on human thinking and behavior if people genuinely adopted a relativist perspective, not just on a theoretical level but in their day-to-day lives?" The consequences would be dire, Stace is convinced, resulting in moral chaos. After all, if morality is truly rootless and subjective and not tied to any universal foundation, then every sort of action would be morally permissible. And once people come to understand and accept this, Stace believes that there is the risk that this will result in the *devolution* of moral values to more primitive, barbaric, and selfish levels. Nor would people be inspired to try to elevate themselves, to become more enlightened, if all moral values (or what are traditionally thought of as immoral values) are of equal validity.

Finally, not only is ethical relativity disastrous in its consequences for moral theory, it cannot be doubted that it must tend to be equally disastrous in its impact upon practical conduct. If men come really to believe that one moral standard has nothing special to recommend it, they might as well then slip down to some lower and easier standard. It is true that for a time, it may be possible, to hold one view in theory and to act practically upon another. But ideas, even philosophical ideas, are not so ineffectual that they can remain forever idle in the upper chambers of the intellect. In the end they seep down to the level of practice. They get themselves acted on. . . .

W. T. Stace, from *The Concept of Morals*

> **For every man by natural necessity desires that which is good for him.**
> **THOMAS HOBBES**

8.4 Egoism as a Universal Principle

The conceptual flaws and logical self-contradictions of ethical relativism have led many philosophers to conclude that it is untenable as an ethical theory. And as W. T. Stace points out, if we abandon ethical relativism, then we are left within some form of ethical absolutism: the notion that at least some moral values are universal and binding on all humans. However, within the general framework of ethical absolutism, there are many possible theories. The first that we shall explore is **ethical egoism**, the belief that the highest moral value for all humans is to pursue their own happiness. This does not mean that you should necessarily be selfish, seeking to take more than your share in life. Rather, it simply expresses the view that all things being equal, your needs and interests should take precedence over the needs and interests of others. For the ethical egoist, "Looking out for #1" is not something to be ashamed about—in fact, it is the best way for you to act in a morally enlightened manner. Nor does it entail being an *egotist*—a person who is arrogant, boastful, and obsessed with his or her self. Instead, the ethical egoist may have friendly, harmonious, and productive relationships with others. It's just that in the final analysis, when our needs and interests are in conflict or competition with those of others, it is our moral obligation to take care of our own needs and interests first. For the ethical egoists, this is a moral value that is binding on all humans.

The ethical egoists recognize that such a view runs counter to the prevailing moral values of many cultures, in which the venerated moral values include altruism, self-sacrifice, empathy, communal responsibility, love, social responsibility to those in need, and a willingness to sacrifice our own needs for the good of the group. Nevertheless, the ethical egoists are convinced that these traditional moral values represent a skewed and unhealthy perspective on how humans ought to think and behave.

Arguments for Egoism

One of the first coherent expressions of the ethical egoist perspective is found in Plato's *Republic*, his monumental exploration of the nature of justice. Plato was not himself, strictly speaking, an ethical egoist, but he gives voice to this view through the person of Glaucon, who tries to convince Socrates that pursuing our own self-interest is our natural condition, and rather than denying this fact, we should embrace it. Glaucon uses a story, "The Myth of Gyges," to make his point.

Ethical egoism The view that we act morally when we pursue our own self-interest.

Plato, from *The Republic,* "The Myth of Gyges"

Glaucon: First, I will state what is commonly held about the nature of justice and its origin; secondly, I shall maintain that it is always practiced with reluctance, not as good in itself, but as a thing one cannot do without; and thirdly, that this reluctance is reasonable, because the life of injustice is much the better life of the two—so people say. . . . Accordingly, I shall set you an example by glorifying the life of injustice with all the energy that I hope you will show later in denouncing it and exalting justice in its stead. Will that plan suit you?

Socrates: Nothing could be better, I replied. Of all subjects this is one on which a sensible man must always be glad to exchange ideas.

Good, said Glaucon. Listen then, and I will begin with my first point: the nature and origin of justice. What people say is that to do wrong is, in itself, a desirable thing; on the other hand, it is not at all desirable to suffer wrong, and the harm to the sufferer outweighs the advantage to the doer. Consequently, when men have had a taste of both, those who have not the power to seize the advantage and escape the harm decide that they would be better off if they made a compact neither to do wrong nor to suffer it. Hence they began to make laws and covenants with one another; and whatever the law prescribed they called lawful and right. This is what right or justice is and how it came into existence; it stands half-way between the best thing of all—to do wrong with impunity—and the worst, which is to suffer wrong without the power to retaliate. So justice is accepted as a compromise, and valued, not as good in itself, but for lack of power to do wrong; no man worthy of the name, who had that power, would ever enter into such a compact with anyone; he would be mad if he did. That, Socrates, is the nature of justice according to this account, and such the circumstances in which it arose.

Glaucon begins his case for ethical egoism with a proposed analysis of the origins of "justice." The version he is presenting has come to be known as the **social contract theory** of political development. This view of humans assumes that we are by nature solitary, aggressive, and competitive. It is in our nature to promote our own interests over those of others, and even inflict harm on them if it will advance our desires. However, although it is our nature to inflict harm in order to advance ourselves, we realize that in such a lawless world we ourselves are vulnerable to being victimized by others. As a result, we enter into a social agreement with others, promising not to hurt or take advantage of them if they won't hurt or take advantage of us. This "compromise," as Glaucon terms it, is not ideal, but it's the best we can do under the circumstances. It would be preferable to us if we could simply bring our own will and desires to bear on others without fear of reprisals or counterattacks.

Glaucon's next point in his argument for ethical egoism is that although people have freely entered into a social contract to escape the danger and instability of the "state of nature," they do so reluctantly. Abiding by the laws of the social contract runs counter to our nature to dominate and exploit others for our own personal advancement. And if we had an opportunity to break these laws without suffering negative consequences, *all of us* would leap at the opportunity to do so. And such behavior would be morally appropriate, because we would simply be acting in accord with our universal nature.

Social contract theory
The view that the main reason people agree to form political communities is out of necessity, because life in a prepolitical "state of nature" would be, though preferable, extremely difficult.

The next point is that men practice it against the grain, for lack of power to do wrong. How true that is, we shall best see if we imagine two men, one just, the other unjust, given full license to do whatever they like, and then follow them to observe where each will be led by his desires. We shall catch the just man taking the same road as the unjust; he will be

Plato, from *The Republic,* "The Myth of Gyges"

moved by self-interest, the end which it is natural to every creature to pursue his good, until forcibly turned aside by law and custom to respect the principle of equality.

Now, the easiest way to give them that complete liberty of action would be to imagine them possessed of the talisman found by Gyges, the ancestor of the famous Lydian. The story tells how he was a shepherd in the King's service. One day there was a great storm, and the ground where his flock was feeding was rent by an earthquake. Astonished at the sight, he went down into the chasm and saw, among other wonders of which the story tells, a brazen horse, hollow, with windows in its sides. Peering in, he saw a dead body, which seemed to be of more than human size. It was naked save for a gold ring, which he took from the finger and made his way out. When the shepherds met, as they did every month, to send an account to the King of the state of his flocks, Gyges came wearing the ring. As he was sitting with the others, he happened to turn the bezel of the ring inside his hand. At once he became invisible, and his companions, to his surprise, began to speak of him as if he had left them. Then, as he was fingering the ring, he turned the bezel outwards and become visible again. With that, he set about testing the ring to see if it really had this power, and always with the same result: according as he turned the bezel inside or out he vanished and reappeared. After this discovery he contrived to be one of the messengers sent to the court. There he seduced the Queen, and with her help murdered the King and seized the throne.

Now suppose there were two such magic rings, and one were given to the just man, the other to the unjust. No one, it is commonly believed, would have such iron strength of mind as to stand fast in doing right or keep his hands off other men's goods, where he could go to the market-place and fearlessly help himself to anything he wanted, enter houses and sleep with any woman he chose, set prisoners free and kill men at his pleasure, and in a word go about among men with the powers of a god. He would behave no better than the other; both would take the same course. Surely this would be strong proof that men do right only under compulsion; no individual thinks of it as good for him personally, since he does wrong whenever he finds he has the power. Every man believes that wrongdoing pays him personally much better, and according to this theory, that is the truth. Granted full license to do as he liked, people would think him a miserable fool if they found him refusing to wrong his neighbors, or to touch their belongings, though in public they would keep up a pretence of praising his conduct, for fear of being wronged themselves. So much for that . . .

< READING CRITICALLY >

Analyzing the Myth of Gyges

- Do you think that most people will break laws and violate traditional moral values if they're confident that they won't be caught? Identify one example that would support this thesis (for example, the looting that takes place during riots) and another example that contradicts it (returning a lost wallet that only you know you found).
- When you hear about someone who could have cheated or lied for their own benefit but refused to, do you consider them, in Glaucon's words, "a miserable fool"? Why or why not?
- If you found yourself in possession of the Ring of Gyges, identify three "immoral" things you might do by making yourself invisible that you ordinarily wouldn't do (for example, walking into a sold-out concert for which you couldn't buy tickets).
- Glaucon states that, "What people say is that to do wrong is, in itself, a desirable thing; on the other hand, it is not at all desirable to suffer wrong, and the harm to the sufferer outweighs the advantage to the doer." Socrates believes just the opposite, stating that "It is better to suffer wickedness than to commit it," and contending that doing wrong "will harm and corrupt that part of ourselves that is improved by just actions and destroyed by unjust actions." Identify which viewpoint you believe makes most sense, and explain your reasons for believing so.

Ethical egoism should not be confused with **psychological egoism**, a theory that purports to describe the way humans necessarily behave. According to psychological egoism, we are driven to pursue our own self-interest by our inborn human nature—we cannot do otherwise. There are serious challenges to the theory of psychological egoism, which we will explore later in the chapter in the work of philosopher James Rachels. For now, however, we are interested in the theory of ethical egoism, which holds that although it may be possible for humans to act in a way that sacrifices their own self-interests, *it is immoral to do so.* The core belief of ethical egoism is that it is our moral obligation to pursue our own self-interest as our first priority, and when we fail to do so, our behavior is ethically inappropriate. One individual who has given a passionate defense of this view is the novelist and essayist **Ayn Rand**.

Ayn Rand is best known for her novels *The Fountainhead* and *Atlas Shrugged* and her ethical philosophy of individualism and "the virtue of selfishness" which they embody. Rand rejects the psychological egoist view that people are compelled to seek their own self-interest. Rather than articulate a *descriptive* theory regarding the way humans are constructed, Rand is proposing a *normative* theory that expresses the way humans *ought* to behave. From her standpoint, it is our moral duty to pursue our own rational self-interest. The "virtue" of altruism that traditional ethical theories and religions recommend is actually a vice, because it encourages people *not* to pursue their own self-interest as their top priority. The following excerpt is from Rand's book *The Virtue of Selfishness.*

Psychological egoism
The view that we are compelled by our psychological makeup always to pursue our self-interest above all else.

Ayn Rand, from *The Virtue of Selfishness*

In popular usage, the word "selfishness" is a synonym of evil; the image it conjures is of a murderous brute who tramples over piles of corpses to achieve his own ends, who cares for no living being and pursues nothing but the gratification of the mindless whims of any immediate moment.

Yet the exact meaning and dictionary definition of the word "selfishness" is: *concern with one's own interests*.

This concept does *not* include a moral evaluation; it does not tell us whether concern with one's own interests is good or evil; nor does it tell us what constitutes man's actual interests. It is the task of ethics to answer such questions.

The ethics of altruism has created the image of the brute, as its answer, in order to make men accept two inhuman tenets: (a) that any concern with one's own interests is evil, regardless of what these interests might be, and (b) that the brute's activities are *in fact* to one's own interest (which altruism enjoins man to renounce for the sake of his neighbors).

For a view of the nature of altruism, its consequences and the enormity of the moral corruption it perpetrates, I shall refer you to *Atlas Shrugged*—or to any of today's newspaper headlines. What concerns us here is altruism's *default* in the field of ethical theory.

There are two moral questions which altruism lumps together into one "package-deal": (1) What are values? (2) Who should be the beneficiary of values? Altruism substitutes the second for the first; it evades the task of defining a code of moral values, thus leaving man, in fact, without moral guidance.

Altruism declares that any action taken for the benefit of others is good, and any action taken for one's own benefit is evil. Thus the *beneficiary* of an action is the only criterion of moral values—and so long as that beneficiary is anybody other than oneself, anything goes.

Hence the appalling immorality, the chronic injustice, the grotesque double standards, the insoluble conflicts and contradictions that have characterized human relationships and human societies throughout history, under all the variants of the altruist ethics.

Ayn Rand (1905–1982). Rand was an American writer who advocated "the virtue of selfishness" in her novels, plays, and short stories. Her most famous works are *The Fountainhead* (1943) and *Atlas Shrugged* (1957).

Observe the indecency of what passes for moral judgments today. An industrialist who produces a fortune, and a gangster who robs a bank are regarded as equally immoral, since they both sought wealth for their own "selfish" benefit. A young man who gives up his career in order to support his parents and never rises beyond the rank of grocery clerk is regarded as morally superior to the young man who endures an excruciating struggle and achieves his personal ambition. A dictator is regarded as moral, since the unspeakable atrocities he committed were intended to benefit "the people," not himself.

Observe what this beneficiary-criterion of morality does to a man's life. The first thing he learns is that morality is his enemy: He has nothing to gain from it, he can only lose; self-inflicted loss, self-inflicted pain and the gray, debilitating pall of an incomprehensible duty is all that he can expect. He may hope that others might occasionally sacrifice themselves for his benefit, as he grudgingly sacrifices himself for theirs, but he knows that the relationship will bring mutual resentment, not pleasure—and that, morally, their pursuit of values will be like an exchange of unwanted, unchosen Christmas presents, which neither is morally permitted to buy for himself. Apart from such times as he manages to perform some act of self-sacrifice, he possesses no moral significance: Morality takes no cognizance of him and has nothing to say to him for guidance in the crucial issues of his life; it is only his own personal, private, "selfish" life and, as such, it is regarded either as evil or, at best, *amoral*.

Since nature does not provide man with an automatic form of survival, since he has to support his life by his own effort, the doctrine that concern with one's own interests is evil means that man's desire to live is evil—that man's life, as such, is evil. No doctrine could be more evil than that.

Yet that is the meaning of altruism, implicit in such examples as the equation of an industrialist with a robber. There is a fundamental moral difference between a man who sees his self-interest in production and a man who sees it in robbery. The evil of a robber does *not* lie in the fact that he pursues his own interest, but in *what* he regards as to his own interest; *not* in the fact that he pursues his values, but in *what* he chooses to value; *not* in the fact that he wants to live, but in the fact that he wants to live on a subhuman level.

> "The achievement of his own happiness is man's highest moral purpose."

Is it ethical to break the law to defend our personal integrity? Gary Cooper in *The Fountainhead*. The protagonist of this film and novel is Howard Roark, a gifted and original architect who refuses to compromise his artistic vision to please others. Roark personifies Rand's moral ideal. When his designs for a huge public works project are modified—and in his mind adulterated—without his permission, he undertakes to destroy the completed structures. How would you evaluate the morality of his decision? Why?

If it is true that what I mean by "selfishness" is not what is meant conventionally, then *this* is one of the worst indictments of altruism: It means that altruism *permits no concept* of a self-respecting, self-supporting man—a man who supports his life by his own effort and neither sacrifices himself nor others. It means that altruism permits no view of men except as sacrificial animals and profiteers-on-sacrifice, as victims and parasites—that it permits no concept of a benevolent coexistence among men—that it permits no concept of *justice*.

If you wonder about the reasons behind the ugly mixture of cynicism and guilt in which most men spend their lives, these are the reasons: cynicism, because they neither practice nor accept the altruist morality—guilt, because they dare not reject it.

To rebel against so devastating an evil, one has to rebel against its basic premise. To redeem both man and morality, it is the concept of "*selfishness*" that one has to redeem.

The first step is to assert *man's right to a moral existence*—that is: to recognize his need of a moral code to guide the course and the fulfillment of his own life. . . . The reasons why man needs a moral code will tell you that the purpose of morality is to define man's proper values and interests, that *concern with his own interests* is the essence of a moral existence, and that *man must be the beneficiary of his own moral actions*.

Since all values have to be gained and/or kept by men's actions, any breach between actor and beneficiary necessitates an injustice: the sacrifice of some men to others, of the actors to the nonactors, of the moral to the immoral. Nothing could ever justify such a breach, and no one ever has. . . .

The Objectivist ethics holds that the actor must always be the beneficiary of his action and that man must act for his own *rational* self-interest. But his right to do so is derived from his nature as man and from the function of moral values in human life—and, therefore is applicable *only* in the context of a rational, objectively demonstrated and validated code of moral principles which define and determine his actual self-interest. It is not a license "to do as he pleases" and it is not applicable to the altruists' image of a "selfish" brute nor to any man motivated by irrational emotions, feelings, urges, wishes or whims. . . . Just as the satisfaction of the irrational desires of others is *not* a criterion of moral values, neither is the satisfaction of one's own irrational desires. Morality is not a contest of whims.

It's a provocative thesis that Rand is defending, and she expresses her view with unrepentant passion. "Selfishness" is not evil—"altruism" is evil. Traditional views of what is morally good and right have inverted the true nature of moral values. Why? According to Nietzsche (Ayn Rand rejects his answer), it is because people who are weak fear and envy the strong individualists in our world. They resent their independence, their passion, their creative visions. These parasitic "second-handers" constrain the strong individualists by creating a perverse system of morality that villainizes the true individual and celebrates the weak altruist devoted to self-sacrifice. In this wrong-headed system, the pursuit of self-interest is branded as "selfishness," whereas the unnatural denial of self-interest is considered to be a saintly virtue. According to Rand, altruism discourages us from fulfilling our greatest potential.

Rand is careful to point out, however, that the ultimate moral value of pursuing one's self-interest means pursuing one's *rational* self-interest. What this means is that the code of ethics that each person is expected to create on his or her own must be an "objectively demonstrated and validated code of moral principles which define and determine his actual self-interest. It is not a license 'to do as he pleases.'" In other words, pursuing your self-interest means creating a value system that is not destructive to yourself, nor is it destructive to others. From Rand's point of view, it is not rational to claim that narcotic use and excessive drinking are your moral values, because these inhibit living a productive, fulfilling life that is truly in your self-interest. Similarly, it is irrational to declare that stealing from others will be your defining moral value in pursuing your self-interest, because such behavior is the antithesis of a strong, independent person achieving his or her creative potentials. Other people are not our enemies, and it is likely that we will have friendly and productive relationships with many people. But we should resist sacrificing our self-interest for the sake of others because such immoral behavior enslaves us to the group will and prevents us from achieving our greatest goals.

< READING CRITICALLY >

Analyzing Rand on the Virtue of Selfishness

- Rand contends that endorsing altruism as a moral value necessarily means condemning the pursuit of one's own self-interest. Do you agree with this point? Why or why not? Provide an example to support your conclusion.

- In her analysis, Rand equates the terms "self-interest" and "selfishness." Do they really mean the same thing? Is it possible to pursue your own self-interest without being selfish, or do these two terms share the same meaning? Provide an example to support your response.

- Rand states, "An industrialist who produces a fortune, and a gangster who robs a bank are regarded as equally immoral, since they both sought wealth for their own selfish benefit. A young man who gives up his career in order to support his parents and never rises beyond the rank of grocery clerk is regarded as morally superior to the young man who endures an excruciating struggle and achieves his personal ambition." Critically evaluate these examples. Can you provide parallels to contemporary figures or people in your own life?

- After endorsing the view that every person must "recognize his need of a moral code to guide the course and fulfillment of his own life," Rand goes on to say "The reasons why man needs a moral code will tell you that the purpose of morality is to define man's proper values and interests, that concern with his own interests is the essence of a moral existence, and that man must be the beneficiary of his own moral actions." Critically evaluate the logic of this position, identifying both arguments that support this position and those that don't.

Arguments Against Egoism

James Rachels
(1941–2003). American moral philosopher who wrote influential articles on applied ethics, especially on the topics of euthanasia and animal rights.

The views of psychological egoism (people necessarily act in their own self-interest) and ethical egoism (people *should* always strive to act in their own self-interest) have been attacked by those who believe that egoism does not represent human's natural inclinations, nor should it be endorsed as a moral value. The philosopher **James Rachels** provides a systematic critique of both of these views in the following article, "Egoism and Moral Skepticism." We begin with his summary and analysis of psychological egoism.

James Rachels, from *Egoism and Moral Skepticism*

Psychological egoism seems to fly in the face of the facts. We are tempted to say: "Of course people act unselfishly all the time. For example, Smith gives up a trip to the country, which he would have enjoyed very much, in order to stay behind and help a friend with his studies, which is a miserable way to pass the time. This is a perfectly clear case of unselfish behavior, and if the psychological egoist thinks that such cases do not occur then he is just mistaken." Given such obvious instances of "unselfish behavior," what reply can the egoist make? There are two general arguments by which he might try to show that all actions, including those such as the one just outlined, are in fact motivated by self-interest. Let us examine these in turn:

The first argument goes as follows. If we describe one person's action as selfish, and another person's action as unselfish, we are overlooking the crucial fact that in both cases, assuming that the action is done voluntarily, *the agent is merely doing what he most wants to do*. If Smith stays behind to help his friend, that only shows that he wanted to help his friend more than he wanted to go to the country. And why should he be praised for his "unselfishness" when he is only doing what he most wants to do? So, since Smith is only doing what he wants to do, he cannot be said to be acting unselfishly.

This argument is so bad that it would not deserve to be taken seriously except for the fact that so many otherwise intelligent people have been taken in by it. First, the argument rests on the premise that people never voluntarily do anything except what they want to do. But this is patently false; there are at least two classes of actions that are exceptions to this generalization. One is the set of actions which we may not want to do, but which we do anyway as a means to an end which we want to achieve; for example, going to the dentist in order to stop a toothache, or going to work every day in order to be able to draw our pay at the end of the month. These classes may be regarded as consistent with the spirit of the egoist argument, however, since the ends mentioned are wanted by the agent. But the other set of actions are those which we do, not because we want to, nor even because there is an end which we want to achieve, but because we feel ourselves *under an obligation* to do them. For example, someone may do something because he has promised to do it, and thus feels obligated, even though he does not want to do it. It is sometimes suggested that in such cases we do the action because, after all, we want to keep our promises; so, even here, we are doing what we want. However, this dodge will not work: if I have promised to do something and if I do not want to do it then it is simply false to say that I want to keep my promise. In such cases we feel a conflict precisely because we do *not* want to do what we feel obligated to do. It is reasonable to think that Smith's action falls roughly into this second category: he might stay behind, not because he wants to, but because he feels that his friend needs help.

But suppose we were to concede, for the sake of the argument, that all voluntary action is motivated by the agent's wants, or at least that Smith is so motivated. Even if this were granted, it would not follow that Smith is acting selfishly or from self-interest. For if Smith wants to do something that will help his friend, even when it means forgoing his own enjoyments, that is precisely what makes him *un*selfish. What else could unselfishness be, if not wanting to help others? Another way to put the same point is to say that it is the *object* of a want that determines whether it is selfish or not. The mere fact that I am acting on *my* wants does not mean that I am acting selfishly; that depends on *what it is* that I want. If I want only my own good, and care nothing of others, then I am selfish; but if I also want other people to be well-off and happy, and if I act on *that* desire, then my action is not selfish. So much for this argument.

The argument and counterarguments Rachels is making here can be summarized in this way:

Egoist Argument 1. Whatever choices people make, they are always doing what they most want to do. So if one person wants to sacrifice a trip to the country to help his friend study, and another person doesn't, both choices are equally selfish because both people are doing what they most want to do.

Are good deeds selfish?
Lincoln claimed that in doing good he was acting selfishly because not doing good would make him suffer. Do you agree that it is selfish to want to help others?

James Rachels,
from *Egoism and Moral Skepticism*

Counterargument 1. We often do things we don't want to do because we have made a promise or feel an obligation. For example, we may have promised our friend, "We will help you study whenever you need us," and now feel that we have to honor that promise even though we would much rather go to the country. This is very different from the person who chooses *not* to honor his promise to his friend, and instead goes to the country instead of helping his friend study.

Counterargument 2. Even if we derive some satisfaction from giving up our trip to the country to help our friend, this is precisely what it means to act "unselfishly"—acting to promote someone else's interests, not just our own. In contrast, the person who breaks his promise and goes to the country is acting only to promote his own interest. The criteria for determining if an action is "selfish" or "unselfish" is the *object* or *consequence* of the action, not the satisfaction it brings the person initiating it.

Rachels then goes on to consider a second argument for psychological egoism.

The second argument for psychological egoism is this. Since so-called unselfish actions always produce a sense of self-satisfaction in the agent[1] and since this sense of satisfaction is a pleasant state of consciousness, it follows that the point of the action is really to achieve a pleasant state of consciousness, rather than to bring about any good for others. Therefore, the action is "unselfish" only at a superficial level of analysis. Smith will feel much better with himself for having stayed to help his friend—if he had gone to the country, he would have felt terrible about it—and that is the real point of the action. According to a well-known story, this argument was once expressed by Abraham Lincoln.

Mr. Lincoln once remarked to a fellow-passenger on an old-time, mud-coach that all men were prompted by selfishness in doing good. His fellow-passenger was antagonizing this position when they were passing over a corduroy bridge that spanned a slough. As they crossed this bridge they espied an old razor-backed sow on the bank making a terrible noise because her pigs had got into the slough and were in danger of drowning. As the old coach began to climb the hill, Mr. Lincoln called out, "Driver, can't you stop just a moment?" Then Mr. Lincoln jumped out, ran back, and lifted the little pigs out of the mud and water and placed them on the bank. When he returned, his companion remarked: "Now, Abe, where does selfishness come in on this little episode?" "Why, bless your soul, Ed, that was the very essence of selfishness. I should have had no peace of mind all day had I gone on and left that suffering old sow worrying over those pigs. I did it to get peace of mind, don't you see?"[2]

This argument suffers from defects similar to the previous one. Why should we think that merely because someone derives satisfaction from helping others this makes him selfish? Isn't the unselfish man precisely the one who *does* derive satisfaction from helping others, while the selfish man does not? If Lincoln "got peace of mind" from rescuing the piglets, does this show him to be selfish, or, on the contrary, doesn't it show him to

---

[1]Or, as it is sometimes said, "It gives him a clear conscience," or "He couldn't sleep at night if he had done otherwise," or "he would have been ashamed of himself for not doing it," and so on.

[2]Frank C. Sharp, *Ethics*, New York, 1928, pp. 74–75. Quoted from the Springfield (Ill.) *Monitor* in the *Outlook*, vol. 56, p. 1059.

be compassionate and good-hearted? (If a man were truly selfish, why should it bother his conscience that *others* suffer—much less pigs?) Similarly, it is nothing more than shabby sophistry to say, because Smith takes satisfaction in helping his friend, that he is behaving selfishly. If we say this rapidly, while thinking about something else, perhaps it will sound all right; but if we speak slowly, and pay attention to what we are saying, it sounds plain silly.

Moreover, suppose we ask *why* Smith derives satisfaction from helping his friend. The answer will be, it is because Smith cares for him and wants him to succeed. If Smith did not have these concerns, then he would take no pleasure in assisting him; and these concerns, as we have already seen, are the marks of unselfishness, not selfishness. To put the point more generally: If we have a positive attitude toward the attainment of some goal, then we may derive satisfaction from attaining that goal. But the *object* of our attitude is *the attainment of that goal*; and we must want to attain the goal *before* we can find any satisfaction in it. We do not, in other words, desire some sort of "pleasurable consciousness" and then try to figure out how to achieve it; rather, we desire all sorts of different things—money, a new fishing-boat, to be a better chess-player, to get a promotion in our work, etc.—and because we desire these things, we derive satisfaction from attaining them. And so, if someone desires the welfare and happiness of another person, he will derive satisfaction from that; but this does not mean that this satisfaction is the object of his desire, or that he is in any way selfish on account of it.

It is a measure of the weakness of psychological egoism that these insupportable arguments are the ones most often advanced in its favor. Why, then, should anyone ever have thought it a true view? Perhaps because of a desire for theoretical simplicity: In thinking about human conduct, it would be nice if there were some simple formula that would unite the diverse phenomena of human behavior under a single explanatory principle, just as simple formulae in physics bring together a great many apparently different phenomena. And since it is obvious that self-regard is an overwhelmingly important factor in motivation, it is only natural to wonder whether all motivation might not be explained in these terms. But the answer is clearly No; while a great many human actions are motivated entirely or in part by self-interest, only by a deliberate distortion of the facts can we say that all conduct is so motivated. This will be clear, I think, if we correct three confusions which are commonplace. The exposure of these confusions will remove the last traces of plausibility from the psychological egoist thesis.

Having countered the arguments advanced by psychological egoism, Rachels now wants to expose the underlying confusions that account for the persistence of this view over the centuries. There are three such confusions:

> *Confusion 1: It is false* to believe that "selfishness" means the same thing as "self-interest."
>
> *Confusion 2: It is false* to say that every action is done *either* from self-interest or from other-regarding motives.
>
> *Confusion 3: It is false* to assume that a concern for one's own welfare is incompatible with any genuine concern for the welfare of others.

James Rachels, from *Egoism and Moral Skepticism*

The first is the confusion of selfishness with self-interest. The two are clearly not the same. If I see a physician when I am feeling poorly, I am acting in my own interest but no one would think of calling me "selfish" on account of it. Similarly, brushing my teeth, working hard at my job, and obeying the law are all in my self-interest but none of these are examples of selfish conduct. This is because selfish behavior is behavior that ignores the interests of others in circumstances in which their interests ought not to be ignored. This concept has a definite evaluative flavor; to call someone "selfish" is not just to describe his action but to condemn it. Thus, you would not call me selfish for eating a normal meal in normal circumstances (although it may surely be in my self-interest); but you would call me selfish for hoarding food while others about are starving.

The second confusion is the assumption that every action is done *either* from self-interest or from other-regarding motives. Thus, the egoist concludes that if there is no such thing as genuine altruism then all actions must be done from self-interest. But this is certainly a false dichotomy. The man who continues to smoke cigarettes, even after learning about the connection between smoking and cancer, is surely not acting from self-interest, not even by his own standards—self-interest would dictate that he quit smoking at once—and he is not acting altruistically either. He *is*, no doubt, smoking for the pleasure of it, but all that this shows is that undisciplined pleasure-seeking and acting from self-interest are very different. This is what led Butler to remark that "The thing to be lamented is, not that men have so great regard to their own good or interest in the present world, for they have not enough."

The last two paragraphs show (*a*) that it is false that all actions are selfish, and (*b*) that it is false that all actions are done out of self-interest. And it should be noted that these two points can be made, and were, without any appeal to putative examples of altruism.

The third confusion is the common but false assumption that a concern for one's own welfare is incompatible with any genuine concern for the welfare of others. Thus, since it is obvious that everyone (or very nearly everyone) does desire his own well-being, it might be thought that no one can really be concerned with others. But again, this is false. There is no inconsistency in desiring that everyone, including oneself *and* others, be well-off and happy. To be sure, it may happen on occasion that our own interests conflict with the interests of others, and in these cases we will have to make hard choices. But even in these cases we might sometimes opt for the interests of others, especially when the others involved are our family or friends. But more importantly, not all cases are like this: Sometimes we are able to promote the welfare of others when our own interests are not involved at all. In these cases not even the strongest self-regard need prevent us from acting considerately toward others.

Once these confusions are cleared away, it seems to me obvious enough that there is no reason whatever to accept psychological egoism. On the contrary, if we simply observe people's behavior with an open mind we may find that a great deal of it is motivated by self-regard, but by no means all of it; and that there is no reason to deny that "the moral institution of life" can include a place for the virtue of beneficence.

Having dispensed with psychological egoism to his satisfaction, Rachels next turns his attention to ethical egoism—the theory that we *ought* to pursue our own self-interest. According to this view, even if we have the ability to act altruistically, the morally correct thing to do is act in our own self-interest.

James Rachels, from *Egoism and Moral Skepticism*

The ethical egoist would say at this point, "Of course it is possible for people to act altruistically, and perhaps many people do act that way—but there is no reason why they *should* do so. A person is under no obligation to do anything except what is in his own interests." This is really quite a radical doctrine. Suppose I have an urge to set fire to some public building (say, a department store) just for the fascination of watching the spectacular blaze: according to this view, the fact that several people might be burned to death provides no reason whatever why I should not do it. After all, this only concerns *their* welfare, not my own, and according to the ethical egoist the only person I need think of is myself.

Of course, advocates of ethical egoism would likely respond that they are advocating *rational* egoism—choices in one's self-interest that can be supported by cogent reasons and compelling evidence. Setting fires on a whim and other acts of senseless violence are clearly *irrational* actions. But even assuming that the ethical egoist is committed to a doctrine of rationality that prevents monstrous actions, the doctrine still faces several serious objections, including the question of whether it is logically consistent. Rachels remarks:

> The rational egoist, then, cannot advocate that egoism be universally adopted by everyone. For he wants a world in which his own interests are maximized; and if other people adopted the egoistic policy of pursuing their own interests to the exclusion of his interests, as he pursues his interests to the exclusion of theirs, then such a world would be impossible. So he himself will be an egoist, but he will want others to be altruists.

James Rachels,
from *Egoism and Moral Skepticism*

But of course, because the ethical egoist believes that pursuing one's self interests is a universal moral value, he *must* recommend that others follow the same mandate, regardless of the consequences. Ethical egoists seem to believe that as long as everyone follows the principles of rationality, that conflicts in self-interest will work themselves out in a harmonious fashion. This confidence is in part based on the belief that the central purpose of government is to protect each individual's right to personal liberty in a way that doesn't infringe on the rights of others. However, even given this basic framework, many areas of potential conflict may still exist between people actively seeking their own self-interest. Ethical egoism does not appear to have any conceptual tools to resolve these conflicts between competing interests.

 Critics of ethical egoism find the approach to be cold, calculating, impersonal—in a word, nonhuman. Rachels expresses his disdain for ethical egoism in the following passage:

> So a non-egoist will accept "It would harm another person" as a reason not to do an action simply because he cares about what happens to that other person. When the egoist says that he does *not* accept that as a reason, he is saying something quite extraordinary. He is saying that he has no affection for friends or family, that he never feels pity or compassion, that he is the sort of person who can look on scenes of human misery with complete indifference, so long as he is not the one suffering. Genuine egoists, people who really don't care at all about anyone other than themselves, are rare. It is important to keep this in mind when thinking about ethical egoism; it is easy to forget just how fundamental to human psychological makeup the feeling of sympathy is. Indeed, a man without any sympathy at all would scarcely be recognizable as a man; and that is what makes ethical egoism such a disturbing doctrine in the first place.

James Rachels,
from *Egoism and Moral Skepticism*

< READING CRITICALLY >

Analyzing Rachels's Critique of Egoism

- Rachels maintains that "wanting" to help someone when it conflicts with our own self-interest is precisely what we mean when we say someone is "unselfish." Do you agree? Why or why not?
- Some philosophers contend that psychological egoism is flawed because it is not "falsifiable"—that is, there is no way to test the theory because it explains all human behavior in terms of self-interest. As a result, there are no standards or tests we can use to distinguish selfish from unselfish behavior, and so the theory is conceptually useless. How would you analyze this objection to psychological egoism?

- In your view, does Rachels successfully undermine ethical egoism? Why or why not?
- Rachels concludes his critique of ethical egoism with an expression of personal contempt and disapproval: "Indeed, a man without any sympathy at all would scarcely be recognizable as a man; and that is what makes ethical egoism such a disturbing doctrine in the first place." Do you find this to be a persuasive argument? Why or why not?
- Would you consider yourself to be an ethical egoist? If so, why? If not, why not?

8.5 Religion and Universal Values

One of the traditional roles of most religions is to provide moral guidelines for believers in that religion. As we saw in our brief overview of religions earlier in the chapter, and as you can no doubt attest to in your own experience, the supernatural/metaphysical dimensions of a religion are intertwined with implications regarding how we should conduct ourselves during this life on earth. To achieve salvation, Nirvana, eternal life, a relationship with the divine, or any other spiritual end-point, we need to live our lives in accordance with certain principles and values.

This relationship between religion and morality is a natural one for several reasons. First, the core purpose of many religions is to serve as a means to achieve ultimate spiritual transformation. And such a spiritual quest necessarily involves what we think, feel, and do. The way we live our lives becomes a vehicle for achieving ultimate spiritual transformation, and our religion provides us with the ethical roadmap.

Second, religion provides a metaphysical grounding for morality. If a person or people develop an ethical system and instruct us to abide by its principles, we can legitimately ask, "Why should I follow your principles? What gives you special legitimacy over any other person to determine ethical guidelines?" However, if an ethical system is grounded in a supernatural creator or what is thought to be a fundamental principle of the universe, then the ethical system speaks with a special authority. "Why should I follow these principles? Because God (or some other metaphysical authority) endorses these principles." That removes moral values from the level of human-to-human debate and raises it to a spiritual level. This does not mean, however, that the believers cannot engage in thinking philosophically about how to apply those moral values to the complex ethical dilemmas of everyday life.

((•—[**Listen** to the **Interview** *Pope Benedict Warns Against Moral Relativism* on **mysearchlab.com**

thinking philosophically

RELIGION AND YOUR ETHICAL VALUES

- If you were raised in a religious tradition, or you are currently involved in a religion, describe the ethical principles and values that are endorsed by your religion. Do you personally agree with all of these ethical beliefs? Why or why not?
- If participants in your religion were to be asked, "Why do you believe these ethical beliefs should be accepted by others?" what would be the response?

Divine Command Theory

The relationship between religion and morality presents a fascinating philosophical question that was first articulated by Plato in his dialogue, the *Euthyphro*, when he posed the question, "Do the gods love piety because it is pious, or is it pious because they love it?" In other words, is a moral value "good" or "right" because God *commands* it to be so, or is the moral value "good" or "right" *independently* of God's commands (though it is presumably *consistent* with divine moral values). You may be asking yourself, "What difference does it make? If it's right, it's right!" Actually, the answer to this seminal question turns out to make quite a profound difference in our approach to both religion *and* ethics.

For example, imagine that you hear about a barbaric murder that has been committed. The murderer, who freely admits his action, announces that "God commanded me to do it: I had no choice." If you believe, in response to Plato's question, that a moral value is "good" or "right" simply because God commands it to be, then you have to at least admit the possibility that the murderer was acting in an ethically appropriate way. On the other hand, if your response to Plato's question is that a moral value is "good" or "right" independently of any of God's commands, then you leave open the possibility of saying something along the lines of, "This barbaric murder is morally deplorable: It violates the ethical principles of virtually every civilized society, and it doesn't matter what 'God' or 'Gods' you think commanded it: What you did was immoral in the worst possible sense. And it is unthinkable that any supernatural deity would condone such an action."

In short, if you ascribe to what in philosophy and religion is known as the **divine command theory**, what is morally right and good (or wrong and evil), is defined simply by God's will. Our independent moral sense of right and wrong, good and bad, is irrelevant. Here are several examples of divine commands. The first is taken from the Old Testament in the Bible, the second from the Qur'an.

And God spoke all these words, saying,

> *I am the Lord your God, who brought you out of the land of Egypt, out of the house of bondage.*
>   *You shall have no other gods before me.*
>   *You shall not make for yourself a graven image. . . . you shall not bow down to them or serve them; for I the Lord your God am a jealous God, visiting the iniquity of the fathers upon the children to the third and the fourth generation of those who hate me, but showing steadfast love to thousands of those who love me and keep my commandments.*

The Holy Bible, Exodus 20: 1–4

It is not righteousness that you turn your faces towards East or West; but it is righteousness to believe in God and the Last Day and the Angels, and the Book, and the Messengers; to spend of your substance, out of love for Him, for your kin, for orphans, for the needy, for the wayfarer, for those who ask; and for the freeing of captives; to be steadfast in prayers, and practice regular charity; to fulfill the contracts which you made; and to be firm and patient in pain (or suffering) and adversity and throughout all periods of panic. Such are the people of truth, the God-conscious.

The Holy Qur'an, 2:177

Divine command theory. According to divine command theory, we act morally when we follow God's commands. In the Jewish and Christian faiths, it is believed that God inscribed the Ten Commandments on stone tablets and gave them to Moses. [The horns on Moses's head are often interpreted as rays of light.]

Divine commands are not intended to be questioned, critically evaluated, or negotiated by the audience for whom they are intended: The commands are intended to be obeyed—period. Once critical judgment is suspended, there is the danger of individuals becoming vulnerable to manipulative leaders claiming to be following God's command—as we see in the case of cults in which people lose their autonomy and sometimes their lives (for example, the mass suicides/murders of the People's Temple or the Branch Davidian cults). On a social level, the belief that it is our spiritual responsibility to suspend our intellectual independence and follow those who claim to interpret divine commands can lead to bloody and destructive wars and persecutions.

One of the more provocative examples of divine command theory is the story of Abraham and his son, Isaac, from the Old Testament. Abraham is revered as a spiritual exemplar for Judaism, Christianity, and Islam. Yet, as recorded in the following passage, Abraham seemed prepared to murder his only and beloved son, Isaac, for the sole reason that God commanded him to.

The Story of Abraham and Isaac, from *The Bible*

After these things God tested Abraham, and said to him, "Abraham!" And he said, "Here am I." He said, "Take your son, your only son Isaac, whom you love, and go to the land of Mori'ah, and offer him there as a burnt offering upon one of the mountains of which I shall tell you." So Abraham rose early in the morning, saddled his ass, and took two of his young men with him, and his son Isaac; and he cut the wood for the burnt offering, and arose and went to the place of which God had told him. On the third day Abraham lifted up his eyes and saw the place afar off. Then Abraham said to his young men, "Stay here with the ass; I and the lad will go yonder and worship, and come again to you." And Abraham took the wood of the burnt offering, and laid it on Isaac his son, and he took in his hand the fire and the knife. So they went both of them together. And Isaac said to his father Abraham, "My father!" And he said, "Here am I, my son." He said, "Behold, the fire and the wood; but where is the lamb for a burnt offering?" Abraham said, "God will provide himself the lamb for a burnt offering, my son" So they went both of them together.

When they came to the place of which God had told him, Abraham built an altar there, and laid the wood in order, and bound Isaac his son, and laid him on the altar, upon the wood. Then Abraham put forth his hand, and took the knife to slay his son. But the angel of the Lord called to him from heaven, and said, "Abraham, Abraham!" And he said, "Here am I." He said, "Do not lay your hand on the lad or do anything to him; for now I know that you fear God, seeing you have not withheld your son, your only son, from me." And Abraham lifted up his eyes and looked, and behold, behind him was a ram, caught in a thicket by his horns; and Abraham went and took the ram, and offered it up as a burnt offering instead of his son. So Abraham called the name of that place The Lord will provide; as it is said to this day, "On the mount of the Lord it shall be provided."

And the angel of the Lord called to Abraham a second time from heaven, and said, "by myself I have sworn, says the Lord, because you have done this, and have not withheld your son, your only son, I will indeed bless you, and I will multiply your descendants as the stars of heaven and as the sand which is on the seashore."

In this chilling and disturbing account (who could not be touched by Isaac's trusting question, "but where is the lamb for a burnt offering?"), the ethical implications have reverberated for centuries. Within the divine command religions for whom Abraham is considered a patriarch and prophet, his willingness to murder his son at God's command is endorsed as revealing Abraham's great faith. But to people outside of the divine command framework, disturbing questions are raised:

- How could Abraham (and others, by implication) be sure that it was the voice of God and not the voice of Satan or mental illness? This is what Jean-Paul Sartre refers to as "the anguish of Abraham."

- Because God is omniscient, and presumably knows precisely what is in Abraham's heart and mind, why does he need to test his faith in this uniquely barbaric way?

- What kind of God would command a believer to murder an innocent person, simply to demonstrate his uncritical willingness to follow His command without question?

- How would you react to what seemed to be a divine command that violated your personal sense of moral rightness?

Natural Law Theory

As we noted, the divine command theory responds to Plato's provocative question ("Do the gods love piety because it is pious, or is it pious because they love it?") with the response that something is "good" or "right" simply because God commands it to be so. Responding to Plato's question with the converse response—namely, that God loves the "good" and "right" *because* it is good and right, *not* simply because God commands it—leads to an entirely different view of the relationship between religion and moral principles. This alternative view, traditionally known as **natural law ethics**, contends that there are universal moral values which people can discover by using their rational, intellectual and emotional capabilities. For those who believe in God, it is reasonable to assume that such moral principles are consistent with God's nature, because God is good and in creating us, God ensured that we were implanted with the "divine spark," the gift of reason. However, the net effect of this view is that whatever is morally "good" and "right" exist independently of God's commands and can be discovered by people using their gift of reason.

> **Natural law ethics** The ethical theory based on the view that universal moral values can be discovered in nature by using the faculty of reason.

There have been centuries of energetic efforts to provide a foundation for moral principles, a grounding that will remove it from the grip of divine command theory, social conditioning, and the shadowland of inscrutable mystery. It was the ancient Greeks who first elaborated this approach by making a distinction between nature (*physis*) and convention (*nomos*). The social conventions of a society are the customs and beliefs, laws, and tastes that are peculiar to that society. That is why when you examine the numerous cultures in the world, past and present, you find a spectacular diversity in the social fabrics of each society: You are observing the social conventions that are relative to each individual society.

Nature, however, embodies the vast realm of truth that exists on a deeper level than social conventions that exist on the surface. These "natural truths" are *not* relative to each society: They are constant from culture to culture, and from age to age. These truths are rooted in the fundamental *nature* of what it means to be human. According to this view, there is a *natural law* that is based on humanity's essential nature and that is universal and binding on all people. We can discover these natural moral truths through reason and reflection, and they have been articulated in the greatest legal and moral philosophies and theological systems of Western culture (and other world cultures as well). The challenge for each individual and culture is to discover this immutable natural law that underlies the specific conventions of any society. It is an effort that the religious thinker **St. Thomas Aquinas** devoted his life to, and that America's founding fathers sought to articulate in the Declaration of Independence and Constitution. "We hold these truths to be self-evident that all men are created equal, that they are endowed by their Creator with certain inalienable rights. . . ."

St. Thomas Aquinas (1225–1274). This medieval thinker championed natural law ethics, in which universal values are to be discovered in nature through reason. In this portrait by Zubarán, Aquinas achieves sainthood in heaven, and his writing is clearly part of his greatness.

((•●—[**Listen** to the **Podcast**
*Anthony Kenny on
Aquinas's Ethics* on
mysearchlab.com

To discover the specifics of the natural law, we need to develop an in-depth understanding of the essential nature of men and women, not simply as they currently *are*, but as they could be if they were fully morally developed. What are the basic requirements of human fulfillment? What are the most enlightened values that humans can aspire to? What are the norms of conduct that foster the most meaningful and productive society? What are the conditions that maximize an individual's freedom and personal growth? What are the moral responsibilities that we have to each other as members of an interdependent human community?

To answer these difficult questions, many people turn to religion. After all, if we are indeed God's creations (whatever your religion's conception of God), designed in God's image, then it makes sense that by understanding our true nature we will be following the path of both moral *and* spiritual enlightenment. In fact, it would be shocking if there was *not* an essential identity between the ethics of our religion and our natural moral intuitions. By following what Thomas Aquinas described as the "dictates of reason," he believes we are able to discover God's ethic encoded in our human nature, in the same way that we are able to display the mysteries of the physical universe through the study of science. In other words, we can use our critical thinking abilities to reveal the essential moral nature of people, the ideal image of fulfilled human potential—and then use this image to inform our moral choices and guide our personal development.

Thomas Aquinas is one of the most significant Christian thinkers of the medieval period. His systematic development of natural law theory was both innovative and influential, especially on the development of ethical theory in the Catholic Church. His most important work is *The Summa Theologica*, in which he attempts to integrate key elements of Aristotle's thinking with Christian theology. Aquinas's metaphysic includes a hierarchy of laws: *Eternal Law* (the uncreated reason of God that guides the universe); *Divine Law* (the law that directs humans to a vision of God and eternal blessedness); *Natural Law* (the moral laws derived from Divine Law that humans can discover through reason); and *Human Law* (the legislation and custom that govern cultures). In an ideal world, human laws would be faithful reflections of natural law, which is directly based on divine law. Of course, the world is not ideal, and human laws are often poor replicas of natural law.

Quoting Aristotle, Aquinas views the purpose of laws to "make men good by habituating them to good works." This is the mainspring of Aristotle's ethical theory: People become virtuous by acting virtuously, and that is why education and proper laws are necessary to help citizens develop virtuous habits. Thus Aquinas portrays human lawgivers as responsible for creating virtuous laws that reflect (or "partake in") the natural law, which in turn reflects the divine law. Of course, medieval society in Western Europe at the time Aquinas was writing was very different from today's world—it was dominated by the Catholic Church, and the rulers—typically kings—were seen to be the representatives of God on earth. Nevertheless, even given this rigid, hierarchical, religiously permeated society, Aquinas recognized that human laws could be "tyrannical" and "perversions" of virtuous laws. Which leads to the question, "What is a citizen's responsibility when confronted with human laws that she considers to be unjust and immoral?" Individuals such as Gandhi and **Dr. Martin Luther King Jr**. believe that in these circumstances civil disobedience is an appropriate response to protest unjust laws.

thinking philosophically

DO YOU BELIEVE IN NATURAL LAWS?

- Identify three ethical principles that you personally believe reflect "natural laws" that are self-evident and that all people ought to ascribe to. If you don't personally believe that there are any such principles, then identify three such ethical principles that are incorporated into one or more religions (such as the Golden Rule).

- For each of the ethical principles that you just identified, describe a moral situation in which the principle would guide you in making an ethically appropriate decision.

- Aquinas ties his natural law ethic to a comprehensive religious theology. However, Aristotle argued that a belief in God is not necessary for the existence of natural law. Which point of view do you agree with? Why?

- "We hold these truths to be self-evident; that all men are created equal; that they are endowed by their creator with certain inalienable rights; and that among these are life, liberty, and the pursuit of happiness. . . ." So begins the Declaration of Independence. Would this statement have the same authority if the phrase "endowed by their creator" were replaced by the phrase "entitled by natural law"? Why or why not?

Natural law ethics confronts the same challenges as all general ethical theories: First, what precisely *are* the ethical principles, and second, how are these general principles translated into specific, concrete ethical guidelines that are useful to us in making complex moral decisions in our lives? Aquinas's first effort is not particularly helpful: *"Good is to be done and pursued, and evil is to be avoided."* This is, presumably, the purpose of any ethical theory. The salient question is, naturally, what exactly is "good" and "evil"? Next, he cites inborn instincts that we find in all animals: "sexual intercourse, education of offspring, and so forth." Again, this is not ethically instructive, for some of the vexing questions ethical theories must deal with is *when* and *where* such inborn behaviors as sexual intercourse or aggression are ethically appropriate. Finally, Aquinas asserts that natural law (as reflected in our natural inclinations) inspires us to know the truth about God and to live in society with others. And to live harmoniously in society with others, we need to "shun ignorance"

Martin Luther King Jr. (1929–1968). King was an American minister and civil rights leader and winner of the Nobel Peace Prize. In the tradition of natural law ethics, Dr. King believed that "one had a moral responsibility to disobey unjust laws," a position that led to his arrest on several occasions. Do you agree with Dr. King's reasoning?

and "avoid offending those among whom one has to live, and other such things regarding the above inclination." This seems to be more akin to common sense and social customs, rather than ethical principles. Of course, Aquinas spells out his concept of natural law in other passages in *The Summa Theologica*, but his struggles in this passage underscore the difficulty of translating general principles into specific precepts.

From the Birmingham jail, where he was imprisoned as a participant in nonviolent demonstrations against segregation, Dr. Martin Luther King Jr. wrote in longhand the passages from the remarkable letter that follows. It was his response to a public statement of concern and caution issued by eight white religious leaders of the South. Like Thomas Aquinas, King believed that there was a natural law containing universal moral principles by which a society could be judged. There are occasions when our commitment to natural law demands civil disobedience against unjust laws, as Dr. King contends in these excerpts from "Letter from a Birmingham Jail: April 16, 1963."

> **" A just law is a man-made code that squares with the moral law or the law of God. "**

Martin Luther King Jr., from *Letter from a Birmingham Jail*

. . . You express a great deal of anxiety over our willingness to break laws. This is certainly a legitimate concern. Since we so diligently urge people to obey the Supreme Court's decision of 1954 outlawing segregation in the public schools, at first glance it may seem rather paradoxical for us consciously to break laws. One may well ask: "How can you advocate breaking some laws and obeying others?" The answer lies in the fact that there are two types of laws: just and unjust. I would be the first to advocate obeying just laws. One has not only a legal but a moral responsibility to obey just laws. Conversely, one has a moral responsibility to disobey unjust laws. I would agree with St. Augustine that "an unjust law is no law at all."

Now, what is the difference between the two? How does one determine whether a law is just or unjust? A just law is a man-made code that squares with the moral law or the law of God. An unjust law is a code that is out of harmony with the moral law. To put it in the terms of St. Thomas Aquinas: An unjust law is a human law that is not rooted in eternal law and natural law. Any law that uplifts human personality is just. Any law that degrades human personality is unjust. All segregation statutes are unjust because segregation distorts the soul and damages the personality. It gives the segregator a false sense of superiority and the segregated a false sense of inferiority. Segregation, to use the terminology of the Jewish philosopher Martin Buber, substitutes an "I–it" relationship for an "I–thou" relationship and ends up relegating persons to the status of things. Hence segregation is not only politically, economically and sociologically unsound, it is morally wrong and awful. Paul Tillich said that sin is separation. Is not segregation an existential expression of man's tragic separation, his awful estrangement, his terrible sinfulness? Thus it is that I can urge men to obey the 1954 decision of the Supreme Court, for it is morally right; and I can urge them to disobey segregation ordinances, for they are morally wrong.

Let us consider a more concrete example of just and unjust laws. An unjust law is a code that a numerical or power majority group compels a minority group to obey but does not make binding on itself. This is difference made legal. By the same token, a just law is a code that a majority compels a minority to follow and that it is willing to follow itself. This is sameness made legal.

Let me give another explanation. A law is unjust if it is inflicted on a minority that, as a result of being denied the right to vote, had no part in enacting or devising the law. Who can say that the legislature of Alabama which set up that state's segregation laws was democratically elected? Throughout Alabama all sorts of devious methods are used to prevent Negroes from becoming registered voters, and there are some counties in which, even though Negroes constitute a majority of the population, not a single Negro is registered. Can any law enacted under such circumstances be considered democratically structured?

Sometimes a law is just on its face and unjust in its application. For instance, I have been arrested on a charge of parading without a permit. Now, there is nothing wrong in having an ordinance which requires a permit for a parade. But such an ordinance becomes unjust when it is used to maintain segregation and to deny citizens the First Amendment privilege of peaceful assembly and protest.

I hope you are able to see the distinction I am trying to point out. In no sense do I advocate evading or defying the law, as would the rabid segregationist. That would lead to anarchy. One who breaks an unjust law must do so openly, lovingly, and with a willingness to accept the penalty. I submit that an individual who breaks a law that conscience tells him is unjust and who willingly accepts the penalty of imprisonment in order to arouse the conscience of the community over its injustice, is in reality expressing the highest respect for law.

Of course, there is nothing new about this kind of civil disobedience. It was evidenced sublimely in the refusal of Shadrach, Meshach and Abednego to obey the laws of Nebuchadnezzar, on the ground that a higher moral law was at stake. It was practiced superbly by the early Christians, who were willing to face hungry lions and the excruciating pain of chopping blocks rather than submit to certain unjust laws of the Roman Empire. To a degree, academic freedom is a reality today because Socrates practiced civil disobedience.

< READING CRITICALLY >

Analyzing King on Universal Values

- King compares his strategy of civil disobedience to the approach of Socrates in trying to rouse the citizens of Athens from their lethargic slumbers. In what ways do you think this comparison is apt?

  Just as Socrates felt that it was necessary to create a tension in the mind so that individuals could rise from the bondage of myths and half-truths to the unfettered realm of creative analysis and objective appraisal, we must see the need for nonviolent gadflies to create the kind of tension in society that will help men rise from the dark depths of prejudice and racism to the majestic heights of understanding and brotherhood.

- King quotes the theologian Reinhold Niebuhr in observing that "groups tend to be more immoral than individuals." Do you agree with this statement? Why or why not?

- The heart of King's philosophical argument is based on an appeal to universal values—a natural law—that transcends all cultures and time periods. Explain what you consider to be the strengths of this argument. Then identify some potential questions or problems that such a view must confront.

  One has not only a legal but a moral responsibility to obey just laws. Conversely, one has a moral responsibility to disobey unjust laws. I would agree with St. Augustine that "an unjust law is no law at all.". . . To put it in the terms of St. Thomas Aquinas: An unjust law is a human law that is not rooted in eternal law and natural law.

8.6 Making Connections: On Becoming an Ethical Person

In this chapter and the next, we examine theories of ethics and moral behavior. But is this merely an academic exercise, or can you make the connection between theory and the choices you make on a daily basis? The following essay, "The Disparity Between Intellect and Character," is by **Robert Coles**, a professor of psychiatry and medical humanities at Harvard University, who has focused much of his work on the moral development of people, especially children. In this essay he explores the question of how someone can be intellectually knowledgeable about ethics and yet not act ethically or be an ethical person, as well as what responsibility the college community has to encourage students to become more ethically enlightened.

Robert Coles (B. 1929). Professor of psychiatry and medical humanities at Harvard who has written extensively on issues in child psychiatry. His five-volume *Children of Crisis* series won the Pulitzer Prize.

Robert Coles, from *The Disparity Between Intellect and Character*

Over 150 years ago, Ralph Waldo Emerson gave a lecture at Harvard University, which he ended with the terse assertion: "Character is higher than intellect." Even then, this prominent man of letters was worried (as many other writers and thinkers of succeeding generations would be) about the limits of knowledge and the nature of a college's mission. The intellect can grow and grow, he knew, in a person who is smug, ungenerous, even cruel. Institutions originally founded to teach their students how to become good and decent, as well as broadly and deeply literate, may abandon the first mission to concentrate on a driven, narrow book learning—a course of study in no way intent on making a connection between ideas and theories on one hand and, on the other, our lives as we actually live them.

Students have their own way of realizing and trying to come to terms with the split that Emerson addressed. A few years ago, a sophomore student of mine came to see me in great anguish. She had arrived at Harvard from a Midwestern, working-class background. She was trying hard to work her way through college, and, in doing so, cleaned the rooms of some of her fellow students. Again and again, she encountered classmates who apparently had forgotten the meaning of *please*, or *thank you*—no matter how high their Scholastic Assessment Test scores—students who did not hesitate to be rude, even crude toward her.

One day she was not so subtly propositioned by a young man she knew to be a very bright, successful premed student and already an accomplished journalist. This was not the first time he had made such an overture, but now she had reached a breaking point. She had quit her job and was preparing to quit college in what she called "fancy, phony Cambridge."

The student had been part of a seminar I teach, which links Raymond Carver's fiction and poetry with Edward Hopper's paintings and drawings—the thematic convergence of literary and artistic sensibility in exploring American loneliness, both its social and its personal aspects. As she expressed her anxiety and anger to me, she soon was sobbing hard. After her sobs quieted, we began to remember the old days of that class. But she had some weightier matter on her mind and began to give me a detailed, sardonic account of college life, as viewed by someone vulnerable and hardpressed by it. At one point, she observed of the student who had propositioned her: "That guy gets all A's. He tells people he's in Group I (the top academic category). I've taken two moral-reasoning courses with him, and I'm sure he's gotten A's in both of them—and look at how he behaves with me, and I'm sure with others."

She stopped for a moment to let me take that in. I happened to know the young man and could only acknowledge the irony of his behavior, even as I wasn't totally surprised by what she'd experienced. But I was at a loss to know what to say to her. A philosophy major, with a strong interest in literature, she had taken a course on the Holocaust and described for me the ironies she also saw in that tragedy—mass murder of unparalleled historical proportion in a nation hitherto known as one of the most civilized in the world, with a citizenry as well educated as that of any country at the time.

Drawing on her education, the student put before me names such as Martin Heidegger, Carl Jung, Paul De Man, Ezra Pound—brilliant and accomplished men (a philosopher, a psychoanalyst, a literary critic, a poet) who nonetheless had linked themselves with the hate that was Nazism and Fascism during the 1930s. She reminded me of the willingness of the leaders of German and Italian universities to embrace Nazi and Fascist ideas, of the countless doctors and lawyers and judges and journalists and schoolteachers, and, yes, even members of the clergy—who were able to accommodate themselves to murderous thugs because the thugs had political power. She pointedly mentioned, too, the soviet Gulag, that expanse of prisons to which millions of honorable people were sent by Stalin and his brutish accomplices—prisons commonly staffed by psychiatrists quite eager to label those victims of a vicious totalitarian state with an assortment of psychiatric names, then shoot them up with drugs meant to reduce them to zombies.

I tried hard, toward the end of a conversation that lasted almost two hours, to salvage something for her, for myself, and, not least, for a university that I much respect, even as I know its failings. I suggested that if she had learned what she had just shared with me at Harvard—why, *that* was itself a valuable education acquired. She smiled, gave me credit for a "nice try," but remained unconvinced. Then she put this tough, pointed, unnerving question to me: "I've been taking all these philosophy courses, and we talk about what's true, what's important, what's *good*. Well, how do you teach people to *be* good?" And she added: "What's the point of *knowing* good, if you don't keep trying to *become* a good person?"

I suddenly found myself on the defensive, although all along I had been sympathetic to her, to the indignation she had been directing toward some of her fellow students, and to her critical examination of the limits of abstract knowledge. Schools are schools, colleges are colleges, I averred, a complaisant and smug accommodation in my voice. Thereby I meant to say that our schools and colleges these days don't take major responsibility for the moral values of their students, but, rather, assume that their students acquire those values at home. I topped off my surrender to the *status quo* with a shrug of my shoulders, to which she responded with an unspoken but barely concealed anger. This she expressed through a knowing look that announced that she'd taken the full moral measure of me.

Suddenly, she was on her feet preparing to leave. I realized that I'd stumbled badly. I wanted to pursue the discussion, applaud her for taking on a large subject in a forthright, incisive manner, and tell her she was right in understanding that moral reasoning

> **What's the point of *knowing* good, if you don't keep trying to *become* a good person?**

thinking philosophically

CAN MORALITY BE LEARNED IN COLLEGE?

- According to Aristotle:

  The ultimate purpose in studying ethics is not as it is in other inquiries, the attainment of theoretical knowledge; we are not conducting this inquiry in order to know what virtue is, but in order to become good, else there would be no advantage in studying it.

  How would Robert Coles respond to this quote? How do you respond to this quote?

- How do you explain the fact that morally evil people can be highly educated in terms of ethics and religion? In other words, how do you account for the "gap" that sometimes occurs between knowledge of ethics and being an ethical person?

- If you were in Robert Coles's position, what would have been your response to the student's concerns regarding the disconnect between ethics and education?

- If you were teaching a course in ethics, what would be your major goals for the course? For example, in addition to exposing students to the major ethical theories in philosophy, would you also want to encourage students to become more thoughtful and enlightened moral individuals?

- Explain how the following thinkers would respond to the student's concern that colleges do not teach students to become more ethical people: Ruth Benedict, Ayn Rand, James Rachels. Do you think that colleges should be responsible for helping students become more ethical individuals?

is not to be equated with moral conduct. I wanted, really, to explain my shrug—point out that there is only so much that any of us can do to affect others' behavior, that institutional life has its own momentum. But she had no interest in that kind of self-justification—as she let me know in an unforgettable aside as she was departing my office: "I wonder whether Emerson was just being 'smart' in that lecture he gave here. I wonder if he ever had any ideas about what to *do* about what was worrying him—or did he think he'd done enough because he'd spelled the problem out to those Harvard professors?"

She was demonstrating that she understood two levels of irony: One was that the study of philosophy—even moral philosophy or moral reasoning—doesn't necessarily prompt in either the teacher or the student a determination to act in accordance with moral principles. And, further, a discussion of that very irony can prove equally sterile—again carrying no apparent consequences as far as one's everyday actions go.

When that student left my office (she would soon leave Harvard for good), I was exhausted and saddened—and brought up short. All too often those of us who read books or teach don't think to pose for ourselves the kind of ironic dilemma she had posed to me. How might we teachers encourage our students (encourage *ourselves*) to take that big step from thought to action, from moral analysis to fulfilled moral commitments? Rather obviously, community service offers us all a chance to put our money where our mouths are; and, of course, such service can enrich our understanding of the disciplines we study. A reading of *Invisible Man* (literature), *Tally's Corner* (sociology and anthropology), or *Childhood and Society* (psychology and psychoanalysis) takes on new meaning after some time spent in a ghetto school or a clinic. By the same token, such books can prompt us to think pragmatically about, say, how the wisdom that Ralph Ellison worked into his fiction might shape the way we get along with the children we're tutoring—affect our attitudes toward them, the things we say and do with them.

Yet I wonder whether classroom discussion, *per se*, can't also be of help, the skepticism of my student notwithstanding. She had pushed me hard, and I started referring again and again in my classes on moral introspection to what she had observed and learned, and my students more than got the message. Her moral righteousness, her shrewd eye and ear for hypocrisy hovered over us, made us uneasy, goaded us.

She challenged us to prove that what we think intellectually can be connected to our daily deeds. For some of us, the connection was established through community service. But that is not the only possible way. I asked students to write papers that told of particular efforts to honor through action the high thoughts we were discussing. Thus goaded to a certain self-consciousness, I suppose, students made various efforts. I felt that the best of them were small victories, brief epiphanies that might otherwise have been overlooked, but had great significance for the students in question.

"I thanked someone serving me food in the college cafeteria, and then we got to talking, the first time," one student wrote. For her, this was a decisive break with her former indifference to others she abstractly regarded as "the people who work on the serving line." She felt that she had learned something about another's life and had tried to show respect for that life.

The student who challenged me with her angry, melancholy story had pushed me to teach differently. Now, I make an explicit issue of the more than occasional disparity between thinking and doing, and I ask my students to consider how we all might bridge that disparity. To be sure, the task of connecting intellect to character is daunting, as Emerson and others well knew. And any of us can lapse into cynicism, turn the moral challenge of a seminar into yet another moment of opportunism: I'll get an A this time, by writing a paper cannily extolling myself as a doer of this or that "good deed"!

Still, I know that college administrators and faculty members everywhere are struggling with the same issues that I was faced with, and I can testify that many students will respond seriously, in at least small ways, if we make clear that we really believe that the link between moral reasoning and action is important to us. My experience has given me at least a measure of hope that moral reasoning and reflection can somehow be integrated into students'—and teachers'—lives as they actually live them.

writing about philosophy: Moral Issues in Multiculturalism

The Assignment

In "Is Multiculturalism Bad for Women?," philosopher Susan Moller Okin argues that multiculturalism confers minority cultures with special group rights and privileges. Moral dilemmas arise when the practices and customs of the minority cultures conflict with the practices and customs of the majority culture. Examples cited by Okin include the marriage of children or marriages that are otherwise coerced; polygamy; clitoridectomy (female genital mutilation); rapists marrying rape victims; kidnap and rape marriages; wife murders for various reasons; mother–child suicide; ritual sacrifice of animals. Some defenders of multiculturalism argue that these practices of cultural minorities should be protected because without these special rights, the minority culture might be threatened with extinction. And cultural extinction would likely undermine the self-respect and freedom of group members.

Research one such example of a "clash of values" and then answer the following questions:

1. What are the arguments and reasons that the minority culture uses to justify the particular practice or custom?

2. What are the arguments and reasons that the majority culture uses to consider the practice or custom to be immoral and/or illegal?

3. What is your informed perspective on this issue? Be sure to explain the justification for your conclusion.

MySearchLab Connections

Watch. Listen. Explore. Read. Mysearchlab is designed just for you. Each chapter features a customized study plan to help you learn and review key concepts and terms. Dynamic visual activities, videos, and readings found in the multimedia library will enhance your learning experience.

Here are a few questions and activities to help you understand this chapter:

1. **Watch** the **Video** *What is Ethics?* on **mysearchlab.com**   What is the focus of moral philosophy?

2. **Watch** the **Video** *Normative Ethics* on **mysearchlab.com**   How does "normative ethics" differ from metaethics and applied ethics?

3. **Listen** to the **Podcast** *Walter Sinnott-Armstrong on Morality Without God* on **mysearchlab.com**   According to Sinnott-Armstrong, what is the foundation of all morality?

4. **Listen** to the **Interview** *Pope Benedict Warns Against Moral Relativism* on **mysearchlab.com**   What is moral relativism?

5. **Listen** to the **Podcast** *Anthony Kenny on Aquinas's Ethics* on **mysearchlab.com**   Explain the influence of Aristotle on Aquinas's development of his own ethical theory.

Your Moral Compass

- The terms *ethics* and *morals* describe how we *ought* to behave, and the rules and standards we *should* employ in the choices we make. The philosophical study of ethics and morals seeks to analyze and evaluate how different patterns of ethics have evolved and are applied by individuals as well as groups and cultures.

- Descriptive ethics is used to describe and analyze current moral and ethical beliefs and behaviors of an individual or a group. Normative ethics analyzes what *ought* to be the moral and ethical beliefs and choices of an individual or group.

[pp. 428–435]

KEY TERM

ethics

Ethical Relativism

- The theory of ethical subjectivism holds that each individual determines what is morally right or wrong, that he or she should determine their own best course of action by following their own moral compass. Some believe that ethical subjectivism can lead to social isolation and moral apathy, a sort of "every man for himself" attitude.

- Cultural relativism is the social correlative to ethical subjectivism. Cultural relativism holds that each culture has its own inherent moral and ethical beliefs, and that people who do not belong to that culture have no "right" to judge or evaluate those beliefs. Although some cultural relativists (including Ruth Benedict and Franz Boas) worked from the perspective of postcolonialist critics, seeking to undo the "civilizing" damage wrought by imperialist Western cultures on non-Western colonized societies, cultural relativism can be very damaging if it simplistically overlooks injustice.

[pp. 435–445]

KEY TERMS

ethical relativism
ethical subjectivism
descriptive ethics
normative ethics
cultural relativism

for further reading, viewing & research

Read the Primary Source on MySearchLab

In addition to the complete texts of readings in this chapter, the companion DVD contains the following related works:

- Aristotle: *Nicomachean Ethics*
- *The Will to Believe*, William James
- Plato: *The Republic*
- *Elements of Moral Philosophy*, James Rachels

Stories and Films

- **Themes:** Developing a moral compass, personal ethics vs. societal norms, universal moral values, ethical relativism vs. absolutism, ethical responses to injustice.

- **Questions to Consider:** In the works listed below, where do you see different value systems coming into conflict? What are the ethical values of the communities each of the characters come from? Are they acting unethically if they defy these values? Is it ethical to respond to injustice through the use of force? Are there universal moral values that emerge in any of the works? Can something that is considered to be unethical in one culture be ethical in another? Do we have an innate sense of right and wrong, or is it learned?

Is violence against another justified if it does not break the ethical code of your culture/community? Does the public have a right to be informed about products that could potentially harm them?

Film

- ***Crash*** (2005) In Los Angeles, the lives of many different people are brought together by a single car crash. The collection of people affected include a police detective with an addict mother, two car thieves, a racist cop, a district attorney and his high maintenance wife, a successful Hollywood director, and a storeowner who is the victim of a hate crime. Issues of race, class, identity, and self-understanding come to the forefront as the characters interact and react to the events.

- ***Do the Right Thing*** (1989) Produced, written, directed by, and starring Spike Lee, this film deals with issues of racial conflict and prejudice in Brooklyn, New York. During one of the hottest days of summer, the tensions in the neighborhood explode into violence.

Ethical Absolutism: Some Moral Values Are Universal

- The converse of relativism is ethical absolutism, which holds that some moral and ethical values apply to all peoples in all circumstances. Although ethical absolutism acknowledges—through descriptive ethics—that different individuals and groups hold different moral and ethical principles, the ethical absolutist (unlike the ethical relativist) does not then hold those beliefs as *normative*—applicable to all people everywhere. However, there is no one "universal code" toward which ethical absolutists can point in support of their perspective. Absolutists argue, based on our own lived experience, that most people conduct themselves *as though there were* such a universal code. Most people, for example, believe that murder is "wrong," and that coming to the aid of someone in distress is "right."

[pp. 445–454]

KEY TERM
ethical absolutism

Egoism as a Universal Principle

- Ethical egoism is the belief that acting in your own best personal interests is the most ethical and moral way to conduct your life. Ethical egoists believe that such traditional community values as altruism, empathy, and social responsibility to those in need actually erode both the personal and the common good. Novelist Ayn Rand went one step further with her theory of rational egoism, which holds that altruism encourages people to *not* pursue their own self-interest, which should be the highest virtuous motivation. She is careful to point out, however, that to act in one's self-interest implies a responsibility to act *rationally*, not to simply satisfy whatever impulses you might be feeling at any particular moment.

[pp. 454–466]

KEY TERMS
ethical egoism
social contract theory
psychological egoism

Religion and Universal Values

- Many individuals and groups set their moral and ethical compass by a specific religious doctrine, in what is known as the divine command theory. Such people believe that what is morally "right" or "wrong" is determined by whatever god(s) they worship. In contrast, natural law ethics holds that there is an eternal, true "human nature" that provides a written moral code for all human beliefs as to what actions are "right" and what are "wrong." There is a long tradition in many religions of working to connect this innate, "natural" facility for determining right and wrong with a divine and unchanging moral principle.

[pp. 466–473]

KEY TERMS
divine command theory
natural law ethics

- ***Gandhi* (1982)** This film portrays the life of Mahatma Gandhi, a small-time lawyer in India who became a political leader, using peaceful means to free India from British colonial rule in the first half of the twentieth century. The film begins with Gandhi's assassination and then flashes back to the beginnings of his political involvement.

- ***The Godfather* (1972)** The first in a series of crime films based on the Mario Puzo novel, this first part chronicles the life of the Corleone Mafia family in New York in the mid-twentieth century. As godfather Don Vito Corleone tries to control the Mafia underworld, we also see the story of his family develop.

- ***The Insider* (1999)** Based on the true story from a 1994 *60 Minutes* episode, this film tells the story of former tobacco executive, Jeffrey Wigand, who agrees to appear on the show to talk about unethical behavior and malpractice in the tobacco industry. On advice from their lawyers and pressure from higher-ups, the show opts not to air the interview.

- ***Monsoon Wedding* (2001)** In modern-day India, a young woman from an upper-class family is about to marry a man she has never meant according to the traditions of arranged marriages. This film follows the celebrations and events leading up to the wedding, and portrays five different romantic entanglements that threaten the limits of class, nation, and morality.

- ***Paradise Now* (2005)** Two Palestinian childhood friends spend their final days together after being recruited as suicide bombers to launch an attack in Israel. After a series of complications, both men reflect on their reasons for participating in the attack, and each must decide whether or not he will go through with it.

- ***Wall Street* (1987)** A motivated stockbroker becomes involved in the Wall Street world of fast money and questionable business deals. As he begins to live out the "Greed is Good" philosophy of another broker, he finds himself torn between this new life and the values with which he was raised.

Literature

- *The Sheltering Sky*, Paul Bowles
- *Medea*, Euripides
- *The Lottery,* Shirley Jackson
- *The Tragical History of Doctor Faustus*, Christopher Marlowe
- *Everything That Rises Must Converge*, Flannery O'Connor
- *Atlas Shrugged,* Ayn Rand
- *The Fountainhead*, Ayn Rand
- *Fathers and Sons*, Ivan Turgenev
- *The Invisible Man*, H. G. Wells

479

Virtue Ethics: Aristotle

Moral rightness is the result of creating a virtuous character by acting in accord with "The Golden Mean."

Deontology: Immanuel Kant

Obeying one's duty, as dictated by "the categorical imperative" is morally right.

what are right actions?

CONSTRUCTING AN ETHICAL THEORY

Existentialist Ethics

Becoming an authentic individual is our moral responsibility.

Søren Kierkegaard

Friedrich Nietzsche

Albert Camus

Utilitarianism: Jeremy Bentham

Actions that promote the greatest happiness for the greatest number of people are morally right.

John Stuart Mill

Higher pleasures have greater worth.

Peter Singer

Utilitarian principles also apply to animals.

Jean-Paul Sartre

Simone de Beauvoir

◀ **Are we all Sisyphus?** This painting depicts the eternal punishment of Sisyphus, a figure from ancient Greek mythology who was condemned to the absurd task of eternally moving a boulder to the top of a mountain only to watch it roll down again. In this chapter, you will learn about the human quest to make morally enlightened choices and create meaningful, purposeful lives.

9.1 Expanding Your Knowledge of Moral Philosophy

The first part of our explorations into the moral realm—Chapter 8—introduced the debate over whether it is possible to find moral truths. We considered the arguments for and against relativism, the idea that what is right depends on the individual or the culture. We examined ethical egoism, in which the individual's interests are placed above all others. Finally, we explored the belief that moral truths come from God or another higher power and that these truths are either given to us in sacred writing or are to be discovered in nature.

In this chapter, we will consider various philosophical attempts to construct an overarching theory that can guide our moral decisions. While several of these theories are compatible with a belief in God and the commandments or other moral laws, they offer alternative ways to evaluate moral actions. By considering the moral reasoning of the philosophers in this chapter, you will open yourself to the human project of creating yourself to be a person of moral value, making morally enlightened choices that express your deepest convictions and highest aspirations.

The most difficult decisions we will face in our lives challenge us to answer the question, "What are right actions?" The philosophers in this chapter approach this question from very different perspectives. For Aristotle, the answer to the question, "What are right actions?" requires another question: "What is the right way to *be*?" The moral quality or *virtue* of the person is fundamental. The Enlightenment philosopher Immanuel Kant focuses on discovering moral *maxims*, asking "Can this law apply to all rational creatures?" The late eighteenth- and nineteenth-century philosophers Jeremy Bentham and John Stuart Mill approach the question of right actions by focusing on *consequences*: "What actions will bring the best outcome?" In the twentieth century, existential philosophers consider the *authenticity* of an action: "Can I accept full responsibility for my choice?" Proponents of the ethics of care consider whether an action expresses empathy and understanding for another. While our survey of moral theories is not exhaustive, it should help you reexamine your own moral compass and make morally enlightened choices.

> **We are not concerned to know what goodness is, but how we are to become good men, for this alone gives the study (of ethics) its practical value.**
> **ARISTOTLE**

Virtue ethics The ethical theory that focuses on the moral quality of individuals rather than their actions.

9.2 Character: Virtue Ethics

The towering Greek philosopher **Aristotle** was a passionate exponent of **virtue ethics**, as were many of the early Greek philosophers. Aristotle was a student of Plato, founded his own school (the Lyceum), wrote prodigiously on a staggering variety of topics, and even tutored a young boy who was to become Alexander the Great. Aristotle set the tone of the virtue ethics approach with his observation that in exploring the moral dimension of experience, "We are discussing no small matter, but how we ought to live," a sentiment that echoed Socrates' commitment to moral action.

Aristotle (384–322 B.C.E.). This ancient Greek philosopher and student of Plato charted a different direction from his teacher. Aristotle made major contributions to metaphysics, ethics, politics, logic, and aesthetics. He is also responsible for conceptualizing the different branches of philosophy.

For Aristotle and other believers in virtue ethics, it is the cultivation of a virtuous *character* that is the goal of ethics, to *become* a virtuous person. The assumption is that genuinely virtuous people will act in morally principled ways as a natural expression of their moral goodness. And these moral actions will in turn strengthen their virtuous nature. Aristotle's particular brand of virtue ethics has had a dominating impact on moral thinking for several thousand years. Aristotle's major work in this area is *The Nicomachean Ethics*, named after his son Nicomachus. Let's explore his central ethical themes as expressed in this enduring treatise, beginning with his views on the nature of moral character and the ultimate goal for which all humans strive.

Aristotle, from *The Nicomachean Ethics*

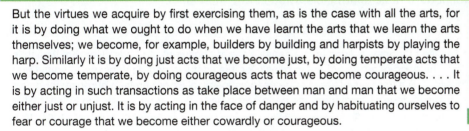

But the virtues we acquire by first exercising them, as is the case with all the arts, for it is by doing what we ought to do when we have learnt the arts that we learn the arts themselves; we become, for example, builders by building and harpists by playing the harp. Similarly it is by doing just acts that we become just, by doing temperate acts that we become temperate, by doing courageous acts that we become courageous. . . . It is by acting in such transactions as take place between man and man that we become either just or unjust. It is by acting in the face of danger and by habituating ourselves to fear or courage that we become either cowardly or courageous.

The concept of *character*, as a "virtuous character," is derived from the Greek word *charakter*, a term that itself comes from the word *charassein*, which means "to make sharp" or "to engrave." And in a sense that is precisely how we form our characters, by gradually etching their outlines and dimensions through the moral choices that we make every day of our lives. Your *moral character* refers to the integrated totality of your moral traits and dispositions, the ways in which you habitually respond when confronted with moral choices. Your character typically displays consistency and coherence because it has been created gradually, inscribed over the totality of your life. This doesn't mean that you can't change or refine your character, only that such changes and refinements are likely to take time as you alter your personal self-portrait by making different choices.

As all knowledge and moral purpose aspires to some good, what is in our view the good at which the political science aims, and what is the highest of all practical goods? As to its name there is, I may say, a general agreement. The masses and the cultured classes

Aristotle, from *The Nicomachean Ethics*

agree in calling it happiness, and conceive that "to live well" or "to do well" is the same thing as "to be happy." But as to the nature of happiness they do not agree, nor do the masses give the same account of it as the philosophers.

Aristotle was a scientist by inclination and training, and so he grounded his inquiry into ethics on empirical observations: What *are* the ultimate aims that people strive for in life? Most people would state that their preeminent goal is to "be happy" and to "live well." Yet people have many different notions of precisely what "being happy" and "living well" actually mean. For Aristotle, one thing that it definitely *doesn't* mean is the hedonistic notion of seeking sensual, unrefined pleasure, which he considered to be "a life fit only for cattle" (foreshadowing John Stuart Mill's warning centuries later against the bankruptcy of a life lived as "a contented pig").

Aristotle, from *The Nicomachean Ethics*

Ordinary or vulgar people conceive (the good) to be pleasure, and accordingly approve a life of enjoyment. . . . Now the mass of men present an absolutely slavish appearance, as choosing the life of brute beasts, but they meet with consideration because so many persons in authority share (such) tastes.

For Aristotle, as for Socrates, devoting your life to acquiring such things as wealth, fame, or public success is as limited a life as seeking pleasure: These goals do not reflect the talents and values that define the human soul. Despite their popularity among people, pleasure, wealth, fame, and success are superficial and transient and will never be able to bring deep and lasting fulfillment.

Aristotle, from *The Nicomachean Ethics*

The life of money-making is in a sense a life of constraint, and it is clear that wealth is not the good of which we are in quest; for it is useful in part as a means to something else. . . . But (the love of fame) appears too superficial for our present purpose; for honor seems to depend more upon the people who pay it than upon the person to whom it is paid, and we have an intuitive feeling that the good is something which is proper to a man himself and cannot be easily taken away from him.

But if these common values in human affairs do not embody "living well," then what does? Aristotle believes that to answer this question, we need to understand the true nature of human "happiness."

Aristotle, from *The Nicomachean Ethics*

> **Inasmuch as happiness is an activity of the soul in accordance with complete or perfect virtue, it is necessary to consider virtue, as this will perhaps be the best way of studying happiness.**

We speak of that which is sought after for its own sake as more final than that which is sought after as a means to something else; we speak of that which is never desired as a means to something else as more final than the things which are desired both in themselves and as means to something else; and we speak of a thing as absolutely final if it is always desired in itself and never as a means to something else.

It seems that happiness pre-eminently answers to this description, as we always desire happiness for its own sake and never as a means to something else, whereas we desire honor, pleasure, intellect, and every virtue, partly for their own sakes (for we should desire them independently of what might result from them) but partly also as being means to happiness, because we suppose they will prove the instruments of happiness. Happiness, on the other hand, nobody desires for the sake of these things, nor indeed as a means to anything else at all. If we define the function of Man as a kind of life, and this life as an activity of soul, or a course of action in conformity with reason, if the function of a good man is such activity or action of a good and noble kind, and if everything is successfully performed when it is performed in accordance with its proper excellence, it follows that the good of Man is an activity of the soul in accordance with virtue or, if there are more virtues than one, accordance with the best and most complete virtue. But it is necessary to add the words "in a complete life." For as one swallow or one day does not make a spring, so one day or a short time does not make a fortunate or happy man. . . .

Inasmuch as happiness is an activity of the soul in accordance with complete or perfect virtue, it is necessary to consider virtue, as this will perhaps be the best way of studying happiness.

In this rich, insightful passage, Aristotle points out that, though we desire pleasure, wealth, fame, and success, we desire them mainly because we hope that they will bring us happiness. Similarly, people often strive to achieve virtues such as honor and intellectual insight, though again the ultimate aim is to be happy.

Happiness, for Aristotle, is expressed in the Greek word *eudaemonia*, which means "actively exercising your soul's powers." What exactly does this mean? It means that achieving happiness necessarily involves fulfilling your distinctive function as a human being, living your life in accordance with reason and virtue. This constitutes the "good life" for you and every other human being.

For Aristotle, every element of the universe has an ultimate goal or purpose, a *raison d'être* (reason for being). This view of the universe is known as **teleological**, a philosophical perspective in which all things are understood in terms of their unique end, purpose, or goal, as Aristotle explains: "Every art and every scientific inquiry, and similarly every action and purpose, may be said to aim at some good. Hence the good has been well defined as that at which all things aim."

Teleological The view that everything has a design or purpose.

The natural principle that drives the teleology of the universe is **entelechy**, a principle that reveals that all events occur according to a natural design. In humans, our entelechy is embodied in our souls, which exist as the "form" of our bodies. What makes the human soul distinctive is its capacity to reason, reflect, and make choices. Thus, achieving your unique purpose in life, and experiencing genuine happiness in the process, means choosing to permit your soul to reach its full potential, to exercise its full powers in accord with reason and virtue (which is based on reason). Fulfilling your human potential is a lifelong project, not a one-time occurrence. As Aristotle so eloquently observes, creating a "complete life" is an evolving process, "For as one swallow or one day does not make a spring, so one day or a short time does not make a fortunate or happy man."

Entelechy The principle that reveals that all events occur according to a natural design. All elements of the universe embody a distinctive essence or potential, the purpose of which is to achieve full expression.

All of these considerations lead Aristotle to conclude that "happiness is an activity of the soul in accordance with complete or perfect virtue." But to understand what this means, we need to develop a clear and concrete sense of what Aristotle has in mind with the term *virtue*.

Aristotle establishes two distinct categories of virtues, "intellectual" and "moral." Intellectual virtues include qualities such as wisdom, knowledge, rationality, clarity of understanding, and cognitive intelligence. Aristotle believes that intellectual virtues are developed through teaching and practice over time. For example, that is the express purpose of your education, from kindergarten to the present—to stimulate and guide you to develop a basic framework of knowledge, as well as the sophisticated thinking and language abilities needed to communicate and use this knowledge in

What are the highest virtues? This sculpture depicts the Christian virtues of faith (the woman holding a beacon), hope (the woman with an anchor), and charity (the woman with poor children). What three virtues do you think are most important?

productive ways. The fact that you can analyze a work of literature, apply a psychological theory, explain the roots of modern consciousness, discuss the implication of the Internet on human affairs, solve a quadratic equation, understand the biochemistry of Alzheimer's disease, interpret a modern painting, or perform any other of a countless number of intellectual operations—all these abilities reflect intellectual virtues you have developed through your educational experiences.

Moral virtues are somewhat different in nature, and they include qualities such as being temperate, just, courageous, compassionate, generous, friendly, and truthful. Moral virtues are also developed over time; but, unlike intellectual virtues that require a great deal of formal instruction, Aristotle believes that moral virtues are mainly developed through consistent and ongoing practice. Becoming a compassionate person necessarily involves engaging in ongoing acts of compassion toward other deserving people. Gradually, acting compassionately becomes a habitual way of thinking and behaving, an important element in the shaping of your character. People who know you *expect* you to be compassionate in appropriate situations because this virtue reflects an intrinsic part of "who" you are.

Certainly this reasoning of Aristotle's seems to make sense on a surface level: "Moral states are the result of activities corresponding to the moral states themselves." It's difficult to take issue with the argument that you become courageous by acting coura-

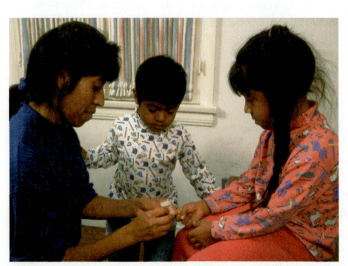

How do we become virtuous? Do you agree with Aristotle that we develop a virtuous character by performing virtuous acts, gradually developing the "habit" of virtue?

geously, honest by acting honestly, and so on. But this formulation also leads immediately to serious questions: What precisely is meant by moral virtues such as *compassion, courage, honesty*? And assuming that we can clearly define these moral virtues, how do we motivate people (and ourselves) to emulate these qualities in our daily lives? Particularly because moral choices often involve agonizing conflicts between competing desires? And how do we encourage people (and ourselves) to commit to these moral virtues over a long period of time, to shape their characters to include them as constitutive elements? Even Aristotle recognizes that simply *knowing* what a moral virtue is or the ethically correct course of action is no guarantee that a person is going to *will* him- or herself to make the morally enlightened choice, as he observes: "Our ability to perform such actions is in no way enhanced by knowing them since the virtues are characteristics (that is, fixed capacities for action, acquired by habit)." Aristotle clearly recognizes the need to address these questions because, after all, it seems almost tautological to observe that "you become moral by being moral." Let's examine how he approaches this apparent dilemma.

> But it may be asked what we mean by saying that people must become just by doing what is just and temperate by doing what is temperate. For if they do what is just and temperate, they are *ipso facto* proved, it will be said, to be just and temperate in the same way as, if they practice grammar and music, they are proved to be grammarians and musicians. . . .
>
> But actions in accordance with virtue are not, for example, justly or temperately performed (merely) because they are in themselves just or temperate. It is necessary that the agent at the time of performing them should satisfy certain conditions, that is, in the first place that he should know what he is doing, secondly that he should deliberately choose to do it and to do it for its own sake, and thirdly that he should do it as an instance of a settled and immutable moral state. If it be a question whether a person possesses any art, these conditions, except indeed the condition of knowledge, are not taken into account; but if it be a question of possessing the virtues, the mere knowledge is of little or no avail, and it is the other conditions, which are the results of frequently performing just or temperate actions, that are not of slight but of absolute importance. Accordingly deeds are said to be just and temperate, when they are such as a just or temperate person would do, and a just and temperate person is not merely one who does these deeds but one who does them in the spirit of the just and the temperate. . . .

Aristotle, from *The Nicomachean Ethics*

" **[A] just and temperate person is not merely one who does these deeds but one who does them in the spirit of the just and the temperate.** "

For Aristotle, the experience of acting morally (compassionately, courageously, truthfully, and so on) counts as an authentic moral action only if the following conditions apply. The person acting should

- *know* what he or she is doing. In other words, if you are acting compassionately, you should be aware of what the moral virtue of compassion is and be aware that you are acting that way.

- *deliberately choose* to do it and *do it for its own sake.* In other words, the compassionate action doesn't really count if the person is not *willing* to do it intentionally. If it's an accidental or unconscious action, it may still have beneficial consequences for the person on the receiving end, but it will not help the person acting to develop compassion as a habitual part of her or his moral character.

- do it as an example of a *settled and immutable moral state.* In other words, authentic moral choices should reflect an established and committed moral character. If the compassionate act is merely a random action inconsistent with the person's underlying character, there is no reason to think that the choice reflects a genuine moral virtue or that we can expect more such compassionate acts on a regular basis.

This further articulation of his position may help Aristotle address some of the questions regarding his ethical approach, but still unarticulated is how we go about defining moral virtues in a precise and persuasive way. Aristotle responds to this challenge with his famous doctrine of the **Golden Mean**, a moral philosophy that is based on the concepts of temperance (moderation), self-discipline, and balance (an approach analogous to the "Middle Way" practiced in Buddhism).

Golden Mean In Aristotle's ethics, the desirable middle between two extremes, one of excess and the other of deficiency.

Aristotle, from *The Nicomachean Ethics*

> First of all, it must be observed that the nature of moral qualities is such that they are destroyed by defect and by excess. We see the same thing happen in the case of strength and of health . . . excess as well as deficiency of physical exercise destroys our strength, and similarly, too much and too little food and drink destroys our health; the proportionate amount, however, produces, increases, and strengthens it. The same applies to self-control, courage, and the other virtues: the man who shuns and fears everything becomes a coward, whereas a man who knows no fear at all and goes to meet every danger becomes reckless. Similarly, a man who revels in every pleasure and abstains from none becomes self-indulgent, while he who avoids every pleasure like a boor becomes what might be called insensitive. Thus we see that self-control and courage are destroyed by excess and deficiency and are preserved by the mean.

> **"Thus we see that self-control and courage are destroyed by excess and deficiency and are preserved by the mean."**

Again the scientist in Aristotle influences him to reason from the physical world to the moral world. How do we determine the appropriate amount of physical exercise in which to engage or the right amount of food and drink to ingest? We reason away from the extremes until we arrive at the optimal amount to promote health and happiness. The danger, Aristotle believes, lies in the extremes: Too much (or too little) exercise, food, or drink can be destructive. Thus we need to avoid the extremes and focus on the ideal balance between them. But we can't use the same rigid standard for everyone: We need to evaluate each situation on its own merits. The ideal amount of exercise (or food or drink) for one person is likely to be very different than for another.

The same principles apply to determining moral virtues. For example, let's take a concept like seeking sensuous pleasure. For many of the hedonists, the "good life" consists in trying to maximize the amount of pleasure that you are receiving. Aristotle, however, believes that this attitude is ruinous. An excessive focus on sensuous pleasure leads to a life of self-indulgence and dissipation. At the other extreme, people who deny themselves any sensuous pleasure are ascetic and often self-righteous boors. The virtuous ideal is the mean between these two extremes: people who fully appreciate sensuous pleasures, but who integrate these pleasures into their lives in healthy and harmonious ways through the exercise of self-discipline and intelligent judgment. Aristotle goes on to elaborate this way of thinking.

Aristotle, from *The Nicomachean Ethics*

> Every science then performs its function well, if it regards the mean and refers the works which it produces to the mean. This is the reason why it is usually said of successful works that it is impossible to take anything from them or to add anything to them, which implies that excess or deficiency is fatal to excellence but that the mean state ensures it. Good artists too, as we say, have an eye to the mean in their works. But virtue, like Nature herself, is more accurate and better than any art; virtue therefore will aim at the mean;—I speak of moral virtue, as it is moral virtue which is concerned with emotions and actions, and it is these which admit of excess and deficiency and the mean. Thus, it is possible to go too far, or not to go far enough, in respect of fear, courage, desire, anger, pity, and pleasure and pain generally, and the excess and the deficiency are alike wrong; but to experience these emotions at the right times and on the right occasions and towards the right persons and for the right causes and in the right manner is the mean or the supreme good, which is characteristic of virtue. Similarly there may be excess, deficiency, or the mean, in regard to actions. But virtue is concerned with emotions and actions, and here excess is an error and deficiency a fault, whereas the mean is successful and laudable, and success and merit are both characteristics of virtue.

It appears then that virtue is a mean state, so far at least as it aims at the mean.

Again, there are many different ways of going wrong; for evil is in its nature infinite, to use the Pythagorean figure, but good is finite. But there is only one possible way of going right. Accordingly, the former is easy and the latter difficult; it is easy to miss the mark but difficult to hit it. This again is a reason why excess and deficiency are characteristics of vice and the mean state a characteristic of virtue.

For good is simple, evil manifold.

Virtue then is a state of deliberate moral purpose consisting in a mean that is relative to ourselves, the mean being determined by reason, or as a prudent man would determine it. It is a mean state firstly as lying between two vices, the vice of excess on the one hand, and the vice of deficiency on the other, and secondly because, whereas the vices either fall short of or go beyond what is proper in the emotions and action, virtue not only discovers but embraces the mean.

> **Again, there are many different ways of going wrong. . . . But there is only one possible way of going right.**

Although Aristotle's Golden Mean approach has a certain commonsense appeal, it's an approach that also raises serious questions. For example, if the ideal virtue—the mean state—varies from person to person, situation to situation, how can we know for certain if we are "hitting the mark," particularly because Aristotle describes how difficult such moral accuracy is? And in the case of conflicting opinions regarding what "hitting the mark" actually means, what standard can we use to decide? One person's pleasure may be another person's self-indulgence and another person's exaggerated self-denial. Or, as the twentieth-century philosopher Bertrand Russell noted in a famous declension:

I am firm.   You are stubborn.   He is pigheaded.

Aristotle tries to address this concern by introducing two proposed criteria: "Virtue then is a state of deliberate moral purpose consisting in a mean that is relative to ourselves, the mean being determined by reason, or as a prudent man would determine it." But this only delays the problem: How precisely do we determine what "reason" is advising or who a "prudent man" is?

Aristotle's alternative response to this question is to provide a more concrete and detailed description of each of the virtues, with the hope that his analysis will resonate with us, that our experience with these concepts of ideal virtues will be consistent with his own. From this point of view, the ultimate determinant of what is morally virtuous is determined by each individual, using his or her accumulated experience and ability to reason to define his or her own personal Golden Mean. As you think through Aristotle's analysis of these moral virtues, ask yourself whether his concepts are consistent with your own, and if not, why not.

But, first, Aristotle wants to point out that not all behaviors or emotions are appropriate for a Golden Mean analysis: Some things are just vices, pure and simple.

How do we discover the Golden Mean? If Aristotle were to speak at your college, what advice do you think he would give to students regarding how best to achieve happiness and "the good life"?

Aristotle, from *The Nicomachean Ethics*

But it is not every action or every emotion that admits of a mean state. There are some whose very name implies wickedness, as for example, malice, shamelessness, and envy, among emotions, or adultery, theft, and murder, among actions. All these, and others like them, are censured as being intrinsically wicked, not merely the excesses or deficiencies of them. It is never possible then to be right in respect of them; they are always sinful. Right or wrong in such actions as adultery does not depend on our committing them with the right person, at the right time or in the right manner; on the contrary it is sinful to do anything of the kind at all. It would be equally wrong then to suppose that there can be a mean state or an excess or deficiency in unjust, cowardly or licentious conduct; for, if it were so, there would be a mean state of an excess or of a deficiency, an excess of an excess and a deficiency of a deficiency. But as in temperance and courage there can be no excess or deficiency because the mean is, in a sense, an extreme, so too in these cases there cannot be a mean or an excess or deficiency, but, however the acts may be done, they are wrong. For it is a general rule that an excess or deficiency does not admit of a mean state, nor a mean state of an excess or deficiency.

But it is not enough to lay down this as a general rule; it is necessary to apply it to particular cases, as in reasonings upon actions, general statements, although they are broader, are less exact than particular statements. For all action refers to particulars, and it is essential that our theories should harmonize with the particular cases to which they apply. We must take particular virtues then from the catalogue of virtues.

In regard to feelings of fear and confidence, courage is a mean state. On the side of excess, he whose fearlessness is excessive has no name, as often happens, but he whose confidence is excessive is foolhardy, while he whose timidity is excessive and whose confidence is deficient is a coward.

In respect of pleasures and pains, although not indeed of all pleasures and pains, and to a less extent in respect of pains than of pleasures, the mean state is temperance, the excess is licentiousness. We never find people who are deficient in regard to pleasures; accordingly such people again have not received a name, but we may call them insensible.

As regards the giving and taking of money, the mean state is liberality, the excess and deficiency are prodigality and illiberality. Here the excess and deficiency take opposite forms; for while the prodigal man is excessive in spending and deficient in taking, the illiberal man is excessive in taking and deficient in spending.

(For the present we are giving only a rough and summary account of the virtues, and that is sufficient for our purpose; we will hereafter determine their character more exactly.)

Aristotle then proceeds to perform a comparable analysis with respect to attitudes toward money, honor and dishonor, the expression of emotions, truthfulness, and even a sense of humor! The following chart summarizes his analysis of the various virtues and vices considered in this passage:

Deficiency/Vice	Mean/Virtue	Excess/Vice
Cowardice	Courage	Foolhardiness
Inhibition	Temperance	Overindulgence
Stinginess	Generosity	Profligacy
Shabbiness	Magnificence	Vulgarity
Standoffishness	Friendliness	Obsequiousness
Shyness	Proper pride	Vanity
Celibacy	Monogamy	Promiscuity
Dullness	Well-roundedness	Wildness
Maliciousness	Righteous indignation	Envy
Sarcasm	Truthfulness	Boastfulness
Boorishness	Wittiness	Buffoonery
Shamelessness	Modesty	Shamefacedness

Being virtuous is a difficult and complicated process, according to Aristotle. Take something like generosity: What is the Golden Mean, the ideal virtuous state? Giving the "right amount" to the "right persons" at the "right time" and for the "right cause." It's no wonder that he ends on the cautionary note that "it is rare and laudable and noble to do well."

It has now been sufficiently shown that moral virtue is a mean state, and in what sense it is a mean state; it is a mean state as lying between two vices, a vice of excess on the one side and a vice of deficiency on the other, and as aiming at the mean in the emotions and actions.

That is the reason why it is so hard to be virtuous; for it is always hard work to find the mean in anything, for example, it is not everybody, but only a man of science, who can find the mean or center of a circle. So too anybody can get angry—that is an easy matter—and anybody can give or spend money, but to give it to the right persons, to give the right amount of it and to give it at the right time and for the right cause and in the right way, this is not what anybody can do, nor is it easy. That is the reason why it is rare and laudable and noble to do well.

Aristotle, from *The Nicomachean Ethics*

For Aristotle, a virtuous life—the way that we ought to live—involves a balanced and harmonious integration of the various behaviors, values, emotions, and attitudes, in accordance with the Golden Mean. But all virtues are not equal, according to Aristotle. The most virtuous life is one devoted to intellectual reflection and contemplation, and it is this life that leads to the greatest possible human happiness, as Aristotle describes in the following passage:

We said that happiness is not a habit or trained faculty. If it were, it would be within the reach of a man who slept all his days and lived the life of a vegetable, or of a man who met with the greatest misfortunes. As we cannot accept this conclusion we must place happiness in some exercise of faculty, as we said before. But as the exercises of faculty are sometimes necessary (*i.e.* desirable for the sake of something else), sometimes desirable in themselves, it is evident that happiness must be placed among those that are desirable in themselves, and not among those that are desirable for the sake of something else: for happiness lacks nothing; it is sufficient in itself. . . .

Now, the exercise of those trained faculties which are proper to him is what each man finds most desirable; what the perfect man finds most desirable, therefore, is the exercise of virtue. Happiness, therefore, does not consist in amusement; and indeed it is absurd to suppose that the end is amusement, and that we toil and moil all our life long for the sake of amusing ourselves. We may say that we choose everything for the sake of something else, excepting only happiness; for it is the end. But to be serious and to labour for the sake of amusement seems silly and utterly childish; while to amuse ourselves in order that we may be serious, as Anacharsis says, seems to be right; for amusement is a sort of recreation, and we need recreation because we are unable to work continuously. Recreation then, cannot be the end; for it is taken as a means to the exercise of our faculties. . . .

But if happiness be the exercise of virtue, it is reasonable to suppose that it will be the exercise of the highest virtue; and that will be the virtue or excellence of the best part of us. Now, that part or faculty—call it reason or what you will—which seems naturally to rule and take the lead, and to apprehend things noble and divine—whether it be itself divine, or only the divinest part of us—is the faculty the exercise of which, in its proper excellence, will be perfect happiness . . . this consists in speculation or theorizing. . . .

. . . It follows that the exercise of reason will be the complete happiness of man, *i.e.* when a complete term of days is added; for nothing incomplete can be admitted into our idea of happiness. But a life which realized this idea would be something more than human; for it would not be the expression of man's nature, but of some divine element in that nature—the exercise of which is as far superior to the exercise of the other kind of virtue,

Aristotle, from *The Nicomachean Ethics*

> as this divine element is superior to our compound human nature. If then reason be divine as compared with man, the life which consists in the exercise of reason will also be divine in comparison with human life. Nevertheless, instead of listening to those who advise us as men and mortals not to lift our thoughts above what is human and mortal, we ought rather, as far as possible, to put off our mortality and make every effort to live in the exercise of the highest of our faculties; for though it be but a small part of us, yet in power and value it far surpasses all the rest. And indeed this part would even seem to constitute our true self, since it is the sovereign and the better part. It would be strange then, if a man were to prefer the life of something else to the life of his true self. Again, we may apply here what we said above—for every being that is best and pleasantest which is naturally proper to it. Since, then, it is the reason that in the truest sense is the man, the life that consists in the exercise of the reason is the best and pleasantest for man—and therefore the happiest.

This is truly a lovely and inspiring vision: living a life based on the mind's best work, its ability to reason, reflect, and contemplate. Such a life enables us to touch the divine, realize our "true self," and achieve the greatest possible happiness.

In the final analysis, the great strengths of Aristotle's ethical vision are tied inevitably to its flaws. Aristotle presents us with a grand and inspiring vision of the "Good Life," a life devoted to fulfilling our most sublime potential as humans in a life that is founded on reason and virtue. He conceives of it as a rich life, which integrates all of the significant dimensions of human ability in an integrated and harmonious whole. And it is a life in which its defining essence, the human soul, strives to soar to transcendent heights, achieving the glorious final end that nature intended.

But an ethical vision drawn on this large a scale cannot help but be imprecise, a risk that Aristotle fully understands and a risk that he is fully prepared to accept. We will leave him with the last word.

Aristotle, from *The Nicomachean Ethics*

> But let us first agree that any discussion on matters of action cannot be more than an outline and is bound to lack precision. . . . And if this is true of our general discussion, our treatment of particular problems will be even less precise, since these do not come under the head of any art which can be transmitted by precept, but the agent must consider on each different occasion what the situation demands, just as in medicine and in navigation. But although this is the kind of discussion in which we are engaged, we must do our best.

< READING CRITICALLY >

Analyzing Aristotle's Virtue Ethics

- Do you agree with Aristotle that the ultimate goal all people strive for is happiness? Why or why not? Describe your concept of "happiness." How does it compare and contrast with that of Aristotle's notion of *eudaemonia*: "actively exercising your soul's powers in accord with virtue and reason"?

- Examine the Golden Mean virtues that Aristotle identifies as displayed in the chart on page 490. Do you agree with his formulations? What changes would you suggest? Create three more moral virtues in the same format:

  Vice (deficient)   Virtue (the mean)   Vice (excess)

- Identify and describe someone you believe to have a virtuous character. What virtuous qualities do they display on a consistent basis? How would you describe your own moral character? What moral virtues do you believe are prominent in your character? Which moral virtues would you like to strengthen?

9.3 Maxims: Duty to Moral Laws

For those advocates of Virtue Ethics like Aristotle, the morally right course of action is determined by individuals of virtuous character: Such people will be able to critically evaluate the unique context of a moral situation and choose an ethically enlightened course of action. The approach of ethical theorists like Immanuel Kant is very different. **Immanuel Kant** was a **deontologist**, a person with an ethical perspective that holds that it is the principle of *duty* that determines the moral value of actions. Deontology is derived from the Greek word *deon*, which means "duty" or "that which is obligatory." Deontologists are intent on discovering the moral duties that all people in all situations should follow. Should you choose to tell a lie to protect a decent person's reputation from being ruined? If the deontologist concludes that telling the truth is a universal duty that all people are obligated to follow (as Kant does), then lying is morally wrong regardless of the consequences.

We examined some of the specifics of Kant's life when we explored his views on the "self" in Chapter 3. What makes Kant such a towering figure in modern philosophy (although he barely topped five feet in real life) was the extraordinary influence he had in so many areas of philosophy: metaphysics, epistemology, and ethics. In fact, the noted American philosopher William Barrett once observed, "Kant can justly be called the father of modern philosophy, for out of him stem nearly all the still current and contending schools of philosophy." Kant's views are stunning in their depth, comprehensiveness, and compelling rationales.

Why was Kant so certain that moral value needed to be based on using our rational faculties to discover moral laws that would be universally binding on all people? Because he was convinced that all other potential foundations for morality were irretrievably flawed. For example, suppose we attempt to ground our moral beliefs in right and wrong in our feelings, impulses, or desires—what Kant calls *inclinations*. How can

Immanuel Kant (1724–1804). A German philosopher considered by many to be the greatest thinker of the eighteenth century, Kant based his moral philosophy on the principle of reason, developing the highly influential concept of the "categorical imperative."

Deontology The ethical view that moral value is determined by fulfilling one's duty.

Is lying always morally wrong? The financier Bernie Madoff lied to many people in bilking them of billions of dollars in an elaborate Ponzi scheme. Do you agree with Kant that lying is wrong in all circumstances? What are some situations in which you believe lying might be ethically justified? Why?

A priori Prior to experience. Often used to describe a proposition, argument, or value that we can be certain is true without empirical verification, something derived from pure reason.

these possibly serve as a consistent and reliable moral guide? These personal inclinations are so subjective that they vary wildly from person to person, culture to culture. Even inclinations that are generally considered admirable—sympathy, empathy, love, caring—are hopeless candidates for establishing a universally binding system of ethical values. Should you choose to tell a lie to protect a decent person's reputation from getting ruined? If you rely on your personal inclinations to instruct you, it's clear that, whatever your conclusion, some people will agree (based on their inclinations) and others will disagree (based on their inclinations). There's simply no way to determine with absolute certainty what the morally right choice is. If we try to apply the virtue ethics approach to the same moral question, we run into the same difficulty. In assessing lying in that situation (or in any situation, for that matter), people may very well arrive at different determinations of "the virtuous" course of action.

What we need, Kant is convinced, is a grounding for morality that is *beyond* the everyday experience of personal inclinations. We need to develop a *metaphysic of morals* that will stand independently of any particular moral belief or custom. Observing the way people make moral choices simply tells us *what* they are doing—it sheds no light on what they *should* be doing. That can only be established by discovering the necessary and universal laws of moral conduct, laws that are **a priori**. A law that is a *priori* is one that we can be certain is true independently of its application to actual empirical experience. And there is only one way that we can discover such necessary and universal moral laws, Kant believes, and that is through the faculty of reason.

> *Thus the moral worth of an action does not lie in the effect expected from it, nor in any principle of action which requires to borrow its motive from its expected effect. For all these effects—agreeableness of one's condition, and even the promotion of the happiness of others—could have been also brought about by other causes so that for this there would have been no need of the will of a rational being; whereas it is in this alone that the supreme and unconditioned good can be found. The preeminent good which we call moral can therefore consist in nothing else than **the conception of law** in itself, which certainly is only possible in a rational being, in so far as this conception, and not the expected effect, determines the will.*

However, to fully appreciate the binding and compelling nature of our universal moral obligations, Kant believes that we must first understand the human "will." It's not enough for people to be told or even understand what their moral obligations are—they need to *choose* to respond to these moral laws. For example, even if you are persuaded that it's morally wrong to lie to protect someone's reputation, you need to *will* yourself to make this choice. There are many times when people *know* what the morally right thing to do is—they simply don't do it, they don't *will* it.

So for Kant, fulfilling your potential as a moral person involves both

- developing a clear understanding of the necessary and universal moral laws that apply to all people in all circumstances, *and*
- developing the "good will" to actually follow these laws.

We can discover these universal laws by using our ability to reason thoughtfully and logically. And it is through our recognition and acceptance of ourselves as rational beings that we develop the "good will" to make choices in our daily lives that reflect these universal duties. But to fully appreciate Kant's complex and compelling views, we need to let him speak for himself.

Immanuel Kant, from *Fundamental Principles of the Metaphysics of Morals*

Nothing can possibly be conceived in the world, or even out of it, which can be called good without qualification, except a Good Will. Intelligence, wit, judgment, and the other *talents* of the mind, however they may be named, or courage, resolution, perseverance, as qualities of temperament, are undoubtedly good and desirable in many respects; but these gifts of nature may also become extremely bad and mischievous if the will which is to make use of them, and which, therefore, constitutes what is called *character*, is not good. It is the same with the *gifts of fortune*. Power, riches, honor, even health, and the general well-being and contentment with one's condition which is called *happiness*, inspire pride, and often presumption, if there is not a good will to correct the influence of these on the mind, and with this also to rectify the whole principle of acting, and adapt it to its end. The sight of a being who is not adorned with a single feature of a pure and good will, enjoying unbroken prosperity, can never give pleasure to an impartial rational spectator. Thus, a good will appears to constitute the indispensable condition even of being worthy of happiness.

There are even some qualities which are of service to this good will itself, and may facilitate its action, yet which have no intrinsic unconditional values, but always presuppose a good will, and this qualifies the esteem that we justly have for them, and does not permit us to regard them as absolutely good. Moderation in the affections and passions, self-control and calm deliberation are not only good in many respects, but even seem to constitute part of the intrinsic worth of the person; but they are far from deserving to be called good without qualification, although they have been so unconditionally praised by the ancients. For without the principles of a good will, they may become extremely bad, and the coolness of a villain not only makes him far more dangerous, but also directly makes him more abominable in our eyes than he would have been without it.

A good will is good, not because of what it performs or effects, not by its aptness for the attainment of some proposed end, but simply by virtue of the volition; that is, it is good in itself, and considered by itself is to be esteemed much higher than all that can be brought about by it in favor of any inclination, nay even of the sum total of all inclinations. Even if it should happen that, owing to special disfavor of fortune, or the niggardly provision of a stepmotherly nature, this will should wholly lack power to accomplish its purpose, if with its greatest efforts it should yet achieve nothing, and there should remain only the good will (not, to be sure, a mere wish, but the summoning of all means in our power), then, like a jewel, it would still shine by its own light, as a thing which has its whole value in itself. Its usefulness or fruitlessness can neither add to nor take away anything from this value. It would be, as it were, only the setting to it the attention of those who are not yet connoisseurs, but not to recommend it to true connoisseurs, or to determine its value.

> **Nothing can possibly be conceived in the world, or even out of it, which can be called good without qualification, except a Good Will.**

It's an inspired argument that Kant is making to ground his moral system in the concept of the "good will." He asks us to consider all the qualities of mind and temperament that we normally value: intelligence, wit, judgment, courage, resolution, perseverance. In the service of a will that is evil, these qualities are stripped of their moral value. Similarly, "gifts of fortune" such as power, riches, honor, health, and happiness—if they characterize the life of a person with a morally deficient will—become instruments of evil rather than good. Kant's point is that it is the "good will" that is the irreducible source of moral value. Other qualities and characteristics that we normally associate with moral goodness are derivative, depending for their moral value on the goodness of the will exercising them. For Kant, even if the good will is ineffectual, unable to achieve its intended goals, it is nevertheless "like a jewel, it would still shine by its own light, as a thing which has its whole value in itself."

Categorical imperative A maxim that commands moral obligation independent of experience or consequences. It is derived from pure reason and always carries overriding value.

Maxim A moral law.

None of the actions being commanded are considered to be *intrinsically* good, to be good *in themselves*. Instead, they are good *only* as a means to something else.

Categorical imperatives are very different, because they command actions that are intrinsically good, *not* actions that are good as a means to something else. They prescribe ways of acting that all rational beings are morally required to follow. But how exactly do we discover categorical imperatives, those moral laws or **maxims**, that command us to fulfill moral obligations that are both necessary and universal? What reason-based moral law could possibly meet these standards? Kant identifies one supreme "categorical imperative" that he believes fulfills this requirement, a universal and necessary moral law that has been a prime element of many modern ethical theories since he first articulated it.

Immanuel Kant, from *Fundamental Principles of the Metaphysics of Morals*

Finally, there is an imperative which commands a certain conduct immediately, without having as its condition any other purpose to be attained by it. This imperative is *categorical*. It concerns not the matter of the action, or its intended result, but its form and the principle of which it is itself a result; and what is essentially good in it consists in the mental disposition, let the consequence be what it may. This imperative may be called that of *morality*. . . .

When I conceive a hypothetical imperative, in general I do not know beforehand what it will contain until I am given the condition. But when I conceive a categorical imperative, I know at once what it contains. For as the imperative contains besides the law only the necessity that the maxims[1] shall conform to this law, while the law contains no conditions restricting it, there remains nothing but the general statement that the maxim of the action should confirm to a universal law, and it is this conformity alone that the imperative properly represents as necessary.

There is therefore but one categorical imperative, namely, this: *Act only on that maxim whereby you can at the same time will that it should become a universal law.*

Since the universality of the law according to which effects are produced constitutes what is properly called *nature* in the most general sense (as to form)—that is, the existence of things so far as it is determined by general laws—the imperative of duty may be expressed thus: *Act as if the maxim of your action were to become by your will a universal law of nature.*

> **Act only on that maxim whereby you can at the same time will that it should become a universal law.**

Kant's formulation of his categorical imperative is conceptually revolutionary. Previous moral theories had tended to focus on

- the *content* of a moral action (e.g., "Thou shalt not kill").
- the *intent* of an action ("Love God and love your neighbor").
- the *character* of the person initiating the action ("Act as a virtuous person would act").

In contrast, Kant focuses on the *logical form* of moral maxims. A moral action is one that a rational person can consistently *universalize* as a moral law applicable to all rational creatures. What determines the moral value of an action is not its content,

---

[1] A "maxim" is a subjective principle of action, and must be distinguished from the *objective principle*, namely, practical law. The former contains the practical rule set by reason according to the conditions of the subject (often its ignorance or its inclinations), so that it is the principle on which the subject acts; but the law is the objective principle valid for every rational being, and is the principle on which it ought to act—that is, an imperative.)

How can we apply the categorical imperative to environmental issues? If you were to apply Kant's categorical imperative, what conclusion would you come to regarding the moral justification of owning a "gas-guzzling" car? Why?

consequences, intention, or the character of the individual acting—it is whether it is logically consistent for the action to be practiced by *all* women and men. For example, should you choose to tell a lie to protect a decent person's reputation from being ruined? Kant's categorical imperative mandates that we ask—and try to answer—the following question to determine what to do: "Is it logically consistent to will that all people in all comparable circumstances tell a lie to protect a decent person's reputation?" If we apply this standard, Kant believes the answer is clear: It is morally wrong to tell a lie in these (or any other) circumstances. Why? Because if we endorsed the moral rightness of telling a lie, then we would never have reason to believe people when they assured us they were telling the truth. For all we know, they might be lying to protect someone's reputation (or some other "worthy" reason), *and* they would be confident that they were taking the morally correct action. But if lying becomes a "morally correct" action, then the concept of "telling the truth" loses all meaning and value. It's precisely because "telling the truth" is often difficult and disturbing that the concept has moral value. But if telling the truth and *not* telling the truth (lying) *both* can be morally right, then both concepts become meaningless. And that would result in a very chaotic—and unlivable—world indeed because we would never be able to depend on the accuracy of what anyone said to us. As a result, telling a lie to protect someone's reputation fails the test of the categorical imperative because if we attempt to universalize it—to *will* that everyone take the same action in similar circumstances—the result is logically inconsistent and so morally wrong.

Kant's "metaphysics of morals" is based on the concept that humans are first and foremost rational creatures, and as such we are necessarily committed to the belief in *logical consistency*. For rational creatures, it is offensive and unacceptable to promote beliefs that are logically *in*consistent—for example, the statements:

A duty to work? Kant argues that we have a duty to develop our natural gifts to be useful rather than idle. Might you argue that relaxed enjoyment could be a categorical imperative? *(Chang W. Lee/The New York Times)*

and resolve to devote their lives merely to idleness, amusement, and propagation of their species—in a word, to enjoyment; but he cannot possibly *will* that this should be a universal law of nature, or be implanted in us as such by a natural instinct. For, as a rational being, he necessarily wills that his faculties be developed, since they serve him, and have been given him for all sorts of possible purposes.

This moral dilemma proposed by Kant is fascinating, as it reflects a very modern consciousness involving the moral value of fulfilling one's human potential. Kant acknowledges the likelihood that even if we universalize the action of choosing a life of self-indulgent enjoyment over hard work and achievement of one's potential, life in some form would continue, as it does with cultures based on more hedonistic principles. But from a *rational* point of view, intentionally universalizing such a principle of moral action is unthinkable. As rational beings, Kant maintains, we necessarily believe that fulfilling our human potential is a morally appropriate course of action, one that provides our lives with meaning and a sense of purpose.

Immanuel Kant, from *Fundamental Principles of the Metaphysics of Morals*

A fourth, who is in prosperity, while he sees that others have to contend with great wretchedness and that he could help them, thinks: What concern is it of mine? Let everyone be happy as Heaven pleases, or as he can make himself; I will take nothing from him nor even envy him, only I do not wish to contribute anything to his welfare or to his assistance in distress! Now no doubt, if such a mode of thinking were a universal law, the human race might very well subsist, and doubtless even better than in a state in which everyone talks of sympathy and good-will, or even takes care occasionally to put it into practice, but, on the other side, also cheats when they can, betrays the rights of me, or otherwise violates them. But although it is possible that a universal law of nature might exist in accordance with that maxim, it is impossible to *will* that such a principle should have the universal validity of a law of nature. For a will which resolved this would contradict itself, inasmuch as many cases might occur in which one would have need of the love and sympathy of others, and in which, by such a law of nature, sprung from his own will, he would deprive himself of all hope and the aid he desires.

Kant's final example deals with the moral sentiments such as empathy, love, caring, sympathy. But Kant's endorsement of the emotions has a logical, not an emotional, foundation. Why is it morally wrong to believe in a selfish, self-absorbed view of our relationships with others? Because it is very likely that there will be times in which we will need and profit from the sympathy and love of others. And if we have already endorsed a detached lack of caring for others as a universal value, then we will be victimized by our own moral value. Thus, such a moral belief contradicts our own self-interest. Of course, although many people would doubtless agree with Kant's conclusion regarding the need to endorse such sentiments as sympathy, love, and concern for others' welfare as moral values, many would also question whether the moral authority of these values is one based purely on the logic of self-interest. Nevertheless, this is Kant's position, and it is certainly consistent with his entire moral system.

A duty to give? Do we have a moral responsibility to share our financial wealth with others?

Interestingly enough, Kant extends his metaphysic of morals to include another version of the categorical imperative that seems much more consistent with traditional moral values involving our relationships with others. *"Act as to treat humanity, whether in your own person or in that of any other, in every case as an end withal, never as means only."* Again, Kant's fundamental concept here is strikingly modern: Because all people possess the same *intrinsic value*, a value that is defined by an ability to understand their options and make autonomous choices, we should always act in a way that respects their inherent dignity as rational agents. Although it's permissible to treat every other element of our experience as a potential *means to an end* (including animals, in Kant's view), we should never treat people instrumentally, as a means to some end we want to achieve. Imagine, for example, that you want to sell something: Is it all right to manipulate people's feelings so that they will buy? Or suppose that your friend is planning to do something that you don't think is in her best interest: Is it permissible to manipulate her thinking indirectly so that she will make a different choice? According to Kant, both of these actions are morally wrong because you are not treating the people involved as *"ends,"* rational agents who are entitled to make their own choices. Instead, you are treating them as *"means" to an end*, even though you may believe that your manipulation is in their best interest. The morally right thing to do is to tell them exactly what you are thinking and then give them the opportunity to reason through the situation and make their own choices.

Of course, we do in fact "use" people all of the time, treating them as means to an end: for example, servers in restaurants, taxi drivers, toll collectors, accountants, doctors, and so on. Kant is well aware of this, and so he is careful to state that we shouldn't use people *solely/merely/only* as ends, for if we do we are in violation of the categorical imperative.

Immanuel Kant, from *Fundamental Principles of the Metaphysics of Morals*

Now I say: man and generally any rational being *exists* as an end in himself, *not merely as a means* to be arbitrarily used by this or that will, but in all his actions, whether they concern himself or other rational beings, but be always regarded at the same time as an end. All objects of the inclinations have only a conditional worth; for if the inclinations and the wants founded on them did not exist, then their object would be without value. But the inclinations themselves, being sources of want, are so far from having an absolute worth for which they should be desired that, on the contrary, it must be the universal wish of every rational being to be wholly free from them. Thus, the worth of any object which is *to be acquired* by our action is always conditional. Beings whose existence depends not on our will but on nature's, have nevertheless, if they are irrational beings, only a relative value as means, and are therefore called *things*: rational beings, on the contrary, are called *persons*, because their very nature points them out as ends in themselves, that is, as something which must not be used merely as means, and so far therefore restricts freedom of action (and is an object of respect). These, therefore are not merely subjective ends whose existence has a worth *for us* as an effect of our action, but *objective ends*, that is, things whose existence is an end in itself—an end, moreover, for which no other can be substituted, which they should subserve *merely* as means, for otherwise nothing whatever would possess *absolute worth*; but if all worth were conditioned and therefore contingent, then there would be no supreme practical principle of reason whatever.

If then there is a supreme practical principle or, in respect of the human will, a categorical imperative, it must be one which, being drawn from the conception of that which is necessarily an end for everyone because it is *an end in itself*, constitutes an *objective* principle of will, and can therefore serve as a universal practical law. The foundation of this principle is: *rational nature exists as an end in itself*. Man necessarily conceives his own existence as being so; so far then this is a *subjective* principle of human actions. But every other rational being regards its existence similarly, just on the same rational principle that holds for me; so that it is at the same time an objective principle from which as a supreme practical law all laws of the will must be capable of being deduced. Accordingly the practical imperative will be as follows: *So act as to treat humanity, whether in thine own person or in that of any other, in every case as an end withal, never as means only. . . .*

> **So act as to treat humanity, whether in thine own person or in that of any other, in every case as an end withal, never as means only.**

The conception of every rational being as one which must consider itself as giving all the maxims of its will universal laws, so as to judge itself and its actions from this point of view—this conception leads to another which depends on it and is very fruitful, namely, that of a *kingdom of ends*.

By a *kingdom* I understand the union of different rational beings in a system by common laws. Now since it is by laws that ends are determined as regards their universal validity, hence, if we abstract from the personal differences of rational beings, and likewise from all the content of their private ends, we shall be able to conceive all ends combined in a systematic whole (including both rational beings as ends in themselves, and also the special ends which each may propose to himself), that is to say, we can conceive a kingdom of ends, which on the preceding principles is possible.

It's a glorious vision of Kant's, the idea of a "kingdom of ends" in which every person is always treated as a person of intrinsic worth. Such a "kingdom" would be governed by laws that ensure the "universal validity" of all people, a harmonious community based on the unassailable rationality of the categorical imperative. Is such a "kingdom of ends" possible? It's a question well worth exploring in Chapter 10, when we consider social and political philosophy.

Yet Kant was not simply concerned with our moral responsibilities toward others: He was equally as interested in the moral responsibilities that we have toward ourselves. In a passage that is eerily prescient of modern psychological theory, Kant makes the claim that we cannot love others more than we love ourselves: In other words, that healthy self-esteem is necessary to act in a morally enlightened fashion toward others.

> *The greatest love I can have for another is to love him as myself. I cannot love another more than I love myself. . . . Our duties towards ourselves (therefore) constitute the supreme condition and the principle of all morality. . . . He who transgresses against himself loses his manliness and becomes incapable of doing his duty toward his fellows.*

One final point needs to be underscored. Some people have tended to view Kant's formulations of the categorical imperative as no more than formalized statements of the Golden Rule: "Do unto others as you would have them do unto you." Kant was aware of such efforts, even while he was alive, and he vigorously rejected all such attempts to reduce the categorical imperative to the Golden Rule.

> *Let it not be thought that the common:* **quod tibi non vis fieri**, *("Do not do unto others what you would not have them do to you.") etc. could serve here as the rule of principle . . . it cannot be a universal law, for it does not contain the principle of duties to oneself, nor of the duties of benevolence to others (for many a one would gladly consent that others should not benefit him, provided only that they might be excused from showing benevolence to them), nor finally that of duties of strict obligation to one another, for on this principle the criminal might argue against the judge who punishes him, etc.*

As admirable as the intent of the Golden Rule may be, Kant finds it insulting that anyone would confuse this imprecise principle with the rational clarity of the categorical imperative. In the span of a few sentences, Kant reels off three ways in which the Golden Rule is conceptually inferior to the categorical imperative.

- First, the Golden Rule makes no mention of the duties we have toward ourselves, to regard ourselves well and strive to fully develop our personal human potential.

- Second, the Golden Rule does not ensure feelings of kindness, consideration, and benevolence to others. Why not? Imagine a person who cares only for him- or herself, lacking any interest in others or desire to have others treat him or her well. For that person the Golden Rule simply means, "I'll leave you alone if you leave me alone"—hardly the foundation of an enlightened moral philosophy. In contrast, the categorical imperative expects such benevolent sentiments to flourish in our efforts to treat others as ends, not simply as means to an end.

- Third, the Golden Rule has the potential for perverting what ought to be understood as rationally based, clearly defined duties toward others. For example, the prisoner before the judge might invoke the Golden Rule to ask for freedom "because if I were judge I would grant you freedom." Again, this is not a moral outcome that the Golden Rule was created to endorse, nor is it an outcome that would be permitted under the categorical imperative.

> ## < READING CRITICALLY >
> ### Analyzing Kant on Duty and Reason
>
> ■ One criticism of Kant's ethical philosophy is that, like other deontology theories, it overemphasizes abstract principles of justice and rationality over subjective emotions such as empathy and love. Do you feel that this criticism is justified? Why or why not? Do you think that Kant's second formulation of the categorical imperative helps address some of these concerns?
>
> ■ Kant's starting point in his ethical analysis is the rational, autonomous individual, from whom he builds toward rationally ordered relationships with other members of the community. Other thinkers, like the German philosopher G. W. F. Hegel, initiate their analysis from the community because they believe that we are fundamentally social beings who naturally exist in a complex web of interconnected relationships. From this vantage point, resting an ethical philosophy on each solitary individual is the exact opposite of the approach that should be taken. Which starting point for an ethical theory makes the most sense to you, the individual or the community? Explain your rationale and provide examples from your own life.
>
> ■ Some people contend that Kant's idea of evaluating moral actions independent of their consequences makes little sense. For example, the family hiding Anne Frank from the Nazis during World War II would have been compelled by Kant's interpretation of the categorical imperative to answer truthfully when asked by the Gestapo, "Are you hiding any Jews in your house?" Do you think this is a valid criticism? How do you think Kant might respond to this criticism (for example, employing the second formulation of the categorical imperative)? Can you think of other examples in which rigidly applying the categorical imperative could result in consequences that most people would consider to be "immoral"?
>
> ■ Some critics of Kant have contended that his approach is unable to provide ethical guidance when two moral principles are in conflict. For example, the Anne Frank example can be seen as involving a conflict between the principles "Do not lie" and "Do not let innocent persons be harmed if you can prevent it." How do you think Kant would respond to this objection?
>
> ■ People with "fanatical" beliefs pose another difficulty for Kant. Couldn't a Kantian terrorist claim to be acting on the basis of the moral imperative to "Destroy all people who don't believe in my 'true' religion"? How would you go about countering such a contention?

Aristippus (c. 435–c. 356 B.C.E.). Ancient Greek philosopher. Follower of Socrates; believed happiness consists in pleasure and is commonly associated with the ethical doctrine of hedonism.

Epicurus (341–270 B.C.E.). Ancient Greek philosopher. Advanced the view in ethics that pleasure is the one sole good and pain is the one sole bad and that one should not seek out pleasures solely but devote oneself to also avoiding pain.

9.4 Consequences: Utilitarianism

Aristotle and Kant thus embody two contrasting approaches to determining the morally right course of action. For Aristotle, the morally right course of action will be determined by the thoughtful reflections of an individual who has carefully cultivated a virtuous character. For Kant, the rigorous application of one or more formulations of the categorical imperative will serve as our unerring guide to determining the ethically correct course of action, which we are morally obligated to follow. Yet two Greek philosophers living at the time of Aristotle, **Aristippus** and **Epicurus**, had a radically different approach to the moral life. They believed that morally enlightened actions were defined not by the moral character of the individual (Aristotle), or by rationally based duty (Kant), but rather by the *consequences* of the action. Further, they both believed that the morally correct course of action was the one that resulted in engendering the greatest amount of pleasure, an ethical approach that became known as **hedonism**, a term derived for the Greek root *hedone*, which means "pleasure."

Hedonism was first identified with Aristippus, who believed that the meaning of life is pleasure, pure and simple. Aristippus argued that if you observe people and what motivates them, it's clear that they seek to enjoy pleasure and avoid pain. Therefore, he concluded, the purpose of life must be to achieve as much intense, sensual pleasure as possible.

Epicurus was the next major figure to advocate hedonism as a way of life. Unlike Aristippus, who made no distinction between different types of pleasure, Epicurus believed that there were "higher" pleasures—such as intellectual pursuits—and "lower" pleasures—such as physical gratifications. Only the higher pleasures could provide optimal pleasure and peace of mind, as he describes in the following passage.

> *Thus when I say that pleasure is the goal of living I do not mean the pleasures of libertines or the pleasures inherent in positive enjoyment, as is supposed by certain persons who are ignorant of our doctrine or who are not in agreement with it or who interpret it perversely. I mean, on the contrary, the pleasure that consists in freedom from bodily pain and mental agitation. The pleasant life is not the product of one drinking party after another or of sexual intercourse with women or of the seafood and other delicacies afforded by a luxurious table. On the contrary, it is the result of sober thinking—namely, investigation of the reasons for every act of choice and aversion and elimination of those false ideas about the gods and death which are the chief source of mental disturbances.*

Epicurus truly lived his philosophy. He created a school—"The Garden," he called it—in which everyone was invited to stop by, socialize, eat and drink well, and discuss philosophy. It was a serene retreat from the noisy bustle of Athens, and what made it even more remarkable was the fact that all people were welcome and treated as equals: women, merchants, slaves, prostitutes, as well as the wealthy and educated men who controlled Athenian society.

The Greatest Happiness for the Greatest Number: Bentham

Epicurus's idyllic Garden was founded on principles that, 2,000 years later, the British philosopher and social reformer **Jeremy Bentham** would have appreciated. Bentham was committed to social equality, democracy, public education, and a universal improvement in the public welfare.

Bentham's writing was aimed at addressing the abuses spawned by the Industrial Revolution in England. He lived at a time when the economy was shifting from one based on family farms to one based on urban manufacturing, creating a new working class that was exploited by industrialists. Children as well as adults toiled long hours in poorly lit, noisy, unventilated factories for paltry wages. Together with his student, John Stuart Mill, Bentham argued for an ethical theory that took the happiness and suffering of the working class into account. Their theory, which came to be known as **utilitarianism**, aimed to promote the greatest good for all people, not just the wealthy. It focused on the social consequences of ethical decisions.

Bentham was a hedonist, believing that humans are not only necessarily governed by pleasure and pain (**psychological hedonism**) but also *should* be governed by pleasure and pain (**ethical hedonism**). But Bentham takes a very different path from Aristippus

Hedonism The view that pleasure is the only thing truly of value. Some hedonists emphasize the "higher" pleasures such as intellectual pursuits.

((•— **Listen** to the **Podcast** *Richard Crisp on Utilitarianism* on **mysearchlab.com**

Jeremy Bentham (1748–1832). Bentham was a British philosopher who developed the moral theory of utilitarianism in response to the ills of industrialization.

Utilitarianism The view that we should act to promote the greatest amount of happiness (and create the least amount of suffering possible) for the greatest number of people.

Psychological hedonism The view that all human desire is necessarily directed to achieving pleasure and avoiding pain.

Ethical hedonism The moral view that human desire and action *ought* to be directed to achieving pleasure and avoiding pain.

John Stuart Mill, from *Utilitarianism*

It is quite compatible with the principle of utility to recognize the fact, that some *kinds* of pleasure are more desirable and more valuable than others. It would be absurd that while, in estimating all other things, quality is considered as well as quantity, the estimation of pleasures should be supposed to depend on quantity alone.

If I am asked, what I mean by difference of quality in pleasures, or what makes one pleasure more valuable than another, merely as a pleasure, except it being greater in amount, there is but one possible answer. Of two pleasures, if there be one to which all or almost all who have experience of both give a decided preference, irrespective of any feeling of moral obligation to prefer it, that is the more desirable pleasure. If one of the two is, by those who are competently acquainted with both, placed so far above the other that they prefer it, even though knowing it to be attended with a greater amount of discontent, and would not resign it for any quantity of the other pleasure which their nature is capable of, we are justified in ascribing to the preferred enjoyment a superiority in quality, so far outweighing quantity as to render it, in comparison, of small account.

This, of course, is a question that must be dealt with in attempting to establish a hierarchy of pleasure. *On what basis* does one declare that the so-called "higher" pleasures have more intrinsic worth than the "lower" pleasures? What is the justification for asserting that the pleasure of drinking an expensive Beaujolais is inherently superior to the pleasure derived from a six-pack of beer? Or that listening to Mozart provides higher quality pleasure than popular music? Or that the joy of attending the opera outclasses attending a sporting event? Mill's response is that the only way to do this is to observe and speak to people who have experienced both "higher" and "lower" pleasures and ask them which they prefer. Mill is confident that the "higher" pleasures will consistently triumph.

Do "higher" pleasures have greater worth? This photograph is from a contemporary production of Verdi's opera, *La Traviata*, which had its premiere during Mill's lifetime. Many people consider opera, classical music concerts, and the theater to be a "higher pleasure."
Do you think that the joy of attending the opera is superior to that of attending a wild party?

Now it is an unquestionable fact that those who are equally acquainted with, and equally capable of appreciating and enjoying, both, do give a most marked preference to the manner of existence which employs their higher faculties. Few human creatures would consent to be changed into any of the lower animals, for a promise of the fullest allowance of a beast's pleasures: no intelligent human being would consent to be a fool, no instructed person would be an ignoramus, no person of feeling and conscience would be selfish and base, even though they should be persuaded that the fool, the dunce, or the rascal is better satisfied with his lot than they are with theirs. They would not resign what they possess more than he for the most complete satisfaction of all the desires which they have in common with him. If they ever fancy they would, it is only in cases of unhappiness so extreme, that to escape from it they would exchange their lot for almost any other, however, undesirable in their own eyes. A being of higher faculties requires more to make him happy, is capable probably of more acute suffering, and certainly accessible to it at more points, than one of an inferior type; but in spite of these liabilities, he can never really wish to sink into what he feels to be a lower grade of existence. . . .

John Stuart Mill,
from *Utilitarianism*

This is certainly a provocative assertion of Mill, and it's one that requires a great deal of careful analysis and investigation. But Mill goes on to say that even if you doubt that the more "elevated" activities provide a qualitatively superior form of pleasure than the less refined activities, nevertheless it is incontrovertible that it is much better to live in a society in which the majority of people pursue the "higher" pleasures than a society dominated by the physical, sensual pleasures.

I have dwelt on this point, as being a necessary part of a perfectly just conception of Utility or Happiness, considered as the directive rule of human conduct. But it is by no means an indispensable condition to the acceptance of the utilitarian standard; for the standard is not the agent's own greatest happiness, but the greatest amount of happiness altogether; and if it may possibly be doubted whether a noble character is always the happier for its nobleness, there can be no doubt that it makes other people happier, and that the world in general is immensely a gainer by it. Utilitarianism, therefore, could only attain its end by the general cultivation of nobleness of character, even if each individual were only benefited by the nobleness of others, and his own, so far as happiness is concerned, were a sheer deduction from the benefit. But the bare enunciation of such an absurdity as this last, renders refutation superfluous.

John Stuart Mill,
from *Utilitarianism*

As a final act, Mill reviews the major themes he has been discussing and then weaves them together into his revised version of utilitarianism.

According to the Greatest Happiness Principle, as above explained, the ultimate end, with reference to and for the sake of which all other things are desirable (whether we are considering our own good or that of other people), is an existence exempt as far as possible from pain, and as rich as possible in enjoyments, both in point of quantity and quality; the test of quality, and the rule for measuring it against quantity, being the preference felt by those who in their opportunities of experience, to which must be added their habits of self-consciousness and self-observation, are best furnished with the means of comparison. This, being, according to the utilitarian opinion, the end of human action, is necessarily also the standard of morality; which may accordingly be defined, the rules and precepts for human conduct, by the observance of which

John Stuart Mill,
from *Utilitarianism*

an existence such as has been described might be, to the greatest extent possible, secured to all mankind, and not of them only, but, so far as the nature of things admits, to the whole sentient creation. . . .

< READING CRITICALLY >

Analyzing Utilitarianism

- Describe a moral decision involving other people that you made recently. Using Bentham's hedonistic calculus as a general guide, calculate what would have been the morally correct choice to make based on the principle of utility. How does this conclusion compare with the choice you actually made?

- Now analyze that same decision using Mill's distinction of "higher" and "lower" pleasures. What ethical conclusion does this method result in? Do you agree with Mill that "higher" pleasures have intrinsically greater value than "lower" pleasures? Why or why not? Use examples to support your conclusion.

- One major criticism of utilitarianism is its potential conflict with the principle of justice: that is, treating an individual unjustly so long as this leads to more overall happiness. For example, suppose the government is planning to execute a person they know to be innocent for the purpose of "setting an example." Create a scenario in which the utilitarians would have to support such an execution.

- In ancient Rome, people were slaughtered in the Coliseum for the entertainment and pleasure of thousands of others. How would the utilitarians analyze this situation?

- Explain why Mill believes that in calculating the greatest good for the greatest number of people it is essential that you "be as strictly impartial as a disinterested and benevolent spectator."

- What do you think about judging the consequences of actions only to determine their moral worth, without reference to an individual's moral values, intentions, or motivations? Describe what role evaluating consequences plays in your moral reasoning. What other factors come into play in your efforts to "do the right thing"?

Consider the Interests of Animals: Singer

Mill's concluding sentence in the last reading makes clear that he believes that the principle of utility should be applied not only to humans but to nonhuman animals as well, ". . . the whole sentient creation." Similarly, Bentham fervently believed that animals as well as humans of all races should be included in the moral community.

The Australian philosopher **Peter Singer** has given this point of view a modern voice, arguing that reason requires that the principle of utility be equally applied to all animals capable of experiencing suffering. The following passages are taken from his influential book, *Animal Liberation*.

Peter Singer (B. 1946). Singer is an Australian philosopher and professor at Princeton University. His writing addresses issues in bioethics, animal rights, and world poverty.

Peter Singer, from *Animal Liberation*

All Animals Are Equal . . . *or why the ethical principle on which human equality rests requires us to extend equal consideration to animals too*

"Animal Liberation" may sound more like a parody of other liberation movements than a serious objective. The idea of "The Rights of Animals" actually was once used to parody the case for women's rights. When Mary Wollstonecraft, a forerunner of today's feminists, published her *Vindication of the Rights of Woman* in 1792, her views were widely regarded as absurd, and before long an anonymous publication appeared entitled *A Vindication of the Rights of Brutes*. The author of this satirical work (now known to have been Thomas Taylor, a distinguished Cambridge philosopher) tried to refute Mary Wollstonecraft's arguments by showing that they could be carried one stage further. If the argument for equality was sound when applied to women, why should it not be applied to dogs, cats, and horses? The reasoning seemed to hold for these "brutes" too; yet to hold that brutes had rights was manifestly absurd. Therefore the reasoning by which this conclusion had been reached must be unsound, and if unsound when applied to brutes, it must also be unsound when applied to women, since the very same arguments had been used in each case.

* * *

. . . *The principle of the equality of human beings is not a description of an alleged actual equality among humans: it is a prescription of how we should treat human beings.* Jeremy Bentham, the founder of the reforming utilitarian school of moral philosophy, incorporated the essential basis of moral equality into his system of ethics by means of the formula: "Each to count for one and none for more than one." In other words, the interests of every being affected by an action are to be taken into account and given the same weight as the like interests of any other being. A later utilitarian, Henry Sidgwick, put the point this way: "The good of any one individual is of no more importance, from the point of view (if I may say so) of the Universe, than the good of any other." More recently the leading figures in contemporary moral philosophy have shown a great deal of agreement in specifying as a fundamental presupposition of their moral theories some similar requirement that works to give everyone's interests equal consideration—although these writers generally cannot agree on how this requirement is best formulated.

It is an implication of this principle of equality that our concern for others and our readiness to consider their interests ought not to depend on what they are like or on what abilities they may possess. Precisely what our concern or consideration requires us to do may vary according to the characteristics of those affected by what we do: concern for the well-being of children growing up in America would require that we teach them to read; concern for the well-being of pigs may require no more than that we leave them with other pigs in a place where there is adequate food and room to run freely. But the basic element—the taking into account of the interests of the being, whatever those interests may be—must, according to the principle of equality, be extended to all beings, black or white, masculine or feminine, human or nonhuman.

* * *

. . . Speciesism—the word is not an attractive one, but I can think of no better term—is a prejudice or attitude of bias in favor of the interests of members of one's own species and against those of members of other species. It should be obvious that the fundamental objections to racism and sexism made by Thomas Jefferson and Sojourner Truth apply equally to speciesism. If possessing a higher degree of intelligence does not entitle one human to use another for his or her own ends, how can it entitle humans to exploit nonhumans for the same purpose?

Many philosophers and other writers have proposed the principle of equal consideration of interests, in some form or other, as a basic moral principle; but not many of them have recognized that this principle applies to members of other species as well as to our own. Jeremy Bentham was one of the few who did realize this. In a forward-looking passage written at a time when black slaves had been freed by the French but in the British dominions were still being treated in the way we now treat animals, Bentham wrote:

> The day may come when the rest of the animal creation may acquire those rights which never could have been withholden from them but by the hand of tyranny. The

> **Speciesism . . . is a prejudice or attitude of bias in favor of the interests of members of one's own species and against those of members of other species.**

French have already discovered that the blackness of the skin is no reason why a human being should be abandoned without redress to the caprice of a tormentor. It may one day come to be recognized that the number of legs, the villosity of the skin, or the termination of the *os sacrum* are reasons equally insufficient for abandoning a sensitive being to the same fate. What else is it that should trace the insuperable line? Is it the faculty of reason, or perhaps the faculty of discourse? But a full-grown horse or dog is beyond comparison a more rational, as well as a more conversable animal than an infant of a day or a week or even a month old. But suppose they were otherwise, what would it avail? The question is not, Can they *reason*? Nor, Can they *talk*? But, Can they *suffer*?

> " The question is not, Can they reason? Nor, Can they talk? But, Can they suffer?
> JEREMY BENTHAM

In this passage Bentham points to the capacity for suffering as the vital characteristic that gives a being the right to equal consideration. The capacity for suffering—or more strictly, for suffering and/or enjoyment or happiness—is not just another characteristic like the capacity for language or higher mathematics. Bentham is not saying that those who try to mark "the insuperable line" that determines whether the interests of a being should be considered happen to have chosen the wrong characteristic. By saying that we must consider the interests of all beings with the capacity for suffering or enjoyment Bentham does not arbitrarily exclude from consideration any interests at all—as those who draw the line with reference to the possession of reason or language do. The capacity for suffering and enjoyment is *a prerequisite for having interests at all*, a condition that must be satisfied before we can speak of interests in a meaningful way. . . .

Racists violate the principle of equality by giving greater weight to the interests of members of their own race when there is a clash between their interests and the interests of those of another race. Sexists violate the principle of equality by favoring the interests of their own sex. Similarly, speciesists allow the interests of their own species to override the greater interests of members of other species. The pattern is identical in each case.

Most human beings are speciesists . . . ordinary human beings—not a few exceptionally cruel or heartless humans, but the overwhelming majority of humans—take an active part in, acquiesce in, and allow their taxes to pay for practices that require the sacrifice of the most important interests of members of other species in order to promote the most trivial interests of our own species.

* * *

It may be objected that comparisons of the sufferings of different species are impossible to make and that for this reason when the interests of animals and humans clash the principle of equality gives no guidance. It is probably true that comparisons of suffering between members of different species cannot be made precisely, but precision is not essential. Even if we were to prevent the infliction of suffering on animals only when it is quite certain that the interests of humans will not be affected to anything like the extent that animals are affected, we would be forced to make radical changes in our treatment of animals that would involve our diet, the farming methods we use, experimental procedures in many fields of science, our approach to wildlife and to hunting, trapping and the wearing of furs, and areas of entertainment like circuses, rodeos, and zoos. As a result, a vast amount of suffering would be avoided.

So far I have said a lot about inflicting suffering on animals, but nothing about killing them. This omission has been

Do zoos and the circus contribute to animal suffering?

deliberate. The application of the principle of equality to the infliction of suffering is, in theory at least, fairly straightforward. Pain and suffering are in themselves bad and should be prevented or minimized, irrespective of the race, sex, or species of the being that suffers. How bad a pain is depends on how intense it is and how long it lasts, but pains of the same intensity and duration are equally bad, whether felt by humans or animals.

The wrongness of killing a being is more complicated. I have kept, and shall continue to keep, the question of killing in the background because in the present state of human tyranny over other species the more simple, straightforward principle of equal consideration of pain or pleasure is a sufficient basis for identifying and protesting against all the major abuses of animals that human beings practice. Nevertheless, it is necessary to say something about killing.

Just as most human beings are speciesists in their readiness to cause pain to animals when they would not cause a similar pain to humans for the same reason, so most human beings are speciesists in their readiness to kill other animals when they would not kill human beings. . . .

This does not mean that to avoid speciesism we must hold that it is as wrong to kill a dog as it is to kill a human being in full possession of his or her faculties. The only position that is irredeemably speciesist is the one that tries to make the boundary of the

> **[M]ost human beings are speciesists in their readiness to kill other animals when they would not kill human beings.**

right to life run exactly parallel to the boundary of our own species. Those who hold the sanctity of life view do this, because while distinguishing sharply between human beings and other animals they allow no distinctions to be made within our own species, objecting to the killing of the severely retarded and the hopelessly senile as strongly as they object to the killing of normal adults.

To avoid speciesism we must allow that beings who are similar in all relevant respects have a similar right to life—and mere membership in our own biological species cannot be a morally relevant criterion for this right. Within these limits we could still hold, for instance, that it is worse to kill a normal adult human, with a capacity for self-awareness and the ability to plan for the future and have meaningful relations with others, than it is to kill a mouse, which presumably does not share all of these characteristics; or we might appeal to the close family and other personal ties that humans have but mice do not have to the same degree; or we might think that

Are we guilty of "speciesism?" Peter Singer believes that most people are speciesists because they support the needless suffering of animals for the most trivial of reasons. Do you agree with his allegation? Why or why not?

it is the consequences for other humans, who will be put in fear for their own lives, that makes the crucial difference; or we might think it is some combination of these factors, or other factors together.

Whatever criteria we choose, however, we will have to admit that they do not follow precisely the boundary of our own species. We may legitimately hold that there are some features of certain beings that make their lives more valuable than those of other beings; but there will surely be some nonhuman animals whose lives, by any standards, are more valuable than the lives of some humans. A chimpanzee, dog, or pig, for instance, will have a higher degree of self-awareness and a greater capacity for meaningful relations with others than a severely retarded infant or someone in a state of advanced senility. So if we base the right to life on these characteristics we must grant these animals a right to life as good as, or better than, such retarded or senile humans.

This argument cuts both ways. It could be taken as showing that chimpanzees, dogs, and pigs, along with some other species, have a right to life and we commit a grave moral

> **Alternatively one could take the argument as showing that the severely retarded and hopelessly senile have no right to life and may be killed for quite trivial reasons, as we now kill animals.**

offence whenever we kill them, even when they are old and suffering and our intention is to put them out of their misery. Alternatively one could take the argument as showing that the severely retarded and hopelessly senile have no right to life and may be killed for quite trivial reasons, as we now kill animals.

Since the main concern of this book is with ethical questions having to do with animals and not with the morality of euthanasia I shall not attempt to settle this issue finally. I think it is reasonably clear, though, that while both of the positions just described avoid speciesism, neither is satisfactory. What we need is some middle position that would avoid speciesism but would not make the lives of the retarded and senile as cheap as the lives of pigs and dogs now are, or make the lives of pigs and dogs so sacrosanct that we think it wrong to put them out of hopeless misery. What we must do is bring nonhuman animals within our sphere of moral concern and cease to treat their lives as expendable for whatever trivial purposes we may have. At the same time, once we realize that the fact that a being is a member of our own species is not in itself enough to make it always wrong to kill that being, we may come to reconsider our policy of preserving human lives at all costs, even when there is no prospect of a meaningful life or of existence without terrible pain.

I conclude, then, that a rejection of speciesism does not imply that all lives are of equal worth. While self-awareness, the capacity to think ahead and have hopes and aspirations for the future, the capacity for meaningful relations with others and so on are not relevant to the question of inflicting pain—since pain is pain, whatever other capacities, beyond the capacity to feel pain, the being may have—these capacities are relevant to the question of taking life. It is not arbitrary to hold that the life a self-aware being, capable of abstract thought, of planning for the future, of complex acts of communication, and so on, is more valuable than the life of a being without these capacities.

< READING CRITICALLY >

Analyzing Singer on Animal Rights

- How does the author, Peter Singer, define *speciesism*? In what way is this concept based on the principles of utilitarianism, both in terms of the principle of utility and the principle of equality?

- According to Singer, "Most human beings are speciesists" because they "take an active part in, acquiesce in, and allow their taxes to pay for practices that require the sacrifice of the most important interests of members of other species in order to promote the most trivial interests of our own species." Explain whether you agree with Singer's conclusion, supporting your analysis with reasons and examples.

- According to Singer, the principle of equality demands that it is our moral obligation to avoid inflicting needless pain on animals, any more than we would inflict it on humans, and that if we followed this principle "we would be forced to make radical changes in our treatment of animals that would involve our diet, the farming methods we use, experimental procedures in many fields of science, our approach to wildlife and to hunting, trapping and the wearing of furs, and areas of entertainment like circuses, rodeos, and zoos. As a result, a vast amount of suffering would be avoided." Do you agree with Singer's conclusion? Why or why not?

- Has reading and reflecting on Singer's article influenced your views on the way we treat animals in our society? If so, what are some areas in which society should reconsider its treatment of animals?

9.5 Authenticity: Existentialist Ethics

The three major moral theories that we have considered to this point—virtue ethics, Kantian deontology, and utilitarianism—each have a different focus in defining and evaluating moral values:

- Virtue ethics: Moral value is determined by cultivating a virtuous *character*.
- Deontology: Moral value is determined by following the *moral rules* (maxims) prescribed by reason.
- Utilitarianism: Moral value is determined by the *consequences of actions*: the greatest happiness for the greatest number.

In contrast to these traditional ethical theories, as well as those ethical views anchored in the specific dictates of various religions, the eclectic theory of **existentialism** takes a much more personal and individual approach to the challenge of making ethical choices. For existentialism the questions are *not*:

- Who is a virtuous person?
- What is my moral duty?
- How can I best apply the principle of utility?

Instead, for existentialism the questions are more along the lines of: How do I live my life authentically? How can I create myself to be a uniquely significant individual? How can I invest my life with meaning while existing in a universe that lacks ultimate meaning? How can I develop an approach to moral responsibility that is grounded in my absolute freedom of choice?

Søren Kierkegaard, Friedrich Nietzsche, Jean-Paul Sartre, Simone de Beauvoir, and Albert Camus are a disparate group of thinkers who share a common commitment to placing the living, concrete individual at the center of all philosophical analysis. Existentialism rose up as a passionate response against a world in which the intrinsic value of the solitary individual was increasingly becoming crushed by the dehumanizing forces of industrial development, the increased pressures to conform to homogeneous social standards, the so-called objective frameworks of modern science. Existentialists saw (and continue to see) the cumulative effect of these influences to be the profound

> **Existentialism** A philosophical and literary movement that focuses on the uniqueness of each human individual as distinguished from abstract universal qualities. Defined by Sartre as "existence precedes essence," meaning that humans create themselves through free choices and are responsible for who they are.

> " **The question is not what am I to believe, but what am I to do?**
> **SØREN KIERKEGAARD** "

Friedrich Nietzsche
We must express our "will to power" by creating our own ethical codes "beyond the good and evil" of social convention.

Soren Kierkegaard
"The crowd is untruth." We must become authentic, responsible individuals.

Existentialist Ethics
Our goal in life is to create ourselves as authentic individuals.

Jean-Paul Sartre
We must create ourselves by accepting our absolute freedom and responsibility. "Existence precedes essence."

Simone de Beauvoir
Acknowledging our interplay with other free people defines us as authentic individuals.

Albert Camus
We must create meaningful lives in an absurd world through courageously free choices.

alienation of the individual. Instead of viewing their work as a personal expression of their individual talents, average individuals become "cogs in the machine," alienated from the process and products of their labor. Instead of crafting themselves to be unique and creative individuals, they become one of the "masses," lumped together with a legion of nameless, faceless people indistinguishable from each other. And instead of viewing themselves as the "crowning jewel" of creation, advancements in science have drained their life spirit, viewing them simply as biological organisms, psychological constructs, historical incidentals, specks in the universe. What can the individual know? He is hopelessly subjective. What value can the individual possess? She is simply an infinitesimal molecule in the cosmic organism.

It was in response to this pervasive diminishment of the individual that existentialist thinkers began to shout, "Enough!" For these thinkers, the starting point for all knowledge and inquiry of the universe, both human and scientific, is subjective human experience: "Truth is subjectivity," Kierkegaard announced, and Sartre echoed this sentiment with the statement, "We must begin from the subjective." *Nothing* is more important than the concrete individual. Without this living, feeling, experiencing person there would be no technology, no social culture, no science or scientific knowledge. Rather than pushing the individual to the margins of the universe, the individual *must* be returned to the central position of honor and focus.

"The Crowd Is Untruth": Kierkegaard

Although existentialism achieved its full development in the twentieth century, there were two philosophers in the nineteenth century who are generally considered to be essential precursors to the existentialist movement: Søren Kierkegaard, a thinker who founded his philosophy on a passionate though highly personal belief in God; and Friedrich Nietzsche, an equally passionate atheist who announced that "God is dead."

The enigmatic and brilliant Danish philosopher **Søren Kierkegaard** was outraged by the destruction of individual values and repulsed by what he considered to be the hypocrisy of political and religious leaders; he despaired of all the individuals who had permitted their souls to become pedestrian and mediocre. His scathing attacks on these "inauthentic" values still reverberate:

> *Let others complain that the age is wicked; my complaint is that it is wretched, for it lacks passion. Men's thoughts are thin and flimsy like lace, they are themselves pitiable like lacemakers. The thoughts of their hearts are too paltry to be sinful. For a worm it might be regarded as a sin to harbor such thoughts, but not for a being made in the image of God. Their lusts are dull and sluggish, their passions sleepy. They do their duty, these shopkeeping souls, but they clip the coin a trifle . . . : they think that even if the Lord keeps ever so careful a set of books, they may still cheat Him a little. Out upon them! This is the reason my soul always turns back to the Old Testament and to Shakespeare. I feel that those who speak there are at least human beings: they hate, they love, they murder their enemies, and curse their descendants throughout all generations, they sin.*

Kierkegaard counted Socrates as his philosophical mentor, and for both thinkers the care of the soul is paramount in human existence: *Everything* else is secondary. We need to cultivate our souls, committing ourselves passionately to the quest of truth and

Søren Kierkegaard (1813–1855). This Danish philosopher challenged much of Christian philosophy while remaining deeply religious. Kierkegaard argued that life has meaning only when people reject the pursuit of pleasure and seek moral truth by looking within and recognizing their connection to the divine.

personal authenticity. We need to fully recognize and accept our personal responsibility in creating ourselves through the choices we make. We need to invest our lives with meaning through our own efforts, fulfilling our unique potential through the power of our minds and the talents of our spirits. These are the core values of the existentialist ethic.

The antithesis of this passionate commitment to creating the "project" of our individual lives is to succumb to the social forces of conformity, permitting the expectations of others to seep into our consciousness, causing us to become weak and insignificant, a tiny inconsequential part of a larger whole. Kierkegaard explains the pernicious and utterly false view that "the crowd" is the ultimate reality to which we should strive to bend our wills, sacrifice our individuality, and become absorbed.

Do crowds steal our individuality? Do you agree with Kierkegaard that people are too willing to sacrifice their individuality to "the crowd," to surrender their identities to the forces of social conformity?

Søren Kierkegaard, from "On the Dedication to 'That Single Individual'"

There is a view of life which holds that where the crowd is, the truth is also, that it is a need in truth itself, that it must have the crowd on its side. There is another view of life; which holds that wherever the crowd is, there is untruth, so that, for a moment to carry the matter out to its farthest conclusion, even if every individual possessed the truth in private, yet if they came together into a crowd (so that "the crowd" received any *decisive*, voting, noisy, audible importance), untruth would at once be let in.

For "the crowd" is untruth. Eternally, godly, christianly what Paul says is valid: "only one receives the prize," [I Cor. 9:24] not by way of comparison, for in the comparison "the others" are still present. That is to say, everyone can be that one, with God's help—but only one receives the prize; again, that is to say, everyone should cautiously have dealings with "the others," and essentially only talk with God and with himself— for only one receives the prize; again, that is to say, the human being is in kinship with, or to be a human is to be in kinship with the divinity. The worldly, temporal, busy, socially-friendly person says this: "How unreasonable, that only one should receive the prize, it is far more probable that several combined receive the prize; and if we become many, then it becomes more certain and also easier for each individually.". . . But the eternal, which vaults high over the temporal, quiet as the night sky, and God in heaven, who from this exalted state of bliss, without becoming the least bit dizzy, looks out over these innumerable millions and knows each single individual; he, the great examiner, he says: only one receives the prize; that is to say, everyone can receive it, and everyone ought to become this by oneself, but only one receives the prize. Where the crowd is, therefore, or where a decisive importance is attached to the fact that there is a crowd, *there* no one is working, living, and striving for the highest end, but only for this or that earthly end; since the eternal, the decisive, can only be worked for where there is one; and to become this by oneself, which all can do, is to will to allow God to help you—"the crowd" is untruth.

Kierkegaard introduces this passage with the theme that he will repeat throughout: "The crowd is untruth." Although there are many people who contend just the opposite—that reality lies in social groups and organizations—Kierkegaard is convinced that "only one receives the prize." Not that he means this in terms of competition with others—when we compare ourselves with others we are by definition letting "the crowd" mentality penetrate our psyches. No, "only one receives the prize" is a mental state, in which you view your project on Earth as striving to achieve "your" prize, the prize that only *you* can achieve. "The crowd" cannot help you in this quest; you must reach your goal by means of your own individual resources.

Søren Kierkegaard,
from "On the Dedication to 'That Single Individual'"

A crowd—not this or that, one now living or long dead, a crowd of the lowly or of nobles, of rich or poor, etc., but in its very concept—is untruth, since a crowd either renders the single individual wholly unrepentant and irresponsible, or weakens his responsibility by making it a fraction of his decision. . . . The untruth is first that it is "the crowd," which does either what only *the single individual* in the crowd does, or in every case what *each single individual* does. For a crowd is an abstraction. . . .

The concept of "the crowd" is a state of consciousness for the individual, not necessarily corresponding to a particular group of people. It's the automatic inclination to view yourself and your life only in terms of others: a family member, an employee, a member of a religion, and so on. When you view yourself *only* as a member of a social group, you implicitly deny your individuality, your unique human distinctness. In so doing you surrender your autonomy, permitting the crowd to make decisions for you, enabling you to temporarily escape from your personal responsibility for your choices. Of course, as Sartre makes clear in Chapter 4, this "escape" is an illusion because you are fully responsible for surrendering your ability to make free choices to the crowd, and you are fully responsible for anything that the crowd chooses to do. For Kierkegaard, surrendering ourselves to the crowd is *inauthentic* and the height of immorality. Moral action begins with "respecting what it means to be human," and concludes with acting on the truth that "everyone can be the one."

Technology has exacerbated the human tendency to subsume themselves to the crowd. In Kierkegaard's time, the power of printed publications like newspapers made it easier for clever leaders to manipulate the thinking of the citizens, fashioning them into a docile crowd to do their bidding. In our day and age, this power to anonymously manipulate large numbers of people has increased exponentially through the electronic mediums of television and the Internet. And the crowd is always vulnerable to the manipulations of "untruths" because untruths play on people's emotions and appeal to their innate desires. Truth, on the other hand, requires thought, understanding, reflection, insight, and critical analysis. In contrast, untruth requires "no previous knowledge, no schooling, no discipline, no abstinence, no self-denial, no honest self-concern, no patient labor!" Untruths are brain candy for the masses, telling them what they want to hear, manipulating them to think and feel precisely what the manipulators want them to. It is in this sense that the crowd, thinking itself strong, is really weak, a herd of unthinking and easily controlled animals, pushed and prodded, stumbling down preordained paths with smiles on their simple faces.

One cannot say that, again with the help of the press, "the truth" can overcome the lie and the error. O, you who say this, ask yourself: Do you dare to claim that human beings, in a crowd, are just as quick to reach for truth, which is not always palatable, as for untruth, which is always deliciously prepared, when in addition this must be combined with an admission that one has let oneself be deceived! Or do you dare to claim that "the truth" is just as quick to let itself be understood as is untruth, which requires no previous knowledge, no schooling, no discipline, no abstinence, no self-denial, no honest self-concern, no patient labor! No, "the truth," which detests this untruth, the only goal of which is to desire its increase, is not so quick on its feet. Firstly, it cannot work through the fantastical, which is the untruth; its communicator is only a single individual. And its communication relates itself once again to the single individual; for in this view of life the single individual is precisely the truth.

Søren Kierkegaard, from "On the Dedication to 'That Single Individual'"

But Kierkegaard believes there is hope. It is a hope that is ignited every time a person rejects the sleeping unreflection of the crowd mentality and insists on being "a single individual," rejecting the mindless tyranny of the crowd and replacing it with the eternal life of the authentic individual. This is the ethical ideal to which every person should aspire.

A crowd is indeed made up of single individuals; it must therefore be in everyone's power to become what he is, a single individual; no one is prevented from being a single individual, no one, unless he prevents himself by becoming many. To become a crowd, to gather a crowd around oneself, is on the contrary to distinguish life from life; even the most well-meaning one who talks about that, can easily offend a single individual. But it is the crowd which has power, influence, reputation, and domination is the distinction of life from life, which tyrannically overlooks the single individual as the weak and powerless one, in a temporal-worldly way overlooks the eternal truth: the single individual.

Søren Kierkegaard, from "On the Dedication to 'That Single Individual'"

The dehumanizing domination of "the crowd," in which uncritical masses of people look outward to political and religious leaders, as well as popular culture, to tell them "who" to be, reflects what Kierkegaard calls "the abstract principle of leveling." With the annihilation of individuality, people are reduced to

How does the media manipulate us? Identify some of the ways that the media are able to manipulate the thinking and behavior of people. Why are people vulnerable to these "untruths"?

abstractions, labels, and categories defined by age, race, marital status, career, socioeconomic status, nationality, educational level, and gender. The net effect of removing the unique and rich qualities from each individual is to place all people on the same abstract level. This is true alienation; and, as Kierkegaard describes it in *The Present Age*, it is profoundly immoral.

> **The abstract principle of leveling . . . like the biting east wind, has no personal relation to any individual, but has only an abstract relationship which is the same for everyone.**

Søren Kierkegaard, from *The Present Age*

The present age tends toward a mathematical equality in which it takes so and so many to make one individual. Formerly the outstanding individual could allow himself everything and the individual in the masses nothing at all. Now everyone knows that so and so many make an individual, and quite consistently people add themselves together (it is called joining together, but that is only a polite euphemism) for the most trivial purposes. Simply in order to put a passing whim into practice a few people add themselves together, and the thing is done—they dare to do it . . . the individual no longer belongs to God, to himself, to his beloved, to his art or to his science; he is conscious of belonging in all things to an abstraction to which he is subjected by reflection . . . .

The abstract principle of leveling . . . like the biting east wind, has no personal relation to any individual, but has only an abstract relationship which is the same for everyone. There no hero suffers for others, or helps them; the taskmaster of all alike is the leveling process, which itself takes on their education. And the man who learns most from the leveling and himself becomes greatest does not become an outstanding man or hero—that would only impede the leveling process, which is rigidly consistent to the end; he himself prevents that from happening because he has understood the meaning of leveling: he becomes a man and nothing else, in the complete equalitarian sense.

We can now more fully appreciate Kierkegaard's pronouncement, "Truth is subjectivity." For several centuries, new discoveries in every branch of science have emboldened certain scientists and philosophers to maintain that the rational and empirical concepts and methodologies of science are "objective" and therefore "truer" and "more real" than the subjective experiences of humans. For Kierkegaard and other existentialists, this notion is dangerous and delusionary. All scientific thought is rooted in the concrete immediacy of lived human experience, without which it wouldn't exist. The world in which each individual lives is infinitely more "real" than any scientific abstraction. Your thoughts and emotions, your quest to understand the purpose of your life and death, your desire to shape your existence through freely originated choices, your passionate commitment to truth, honesty, and authenticity—these are the building blocks of the human universe. Scientific thought simply reflects an abstracted version of the ground of its reality—to argue that it is more "real" than the direct experience of the living individual who gave rise to it makes as little sense as assuming that a sophisticated computer is "more real" than the individual human mind that created it, or that a motion picture is "more real" than the life experiences on which it is based. Kierkegaard makes this point eloquently in his *Concluding Unscientific Postscript*:

All logical thinking employs the language of abstraction. . . . It is easier to indulge in abstract thought than it is to exist. . . .

The difficulty that inheres in existence, with which the existing individual is confronted, is one that never really comes to expression in the language of abstract thought, much less receives an explanation. . . . Abstract thought ignores the concrete and the temporal, the existential process, the predicament of the existing individual arising from his being a synthesis of the temporal and the eternal situated in existence. . . .

Existing is ordinarily regarded as no very complex matter, much less an art, since we all exist; but abstract thinking takes rank as an accomplishment. But to really exist . . . that is truly difficult.

> **But to really exist . . . that is truly difficult.**
> **SØREN KIERKEGAARD**

To "really exist," for Kierkegaard, is a lifelong challenge and evolutionary process. He identifies "Three Stages on Life's Way" through which every person must pass to become an authentic individual and "really exist":

- *Aesthetic Stage:* This is the stage of life in which people are absorbed in pursuing the beautiful and pleasurable dimensions of life, living for the moment, led by emotions and sensuous passions. Although powerfully seductive, a life devoted to simply pursuing pleasurable experience after pleasurable experience is ultimately dissatisfying. Kierkegaard describes his own experience in the aesthetic stage as a vain search for anchorage on a "boundless sea of pleasure," an existence in which he had "tasted the fruit of the tree of knowledge . . . but the pleasure did not outlast the sea of pleasure." Kierkegaard concludes that a hedonistic life devoted solely to the pursuit of pleasure is devoid of genuine meaning and ultimately filled with emptiness and dread.

- *Ethical Stage:* Dissatisfaction with the excesses of the aesthetic stage typically motivates people to seek a life guided by moral standards and ethical values. Moral codes provide people with a structure that was lacking in the aesthetic stage. Such codes provide them with a clear listing of "dos" and "don'ts," of values to live by, of virtuous people to aspire to. But for Kierkegaard, this stage is ultimately unsatisfactory as well. Too often people look outside themselves for moral guidance and define themselves in terms of the values of others, "the crowd." The ethical stage is a necessary but transitory stage in an individual's quest for ultimate meaning, an authentic existence that can only be realized in the *religious stage*. In fact, as far as ethical beliefs are concerned, Kierkegaard contends, "The important thing is not what you may think is precisely right or wrong. What matters is that you choose to have an opinion at all on what is right or wrong."

- *Religious Stage:* Unlike the previous life stages, which are characterized by a distinct set of beliefs and behavior that are easily identifiable, the religious stage is characterized by a highly personal, subjective, and nonrational "leap of faith." And because it is beyond reason and objective analysis, it is impossible by its nature to communicate it in any precise fashion. For Kierkegaard this is the realm of *subjective truth*, an existence in which people become profoundly aware of their individuality and relationship to the divine. This is an area of Kierkegaard's thought that is examined more fully in Chapter 7, "Is There a Spiritual Reality?"

< READING CRITICALLY >

Analyzing Kierkegaard on Authenticity

- For Kierkegaard, the moral goal in life is to achieve *authenticity*, a state in which you fully and honestly accept your existential predicament: your freedom to choose your destiny, your independence of outside groups or individuals in defining your "self," your willingness to confront the uncertainties of the cosmos—including death and the meaning of life—with courage and resilience. With this as a criterion, evaluate to what extent you are living what Kierkegaard would consider an "authentic" life.

- Reflect on the forces that existentialists believe have alienated modern men and women, including the increasing dominance of technology; the complex size and structures of many businesses, bureaucracies, and social organizations; the manipulation by the media. In what ways have these forces affected you and the way you see yourself? For example, do you sometimes feel that you are being treated more as a Social Security number or a statistic than as a human being? Do you feel that you are seen by others primarily in terms of abstract categories rather than as a uniquely valuable individual? Do you sometimes feel that it's difficult to forge meaningful relationships with other people in the professional or social groups of which you are a member? Have you felt disconnected from the jobs that you have had, being treated like a "cog" in a machine, or an impersonal paper-pusher?

- Consider society as a whole. To what extent do you believe that Kierkegaard's and Socrates' condemnations are on target?

> Let others complain that the age is wicked; my complaint is that it is wretched, for it lacks passion. Men's thoughts are thin and flimsy like lace, they are themselves pitiable like lacemakers. The thoughts of their hearts are too paltry to be sinful. For a worm it might be regarded as a sin to harbor such thoughts, but not for a being made in the image of God. Their lusts are dull and sluggish, their passions sleepy. They do their duty, these shopkeeping souls. . . . *Kierkegaard*

> You, my friend,—a citizen of the great and mighty and wise city of Athens,—are you not ashamed of heaping up the greatest amount of money and honour and reputation, and caring so little about wisdom and truth and the greatest improvement of the soul, which you never regard or heed at all? *Socrates*

Friedrich Nietzsche
(1844–1900). Nietzsche was a German philosopher who challenged the ideals of Western philosophy, including science, morality, and the notion of God.

Beyond Good and Evil: Nietzsche

Kierkegaard's passionate conviction that the "leveling" influences of society have inhibited the development of the "hero" and the "outstanding man" express core themes in the thinking of **Friedrich Nietzsche**, a German philosopher whose writings were enigmatic, passionate, poetic, disturbing, inspiring, and open to varied interpretations. He was in many ways an outsider with respect to his culture, his philosophical tradition, and his personal life. At the heart of his philosophy, he glorified the individual self in all of its power and nobility. For Nietzsche, all of life is governed by a primal force, the *will to power*—"the will to grow, spread, seize, become predominant"—that is manifest in all living things. The *will to power* finds its highest expression in humankind in our universal desire to control others and impose our values on them. Thus the ultimate moral good is an individual's striving to exert his or her *will to power* to the fullest possible extent.

This conviction set Nietzsche at odds with the prevailing Christian and Judeo-Christian morality of his time (and to a certain extent, our time as well), which trumpeted the virtues of compassion, self-sacrifice, meekness, humility, pity, dependency, and a denial of self. He found these qualities to be a gross violation and perversion of the natural life principle of *will to power*. For Nietzsche, these traditionally "good" values were in fact contemptible, destructive, and socially toxic. Why? Because these so-called virtues were in fact the product of a conspiracy of the weak and powerless designed to constrain the strong and powerful individuals in a web of moral restrictions. Instead of encouraging individuals to fulfill their glorious potential through the unrestrained expression of their *will to power*, this perverted moral code of the weak and powerless exhorted people to serve and devote themselves to others, particularly the weak and incompetent. For Nietzsche, the pervasive domination of this Christian "slave morality" perpetrated by the decadent, sheeplike herds of resentful weaklings was an evolutionary catastrophe. He was convinced that humans were destined to evolve to higher forms of being, the *übermensch* (the "overman"), but that this "slave morality"—with its values of humility, self-sacrifice, compassion, and equality—was threatening to weaken the human spirit and prevent the best and strongest individuals from becoming strong and dominant. The Judeo-Christian slave morality represented a moral *de*volution in its rejection of the ancient virtues of nobility and devotion to the growth of self rather than subjugation to others. As he exclaims in his book *Daybreak*:

● Watch the **Video**
*Human, All
Too Human* on
mysearchlab.com

> How the overall moral judgments have shifted! The great men of antique morality, Epictetus for instance, knew nothing of the now normal glorification of thinking of others, of living for others; in the light of our moral fashion they would have to be called downright immoral, for they strove with all their might **for** their ego and **against** feeling with others (that is to say, with the sufferings and moral frailties of others). Perhaps they would reply to us: "If you are so boring or ugly an object to yourself, by all means think of others more than yourself! It is right you should."

For Nietzsche, the role of the overman is to *create* values, not to conform to the decadent and life-denying values of the slave morality. Ironically, he considered Jesus to be a supreme example of the overman, an individual of great power, influence, and originality. However, he considered the religion and moral system that was based on Jesus' life and teachings to be a distorted version of his true message ("The last Christian died on the cross," he said). Christianity is a religion that warns against the sins of ambition, pride, and domination, precisely those qualities that Nietzsche found to be the purest expression of the *will to power*. He found obscene the Christian concepts of devoting ourselves to God, becoming empty vessels for God's will, pursuing the values of loving our neighbors, and humbly caring for the meek. For Nietzsche, devoting ourselves to God is a wasted effort because, as he declared, "God is dead." Not literally dead, of course: What he meant was that the concept of God as an all-powerful dominant entity was being eroded by modern

Is God "dead"? Nietzsche on Christ. Nietzsche claimed that Jesus was an overman but that his followers instead promoted the values of the slave morality. Which values do you find more compelling—those of the pride, strength, and ambition or those of humility, self-sacrifice, and compassion?

consciousness, the evolving influence of scientific progress, and the increasing faith in humankind's abilities to solve humankind's problems without divine intervention. In one of the most memorable passages in contemporary philosophy, Nietzsche articulates his prophecy of the death of God in the form of a parable:

> "
> **God is dead. God remains dead. And we have killed him.**
> "

Friedrich Nietzsche, from *The Gay Science*

The madman. —have you not heard of the madman who lit a lantern in the bright morning hours, ran to the market place, and cried incessantly: "I seek God! I seek God!"—As many of those who did not believe in God were standing around just then, he provoked much laughter. Has he got lost? asked one. Did he lose his way like a child? asked another. Or is he hiding? Is he afraid of us? Has he gone on a voyage? Emigrated?—Thus they yelled and laughed.

The madman jumped into their midst and pierced them with his eyes. "Whither is God?" he cried; "I will tell you. *We have killed him*—you and I. All of us are his murderers. But how did we do this? How could we drink up the sea? Who gave us the sponge to wipe away the entire horizon? What were we doing when we unchained the earth from its sun? Whither is it moving now? Whither are we moving? Away from all suns? Are we not plunging continually? Backward, sideward, forward, in all directions? Is there still any up or down? Are we not straying as through an infinite nothing? Do we not feel the breath of empty space? Has it not become colder? Is not night continually closing in on us? Do we not need to light lanterns in the morning? Do we hear nothing as yet of the noise of the gravediggers who are burying God? Do we smell nothing yet of the divine decomposition? Gods, too, decompose. God is dead. God remains dead. And we have killed him."

The implications of the death of God are profound: No longer can humans depend on a supernatural being to provide purpose to their lives and a moral code to live by. We can no longer consider ourselves "children of God," our supernatural "father," needing his forgiveness to cleanse us of "original sin." Nietzsche believes it is now up to us humans to create meaning in life and a moral code to live by. The brave and fearless overmen welcome this challenge; the weak and insecure "undermen" fear and resist it.

Friedrich Nietzsche, from *The Gay Science*

The greatest recent event—that "God is dead," that the belief in the Christian god has become unbelievable—is already beginning to cast its first shadows. . . . The event itself is far too great, too distant, too remote for the multitude's capacity for comprehension even for the tidings of it to be thought of as having *arrived* as yet. Much less may one suppose that many people know as yet *what* this event really means—and how much must collapse now that (the possibility of) faith has been undermined because it was built upon this faith (in God's existence), propped up by it, grown into it; for example, the whole of our morality.

The weak "doglike" people seek to establish a social order in which everyone is considered equal, whether they are or not. The slave mentality envies and resents these superior individuals. The weak yearn to be like them, but they lack the strength and determination, so they first deny that *anyone* is superior. In his strikingly original narrative, *Thus Spake Zarathustra*, a combination of prose and poetry "spoken" as a character based on a Persian prophet, Nietzsche give voice to this idea:

> You higher men learn this from me: in the market place nobody believes in higher men. And if you want to speak there, very well! But the mob blinks: "We are all equal." "You higher men"—thus blinks the mob—"there are no higher men, we are all equal, man is man; before God we are all equal."
>
> Before God! But now this God has died. And before the mob we do not want to be equal. You higher men, go away from the market place!

This "marketplace" mentality inhibits individuals' pursuit of excellence and leads to the creation of a slave morality that is designed to completely submerge the individual in tradition, conformity, and devotion to the "greater good." But because the group is based on fear and insecurity, it is distrustful of outsiders in any form, and it demands unthinking allegiance to the will of the group. Rather than the open, honest, and natural expression of each individual's *will to power*, this life-affirming instinct becomes a perverted surrender to the group identity. As Nietzsche notes in *Towards a Genealogy of Morals*, the individual is lost, a human sacrifice to fear and weakness:

> The slaves' revolt in morals begins with this, that **ressentiment** itself becomes creative and gives birth to values: the **ressentiment** of those who are denied the real reaction, that of the deed, and who compensate with an imaginary revenge. Whereas all noble morality begins out of a triumphant affirmation of oneself, slave morality immediately says No to what comes from outside, to what is different, to what is not oneself: and **this** No is its creative deed. This reversal of the value-positing glance—this **necessary** direction outward instead of back to oneself—is of the nature of **ressentiment**: to come into being, slave morality requires an outside world, a counterworld; physiologically speaking, it requires external stimuli in order to react at all: its action is always at bottom a reaction.

Nietzsche ties together these themes in the following passages from his book, *Beyond Good and Evil*. For Nietzsche, the value-creating *ubermensch* exists "beyond" good and evil: proud, fierce, courageous, bold, independent, glorious, noble. She is the master of morality, not its victim. She has been able to overcome her own doubts and weaknesses, vanquishing obstacles in the path to full development as an individual.

Friedrich Nietzsche, from *Beyond Good and Evil*

Refraining mutually from injury, violence, and exploitation and placing one's will on a par with that of someone else—this may become, in a certain rough sense, good manners among individuals if the appropriate conditions are present (namely, if these men are actually similar in strength and value standards and belong together in *one* body). But as soon as this principle is extended, and possibly even accepted as the *fundamental principle of society*, it immediately proves to be what it really is—a will to the *denial* of life, a principle of disintegration and decay.

Here we must beware of superficiality and get to the bottom of the matter, resisting all sentimental weakness: life itself is *essentially* appropriation, injury, overpowering of what is alien and weaker; suppression, hardness, imposition of one's own forms, incorporation and at least, at its mildest, exploitation—but why should one always use those words in which a slanderous intent has been imprinted for ages?

Even the body within which individuals treat each other as equals, as suggested before—and this happens in every healthy aristocracy—if it is a living and not a dying body, has to do to other bodies what the individuals within it refrain from doing to each other: it will have to be an incarnate will to power, it will strive to grow, spread, seize, become predominant—not from any morality or immorality but because it is *living* and because life simply *is* will to power. But there is no point on which the ordinary consciousness of Europeans resists instruction as on this: everywhere people are now raving, even under scientific disguises, about coming conditions of society in which "the exploitative aspect" will be removed—which sounds to me as if they promised to invent a way of life that would dispense with all organic functions. "Exploitation" does not belong to a corrupt or imperfect and primitive society: it belongs to the *essence* of what lives, as a basic organic function; it is a consequence of the will to power, which is after all the will of life.

If this should be an innovation as a theory—as a reality it is the *primordial fact* of all history: people ought to be honest with themselves at least that far.

For Nietzsche, the cardinal Christian values of refraining from injury, violence, and exploitation are not intrinsically negative—among superior individuals they may actually be viewed as "good manners." The problem comes when these values are elevated to a universal status, dominating the relations between all people—weak and strong—in all circumstances. When universalized, these values of compassion, kindness, and empathy have the cumulative effect of denying life and the fundamental principle that powers all life—the *will to power*. Although conventional society condemns "exploitation" as an evil, Nietzsche views it as a necessary consequence of the *will to power* that is essential for the survival of the species. Evolutionary development is based on strong individuals making full use of their powers, unconstrained by a false and corrosive belief in equality.

> ## < READING CRITICALLY >
> ### Analyzing Nietzsche on Morality
>
> - Nietzsche grounds his religious and moral philosophy on what he considers to be a basic principle found at the core of life—"an incarnate will to power, it will strive to grow, spread, seize, become predominant—not from any morality or immorality but because it is *living* and because life simply *is* will to power." Do you agree with this characterization of a basic life force? Why or why not?
> - What does Nietzsche mean by his arresting pronouncement that "God is dead"? What are his reasons for coming to this conclusion?
> - Exploitation and domination are natural consequences of the *will to power*, according to Nietzsche. Rather than see them as "immoral," we should recognize them as essential attributes of the strong and noble individual. Critically evaluate this view and provide an example of your perspective.
> - Because the majority of individuals are weak, insecure, and lacking in determination, Nietzsche believes that they conspire to create a system of values to drag down superior individuals and keep them in check. Have you ever personally experienced a situation in which you distinguished yourself in some way, only to find yourself the target of envy and criticism from others? If so, does this experience support Nietzsche's thesis regarding the "slave morality"?
> - Nietzsche voiced contempt for Kant's moral theory because he believed that using rational duty as the sole criterion for conduct promoted mindless

conformity among people. Instead, he believed that individuals must follow their natural passions and instincts for life: Otherwise, they are doomed to become faceless members of the human "herd." In *Twilight of the Idols* he observes: "(Virtue) must be our own invention, our most necessary self-expression. . . . The fundamental laws of self-preservation and growth demand . . . that everyone invent his own virtue, his own categorical imperative. A people perishes when it confuses its duty with duty in general." Do you think Nietzsche's point has merit? Support your analysis with specific examples from contemporary culture.

Authenticity and Ethical Responsibility: Sartre

Jean-Paul Sartre
(1905–1980). This French philosopher, novelist, playwright, and literary critic was a leading figure in twentieth-century existentialism.

Jean-Paul Sartre's approach to ethics was based on the same fundamental themes as Kierkegaard's, though he was writing nearly a century later in a very different world. We explored Sartre's views in some detail in Chapter 4, "Are You Free?" As with Kierkegaard, Sartre believes that becoming an authentic individual is the ethical ideal we should strive to achieve. And authenticity means fully accepting the fact that we are "condemned to be free," completely responsible for every action we take in life. We create ourselves through our daily choices, and those choices are free: We are without excuse.

Jean-Paul Sartre, from *Existentialism Is a Humanism*

Atheistic existentialism, which I represent, is more coherent. It states that if God does not exist, there is at least one being in whom existence precedes essence, a being who exists before he can be defined by any concept, and that this being is man, or, as Heidegger says, human reality. What is meant here by saying that existence precedes essence? It means that, first of all, man exists, turns up, appears on the scene, and, only afterward, defines himself. If man, as the existentialist conceives him, is indefinable, it is because at first he is nothing. Only afterward will he be something, and he himself will have made what he will be. Thus, there is no human nature, since there is no God to conceive it. Not only is man what he conceives himself to be, but he is also only what he wills himself to be after this thrust toward existence.

Man is nothing else but what he makes of himself. Such is the first principle of existentialism. It is also what is called subjectivity, the name we are labeled with when charges are brought against us. But what do we mean by this, if not that man has a greater dignity than a stone or table? For we mean that man first exists, that is, that man first of all is the being who hurls himself toward a future and who is conscious of imagining himself as being in the future.

But if existence really does precede essence, man is responsible for what he is. Thus, existentialism's first move is to make every man aware of what he is and to make the full responsibility of his existence rest on him. And when we say that a man is responsible for himself, we do not only mean that he is responsible for his own individuality, but that he is responsible for all men. . . .

> **Man is nothing else but what he makes of himself.**

For Sartre, our choices are entirely free, and we can depend only on ourselves to determine the "right" choice to make because God does not exist, and there are no absolute moral codes that apply to all people. This means that there are no reliable guidelines to instruct us as to what we should do. We are alone, abandoned in a callous and uncaring universe, with only ourselves as resources.

But isn't this a potentially dangerous theory? After all, if we give people unlimited license to choose whatever they want, as long as they accept responsibility for their choices, how can we condemn the actions of evil people like Hitler and Stalin? When confronted regarding their moral evil, couldn't they respond: "I'm an existentialist: My choices are completely free, and I accept responsibility for them. So you have no grounds for condemning me." This is a potentially devastating issue for Sartre, and he is clearly aware of its threat. Sartre himself was a person of strong moral principles, which led him to become a fighter for the French Resistance during World War II, following the invasion of France by Nazi Germany. For Sartre, choosing freely and accepting one's responsibility is not a solely individual project: It takes place in a social context and embodies an enlightened sense of moral responsibility to humanity as a whole.

Jean-Paul Sartre,
from *Existentialism Is a Humanism*

"
When we say that man chooses his own self, we mean that every one of us does likewise; but we also mean by that in making this choice he also chooses all men.
"

When we say that man chooses his own self, we mean that every one of us does likewise; but we also mean by that that in making this choice he also chooses all men. In fact, in creating the man that we want to be, there is not a single one of our acts which does not at the same time create an image of man as we think he ought to be. To choose to be this or that is to affirm at the same time the value of what we choose, because we can never choose evil. We always choose the good, and nothing can be good for us without being good for all.

. . . If we grant that we exist and fashion our image at one and the same time, the image is valid for everybody and for our whole age. Thus, our responsibility is much greater than we might have supposed, because it involves all mankind. . . . if I want to marry, to have children; even if this marriage depends solely on my own circumstances or passion or wish, I am involving all humanity in monogamy and not merely myself. Therefore, I am responsible for myself and for everyone else. I am creating a certain image of man of my own choosing. In choosing myself, I choose man.

In an effort to save his theory from charges of amorality, Sartre is invoking a bold blend of Immanuel Kant and Plato. Kant, as we saw on page 498, founded his ethical theory on what he termed his categorical imperative: "Act as if the maxim of your action were to become by your will a universal law of nature." In other words, Kant is suggesting that the standard we use in making moral decisions is to ask ourselves: "Would I be rationally able to endorse *everyone* making the same choice as I?" For example, if you're thinking about purchasing a term paper online and submitting it as your own, you would have to endorse as a rational law *everyone* doing exactly the same thing. Sartre seems to be trying to attach his theory of free choice to this same "universalizing" concept when he states:

> When we say that man chooses his own self, we mean that every one of us does likewise; but we also mean by that that in making this choice he also chooses all men. In fact, in creating the man that we want to be, there is not a single one of our acts which does not at the same time create an image of man as we think he ought to be.

When you make a choice, according to Sartre, you are not simply creating and defining yourself as a person—you are also creating and defining your image of the way all humans *should* be. So if you choose to cheat in school, you are by implication suggesting that all humans should act exactly the same way. It's a fascinating approach to ethical choice, combining a belief in absolute freedom with a Kantian responsibility to universalize our choices with an implicit endorsement that all men and women make the choice that you are making.

Despite the surface similarities, however, Sartre believed that his approach to ethics was fundamentally different from Kant's. For Kant, obeying the categorical imperative is an absolute duty grounded on the primacy of reason: We are in essence rational creatures, so we cannot help but recognize our responsibility to universalize our choices with logical consistency. For Sartre, there are no absolute moral standards or duties that transcend the individual: Our choices rest solely on our own shoulders, guided by our own spontaneous and unfettered ability to choose freely. Yet if this is truly the case, what is Sartre's rationale for contending that when we choose for ourselves we implicitly "choose for all men"?

Sartre also seems to be invoking Plato's ethical perspective that no person does evil intentionally. Plato was convinced that people act immorally due to ignorance. When you educate people and show them a more enlightened path, they cannot help but take it. Sartre seems to be making the same point when he states, "To choose to be this or that is to affirm at the same time the value of what we choose, because we can never choose evil. We always choose the good, and nothing can be good for us without being good for all."

Sartre realized that many people are terrified by the prospect of such absolute freedom and complete responsibility. Their response is to flee, to escape from this life sentence of freedom and responsibility. This refusal to accept responsibility creates *inauthenticity*. Inauthentic individuals deny their freedom, attempt to surrender their freedom to others, passively let outside forces shape their lives, or pretend that the formation of their characters was beyond their control. They lack the courage to accept themselves as self-creators, creating a false image of themselves that they present to the world as real, a mask concealing their weak and trembling selves. And they refuse to acknowledge their awesome responsibility of legislating for all humankind by the choices that they make.

Listen to the **Podcast**
Sebastian Gardner on Sartre's Bad Faith on
mysearchlab.com

The existentialists say at once that man is anguish. What that means is this: the man who involves himself and who realizes that he is not only the person he chooses to be, but also a law-maker who is, at the same time, choosing for all mankind as well as himself, cannot help escape the feeling of his total and deep responsibility. Of course, there are many people who are not anxious; but we claim that they are hiding their anxiety, that they are fleeing from it. Certainly, many people believe that when they do something, they themselves are the only ones involved, and when someone says to them, "What if everyone acted that way?" they shrug their shoulders and answer, "Everyone doesn't act that way." But really, one should always ask himself, "What would happen if everybody looked at things that way?" There is no escaping this disturbing thought except by a kind of double-dealing. A man who lies and makes excuses for himself by saying "not everybody does that," is someone with an uneasy conscience, because the act of lying implies that a universal value is conferred upon the lie.

Jean-Paul Sartre, from *Existentialism Is a Humanism*

> **The existentialists say at once that man is anguish.**

All such efforts to escape from freedom and responsibility are doomed because we are "condemned" to be free. Our efforts to escape succeed only in creating inauthentic selves with no hope of living meaningful lives. The only way to live a genuinely authentic life is to embrace your freedom, acknowledge your responsibility, and face the profound existential emotions of abandonment, anguish, and despair with uncommon courage. (These are the views of the "early" Sartre. The "later" Sartre, influenced by Marxism, qualified his extreme notion of freedom.)

Sartre provides a real-world example to illustrate the general framework that he is proposing. His example is set during World War II, after Nazi Germany had invaded France. A certain percentage of the French population became "collaborators," cooperating with the occupying Germans, whereas others continued to fight against the Germans in the French Resistance, of which Sartre himself was a member. But before describing the example, he first provides us with a memorable restatement of his central thesis regarding human freedom.

Jean-Paul Sartre,
from *Existentialism Is a Humanism*

That is the idea I shall try to convey when I say that man is condemned to be free. Condemned, because he did not create himself, yet, in other respects he is free; because, once thrown into the world, he is responsible for everything he does. The existentialist does not believe in the power of passion. He will never agree that a sweeping passion is a ravaging torrent which fatally leads a man to certain acts and is therefore an excuse. He thinks that man is responsible for his passion. . . .

To give you an example which will enable you to understand abandonment better, I shall cite the case of one of my students who came to see me under the following circumstances: his father was on bad terms with his mother, and, moreover, was inclined to be a collaborationist; his older brother had been killed in the German offensive of 1940, and the young man, with somewhat immature but generous feelings, wanted to avenge him. His mother lived alone with him, very much upset by the half-treason of her husband and the death of her older son; the boy was her only consolation.

The boy was faced with the choice of leaving for England and joining the Free French Forces—that is, leaving his mother behind—or remaining with his mother and helping her to carry on. He was fully aware that the woman lived only for him and that his going-off—and perhaps his death—would plunge her into despair. He was also aware that every act that he did for his mother's sake was a sure thing, in the sense that it was helping her to carry on, whereas every effort he made toward going off and fighting was an uncertain move which might run aground and prove completely useless; for example, on his way to England he might, while passing through Spain, be detained indefinitely in a Spanish camp; he might reach England or Algiers and be stuck in an office at a desk job. As a result, he was faced with two very different kinds of action: one, concrete, immediate, but concerning only one individual; the other concerned an incomparably vaster group, a national collectivity, but for that very reason was dubious, and might be interrupted en route. And, at the same time, he was wavering between two kinds of ethics. On the one hand, an ethics of sympathy, of personal devotion; on the other, a broader ethics, but one whose efficacy was more dubious. He had to choose between the two.

Who could help him choose? Christian doctrine? No. Christian doctrine says, "Be charitable, love our neighbor, take the more rugged path, etc., etc." But which is the more rugged path? Whom should he love as a brother? The fighting man or his mother? Which does the greater good, the vague act of fighting in a group, or the concrete one of helping a particular human being to go on living? Who can decide *a priori*? Nobody. No book of ethics can tell him. The Kantian ethics says, "Never treat any person as a means, but as an end." Very well, if I stay with my mother, I'll treat her as an end and not

Would you risk your life to free your country? Soldiers of the Free French Forces. Sartre presents the dilemma of a young man who must choose between staying with his mother or joining the fight to liberate France from the Nazis. Which choice would you make?

as a means; but by virtue of this very fact I'm running the risk of treating the people around me who are fighting, as means; and, conversely, if I go to join those who are fighting, I'll be treating them as an end, and, by doing that, I run the risk of treating my mother as a means.

What makes this a fascinating example is that it involves choosing between two morally desirable outcomes: the personal value of staying with a loved one who needs us versus the social value of fighting to defeat a terrible enemy who has occupied one's homeland and threatens increasingly monstrous evil. Sartre's point is that there are no moral codes that will instruct him in clear and unambiguous terms what the morally "right" choice is. This is something he must decide for himself. Moral codes and rules are too general to provide guidance in specific situations like this. Whichever alternative he chooses can be justified on moral grounds as a "good" thing, but there is no way of determining the "best" choice outside of his own independent thinking and thoughtful action. His choice is totally free, and he is completely responsible for it.

Does that mean that we should trust our moral "instincts," our ethical "emotions," our "conscience"? Sartre thinks not.

If values are vague, and if they are always too broad for the concrete and specific case that we are considering, the only thing left for us is to trust our instincts. That's what this young man tried to do; and when I saw him, he said, "In the end, feeling is what counts. I ought to choose whichever pushes me in one direction. If I feel that I love my mother enough to sacrifice everything else for her—my desire for vengeance, for action, for adventure—then I'll stay with her. If, on the contrary, I feel that my love for my mother isn't enough, I'll leave."

But how is the value of a feeling determined? What gives his feeling for his mother value? Precisely the fact that he remained with her. I may say that I like so-and-so well enough to sacrifice a certain amount of money for him, but I may say so only if I've done it. I may say "I love my mother well enough to remain with her" if I have remained with her. The only way to determine the value of this affection is, precisely, to perform an act which confirms and defines it. But, since I require this affection to justify my act, I find myself caught in a vicious circle.

Jean-Paul Sartre, from *Existentialism Is a Humanism*

Sartre contends that our moral instincts, emotions, "conscience" are notoriously unreliable and difficult to interpret. We discover which instinct or emotion is stronger by what alternative we choose, but then it is too late to use this instinct or emotion as a guide. That's why Sartre describes this sort of reasoning as a "vicious circle." What's more, it's often difficult to discern the "strength" of emotions and instincts when they are in conflict with one another, and it is also difficult to differentiate "authentic" emotions from "false" emotions. The net result? We cannot discover moral guidance by trying to follow our moral instincts and emotions, any more than we can look to external moral codes for moral direction.

What about seeking the guidance of wise and morally upright people? This approach isn't going to work either, according to Sartre.

You will say, "At least, he did go to a teacher for advice." But if you seek advice from a priest, for example, you have chosen this priest; you already knew, more or less, just about what advice he was going to give you. In other words, choosing your adviser is involving yourself. The proof of this is that if you are a Christian, you

Jean-Paul Sartre, from *Existentialism Is a Humanism*

will say, "Consult a priest." But some priests are collaborating, some are just marking time, some are resisting. Which to choose? If the young man chooses a priest who is resisting or collaborating, he has already decided on the kind of advice he's going to get. Therefore, in coming to see me he knew the answer I was going to give him, and I had only one answer to give: "You're free, choose, that is invent." No general ethics can show you what is to be done, there are no omens in the world. The Catholics will reply, "But there are." Granted—but, in any case, I myself choose the meaning they have.

Sartre's point is that we cannot rely on other people for moral instruction because by selecting the person we are going to for advice, we ourselves are already making the choice of which alternative to select. We know what their values and biases are, and we can be fairly certain of what advice they will give us. It's the same in nonmoral circumstances. Suppose you are engaged in a romantic relationship and are trying to decide whether to continue or to break up. You undoubtedly have a pretty good idea what each of your friends or family will advise you to do, so by selecting the individuals you will ask for advice, you are already reflecting which choice you really want to make. In the final analysis, this is your choice and your choice alone, for which you are fully responsible.

< READING CRITICALLY >

Analyzing Sartre on Moral Responsibility

- Explain what Sartre means when he states, "We are condemned to be free," and as a result our "existence" precedes our "essence."

- Sartre believes that our freedom is absolute and that we achieve authenticity by accepting our freedom and the responsibility that goes along with it. Identify some of the ways in which Sartre believes people behave inauthentically by trying to "escape" from their freedom.

- "In fact, in creating the man that we want to be, there is not a single one of our acts which does not at the same time create an image of man as we think he ought to be. To choose to be this or that is to affirm at the same time the value of what we choose, because we can never choose evil. We always choose the good, and nothing can be good for us without being good for all." Explain what Sartre means in this passage.

- How does Sartre respond when the young man comes to him for advice regarding an ethical dilemma he is facing? How would you respond if the young man came to you with the same question? Explain your reasoning.

Simone de Beauvoir (1908–1986). A French existentialist philosopher and feminist, in *The Second Sex* (1949), de Beauvoir argued that women, historically subordinate to men, have been relegated to the category of the Other Sex.

Our Interplay with Others Defines Us: de Beauvoir

Another powerful voice for existentialism is **Simone de Beauvoir**. A philosopher and novelist, she had an intimate and enduring relationship with Jean-Paul Sartre that spanned most of their adult lives. As revealed in the following excerpt from her book *The Ethics of Ambiguity*, de Beauvoir brought a distinct but complementary perspective to the ethical questions that existentialism confronts.

Simone de Beauvoir, from *Ethics of Ambiguity*

There is no way for a man to escape from this world. It is in this world that—avoiding the pitfalls we have just pointed out—he must realize himself morally. Freedom must project itself toward its own reality through a content whose value it establishes. An end is valid only by a return to the freedom which established it and which willed itself through this end. But his will implies that freedom is not to be engulfed in any goal; neither is it to dissipate itself vainly without aiming at a goal. It is not necessary for the subject to seek to be, but it must desire that there *be* being. To will oneself free and to will that there be *being* are one and the same choice, the choice that man makes of himself as a presence in the world. We can neither say that the free man wants freedom in order to desire being, nor that he wants the disclosure of being by freedom. These are two aspects of a single reality. And whichever be the one under consideration, they both imply the bond of each man with all others.

In this passage de Beauvoir grapples with the mystery of freedom, which, like Sartre, she considers to be radical in nature and central to human experience. Freedom is the source of all value in human experience: As it projects itself outward through intention and action, it confers value. So, for example, when you choose to pursue your education in college, you are at the same time conferring value on your choice. This pursuit has value to you not because someone else *says* it's important but because you *chose* to pursue it as an end. At the same time, de Beauvoir maintains that the act of choosing freely also reveals a desire on our part that there be a world in which our choices can have meaning, a world populated with other freely choosing agents.

Simone de Beauvoir, from *Ethics of Ambiguity*

This bond does not immediately reveal itself to everybody. A young man wills himself free. He wills that there be being. This spontaneous liberality which casts him ardently into the world can ally itself to what is commonly called egoism. Often the young man perceives only that aspect of his relationship to others whereby others appear as enemies. In the preface to *The Inner Experience* Georges Bataille emphasizes very forcefully that each individual wants to be All. He sees in every other man and particularly in those whose existence is asserted with most brilliance, a limit, a condemnation of himself. "Each consciousness," said Hegel, "sees the death of the other." And indeed at every moment others are stealing the whole world away from me. The first movement is to hate them. But his hatred is naïve, and the desire immediately struggles against itself. If I were really everything there would be nothing beside me; the world would be empty. There would be nothing to possess, and I myself would be nothing. If he is reasonable, the young man immediately understands that by taking the world away from me, others also give it to me, since a thing is given to me only by the movement which snatches it from me. To will that there be being is also to will that there be men by and for whom the world is endowed with human significations. One can reveal the world only on a basis revealed by other men. No project can be defined except by its interference with other projects. To make being "be" is to communicate with others by means of being.

Our freedom, which defines our existence, only has meaning in relationship to others who are exercising their freedom of choice. Even when the initial impulse of someone is to control and dominate everything—in the same way that immature people may seek to have the world revolve entirely around *them*—there is the rapid realization that we need other people for our own lives to have meaning. Even when others make choices that challenge or interfere with our own choices, we recognize that the only way we can define ourselves as humans is through our interaction with others.

Simone de Beauvoir, from *Ethics of Ambiguity*

> This truth is found in another form when we say that freedom cannot will itself without aiming at an open future. The ends which it gives itself must be unable to be transcended by any reflection, but only the freedom of others can extend them beyond our life. I have tried to show in *Pyrrhus and Cineas* that every man needs the freedom of other men and, in a sense, always wants it, even though he may be a tyrant; the only thing he fails to do is to assume honestly the consequences of such a wish. Only the freedom of others keeps each one of us from hardening in the absurdity of facticity. And if we are to believe the Christian myth of creation, God himself was in agreement on this point with the existentialist doctrine since, in the words of an anti-fascist priest, "He had such respect for man that He created him free."

We need other people to become fully human, and this is the existential basis for morality. The essence of being human is to be continually exercising our freedom of choice, projecting ourselves into the future, transcending ourselves, continually evolving. This is only possible through our interplay with others, who are striving to achieve the same significance for themselves through the choices they make. If we were completely alone, solitary in an empty world, our dynamic humanity would become hardened into "facticity"—a "thingness" created by our objective circumstances, sapped of its life and spirit.

In defining his freedom-based ethic, Sartre argued that in choosing for ourselves we are choosing for all humanity. De Beauvoir provides a compelling rationale for this view by displaying the intimate and essential connection that we have to all men and women: Our existence can have meaning only in relationship to the existence of others. Our freedom to choose can exist only in relation to the freedom of choice exercised by others. Thus the choices we make as we define who we are must necessarily reflect the kinds of choices that we believe all men and women should make, for we are connected to one another in ways that are profound and inescapable.

< READING CRITICALLY >

Analyzing de Beauvoir on Moral Choices

- Simone de Beauvoir believes that in creating ourselves through our free choices we initially desire to be "All" but gradually recognize that we need to exist in a world of other free agents to fully realize ourselves. What do you think she means by this? Do you agree with her? Why or why not?

- According to de Beauvoir, "freedom cannot will itself without aiming at an open future. The ends which it gives itself must be unable to be transcended by any reflection, but only the freedom of others can extend them beyond our life." Explain what you believe she means by this assertion and provide an example from your own life that either confirms or disconfirms it.

Courage Is the Highest Value: Camus

Albert Camus was a friend and associate of Jean-Paul Sartre and Simone de Beauvoir. Camus was a French writer of powerful plays and novels with existentialist themes, including such well-known works as *The Stranger* and *The Plague*. One of Camus' most haunting works is his essay "The Myth of Sisyphus," an analysis of human existence based on the ancient Greek myth. Sisyphus is condemned by the gods to eternally push a huge stone up a hill in Hades, only to watch it roll all the way down the slope once he nears the top. For Camus, Sisyphus's fate is emblematic of the human condition. Our lives are doomed to the same sort of *absurd* existence, living our lives in an "unintelligible and limited universe" devoid of intrinsic meaning. We make choices and engage in activities with the inescapable specter that they are ultimately without purpose. Yet Camus believes that, even in the midst of an absurd world, meaning is possible through critical reflection and courageously free choices.

Albert Camus (1913–1960). A French existentialist known for essays and novels, Camus dealt with what he felt was the absurd situation of human beings in which the world is essentially irrational, yet we still need to find meaning within it.

Here is Camus' account of the myth, followed by his thoughts regarding the implications of the myth for human existence. As we will see, Camus believes that "There is but one truly serious philosophical problem, and that is suicide," and he also believes that even in the face of a universe that lacks ultimate purpose or meaning, suicide is a betrayal of existentialist ethics. The greatest challenge for each of us is to discover meaning in an absurd world, a conviction revealed even more explicitly in the following comment:

> To lose one's life is a little thing and I shall have the courage to do so if it is necessary; but to see the meaning of this life dissipated, to see our reason for existing disappear, that is what is unbearable. One cannot live without meaning.

Camus, from *The Myth of Sisyphus*

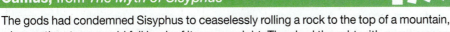

The gods had condemned Sisyphus to ceaselessly rolling a rock to the top of a mountain, whence the stone would fall back of its own weight. They had thought with some reason that there is no more dreadful punishment than futile and hopeless labor.

If one believes Homer, Sisyphus was the wisest and most prudent of mortals. According to another tradition, however, he was disposed to practice the profession of highwayman. I see no contradiction in this. Opinions differ as to the reasons why he became the futile laborer of the underworld. To begin with, he is accused of a certain levity in regard to the gods. He stole their secrets. Aegina, the daughter of Aesopus, was carried off by Jupiter. The father was shocked by that disappearance and complained to Sisyphus. He, who knew of the abduction, offered to tell about it on condition that Aesopus would give water to the citadel of Corinth. To the celestial thunderbolts he preferred the benediction of water. He was punished for this in the underworld. Homer tells us also that Sisyphus had put Death in chains. Pluto could not endure the sight of his deserted, silent empire. He dispatched the god of war, who liberated Death from the hands of her conqueror.

It is said that Sisyphus, being near to death, rashly wanted to test his wife's love. He ordered her to cast his unburied body into the middle of the public square. Sisyphus woke up in the underworld. And there, annoyed by an obedience so contrary to human love, he obtained from Pluto permission to return to earth in order to chastise his wife. But when he had seen again the face of this world, enjoyed water and sun, warm stones and the sea, he no longer wanted to go back to the infernal darkness. Recalls, signs of anger, warnings were of no avail. Many years more he lived facing the curve of the gulf, the sparkling sea, and the smiles of earth. A decree of the gods was necessary. Mercury came and seized the impudent man by the collar and, snatching him from his joys, led him forcibly back to the underworld, where his rock was ready for him.

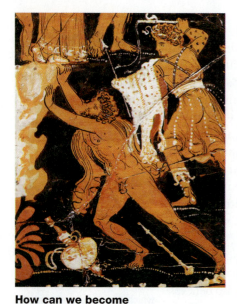

How can we become "absurd heroes"? The punishment of Sisyphus.
This Greek vase from 330 B.C.E. depicts Sisyphus as he pushes his rock uphill in the underworld, an image that had meaning for the twentieth-century philosopher Camus.

You have already grasped that Sisyphus is the absurd hero. He is, as much through his passions as through his torture. His scorn of the gods, his hatred of death, and his passion for life won him that unspeakable penalty in which the whole being is exerted toward accomplishing nothing. This is the price that must be paid for the passions of this earth. Nothing is told us about Sisyphus in the underworld. Myths are made for the imagination to breathe life into them. As for this myth, one sees merely the whole effort of a body straining to raise the huge stone, to roll it, and push it up a slope a hundred times over; one sees the face screwed up, the cheek tight against the stone, the shoulder bracing the clay-covered mass, the foot wedging it, the fresh start with arms outstretched, the wholly human security of two earth-clotted hands. At the very end of his long effort measured by skyless space and time without depth, the purpose is achieved. Then Sisyphus watches the stone rush down in a few moments toward that lower world whence he will have to push it up again toward the summit. He goes back down to the plain.

It is during that return, that pause, that Sisyphus interests me. A face that toils so close to stones is already stone itself! I see that man going back down with a heavy yet measured step toward the torment of which he will never know the end. That hour like a breathing-space which returns as surely as his suffering, that is the hour of consciousness. At each of those moments when he leaves the heights and gradually sinks toward the lairs of the gods, he is superior to his fate. He is stronger than his rock.

If this myth is tragic, that is because its hero is conscious. Where would his torture be, indeed, if at every step the hope of succeeding upheld him? The workman of today works everyday in his life at the same tasks, and his fate is no less absurd. But it is tragic only at the rare moments when it becomes conscious. Sisyphus, proletarian of the gods, powerless and rebellious, knows the whole extent of his wretched condition: it is what he thinks of during his descent. The lucidity that was to constitute his torture at the same time crowns his victory. There is no fate that cannot be surmounted by scorn.

If the descent is thus sometimes performed in sorrow, it can also take place in joy. This word is not too much. Again I fancy Sisyphus returning toward his rock, and the sorrow was in the beginning. When the images of earth cling too tightly to memory, when the call of happiness becomes too insistent, it happens that melancholy arises in man's heart: this is the rock's victory, this is the rock itself. The boundless grief is too heavy to bear. These are our nights of Gethsemane. But crushing truths perish from being acknowledged. Thus, Oedipus at the outset obeys fate without knowing it. But from the moment he knows, his tragedy begins. Yet at the same moment, blind and desperate, he realizes that the only bond linking him to the world is the cool hand of a girl. Then a tremendous remark rings out: "Despite so many ordeals, my advanced age and the nobility of my soul make me conclude that all is well." Sophocles' Oedipus, like Dostoevsky's Kirilov, thus gives the recipe for the absurd victory. Ancient wisdom confirms modern heroism.

One does not discover the absurd without being tempted to write a manual of happiness. "What! by such narrow ways—?" There is but one world, however. Happiness and the absurd are two sons of the same earth. They are inseparable. It would be a mistake to say that happiness necessarily springs from the absurd discovery. It happens as well that the feeling of the absurd springs from happiness. "I conclude that all is well," says Oedipus, and that remark is sacred. It echoes in the wild and limited universe of man. It teaches that all is not, has not been, exhausted. It drives out of this world a god who had come into it with dissatisfaction and a preference for futile suffering. It makes of fate a human matter, which must be settled among men.

All Sisyphus' silent joy is contained therein. His fate belongs to him. His rock is a thing. Likewise, the absurd man, when he contemplates his torment, silences all the idols. In the universe suddenly restored to its silence, the myriad wondering little voices of the earth rise up. Unconscious, secret calls, invitations from all the faces, they are the necessary reverse and price of victory. There is no sun without shadow, and it is essential to know the night.

The absurd man says yes and his efforts will henceforth be unceasing. If there is a personal fate, there is no higher destiny, or at least there is but one which he concludes is inevitable and despicable. For the rest, he knows himself to be the master of his days. At that subtle moment when man glances backward over his life, Sisyphus returning toward his rock, in that slight pivoting he contemplates that series of unrelated actions which become his fate, created by him, combined under his memory's eye and soon sealed by his death. Thus, convinced of the wholly human origin of all that is human, a blind man eager to see who knows that the night has no end, he is still on the go. The rock is still rolling.

I leave Sisyphus at the foot of the mountain! One always finds one's burden again. But Sisyphus teaches the higher fidelity that negates the gods and raises rocks. He too concludes that all is well. This universe henceforth without a master seems to him neither sterile nor futile. Each atom of that stone, each mineral flake of that night filled mountain, in itself forms a world. The struggle itself toward the heights is enough to fill a man's heart. One must imagine Sisyphus happy.

> **The struggle itself toward the heights is enough to fill a man's heart. One must imagine Sisyphus happy.**

< READING CRITICALLY >

Analyzing the Myth of Sisyphus

- For Camus, Sisyphus is the *absurd hero* because of "his scorn of the gods, his hatred of death, and his passion for life." His existence is absurd because he pays for his passions by suffering "that unspeakable penalty in which the whole being is exerted toward accomplishing nothing." Why do you think Camus considers Sisyphus to be a "hero"? If Sisyphus is a model for human existence, how does Camus believe that we can also become heroes? Why do you think Camus believes that Sisyphus, at these moments of consciousness, "is superior to his fate . . . stronger than his rock"?

- For Camus, "Crushing truths perish from being acknowledged," liberating us to discover meaning and happiness. "Ancient wisdom confirms modern heroism" in the remarkable words of Oedipus, "Despite so many ordeals, my advanced age and the nobility of my soul make me conclude that all is well." What does Camus believe we have to do, as modern men and women living in an absurd world, so we can also conclude that "all is well"?

- Camus believes that despite his eternal torment, Sisyphus is joyful because "His fate belongs to him." "The universe henceforth without a master seems to him neither sterile nor futile. Each atom of that stone, each mineral flake of that night filled mountain, in itself forms a world. The struggle itself toward the heights is enough to fill a man's heart. One must imagine Sisyphus happy."

Reflect on your own life: Even if you were to conclude that there is no benevolent God or ultimate purpose to life, do you think that your life could still be meaningful and happy? Why or why not?

9.6 Empathy: The Ethics of Care

The major ethical theories we have considered to this point all tend to focus on the person contemplating a moral choice—in other words, *you*. Certainly the interests of others and the impact of your choices on them is a relevant consideration in your moral deliberations (in the case of utilitarianism, it is the major focus), but *you* are the agent who is center stage.

But there is another ethical tradition that considers the needs and interests of others to be the primary focus of moral reasoning. The term *ethics of care* is sometimes used to designate this loose confederation of other-centered theories that emphasize the role of others in our moral relationships and includes such diverse people as

Nel Noddings (B. 1929). This American feminist philosopher writes on issues surrounding ethics and the philosophy of education. In *Caring: A Feminine Approach to Ethics and Moral Education* (1984) and *Women and Evil* (1989), Noddings argues that ethics should be founded on caring and interpersonal relationships.

Jesus, David Hume, and Nel Noddings. **Nel Noddings** is a contemporary American philosopher who has devoted her work to the concept of "care ethics," which holds sympathy and caring to be the most important virtues. Noddings believes that morality is rooted in "natural caring," a primal emotional response. Our moral obligations are not created through the rational logic of the categorical imperative or the calculations of the utilitarian calculus: Our moral obligations are instead created by the *caring response.* Noddings articulates her views on the caring response in the following passages from her work *Caring: A Feminine Approach to Ethics and Moral Education.*

Nel Noddings, from *Caring: A Feminine Approach to Ethics and Moral Education*

What Does It Mean to Care?

Our dictionaries tell us that "care" is a state of mental suffering or of engrossment: to care is to be in a burdened mental state, one of anxiety, fear, or solicitude about something or someone. Alternatively, one cares for something or someone if one has a regard for or inclination toward that something or someone. If I have a regard for you, what you think, feel, and desire will matter to me. . . .

 When I look at and think about how I am when I care, I realize that there is invariably this displacement of interest from my own reality to the reality of the other. . . . I am suggesting that we do not see only the direct possibilities for becoming better than we are when we struggle toward the reality of the other. We also have aroused in us the feeling, "I must do something." When we see the other's reality as a possibility for us, we must act to eliminate the intolerable, to reduce the pain, to fill the need, to actualize the dream. When I am in this sort of relationship with another, when the other's reality becomes a real possibility for me, I care. Whether the caring is sustained, whether it lasts long enough to be conveyed to the other, whether it becomes visible in the world, depends upon my sustaining the relationship or, at least, acting out of concern for my own ethicality as though it were sustained.

 The act of *caring*, for Noddings, involves a full-fledged empathy that is both cognitive as well as emotional. In Noddings' terms, there is a "displacement of interest from my own reality to the reality of the other," moving us out of our unconscious absorption in our own frame of reference to that of another. When we "care" in this deep and meaningful way, "the other's reality becomes a real possibility for me," a reality that we connect to on an existential level. Of course, the act of caring does not necessarily entail action—it is a *prelude* to action. For example, you may encounter someone who has just experienced a personal tragedy, which in turn evokes a caring response in you—"your heart goes out to her"—and yet you may take no overt action. Or, as is frequently the case, your caring response may be a prelude to action, motivating you to offer to the person words of comfort and support, share your own similar experiences, or place a consoling hand on her arm. As Noddings expresses it: "Whether the caring is sustained, whether it lasts long enough to be conveyed to the other, whether it becomes visible in the world, depends upon my sustaining the relationship. . . ."

Nel Noddings, from *Caring: A Feminine Approach to Ethics and Moral Education*

In this latter case, one in which something has slipped away from me or eluded me from the start but in which I strive to regain or to attain it, I experience a genuine caring for the self. This caring for self, for the *ethical* self, can emerge only from a caring for others. But a sense of my physical self, a knowledge of what gives me pain and pleasure, precedes my caring for others. Otherwise, their realities as possibilities for my own reality would mean nothing to me. When we say of someone, "He cares only for himself," we mean that, in our deepest sense, he does not care at all. He has only a sense of that physical self—of what gives him pain and pleasure.

Whatever he sees in others is pre-selected in relation to his own needs and desires. He does not see the reality of the other as a possibility for himself but only as an instance of what he has already determined as self or not-self. Thus, he is ethically both zero and finished. His only "becoming" is a physical becoming.

The caring response, Noddings believes, is originally directed toward others. Once we have developed the ability to empathize with others, welcoming "their realities as possibilities for me," we are then equipped to direct this same caring toward ourselves in our desire to cultivate our own ethically enlightened character. But people who have not developed the ability to genuinely care for others cannot really care for themselves in an ethical sense. They lack the understanding of what empathetic caring is all about. They are absorbed in themselves, submerged in their own reality, living in a dualistic universe that is divided between "self" and "not-self." Such a person "does not see the reality of the other as a possibility for himself but only as an instance of what he has already determined as self or not-self." As a result, the potential for ethical growth does not exist, only physical, sensual growth—hedonistic attempts to maximize his own pleasures and diminish his pains. This morally empty existence is "both zero and finished."

What is "natural caring"?
Do you agree with Noddings that acting ethically involves the "caring" response in which there is a "displacement of interest from my own reality to the reality of others"? Why?

According to Noddings, we can be generally caring people and yet not behave in a caring way in a given situation. Even when well intentioned, if we are intent on imposing our own ideas *before* attempting to achieve a deep and empathetic understanding of what the other person is thinking and feeling—then we are not "caring" in an authentic way. To achieve genuine caring, we have to bracket our own immediate reactions to the situation and make every effort to understand and appreciate *their* reactions to the situation. Then we are in a position, through genuine caring, to "struggle together."

Apprehending the other's reality, feeling what he feels as nearly as possible, is the essential part of caring from the view of the one-caring. For if I take on the other's reality as possibility and begin to feel its reality, I feel, also, that I must act accordingly; that is, I am impelled to act as though in my own behalf, but in behalf of the other. Now, of course, this feeling that I must act may or may not be sustained. I must make a commitment to act. The commitment to act in behalf of the cared-for, a continued interest in his reality throughout the appropriate time span, and the continual renewal of commitment over this span of time are the essential elements of caring from the inner view.

As I think about how I feel when I care, about what my frame of mind is, I see that my caring is always characterized by a move away from self. Yet not all instances of caring are alike even from the view of one-caring. Conditions change, and the time spanned by caring varies. While I care for my children throughout our mutual lifetimes, I may care only momentarily for a stranger in need. The intensity varies. I care deeply for those in my inner circles and more lightly for those farther removed from my personal life. Even with those close to me, the intensity of caring varies; it may be calm and steady most of the time and desperately anxious in emergencies. . . .

I reject the notion of universal caring—that is, caring for everyone—on the grounds that it is impossible to actualize and leads us to substitute abstract problem solving and mere talk for genuine caring. Many of us think that it is not only possible to care for everyone but morally obligatory that we should do so. We can, in a sense that will need elaboration, "care about" everyone; that is, we can maintain an internal state of readiness to try to care for whoever crosses our path. But this is different from the caring-for to which we refer when we use the word "caring." If we are thoughtful persons, we know that the difference is great, and we may even deliberately restrict our contacts so that the caring-for of which we are capable does not deteriorate to mere verbal caring-about. . . .

Nel Noddings, from *Caring: A Feminine Approach to Ethics and Moral Education*

Genuine caring suggests *acting* on our feelings. When we "take on the other's reality as a possibility and begin to feel its reality," the next natural step is to try to do something to express our caring *because it feels as if we're doing it for ourselves* because the boundary between our "self" and the other "self" is being erased. Of course, as Noddings points out, we need to *commit* ourselves to action if our caring is going to be expressed and sustained in a meaningful way.

Noddings makes the further point that not all caring is alike: Caring varies from person to person, relationship to relationship. Appropriate caring toward one person would be inappropriate caring toward another. In addition, Noddings believes that *universal caring* is an empty concept. On a practical level, it's impossible to genuinely care for more than a finite number of people. Those who claim to "care for everyone" are "merely talking" or retreating into abstract analyses. What could it possibly mean to say that you "care for everyone," the vast majority of whom you don't know personally and will never meet? The only possible meaning is that *if* you were to meet them, *then* you would be prepared to enter into a caring relationship with them. Otherwise, "caring for everyone" is simply an empty use of language.

Noddings goes on to advance the idea that to qualify as a moral response, two types of "caring" must be present. The foundation of morality is the natural caring that occurs in humans toward children, parents, and other close family members. Such natural caring may also extend to intimate romantic relationships, as well as close friendships. But the *natural caring* in all of these instances is not, Noddings believes, *ethical caring*. Ethical caring necessarily involves natural caring but takes it one step further, directing your caring toward individuals to whom you do not naturally experience caring feelings. Thus, caring for a homeless individual, coming to the aid of a stranger in need, donating your time to a soup kitchen—all of these would qualify as ethical actions. Although they assume the existence of natural caring, they extend beyond it to include people we wouldn't naturally care about.

Nel Noddings, from *Caring: A Feminine Approach to Ethics and Moral Education*

> **The** epithets sociable, good-natured, humane, merciful, grateful, friendly, generous, beneficent, or their equivalents, are know in all languages, and universally express the highest merit, which human nature is capable of attaining.
> **DAVID HUME**

From Natural to Ethical Caring

David Hume long ago contended that morality is founded upon and rooted in feeling—that the "final sentence" on matters of morality, "that which renders morality an active virtue—this final sentence depends on some internal sense or feeling, which nature has made universal in the whole species. For what else can have an influence of this nature?"

What is the nature of this feeling that is "universal in the whole species"? I want to suggest that morality as an "active virtue" requires two feelings and not just one. The first is the sentiment of natural caring. There can be no ethical sentiment without the initial, enabling sentiment. In situations where we act on behalf of the other because we want to do so, we are acting in accord with natural caring. A mother's caretaking efforts in behalf of her child are not usually considered ethical but natural. Even maternal animals take care of their offspring, and we do not credit them with ethical behavior.

Recognizing that ethical caring requires an effort that is not needed in natural caring does not commit us to a position that elevates ethical caring over natural caring. Kant has identified the ethical with that which is done out of duty and not out of love, and that distinction in itself seems right. But an ethic built on caring strives to maintain the caring attitude and is thus dependent upon, and not superior to, natural caring. The source of ethical behavior is, then, in twin sentiments—one that feels directly for the other and one that feels for and with that best self, who may accept and sustain the initial feeling rather than reject it.

Does this distinction between "natural caring" and "ethical caring" make sense? A number of philosophers have criticized Noddings for suggesting that she artificially limits the concept of ethical caring. Does her view mean, for example, that a self-sacrificing action directed toward a friend doesn't count as an "ethical action" because it is the product of natural caring? That seems rather silly and at serious variance from common understanding of moral motivations and actions.

The ethical North Star for Noddings is an *ethical ideal*: the image of the best of ourselves when we are caring and being cared for, deeply and authentically. It is this ethical ideal that we strive for when we experience the call of moral obligation, the "I must." She believes this to be in sharp contrast with ethical approaches based on general principles, either specific pronouncements like "Thou shalt not. . . ," or more general principles like Kant's categorical imperative ("Act only on that maxim whereby thou canst at the same time will that it should become a universal law"). Her criticism of such universalizing principles is that they are unworkable in practical terms. Every moral situation is unique, with its own special circumstances. We cannot assume that other people will confront moral choices that are sufficiently similar to our own for the maxim to have meaning.

> ## < READING CRITICALLY >
> ### Analyzing Noddings on the Ethics of Care
> - The ethics of care is based on *empathy*, a complex intellectual and emotional identification with another person. Think of a recent situation in which you felt empathy toward someone else and describe what the experience felt like as specifically as you can.
> - In your own words, explain what you think Noddings means by the concept of "grasping the reality of the other as a possibility for myself."
> - Reflect on several of the moral decisions that you have made recently. What role has the ethics of care played in your moral reasoning?

9.7 Making Connections: Your Moral Compass Revisited

The ultimate goal of moral philosophy is for us to use these moral theories to calibrate accurately our moral compasses, sharpen our moral intuitions, and refine our moral consciences. In this way, when we are faced with moral decisions and ethical issues, we will be able to choose confidently, with decisions that are wise, enlightened, and justified. It is now your opportunity to sort through these theories and consider how they might inform your existing moral compass. How might you synthesize the diverging philosophical views we have examined? Which theories make the most sense to you? This is not to suggest that you need to abandon the moral beliefs that you have developed through your experiences and your reflections on these experiences. Rather, you ought to critically evaluate these—and other ethical theories—to see which of them you may want to use to refine your existing moral values.

The moral theories that we have considered in this chapter each have a different focus in defining and evaluating moral values:

Virtue Ethics: Moral value is determined by cultivating a virtuous *character*.

Deontology: Moral value is determined by following the moral rules (*maxims*) prescribed by reason.

Utilitarianism: Moral value is determined by the *consequences* of actions: the greatest happiness for the greatest number.

What is your moral compass? Every day we are faced with questions about our moral responsibility to our friends and family, our community, and those who are suffering in distant lands. How will you decide what is the right thing to do?

Existentialism: Moral value is determined by the *authenticity* of actions: by acknowledging and accepting our freedom to create our lives and the moral values that define them.

Ethics of Care: Ethics of care moral value is determined by an *empathic caring* response to one other.

However, when we turn an analytical lens to the way these theories actually function in human experience, we see that they are not mutually exclusive and that our project of constructing an enlightened moral compass may in fact make use of a number of different theories. The truth is that in the practical application of each of these theories, the moral elements of *consequences, maxims,* and *character* are dynamically interrelated. For example, in virtue ethics, it is by the repeated and habitual choosing of morally enlightened *actions* that we develop the habits of thought and patterns of behaving that gradually shape our moral character. And the moral virtues themselves reflect *moral maxims* that serve as guides.

The same dialectical relationships between *consequences, maxims,* and *character* are also found in utilitarian theory. After all, expecting people to act consistently to promote the principle of utility assumes that their characters are sufficiently virtuous to provide an ongoing desire to do so. For Mill, embodying the utilitarian spirit means more than simply applying the hedonic calculus in an impersonal, mechanical fashion. Instead, the principle of utility implies a genuine concern for others and a desire to enrich the lives of those less fortunate.

We also find these same interconnections between *consequences, maxims,* and *character* in the deontology of Immanuel Kant. In fact, Kant (as we saw) begins his foundational ethical work with an impassioned description of "the good will" as an essential dimension of any enlightened morality. Without a fully developed and authentically grounded "good will," there is no reason to think that people will use the categorical or any other moral maxim.

And when we turn our attention to existentialist ethics, we find that creating ourselves as authentic individuals necessarily involves *consequences* and *character* as well. Our moral values as individuals are defined by the reflectively chosen actions that we take with the full awareness that we are responsible for the consequences of these free choices.

However, a word of caution is in order. Although there are undeniable areas of overlap and connection among the major ethical theories, there are also significant areas of contrast. Each ethical theory identifies different fundamental values; they have different priorities in terms of which values take precedence: virtue, utility, maxims, or authenticity. Thus, in analyzing complex ethical situations, each theory is likely to provide a very different analysis in terms of moral reasoning and may end up with very different conclusions regarding the ethically appropriate course of action.

Once you have developed a clear understanding of your moral code, the struggle has just begun. Becoming a morally enlightened person—a person of character and integrity—requires not just an insightful moral compass but also the commitment to use the compass to navigate the way through the storms and shoals of your moral life. As a reflective critical thinker, you will be conscious of the choices you are making and the reasons you are making them, and you will learn from experience, refining your code of ethics and improving your moral choices through self-exploration. Achieving moral enlightenment is an ongoing process, but it is a struggle that cannot be avoided if you are to live a life of purpose and meaning, created by a self that is authentic and, as Aristotle would say, great-souled.

writing about philosophy: Analyzing Moral Choices in a Film or Novel

The Assignment

Films and novels can be excellent vehicles for applying ethical theories and thinking through complex moral situations. For example, the existentialist philosophers we examine in this chapter all wrote creative works to elaborate their ideas and also point out existentialist themes in literature written by others. In contrast to the simple, bare-bones moral examples that are typically found in textbooks, films, and novels can present moral choices as we often experience them: multileveled, entangling, unstructured, and ambiguous.

For this assignment, select a film or novel with which you are familiar that provides a rich moral context for analysis. Focus on one or two of the characters and think philosophically about the moral choices that they are making, addressing questions such as

- What are the moral choices that the character(s) is (are) making?
- How do they justify their choices? To what moral theories or principles are they appealing?
- How would various moral theories evaluate their choices? How would *you* evaluate their choices? What is your moral reasoning in reaching this conclusion?

MySearchLab Connections

Watch. Listen. Explore. Read. Mysearchlab is designed just for you. Each chapter features a customized study plan to help you learn and review key concepts and terms. Dynamic visual activities, videos, and readings found in the multimedia library will enhance your learning experience.

Here are a few questions and activities to help you understand this chapter:

1. **Listen** to the **Interview** *The Philosophy of Choosing Between Bad Options* on **mysearchlab.com** What is Kant's "categorical imperative"?

2. **Listen** to the **Podcast** *Richard Crisp on Utilitarianism* on **mysearchlab.com** Why is utilitarianism properly categorized as an ethical theory?

3. **Listen** to the **Podcast** *Richard Reeves on Mill's On Liberty* on **mysearchlab.com** In Mill's view, what are the acceptable limits on individual freedom?

4. **Watch** the **Video** *Human, All Too Human* on **mysearchlab.com** Explain Nietzche's concept of the "will to power".

5. **Listen** to the **Podcast** *Sebastian Gardner on Sartre's Bad Faith* on **mysearchlab.com** According to Sartre, what role does our past play in constituting who we are?

visual summary

Expanding Your Knowledge of Moral Philosophy

- Moral theories are designed to help us refine our moral compasses so that we can make informed choices in moral situations. Each theory embodies a distinctive approach to the complex realm of moral experience.

[p. 482]

Maxims: Duty to Moral Laws

- *Deontologists* like Immanuel Kant focus on the notion of duty or obligation as the measure of ethically correct conduct. For a deontologist, moral value is determined by following the moral maxims prescribed by reason. Kant believed that the work of philosophy was to uncover those moral laws that are true independently of experience—*a priori*—and therefore binding on all people.

- Kant identified the supreme moral law that all rational beings are required to follow as the Categorical Imperative: *"Act as if the maxim of your action were to become by your will a universal law of nature."* An ethically enlightened person implements the Categorical Imperative by exercising his or her "good will."

[pp. 493–506]

Character: Virtue Ethics

- *Virtue ethics* hold that the moral character of the person performing an action determines the moral value of that action. Aristotle laid the groundwork for *virtue ethics* in *The Nicomachean Ethics*.

- Aristotle's view of the world is teleological, assuming that everything has a unique end, purpose, or goal. Driving that teleology is *entelechy*, the principle that reveals the natural design that governs things and motivates them to fully express their essence or potential. Aristotle believes that it is natural for all humans to strive to realize their full potential as reasonable, happy, virtuous people.

- Aristotle divides virtues into two broad categories, intellectual and moral. To truly act morally, people need to know *why* they are acting, deliberately choose to take the morally correct action, and perform the action for its own sake. The repetition of these moral actions gradually builds a consistent moral character. Aristotle's "Golden Mean" defines this consistent moral character as founded on temperance, self-discipline, and balance.

[pp. 482–492]

KEY TERMS
virtue ethics
teleological
entelechy
Golden Mean

KEY TERMS
deontology
a priori
hypothetical imperative
categorical imperative
maxim

for further reading, viewing & research

Read the Primary Source on MySearchLab

- *The Nicomachean Ethics*, Aristotle
- *Fundamental Principles of the Metaphysics of Morals*, Immanuel Kant
- *An Introduction to the Principles of Morals and Legislation*, Jeremy Bentham
- *Utilitarianism,* John Stuart Mill
- *Animal Liberation*, Peter Singer
- *That Single Individual*, Søren Kierkegaard
- *The Gay Science and Beyond Good and Evil*, Friedrich Nietzsche
- *Existentialism Is a Humanism*, Jean-Paul Sartre
- *Ethics of Ambiguity*, Simone de Beauvoir
- *The Myth of Sisyphus*, Albert Camus
- *Caring: A Feminist Approach to Ethics and Moral Education*, Nell Noddings

Films

- ***Dead Man Walking*** (1995) What are the ethical arguments for and against the death penalty? After receiving a letter from a convicted murderer on death row, a nun agrees to be his spiritual advisor. Her experience prompts her to both protest capitol punishment and begin an organization to give support to the families of victims of violence.

- ***An Inconvenient Truth*** (2006) What are our responsibilities in terms of the environment? Al Gore's documentary addresses the scientific causes as well as the social and political factors that support and inhibit a decrease in global warming.

- ***Maria, Full of Grace*** (2004) Are the women hired by drug traffickers to act as drug mules ethically culpable for the lives that the drugs destroy? This film follows a young Colombian girl who becomes a drug mule in an attempt to escape the desperate circumstances of her life. When she arrives in the United States, she struggles to survive and to live a life of "grace."

- ***Saving Private Ryan*** (1998) When three brothers are killed in World War II, the U.S. government sends a squad on a risky mission to rescue the fourth brother, Private James Ryan. As the men search for Ryan,

Consequences: Utilitarianism

- *Utilitarianism,* as developed by Jeremy Bentham and John Stuart Mill, is a socially conscious approach to hedonism that holds *that the greatest good is to promote happiness and alleviate suffering for the greatest number of people.* A society in which all people have the opportunity to pursue the higher pleasures, and which that works to promote social justice, would conform to this *principle of utility:* Act always to promote the greatest happiness for the greatest number.

- In contemporary philosophy, the ethicist Peter Singer's concept of "speciesism" holds that humanity's willingness to allow the suffering of some species in order to make the lives of people easier and more pleasurable is morally wrong.

[pp. 506–522]

KEY TERMS

hedonism

utilitarianism

psychological hedonism

ethical hedonism

KEY TERM

existentialism

Authenticity: Existentialist Ethics

- *Existentialist ethics* holds that an authentic life is lived according to the free choices that you make.

- For Søren Kierkegaard, the individual's recognition of choice and responsibility is paramount. Rather than succumbing to the values of "the crowd," we must create ourselves as unique individuals, and develop a personal relationship with the Divine through a "leap of faith."

- For Friedrich Nietzsche, all of life is governed by a primal force, the *will to power*—"the will to grow, spread, seize, become predominant"—that is manifest in all living things. The ultimate moral good is an individual's striving to exert his or her will to power to the fullest possible extent.

- Jean-Paul Sartre's ethics also reinforce the primacy of the individual and his absolute freedom in the absence of a "God" or other universalizing moral force, but Sartre underscores that the moral choices we make are not just for ourselves in isolation, but for all humankind.

- Simone de Beauvoir contended that our freedom, which defines our existence, has meaning only in relationship to others who are exercising their freedom of choice.

- For Albert Camus, most of us live in a way that is "unintelligible and limited" until we make free choices that are courageous and work to discover meaning in an otherwise absurd universe.

[pp. 523–545]

Empathy: The Ethics of Care

- The *ethics of care*, associated with the work of feminist philosopher Nel Noddings, holds that our individual ethical actions are motivated by what she defines as a "caring response" rooted in "natural caring."

[pp. 545–549]

KEY TERM

ethics of care

visual summary

---

the dangers of the mission increase, and the question arises: Is one life worth the risk?

- ***Sophie's Choice* (1982)** Whom would you save? Based on the novel by William Styron, this film tells the story of Sophie, a Holocaust survivor living in the United Sates who is haunted by her past. When a young writer befriends Sophie, the truth of her history emerges, as does the unbearable decision she was forced to make in a concentration camp.

- ***Super Size Me* (2004)** What are the responsibilities of business to the health of its customers? Director Morgan Spurlock documents thirty days in which he only eats McDonald's food. He explores the physical and psychological effects of his experiment and raises ethical questions regarding the role of America's commercial food industry in contributing to obesity.

Literature

- ***The Plague,*** Albert Camus. This novel traces the reaction of a small French community struck by a plague epidemic. As infection and hysteria spread through the quarantined village, people are forced to make ethically complex decisions regarding care for others, self-preservation, and the needs of the community as a whole.

- ***The Second Sex,*** Simone de Beauvoir. This seminal work re-examines history from a feminist perspective and describes a type of "feminist existentialism." As de Beauvoir attempts to uncover the cause of gender inequality, she analyzes the way in which women have been portrayed as the "Other" in myth, history, science, literature, and psychology.

- ***The Brothers Karamazov,*** Fyodor Dostoevsky. When a landowner is murdered in nineteenth-century Russia, all of his sons become suspects. In a potentially godless and meaningless world, the question of culpability becomes ethically ambiguous. Other philosophical ideas explored include free will and responsibility, the nature of sin and redemption, collective guilt, the conflict between faith and doubt, and the potential dangers of extreme rationalism.

- ***For Whom the Bell Tolls,*** Ernest Hemingway. A young American participating in the Spanish Civil War as an explosives expert is given the task of blowing up a bridge. His sense of duty is challenged by the ethics of performing this covert operation, as well as his desire and the desire of his comrades to preserve their own lives. The novel raises questions about self-sacrifice for a greater good, the achievement of ideological ends through violent means, the ethics of suicide, and the ethics of war.

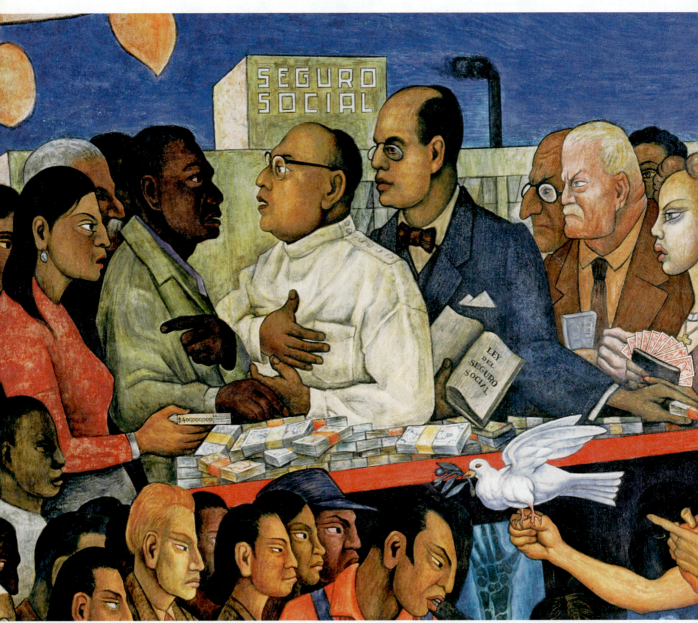

(Schalkwijk / Art Resource, NY / © 2011 Banco de México Diego Rivera Frida Kahlo Museums Trust, Mexico, D.F. / Artists Rights Society (ARS), New York.)

Classical theories of society.

Confucius

Plato

Aristotle

Justice depends on a social contract.

John Rawls
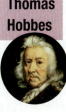

John Locke

Thomas Hobbes

what is social justice?

CREATING A JUST STATE

Justice is based on need and ability.

Karl Marx
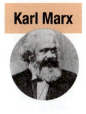

Friedrich Engels

Justice is what promotes gender equality.

Susan Moller Okin

Justice is what promotes the general welfare.

John Stuart Mill

chapter **10**

◄ **Can we create a just society?** Diego Rivera's mural, *The History of Medicine in Mexico*, and the *People Demanding Health*, dramatizes the struggle of the poor for access to a health care system that favors the rich. The issues of human rights, economic and social justice, and government responsibility, are some of the central issues addressed in this chapter on social and political philosophy.

PHILOSOPHERS AND THINKERS IN THIS CHAPTER	
Confucius	551–479 B.C.E.
Plato	428–347 B.C.E.
Aristotle	384–322 B.C.E.
Thomas Hobbes	1588–1679
John Locke	1632–1704
David Hume	1711–1776
Thomas Jefferson	1743–1826
John Stuart Mill	1806–1873
Karl Marx	1818–1883
Friedrich Engels	1820–1895
John Rawls	1921–2002
Susan Moller Okin	1946–2004

10.1 Elements of a Just Society

Imagine that you were given the project of creating a society based on the principle of justice: How would you go about it and how would you justify your proposed state? This is a question to which you may have given some thought during a recent local or national election. Although your political interest and involvement may typically focus on specific social issues—health care, government spending, educational issues, foreign policy—political philosophy requires you to question the system as a whole. Of course, if you emigrated from another country with another political structure, your experiences would give you a very different perspective than those of us who have never lived within another political regime.

In designing your ideal "just society," you will have to grapple with a number of questions that philosophers and others have been struggling with for thousands of years:

Distributive justice
Theory of justice dealing with how society's wealth, opportunity, and power should be distributed.

Retributive justice Theory of justice dealing with how societies should treat those who violate laws.

- *Questions of justice:* What exactly *is* a "just society"? How can we be fair to all the citizens in terms of distribution of wealth, opportunity, and power (**distributive justice**)? Should a society treat everyone equally? How should people who have violated society's laws be treated (**retributive justice**)? What is the core meaning of the concept of "justice"?

- *Questions of law:* What is the justification for a society and its laws? Are there "natural laws" on which "civic laws" should be based? Should citizens be expected to obey a society's laws even if they believe the laws to be unjust? When is "civil disobedience" justified?

- *Questions of public interest:* Does society have a responsibility to protect and support its less advantaged members? To what extent should individual citizens be expected to sacrifice their individual interests to support the general public interest? To what extent should the state promote the well-being of its citizens through public education, medical services, low-cost housing, welfare support, low-interest loans, and subsidies for businesses? To what extent should the state create and enforce regulations in employee safety, drug and medical safety, ethical practices in business, equal opportunity for citizens?

- *Questions of duty:* For what obligations and duties are the citizens of the state responsible?

- *Questions of rights:* To what individual rights are citizens entitled? In addition to the civil rights of a society, are there basic human rights that citizens of all societies are entitled to?

- *Questions of freedom:* On what basic freedoms is society based? To what individual freedoms should each citizen be entitled? Under what circumstances should personal liberty be limited?

- *Questions of power and influence:* How should power be acquired and administered? In what ways can citizens influence the policies and laws?

Responses to these questions form the basic "ingredients" of a community; and, because these questions can be answered in many different ways, there have been many different kinds of social/political communities in human history. That is what

Why do people struggle for freedom? This mural depicts the history of Mexico as the clash of brutal European forces against the indigenous population. Do you think it is ever right for one society to attempt to reshape another in its own image?

the study of social and political philosophy is all about: the ways these different themes weave together to form various communities and the overarching question of whether some communities are more ideal than others. The "Thinking Philosophically" activity on page 558 gives you an opportunity to reflect on and analyze the ingredients of the society in which we live from *your* perspective (which may be somewhat different from the perspectives of others in the same society). If you have lived in a different social and political system, your professor may ask you to use that society as the subject of your analysis to provide a richer, more varied understanding of these themes for the class as a whole.

The themes that you explored in this "Thinking Philosophically" activity are the threads that are woven into the fabric of social communities. Since the time of Plato and Aristotle, philosophers and other thinkers have constructed theories to both explain the nature of society and to recommend how an "ideal" society *ought* to be constructed. Thus social and political philosophies are *normative* as well as descriptive, because they embody values that the authors believe should be reflected in an ideal society. This parallels the way that moral theories are designed to both describe the way individuals behave and also how they *ought* to behave. In fact, political philosophies involve applying moral values to the context of larger social communities, defined by their common culture and political institutions. Concepts such as "justice," "fairness," "rights," "duties," "equality," and "political freedom" are essentially moral concepts characterizing societies of people. And just like moral concepts that characterize our personal relationships with one another, these moral concepts need to be defined, justified, and critically

Is there a social obligation to help less fortunate members of society? Treatment of the homeless is one of the contested issues in our society. To what extent do you think we have an obligation to help the homeless, including those who suffer from drug or alcohol addiction? Should the help come from individuals or from the government?

thinking philosophically

EXAMINING OUR SOCIETY

Reflect on the social and political structure of the society in which we live by responding to the following questions:

- *Issues of justice:* In what ways does our society distribute resources to its citizens? make opportunities for education and to acquire available resources? treat people equally and unequally? practice what you would consider to be the principles of justice?

- *Issues of law:* In what ways does our society justify its existence and its laws? practice "civic laws" based on "natural laws" that are thought to apply to all humans in all societies? apply laws fairly to people, regardless of their wealth, social status, gender, or racial identity? treat people who disagree with and disobey its laws? treat people who engage in "civil disobedience" (for example, those who act disruptively to protest social policies or war policies with which they disagree)?

- *Issues of public interest:* In what ways does our society support the well-being of its less advantaged citizens (for example, those who are poor, elderly, unemployed, sick, abused, or neglected)? expect citizens to sacrifice their individual interests to support the general interest (for example, paying taxes)? help those who are unable to help themselves? promote the general good through regulations and economic support?

- *Issues of duty:* What specific obligations and duties are citizens in our society responsible for performing (for example, serving on juries)?

- *Issues of rights:* What individual rights do citizens in our society expect to have (for example, the right to practice the religion of their choice)? What rights are considered to be "universal" in the sense that they are rights that all people in all societies should enjoy?

- *Issues of freedom:* What basic freedoms are guaranteed for all citizens (for example, freedom to express our views without being arrested or harassed)? In what areas are personal freedoms limited?

- *Issues of power and influence:* How is power acquired and administered? What can citizens do to influence social policies and laws?

evaluated. Our study of ethics from Chapters 8 and 9 thus forms the philosophical foundation for understanding and evaluating social and political theories.

In this chapter, we will explore and critically evaluate the most prominent social and political theories that have been proposed in Western culture, while also considering the ancient Chinese philosophy of Confucius. Our ultimate goal is to develop an in-depth understanding of these core concepts so that we are in a position to develop our own integrated vision of what an ideal society ought to be. This will be a vision that we can use to inform our own actions, as we work to make the society in which we live more enlightened and morally sound. In pursuing this utopian goal, we might aspire to be what the philosopher Roderick Firth calls an "Ideal Observer": someone who is knowledgeable, imaginative, objective, and consistent. Such an approach encourages us to conceive of a society that ensures justice for others as well as ourselves.

10.2 Classical Theories of Society: Confucius, Plato, and Aristotle

Writing nearly 2,500 years ago, the three thinkers in this section took up the question of how society should be organized and governed rather than uncritically accepting the social and political structures of their times. And, despite the uniqueness of each of their perspectives, core ideas regarding virtue, justice, and the common good emerge. At the same time, even discounting their specific social milieus, there are also significant differences in their conceptions of the ideal society. As you read about and reflect on their ideas, take particular note of what ways our current societies reflect their views and in what ways our current societies would be enhanced if they reflected their views to a greater extent.

Society Should Be Based on Virtue: Confucius

Nearly 100 years before Plato and Aristotle laid the foundation for Western thought, a remarkable thinker named **Confucius** developed a view of an enlightened society based on virtue and social order that was destined to have a dominant effect on

Confucius
Society should be based on virtue.

Plato
Society should be based on function and harmony.

Classical Theories of Society

Aristotle
Society is the natural state of man.

Confucius (551–479 B.C.E.). This Chinese philosopher was esteemed as the "Greatest Master." His teachings were aimed at bringing harmony to society through an emphasis on virtue.

Chinese culture for centuries to come. Confucius—the Latinized name of Kong Fuzi or Master Kong—was a legendary teacher whose teachings were collected by his students in *The Analects* in the form of epigrams, or pithy sayings. Growing up in poverty, Confucius was self-educated and entered government service when he was in his early twenties. His ambitious hope was to reshape and restructure Chinese society based on philosophically enlightened values. He was not successful in realizing his dream during his life, but his ideas became a powerfully effective force in Chinese society in the generations to come.

As with many political philosophers, Confucius's ideas were a direct response to the social conditions of his times, a period dominated by political confusion that would eventually lead (after Confucius's death) to the Period of the Warring States. Confucius was convinced that the only path out of this violent and chaotic state was by establishing a social order based on a commitment to "humanity" or benevolence, the conscientious practice of social customs, and the widespread adherence to moral principles. As a teacher, Confucius (the "Master") tried to effect political harmony by cultivating moral harmony within each individual:

> *2:3 The Master said, "If the people be led by laws and uniformity sought to be given them by punishments, they will try to avoid the punishment, but have no sense of honor or shame. If they be led by virtue, and uniformity sought to be given them by the rules of propriety, they will have the sense of honor and respect, and moreover will become good."*

Philosophically, Confucianism can be characterized as **ethical humanism**, an ethical perspective based not on religion but on the belief that human intelligence is capable of promoting human welfare and dignity in a way that conforms to our essential human nature:

> *4:15 The Master went out, and the other disciples asked, saying, "What do his words mean?" Zang said, "The doctrine of our master is to be true to the principles of our nature and the benevolent exercise of them to others,—this and nothing more."*

But how do we discover "the principles of our nature"? To fully realize our enlightened human nature, we must develop general virtue or **ren**—a humane principle rooted in empathy and feeling for others. The Chinese character for ren is composed

○─| **Watch** the **Interview** *The Authentic Confucius* on **mysearchlab.com**

Ethical humanism An ethical perspective based on the belief that human intelligence is capable of promoting human welfare and dignity in a way that conforms to our essential nature.

Ren A humane principle rooted in empathy and feeling for others.

Zhong-yong A state of harmony achieved through the practice of virtue.

Li The rules of propriety or moral customs of a society.

of "two" and "man," symbolizing the close relationship between men. Virtue should be our ultimate guiding principle.

> *4:5 "The superior man does not, even for the space of a single meal, act contrary to virtue. In moments of haste, he cleaves to it. In seasons of danger, he cleaves to it."*

Confucius believes that this pure and all-encompassing virtue is the key to inner peace, harmonious relationships, and enlightened social orders. The heart of this virtue is reciprocity, the principle that we should treat others the same way we wish to be treated.

> *15:23 Zigong asked, saying, "Is there one word which may serve as a rule of practice for all one's life?" The Master said, "Is not RECIPROCITY such a word? What you do not want done to yourself, do not do to others."*

Becoming virtuous requires self-restraint and a commitment to living our lives according to **zhong-yong**, the Golden Mean, which has been variously translated as moderation, normality, and universal moral law. The literal meaning is "centrality and universality," which are generally equated with "equilibrium" and "harmony." This concept is explored in *The Doctrine of the Mean*, a text that some scholars believe was written by Confucius's grandson:

> *Before the feelings of pleasure, anger, sorrow and joy are aroused it is called equilibrium (**zhong, centrality, mean**). When these feelings are aroused and each and all attain due measure and degree, it is called harmony. Equilibrium is the great foundation of the world, and harmony its universal path. When equilibrium and harmony are realized to the highest degree, heaven and earth will attain proper order and all things will flourish.*

The practice of virtue is thus a total commitment to a life of benevolent generosity, equilibrium and harmony, and conscientious self-restraint in all dimensions of our selves.

> *12:1 Yan Yuan asked about perfect virtue. The Master said, "To subdue one's self and return to propriety, is perfect virtue. If a man can for one day subdue himself and return to propriety, all under heaven will ascribe perfect virtue to him."*

In conjunction to the general commitment to the principles of virtue, Confucius also believed that achieving our full humanity entails following **li**, the "rules of propriety" or the moral customs of one's society that provide specific guidance. Li includes all of the rites, customs, moral precepts, conventions, etiquette, and good manners of a society. By mastering and practicing li, all human relationships are enhanced in a benevolent way, a state which ultimately results in a harmonious society

Are bureaucrats required for a good and orderly government?
The legacy of Confucian thought continued for centuries in the form of civil service examinations that scholar-bureaucrats had to pass to gain governance posts.

based on a good and orderly government. Thus both the individuals and the leaders of the state have a responsibility in creating an enlightened society founded on virtue.

> *6:25 The Master said, "The superior man, extensively studying all learning and keeping himself under the restraint of the rules of propriety, may thus likewise not overstep what is right."*
>
> *2:1 The Master said, "He who exercises government by means of his virtue may be compared to the north polar star, which keeps its place and all the stars turn towards it."*

< READING CRITICALLY >

Analyzing Confucius on the Social Order

- Both Confucius and Aristotle feature the concepts of virtue and of the "Golden Mean" as integral parts of their philosophies. How are they similar and different? (Aristotle's virtue ethics are covered in Section 9.2.)
- Do you agree that Confucius's concept of li, the "rules of propriety," could lead to a more harmonious society? What are the advantages and disadvantages? Would this concept work in a modern, multicultural society?

Listen to the **Audiobook** *Plato The Republic by Nigel Warburton* on **mysearchlab.com**

Society Should Be Based on Function and Harmony: Plato

Plato (427–347 B.C.E.). An ancient Greek philosopher of extraordinary significance in the history of ideas, Plato not only preserved Socrates' teachings for future generations but contributed original ideas on a wide range of issues such as morality, politics, metaphysics, and epistemology.

The first comprehensive social theory based on the concept of "justice" was developed by **Plato**, and his vision is fully articulated in his monumental work, *The Republic*. The title of the work in Greek is "Politeia" which is derived from the word *polis*, a term that roughly corresponds to the modern term "city-state." An ancient Greek *politeia* was considered to be a way of life, so a more precise translation would be "how we live as people." Although his home of Athens had developed a governing structure based on **democratic** principles (not fully however—the right to vote in Athens was reserved for free men, excluding women and the large number of slaves and servants who formed the infrastructure of the society), Plato rejected it as an ideal model of a "just" society. Why? Because he felt that ordinary citizens were too easily swayed by appeals to irrational emotions and illogical arguments. He had witnessed firsthand the destructive power of an irrational group of citizens when they condemned his mentor and friend Socrates to death. For Plato, the unwarranted killing of such a wise and ethically principled person was a profoundly traumatic event that convinced him that the general population could never be trusted to vote or rule with reason and wisdom.

Instead, Plato concluded that an ideal society must be a type of intellectual aristocracy, a political form in which society is governed by a limited number of individuals who are considered to be uniquely qualified because of their intellectual abilities. For Plato, this meant that society should be ruled by the wisest and most enlightened of people: the philosopher-kings. These would be people who had dedicated themselves to achieving authentic wisdom through enlightened education and hard work. It was to train such wise leaders (among other reasons) that he created his Academy for philosophical study, a school in which he taught citizens of Athens for the remaining forty years of his life. (Plato's Academy continued for an astonishing 873 years after his death!)

Democracy A system of government in which rulers are elected by a broad representation of society's members for specified terms of office.

Philosopher-King?
Many people consider the British statesman Winston Churchill (1874–1965) to be an exemplar of the philosopher-king—one who can combine enlightened thinking with superior leadership abilities. Is there a philosopher-king in our times?

Plato did not believe that all people are created with equal abilities: Instead, he believed that each person has unique strengths and talents that must be used in an appropriate way. People, he concluded, fall into one of three general categories:

- Workers (craftspeople, farmers, artisans, shopkeepers)
- Guardians (soldiers, police, firefighters)
- Philosopher-kings

A just state is one in which all the groups perform their unique functions in exemplary fashion and all members of society work together harmoniously. Plato believed that the three types of people correspond to the three fundamental parts of the soul: appetite, spirit, and reason. As we saw in Chapter 3, Plato uses the metaphor of a chariot and driver to explain the soul's functioning: The driver is "reason," working to control and direct the two powerful horses, "spirit" and "appetite."

> So the reason ought to rule, having the ability and foresight to act for the whole, and the spirit ought to obey and support it. And this concord between them is effected, as we said, by a combination of intellectual and physical training, which tunes up the reason by intellectual training and tones down the crudeness of natural high spirits by harmony and rhythm.

In a virtuous person, the three elements of the soul function together in a smoothly integrated and productive way. Thus for Plato, the virtuous soul and the just state are mirrors of one another, and they both reflect the "cardinal virtues" characteristic of a good society and a truly happy individual (Figure 10.1).

Elements of a *Virtuous* Soul	Elements of Soul	Functions	Elements of State	Elements of *Just* State
Wisdom	Reason	Rule	Philosopher-Kings	Wisdom
Courage	Spirit	Guard	Guardians	Courage
Temperance	Appetites	Nourish	Workers	Temperance

Figure 10.1 The Virtuous Soul and Just State

Justice exists in the state and the individual when all the elements perform their distinctive function and work together as a smoothly articulated and balanced whole. In contrast, injustice occurs when the parts of the state or the individual fail to perform the functions for which they were designed, or they fail to work with the other members in a harmonious way. Plato explores these central themes in the following exchange between Socrates and Glaucon in *The Republic*:

Plato, from *The Republic*

I [Socrates] think that justice is the very thing, or some form of the thing which, when we were beginning to found our city, we said had to be established throughout. We stated, and often repeated, if you remember, that everyone must pursue one occupation of those in the city, that for which his nature best fitted him.

Yes, we kept saying that.

Further, we have heard many people say, and have often said ourselves, that justice is to perform one's own task, and not to meddle with that of others.

We have said that.

This then, my friend, I said, when it happens, is in some way justice, to do one's own job. And do you know what I take to be a proof of this?

No, tell me.

I think what is left over of those things we have been investigating, after moderation and courage and wisdom have been found, was that which made it possible for those three qualities to appear in the city and to continue as long as it was present. We also said that what remained after we found the other three was justice.

It had to be.

And surely, I said, if we had to decide which of the four will make the city good by its presence, it would be hard to judge whether it is a common belief among the rulers and the ruled, or the preservation among the soldiers of a law-inspired belief as to the nature of what is, and what is not, to be feared, or the knowledge and guardianship of the rulers, or whether it is, above all, the presence of this fourth in child and woman, slave and free, artisan, ruler and subject, namely that each man, a unity in himself, performed his own task and was not meddling with that of others.

How could this not be hard to judge?

It seems then that the capacity for each in the city to perform his own task rivals wisdom, moderation and courage as a source of excellence for the city.

It certainly does.

You would then describe justice as a rival to them for excellence in the city?

Most certainly.

Look at it this way and see whether you agree: you will order your rulers to act as judges in the courts of the city?

Surely.

And will their exclusive aim in delivering judgment not be that no citizen should have what belongs to another or be deprived of what is his own?

That would be their aim.

That being just?

Yes.

In some way then possession of one's own and the performance of one's own task could be agreed to be justice.

That is so.

Consider then whether you agree with me in this: if a carpenter attempts to do the work of a cobbler, or a cobbler that of a carpenter, and they exchange their tools and the esteem that goes with the job, or the same man tries to do both, and all the other exchanges are made, do you think that this does any great harm to the city?

No.

But I think that when one who is by nature a worker or some other kind of moneymaker is puffed up by wealth, or by the mob, or by his own strength, or some other such thing, and attempts to enter the warrior class, or one of the soldiers tries to enter the group of counselors or guardians, though he is unworthy of it, and these exchange their tools and the public esteem, or when the same man tries to perform all these jobs together, then I think you will agree that these exchanges and this meddling bring the city to ruin.

They certainly do.

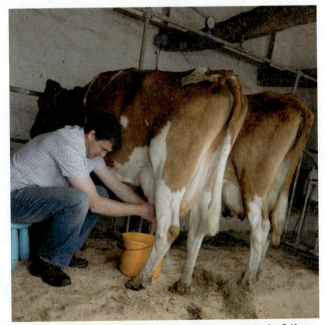

What would you wish your social placement to be? If you were a citizen in Plato's ideal state, how would you respond on receiving the news that you were expected to be a farmer because that career best matched your abilities?

> The meddling and exchange between the three established orders does very great harm to the city and would most correctly be called wickedness.
> Very definitely.
> And you would call the greatest wickedness worked against one's own city injustice?
> Of course.
> That then is injustice. And let us repeat that the doing of one's own job by the money-making, auxiliary, and guardian groups, when each group is performing its own task in the city, is the opposite, it is justice and makes the city just.
> I agree with you that this is so.

Plato's theory of the state is both structured and hierarchical. Once people have been sorted into their respective groups, based on their intrinsic talents, they are typically expected to remain in those social classes and work toward the good of the entire society. This may entail subsuming their own personal interests and preferences so that society as a whole may flourish. Although Plato found it acceptable for people to move *within* their social class, he cautioned that trying to move to *another* social class would do harm to society as a whole, contributing to an unjust society. And because society and its citizens have a close, reciprocal relationship with one another, such "wicked" behavior would also threaten the happiness of the citizens. One area in which Plato considered social mobility to be possible was in the search for members of the ruling class, those men and women who were identified through a type of education as being intellectually superior. In this regard, Socrates himself was a model, coming from a father who was a sculptor and a mother who was a midwife to become the most revered thinker in Athens.

Egalitarian Characterized by a belief that people are intrinsically equal.

For many people in the modern era who are committed to **egalitarian** values (everyone is intrinsically equal) and *democratic* principles (all people should have an equal voice in governing), Plato's ideas may seem wrongheaded and even offensive. But it is important to realize that Plato's social and political views are a direct outgrowth of his entire metaphysic and epistemology (which we explored in Chapter 5) as well as witnessing "democracy" execute his mentor Socrates. For Plato's hierarchy is not based on elitist or aristocratic principles but is rather a hierarchy of wisdom and enlightenment, at least for the ruling leaders. He believed that all people should strive to achieve a rationally based understanding of the essence of truth and goodness. Using his Allegory of the Cave as a framework, he urged that each person should escape from the enslavement of unreality, and then seek to free the minds of those still submerged in the world of appearances.

The people who are best equipped to rule are those who have earned the right through the development of their rational intellects. In principle, this system of intellectual merit would not exclude anyone based on gender, race, or social class: The sole criterion would be one's developed wisdom. Of course, the practical application of such an ideal would likely be very different, as everyone in Athens, like now, did not have equal educational opportunities to reach higher stages of enlightenment. Nevertheless, Plato was clear in his belief that women were as qualified as men to be rulers and ought to share the same education as men to prepare them.

Plato believed that for individuals to lead virtuous lives and attain happiness, they needed to conform to their intrinsic natures and fulfill their unique potentials, goals that could be achieved only within the context of a just, rationally ordered state. The natural order is for people of wisdom to lead society, people of courage to protect its interests, and people of temperance to provide the basic nourishing needs of the community. Plato's ideal society is based on the concept of cooperation, a state in which all people fulfill their distinctive functions, fully committed to the general interests of society as a whole.

< READING CRITICALLY >

Analyzing Plato on Social Harmony

- Plato's concern about democratic forms of government was that many citizens are ill-informed about important issues and vulnerable to being manipulated by those in power. When you examine the current state of affairs in our society, do you believe that there is evidence to support Plato's concern? If so, what solutions would you propose?

- One of the major critiques of Plato's ideas about social justice is that the Athenian system was dependent on a large slave population for its functioning, individuals who are left out of Plato's conception of an ideal state. How do you think Plato would respond to the criticism that his ideas lack validity because of his acceptance of slavery? (The same question can be posed to the founding fathers of America who, like Thomas Jefferson, supported the institution of slavery while advocating "inalienable rights" of life, liberty, and the pursuit of happiness for everyone else.)

- Critically evaluate Plato's basic assumption that people fall into one of three classes: guardians, warriors, or workers. For example, do such natural classes exist? How would one go about determining which group people should be placed in? At what point in a person's life do his or her abilities become clearly delineated? Is it possible for people to develop abilities later in life that may not have been obvious earlier on? Is there a danger of prematurely classifying people and creating a "self-fulfilling prophecy" for their destinies? Who would make the decision?

- Many people assume "egalitarianism" as a core value today, the idea that every person is created equal and that everyone is entitled to certain basic rights and freedoms. How would you go about defending this point of view to Plato?

Society Is the Natural State of Humanity: Aristotle

Many theories of social justice begin with the idea that the state is the result of individuals coming together to form an organized society for their mutual benefit. We will see this perspective fully expressed in the upcoming sections in which various philosophers view society as a "social contract" freely entered into by independent and fully informed people.

Aristotle's view is the complete opposite: He believes that "man is a political creature" by nature and that existing in social communities is our natural state. In fact, we can exist as fully formed individuals only through our social relationships with others. Our self-identity is at its core a social identity, shaped by the network of people who form our social community, and within which we are embedded. This is the argument that Aristotle makes in the following passage from his work, *Politics.*

Aristotle (384–322 B.C.E.). An ancient Greek philosopher and student of Plato who charted a direction different from his teacher, Aristotle made major contributions to metaphysics, ethics, politics, logic, and aesthetics. He is also responsible for conceptualizing the different branches of philosophy.

Aristotle, from *Politics*

He who thus considers things in their first growth and origin, whether a state or anything else, will obtain the clearest view of them. In the first place there must be a union of those who cannot exist without each other; namely, of male and female, that the race may continue (and this is a union which is formed, not of deliberate purpose, but because, in common with other animals and with plants, mankind have a natural desire to leave behind them an image of themselves. . . . Out of these two relationships between man and woman . . . the first thing to arise is the family. . . . But when several families are united, and the association aims at something more than the supply of daily needs, the first society to be formed is the village. And the most natural form of the village appears to be that of a colony from the family, composed of the children and grandchildren, who are said to be suckled "with the same milk." . . . When several villages are united in a single complete community, large enough to be nearly or quite self-sufficing, the state comes into existence, originating in the bare needs of life, and continuing in existence for the sake of a good life. And therefore, if the earlier forms of society are natural, so is the state, for it is the end of them, and the nature of a thing is its end. For what each thing is when fully developed, we call its nature, whether we are speaking of a man, a horse, or a family. . . . Hence it is evident that the state is a creation of nature, and that man is by nature a political animal. And he who by nature and not by mere accident is without a state, is either a bad man or above humanity. . . .

Humans are naturally social creatures—"political animals"—in the same way that many other species instinctively form herds or packs. But humans have abilities that transcend those of other animals. Our ability to use language enables us to think and communicate in complex, symbolic, and abstract ways. (Experiments have led some researchers to conclude that higher primates have some ability to think and use language as well.) And these thinking and language abilities enable humans to reflect on their social communities and evaluate them in terms of concepts such as "just" and "unjust," "good" and "evil."

Aristotle, from *Politics*

Now, that man is more of a political animal than bees or any other gregarious animals is evident. Nature, as we often say, makes nothing in vain, and man is the only animal whom she has endowed with the gift of speech. And whereas mere voice is but an indication of pleasure or pain, and is therefore found in other animals (for their nature attains to the perception of pleasure and pain and the intimation of them to one another, and no further), the power of speech is intended to set forth the expedient and inexpedient, and therefore likewise the just and the unjust. And it is a characteristic of man that he alone has any sense of good and evil, of just and unjust, and the like, and the association of living beings who have this sense makes a family and a state.

Do the state's interests come first? According to Aristotle, the state is "prior to the individual," suggesting that the public interest of the community takes precedence over the interests of a few individuals. For example, imagine the state wants to construct a new road to alleviate traffic congestion and that the proposed route runs right through a neighborhood where you and other families have lived for decades. What would your reaction be?

For Aristotle, the fact that the state is "prior to the individual" means that humans can achieve their full potential only through their social existence. In fact, Aristotle believed that any individual who *can* exist independently of human community must either be a "beast or a god." In addition, the conviction that the state is prior to the individual means that the interests of the individual are secondary to the interests of the entire community, in the same way that the whole body takes precedence over any individual body parts. For humans to achieve their potential, they must work cooperatively with others to achieve virtue for themselves and for their community, "for justice is the bond of men in states, for the administration of justice . . . is the principle of order in political society."

Aristotle, from
Politics

Further, the state is by nature clearly prior to the family and to the individual, since the whole is of necessity prior to the part; for example, if the whole body be destroyed, there will be no foot or hand, except in an equivocal sense, as we might speak of a stone hand; for when destroyed the hand will be no better than that. But things are defined by their working and power; and we ought not to say that they are the same when they no longer have their proper quality, but only that they have the same name. The proof that the state is a creation of nature and prior to the individual is that the individual, when isolated, is not self-sufficing; and therefore he is like a part in relation to the whole. But he who is unable to live in society, or who has no need because he is sufficient for himself, must be either a beast or a god: he is no part of a state. A social instinct is implanted in all men by nature, and yet he who first founded the state was the greatest of benefactors. For man, when perfected, is the best of animals, but, when separated from law and justice, he is the worst of all; since armed injustice is the more dangerous, and he is equipped at birth with arms, meant to be used by intelligence and virtue, which he may use for the worst ends. Wherefore, if he have not virtue, he is the most unholy and the most savage of animals, and the most full of lust and gluttony. But justice is the bond of men in states, for the administration of justice, which is the determination of what is just, is the principle of order in political society.

> **But he who is unable to live in society, or who has no need because he is sufficient for himself, must be either a beast or a god: he is no part of a state.**

Like Plato, Aristotle believes that different people have different potentials to fulfill (their distinctive *entelechy*), and he also agrees that slaves are fulfilling their distinctive purpose in life, a view that people today would find offensive and profoundly immoral. Nor does Aristotle accord women a status comparable to free men.

Although we may find certain dimensions of Plato's and Aristotle's social and political philosophies unacceptable—in particular their endorsement of the institution of slavery and the inferior status of women—we must also recognize their lasting contributions to our thinking regarding our social and political lives:

- Both Plato and Aristotle proposed comprehensive theories that were built around the concept of "justice" for the first time in recorded Western history.
- Both Plato and Aristotle affirmed the idea that members of a category must be treated as equals, a principle that forms the bedrock of many modern concepts of justice. The difference is that many people today believe that *all* people are equal in the most fundamental sense and that they therefore deserve equal consideration.
- Aristotle articulated the concept of distributive justice, endorsing the notion that wealth and goods should be fairly distributed among the members of society.
- Aristotle also recognized that the poor and disadvantaged members of society required special protection in a just society, to ensure that their basic needs were taken care of.

So as with many circumstances in life, it is helpful for us to retain the core ideas that we find useful and applicable to our thinking about our social and political lives, while discarding the elements (such as slavery) that we find to be morally indefensible and conceptually wrongheaded.

< READING CRITICALLY >

Analyzing Aristotle on Community

- Aristotle believes that humans are first and foremost social creatures who can fulfill their potential only as members of a social community and that anyone who could exist independently of human community must be either a "beast or a god." Do you agree? Why or why not?
- Aristotle believed that slaves were fulfilling their natural function in society by promoting the general interest for all. He also argued that if slaves were freed, they would be unhappy and unable to cope with the challenges of living. What arguments would you make to convince him that his view of slaves is unjust?
- Aristotle also believed that women should not be considered the equals of men and that fulfilling their potential meant recognizing and accepting their secondary status. What arguments would you make to convince Aristotle that his view is mistaken? How might he respond?
- Justice, for Aristotle, is the result of each person fulfilling his or her natural potential, which would result in a hierarchical but cooperative society. Critically evaluate this definition of "justice."

10.3 Justice Depends on a Social Contract: From Hobbes and Locke to Rawls

Plato and Aristotle both envisioned an ideal society as one based on the assumption that justice was the natural result of each citizen performing his or her natural function, no matter what that person's position in the social hierarchy. They grounded their social and political visions in their metaphysical beliefs: Plato's quest for rational enlightenment and wisdom and Aristotle's belief in the purposeful nature of every dimension of the universe.

The Middle Ages in Europe was dominated by the influence of religion. The ruling monarchs often sought to establish their authority by claiming they ruled by "divine right," supported by the full force of God's will. Thus the state and the rulers came to be seen as an integral part of God's kingdom on earth. As in Plato and Aristotle's theories, this religiously ordained and authoritarian system was structured and hierarchical. Whether your destiny was to be a slave, serf, landowner, knight, or king, you were expected to embrace your fate willingly and without question, as the natural expression of God's will.

Thomas Hobbes
We need a social contract to coexist peacefully and avoid a life that is "nasty, brutish, and short."

John Locke
The social contract protects natural rights of life, liberty, health, and property.

Social Contract

John Rawls
The "state of nature" is a conceptual tool to implement "the veil of ignorance."

With this as background, we can better appreciate the revolutionary thinking of the seventeenth-century British philosophers Thomas Hobbes, John Locke, and David Hume. Collectively, these thinkers developed views regarding the origins of the state and the nature of social justice that represented a radical departure from the political theories up until that time. Although there were important differences in their philosophical ideas, they all agreed on the following core political beliefs:

- *All members of society are intrinsically equal*, a sharp contrast to Plato and Aristotle's belief that people were naturally *un*equal, based on their natural talents and abilities.
- *Individuals willingly enter into a "social contract" with one another to promote a better quality of life for themselves*, the direct opposite of Aristotle's conviction that individuals are naturally social creatures.
- *Justice (and other laws) only comes into existence with the formation of the social contract* (Locke has a somewhat different view in this case).
- *Justice is viewed as pursuing the* public interest, *enforced by the authority of the ruling members of the community*. For Plato and Aristotle, on the other hand, justice results from each individual fulfilling his or her special social function in a cooperative fashion.

The philosophers whom we will examine in this section—Hobbes, Locke, and the contemporary philosopher John Rawls—will elaborate on this notion that government should be based on **social contract**, an agreement between people and their rulers or among the people in a community.

We Need a Social Contract to Coexist: Hobbes

We begin our analysis of social contract theory by exploring the influential ideas of **Thomas Hobbes**. Unlike Aristotle's belief in the original primacy of the social community, Hobbes contends that humans begin in the "state of nature," unconstrained by laws or social agreements. Because Hobbes believes that humans are by nature selfish, destructive, and unprincipled, living in the state of nature is very unpleasant indeed: "A war of all against all" is how Hobbes describes it (which mirrored the political unrest that was occurring at this time in England). And the consequence is that our lives in the state of nature are "nasty, brutish, and short."

What is the remedy? Because humans are capable of reason, they recognize that the only way to improve the quality of their lives is to enter into a cooperative partnership with their competitors, a social contract in which they will agree to surrender some of their autonomy to create a safe and productive environment in which to live. This cooperative peace is enforced by laws and a justice system that the individual members have endorsed and ceded power to. And once this central political authority has been established, its actions should not be questioned. Thus the legitimacy of the state is based on the consent of the governed, in the same way that members of an organization might elect a leader to control and direct the group's activities.

The following selection is from Hobbes's 1651 work, *Leviathan*: The title refers to a mythological sea creature that symbolized evil. Hobbes uses this image to symbolize his belief in the need for a strong, authoritative central government that has the power to maintain control and order in the face of political turmoil.

Social contract An agreement either between the people and their ruler or among the people in a community.

Thomas Hobbes (1588–1679). This British philosopher was a thoroughgoing materialist who tried to reconcile free will with materialism. He is best known for his social contract theory, which advocates the transfer of power to an absolute sovereign.

Thomas Hobbes, from *Leviathan*

Chapter XIII: Of the Natural Condition of Mankind as Concerning Their Felicity and Misery

Nature hath made men so equal in the faculties of body and mind as that, though there be found one man sometimes manifestly stronger in body or of quicker mind than another, yet when all is reckoned together the difference between man and man is not so considerable as that one man can thereupon claim to himself any benefit to which another may not pretend as well as he. For as to the strength of body, the weakest has strength enough to kill the strongest, either by secret machination or by confederacy with others that are in the same danger with himself.

And as to the faculties of the mind, setting aside the arts grounded upon words, and especially that skill of proceeding upon general and infallible rules, called science, which very few have and but in few things, as being not a native faculty born with us, nor attained, as prudence, while we look after somewhat else, I find yet a greater equality amongst men than that of strength. For prudence is but experience, which equal time equally bestows on all men in those things they equally apply themselves unto. That which may perhaps make such equality incredible is but a vain conceit of one's own wisdom, which almost all men think they have in a greater degree than the vulgar; that is, than all men but themselves, and a few others, whom by fame, or for concurring with themselves, they approve. For such is the nature of men that howsoever they may acknowledge many others to be more witty, or more eloquent or more learned, yet they will hardly believe there be many so wise as themselves; for they see their own wit at hand, and other men's at a distance. But this proves rather that men are in that point equal, than unequal. For there is not ordinarily a greater sign of the equal distribution of anything than that every man is contented with his share.

Hobbes articulates an extraordinary viewpoint. Flying in the face of 2,000 years of hierarchical thinking, Hobbes uses the tools of reason and common sense to conclude that, in general terms, humans are more similar than different, more equal than unequal—physically and intellectually. The proof of this? All people consider themselves to be wiser than all others, pleased with the natural talents they have been awarded. And "there is not ordinarily a greater sign of the equal distribution of anything than that every man is contented with his share." And though they may vary in physical size and strength, weapons, alliances with others, and the element of surprise render them an equally lethal threat to one another.

Thomas Hobbes, from *Leviathan*

> **Again,** men have no pleasure (but on the contrary a great deal of grief) in keeping company where there is no power able to overawe them all.

From this equality of ability arises equality of hope in the attaining of our ends. And therefore if any two men desire the same thing, which nevertheless they cannot both enjoy, they become enemies; and in the way to their end (which is principally their own conservation, and sometimes their delectation only) endeavour to destroy or subdue one another. And from hence it comes to pass that where an invader hath no more to fear than another man's single power, if one plant, sow, build, or possess a convenient seat, others may probably be expected to come prepared with forces united to dispossess and deprive him, not only of the fruit of his labour, but also of his life or liberty. And the invader again is in the like danger of another.

And from this diffidence of one another, there is no way for any man to secure himself so reasonable as anticipation; that is, by force, or wiles, to master the persons of all men he can so long till he see no other power great enough to endanger him: and this is no more than his own conservation requires, and is generally allowed. . . .

Again, men have no pleasure (but on the contrary a great deal of grief) in keeping company where there is no power able to overawe them all. For every man looks that his companion should value him at the same rate he sets upon himself, and upon all signs of contempt or undervaluing naturally endeavours, as far as he dares (which amongst them that have no common power to keep them in quiet is far enough to make them destroy each other), to extort a greater value from his contemners, by damage; and from others, by the example. So that in the nature of man, we find three principal causes of quarrel. First, competition; secondly, diffidence; thirdly, glory. The first makes men invade for gain; the second, for safety; and the third, for reputation. The first use violence, to make themselves masters of other men's persons, wives, children, and cattle; the second, to defend them; the third, for trifles, as a word, a smile, a different opinion, and any other sign of undervalue, either direct in their persons or by reflection in their kindred, their friends, their nation, their profession, or their name. Hereby it is manifest that during the time men live without a common power to keep them all in awe, they are in that condition which is called war; and such a war as is of every man against every man. For war consists not in battle only, or the act of fighting, but in a tract of time, wherein the will to contend by battle is sufficiently known: and therefore the notion of time is to be considered in the nature of war, as it is in the nature of weather. For as the nature of foul weather lies not in a shower or two of rain, but in an inclination thereto of many days together: so the nature of war consists not in actual fighting, but in the known disposition thereto during all the time there is no assurance to the contrary. All other time is peace.

What are the proper roles of government?
The frontispiece from Hobbes's *Leviathan* includes symbols of power and government. One of the symbols is a bishop's cap, known as a miter. Do you think that religion should play a role in government?

For most people, equality among people is viewed as a positive and enlightened perspective. But Hobbes sees it differently. Because we all want the same things, and we all have roughly equal abilities and pose equal threats to one another, the result is a free-for-all, a war of all against all. And even when we are not actually engaged in conflict, we are *worried* about being engaged in conflict. This preoccupation with our personal safety precludes the possibility of social cooperation and all of the constructive creations that grow out of such cooperation. It's every person for him- or herself, and this results in a very primitive style of living indeed.

Whatsoever therefore is consequent to a time of war, where every man is enemy to every man, the same consequent to the time wherein men live without other security than what their own strength and their own invention shall furnish them withal. In such condition there is no place for industry, because the fruit thereof is uncertain: and consequently no culture of the earth; no navigation, nor use of the commodities that may be imported by sea; no commodious building; no instruments of moving and removing such things as require much force; no knowledge of the face of the earth; no account of time; no arts; no letters; no society; and which is worst of all, continual fear, and danger of violent death; and the life of man, solitary, poor, nasty, brutish, and short.

    It may seem strange to some man that has not well weighed these things that Nature should thus dissociate and render men apt to invade and destroy one another: and he may therefore, not trusting to this inference, made from the passions, desire perhaps to have the same confirmed by experience. Let him therefore consider with himself: when taking a journey, he arms himself and seeks to go well accompanied; when going to

Thomas Hobbes,
from *Leviathan*

Do people require laws to live together harmoniously? Do you agree with Hobbes that without laws and police to control us, people would return to a violent state of nature, a "war of all against all"?

sleep, he locks his doors; when even in his house he locks his chests; and this when he knows there be laws and public officers, armed, to revenge all injuries shall be done him; what opinion he has of his fellow subjects, when he rides armed; of his fellow citizens, when he locks his doors; and of his children, and servants, when he locks his chests. Does he not there as much accuse mankind by his actions as I do by my words? But neither of us accuse man's nature in it. The desires, and other passions of man, are in themselves no sin. No more are the actions that proceed from those passions till they know a law that forbids them; which till laws be made they cannot know, nor can any law be made till they have agreed upon the person that shall make it.

It may peradventure be thought there was never such a time nor condition of war as this; and I believe it was never generally so, over all the world: But though there had never been any time wherein particular men were in a condition of war one against another, yet in all times kings and persons of sovereign authority, because of their independency, are in continual jealousies, and in the state and posture of gladiators, having their weapons pointing, and their eyes fixed on one another; that is, their forts, garrisons, and guns upon the frontiers of their kingdoms, and continual spies upon their neighbours, which is a posture of war. But because they uphold thereby the industry of their subjects, there does not follow from it that misery which accompanies the liberty of particular men.

Hobbes readily acknowledges that we may never have actually existed in such a "state of nature," but this doesn't matter. We see the reality of people's competitive and destructive natures in the way we behave in current society: We lock our doors, protect our possessions and family, and take consolation in the existence of laws and police to enforce the laws. As Hobbes notes, doesn't each person "accuse mankind by his actions as I do by my words"? In addition, if we look at the history of civilization, we find that it is an unrelenting account of wars, invasions, threats, and destruction. Not that people—or countries—should be blamed for their behavior, according to Hobbes. These competitive and destructive impulses are simply a part of our human nature, wired into our brains since birth. It is only when humans come together to make peace with one another, create laws, and establish a central authority to enforce the laws that the moral concepts of "justice" and "injustice" come into existence. Before this point is reached, however, "force" and "fraud" are the two cardinal virtues in the war of all against all.

Thomas Hobbes,
from *Leviathan*

To this war of every man against every man, this also is consequent; that nothing can be unjust. The notions of right and wrong, justice and injustice, have there no place. Where there is no common power, there is no law; where no law, no injustice. Force and fraud are in war the two cardinal virtues. Justice and injustice are none of the faculties neither of the body nor mind. If they were, they might be in a man that were alone in the world, as well as his senses and passions. They are qualities that relate to men in society, not in solitude. It is consequent also to the same condition that there be no propriety, no dominion, no mine and yours distinct; but only that to be every man's that he can get, and for so long as he can keep it. And thus much for the ill condition which man by mere nature is actually placed in; though with a possibility to come out of it, consisting partly in the passions, partly in his reason.

The passions that incline men to peace are: fear of death; desire of such things as are necessary to commodious living; and a hope by their industry to obtain them. And reason suggests convenient articles of peace upon which men may be drawn to agreement. These articles are they which otherwise are called the laws of nature. . . .

Weary from this ongoing conflict, threat, and competition, the rational part of our nature enables us to understand that we need to create a political structure that will enable us to live cooperatively and harmoniously with one another. And so we enter into a social contract with others, agreeing to laws and a central governing authority in order to ensure peaceful coexistence.

Chapter XIV: Of the First and Second Natural Laws, and of Contracts

The right of nature, which writers commonly call *jus naturale*, is the liberty each man hath to use his own power as he will himself for the preservation of his own nature; that is to say, of his own life; and consequently, of doing anything which, in his own judgement and reason, he shall conceive to be the aptest means thereunto.

By liberty is understood, according to the proper signification of the word, the absence of external impediments; which impediments may oft take away part of a man's power to do what he would, but cannot hinder him from using the power left him according as his judgement and reason shall dictate to him.

A law of nature, *lex naturalis*, is a precept, or general rule, found out by reason, by which a man is forbidden to do that which is destructive of his life, or takes away the means of preserving the same, and to omit that by which he thinks it may be best pre-served. For though they that speak of this subject use to confound *jus* and *lex*, right and law, yet they ought to be distinguished, because right consists in liberty to do, or to forbear; whereas law determines and binds to one of them: so that law and right differ as much as obligation and liberty, which in one and the same matter are inconsistent.

And because the condition of man (as hath been declared in the precedent chapter) is a condition of war of every one against every one, in which case every one is governed by his own reason, and there is nothing he can make use of that may not be a help unto him in preserving his life against his enemies; it follows that in such a condition every man has a right to every thing, even to one another's body. And therefore, as long as this natural right of every man to every thing endures, there can be no security to any man, how strong or wise soever he be, of living out the time which nature ordinarily allows men to live. And consequently it is a precept, or general rule of reason: that every man ought to endeavour peace, as far as he has hope of obtaining it; and when he cannot obtain it, that he may seek and use all helps and advantages of war. The first branch of which rule contains the first and fundamental law of nature, which is: to seek peace and follow it. The second, the sum of the right of nature, which is: by all means we can to defend ourselves.

From this fundamental law of nature, by which men are commanded to endeavour peace, is derived this second law: that a man be willing, when others are so too, as far forth as for peace and defense of himself he shall think it necessary, to lay down this right to all things; and be contented with so much liberty against other men as he would allow other men against himself. For as long as every man holds this right, of doing anything he likes; so long are all men in the condition of war. But if other men will not lay down their right, as well as he, then there is no reason for anyone to divest himself of his: for that were to expose himself to prey, which no man is bound to, rather than to dispose himself to peace. This is that law of the gospel: Whatsoever you require that others should do to you, that do ye to them.

Thomas Hobbes,
from *Leviathan*

Is law enforcement necessary to keep the peace? Hobbes believed that people enter into a social contract enforced by a central authority to ensure everyone's safety. Do you agree that this is a primary motivation of social communities?

Thus humans, to extricate themselves from the vicious cycle of war against everyone, agree to seek peace with one another. But it is an uneasy peace, dependent on the consistent intentions of others not to breach the agreement. And so Hobbes is quick to point out that even after agreeing to the social contract, people still retain the right to defend themselves against any and all attacks from their fellow citizens. For Hobbes, the social community is essentially a collection of hostile and untrustworthy individuals, reluctantly drawn together to promote their individual interests. Although cooperative projects with others are pursued to enjoy the mutual benefits such projects produce, it is still prudent for us to keep looking over our shoulders to ensure that we don't make the mistake of being too trustful.

< READING CRITICALLY >

Analyzing Hobbes on the Social Contract

- In sharp contrast to Aristotle's view that humans are naturally social and political animals, Hobbes believes that being alone is our natural state and that we form social relationships only out of necessity and personal self-interest. Identify which viewpoint you find more compelling and explain your reasoning.

- Hobbes believes that people are naturally competitive with one another and that, in the absence of laws to keep these impulses in check, we would do whatever it takes to gain wealth, power, and glory. Try to imagine a society in which there were no laws or police or justice system to protect people from one another. Describe what you think would happen to society and our social relationships over the period of a year.

- Have you ever been in a situation in which the normal social rules broke down? For example, in the middle of an out-of-control mob, a panic situation involving other people, or a competitive activity in which people's emotions got out of hand? Describe what it felt like to be in this situation and analyze its dynamics from Hobbes's point of view.

- Hobbes believes that his rather pessimistic views are supported by our experiences: We take extraordinary precautions to protect ourselves and our possessions, and when we look at world events, we see ongoing examples of war, oppression, cruelty, competition, hatred, and genocide. Do you think that this is a persuasive argument for Hobbes's view of human nature? Why or why not?

- According to Hobbes, the ideas of "justice" and "injustice" only come into existence when laws are created: They have no natural existence or authority. Do you agree with this perspective? Why or why not?

The Social Contract Protects Natural Rights: Locke

John Locke (1632–1704). Locke was a British philosopher and physician who laid the groundwork for modern political theory with his concept of "inalienable personal rights."

John Locke, a younger contemporary of Thomas Hobbes, agreed with him that the concept of a social contract was the most intelligent way to explain the origins of the political state and to justify its authority, an authority derived from the voluntary consent of the governed. But Locke's views were significantly different from Hobbes's in other respects. To begin with, Locke had a decidedly more optimistic view of human nature than Hobbes. Rather than viewing the "state of nature" as a "war of all against all," Locke believed that humans are governed by certain "natural laws" that made them free, rational, and social creatures. As God's creations, all people are entitled to "inalienable" (that is, nontransferable) rights, including the rights to life, liberty, health, and property. No other person has the authority to threaten or remove any of these God-given rights.

Nevertheless, despite the advantages of living in the "state of nature" as free and independent individuals, humans find it advantageous to come together and form a political state to ensure that their natural rights will be protected by laws and the authority of the government. As with Hobbes, this social contract is freely consented to. For Locke, however, the state is the "servant" of the people; and, if the state fails to live up to the terms of the agreement, it can be "dismissed" through revolution. Hobbes disagrees, believing that once contracted for, the authority of the state can never be questioned.

Locke's views had a profound and far-reaching influence on the political thinking and events of the time. In fact, his fundamental concepts of inalienable rights formed the basis of America's Declaration of Independence as well as its Constitution and Bill of Rights, a relationship we shall explore further in the pages ahead.

The following passages are taken from his influential work, *The Second Treatise of Civil Government*, written in 1690.

Listen to the
Audiobook *Locke's Second Treatise* by *Nigel Warburton* on
mysearchlab.com

John Locke, from *The Second Treatise of Civil Government*

CHAP. II. Of the State of Nature.

Sec. 4. To understand political power right, and derive it from its original, we must consider, what state all men are naturally in, and that is, a state of perfect freedom to order their actions, and dispose of their possessions and persons, as they think fit, within the bounds of the law of nature, without asking leave, or depending upon the will of any other man.

A state also of equality, wherein all the power and jurisdiction is reciprocal, no one having more than another; there being nothing more evident, than that creatures of the same species and rank, promiscuously born to all the same advantages of nature, and the use of the same faculties, should also be equal one amongst another without subordination or subjection, unless the lord and master of them all should, by any manifest declaration of his will, set one above another, and confer on him, by an evident and clear appointment, an undoubted right to dominion and sovereignty. . . .

Sec. 6. But though this be a state of liberty, yet it is not a state of licence: though man in that state has an uncontroullable liberty to dispose of his person or possessions, yet he has not liberty to destroy himself, or so much as any creature in his possession, but where some nobler use than its bare preservation calls for it. The state of nature has a law of nature to govern it, which obliges every one: and reason, which is that law, teaches all mankind, who will but consult it, that being all equal and independent, no one ought to harm another in his life, health, liberty, or possessions: for men being all the workmanship of one omnipotent, and infinitely wise maker; all the servants of one sovereign master, sent into the world by his order, and about his business; they are his property, whose workmanship they are, made to last during his, not one another's pleasure: and being furnished with like faculties, sharing all in one community of nature, there cannot be supposed any such subordination among us, that may authorize us to destroy one another, as if we were made for one another's uses, as the inferior ranks of creatures are for our's. Every one, as he is bound to preserve himself, and not to quit his station wilfully, so by the like reason, when his own preservation comes not in competition, ought he, as much as he can, to preserve the rest of mankind, and may not, unless it be to do justice on an offender, take away, or impair the life, or what tends to the preservation of the life, the liberty, health, limb, or goods of another.

Sec. 7. And that all men may be restrained from invading others rights, and from doing hurt to one another, and the law of nature be observed, which willeth the peace and preservation of all mankind, the execution of the law of nature is, in that state, put into every man's hands, whereby every one has a right to punish the transgressors of that law to such a degree, as may hinder its violation: for the law of nature would, as all other laws that concern men in this world be in vain, if there were no body that in the state of nature had a power to execute that law, and thereby preserve the innocent and restrain offenders. And if any one in the state of nature may punish another for any evil he has done, every one may do so: for in that state of perfect equality, where naturally there is no superiority or jurisdiction of one over another, what any may do in prosecution of that law, every one must needs have a right to do.

Notice how idyllic and rational Locke's "state of nature" is when contrasted with Hobbes's violent and perilous war of all against all. Locke's state is one of "perfect freedom to order their actions and dispose of their possessions and persons as they see fit," governed by the "law of nature." It's a state "of equality, wherein all the power and jurisdiction is reciprocal, no one having more than another." Unlike the ideas expressed by Hobbes, Locke's "state of nature" has a rational structure to it, ordained by God the Creator and manifest in the law of nature "which obliges every one: and reason, which is that law, teaches all mankind, who will but consult it, that being all equal and independent, no one ought to harm another in his life, health, liberty, or possessions." In fact, not only does the law of nature prohibit individuals from harming others, but it exhorts us to actively preserve their well-being.

Yet Locke recognizes that despite the law of nature, some individuals may still invade the rights of others and even try to hurt them. In this case, each person is a government to him- or herself, with the right to administer the law of nature and punish the transgressors to protect the innocent and preserve the peace.

But if the "state of nature" is such a utopian paradise, then what is the incentive for people to come together and constitute a formal political state? Locke addresses this question directly:

John Locke,
from *The Second Treatise of Civil Government*

CHAP. IX. Of the Ends of Political Society and Government.

Sec. 123. If man in the state of nature be so free, as has been said; if he be absolute lord of his own person and possessions, equal to the greatest, and subject to no body, why will he part with his freedom? why will he give up this empire, and subject himself to the dominion and controul of any other power? To which it is obvious to answer, that though in the state of nature he hath such a right, yet the enjoyment of it is very uncertain, and constantly exposed to the invasion of others: for all being kings as much as he, every man his equal, and the greater part no strict observers of equity and justice, the enjoyment of the property he has in this state is very unsafe, very unsecure. This makes him willing to quit a condition, which, however free, is full of fears and continual dangers: and it is not without reason, that he seeks out, and is willing to join in society with others, who are already united, or have a mind to unite, for the mutual preservation of their lives, liberties and estates, which I call by the general name, property.

Sec. 124. The great and chief end, therefore, of men's uniting into commonwealths, and putting themselves under government, is the preservation of their property. To which in the state of nature there are many things wanting.

First, There wants an established, settled, known law, received and allowed by common consent to be the standard of right and wrong, and the common measure to decide all controversies between them: for though the law of nature be plain and intelligible to all rational creatures; yet men being biassed by their interest, as well as ignorant for want of study of it, are not apt to allow of it as a law binding to them in the application of it to their particular cases.

> "The great and chief end, therefore, of men's uniting into commonwealths, and putting themselves under government, is the preservation of their property."

Sec. 125. Secondly, In the state of nature there wants a known and indifferent judge, with authority to determine all differences according to the established law: for every one in that state being both judge and executioner of the law of nature, men being partial to themselves, passion and revenge is very apt to carry them too far, and with too much heat, in their own cases; as well as negligence, and unconcernedness, to make them too remiss in other men's.

Sec. 126. Thirdly, In the state of nature there often wants power to back and support the sentence when right, and to give it due execution. They who by any injustice offended, will seldom fail, where they are able, by force to make good their injustice; such resistance many times makes the punishment dangerous, and frequently destructive, to those who attempt it.

Sec. 127. Thus mankind, notwithstanding all the privileges of the state of nature, being but in an ill condition, while they remain in it, are quickly driven into society. Hence it comes to pass, that we seldom find any number of men live any time together in this state. The inconveniences that they are therein exposed to, by the irregular and uncertain exercise of the power every man has of punishing the transgressions of others, make them take sanctuary under the established laws of government, and therein seek the preservation of their property. It is this makes them so willingly give up every one his single power of punishing, to be exercised by such alone, as shall be appointed to it amongst them; and by such rules as the community, or those authorized by them to that purpose, shall agree on. And in this we have the original right and rise of both the legislative and executive power, as well as of the governments and societies themselves.

In contemplating the need for a social contract, Locke's "state of nature" suddenly seems less idyllic than initially proposed. In fact, although everyone is equal ("all being kings as much as he, every man his equal") the "greater part" of them are *not* "strict observers of equity and justice." As a result, "this state is very unsafe, very unsecure," and it is "full of fears and continual dangers." It seems that Locke's utopian paradise has become more like Hobbes's jungle. Faced with these unpleasant drawbacks of being a "king" among "kings," individuals reason that it would be in their self-interest to form a political state for the express purpose of ensuring that God's law of nature is effectively administered. Specifically:

- The provisions of the law of nature need to be clearly articulated because, in the "state of nature," people's inherent biases skew their understanding of the law.
- Judges need to be appointed to arbitrate in the case of different interpretations of the law, again because people are "partial to themselves" and "passion and revenge" too often replace rational evaluation.
- There needs to be sufficient power to enforce the law, because offenders rarely accept their punishments passively.

Thus individuals voluntarily enter into a social contract with others, constituting a government (by majority vote) that will effectively carry out these responsibilities, and ensuring that all citizens will receive equal, fair, impartial treatment and have their fundamental rights (granted under the law of nature) protected.

Locke believed that it was important to create different branches of government that would have distinct powers and responsibilities:

- A legislative branch, to create and interpret laws;
- An executive branch, to implement the laws;
- A federative branch, responsible for making war and peace.

Baron de Montesquieu
(1689–1755). This Enlightenment philosopher extensively and systematically studied the social and political affairs of his time and dealt with the themes of toleration, moderation, and freedom in his writings.

Of course, the first two branches are identical to those of the U.S. government, and although Locke believed that judges should play a prominent role in government, he did not propose the judiciary as a distinct branch. This was the unique contribution of **Baron de Montesquieu**, who is often considered the ideological cofounder of the American Constitution, along with John Locke.

Thus for Locke, the formation of the social contract is just the beginning of his philosophical thinking, not the culmination as it was for Hobbes. Locke is intent on exploring what form this government should take, what rights it should protect, and what should be justifiable conditions for its dissolution. At the center of his thinking of human rights is the concept of "property," a term that for him extends far beyond the idea of material possessions to include one's body and the products of one's labor (what "he has mixed his labour with").

John Locke,
from *The Second Treatise of Civil Government*

CHAP. V. Of Property.

Sec. 27. Though the earth, and all inferior creatures, be common to all men, yet every man has a property in his own person: this no body has any right to but himself. The labour of his body, and the work of his hands, we may say, are properly his. Whatsoever then he removes out of the state that nature hath provided, and left it in, he hath mixed his labour with, and joined to it something that is his own, and thereby makes it his property. It being by him removed from the common state nature hath placed it in, it hath by this labour something annexed to it, that excludes the common right of other men: for this labour being the unquestionable property of the labourer, no man but he can have a right to what that is once joined to, at least where there is enough, and as good, left in common for others.

Sec. 28. He that is nourished by the acorns he picked up under an oak, or the apples he gathered from the trees in the wood, has certainly appropriated them to himself. No body can deny but the nourishment is his. I ask then, when did they begin to be his? when he digested? or when he ate? or when he boiled? or when he brought them home? or when he picked them up? and it is plain, if the first gathering made them not his, nothing else could. That labour put a distinction between them and common: that added something to them more than nature, the common mother of all, had done; and so they became his private right. And will any one say, he had no right to those acorns or apples, he thus appropriated, because he had not the consent of all mankind to make them his? Was it a robbery thus to assume to himself what belonged to all in common? If such a consent as that was necessary, man had starved, notwithstanding the plenty God had given him. We see in commons, which remain so by compact, that it is the taking any part of what is common, and removing it out of the state nature leaves it in, which begins the property; without which the common is of no use. And the taking of this or that part, does not depend on the express consent of all the commoners. Thus the grass my horse has bit; the turfs my servant has cut; and the ore I have digged in any place, where I have a right to them in common with others, become my property, without the assignation or consent of any body. The labour that was mine, removing them out of that common state they were in, hath fixed my property in them.

Sec. 51. And thus, I think, it is very easy to conceive, without any difficulty, how labour could at first begin a title of property in the

Should citizens have the right to protest government policies? In contrast to Hobbes, Locke believed that citizens have the right to protest the policies and even dissolve a government which is not ensuring the "life, liberty and property" of its citizens. Do you agree with Hobbes or with Locke?

common things of nature, and how the spending it upon our uses bounded it. So that there could then be no reason of quarrelling about title, nor any doubt about the largeness of possession it gave. Right and conveniency went together; for as a man had a right to all he could employ his labour upon, so he had no temptation to labour for more than he could make use of. This left no room for controversy about the title, nor for encroachment on the right of others; what portion a man carved to himself, was easily seen; and it was useless, as well as dishonest, to carve himself too much, or take more than he needed.

Locke's concept of the "right to property" thus represents a core value: We have the right to our own body, meaning the freedom to live our lives and pursue our happiness freely, without arbitrary interference from other individuals or from the state. We also have the right to own property, a significant claim in Locke's time when much of a person's value was defined by the property he owned (or didn't own). Locke was not advocating that everyone should own the *same* amount of property, only that every person be entitled to own *some* property. The amount of property you own depends on your ingenuity and industriousness, qualities that came to be associated with the "Protestant work ethic." And finally, we have the right to reap the benefits that our labor produces. It is a violation of our benefits to be expected to work without receiving a proportionate share of what our labor produces.

Locke's ideas were truly revolutionary when he wrote them, and they remain revolutionary today in many parts of the world. His ideas are surely inconsistent with slavery, as well as the exploitation of underpaid workers. The political leaders in America were very familiar with Locke's writings (along with Montesquieu's), and **Thomas Jefferson** was a particularly avid student of his ideas. This is clear when we compare Locke's declaration of the "inalienable rights of life, liberty, and the right to own property," with this famous sentence of the Declaration of Independence, composed by Thomas Jefferson: "We hold these truths to be self-evident, that all men are created equal, that they are endowed by their Creator with certain unalienable Rights, that among these are Life, Liberty and the pursuit of Happiness."

Locke's ideas were also instrumental in shaping the rationale for America's rebellion against the government of England, as we can see in the following passages regarding the conditions for the dissolution of the social contract.

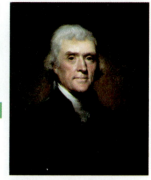

Thomas Jefferson
(1743–1826). Jefferson was an American statesman and advocate of the social contract and natural rights of humans who composed the Declaration of Independence.

CHAP. XIX. Of the Dissolution of Government.

Sec. 222. The reason why men enter into society, is the preservation of their property; and the end why they chuse and authorize a legislative, is, that there may be laws made, and rules set, as guards and fences to the properties of all the members of the society, to limit the power, and moderate the dominion, of every part and member of the society: for since it can never be supposed to be the will of the society, that the legislative should have a power to destroy that which every one designs to secure, by entering into society, and for which the people submitted themselves to legislators of their own making; whenever the legislators endeavour to take away, and destroy the property of the people, or to reduce them to slavery under arbitrary power, they put themselves into a state of war with the people, who are thereupon absolved from any farther obedience, and are left to the common refuge, which God hath provided for all men, against force and violence. Whensoever therefore the legislative shall transgress this fundamental rule of society; and either by ambition, fear, folly or corruption, endeavour to grasp themselves, or put into the hands of any other, an absolute power over the lives, liberties, and estates of the

John Locke,
from *The Second Treatise of Civil Government*

people; by this breach of trust they forfeit the power the people had put into their hands for quite contrary ends, and it devolves to the people, who have a right to resume their original liberty, and, by the establishment of a new legislative, (such as they shall think fit) provide for their own safety and security, which is the end for which they are in society. . . .

If we compare Locke's passages with the opening paragraphs of the Declaration of Independence, the ideological debt owed to Locke is clear.

Thomas Jefferson et al., from *The Declaration of Independence: A Transcription*

***IN CONGRESS**, July 4, 1776.*

The unanimous Declaration of the thirteen United States of America.
When in the Course of human events, it becomes necessary for one people to dissolve the political bands which have connected them with another, and to assume among the powers of the earth, the separate and equal station to which the Laws of Nature and of Nature's God entitle them, a decent respect to the opinions of mankind requires that they should declare the causes which impel them to the separation.

We hold these truths to be self-evident, that all men are created equal, that they are endowed by their Creator with certain unalienable Rights, that among these are Life, Liberty and the pursuit of Happiness.—That to secure these rights, Governments are instituted among Men, deriving their just powers from the consent of the governed,—That whenever any Form of Government becomes destructive of these ends, it is the Right of the People to alter or to abolish it, and to institute new Government, laying its foundation on such principles and organizing its powers in such form, as to them shall seem most likely to effect their Safety and Happiness. Prudence, indeed, will dictate that Governments long established should not be changed for

Signing of the Declaration of Independence.
What are the key principles of the Declaration of Independence? To what extent do you believe these principles are reflected in our society today?

light and transient causes; and accordingly all experience hath shewn, that mankind are more disposed to suffer, while evils are sufferable, than to right themselves by abolishing the forms to which they are accustomed. But when a long train of abuses and usurpations, pursuing invariably the same Object evinces a design to reduce them under absolute Despotism, it is their right, it is their duty, to throw off such Government, and to provide new Guards for their future security. — Such has been the patient sufferance of these Colonies; and such is now the necessity which constrains them to alter their former Systems of Government. The history of the present King of Great Britain is a history of repeated injuries and usurpations, all having in direct object the establishment of an absolute Tyranny over these States. To prove this, let Facts be submitted to a candid world.

< READING CRITICALLY >

Analyzing Locke on Natural Rights

- Locke believes that even when people do not live in organized societies with laws and justice systems, they are nevertheless bound by the "law of nature," reflecting God's will. Do you agree with this view? Why or why not? If so, what values and stipulations are a part of the law of nature?

- As the "servant" of the people, Locke believed that the political state should be rebelled against and dissolved if it fails to perform its functions under the social contract. What functions would your government have to fail to perform for you to support the idea of rebelling against it?

- Locke believes that all people retain the right to control their own bodies and are entitled to a fair share of whatever they produce through their own labor. Do you agree with this view? Why or why not? Can you think of any exceptions to this perspective (for example, someone contemplating suicide)?

- Thomas Jefferson changed Locke's statement of inalienable rights from "Life, liberty and property" to "Life, liberty and the pursuit of happiness." How does the meaning of these two formulations differ? Which one do you think is more appropriate for the Declaration of Independence? Why?

The State of Nature: Assumptions and Questions

Hobbes's and Locke's differing versions of social contract theory reflect their views on human nature. Hobbes has a decidedly pessimistic view of human nature, in which a government must be formed to protect us from each other. Locke's view of humans is more hopeful: Government supports our innate desires for equality, freedom, and tolerance. Nevertheless, Locke also believes that humans are sufficiently competitive and dangerous to one another that a central government is required to ensure social order and protect the intrinsic rights of each individual. The influential French political philosopher **Jean-Jacques Rousseau** has an even more positive view of humans, believing that we are naturally compassionate. Although it's true that this natural compassion is repressed or distorted by social conditioning, it nevertheless forms an important part of our human nature:

> It is this compassion that hurries us without reflection to the relief of those who are in distress: it is this which in a state of nature supplies the place of laws, morals, and virtues, with the advantage that none are tempted to disobey its gentle voice: it is this

Jean-Jacques Rousseau (1712–1778). An Enlightenment philosopher who maintained that society and culture corrupted the inherent goodness of humanity and restricted the freedom people enjoy in the state of nature; offered up a version of the social contract that was much different from his contemporaries.

David Hume (1711–1776). His skeptical examinations of religion, ethics, and history were to make this Scottish philosopher a controversial eighteenth-century figure.

which will always prevent a sturdy savage from robbing a weak child or a feeble old man of the sustenance they may have with pain and difficulty acquired, if he sees a possibility of providing for himself by other means.

Other philosophers have questioned the whole concept of "the state of nature." Foremost among these was **David Hume**, who used his demolition logic to assault what he considers to be the fanciful notion of the "state of nature" and the "social contract,' as he makes scornfully clear in the following passage:

(Some) philosophers . . . assert . . . that government in its earliest infancy arose from consent, or rather the voluntary acquiescence of the people. . . . They affirm that all men are born equal and owe allegiance to no prince or government, unless bound by the obligation and sanction of a promise. . . .

But would these reasoners look abroad into the world, they would meet with nothing that, in the least, corresponds to their ideas. . . . On the contrary, we find everywhere princes who claim their subjects as their property and assert their independent right of sovereignty, from conquest or succession. We find also, everywhere, subjects who acknowledge this right in their prince. . . . Were you to preach, in most parts of the world, that political connections are founded altogether on voluntary consent or a mutual promise, the magistrate would soon imprison you, as seditious, for loosening the ties of obedience; if your friends did not before shut you up as delirious, for advancing such absurdities. . . . Almost all the governments which exist at present, or of which there remains any record in history, have been founded originally either on usurpation or conquest or both, without any pretense of a fair consent or voluntary subjection of the people.

"Take a dose of reality!" Hume seems to be saying to these "social contractors," with his typical biting sarcasm. "Look at the governments in the world and their history!" There is absolutely no evidence of people coming together by common consent to form a social contract from some imagined "state of nature." Quite the contrary: The history of political states is one of conquest and succession, in which the consent of the governed plays absolutely no role. The state of nature and social contract are no more than the fictional creations of philosophers' overwrought imaginations.

John Locke, however, had already anticipated at least a portion of Hume's frontal assault in acknowledging that the state of nature may not have actually existed in fact. And even if citizens had never had the opportunity to give their explicit *prior consent* for the existence, authority, and power of the state, they nevertheless have the opportunity to give their *tacit consent* by choosing to live in society and accept the social/political structure that it provides. In other words, by choosing to live in a society, use its services, and accept its protections, you are confirming your voluntary consent to the state. For Locke, this fulfills his conditions for a legitimate government, one that is based on the recognition that because people are "by nature all free, equal and independent, no one can be . . . subjected to the political power of another without his consent."

Does this meet Hume's objections? Hume would likely say "no." For if we interview citizens of various countries—particularly those in authoritarian regimes, which dominated the landscape in Hume's time—it is probable that they would deny they were making a free, voluntary choice to live in that particular political system. In truth, they would probably respond, "What choice do we have?" In any case, Hume's critique was devastating enough that a serious updating of the social contract theory did not occur until the twentieth century in the person of the philosopher John Rawls.

The State of Nature Is a Conceptual Tool: Rawls

John Rawls picked up the torch of social contract theory, which had been discarded for over 200 years following Hume's withering critique, and gave it a decidedly modern interpretation in his influential book, *A Theory of Justice* (1972). Rawls agreed with Hume that the notion of people living in a "state of nature" and then assembling to enter into a "social contract" were historical fictions. Nevertheless, Rawls believed that we could still make productive use of these concepts by viewing them as theoretical constructs for understanding the nature, purpose, and authority of government and the state. For example, we can pose the question, "If we were living in the 'state of nature' and wanted to enter into an agreement with others to create a social/political community, *what kind of social/political system would we create?*" Imagining ourselves in this situation provides us with the opportunity to identify the values we believe are integral to an enlightened society and to begin thinking about what form such a society would take. Rather than speculate about what social contract people *actually consented* to, we can entertain the question of what type of social/political state we *would consent* to. Once we have constructed a clear model of such a society, we can then go about the business of trying to reshape our current society into one that more closely approximates our ideal society.

John Rawls (1921–2002). An American philosopher who made major contributions to political philosophy, Rawls suggested that the principles of justice be chosen behind a "veil of ignorance," in which no one knows his or her social status, assets and abilities, intelligence and strengths.

Rawls believes that the primary value of society is that it be based on justice. But his concept of justice is very different than that of Plato and Aristotle, for example, who envisioned a just state as one in which every person happily performed his or her appropriate function, whether slave, merchant, soldier, or king. For Rawls, the concept of "justice" is necessarily tied to the concept of "fairness." For a society to be truly *just*, it must be truly *fair*. After all, he reasons, wouldn't anyone about to enter into a social contract with others want to be assured that he or she would be treated fairly with respect to political rights and economic responsibilities? Surely the answer is an emphatic "yes." Who would choose to be a slave, a pauper, an exploited worker, or the target of unfair, discriminatory treatment?

If we assume that all people emerging from the "state of nature" would want to be guaranteed fair treatment and equal opportunities, what is the best way to conceive of what such a state would look like? It is in response to this question that Rawls introduces a simple but powerful concept, the "Veil of Ignorance." Imagine that in devising an ideal society that you had no idea *who* exactly you would be in this new society. Everything about you would be hidden behind a "veil of ignorance" that would conceal your gender, age, race, talents, education, parents—everything that defines you as an individual. In this case, Rawls asks, on what principles would you want this new society to be founded? Rawls is confident that most—perhaps all—people will want to be assured that they will be guaranteed fair treatment and equal opportunities, whatever their situation turns out to be. It is analogous to asking you to divide up a pie for dessert with the proviso that you do not know which piece you will be receiving: You will likely make every effort to ensure that the pieces are exactly equal so that you don't end up getting shortchanged!

In the following passages from *A Theory of Justice*, Rawls explores these themes and also goes on to identify the core principles that a just and fair society will embody.

John Rawls, from *A Theory of Justice*

The Main Idea of the Theory of Justice

My aim is to present a conception of justice which generalizes and carries to a higher level of abstraction the familiar theory of the social contract as found, say, in Locke, Rousseau, and Kant. In order to do this we are not to think of the original contract as one to enter a particular society or to set up a particular form of government. Rather, the guiding idea is that the principles of justice for the basic structure of society are the original agreement. They are the principles that free and rational persons concerned to further their own interests would accept in an initial position of equality as defining the fundamental terms of their association. These principles are to regulate all further agreements; they specify the kinds of social cooperation that can be entered into and the forms of government that can be established. This way of regarding the principles of justice I shall call justice as fairness.

Thus we are to imagine that those who engage in social cooperation choose together in one joint act, the principles which are to assign basic rights and duties and to determine the division of social benefits. Men are to decide in advance how they are to regulate their claims against one another and what is to be the foundation charter of their society. Just as each person must decide by rational reflection what constitutes his good, that is, the system of ends which it is rational for him to pursue, so a group of persons must decide once and for all what is to count among them as just and unjust. The choice which rational men would make in this hypothetical situation of equal liberty, assuming for the present that this choice problem has a solution, determines the principles of justice.

In justice as fairness the original position of equality corresponds to the state of nature in the traditional theory of the social contract. This original position is not, of course, thought of as an actual historical state of affairs, much less as a primitive condition of culture. It is understood as a purely hypothetical situation characterized so as to lead to a certain conception of justice. Among the essential features of this situation is that no one knows his place in society, his class position or social status, nor does anyone know his fortune in the distribution of natural assets and abilities, his intelligence, strength and the like. I shall even assume that the parties do not know their conceptions of the good or their special psychological propensities. The principles of justice are chosen behind a veil of ignorance. This ensures that no one is advantaged or disadvantaged in the choice of principles by the outcomes of natural chance or the contingency of social circumstances. Since all are similarly situated and no one is able to design principles to favor his particular condition, the principles of justice (for society and government) are the result of a fair agreement or bargain. For given the circumstances of the original position, the symmetry of everyone's relations to each other, this initial situation is fair between individuals as moral persons, that is, as rational beings with their own ends and capable, I shall assume, of a sense of justice. The original position is, one might say, the appropriate initial status quo, and thus the fundamental agreements reached in it are fair. This explains the propriety of the name "justice as fairness": it conveys the idea that the principles of justice are agreed to in an initial situation that is fair. The name does not mean that the concepts of justice and fairness are the same, any more than the phrase "poetry as metaphor" means that the concept of poetry and metaphor are the same.

Rawls believes—along with Hobbes and Locke—that humans are fundamentally *rational* creatures who are interested in using their reasoning abilities to enter into a mutually productive social relationship with others. Hobbes believed this rationally chosen social contract was necessary to curb and control our intrinsic aggressive and destructive impulses. Locke believed that humans entered into a social contract to formalize and enforce the divinely inspired Law of Nature. Rawls has a different perspective. He believes that we should use the idea of the social contract as a conceptual tool for determining how best to construct a fair and just society. And to achieve this end, he suggests that we employ a veil of ignorance to develop the fundamental principles of justice on which society should be built. He believes that this process will result in a fair and impartial analysis because the veil will ensure that "no one knows his place in society, his class position or social status, nor does anyone know his fortune in the distribution of natural assets and abilities, his intelligence, strength and the like." And because we can't be sure what social position we will occupy in society, we have no choice but to create a system that will ensure that we are treated fairly and justly no matter *who* we are. It is a fascinating proposal: The "Thinking Philosophically" box gives us the opportunity to try it out.

Of course, Rawls has his own ideas regarding the fundamental principles of justice that ought to form the basis of society that he identifies in the following passages. As you read them, compare your principles of justice with the ones he endorses.

> ### thinking philosophically
>
> ## CREATING A JUST SOCIETY
>
> We began this chapter with the challenge: "Imagine that you were given the project of creating a society based on the principle of justice: How would you go about it and how would you justify your proposed state?" Using Rawls's concept of the "veil of ignorance," identify what principles of justice you would base your society on in the areas of
>
> - Rights and liberties
> - Economic opportunity
> - Education
> - Allocation of wealth and property
> - Health care
> - Political representation
> - Other areas you believe are important

Two Principles of Justice

John Rawls, from *A Theory of Justice*

I shall now state in a provisional form the two principles of justice that I believe should be chosen in the original position. In this section I wish to make only the most general comments, and therefore the first formulation of these principles is tentative. . . .

The first statement of the two principles reads as follows.

First: each person is to have an equal right to the most extensive basic liberty compatible with a similar liberty for others.

Second: social and economic inequalities are to be arranged so that they are both (a) reasonably expected to be to everyone's advantage, and (b) attached to positions and offices open to all. . . .

By way of general comment, these principles primarily apply, as I have said, to the basic structure of society. They are to govern the assignment of rights and duties and to regulate the distribution of social and economic advantages. As their formulation suggests, these principles presuppose that the social structure can be divided into two more or less distinct parts, the first principle applying to the one, the second to the other. They distinguish between those aspects of the social system that define and secure the equal liberties of citizenship and those that specify and establish social and economic inequalities. The basic liberties of citizens are, roughly speaking, political liberty (the right to vote and to be eligible for public office) together with freedom of speech and assembly; liberty of conscience and freedom of thought; freedom of the person along with the right to hold (personal) property; and freedom from arbitrary arrest and seizure as defined by the concept of the rule of law. These liberties are all required to be equal by the first principle, since citizens of a just society are to have the same basic rights.

The second principle applies, in the first approximation, to the distribution of income and wealth and to the design of organizations that make use of differences in authority and responsibility, or chains of command. While the distribution of wealth and income

> need not be equal, it must be to everyone's advantage, and at the same time, positions of authority and offices of command must be accessible to all. One applies the second principle by holding positions open, and then, subject to this constraint, arranges social and economic inequalities so that everyone benefits.

Rawls thus identifies two cardinal principles on which a just society should be based. The first deals with the "basic liberties" of citizens, and he believes that every person should have the maximum amount of freedom that is compatible with the freedom for all. This includes

- voting and being eligible to run for office.
- freedom of speech and assembly.
- freedom of conscience and thought.
- freedom of the person and the right to hold property.
- freedom from arbitrary arrest and seizure.

The second principle deals with economic issues and states that each person should have an equal opportunity to seek careers and economic opportunities. This means that every position should be open to all people and that the sole criterion for determining which people are selected for these positions is their qualifications. But this principle also means that all people should have an equal opportunity for the education and training that would enable them to develop the qualifications required. In other words, it is an empty promise to tell people that jobs or careers are open to all qualified candidates and then not ensure that people have an equal opportunity to *develop* those qualifications.

Rawls is not advocating a social model in which everybody is entitled to exactly the same amount of wealth and income: rather, simply that people have an *equal opportunity* to acquire such wealth and income. And he also recognizes that it is sometimes in the interest of society to have economic *inequalities*. For example, if everyone is going to earn the same amount of salary, no matter how hard he or she works, there will be little incentive for each to put forth his or her best effort. It would be analogous to telling students in a class that everyone was going to receive an "A" no matter what that student's performance in the class. What do you think would be the result of such a policy? Similarly, for a society to achieve its greatest productivity, people should be rewarded for their dedication, ingenuity, and all the other qualities that are a part of being successful.

However, Rawls also recognizes that not everyone is equally talented, and some members of society are at a disadvantage due to disabilities, age, and any number of other variables. So he adds the proviso that any economic inequalities should be for everyone's benefit. In practice, this means that such inequalities as incentives should enrich society as a whole by rewarding excellent performance. And it also means that a just society not merely provides a safety net (a minimum for the worst off) but that it distributes social goods unequally so as to *maximize* the status of those worst off— society makes their unequal status the best that it could be. To sum up, Rawls's two principles of a just society are:

- Each person should have the greatest amount of political freedom that is compatible with equal freedom for all citizens.
- Economic wealth and income should provide everyone with an equal opportunity to secure all positions. In addition, any economic inequalities (such as incentives for superior performance) should be designed to benefit all people in society, including the least advantaged persons.

> **< READING CRITICALLY >**
>
> ### Analyzing Rawls on Justice and Equality
>
> ■ Do you agree with Rawls's idea that economic wealth and income should provide everyone with an equal opportunity to secure all positions? Why or why not? How would you ensure that everyone has a chance to be equally educated or trained for all positions?
>
> ■ Do you agree with Rawls's idea that there should be economic equalities as long as they benefit society as a whole? Why or why not? Have you ever been in a situation in which there were no incentives for superior performance? If so, how did people respond under those circumstances?
>
> ■ Do you agree with Rawls's idea that there should be a system of public welfare that ensures a basic standard of living for everyone in society, no matter how disadvantaged? Why or why not? Identify some of the challenges of creating and administering such a public welfare system.
>
> ■ Rawls's colleague at Harvard, the philosopher **Robert Nozick**, believed that liberty and individual rights are so powerful that creating a safety net for less advantaged members of society is illegitimate. The government has no right to transfer property from some individuals (the rich) to other individuals (the poor). Instead, a society should rely on gifts and charity that is freely donated to support needy members of society. This is liberalism in its purest form, and is also characterized as libertarianism. He explains in this passage from his influential book, *Anarchy, State, and Utopia* (1975):
>
> > Benefits and burdens are distributed justly when society allows every individual the freedom to do what he chooses to do for himself or for others, the freedom to keep what he makes for himself or what others choose to give him, and the freedom to keep what he has or give it to whomever he chooses.
>
> ■ Critically evaluate Nozick's point of view by citing the reasons that might be used to support it as well as reasons opposed to it. What do you think would be the practical outcome for the less advantaged members of society if Nozick's philosophy were implemented?

10.4 Justice Is Based on Need and Ability: Marx and Engels

Liberalism is a sociopolitical theory that emphasizes the liberty, rights, and responsibilities of the individual, and as a consequence it is also tied to the concept of social contract as reflected in the views of Hume, Locke, and Rawls. For liberalism, a just society is one in which individuals are free to pursue their own interests and achieve their own goals. The role of government is to ensure that individuals' rights are protected so that they can pursue their free choices without interference from others. Modern liberalism, as reflected in the views of philosophers such as John Rawls, recognizes that an individual's freedom of choice may be limited by other factors, such as lack of wealth, inadequate education, and social discrimination. In the previous section, we saw how Rawls attempts to compensate for these inhibiting factors by endorsing a principle of equal economic opportunity, as well as a social welfare safety net for those less advantaged members of society. Nevertheless, the emphasis for liberalism remains on the liberty, rights, and responsibilities of the individual.

Robert Nozick (1938–2002) Nozick was a political philosopher. In *Anarchy, State, and Utopia* (1975), he took a libertarian position and argues that only a "minimal state" is justified.

Utopia An ideal place, state, or society.

Liberalism Political theory that champions the liberty, rights, and responsibilities of the individual.

Socialism The belief that society's resources belong to all members and should be shared with everyone.

Capitalism Social organization based on the free-market exchange of goods and services.

Communism Social organization based on communal ownership of resources and communal self-government.

Karl Marx (1818–1883). Marx was a German philosopher and economist whose writings laid the groundwork for socialism.

((•—[**Listen** to the **Radio**
How Marx's General Helped Lead the Revolution on **mysearchlab.com**

Georg Hegel (1770–1831). This nineteenth-century German philosopher wrote extensively on subjects from logic to politics. His dialectical view of the way in which history progresses influenced Marx and many other philosophers who followed him.

Socialism is the sociopolitical philosophy that is the major competitor to liberalism. For socialism, a just society is one in which the wealth and property produced by society belongs to everyone and ought to be shared with everyone. In sharp contrast to liberalism's emphasis on the rights of the individual, socialism takes as its starting point the welfare of the entire community of individuals, and its central theme is captured in Karl Marx's slogan, "From each according to his abilities, to each according to his needs." Liberalism and socialism are the two predominant ideologies in the modern world, and most modern societies are a version of one or the other or some blending of the two. In general, societies that are characterized as **capitalist** are considered built on the principles of liberalism. In contrast, societies characterized as **communist** or Marxist are considered built on the principles of socialism.

Karl Marx is the political theorist who is considered to be the architect of modern socialism, and his views have had a profound and far-reaching impact. Marx grew up in Germany, a philosophy student who aspired to be a philosophy professor. However, his "radical" political views prevented him from pursuing this career, and so he became a political journalist. But his political views continued to cause him problems. In his first position as editor of the *Rhineland Gazette*, he launched a campaign against Christian religion and the Christian state, which resulted in the state censor closing the newspaper down. This same pattern was repeated in subsequent journalistic positions, and he was forced to move throughout Europe as his publications were banned by one government after another. He ultimately settled in London in 1849, where he devoted the rest of his life to writing books and articles on the topics of philosophy, history, politics, and economics that would come to have such an extraordinary impact on the world. Marx fervently believed that ideas should be alive, with real-world consequences, a view captured in his statement that "the philosophers have only *interpreted* the world, in various ways; the point is to *change* it." Marx believed that this change is best accomplished through social and political action. On a personal level, the fact that two of his children died at least in part as the result of poverty and disease doubtless helped fuel his passionate defense of his views.

Marx was drawn to the ideas of **Georg Hegel**, who believed that history unfolds according to certain laws, following a logic that Hegel described as *dialectical*. The dialectical development of historical events means that a current state of affairs (the *thesis*) inevitably creates its opposite (the *antithesis*), which finds ultimate resolution in a state of affairs (the *synthesis*) that both includes and transcends both of these elements. Marx believed that we can see this dialectical movement of history at work in the class struggles that have characterized every historical period. At the time he was writing, he considered the class struggle to be between the *bourgeoisie* and the *proletariat*. The bourgeoisie are those people in control of economic forces: the owners of industrial production (businesses and factories) and the employers of people who work for wages. The proletariat are the wage-earning workers, who typically own no property and who are at the mercy of the owners and employers.

In terms of the current dialectic of history, the bourgeoisie represent the *thesis* element, whereas the large angry, disillusioned, and exploited class of workers represent the *antithesis*. Marx believed that it was only a matter of time before the downtrodden proletariat would rise up in revolt against their bourgeoisie exploiters, creating a new economic and social order—the *synthesis*—in which the workers would control the means of production and share equally in the *capital* (goods, services, money) that their efforts produce. This new synthesis would find its social/political form in communism. For Marx, this dialectical process is not speculative: It will necessarily occur because the laws of history are "tendencies working with iron necessity towards inevitable results."

Marx was convinced that the economic structure (in terms of the means of production) of a society is the dominant force that shapes the community's social relationships, political processes, and spiritual values. He states: "The ideas of the ruling class are in every epoch the ruling ideas: The class which has the means of production at its disposal, has control at the same time over the means of mental production." Marx's most famous articulation of his views is to be found in the *Manifesto of the Communist Party*, which he coauthored with **Friedrich Engels** in 1848. The *Manifesto* is a passionate and influential document that merits close scrutiny.

Karl Marx and Friedrich Engels, from *Manifesto of the Communist Party*

A spectre is haunting Europe—the spectre of communism. All the powers of old Europe have entered into a holy alliance to exorcise this spectre: Pope and Tsar, Metternich and Guizot, French Radicals and German police-spies. . . .

Two things result from this fact:

I. Communism is already acknowledged by all European powers to be itself a power.

II. It is high time that Communists should openly, in the face of the whole world, publish their views, their aims, their tendencies, and meet this nursery tale of the spectre of communism with a manifesto of the party itself.

To this end, Communists of various nationalities have assembled in London and sketched the following manifesto, to be published in the English, French, German, Italian, Flemish and Danish languages.

I—Bourgeois and Proletarians

(By *bourgeoisie* is meant the class of modern capitalists, owners of the means of social production and employers of wage labor. By *proletariat*, the class of modern wage laborers who, having no means of production of their own, are reduced to selling their labor power in order to live.) Note by Engels—1888 English edition

The history of all hitherto existing society is the history of class struggles.

Freeman and slave, patrician and plebeian, lord and serf, guild-master and journeyman, in a word, oppressor and oppressed, stood in constant opposition to one another, carried on an uninterrupted, now hidden, now open fight, a fight that each time ended, either in a revolutionary reconstitution of society at large, or in the common ruin of the contending classes.

In the earlier epochs of history, we find almost everywhere a complicated arrangement of society into various orders, a manifold gradation of social rank. In ancient Rome we have patricians, knights, plebeians, slaves; in the Middle Ages, feudal lords, vassals, guild-masters, journeymen, apprentices, serfs; in almost all of these classes, again, subordinate gradations.

The modern bourgeois society that has sprouted from the ruins of feudal society has not done away with class antagonisms. It has but established new classes, new conditions of oppression, new forms of struggle in place of the old ones.

Our epoch, the epoch of the bourgeoisie, possesses, however, this distinct feature: it has simplified class antagonisms. Society as a whole is more and more splitting up into two great hostile camps, into two great classes directly facing each other—bourgeoisie and proletariat. . . .

Friedrich Engels (1820–1895). This German philosopher and social scientist wrote about the horrors of factory working conditions in England before befriending Karl Marx. Engels cowrote the *Communist Manifesto* with Marx and also edited parts of Marx's *Das Kapital*.

Is there a continuing social struggle between the oppressors and the oppressed as there was in medieval times between the serfs and the lords? According to Marx and Engels, economic history is best understood as an ongoing struggle between the oppressors and the oppressed—"freeman and slave, patrician and plebeian, lord and serf, guild-master and journeyman"—a fight that inevitably ends "either in a revolutionary reconstitution of society at large, or in the common ruin of the contending classes."

Marx and Engels begin their *Manifesto*—a word that means a proclamation or declaration of principles—by first describing the social context. This document is being issued by a gathering of communists who have assembled in London for the express purpose of stating their beliefs and intentions, mobilizing the proletariat of all nations, and warning all governments that a social and economic revolution is coming. History is best understood, they argue, as a sequence of class struggles between the oppressors and the oppressed, a dynamic process that in all cases results either in a "revolutionary reconstitution" of society or the "common ruin" of all parties. The latest incarnation of this class struggle is between the bourgeoisie and the proletariat, the two social groups that have been created and shaped by the evolution of modern industry. The preceding era—the Middle Ages—was a feudal society in which the hierarchy of classes included feudal lords, vassals, guildmasters, journeymen, apprentices, and serfs. The development of improved manufacturing methods, combined with the discovery of new trade markets in America and Asia, fueled an industrial explosion that spelled doom for the previous feudal society. It also created the latest version of class warfare between the owners of these manufacturing and trade industries—the *bourgeoisie*—and the "industrial armies" that they employ—the workers or *proletariat*. In the judgment of the Communists, this economic revolution wreaked havoc on the social relationships, political processes, and spiritual values of nations that it touched and contaminated.

Karl Marx and Friedrich Engels, from *Manifesto of the Communist Party*

The bourgeoisie cannot exist without constantly revolutionizing the instruments of production, and thereby the relations of production, and with them the whole relations of society. Conservation of the old modes of production in unaltered form, was, on the contrary, the first condition of existence for all earlier industrial classes. Constant revolutionizing of production, uninterrupted disturbance of all social conditions, everlasting uncertainty and agitation distinguish the bourgeois epoch from all earlier ones. All fixed, fast frozen relations, with their train of ancient and venerable prejudices and opinions, are swept away, all new-formed ones become antiquated before they can ossify. All that is solid melts into air, all that is holy is profaned, and man is at last compelled to face with sober senses his real condition of life and his relations with his kind.

The need of a constantly expanding market for its products chases the bourgeoisie over the entire surface of the globe. It must nestle everywhere, settle everywhere, establish connections everywhere.

The bourgeoisie has, through its exploitation of the world market, given a cosmopolitan character to production and consumption in every country. To the great chagrin of reactionaries, it has drawn from under the feet of industry the national ground on which it stood. All old-established national industries have been destroyed or are daily being destroyed. They are dislodged by new industries, whose introduction becomes a life and death question for all civilized nations, by industries that no longer work up indigenous raw material, but raw material drawn from the remotest zones; industries whose products are consumed, not only at home, but in every quarter of the globe. In place of the old wants, satisfied by the production of the country, we find new wants, requiring for their satisfaction the products of distant lands and climes. In place of the old local and national seclusion and self-sufficiency, we have intercourse in every direction, universal inter-dependence of nations. And as in material, so also in intellectual production. The intellectual creations of individual nations become common property. National one-sidedness and narrow-mindedness become more and more impossible, and from the numerous national and local literatures, there arises a world literature.

The bourgeoisie, by the rapid improvement of all instruments of production, by the immensely facilitated means of communication, draws all, even the most barbarian, nations into civilization. The cheap prices of commodities are the heavy artillery with which it forces the barbarians' intensely obstinate hatred of foreigners to capitulate. It compels all nations, on pain of extinction, to adopt the bourgeois mode of production; it compels them to introduce what it calls civilization into their midst, i.e., to become bourgeois themselves. In one word, it creates a world after its own image. . . .

The bourgeoisie, during its rule of scarce one hundred years, has created more massive and more colossal productive forces than have all preceding generations together. Subjection of nature's forces to man, machinery, application of chemistry to industry and agriculture, steam navigation, railways, electric telegraphs, clearing of whole continents for cultivation, canalization of rivers, whole populations conjured out of the ground—what earlier century had even a presentiment that such productive forces slumbered in the lap of social labor?

Did industrial development make possible exploitation on a larger scale? According to Karl Marx, "The bourgeoisie . . . created more massive and more colossal productive forces than have all preceding generations together," signaling the end of feudal society and the beginning of the progressive exploitation of the working class. Do you agree with his analysis?

For Marx and Engels, the evolution of a feudal society to one based on capitalism, free competition, and free trade is just one more step in the necessary evolution of human history, having profound repercussions. Although they do not explicitly mention the relationship of free trade and capitalism to Enlightenment values and intellectual freedom, they do cite the following progressive advancements of capitalism:

- Capitalism has encouraged the invention of consistently superior modes of production (as well as the invention of new products), rather than staying with the "conservation of the old modes of production in unaltered form."

- Capitalism has encouraged the creation of new forms of thinking, replacing the "ancient and venerable prejudices and opinions" of feudal society.

- Capitalism and free trade have encouraged globalization and world literature, a "universal inter-dependence of

How is child labor evidence of bourgeois exploitation, according to Marx? Marx and Engels believed that the Industrial Revolution, in addition to causing the migration of people from rural locations to cities, also forced the working class to "sell themselves piecemeal . . . a commodity, like every other article of commerce." This left them—and their children—vulnerable to terrible exploitation at the hands of the owners of capital, the bourgeoisie capitalists.

nations," replacing "national seclusion and self-sufficiency," as well as "national one-sidedness and narrow-mindedness."

- Capitalism has created enormous cities that "rescued a considerable part of the population from the idiocy of rural life."
- Capitalism has "centralized the means of production, and has concentrated property in a few hands," which has resulted in political centralization, replacing a decentralized political structure.
- Capitalism, in the short span of one hundred years, has created "massive" and "colossal" productive forces in the areas of machinery, improved methods of farming, steam navigation, railways, and electric telegraphs.

Thus capitalism, free trade, and free competition remade the world in a very short span of time, creating a new society and culture, controlled economically and politically by the human instruments of capitalism, the bourgeois. The next stage in the evolution of capitalism and its bourgeoisie creators reveals that the seeds for their self-destruction have already been sown—by the same elements that have contributed to their rapid growth and marketplace hegemony.

Marx and Engels believed that, like Dr. Frankenstein, the bourgeoisie have created a monster that they can no longer control, as the forces of capitalism run amok. Free competition, free trade, and the limitless greed of the capitalists create "the epidemic of over-production." They have created a production machine that is too efficient, the consequence of "too much civilization, too much means of subsistence, too much industry, too much commerce." There simply are not enough buyers for the products. What to do? There are two answers: Lay off or fire the workers until production matches demand, or create new markets through aggressive sales and trade initiatives. Capitalism has become an economic system out of control with an appetite for growth that is so rapacious that it is ultimately forced to feed on itself. Capitalism's failure to control the growth of its modes of production has the unintended effect of creating a new class of citizens who will ultimately spell capitalism's downfall—the army of the **proletariat**.

Karl Marx and Friedrich Engels,
from *Manifesto of the Communist Party*

But not only has the bourgeoisie forged the weapons that bring death to itself; it has also called into existence the men who are to wield those weapons—the modern working class—the proletarians.

In proportion as the bourgeoisie, i.e., capital, is developed, in the same proportion is the proletariat, the modern working class, developed—a class of laborers, who live only so long as they find work, and who find work only so long as their labor increases capital. These laborers, who must sell themselves piecemeal, are a commodity, like every other article of commerce, and are consequently exposed to all the vicissitudes of competition, to all the fluctuations of the market.

Owing to the extensive use of machinery, and to the division of labor, the work of the proletarians has lost all individual character, and, consequently, all charm for the workman. He becomes an appendage of the machine, and it is only the most simple, most monotonous, and most easily acquired knack, that is required of him. Hence, the cost of production of a workman is restricted, almost entirely, to the means of subsistence that he requires for maintenance, and for the propagation of his race. But the price of a commodity, and therefore also of labor, is equal to its cost of production. In proportion, therefore, as the repulsiveness of the work increases, the wage decreases. What is more, in proportion as the use of machinery and division of labor increases, in the same proportion the burden of toil also increases, whether by prolongation of the working hours, by the increase of the work exacted in a given time, or by increased speed of machinery, etc.

Proletariat The class of people who, lacking resources and the means of production, sell their labor.

Modern Industry has converted the little workshop of the patriarchal master into the great factory of the industrial capitalist. Masses of laborers, crowded into the factory, are organized like soldiers. As privates of the industrial army, they are placed under the command of a perfect hierarchy of officers and sergeants. Not only are they slaves of the bourgeois class, and of the bourgeois state; they are daily and hourly enslaved by the machine, by the overlooker, and, above all, in the individual bourgeois manufacturer himself. The more openly this despotism proclaims gain to be its end and aim, the more petty, the more hateful and the more embittering it is.

Are we merely cogs in the wheels of society? Charlie Chaplin in *Modern Times*. Chaplin's film, created half a century after Marx's death, satirizes factory life. It illustrates Marx's idea of workers as "slaves of the bourgeois state" who "are daily and hourly enslaved by the machine."

Capitalism, with its industrialized means of production and voracious appetite for growth, needs an army of workers to run its factories. But these workers are not valued as human beings: They are merely seen as "appendages of the machine." These workers, the proletariat, "must sell themselves piecemeal, are a commodity, like every other article of commerce, and are consequently exposed to all the vicissitudes of competition, to all the fluctuations of the market." And unlike previous eras, when individuals developed expertise in various areas and took pride in the products that they produced, the division of labor has reduced their activities to simple, mindless tasks that have no personal meaning and provide no satisfaction. Instead of taking pride in the crops they have grown, the clothes they have fashioned, the furniture they have built, the bread they have baked, they are now reduced to "repulsive" repetitive tasks in crowded, noisy factories, working excessive hours for low wages. In Marx's terms, they have become profoundly *alienated* from the product of their labor, an alienation that seeps into every area of their lives, as we will see later in the chapter.

Thus the proletariat become objects to be manipulated by the bourgeoisie, at the mercy of market forces, performing tasks that rob them of their sense of human value and self-esteem.

But although the proletariat are powerless as individuals, they have—potentially—immense power as an organized group. Marx and Engels next describe their idealized vision of the future, as the downtrodden proletariat rise up as a powerful army and take their vengeance on their despised tormenters, the bourgeoisie.

The proletariat goes through various stages of development. With its birth begins its struggle with the bourgeoisie. At first, the contest is carried on by individual laborers, then by the work of people of a factory, then by the operative of one trade, in one locality, against the individual bourgeois who directly exploits them. They direct their attacks not against the bourgeois condition of production, but against the instruments of production themselves; they destroy imported wares that compete with their labor, they smash to pieces machinery, they set factories ablaze, they seek to restore by force the vanished status of the workman of the Middle Ages.

At this stage, the laborers still form an incoherent mass scattered over the whole country, and broken up by their mutual competition. If anywhere they unite to form more compact bodies, this is not yet the consequence of their own active union, but of the union of the bourgeoisie, which class, in order to attain its own political ends, is compelled to set the whole proletariat in motion, and is moreover yet, for a time, able to do

Karl Marx and Friedrich Engels, from *Manifesto of the Communist Party*

In assessing Marx's vision of the future, is a proletarian revolt still possible? Marx believed that exploited workers would band together to form ever-widening and more powerful unions, culminating in a proletarian revolt. To what extent was his prediction accurate? Inaccurate?

❝ **But with the development of industry, the proletariat not only increases in number; it becomes concentrated in greater masses, its strength grows, and it feels that strength more.** ❞

so. At this stage, therefore, the proletarians do not fight their enemies, but the enemies of their enemies, the remnants of absolute monarchy, the landowners, the non-industrial bourgeois, the petty bourgeois. Thus, the whole historical movement is concentrated in the hands of the bourgeoisie; every victory so obtained is a victory for the bourgeoisie.

But with the development of industry, the proletariat not only increases in number; it becomes concentrated in greater masses, its strength grows, and it feels that strength more. The various interests and conditions of life within the ranks of the proletariat are more and more equalized, in proportion as machinery obliterates all distinctions of labor, and nearly everywhere reduces wages to the same low level. The growing competition among the bourgeois, and the resulting commercial crises, make the wages of the workers ever more fluctuating. The increasing improvement of machinery, ever more rapidly developing, makes their livelihood more and more precarious; the collisions between individual workmen and individual bourgeois take more and more the character of collisions between two classes. Thereupon, the workers begin to form combinations (trade unions) against the bourgeois; they club together in order to keep up the rate of wages; they found permanent associations in order to make provision beforehand for these occasional revolts. Here and there, the contest breaks out into riots.

Now and then the workers are victorious, but only for a time. The real fruit of their battles lie not in the immediate result, but in the ever expanding union of the workers. This union is helped on by the improved means of communication that are created by Modern Industry, and that place the workers of different localities in contact with one another. It was just this contact that was needed to centralize the numerous local struggles, all of the same character, into one national struggle between classes. But every class struggle is a political struggle. And that union, to attain which the burghers of the Middle Ages, with their miserable highways, required centuries, the modern proletarians, thanks to railways, achieve in a few years.

This organization of the proletarians into a class, and, consequently, into a political party, is continually being upset again by the competition between the workers themselves. But it ever rises up again, stronger, firmer, mightier. It compels legislative recognition of particular interests of the workers, by taking advantage of the divisions among the bourgeoisie itself. . . .

Of all the classes that stand face to face with the bourgeoisie today, the proletariat alone is a genuinely revolutionary class. The other classes decay and finally disappear in the face of Modern Industry; the proletariat is its special and essential product. . . .

All previous historical movements were movements of minorities, or in the interest of minorities. The proletarian movement is the self-conscious, independent movement of the immense majority, in the interest of the immense majority. The proletariat, the lowest stratum of our present society, cannot stir, cannot raise itself up, without the whole superincumbent strata of official society being sprung into the air.

Though not in substance, yet in form, the struggle of the proletariat with the bourgeoisie is at first a national struggle. The proletariat of each country must, of course, first of all settle matters with its own bourgeoisie.

In depicting the most general phases of the development of the proletariat, we traced the more or less veiled civil war, raging within existing society, up to the point where that war breaks out into open revolution, and where the violent overthrow of the bourgeoisie lays the foundation for the sway of the proletariat.

Hitherto, every form of society has been based, as we have already seen, on the antagonism of oppressing and oppressed classes. But in order to oppress a class, certain conditions must be assured to it under which it can, at least, continue its slavish existence. The serf, in the period of serfdom, raised himself to membership in the commune, just as the petty bourgeois, under the yoke of the feudal absolutism, managed to develop into a bourgeois. The modern laborer, on the contrary, instead of rising with the process of industry, sinks deeper and deeper below the conditions of existence of his own class. He becomes a pauper, and pauperism develops more rapidly than population and wealth. And here it becomes evident that the bourgeoisie is unfit any longer to be the ruling class in society, and to impose its conditions of existence upon society as an overriding law. It is unfit to rule because it is incompetent to assure an existence to its slave within his slavery, because it cannot help letting him sink into such a state, that it has to feed him, instead of being fed by him. Society can no longer live under this bourgeoisie, in other words, its existence is no longer compatible with society.

The essential conditions for the existence and for the sway of the bourgeois class is the formation and augmentation of capital; the condition for capital is wage labor. Wage labor rests exclusively on competition between the laborers. The advance of industry, whose involuntary promoter is the bourgeoisie, replaces the isolation of the laborers, due to competition, by the revolutionary combination, due to association. The development of Modern Industry, therefore, cuts from under its feet the very foundation on which the bourgeoisie produces and appropriates products. What the bourgeoisie therefore produces, above all, are its own grave-diggers. Its fall and the victory of the proletariat are equally inevitable.

> **What the bourgeoisie therefore produces, above all, are its own grave-diggers.**

Marx and Engels were certain that the dialectical forces of history would cause the ultimate overthrow of capitalism and the bourgeoisie by the proletariat masses, resulting in a new economic, social, political era. This conclusion was seen to be the end result of an inevitable process in which the seeds for the destruction of capitalism were sown at its creation. "What the bourgeoisie therefore produces, above all, are its own grave-diggers. Its fall and the victory of the proletariat are equally inevitable."

Marx and Engels believed that this ultimate conclusion would be the end product of a sequence of well-defined developmental stages. In the initial stages of capitalism, the proletariat become, as we have noted, exploited and alienated extensions of the bourgeoisie modes of production. As the proletariat grow in numbers, their rage grows as well. They direct this rage not toward the bourgeoisie

Will the workers of the world unite to form an ideal society? This Soviet poster asserts that "Soviet power is key to the eternal union of peasants and factory workers." Would Marx and Engels agree that state power is needed to cause the ultimate overthrow of capitalism and triumph by the workers?

but against the instruments of production: "They destroy imported wares that compete with their labor, they smash to pieces machinery, they set factories ablaze, they seek to restore by force the vanished status of the workman of the Middle Ages."

Of course, we know now that such an attack against the instruments of production rarely occurred. However, Marx and Engels were right on one count: In difficult economic times, workers often direct their anger toward imported products that threaten their economic well-being, an isolationist tendency that continues to this day. It is typically blue-collar workers who are most vocal in their support of trade barriers to protect their livelihoods.

However, Marx and Engels's vision of the future was more accurate with their vision of the next developmental stage, which involves the potent coalescence of several factors:

- The proletariat increase in number, become concentrated in greater masses, and grow in strength.
- The work of the proletariat becomes more mindless, their wages lower, and their economic stability less secure, reflecting the fluctuations of the commercial crises created by the bourgeoisie.
- Sensing their strength, the proletariat organize into unions and initiate direct confrontations with the bourgeoisie, erupting in occasional riots.
- Improved communication and transportation systems enable the proletariat to organize themselves in ever widening circles of membership.

Many of these predictions have in fact occurred in many parts of the world since the time of Marx and Engels. However, in only a few instances have these factors resulted in the "open revolution" and "violent overthrow" of the bourgeoisie and their capitalistic system occurred. Why not?

At least one key assumption made by Marx and Engels appears, in retrospect, to be fatally flawed. They were convinced that the schism between the bourgeoisie and the proletariat would become greater, increasing the distance between the oppressors and the oppressed in every way: economically, socially, and politically. They were convinced that "The modern laborer . . . instead of rising with the process of industry, sinks deeper and deeper below the condition of existence of his own class. He becomes a pauper, and pauperism develops more rapidly than population and wealth." Instead of this scenario occurring, the reverse scenario has occurred in most industrialized countries. Rather than eroding, the economic and social status of the proletariat has often risen, powered by the strength of their unions and the democratic political systems within which they exist. In addition, as we noted in our discussion of Rawls, liberal economies have also intervened to improve the lives of the workers and more disadvantaged members of society through the creation of public education, economic opportunities, avenues of social advancement, the protection of workers through government legislation, and the creation of welfare safety nets to ensure a minimum standard of living and health care.

Most disturbingly, in those countries in which genuine revolutions took place—such as Russia, China, North Korea, and Cuba—the idealized rule of the proletariat predicted by Marx and Engels did not occur. Rather than creating classless societies based on the communal rule of the proletariat, the aristocratic and bourgeoisie ruling classes were instead replaced by tyrants and dictators who created violent and repressive regimes that were often as bad as or worse than the ones they overthrew.

10.5 Justice Is What Promotes the General Welfare: Mill

We first encountered the thinking of **John Stuart Mill** in Chapter 8 when we explored the utilitarian perspective on ethics: We determine moral "rightness" or "goodness" by calculating which course of action will bring about the greatest happiness for the greatest number of people (and conversely, which course of action will result in the avoidance of unhappiness for the greatest number of people). Not surprisingly, Mill's views on social justice and liberty are based directly on his ethical theory. Justice on the social and political level is what best promotes the well-being and public interest of the greatest number of citizens. So, for example, does the principle of justice require that a society create a financial and medical "safety net" for its disadvantaged citizens? Mill believes that the answer can be determined with certainty by calculating whether such a policy will maximize social benefits for the majority of citizens, and minimize social harms. The core principle of social justice is, in Mill's terms, the principle of **social utility**.

Mill recognizes that viewing justice as being equivalent to social utility—that is, calculating the maximum social benefits—does not capture the intuitive conviction and moral passion that most people associate with justice. To his credit, Mill acknowledges that, for most people, the concept of justice has a uniquely imperative power. It is a

John Stuart Mill (1806–1873). This British philosopher and student of Jeremy Bentham expanded on Bentham's concept of utilitarianism. Mill took into account the quality, not just the quantity, of pleasure when determining the morality of an action.

Social utility The principle advanced by utilitarians that justice is produced by the form of government that creates the greatest social benefit for the greatest number of people.

How does the hedonistic calculus deal with the injustice of slavery? Mill believed that we could define "social justice" by using the hedonistic calculus to calculate what policy brings "the greatest happiness to the greatest number of people." Using this approach, would slavery be considered just or unjust? Why?

((•●—| **Listen** to the **Audiobook** *John Stuart Mill Utilitarianism by Nigel Warburton* on **mysearchlab.com**

concept so fundamental to our way of thinking that it is commonly thought to be a primal instinct. But Mill astutely points out that, simply because there are primal emotions associated with the concept of justice, that is no guarantee that these emotional inclinations or "natural" feelings are enlightened or appropriate. In many cultures past and present, for example, it seemed self-evident to citizens that slavery, human sacrifice, or systematic oppression were an essential part of the natural order and so were "just." The problem is, Mill believes, that when beliefs are founded on strong subjective feelings, people tend to believe that they represent "a revelation of objective reality."

Emotions may be powerful, Mill contends, but emotions often need the guiding light of higher reason to become fully enlightened. One of the major differences between humans and other animals is that we can apply our intellect to arriving at the most enlightened conclusions, whether or not our emotions or instincts are in accord. However, once our reasoning abilities elevate our understanding, our emotions and instincts often follow along behind. For example, once you fully understand the immorality of slavery on an intellectual level, you will likely come to *feel* that slavery is wrong and your instinctive reactions to related issues will probably get reshaped as well. (Mill, by the way, was a passionate abolitionist and supported the Union during the Civil War.)

Mill knows that the idea of calculating the maximum benefits to the general population is not a concept of justice that people are likely to become passionate about. But he wants to argue that if we apply our reasoning ability, this is precisely the conclusion that we will arrive at. But how can we test this idea? Mill proposes the following: Let's examine the various common definitions of *justice* and *injustice* and attempt to determine if there is a core meaning—emotional or intellectual or both—that is common to the primary uses of the concept. If there is a common set of qualities that are different from Mill's principle of social utility, then he is willing to accept the conclusion, even though it has the consequence of undermining his entire approach to social justice. Is this likely to happen? A modicum of skepticism would not be misplaced in this instance!

Mill considers five different meanings of justice and in each case attempts to demonstrate that they are meanings that do not stand on their own but instead rely on the principle of social utility (or "expediency" as he calls it) in their actual application:

- *Justice means not depriving someone of his personal liberty, property, or possession which belongs to him by law.* But, Mill notes, there are laws that we consider to be "bad" or "unjust" in our society or other societies. For example, consider societies in which the law permits slavery to exist; an entire group of people is deprived of liberty. Mill contends that to brand a law "unjust," we appeal to a principle like that of social utility: The law is unjust because it diminishes the general welfare of that society.

- *Justice means not disobeying any law in society, even if you disagree with it or consider it to be unjust.* This was Socrates' belief: He accepted the judgment against him even though he thought it to be unjust because he believed that accepting the judgments of a society's legal system was the obligation of citizens who chose to live in a certain society. But there are legitimate perspectives on both sides of this issue:

Some contend that it is our moral obligation to contest unethical laws because they threaten the general welfare of the state. Others maintain that if laws are not consistently respected and obeyed, then the foundation of the state will be undermined, which will threaten the general welfare of the state. In both cases, the issue turns on the question of social utility.

- *Justice means each person receiving the good or evil that they deserve.* But what is the basis for such a definition? And how is one to determine when someone "deserves" good or evil? And what would be the appropriate amount of good or evil? To answer these questions, we need to appeal to an independent principle, such as the principle of social utility: For example, it is in the interest of the general welfare for there to be a proportionate awarding of rewards and punishments to members of society.

- *Justice means honoring agreements and telling the truth.* But what about examples in which telling the truth will result in great harm coming to innocent people? Or when keeping an agreement that was deceptive in nature will result in the financial ruin of many decent people? Mill notes that this principle can be overridden by other considerations, determined by principles like that of social utility.

- *Justice means acting impartially, not showing preference.* Obviously this is not a meaning that applies in our personal lives, Mill contends, because we are expected to show favor toward our family and friends, providing our action doesn't violate some other duty. And on a social level, such as the judicial system, impartiality is desirable directly because of the principle of social utility: A fair and impartial judicial system is essential in order to promote the general welfare.

- *Justice means treating others with equality.* This is a natural extension of the previous definition. But what exactly does this mean? After all, people are surely not equal to one another; nor are they always deserving of equal treatment. For example, suppose one person is hard-working and conscientious and another is lazy and unreliable: Should they both receive equal compensation? Like the other definitions, justice as equality varies from person to person, situation to situation. Ultimately, it is by appealing to principles like that of social utility that people decide when to treat others equally and when to treat them unequally.

Is justice really blind?
Mill described impartiality as an important aspect of justice. Do you think that our justice system is fair and impartial? What evidence supports your position?

---

thinking philosophically

ANALYZING MILL'S CONCEPT OF JUSTICE

- In analyzing the concept of justice, Mill distinguishes between the conceptual meaning of the term and the emotions associated with the idea of justice. What is the conceptual meaning of *your* concept of justice? What emotions do you associate with your idea of justice? Are these two dimensions of your notion of justice consistent?

- Are any of Mill's five different definitions of justice also a part of your definition of justice? Mill believes that these definitions ultimately depend on the principle of social utility. Do you agree?

- John Rawls, whose ideas we encountered earlier in this chapter, articulates the following criticism of a utilitarian approach to social justice. Evaluate his argument:

> Justice is the first virtue of social institutions, as truth is of systems of thought. A theory however elegant and economical must be rejected or revised if it is untrue; likewise laws and institutions no matter how efficient and well-arranged must be reformed or abolished if they are unjust. Each person possesses an inviolability founded on justice that even the welfare of society as a whole cannot override. For this reason justice denies that the loss of freedom for some is made right by a greater good shared by others. It does not allow that the sacrifices imposed on a few are outweighed by the larger sum of advantages enjoyed by many. Therefore in a just society the liberties of equal citizenship are taken as settled; the rights secured by justice are not subject to political bargaining or to the calculus of social interests. The only thing that permits us to acquiesce in an erroneous theory is the lack of a better one; analogously, an injustice is tolerable only when it is necessary to avoid an even greater injustice. Being first virtues of human activities, truth and justice are uncompromising.

In sum, Mill's concept of justice involves two elements:

- A rule of conduct common to all humankind and intended for their good.
- The sentiment that punishment may be suffered by those who infringe upon the rule, because this is in the interest of both individuals and society as a whole.

Thus, according to Mill, both dimensions of justice necessarily involve the principle of social utility, a conclusion that ensures the fact that Mill will not have to abandon his lifelong utilitarian principles!

With his concept of justice firmly grounded on the principle of social utility, Mill believes he can now explore his real passion, *individual liberty*. The ultimate purpose of government and its laws is to allow individuals to fully realize themselves through their free, unconstrained choices. Mill is convinced that the principle of social utility that forms the foundation of his philosophy—promoting the public welfare for the greatest number of citizens—is best achieved by maximizing the individual liberty of each member of the community. Mill argued this view in the highly influential essay *On Liberty*, to which we will next turn our attention.

((•— **Listen** to the **Podcast**
Richard Reeves on Mill's On Liberty on **mysearchlab.com**

" **Over himself, over his own body and mind, the individual is sovereign.** "

John Stuart Mill, from *On Liberty*

Chapter 1: Introductory

The object of this Essay is to assert one very simple principle, as entitled to govern absolutely the dealings of society with the individual in the way of compulsion and control, whether the means used be physical force in the form of legal penalties, or the moral coercion of public opinion. That principle is, that the sole end for which mankind are warranted, individually or collectively, in interfering with the liberty of action of any of their number, is self-protection. That the only purpose for which power can be rightfully exercised over any member of a civilized community, against his will, is to prevent harm to others. His own good, either physical or moral, is not a sufficient warrant. He cannot rightfully be compelled to do or forbear because it will be better for him to do so, because it will make him happier, because, in the opinions of others, to do so would be wise, or even right. These are good reasons for remonstrating with him, or reasoning with him, or persuading him, or entreating him, but not for compelling him, or visiting him with any evil in case he do otherwise. To justify that, the conduct from which it is desired to deter him, must be calculated to produce evil to some one else. The only part of the conduct of any one, for which he is amenable to society, is that which concerns others. In the part which merely concerns himself, his independence is, of right, absolute. Over himself, over his own body and mind, the individual is sovereign.

It is, perhaps, hardly necessary to say that this doctrine is meant to apply only to human beings in the maturity of their faculties. We are not speaking of children, or of young persons below the age which the law may fix as that of manhood or womanhood. Those who are still in a state to require being taken care of by others, must be protected against their own actions as well as against external injury.

"Over himself, over his own body and mind, the individual is sovereign." Mill could not have stated his core belief more clearly. *Whatever* an individual chooses to do is his or her absolute and irrevocable right, *provided it does not interfere or harm others*. Even if we are convinced that people are acting foolishly, self-destructively, or recklessly, we have no right to intervene and compel them to do otherwise—provided that they pose no threat to others. We may certainly attempt to persuade and reason with them, but beyond that we must respect their autonomy to freely choose.

Mill is quick to point out that even though it may be tempting to ground his concept of liberty by viewing it as an abstract, inalienable "right" (as Locke and Jefferson do), he has no interest in doing so. As noted in the previous section, Mill believes that all notions of "justice" and "rights" are ultimately reducible to the principle of social utility. People should be permitted and encouraged to exercise their full liberty *because this is the best way to promote the general welfare of most citizens.* Mill is convinced that we need to view human potential in the broadest possible way—"the permanent interests of man as a progressive being." Our human identities and possibilities are defined in large measure by our ability to make free choices. It is through unfettered and unconstrained "individual spontaneity" that we create ourselves, shape our destinies, and fulfill our unique potential, both individually and collectively.

Nevertheless, despite this powerful and passionate vision, Mill believes that such freedom does not exist in isolation: It is necessarily accompanied by social responsibilities and obligations toward others. Of course, the most obvious obligation is not to interfere with the free choices of others, and to do so means being punished by legal remedies or being subjected to social disapproval. But, in addition, Mill believes that "There are also many positive acts for the benefit of others, which he may rightfully be compelled to perform." Such obligations include participating in the legal process, bearing one's fair share in the common defense of the community, saving a fellow-creature's life, protecting the defenseless against abuse or exploitation, and so on.

The essence of liberty for Mill is the freedoms that ought to naturally accrue to every citizen. Mill identifies three such areas:

- The freedom to think, express, and publish one's opinions on all subjects, including scientific, moral, and religious.
- The freedom to plan one's life and pursue one's goals without interference from others (providing our actions do not cause others harm).
- The freedom to unite with others for any purpose not involving harm to others.

Mill then sums up his views on social liberties with the following memorable and uncompromising statement:

No society in which these liberties are not, on the whole, respected, is free, whatever may be its form of government; and none is completely free in which they do not exist absolute and unqualified. The only freedom which deserves the name, is that of pursuing our own good in our own way, so long as we do not attempt to deprive others of theirs, or impede their efforts to obtain it. Each is the proper guardian of his own health, whether bodily, or mental and spiritual. Mankind are greater gainers by suffering each other to live as seems good to themselves, than by compelling each to live as seems good to the rest.

John Stuart Mill,
from *On Liberty*

And he concludes this section with a sobering warning that is as relevant today as in centuries past: In the ongoing tension between the freedom of the individual and the rights of society, there is a perennial tendency to "strengthen society, and diminish the power of the individual." It is our human responsibility to jealously guard the individual liberties (described above) in the face of all efforts to limit or abandon them.

Apart from the peculiar tenets of individual thinkers, there is also in the world at large an increasing inclination to stretch unduly the powers of society over the individual, both by the force of opinion and even by that of legislation: and as the tendency of all the changes taking place in the world is to strengthen society, and diminish the power

John Stuart Mill,
from *On Liberty*

of the individual, this encroachment is not one of the evils which tend spontaneously to disappear, but, on the contrary, to grow more and more formidable. The disposition of mankind, whether as rulers or as fellow-citizens, to impose their own opinions and inclinations as a rule of conduct on others, is so energetically supported by some of the best and by some of the worst feelings incident to human nature, that it is hardly ever kept under restraint by anything but want of power; and as the power is not declining, but growing, unless a strong barrier of moral conviction can be raised against the mischief, we must expect, in the present circumstances of the world, to see it increase.

Mill continues his passionate defense of liberty with a remarkable exhortation to live an examined life in the Socratic tradition, rather than an "ape-like one of imitation."

John Stuart Mill, from *On Liberty*

Chapter III: Of Individuality, as One of the Elements of Well-Being

He who lets the world, or his own portion of it, choose his plan of life for him, has no need of any other faculty than the ape-like one of imitation. He who chooses his plan for himself, employs all his faculties. He must use observation to see, reasoning and judgment to foresee, activity to gather materials for decision, discrimination to decide, and when he has decided, firmness and self-control to hold to his deliberate decision. And these qualities he requires and exercises exactly in proportion as the part of his conduct which he determines according to his own judgment and feelings is a large one. It is possible that he might be guided in some good path, and kept out of harm's way, without any of these things. But what will be his comparative worth as a human being? It really is of importance, not only what men do, but also what manner of men they are that do it. Among the works of man, which human life is rightly employed in perfecting and beautifying, the first in importance surely is man himself. Supposing it were possible to get houses built, corn grown, battles fought, causes tried, and even churches erected and prayers said, by machinery—by automatons in human form—it would be a considerable loss to exchange for these automatons even the men and women who at present inhabit the more civilized parts of the world, and who assuredly are but starved specimens of what nature can and will produce. Human nature is not a machine to be built after a model, and set to do exactly the work prescribed for it, but a tree, which requires to grow and develope itself on all sides, according to the tendency of the inward forces which make it a living thing. . . .

Mill's concepts of self-determination and human well-being are both classical and contemporary. The ancient Greek concept of happiness—*eudaemonia*—refers to the full exercise of the soul's powers, a concept akin to Mill's notion of each person's responsibility to choose a life plan rather than letting it be chosen for us by others. Such a project can only be undertaken by thinking critically in the fullest sense, using our abilities to observe, reason, judge, discriminate, decide, and commit ourselves to a course of action with steadfastness.

Of course, individuals pursue their life plans within the structure of a social community. Although Mill does not believe that a social contract was ever voluntarily entered into by members of a society, he nevertheless believes that by choosing to remain in a social community, we commit ourselves to membership and the rights and responsibilities that go along with it. In return for society's protection so that we can live our lives freely, citizens reciprocate this protection by not impeding the rights of others to live freely. In addition, citizens are expected to do their fair share in defending the community from threats to its well-being, whether external or internal.

Is social welfare more important than individuality liberty? According to Mill, "Over himself, over his own body and mind, the individual is sovereign." But what is the appropriate balance when the desires of the individual conflict with the social welfare in cases like the over-harvest of natural resources or issues of public safety?

These are expectations for the individual citizens that are enforceable by law. However, Mill believes that there may be other forms of misconduct that detract from the general welfare yet do not rise to the level of legal sanctions. For example, acting rudely, failing to help others in need, speaking to others in an insulting manner—though these and other like behaviors may not merit arrest, fines, or incarceration, the community can nevertheless exercise social control through social disapproval and communal condemnation.

With all other actions, Mill suggests that individuals should, in general, be left alone to pursue their interests and choose their lives. And yet he entertains the intriguing argument that virtually *all* actions we take affect others in some way or other, often negatively. As Mill expresses this point of view: "No person is an entirely isolated being: it is impossible for a person to do anything seriously or permanently hurtful to himself without mischief reaching at least to his near connexions, and often far beyond them." Ought these actions to be condemned as well?

The distinction here pointed out between the part of a person's life which concerns only himself, and that which concerns others, many persons will refuse to admit. How (it may be asked) can any part of the conduct of a member of society be a matter of indifference to the other members? No person is an entirely isolated being; it is impossible for a person to do anything seriously or permanently hurtful to himself, without mischief reaching at least to his near connexions, and often far beyond them. If he injures his property, he does harm to those who directly or indirectly derived support from it, and usually diminishes, by a greater or less amount, the general resources of the community. If he deteriorates his bodily or mental faculties, he not only brings evil upon all who depended on him for any portion of their happiness, but disqualifies himself for rendering the services which he owes to his fellow-creatures generally; perhaps becomes a burthen on their affection or benevolence; and if such conduct were very frequent, hardly any offence that is committed would detract more from the general sum of good. Finally, if by his vices or follies a person does no direct harm to others, he is nevertheless (it may be said) injurious by his example; and ought to be compelled to control himself, for the sake of those whom the sight or knowledge of his conduct might corrupt or mislead.

John Stuart Mill,
from *On Liberty*

Mill's argument can be summarized in this way: Because our lives are necessarily interwoven with the lives of others in society, virtually all negative actions that we take are liable to have a negative impact on the welfare of others, thus violating Mill's principle of general utility. For example, if you choose to damage or destroy property that you own (closing down a business, for example) you will likely harm those who are benefiting from the business, and you are also diminishing the general resources of the community. Or if you allow your health to deteriorate through neglect, you are causing pain to those who care for you, and you are also diminishing your ability to contribute your fair share to the community. Finally, if you engage in such vices as substance abuse or reckless spending, you are damaging the community by acting as a poor example that might influence others. Do these examples prove that people are never completely free to make autonomous choices, without first taking into account the general welfare of the community?

How does Mill respond to this argument? Although he fully acknowledges that the private choices of individuals often cause pain to those close to them, and perhaps even minimal damage to the community as a whole, Mill doesn't believe that this justifies the state stepping in to impose the principle of general utility. If someone becomes addicted to alcohol or gambling, it may very well be appropriate for friends and acquaintances to express their social disapproval, but that doesn't mean that the person's conduct ought to be seen as illegal. Of course, if a person is drunk while flying a commercial airplane or presiding over a court case, that conduct may merit legal sanctions because the individual is threatening the welfare of others while performing in an official capacity.

But as a staunch supporter of individual liberty, Mill strongly believes that the greater danger to a community comes from too much interference in the lives of citizens, not too little. In Mill's view, people are much too willing to impose their views and values on others, thus threatening the right to live our lives as freely as we wish, a fundamental right to which we are all entitled.

John Stuart Mill, from *On Liberty*

But the strongest of all the arguments against the interference of the public with purely personal conduct, is that when it does interfere, the odds are that it interferes wrongly, and in the wrong place. On questions of social morality, of duty to others, the opinion of the public, that is, of an overruling majority, though often wrong, is likely to be still oftener right; because on such questions they are only required to judge of their own interests; of the manner in which some mode of conduct, if allowed to be practised, would affect themselves. But the opinion of a similar majority, imposed as a law on the minority, on questions of self-regarding conduct, is quite as likely to be wrong as right; for in these cases public opinion means, at the best, some people's opinion of what is good or bad for other people; while very often it does not even mean that; the public, with the most perfect indifference, passing over the pleasure or convenience of those whose conduct they censure, and considering only their own preference. There are many who consider as an injury to themselves any conduct which they have a distaste for, and resent it as an outrage to their feelings; as a religious bigot, when charged with disregarding the religious feelings of others, has been known to retort that they disregard his feelings, by persisting in their abominable worship or creed. But there is no parity between the feeling of a person for his own opinion, and the feeling of another who is offended at his holding it; no more than between the desire of a thief to take a purse, and the desire of the right owner to keep it. And a person's taste is as much his own peculiar concern as his opinion or his purse. It is easy for any one to imagine an ideal public, which leaves the freedom and choice of individuals in all uncertain matters undisturbed, and only requires them to abstain from modes of conduct which universal experience has condemned. But where has there been seen a public which set any such limit to its censorship? or when does the public trouble itself about universal experience? In its interferences with personal conduct it is seldom thinking of anything but the enormity of acting or feeling differently from itself; and this standard of judgment, thinly disguised, is held up to mankind as the dictate of religion and philosophy, by nine-tenths of all moralists and speculative writers. These teach that things are right because they are right; because we feel them to be so. They tell us to search in our own minds and hearts for laws of conduct binding on ourselves and on all others. What can the poor public do but apply these instructions, and make their own personal feelings of good and evil, if they are tolerably unanimous in them, obligatory on all the world?

< READING CRITICALLY >

Analyzing Mill on Liberty

- Critically evaluate the following statement:

  The only freedom which deserves the name, is that of pursuing our own good in our own way, so long as we do not attempt to deprive others of theirs, or impede their efforts to obtain it. Each is the proper guardian of his own health, whether bodily, or mental and spiritual. Mankind are greater gainers by suffering each other to live as seems good to themselves, than by compelling each to live as seems good to the rest.

- Do you agree with Mill's concern and warning that there is a perennial tendency to "strengthen society and diminish the power of the individual"? Provide examples from our current culture to support your response.

- Explain what Mill means in the following passage. Do you agree? Why or why not?

  He who lets the world, or his own portion of it, choose his plan of life for him, has no need of any other faculty than the ape-like one of imitation. He who chooses his plan for himself, employs all his faculties. He must use observation to see, reasoning and judgment to foresee, activity to gather materials for decision, discrimination to decide, and when he has decided, firmness and self-control to hold to his deliberate decision.

10.6 Justice Is What Promotes Gender Equality: Okin

For many of the (male) political philosophers—including John Locke and John Stuart Mill—a democratic society is one where the government rests on the freely given consent of the governed. This "free consent" is at the heart of the social contract between the citizens and the government that they constitute and support. But women have legitimately asked where they fit in this equation. Historically, women have been denied equal rights to men in virtually every arena—economic, political, and social—and this inequality persists to this day in many societies. In most instances, the "free consent" of political theories applies only to men, not women.

At the core of this disparity is the distinction between the public and private spheres of life. Women have traditionally been responsible to the area of private life: raising children and maintaining a home. This has enabled men to function freely in the public sphere, pursuing careers and political involvement. Even when women have entered the workforce (as they have increasingly), they are still expected to assume the

Susan Moller Okin (1946–2004). This American philosopher is known as one of the most important thinkers in the field of gender and political theory.

major responsibility for domestic life. This inhibits their ability to compete equally in the public world, where entrenched attitudes also serve to discriminate against them. For example, even when women perform exactly the same jobs as men, they are typically paid less. And their career advancement is often restricted because it is assumed that they will be primarily responsible for child care and maintaining a home. Over 50 percent of marriages end in divorce in this country, and in 90 percent of those cases women end up with the primary custody of the children. So for women to achieve a just society, this deep and pervasive inequality based on gender roles must be eradicated and replaced with a social structure that is truly based on equality. This is the only way that they will be able to achieve parity in both economic and political power.

Susan Moller Okin was a twentieth-century political philosopher who wrote extensively on this subject. The following passages are taken from her book *Justice, Gender, and the Family.*

Susan Moller Okin, from *Justice, Gender, and the Family*

Introduction: Justice and Gender

We as a society pride ourselves on our democratic values. We don't believe people should be constrained by innate differences from being able to achieve desired positions of influence or to improve their well-being; equality of opportunity is our professed aim. The Preamble to our Constitution stresses the importance of justice, as well as the general welfare and the blessings of liberty. The Pledge of Allegiance asserts that our republic preserves "liberty and justice for all."

Yet substantial inequalities between the sexes still exist in our society. In economic terms, full-time working women (after some very recent improvement) earn on average 71 percent of the earnings of full-time working men. One-half of poor and three-fifths of chronically poor households with dependent children are maintained by a single female parent. The poverty rate for elderly women is nearly twice that for elderly men. On the political front, two out of a hundred U.S. senators are women, one out of nine justices seems to be considered sufficient female representation on the Supreme Court, and the number of men chosen in each congressional election far exceeds the number of women elected in the entire history of the country. Underlying and intertwined with all these inequalities is the unequal distribution of the unpaid labor of the family.

Are women still the victims of pervasive gender discrimination in our society? The United States Supreme Court in the early 1980s. When Okin wrote *Justice, Gender, and Society*, only one Supreme Court justice and two U.S. senators were women. As of this writing, sixteen U.S. senators are women, but there are still only two women on the Supreme Court. Do you think that this lack of equal representation hurts women?

An equal sharing between the sexes of family responsibilities, especially child care, is "the great revolution that has not happened." Women, including mothers of young children, are, of course, working outside the household far more than their mothers did. And the small proportion of women who reach high-level positions in politics, business, and the professions command a vastly disproportionate amount of space in the media, compared with the millions of women who work at low-paying, dead-end jobs, the millions who do part-time work with its lack of benefits, and the millions of others who stay home performing for no pay what is frequently not even acknowledged as work. Certainly, the fact that women are doing more paid work does not imply that they are more equal. It is often said that we are living in a postfeminist era. This claim, due in part to the distorted emphasis on women who have "made it," is false, no matter which of its meanings is intended. It is certainly not true that feminism has been vanquished, and equally untrue that it is no longer needed because its aims have been fulfilled. Until there is justice within the family, women will not be able to gain equality in politics, at work, or in any other sphere.

. . . [T]he typical current practices of family life, structured to a large extent by gender, are not just. Both the expectation and the experience of the division of labor by sex make women vulnerable. As I shall show, a cycle of power relations and decisions pervades both family and workplace, each reinforcing the inequalities between the sexes that already exist within the other. Not only women, but children of both sexes, too, are often made vulnerable by gender-structured marriage. One-quarter of children in the United State now live in families with only one parent—in almost 90 percent of cases, the mother. Contrary to common perceptions—in which the situation of never-married mothers looms largest—65 percent of the single-parent families are a result of marital separation or divorce. Recent research in a number of states has shown that, in the average case, the standard of living of divorced women and the children who live with them plummets after divorce, whereas the economic situation of divorced men tends to be better than when they were married.

A central source of injustice for women these days is that the law, most noticeably in the event of divorce, treats more or less as equals those whom custom, workplace discrimination, and the still conventional division of labor within the family have made very unequal. Central to this socially created inequality are two commonly made but inconsistent presumptions: that women are primarily responsible for the rearing of children; and that serious and committed members of the workforce (regardless of class) do not have primary responsibility, or even shared responsibility, for the rearing of children. The old assumption of the workplace, still implicit, is that workers have wives at home. It is built not only into the structure and expectations of the workplace but into other crucial institutions, such as schools, which make no attempt to take account, in their scheduled hours or vacations, of the fact that parents are likely to hold jobs.

Now, of course, many wage workers do not have wives at home. Often, they *are* wives and mothers, or single, separated, or divorced mothers of small children. But neither the family nor the workplace has taken much account of this fact. Employed wives still do by far the greatest proportion of unpaid family work, such as child care and housework. Women are far more likely to take time out of the workplace or to work part-time because of family responsibilities than are their husbands or male partners. And they are much more likely to move because of their husbands' employment needs or opportunities than their own. All these tendencies, which are due to a number of factors, including the sex segregation and discrimination of the workplace itself, tend to be cyclical in their effects: wives advance more slowly than their husbands at work and thus gain less seniority, and the discrepancy between their wages increases over time. Then, because both the power structure of the family and what is regarded as consensual "rational" family decision making reflect the fact that the husband usually earns more, it will become even less likely as time goes on that the unpaid work of the family will be shared between the spouses. Thus the cycle of inequality is perpetuated. Often hidden from view within a marriage, it is in the increasingly likely event of marital breakdown that the socially constructed inequality of married women is at its most visible.

This is what I mean when I say that gender-structured marriage *makes* women vulnerable. These are not matters of natural necessity, as some people would believe. Surely nothing in our natures dictates that men should not be equal participants in the rearing of their children. Nothing in the nature of work makes it impossible to adjust it to the fact that people are parents as well as workers. That these things have not happened is part of the historically, socially constructed differentiation between the sexes that feminists have

How to balance home and work? Okin believed that women could better balance work and family if there was equality in gender roles and responsibilities. Do you agree? Why?

come to call *gender*. We live in a society that has over the years regarded the innate characteristic of sex as one of the clearest legitimizers of different rights and restrictions, both formal and informal. While the legal sanctions that uphold male dominance have begun to be eroded in the past century, and more rapidly in the last twenty years, the heavy weight of tradition, combined with the effects of socialization, still works powerfully to reinforce sex roles that are commonly regarded as of unequal prestige and worth. The sexual division of labor has not only been a fundamental part of the marriage contract, but so deeply influences us in our formative years that feminists of both sexes who try to reject it can find themselves struggling against it with varying degrees of ambivalence. Based on this linchpin, "gender"—by which I mean *the deeply entrenched institutionalization of sexual difference*—still permeates our society. . . .

This last sentence is the cornerstone of Okin's critique of the fundamentally unjust nature of our society. The society is unjust to women because of "the deeply entrenched institutionalization of sexual difference" that permeates our society at every level, an inequality she designates with the term *gender*. According to Okin, our society is founded on a profound hypocrisy. On the surface, lip service is paid to the equality of the sexes and the concept that every individual has an equal opportunity to success, no matter what her or his gender. But on a deeper level, this concept of gender equality is a sham. Woven into the culture and the psyches of society's members is the presumption that women will have the primary responsibility for child care and maintaining the home, and in fact this turns out to be the fact in the overwhelming number of cases. And the effects of this deeper unequal reality are devastating: Women are prevented from competing on equal footing in the career arena, and they are discriminated against when they try to do so. In the majority of marriages, it is assumed that they will be the primary child caring parent, inhibiting their development of a professional career. And if the marriage ends in divorce, as marriages do over fifty percent of the time, women find themselves with custody of the children in ninety percent of the cases and lacking a professional career sacrificed during the years of raising children and maintaining the home. The net result? The standard of living declines in most cases for divorced and separated women and their children, while the standard of living for divorced and separated men is maintained or increases. What can be done to address this seemingly intractable gender injustice? Okin believes nothing short of radically restructuring the gender roles of women and men will create meaningful justice for women.

Susan Moller Okin,
from *Justice, Gender, and the Family*

Introduction: Justice and Gender

The Personal as Political

"The personal is political" is the central message of feminist critiques of the public/domestic dichotomy. It is the core idea of most contemporary feminism. Though many of those who fought in the nineteenth and early twentieth centuries for suffrage and for the abolition of the oppressive legal status of wives were well aware of the connections between women's political and personal dominations by men, few pre-1960s feminists questioned women's special role in the family. While arguing for equal rights, such as the vote or access to education, most accepted the prevailing assumption that women's class association with and responsibility for the care of the family was natural and inevitable.

The earliest claims that the personal is political came from those radical feminists of the 1960s and 1970s who argued that, since the family was at the root of women's oppression, it must be "smashed." The anti-family nature of some early radical feminism has been exaggerated and exploited both by antifeminists and by those who have been termed "conservative" or "backlash" feminists. They have focused on it in order to attack all, or all but their own version, of feminism. But most contemporary feminists, while critiquing the gender-structured family, have not attacked all varieties of family. Many advocate that "family" be defined so as to include any intimately connected and committed group, specifically endorsing homosexual marriage; most, certainly, refuse to accept that the choice must be between accepting women's double burden and abolishing the family. We refuse to give up on the institution of the family, and refuse to accept the division of labor between the sexes as natural and unchangeable. More and more, as the extent to which gender is a social construction has become understood, feminists have come to recognize how variable are the potential forms and practices of family groups. The family is in no way inevitably tied to its gender structure, but until this notion is successfully challenged, and nontraditional groupings and divisions of labor are not only recognized but encouraged, there can be no hope of equality for women in either the domestic or the public sphere.

Do we need a more inclusive definition of family?
According to Okin, many feminists believe that the traditional gender-structured idea of "family" should be redefined to include "any intimately connected and committed group, specifically endorsing homosexual marriage." Do you agree? Why?

Thus feminists have turned their attention to the politics of what had previously been regarded—and, as I have shown, still is seen by most political theorists—as paradigmatically *non*political. That the personal sphere of sexuality, of housework, of child care and family life *is* political became the underpinning of most feminist thought. Feminists of different political leanings and in a variety of academic disciplines have revealed and analyzed the multiple interconnections between women's domestic roles and their inequality and segregation in the workplace, and between their socialization in gendered families and the psychological aspects of their oppression. We have strongly and persistently challenged the long-standing underlying assumption of almost all political theories: that the sphere of family and personal life is so separate and distinct from the rest of social life that such theories can justifiably assume but ignore it.

As my argument so far has made clear, however, these feminist arguments have not been acknowledged by most contemporary political theorists writing about justice. In discussing some of the central feminist arguments about the essentially political nature of personal life and of the family in particular, I shall establish that domestic life needs to be just and to have its justice reinforced by the state and its legal system. In the circumstances of the division of labor that is practiced within the vast majority of households in the United States today, women are rendered vulnerable by marriage and especially by motherhood, and there is great scope for unchecked injustice to flourish.

The interconnections between the domestic and the nondomestic aspects of our lives are deep and pervasive. Given the power structures of both, women's lives are far more detrimentally affected by these interconnections than are men's. Consider two recent front-page stories that appeared on subsequent days in the *New York Times*. The first was about a tiny elite among women: those who work as lawyers for the country's top law firms. If these women have children with whom they want to spend any time, they find themselves off the partnership track and instead, with no prospects of advancement, on the "mommy track." "Nine-to-five" is considered part-time work in the ethos of such firms, and one mother reports that, in spite of her twelve-hour workdays and frequent work on weekends, she has "no chance" of making partner. The article fails to mention that these women's children have fathers, or that most of the men who work for the same prestigious law firms also have children, except to report that male lawyers who take parental leave are seen as "wimp-like." The sexual division of labor in the family, even in these cases where the women are extremely well qualified, successful, and potentially influential, is simply assumed.

An unfair distribution of labor? Okin contends that too often women with full-time careers are still expected to assume a disproportionate amount of the responsibility for child rearing and homemaking. Do your observations support this view?

The next day's *Times* reported on a case of major significance for abortion rights, decided by a Federal Appeals Court in Minnesota. The all-male panel of judges ruled 7 to 3 that the state may require a woman under eighteen years who wishes to obtain an abortion to notify *both* her parents—even in cases of divorce, separation, or desertion—or to get special approval from a state judge. The significance of this article is amplified when it is juxtaposed with the previous one. For it shows us how it is that those who rise to the top in the highly politically influential profession of law are among those who have had the least experience of all in raising children. There is a high incidence of recruitment of judges from those who have risen to partnership in the most prestigious law firms. Other judges are often drawn from the equally highly competitive field of academic law, which also places its greatest demands (those of the tenure hurdle) on lawyers during the child-rearing years, and therefore discriminates against those who participate in parenting. Those who are chosen, therefore, would seem to be those least well informed to make decisions about abortion, especially in cases involving relations between teenage girls and their parents. Here we find a systematically built-in absence of mothers (and presumably of "wimp-like" participating fathers, too) from high-level political decisions concerning some of the most vulnerable persons in society—women, disproportionately poor and black, who become pregnant in their teens, and their future children. It is not hard to see here the ties between the supposedly distinct public and domestic spheres.

This is but one example of what feminists mean by saying the "the personal is political," sometimes adding the corollary "the political is personal." It is because of this claim, of course, that the family became and has remained central to the politics of feminism and to feminist theory. Contemporary feminism poses a significant challenge to the long-standing and still-surviving assumption of political theories that the sphere of family and personal life is sharply distinct from the rest of social and political life, that the state can and should restrain itself from intrusion into the domestic sphere, and that political theories can therefore legitimately ignore it. In contrast, both challenging and aiming to restructure the public/domestic dichotomy are fundamental to the feminist enterprise.

Conclusion: Toward a Humanist Justice

The family is the linchpin of gender, reproducing it from one generation to the next. As we have seen, family life as typically practiced in our society is not just, either to women or to children. Moreover, it is not conducive to the rearing of citizens with a strong sense of justice. In spite of all the rhetoric about equality between the sexes, the traditional or quasi-traditional division of family labor still prevails. Women are made vulnerable by constructing their lives around the expectation that they will be primary parents; they become more vulnerable within marriages in which they fulfill this expectation, whether or not they also work for wages; and they are most vulnerable in the event of separation or divorce, when they usually take over responsibility for children without adequate support from their ex-husbands. Since approximately half of all marriages end in divorce, about half of our children are likely to experience its dislocations, often made far more traumatic by the socioeconomic consequences of both gender-structured marriage and divorce settlements that fail to take account of it. I have suggested that, for very important reasons, the family *needs* to be a just institution, and have shown that contemporary theories of justice neglect women and ignore gender. How can we address this injustice?

This is a complex question. It is particularly so because we place great value on our freedom to live different kinds of lives, there is no current consensus on many aspects of gender, and we have good reason to suspect that many of our beliefs about sexual difference and appropriate sex roles are heavily influenced by the very fact that we grew up in a gender-structured society. All of us have been affected, in our very psychological structures, by the fact of gender in our personal pasts, just as our society has been deeply affected by its strong influence in our collective past. Because of the lack of shared meanings about gender, it constitutes a particularly hard case for those who care deeply about both personal freedom and social justice. The way we divide the labor and responsibilities in our personal lives seems to be one of those things that people should be free to work out for themselves, but because of its vast repercussions it belongs clearly within the scope of things that must be governed by principles of justice. Which is to say, in the language of political and moral theory, that it belongs both to the sphere of "the good" and to that of "the right."

I shall argue here that any just and fair solution to the urgent problem of women's and children's vulnerability must encourage and facilitate the equal sharing by men and women of paid and unpaid work, of productive and reproductive labor. We must work toward a future in which all will be likely to choose this mode of life. A just future would be without gender. In its social structures and practices, one's sex would have no more relevance than one's eye color or the length of one's toes. No assumptions would be made about "male" and "female" roles; childbearing would be so conceptually separated from child rearing and other family responsibilities that it would be a cause for surprise, and no little concern, if men and women were not equally responsible for domestic life or if children were to spend much more time with one parent than the other. It would be a future in which men and women participated in more or less equal numbers in every sphere of life, from infant care to different kinds of paid work to high-level politics. Thus it would no longer be the case that having no experience of raising children would be the practical prerequisite for attaining positions of the greatest social influence. Decisions about abortion and rape, about divorce settlements and sexual harassment, or about any other crucial social issues would not be made, as they often are now, by legislatures and benches of judges overwhelmingly populated by men whose power is in large part due to their advantaged position in the gender structure. If we are to be at all true to our democratic ideals, moving away from gender is essential. Obviously, the attainment of such a social world requires major changes in a multitude of institutions and social settings outside the home, as well as within it. Such changes will not happen overnight. Moreover, any present solution to the vulnerability of women and children that is just and respects individual freedom must take into account that most people currently live in ways that are greatly affected by gender, and most still favor many aspects of current gendered practices. Sociological studies confirm what most of us already infer from our own personal and professional acquaintances: there are no currently shared meanings in this country about the extent to which differences between the sexes are innate or environmental, about the appropriate roles of men and women, and about which family forms and divisions of labor are most beneficial for partners, parents, and children. There are those, at one extreme, for whom the different roles of the two sexes, especially as parents, are deeply held tenets of religious belief. At the other end of the spectrum are those of us for whom the sooner all social differentiation between the sexes vanishes, the better it will be for all of us. And there are a thousand varieties of view in between. Public policies must respect people's views and choices. But they must do so only insofar as it can be ensured that these choices do not result, as they now do, in the vulnerability of women and children. Special protections must be built into our laws and public policies to ensure that, for those who choose it, the division of labor between the sexes does not result in injustice. In the face of these difficulties—balancing freedom and the effects of past choices against the needs of justice—I do not pretend to have arrived at any complete or fully satisfactory answers. But I shall attempt in this final chapter to suggest some social reforms, including changes in public policies and reforms of family law, that may help us work toward a solution to the injustices of gender.

Marriage has become an increasingly peculiar contract, a complex and ambiguous combination of anachronism and present-day reality. There is no longer the kind of agreement that once prevailed about what is expected of the parties to a marriage. Clearly, at least

> A just future would be one without gender. In its social structures and practices, one's sex would have no more relevance than one's eye color or the length of one's toes.

Should society strive to achieve equality in the family? Okin believes that a genuine "humanist justice" would involve doing away with traditional male and female roles and replacing them with a gender-neutral approach to family responsibilities. Do you think this is a realistic goal?

in the United States, it is no longer reasonable to assume that marriage will last a lifetime, since only half of current marriages are expected to. And yet, in spite of the increasing legal equality of men and women and the highly publicized figures about married women's increased participation in the labor force, many couples continue to adhere to more or less traditional patterns of role differentiation. As a recent article put it, women are "out of the house but not out of the kitchen." Consequently, often working part-time or taking time out from wage work to care for family members, especially children, most wives are in a very different position from their husbands in their ability to be economically self-supporting. This is reflected, as we have seen, in power differentials between the sexes within the family. It means also, in the increasingly common event of divorce, usually by mutual agreement, that it is the mother who in 90 percent of cases will have physical custody of the children. But whereas the greater need for money goes one way, the bulk of the earning power almost always goes the other. This is one of the most important causes of the feminization of poverty, which is affecting the life chances of ever larger numbers of children as well as their mothers. The division of labor within families has always adversely affected women, by making them economically dependent on men. Because of the increasing instability of marriage, its effects on children have now reached crisis proportions.

Some who are critical of the present structure and practices of marriage have suggested that men and women simply be made free to make their own agreements about family life, contracting with each other, much as business contracts are made. But this takes insufficient account of the history of gender in our culture and our own psychologies, of the present substantive inequalities between the sexes, and, most important, of the well-being of the children who result from the relationship. As has long been recognized in the realm of labor relations, justice is by no means always enhanced by the maximization of freedom of contract, if the individuals involved are in unequal positions to start with. Some have even suggested that it is consistent with justice to leave spouses to work out their own divorce settlement. By this time, however, the two people ending a marriage are likely to be far *more* unequal. Such a practice would be even more catastrophic for most women and children than is the present system. Wives in any but the rare cases in which they as individuals have remained their husbands' socioeconomic equals could hardly be expected to reach a just solution if left "free" to "bargain" the terms of financial support or child custody. What would they have to bargain *with*?

There are many directions that public policy can and should take in order to make relations between men and women more just. In discussing these, I shall look back to some of the contemporary ways of thinking about justice that I find most convincing. I draw particularly on Rawls's idea of the original position and Walzer's conception of the complex equality found in separate spheres of justice, between which I find no inconsistency. I also keep in mind critical legal theorists' critique of contract, and the related idea, suggested earlier, that rights to privacy that are to be valuable to all of us can be enjoyed only insofar as the sphere of life in which we enjoy them ensures the equality of its adult members and protects children. Let us begin by asking what kind of arrangements persons in a Rawlsian original position would agree to regarding marriage, parental and other domestic responsibilities, and divorce. What kinds of policies would they agree to for other aspects of social life, such as the workplace and schools, that affect men, women, and children and relations among them? And let us consider whether these arrangements would satisfy Walzer's separate spheres test—that inequalities in one sphere of life not be allowed to overflow into another. Will they foster equality within the sphere of family life? For the protection of the privacy of a domestic sphere in which inequality exists is the protection of the right of the strong to exploit and abuse the weak.

Let us first try to imagine ourselves, as far as possible, in the original position, knowing neither what our sex nor any other of our personal characteristics will be once the veil of ignorance is lifted. Neither do we know our place in society or our particular conception of the good life. Particularly relevant in this context, of course, is our lack of knowledge of our beliefs about the characteristics of men and women and our related convictions about the appropriate division of labor between the sexes. Thus the positions we represent must include a wide variety of beliefs on these matters. We may, once the veil of ignorance is lifted, find ourselves feminist men or feminist women whose conception of the good life includes the minimization of social differentiation between the sexes. Or we may find ourselves traditionalist men or women, whose conception of the good life, for religious or other reasons, is bound up in an adherence to the conventional division of labor between the sexes. The challenge is to arrive at and apply principles of justice having to do with the family and the division of labor between the sexes that can satisfy these vastly disparate points of view and the many that fall between.

There are some traditionalist positions so extreme that they ought not be admitted for consideration, since they violate such fundamentals as equal basic liberty and self-respect. We need not, and should not, that is to say, admit for consideration views based on the notion that women are inherently inferior beings whose function is to fulfill the needs of men. Such a view is no more admissible in the construction of just institutions for a modern pluralist society than is the view, however deeply held, that some are naturally slaves and others naturally and justifiably their masters. We need not, therefore, consider approaches to marriage that view it as an inherently and desirably hierarchical structure of dominance and subordination. Even if it were conceivable that a person who did not know whether he or she would turn out to be a man or a woman in the society being planned would subscribe to such views, they are not admissible. Even if there were no other reasons to refuse to admit such views, they must be excluded for the sake of children, for everyone in the original position has a high personal stake in the quality of childhood. Marriages of dominance and submission are bad for children as well as for their mothers, and the socioeconomic outcome of divorce after such a marriage is very likely to damage their lives and seriously restrict their opportunities.

With this proviso, what social structures and public policies regarding relations between the sexes, and the family in particular, would we agree on in the original position? I think we would arrive at a basic model that would absolutely minimize gender. . . . We would also, however, build in carefully protective institutions for those who wished to follow gender-structured modes of life. . . .

< READING CRITICALLY >

Analyzing Okin on Gender Equality

- Susan Moller Okin makes the compelling point that, in contrast to the democratic ideals of justice and equality, women in our culture (and most others as well) are in fact treated *un*justly and *un*equally. Based on your personal experience, either in this culture or one in which you have lived, identify areas in which you believe women have not been treated fairly by the social institutions.

- According to Okin, much of women's unequal status can be traced to their traditional role in the family. Explain the reasoning Okin uses to support this position. Do you agree with her?

- Okin believes that marital divorce and separation (about 50 percent of all marriages) make women and their children extremely vulnerable, both economically and socially. Do you agree with her analysis? Why or why not?

- The gender roles for men and women in our culture (and other cultures as well) are not necessary or preordained, according to Okin. Instead, these gender roles are "social constructions," and as a result they can be *re*constructed more justly and equally. What does it mean to say that gender roles are "social constructions"? What are some of the ways that these roles could be "reconstructed"?

YOUR IDEAL SOCIETY

Consider the following questions as you envision the "ideal society" in which you'd like to live. Approaches to this assignment and a sample response can be found in the "Writing About Philosophy" section on the next page.

- *Issues of justice:* In what ways will your society distribute wealth to its citizens? In what ways will it make opportunities for education and to acquire wealth available? To what extent will people be treated equally? In what ways will you consider your society to be "just"?

- *Issues of law:* How will your society justify its existence and its laws? To what extent will its "civic laws" be based on "natural laws" that are thought to apply to all humans in all societies? To what extent will the laws be applied fairly to people, regardless of their wealth, social status, gender, or racial identity? How will your society treat people who disagree with and disobey its laws? How will people who engage in "civil disobedience" be treated (for example, those who act disruptively to protest social policies or war policies with which they disagree)?

- *Issues of public interest:* In what ways will your society support the well-being of those less advantaged citizens (for example, those who are poor, elderly, unemployed, sick, abused, or neglected)? In what ways will citizens be expected to sacrifice their individual interests to support the general interest (for example, paying taxes)? In what ways will your society help those who are unable to help themselves? How will it promote the general good through regulations and economic support?

- *Issues of duty:* What specific obligations and duties will citizens in your society be responsible for performing (for example, serving on juries)?

- *Issues of rights:* What individual rights will citizens in your society be expected to have (for example, the right to practice the religion of their choice)? What rights will your society consider to be "universal" in the sense that they are rights that all people in all societies should enjoy?

- *Issues of freedom:* What will be the basic freedoms that your society guarantees for all of its citizens (for example, freedom to express their views without being arrested or harassed)? In what areas will personal freedoms be limited in your society?

- *Issues of power and influence:* How will power be acquired and administered in your society? How will citizens be able to influence social policies and laws?

10.7 Making Connections: An Ideal Society

This chapter began with the challenge for you to reflect on the social and political "ingredients" that constitute the particular "recipe" of our culture. This activity was designed to encourage you to step back and examine our culture from a more analytical perspective. Since that point, you have had an opportunity to explore the way influential thinkers from the past 2,500 years have grappled with these same issues. And you have likely been constructing in your own mind the kind of ideal society in which you would like to live.

Confucius was convinced that the only way to avoid the natural violence and chaos of social unrest was by establishing a social order based on a commitment to "humanity" or benevolence, the conscientious practice of social customs, and the widespread adherence to moral principles. As a teacher, Confucius (the "Master") tried to effect political harmony by cultivating moral harmony within each individual. Philosophically, Confucius's "ethical humanism" is based on the belief that human intelligence is capable of promoting human welfare and dignity in a way that conforms to our essential human natures.

For Plato, such an ideal society would be based on matching the unique talents of each individual to the social responsibilities required for people to live together: leaders (philosopher-kings), guardians, and workers. The central criterion for evaluating a society is how harmoniously and productively all of its various elements function together. Aristotle endorsed this general approach to constructing an ideal society, founding his theory on the belief that humans are naturally communal animals and that each person should seek happiness by discovering and fulfilling his or her own unique purpose (*entelechy*). Both Plato and Aristotle rejected the idea that an ideal society is egalitarian (the belief that people are intrinsically equal) or democratic (the belief that each person should have an equal voice in governing).

Leaping ahead a few thousand years, egalitarianism and democracy *are* the concerns of thinkers such as Thomas Hobbes, John Locke, and John Rawls. Beginning with the concept of a "state of nature"—either real or imagined—these philosophers developed the notion of a "social contract" that individuals voluntarily enter into with one another to ensure their safety and individual rights. What form should such a society take? Rawls suggests that we imagine that we are behind a "veil of ignorance," not knowing who we will be in the new society—what sort of society would we wish for that would guarantee ourselves an equal opportunity regardless of our gender, race, culture, or social pedigree? Rawls suggests it would be a society based on political freedom and equal economic opportunities for all, with a social safety net for less advantaged members of society.

Karl Marx and Friedrich Engels approach the development of an ideal society from the opposite extreme. Rather than focusing on individual rights as primary, as liberalism does, they believed that the needs of the social community taken as a whole were primary. Thus all individuals are expected to willingly contribute whatever talents they have, while all goods and wealth are divided equally among society's members, regardless of their social station in life. Marx and Engels believed that the creation of such a socialist society was inevitable, produced by the inexorable dialectic of historical forces.

John Stuart Mill returned our focus to the concept of individual rights, echoing many of the ideas of John Locke and the founders of the United States, as articulated in the Declaration of Independence and the Constitution. Yet the eloquent and powerful statement that all people are "endowed by their Creator with certain unalienable rights," which include "Life, Liberty and the pursuit of Happiness" was in seemingly sharp contradiction to the legal existence of slavery in America at this time. The fact is that slaves were seen primarily as "property" and not members of the "moral community" and thus not deserving of these "inalienable rights."

And Susan Moller Okin reminds us that neither have women historically been accorded the same basic human rights as men, even in the United States, where they did not receive the right to vote until the early twentieth century. And even more profoundly, the gender role division that expects women to be responsible for the "personal sphere" of child rearing and homemaking, and men to be responsible for the "public" sphere of careers and politics, has resulted in unequal treatment of women throughout society. Okin appeals to Rawls's veil of ignorance to argue that a truly ideal society would reshape both the private and public spheres so that all responsibilities would be divided in an equal, gender-neutral fashion.

As citizens of a particular society, we each have a solemn responsibility to reflect and think clearly about these critical issues and to assume our share of the responsibility to help our society become more enlightened, more like the "ideal society" in which we would each like to live.

writing about philosophy: Your Ideal Society

The Assignment

This assignment is based on the "Thinking Philosophically" box on page 617. As you consider the answers to those questions, think about the experiences you have had in our society and where you have felt a sense of injustice. Also consider your experiences with other societies and what struck you as better or worse in terms of citizens' rights and responsibilities and the way that the government provides for and controls its citizens. In the paper below, the student describes how her beliefs evolved in response to current events and then compares her ideas about the ideal society to those of the philosophers in this chapter.

 **Student Essay**

WHERE DO I STAND?
by Sue Martin

There are certain political assumptions I thought were universally accepted since their inception. My first assumption crumbled during the war in Yugoslavia in the early 1990s when Serbs tried to annihilate Muslim neighbors with whom they had lived for centuries. I had thought it was a truth universally held since the Enlightenment that all people were considered equal under the law, especially in a European nation where different ethnic groups had coexisted since the Middle Ages. I had vaguely heard that Tito had kept disparate groups under fierce control so that they would not attack each other after WWII, but I had assumed that by the 1990s all such ethnic rivalry had died out. The depth of my naiveté was revealed as increasingly horrific stories and photographs of bloodshed, concentration camps, and mass graves came out of Yugoslavia. It would never have occurred to me that citizens of the same political state would perpetuate ancient hates rather than work together, yet this is what people in Yugoslavia demonstrated less than two decades ago.

Another assumption I had was that all people born in a country were automatically citizens of that country and therefore equal under the law. Sometime in the 90s I read an essay in *The New York Review of Books* by an Israeli author who compared Palestinians in refugee camps to Jews in concentration camps. I was stunned. Why were Palestinians being kept behind barbed wire? Why were they not granted full citizenship? How could the Israelis have resorted to the very violation of human rights they themselves had undergone during World War II? The demographic argument that Israel would cease to be a Jewish state if it allowed Palestinians full citizenship made me question the legitimacy, the viability, and the fairness of a state based on religion.

On 9/11/01 I lost my assumption that the United States was impregnable. Someone clever and organized had achieved a stunning blow to our sense of secure isolation, and we Americans had to admit we were no longer safer than other people. But the question arose: Why did this attack occur? I ran to read books on fundamentalism, the history of the Middle East, anything that might give me clues as to whom we were dealing with and what their motives were.

More recently, I find myself losing my assumption that the United States still stands as the embodiment of a fair and just society. I am stunned and disturbed by events that suggest that we are declining politically, economically, and morally.

The U.S. Congress appears to be held hostage by an extremist group which stalls progress. Not only the U.S.'s, but the world's economy appears precarious. China aside, markets in Europe and Asia, as well in the U.S., are dropping deeper into a recession. Financial corruption has not been countered by government regulation since Bernard Madoff's 2008 hedge fund Ponzi scheme, which robbed investors of 50 billion dollars, or the 2008 financial crisis caused by risky loans and mortgages, which resulted in the loss of trillions of dollars, the loss of millions of jobs, and in widespread hardship.

On January 21, 2010, the Supreme Court ruled that a corporation was to be considered an individual for purposes of campaign finance. This interpretation could lead to corporate purchase of the country's highest government offices. An overt and growing disparity between rich and poor is exemplified by current tax laws that permit the wealthier to pay less proportionately than the poor.

Recent hurricanes, tornadoes, and tsunamis suggest that it is not only natural causes which generate horrendous destruction and loss of life, but a complex set of human-generated factors as well. The evidence builds against we, ourselves, but no one seems willing to legislate any response.

When I try to imagine how these problems might be solved, I am stymied. What policy or conception should be established first for a livable, just world? How do I weight all the factors when they are huge and shift so quickly? What would be fair, what would work, and where do I stand in a world where every purpose, cause, and right seem to be in question?

Looking back over the events of the past two decades, the first rule I would establish to set up a free yet peaceful society would follow John Stuart Mill's definition of personal liberty: "Over himself, over his own body and mind, the individual is sovereign … the only purpose for which power can be rightfully exercised over any member of a civilized community, against his will, is to prevent harm to others." In other words, a person has the right to do anything, provided it does not harm anyone else.

Second, I would establish that everyone is equal under the law. I don't think Plato would agree with this idea. According to the dialogue quoted earlier, Plato affirms that "possession of one's own and the performance of one's own task could be agreed to be justice," implying that one should accept one's station and thus not strive for change or demand equal consideration with someone higher in rank before the law. Aristotle, by contrast, senses the vital importance of law as a means to protect individual rights when he says, "For man, when perfected, is the best of animals, but, when separated from law and justice, he is the worst of all; since armed injustice is the more dangerous, and he is equipped at birth with arms, meant to be used by intelligence and virtue, which he may use for the worst ends…. But justice is the bond of men in states, for the administration of justice, which is the determination of what is just, is the principle of order in political society."

Aristotle acknowledges that there can be no order in society without some system of laws, and though he does not directly say so, the quote above leads one to understand that there can be no fair and honest judgment of people accused of breaking the law, if all are not considered equal before the law. As soon as someone puts him- or herself above the law, there is always the risk that that person might act cruelly to others without means of being stopped. Aristotle recognizes that people must be stopped if and when they use arms "for the worst ends" and that justice, rather than military force, is the most desirable and effective way to maintain order in an ongoing society. Mill puts the idea clearly when he says: "…[I]t is, by universal

■ ■ ■   **Student Essay** (continued)

admission, inconsistent with justice to be partial; to show favour or preference to one person over another, in matters to which favour and preference do not properly apply."

One major impact of establishing equality before the law is that second-class citizenship cannot occur. Different points of view must be tolerated as well as different ways of life, different practices and beliefs, and dissenters' ideas. Everyone becomes protected from a misuse of power. The Declaration of Independence reflects the concept of equality under the law indirectly when it states that, "Governments… [derive] their just powers from the consent of the governed," as society gives power to rulers by electing them, and may transfer it to others at new elections.

Another example of second-class citizenship is pointed out by Susan Moller Okin, who argued that "… any just and fair solution to the urgent problem of women's and children's vulnerability must encourage and facilitate the equal sharing by men and women of paid and unpaid work, of productive and reproductive labor." Just as no two people should be treated differently under the law they should not be paid differently due to a difference in gender, or sexual orientation, in my opinion, ignored for uncompensated work in and around the home, or treated unfairly in a divorce settlement.

I'm not sure how men and women are to be encouraged to share uncompensated work or reproductive labor, by which phrases I believe Okin means housework and child care, but perhaps through equal pay and a universal focus on concern for offspring men might work less and choose to help more with marketing, house cleaning, and child rearing. I cannot speak to the degree to which men in a heterosexual relationship, or a person of any sexual orientation in a couple, for that matter, might assume more domestic responsibilities, but an increasing number of American households contain two wage-earning adults. I agree that equal pay for equal work and monetary compensation in a divorce to cover the cost of child rearing should be established by law. Okin points out the enormous, unfair load underpaid women and divorced mothers carry when just compensation is not sustained. The need for parity is so obvious that I would hope the pervasive problem of unfair compensation due to gender and inequitable divorces would be rectified soon. I appreciate Okin's application of John Rawls's veil of ignorance in considering the "appropriate division of labor" in a domestic arrangement. The laws one establishes for marriage and child rearing must be fair according to a universal principle, which supersedes any traditional, religious, or fundamentalist practice.

I realize, as I look over my initial choices of laws for a just society above, that my perspective is distinctly liberal, that is to say, it concentrates on the liberty, rights, and responsibilities of the individual. I believe that socialism to some degree is necessary in the age we live in; however, for without a collective, centralized effort to provide housing, food, health care, and education, our country would be vastly diminished and our conduct inhumane.

Education is a case in point. We need it to compete in our increasingly difficult job market. John Rawls's theory of justice includes a second principle which states that "each person should have an equal opportunity to seek careers and economic opportunities." This claim extends far beyond the basic protection of individual rights established by Aristotle, "Justice … is the principle of order in political society," and elaborated on by Locke, "… [A]ll [being] equal and independent , no one ought to harm another in his life, health, liberty, or possessions…." Rawls's second principle applies justice not to the individual in society but to society as a whole and thus opens up a whole new realm of possible application of civil liberties.

If Rawls is right, that each person should have not only "the right to pursue Life, Liberty and the pursuit of Happiness" (Thomas Jefferson), but also "the equal opportunity to seek careers and economic opportunities", then one could not sit quietly while millions of American school children got a bad education. It would be each child's right to demand better schooling in order to be better qualified for employment, and funds would have to be provided to help. One could further employ Rawls's principle as regards "economic opportunities." The social impact of this ruling would be enormous. Millions of Americans could claim that they have been undereducated or mistreated in their career paths and thus deprived of economic opportunity. How could such claims be handled?

I do not have an answer to this enormous question, but I am impressed by Rawls's attempt to try to create some legal response to the open-ended question of economic unfairness in a society. There have always been rich and poor, but Rawls is the first person I've ever seen try to deal with managing some level of comprehensive fairness while acknowledging that there will never be an equal distribution of wealth.

Though some people take exception to the mixing of democratic and socialist practices, I do not find a contradiction between giving the individual the right to choose his or her employment and providing care for someone who requires it. Pragmatically speaking, there is enough money for many social needs in this country, if it is carefully managed, and the constant tension between allowing people liberty at their own risk and support at the risk of losing autonomy is, in my opinion, a necessary and a healthy one to maintain.

Robert Nozick would disagree. He believed that "creating a safety net for less advantaged members of society is illegitimate." Charity is to be used instead. "Benefits and burdens are distributed justly when society allows every individual the freedom to do what he chooses to do for himself or for others, the freedom to keep what he makes for himself or what others choose to give him, and the freedom to keep what he has or give it to whomever he chooses."

I disagree with Mr. Nozick. To claim that burdens and benefits are justly distributed by individual efforts is to assume that Confucius's belief in the innate good conduct of individuals operates sufficiently to cover the cost of our national needs. Many Americans give to charity. Eighty-nine percent of American households made charitable contributions in 2000. I believe, however, that a degree of provision in the form

■ ■ ■ **Student Essay** *(continued)*

of taxes for others in society should be mandated by law to ensure the public weal, as is currently done in the United States and other nations around the world.

Perhaps a more creative application of taxes is needed to improve health, education, and welfare programs in our country. Geoffrey Canada's Harlem Children's Zone Project, a multifaceted program of support for young children, their parents, and their neighborhood is an example of insightful, comprehensive, and effective assistance to ensure success in school and into the job market. Twenty-eight percent of the Harlem Children's Zone Project is funded by the government. Samuel Johnson once said, "A decent provision for the poor is the true test of civilization." The quote has haunted me since I first read it, for no matter what philosophical justification I may give as to why people should find the means to support themselves, the specter of indigent people who cannot, for whatever reason, take care of themselves, cries out to me for some systematic means of help, and our government is the best organization to provide such care because it draws from everyone's revenue.

Up until now I have considered only the needs of a single society. What about international relations? Of course I accept, as Hobbes says, that, "… the first and fundamental law of nature … is: to seek peace and follow it. The second, the sum of the right of nature … is: by all means we can to defend ourselves." In other words, if one is attacked, one is allowed to defend oneself. But what happens when an invasion occurs? What right does a country have to stay once it has subdued a country that was attacking it? What if the invading country was not being attacked? I know that from time immemorial countries have taken each other's territories; that is how countries grow, and no one would expect Australia to give the continent back to the Aborigines, or the Brazilians to move to Portugal, but is the taking of someone else's land right? Is it fair?

The *Communist Manifesto* looks rather naive when one realizes that many of its proclamations did not come true. The Soviet Union ultimately fell, no world revolution against capitalism occurred, and many workers were glad to become part of the modern world with the benefits it offered. However, the *Manifesto*'s global proposal that, "[t]he Proletarians have nothing to lose but their chains. They have a world to win. Proletarians of all countries, unite!" inspires the reader by suggesting that a global cause might unite people as a local or national one once did.

Trade unions emerged as workers realized that there was force in numbers, as such movements as the Arab Spring, the Tea Party, and Outlaw Wall Street have recently emerged, aided by sophisticated global communication provided by cell phones and the Internet. If one day a global, rather than simply a national, identity emerges, should not then nations, like individuals, be considered equal under the law? The concept of an identity beyond national, religious, or historical experience was first proposed by Baruch Spinoza, a Marrano Jew living in Amsterdam during a century of religious wars who thought of himself, not as Jew or a Dutchman, but as a rational individual. Is it possible that people today might conceive of themselves beyond their national identities, and thus find common ground, rather than abject strife, with those who do not share their political philosophy? Over periods of time much longer than a lifetime, or even generations, change, growth, and understanding can and do occur.

Are there certain precepts, despite cultural differences, which nonetheless all must obey for the good of the international body politic? Of course. We could not permit murder, theft, fraud, and harassment in any society. Are such precepts always readily accepted and easily enforced? No. Herein lies one tragedy of human existence, that we as countries as well as individuals must struggle to understand what we value most and how best to protect it, though the conflict may take beyond our lifetime to resolve.

Perhaps the most looming example of a sustained conflict is our impact on the planet. If one only considers one's own rights and actions, the world as a whole may be made uninhabitable by humans. I think of cars, nonrecyclable garbage, and toxic wastes which now threaten our air and water and, by extension, ourselves. We as human beings, not just Americans, are beginning to feel the negative effects of acting solely in our immediate self-interest. We are not capable of curbing our destructive actions individually. Accommodation to a less polluting lifestyle would require the participation of people, industries, organizations, and government agencies throughout the country and the world. I believe ultimately that the concerted efforts of governments, including our own, will be needed to help alter human action and improve the world's environment. The question is will such action be mandated by law, and if so, will social justice then consist in violating the rights of the individual to ensure the survival of the group, or will it rely on voluntary participation and perhaps risk failure and the demise of the human race?

More immediate than global warming is the downward spiraling of the economy, and the fear that one's children and grandchildren will suffer a severe turn of circumstances that no application of justice may prevent. I do not understand the complex series of events which have led to our current economic distress, nor am I sure what changes in fiscal policy might improve our financial sector and the U.S. economy as a whole. I notice only Marx and Engels within this chapter focus specifically on the relationship between social justice and the economy.

Economic security is an individual pursuit as much as life and liberty. We all hope to avoid joblessness, poverty, and the lack of a future. Locke's pursuit of happiness could not exist if money were not part of the equation. Economic security has never been called a right because it is not something which can be guaranteed by law. The economy is precarious by nature and beyond anyone's control. Marx and Engels predicted certain outcomes from the confrontation of the working class and the upper class, but history has shown that in most industrialized countries the proletariat has gained stature and economic strength without attacking the bourgeois, and in countries where a revolution has occurred, authoritarian regimes now rule. A free market, with the incentive to make a profit, has proven in general more effective than controlled means in fostering economic development. Just as John Rawls opened up the idea

■ ■ ■ **Student Essay** *(continued)*

that equal opportunity to a good education should be provided to all in a society, perhaps equal opportunity to employment and to a secure existence should be mandated as well. I don't know what this mandate would look like, but it seems to me a logical extension of Rawls's extended consideration of equal opportunity.

The world is currently gripped in an economic crisis of deepening impact. International political upheaval may come at any time, quickened through modern technology. The planet's ability to sustain life, given unchecked human activity, is in question. Where is justice, and how can it be maintained? I believe one must begin with the examination of existing laws, their application or reinterpretation, and the legislating of new laws if necessary in response to new circumstances. Though our world is changing, yet the law, some accepted standard of judgment under which all parties may speak and be considered impartially, must be preserved to maintain fairness, protect the rights of the individual, and support society.

I believe furthermore that we have a moral responsibility as a country to take care of ourselves and, by extension, our world. The needs of the community may grow increasingly at odds with the rights of the individual, and each generation will have to weigh what steps to take to balance personal freedom with public welfare, but if one begins with the cornerstone that all are equal under the law, I believe the foundation will hold.

Work Cited

Chaffee, John. *The Philosopher's Way: Thinking Critically About Profound Ideas*. Upper Saddle River, NJ: Pearson/Prentice Hall, 2010.

My**Search**Lab Connections

Watch. Listen. Explore. Read. Mysearchlab is designed just for you. Each chapter features a customized study plan to help you learn and review key concepts and terms. Dynamic visual activities, videos, and readings found in the multimedia library will enhance your learning experience.

Here are a few questions and activities to help you understand this chapter:

1. **Watch** the **Interview** *The Authentic Confucius* on **mysearchlab.com**   How did the social unrest in China impact the development of Confucius's philosophical beliefs?

2. **Listen** to the **Audiobook** *Plato The Republic by Nigel Warburton* on **mysearchlab.com**   Do you agree with Socrates that justice is "intrinsically valuable"? Explain.

3. **Listen** to the **Audiobook** *Locke's Second Treatise by Nigel Warburton* on **mysearchlab.com** According to Locke, how would people behave in the state of nature?

4. **Listen** to the **Radio** *How Marx's General Helped Lead the Revolution* on **mysearchlab.com**   Explain how Engels came to adopt a Marxist worldview.

5. **Listen** to the **Audiobook** *John Stuart Mill Utilitarianism by Nigel Warburton* on **mysearchlab.com** Explain the differences between the utilitarism theories of Bentham and Mill with respect to their treatment of "pleasures".

6. **Listen** to the **Podcast** *Richard Reeves on Mill's On Liberty* on **mysearchlab.com**   What is the "single truth" at the heart of *On Liberty?* Explain.

Elements of a Just Society

- Philosophers interested in political and social constructions explore questions about the following broad topics: justice, law, public interest, duty, rights, freedom, and power and influence. Social and political philosophies are both *normative*, in that they propose ideal societies, and *descriptive*, in that they offer critical analysis of how a specific political system actually functions (or doesn't!).

[pp. 556–558]

Classical Theories of Society: Confucius, Plato, and Aristotle

- The Chinese philosopher Confucius believed that an ideal state could only be achieved by a commitment to the principles of virtue, both by the leaders and the citizens. Achieving our full humanity entails following the "rules of propriety."

- Plato's political philosophy was the first to be based on the concept of justice, aspiring to the ideals of function and harmony. Such a society would be ruled by carefully educated philosopher-kings, who would preside over a society of workers and guardians.

- Aristotle believed that humans are inherently "political," social animals who achieve their individual potential only through social interaction. For him, the state is "prior to the individual," meaning that the interests of the community take precedence over the interests of the individual citizens.

[pp. 558–568]

KEY TERMS
distributive justice
retributive justice

KEY TERMS
ethical humanism
ren
zhong-yong
li
democracy
egalitarianism

Justice Depends on a Social Contract: From Hobbes and Locke to Rawls

- In stark contrast to Aristotle, Thomas Hobbes believed that humans are fundamentally predisposed to selfishness and destruction, living originally in a violent "state of nature," unrestrained by laws or moral discipline. To improve their lives, humans agree to enter into "social contracts," by which they surrender some of their personal autonomy to a governing authority in exchange for order and protection.

visual summary

for further reading, viewing & research

Read the Primary Source on MySearchLab

- *The Analects*, Confucius
- *The Republic*, Plato
- *Politics*, Aristotle
- *Leviathan*, Thomas Hobbes
- *The Second Treatise of Government*, John Locke
- *Manifesto of the Communist Party*, Karl Marx and Friedrich Engels
- *On Liberty*, John Stuart Mill

Films

- *A Dry White Season* (1989) How should people respond to an unjust state? Ben Du Doit is a schoolteacher in South Africa during the apartheid movement who witnesses the results of a murder committed by the corrupt government police. Du Doit puts himself at risk when he stands up to the prejudiced and oppressive government by attempting to reveal their inhumane actions. The novel by Andre Brink is also recommended.

- *A Clockwork Orange* (1971) How should a society treat its criminals? In a near-distant future, an adolescent gang member accused of numerous rapes and violent attacks agrees to try a controversial aversion therapy in order to shorten his jail sentences. The results of the therapy are essentially brainwashing, and he emerges from the hospital a very different person from the one who entered it. The novel by Anthony Burgess is also recommended.

- *A Few Good Men* (1992) What happens when national security conflicts with the ethical treatment of the individual? How might utilitarianism clash with human rights? Based on the play of the same name, this courtroom thriller deals with a Navy lawyer hired to defend two marines accused of murdering another marine.

- *Hotel Rwanda* (2004) What happens when a government fails to protect its people? In this historical film, a single man uses his social position, charisma, and intelligence to save thousands of people from the Rwandan genocide.

- *Lord of the Flies* (1963 and 1990) Are humans fundamentally predisposed to selfishness, destruction, and

- John Locke, a contemporary of Hobbes, took a more optimistic view of human nature. Humans, he said, are governed by certain "natural laws" inherent to us as God's creation. These natural laws include the rights to life, liberty, health, and property. A just society respects and protects each citizen's natural rights; humans willingly enter into social contracts in order to create a just society with a central authority. Unlike Hobbes, Locke believed that the authority of the state could be questioned, challenged, or even changed.

- Using examples of repressive, violent, and unjust regimes throughout history, David Hume argued that political states have little interest in the rights of individual citizens.

- Modern liberalism, as exemplified by John Rawls, is founded on the assumption that all citizens are entitled to equal opportunities to achieve their maximum potential. Rawls suggests that to conceive of a fair and just society, we need to assume a "veil of ignorance" regarding our own standing and situation within that idealized society.

[pp. 568–587]

Justice Is Based on Need and Ability: Marx and Engels

- Marxism, as articulated by Karl Marx and Friedrich Engels, is a social, economic, and political system based on the socialist ideal of "from each according to his abilities, to each according to his needs." If liberalism privileges the rights and freedoms of the individual, socialism (and communism) emphasizes the duty of a society to maintain as a preeminent value what is best for *all* of its citizens. Marx and Engels conceived of history as *dialectical*—that is, each historical state of events creates, or leads to, its opposite, which in turn results in a synthesis which that unites and transcends the two conflicting forces.

[pp. 587–597]

Justice Is What Promotes the General Welfare: Mill

- For John Stuart Mill, the touchstone for creating a society based on social justice and individual liberty is the concept of social utility. A rational critique of the concept of justice will lead us to understand it as that which calculates and implements the maximum good for the maximum amount of people.

[pp. 597–605]

Justice Is What Promotes Gender Equality: Okin

- Feminist sociopolitical philosophy focuses on the traditional disparity between the sexes when it comes to social duties and obligations. Feminist philosophers such as Susan Moller Okin call for a reconsideration of traditional gender roles to more fully and equitably distribute justice and equality to all members of society.

[pp. 605–614]

KEY TERMS
social contract
utopia

KEY TERMS
liberalism
socialism
capitalism
communism
proletariat

KEY TERM
social utility

---

a kind of crude "state of nature"? Based on the allegorical novel by William Golding, these two film versions chronicle the events that occur when a group of military students are stranded on an island after a plane crash.

- **Welcome to Sarajevo** (1997) Does a country ever have an ethical right and/or responsibility to intercede in the affairs of another country? A British journalist travels to Sarajevo at the beginning of the Bosnian War, where he encounters firsthand the suffering of the people there. He also discovers an orphanage near the front line and attempts to rescue one of the children by taking her back to England with him.

Literature

- **Things Fall Apart,** Chinua Achebe. This classic work by the Nigerian author explores the effects of colonialism and Christianity on an African community. Its protagonist, one of the community leaders, is both sympathetic and cruel in his attempt to adhere to traditional values. The novel is an illuminating reflection on the complexities that arise when different cultures, world views, moral codes, and belief systems are in conflict.

- **Notes from Underground,** Fyodor Dostoevsky. This is the fictional memoir of an alienated individual who has removed himself entirely from society. The novel is an attack on the rational egoism and utopianism in nineteenth-century Russia, and explores the alienation and paralysis that emerge in a world void of moral or religious absolutes.

- **1984,** George Orwell. This dystopian novel imagines a futuristic world in which the government has become a totalitarian regime. Its protagonist is a civil servant who is responsible for falsifying documents and literature in order to support the regime's propaganda.

- **Harvest Home,** Thomas Tryon. A family abandons urban life in an attempt to return to the land. They join a seemingly idyllic farming community and subsequently become aware of and ensnared by the horrific cultish practices of the community members.

- **All the King's Men,** Robert Penn Warren. Based in part on true events, this novel recounts the political rise and fall of a politician in the South in the 1930s. Narrated by this politician's right-hand man, who is privy to all of the corrupt practices of the politician, the work raises questions about free will, political ethics, nihilism, and individual responsibility and duty.

credits

Text Credits

Chapter 1

p. 7 — Perictione, Quoted in *A History of Women Philosophers*, ed. Mary Ellen Waithe (Boston: Martinus Nijhoff, 1987). Reprinted by permission of Springer Science & Business Media.

pp. 38–40 — Bertrand Russell, *The Problems of Philosophy* (Oxford: Oxford University Press, 1912). Copyright © 1912. Reprinted by permission of Oxford University Press.

pp. 41–43 — From *Man's Search for Meaning* by Frankl, Viktor E. Copyright © 1959, 1962, 1984, 1992 by Viktor E. Frankl. (Boston: Beacon Press, 1959).

Chapter 2

p. 51 — From *Hesiod and Theognis*, Translated by Dorothea Wender. Translation and Introduction © 1973, Dorothea Wender. Reprinted by permission of Penguin Group, UK, and the Estate of Dorothea Wender.

p. 52 — Excerpts from *The Iliad*, trans. Robert Fagles, Edited by Bernard Knox. Copyright © Robert Fagles. (New York: Penguin Books, USA, Inc., 1990).

pp. 56–57 — From Karl Jaspers, *Basic Philosophical Writings—Selections*. Ed., trans., and with introductions by Edith Ehrlich, Leonard H. Ehrlich, and George B. Pepper. (Athens, OH: Ohio University Press), pp. 382–387. Reprinted by permission of Hans Saner.

pp. 59, 60, 61, 68, 73–86, 88–90 — Excerpts from Plato, *The Apology*, from *The Dialogues of Plato*, trans. Benjamin Jowett (1896).

pp. 63–66 — From *The Republic*, by Plato. Translated by H. D. P. Lee. Copyright © H. D. P. Lee, 1955, 1974, 1987. Reprinted by permission of Penguin Group, UK.

p. 92 — I. F. Stone, *The Trial of Socrates* (New York: Little, Brown and Company, 1988).

Chapter 3

pp. 104–105 — HAMILTON, EDITH; THE COLLECTED DIALOGUES OF PLATO, INCLUDING THE LETTERS. © 1961 Princeton University Press, 1989 renewed Reprinted by permission of Princeton University Press.

p. 105 — Excerpt from *The Symposium*, by Plato, trans. Benjamin Jowett. (London: Oxford University Press, 1892).

pp. 108–109 — Excerpts from *Phaedrus*, The Chariot Analogy, by Plato, trans. Benjamin Jowett. (London: Oxford University Press, 1892).

p. 112 — Excerpts from "Discourse on Method," by Rene Descartes, from *The Philosophical Works of Descartes*, translated by Elizabeth Haldane and GRT Ross. (London: Oxford University Press, 1911–1912)

pp. 113–117 — Excerpts from "Meditations on First Philosophy," by Rene Descartes, from *The Philosophical Works of Descartes*, translated by Elizabeth Haldane and GRT Ross. (London: Cambridge University Press, 1911–1912).

pp. 124–126 — David Hume, "On Personal Identity" from *A Treatise on Human Nature* by David Hume, ed. by L. A. Selby–Bigge (London: Oxford University Press, 1975).

pp. 127 — BECK, LEWIS WHITE, PROLEGOMENA TO ANY FUTURE METAPHYSICS: KANT, 1st Ed., © 2004. Reprinted and Electronically reproduced by permission of Pearson Education, Inc., Upper Saddle River, New Jersey.

pp. 128–130 — From Immanuel Kant, *Critique of Pure Reason*. Translated by Norman Kemp Smith. Copyright © 1991 Palgrave Macmillan. Reproduced with permission of Palgrave Macmillan.

p. 132 — Sigmund Freud, Excerpt from "An Outline of Psychoanalysis," *International Journal of Psycho-Analysis*, 21:27–84., John Wiley & Sons, Ltd. Reprinted by permission of John Wiley & Sons, Ltd.

p. 136 — Alasdair MacIntyre, *The Unconscious* (London: Routledge & Kegan Paul Ltds., 1958). Copyright © 1958, 2004 Alasdair MacIntyre. Reprinted by permission of Taylor and Francis Group, Ltd.

p. 137   Norman Cameron, *Personality Development and Psychopathology* (Boston: Houghton Mifflin & Co., 1985)

pp. 138–141   *The Concept of Mind* by Ryle, Gilbert. Copyright 1949. Reproduced with permission of BARNES & NOBLE BOOKS—IMPORTS in the format Textbook and Other Book via Copyright Clearance Center.

p. 144   Excerpts from The Mind-Body Problem, from The Language of Thought, The Modularity of Mind, and Psychosemantics. Reproduced with permission. Copyright © 1981 by Scientific American, Inc. All rights reserved.

pp. 148–150   "On Eliminative Materialism." From Churchland, Paul M., *Matter and Consciousness, revised edition: A Contemporary Introduction to the Philosophy of Mind*, pp. 43–49. © 1988 Massachusetts Institute of Technology, by permission of The MIT Press.

p. 156   Excerpt from "Within a Budding Grove" from *In Search of Time Lost,* by Marcel Proust. Translated by C. K. Scott Moncrieff and Terence Kilmartin, translation revised by D. J. Enright. (New York: Random House, 2003).

pp. 156–157   Maurice Merleau–Ponty, *Phenomenology of Perception* trans. Colin Smith (New York: Routledge & Kegan Paul, 1962).

p. 158   Excerpt from "Waking from Sleep" from *In Search of Time Lost*, by Marcel Proust. Translated by C. K. Scott Moncrieff and Terence Kilmartin, translation revised by D. J. Enright. (New York: Random House, 2003)

p. 160   Milindapan'ha, ed. V. Trenckner (Williams and Norgate, 1880).

p. 162   Excerpt from Aristotle, *Politics*, translated by Benjamin Jowett. (London: Oxford University Press, 1905).

Chapter 4

pp. 176–177   John Stuart Mill, "On Causation and Necessity" quoted in the introduction to *A Modern Introduction to Philosophy: Readings from Classical andContemporary Sources*, ed. by P. Edwards & Pap (New York: Free Press, 1967).

p. 177   Clarence Darrow, "The Crime of Compulsion," in *Attorney for the Damned*, ed. Arthur Weinberg (New York: Simon and Schuster, 1957).

p. 177   *The Rubaiyat* of Omar Khayyam.

pp. 178–183   Paul Henry Thiry, *Baron d'Holbach, The System of Nature*, Vol. I, Chapters 11 and 12, translated by H. D. Robinson (1853).

pp. 185–189   "Is Determinism Inconsistent with Free Will", pages 248–258 (entire) from *Religion and the Modern Mind*, by W. T. Stace. Copyright 1952 by W. T. Stace, renewed © 1980 by Blanche Stace. Reprinted by permission of Harper Collins Publishers and the Estate of W. T. Stace.

pp. 190, 194–202   William James, *Will to Believe and Other Essays in Popular Philosophy* (New York: Dover Publications, 1960).

p. 191   Moritz Schlick, *Problems of Ethics*, trans. David Rynin (New York: Prentice Hall, 1939).

p. 192   Daniel Dennett, *Freedom Evolves* (New York: Viking, 2003).

pp. 204–205, 207–212   Excerpts from "Existentialism is a Humanism," from *Existentialism and Human Emotion*, by Jean-Paul Sartre. Translated by Bernard Frechtman. Copyright © 1957 Philosophical Library. Reprinted by permission of the Philosophical Library, New York.

p. 213   Jean Grimshaw, "Autonomy and Identity in Feminist Thinking" from *Feminist Perspectives in Philosophy*, Griffiths, Morwenna, and Margaret Whitford, eds., pp. 90–95. Copyright © 1988 Indiana University Press. Reprinted with permission of Indiana University Press.

p. 217   Erich Fromm, *Escape From Freedom* (New York: Henry Holt & Co., 1994).

p. 222   Viktor Frankl, *Man's Search for Meaning* (New York: Pocket Books, 1997).

Chapter 5

pp. 205–209   Plato, *Republic,* Translated by G. M. A. Grube. Copyright © 1974 by Hackett Publishing Company, Inc. Reprinted by permission of Hackett Publishing Company, Inc. All rights reserved.

p. 239   Charles Dickens, *Hard Times* (New York: Bantam, 1981).

p. 240 — Excerpt from "Metaphysics," by Aristotle. From *The Philosophy of Aristotle*, Edited by Renford Bambrough, Translated by A. E. Wardman and J. L. Creed. (New York: New American Library, 1963).

p. 240 — Plato, "Timaeus," from *The Dialogues of Plato*, trans. Benjamin Jowett. (London: Oxford University Press, 1896).

p. 243 — Plato, *Meno*, trans. G. M. A. Grube. (Cambridge, MA: Hackett Publishing, 1976).

p. 250 — Aristotle, "Metaphysics," in W. T. Jones, *The Classical Mind*, 2nd ed. (New York: Harcourt Brace Jovanovich, 1970).

pp. 253–254 — Excerpts from "Metaphysics," by Aristotle. Translated by Philip Wheelwright. Westerville, OH: Odyssey Press (1951).

pp. 254–255 — Excerpts from "Metaphysics" by Aristotle. Translated by Hugh Tredennick. Cambridge, M.A.: Harvard University Press (1933).

pp. 257–267 — Excerpts from "Meditations on First Philosophy" by René Descartes from *The Philosophical Works of Descartes*, Vol. 1, edited by Elizabeth S. Haldane and G. R. T. Ross, (London: Cambridge University Press, 1911–1912).

p. 260 — Excerpt from *Chuang–Tzu: Taoist Philosopher and Chinese Mystic*. Translated by Herbert A. Giles. (London: George Allen and Unwin, 1961/1889).

Chapter 6

pp. 283–287 — Bertrand Russell, *The Problems of Philosophy*. Copyright © 1959 Oxford University Press. Reprinted by permission of Oxford University Press.

pp. 283–287, 288–290, 293–299 — John Locke, *An Essay Concerning Human Understanding*, 1689, ed. A. C. Fraser (Oxford: Clarendon Press, 1894).

pp. 290–292 — Gottfried Wilhelm von Leibniz, from *New Essays Concerning Human Understanding*, translated by Alfred Gideon Langley. (Chicago, IL: Open Court Publishing Company, 1949).

pp. 300–304 — George Berkeley, from TREATISE CONCERNING THE PRINCIPLES OF HUMAN KNOWLEDGE, 1st ed. (Upper Saddle River, NJ: Pearson Education, Inc., 1900).

pp. 304–305 — Msgr Ronald Knox, "There was a young man who said, "God."" Copyright by the Earl of Oxford and Asquith. Reprinted by permission of A.P.Watt Ltd.

p. 306 — Bertrand Russell, *A History of Western Philosophy* (New York: Simon and Schuster, 1945).

pp. 306–314 — David Hume, from *An Enquiry Concerning Human Understanding*, 2nd Edition edited by L. A. Selby–Bigge (1902).

pp. 316–319; 321 — Immanuel Kant, PROLEGOMENA TO ANY FURTHER METAPHYSICS. Translated by Lewis White Beck. Copyright © 1957 Lewis White Beck. Reprinted by permission of the Estate of Lewis White Beck.

pp. 316–319; 321 — BECK, LEWIS WHITE, PROLEGOMENA TO ANY FUTURE METAPHYSICS: KANT, 1st Ed., © 2004. Reprinted and Electronically reproduced by permission of Pearson Education, Inc., Upper Saddle River, New Jersey.

p. 321 — David Hume, from *An Enquiry Concerning Human Understanding*, 2nd Edition, edited by L. A. Selby–Bigge (1902).

pp. 321–324 — Keiji Nishitani, RELIGION AND NOTHINGNESS, Translated and Edited by Jan Van Bragt. Copyright © 1983, Keiji Nishitani. Reprinted by permission of the University of California Press and the Estate of Keiji Nishitani.

pp. 324–326, 328, 332 — Kant, Immanuel. From *Critique of Pure Reason*, Translated by Norman Kemp-Smith. Copyright © 1929, Palgrave Macmillan. Reprinted Kant, Immanuel. From *Critique of Pure Reason*, Translated by Norman Kemp-Smith. Copyright © 1929, Palgrave Macmillan. Reprinted by permission.

p. 334 — From *The New York Times*, February 22, 1965. © 1965 The New York Times. All rights reserved. Used by permission and protected by the Copyright Laws of the United States. The printing, copying, redistribution, or retransmission of this Content without express written permission is prohibited.

p. 334 — "The Violent End of the Man Called Malcolm." From the March 5, 1965 LIFE Magazine. Copyright © 1965 The Picture Collection Inc. Reprinted with permission. All rights reserved.

p. 335 — Thomas Skinner, "I Saw Malcolm Die," *The New York Post*, February 22, 1965,

p. 1. Copyright © 1965. Reprinted by permission of the New York Post.

pp. 337–344 From "Love and Knowledge: Emotion in Feminist Epistemology" by Alison M. Jaggar, INQUIRY, January 1, 1989. Copyright © 1989 Routledge. Reprinted by permission of the publisher (Taylor & Francis Group, http://www.informaworld.com) and the author.

Chapter 7

p. 354 "Religion and Science" by Albert Einstein first appeared in *The New York Times Magazine* on November 9, 1930, pp. 1–4. Reprinted by permission of the Albert Einstein Archives, Hebrew University of Jerusalem.

pp. 356–359 STRENG, FREDERICK J.; LLOYD, CHARLES L.; ALLEN, JAY T., WAYS OF BEING RELIGIOUS, 1st Ed., © 1973. Reprinted and Electronically reproduced by permission of Pearson Education, Inc., Upper Saddle River, New Jersey.

pp. 360–362 Ludwig Feuerbach, from *The Essence of Christianity*, translated by George Eliot. Gloucester, MA: Peter Smith Publishers (reprint of 1854 ed.).

pp. 377–380 Reprinted by permission of Open Court Publishing Company, a division of Carus Publishing Company, Chicago, IL, from *St. Anselm's Basic Writings*, 2nd ed. Translated by S. N. Deane. Copyright © 1962 by Open Court Publishing Company.

pp. 381–383 Thomas Aquinas, *Summa Theologica* (Benziger Bros. Edition, 1947). Translated by Fathers of the English Dominican Province.

p. 384 William Paley, *Natural Theology*, (1822).

p. 385 From *Why I Am Not a Christian* by Bertrand Russell. Copyright © 1957 by George Allen & Unwin Ltd.

pp. 386–387 BECK, LEWIS WHITE, KANT: CRITIQUE OF PRACTICAL REASON, 1st Ed., © 1956. Reprinted and Electronically reproduced by permission of Pearson Education, Inc., Upper Saddle River, New Jersey.

pp. 389–390 J. L. Mackie, "Evil and Omnipotence" from *Mind*, 1955, Volume 64, April 1, 1955, pp. 200–212. Copyright © 1955

Mind Association. Reprinted by permission of Oxford University Press.

pp. 395–398 John H. Hick, from *Philosophy of Religion*, 1st ed., © 1963, reproduced by permission of Pearson Education, Inc., Upper Saddle River, NJ.

pp. 399–400 Edward Madden and Peter Hare, "A Critique of Hick's Theodicy," from *Evil and the Concept of God* (A Monograph in The Bannerstone Division of American Lectures in Philosophy) (American Lecture Series, Publication Number 706). Reprinted by permission of the publisher in the formats Textbook and Other Book, via Copyright Clearance Center.

pp. 402–404 Pascal, Blaise. "A Wager" from *Thoughts [Pensees]* by Blaise Pascal, trans. by W. F. Trotter, New York: P. F. Collier & Son, 1910.

pp. 405–409 W. K. Clifford, from "The Ethics of Belief" reprinted from W. K. Clifford, *Lectures and Essays*, Vol. 2, London: Macmillan, 1879, pp. 177–188.

pp. 409, 411–418 William James, from *The Will to Believe* (New York: Longmans, Green, 1897).

pp. 419–420 KIERKEGAARD, SØREN; PHILOSOPHICAL FRAGMENTS/JOHANNES CLIMACUS. © 1985 Princeton University Press. Reprinted by permission of Princeton University Press.

pp. 420–421 KIERKEGAARD, SØREN; CONCLUDING UNSCIENTIFIC POSTSCRIPT TO PHILOSOPHICAL FRAGMENTS (2 vols). © 1992 Princeton University Press. Reprinted by permission of Princeton University Press.

pp. 422–423 STRENG, FREDERICK J.; LLOYD, CHARLES L.; ALLEN, JAY T., WAYS OF BEING RELIGIOUS, 1st Ed., © 1973. Reprinted and Electronically reproduced by permission of Pearson Education, Inc., Upper Saddle River, New Jersey.

Chapter 8

p. 430 M. Scott Peck, *The Road Less Traveled*, (Touchstone Books, 2003).

p. 437 Mohandas Gandhi, *All Men Are Brothers* (New York: Columbia University Press, 1958).

pp. 441–445 "Anthropology and the Abnormal," Ruth Benedict, THE JOURNAL OF GENERAL PSYCHOLOGY, January 1, 1934,

Chapter 9

pp. 533–534   1995 by Mrs. Hazel Kaufmann. Reprinted by permission of Random House, Inc.

pp. 533–534   Friedrich Nietzsche, *Beyond Good and Evil*, trans. Walter Kaufmann (New York: Random House, 1966). Copyright © 1967 by Walter Kaufmann, Copyright renewed 1995 by Mrs. Hazel Kaufmann. Reprinted by permission of Random House, Inc.

pp. 535–540   Jean–Paul Sartre, from *Existentialism and Human Emotion*, trans. Bernard Frechtman (NY: Philosophical Library, 1957). Reprinted by permission of Philosophical Library, New York.

pp. 541–542   Simone de Beauvoir, from *The Ethics of Ambiguity*, trans. Bernard Frechtman. Copyright © 1948 by Philosophical Library, Inc. Reprinted bypermission of Philosophical Library, New York.

pp. 543–545   From *The Myth of Sisyphus* by Albert Camus, trans. by Justin O'Brien, translation copyright © 1955, copyright renewed 1983 by Alfred A. Knopf, a division of Random House, Inc. Used by permission of Alfred A. Knopf, a division of Random House, Inc., and Penguin Press. Published in French as Le Mythe de Sisyphe, copyright © 1942 by Editions Gallimard. www.gallimard.fr.

pp. 546–548   From CARING: A FEMININE APPROACH TO ETHICS AND MORAL EDUCATION, by Nel Noddings. Copyright © 2003, The Regents of the University of California. Reprinted by permission of the University of California Press.

Chapter 10

pp. 559–561   Confucius, The Analects, in T*he Chinese Classics*, vol. 1, ed. and trans. James Legge (Oxford: Clarendon, 1893).

pp. 562–564   Plato, REPUBLIC, Translated by G. M. A. Grube. Copyright © 1983 by Hackett Publishing Company, Inc. Reprinted by permission of Hackett Publishing Company, Inc. All rights reserved.

pp. 566–568   Aristotle, *Politics*, trans. Benjamin Jowett (1896).

pp. 570–573   Thomas Hobbes, *Leviathan* (New York: Hafner, 1926).

pp. 575–580   John Locke, *The Second Treatise of Civil Government* (New York: Hafner, 1947).

p. 582   David Hume, "Of the Original Contract," in *Essays, Moral, Political, and Literary* (New York: Ward, Lock).

pp. 584–586   Reprinted by permission of the publisher from A THEORY OF JUSTICE by John Rawls, pp. 11–13, Cambridge, Mass.: The Belknap Press of Harvard University Press, Copyright © 1971, 1999 by the President and Fellows of Harvard College.

p. 587   Robert Nozick, ANARCHY, STATE AND UTOPIA (New York: Basic Books, 1974).

pp. 589–595   Karl Marx and Friedrich Engels, *Manifesto of the Communist Party* (1888).

pp. 600–605   John Stuart Mill, from *On Liberty*, (London: Longmans, 1859).

pp. 606–613   Susan Moller Okin, from *Justice, Gender and the Family*. Copyright © 1991 by Susan Moller Okin. Reprinted by permission of Basic Books, a member of the Perseus Books Group.

pp. 524, 530   Excerpt from *Either/Or*, by Søren Kierkegaard. Translated by Alastair Hannay. (New York: Penguin, 1992).

Photo Credits

Chapter 1

p. 2   McPHOTO/Alamy

p. 3   McPHOTO/Alamy

p. 5   Moviestore collection Ltd/Alamy

p. 9   TERRY SCHMITT/UPI/Newscom

p. 10   Andrey Arkusha/Shutterstock

p. 29   David Keeler/Getty Images Entertainment/Getty Images

p. 35   REUTERS/Zohra Bensemra

p. 36   Schalkwijk/Art Resource, NY/© 2011 Banco de México Diego Rivera Frida Kahlo Museums Trust, Mexico, D.F./ Artists Rights Society (ARS), New York

p. 37   CREMASTER 3: Five Points of Fellowship, 2002 C-print in acrylic frame 54 × 44 inches Copyright Matthew Barney Courtesy Gladstone Gallery, New York and Brussels

p. 38   Erich Auerbach/Hulton Archive/Getty Images

p. 41   Bettmann/CORBIS

p. 46 top right   Moviestore collection Ltd/Alamy

p. 46 bottom   Mary Evans/DREAMWORKS SKG/Ronald Grant/Everett Collection (10400040)

Chapter 8

Chapter 9

index